UNCEASING MILITANT

THE JOHN HOPE FRANKLIN
SERIES IN AFRICAN AMERICAN
HISTORY AND CULTURE

*Waldo E. Martin Jr. and
Patricia Sullivan, editors*

UNCEASING
MILITANT

THE LIFE OF MARY CHURCH TERRELL

Alison M. Parker

THE UNIVERSITY OF NORTH CAROLINA PRESS

CHAPEL HILL

Publication of this book was supported in part
by a generous gift from Florence and James Peacock.

Designed by April Leidig
Set in Garamond by Copperline Book Services, Inc.
Manufactured in the United States of America

The University of North Carolina Press has been a
member of the Green Press Initiative since 2003.

Jacket illustrations: portrait of Mary Church Terrell in hat and gown and
photograph of Terrell picketing in 1952, courtesy Oberlin College Archives.

Library of Congress Cataloging-in-Publication Data
Names: Parker, Alison M. (Alison Marie), 1965– author.
Title: Unceasing militant : the life of Mary Church Terrell / Alison M. Parker.
Other titles: John Hope Franklin series in African American history and culture.
Description: Chapel Hill : The University of North Carolina Press, [2020] |
Series: The John Hope Franklin series in African American history and culture |
Includes bibliographical references and index.
Identifiers: LCCN 2020024350 | ISBN 9781469659381 (cloth ; alk. paper) |
ISBN 9781469659398 (ebook)
Subjects: LCSH: Terrell, Mary Church, 1863–1954. | National Association of
Colored Women (U.S.)—Biography. | African American women social reformers—
Biography. | African American women civil rights workers—Biography.
Classification: LCC E185.97.T47 P37 2021 | DDC 323/.092 [B]—dc23
LC record available at https://lccn.loc.gov/2020024350

In loving memory of
my beloved mother
Joanne Johnson Parker
(1933–2019)
and
beloved mother-in-law
Carol Lamar Blake
(1943–2019)

CONTENTS

FIGURES

UNCEASING MILITANT

Introduction

Mary ("Mollie") Church began her life in an era of cruelty, tumult, and hope. She was born on September 23, 1863, in Memphis, Tennessee, some ten months after Abraham Lincoln issued the Emancipation Proclamation. In spite of having been born into slavery, she grew up in a privileged household. She learned to use her class privilege, education, light skin color, and cross-class and cross-race connections tactically to work on a wide range of social justice and civil rights issues. From young adulthood on, Mollie Church Terrell became an educator, journalist, public speaker, organizer, and civil rights activist. She brought her energy, leadership, and determination through to the post–World War II Civil Rights Movement. After winning a 1953 legal challenge to District of Columbia segregation in the Supreme Court, Terrell lived just long enough to see the Court issue its 1954 landmark decision in *Brown v. Board of Education*.[1]

Unabashedly ambitious and passionate about social justice, Terrell claimed that she would have run for a U.S. Senate seat to pursue her civil rights agenda if not for the barriers that blocked African American women from attaining such positions of political power. In spite of such limitations, by the time of her death in 1954, Terrell had become one of the most prominent black women in the nation. One of the first African American women to earn a four-year bachelor's degree in 1884 from Oberlin College, Mollie Church taught at Wilberforce University and then moved to Washington, D.C., to teach in the well-respected M Street Colored High School. In the 1890s, her role as an educator led to her appointment as the first black woman on the District of Columbia's board of education. In 1896 she was elected as first president of the National Association of Colored Women (NACW), and in the first two decades of the twentieth century, Terrell helped found the National Association for the Advancement of Colored People (NAACP). She became a paid speaker on the black and white lecture circuits, published newspaper articles, served as the only African American delegate to two international women's conventions in Europe (which she addressed in fluent German and French), picketed the

White House for woman suffrage, helped create the Woman Wage Earners' Association during World War I, and was a founding member of the International Council of Women of the Darker Races. In the 1930s, she was active in the NAACP's Washington, D.C., branch, joined with the Communist Party's International Labor Defense on behalf of the Scottsboro Nine, worked as a clerk in Democratic New Deal agencies, and campaigned for Republican Party candidates. In the 1940s, she helped A. Philip Randolph organize the March on Washington Movement, initiated a lawsuit to integrate the American Association of University Women, and supported striking black cafeteria workers who were resisting signing anticommunist pledges. In the late 1940s and early 1950s, Terrell spoke before congressional committees in favor of the Equal Rights Amendment. She also chaired two important committees affiliated with the Civil Rights Congress (CRC), a communist front organization. One committee demanded freedom for a black sharecropper, Rosa Lee Ingram, and her sons, who had struck out in self-defense but had been convicted of murdering her white male assailant. The other committee's direct-action protests and legal challenges successfully dismantled segregation in the nation's capital the year before *Brown v. Board of Education*. Over her long life, Mollie Church Terrell's range of activism and alliances was extraordinary, and yet she has never before been the subject of a full-length scholarly biography.[2]

Unceasing Militant tells a comprehensive life story of a woman who inhabited many worlds and whose life provides a timeline of civil rights activism from the 1890s through 1954. Flexible about her activist approaches, she moved back and forth from moral suasion to militant action on a case-by-case basis, always in service of her unflinching commitment to equal rights. In the 1890s, for example, she was likely to be organizing a meeting of an African American literary society, attending a black women's club meeting, lobbying against lynching, and participating in a suffrage meeting. In the 1930s, she was likely to be playing bridge with friends, attending a union gathering, eating at an interfaith luncheon, still lobbying Congress for antilynching legislation, and attending an evening meeting of the NAACP. Terrell always approached the problems confronting African Americans and women from a number of angles at once, and her varied activities demonstrate her indefatigable energy as well as the value she placed on participating in multiple overlapping reform groups to achieve her goals of equality and justice for all.

Mollie Church Terrell's life spanned nine decades, but the decades of the 1920s through the late 1940s are particularly underexplored by historians. Even her leadership of the D.C. anti-discrimination fight and of the Ingram case fell off historians' radar until recently.[3] This interrupted narrative misses several crucial decades, especially the interwar era when she took part in the International Council of Women of the Darker Races of the World, wrote a column for the *Chicago Defender*, and worked on Republican Party senate and presidential campaigns. During those years she also nursed her husband through a multiyear illness, grieved his death, adapted to widowhood, entered into a love affair, and focused more attention on earning an income as a freelance journalist, speaker, and employee in Republican campaigns. After women won the right to vote at the national level in 1920, Terrell fully engaged in partisan politics. She relished the paid Republican National Committee (RNC) leadership positions from which she encouraged African American women to vote Republican. She pushed hard to keep the Grand Old Party true to its claim to be the "party of Lincoln," even when she could see that it was failing to do so. Terrell continued to fight against the disfranchisement of all African Americans, especially in the South.

The last period of Terrell's life, from the late 1940s through her death in 1954, does not represent a dramatic departure for her. Despite her age, she remained a militant activist who settled for nothing short of full equality and full citizenship. The anticommunist hysteria of the Red Scare gave her pause when she received pushback from white women in the American Association of University Women and from black and white anticommunist liberals who opposed working with activists on the left. Yet the fear mongering did not stop her from taking on leadership roles in the D.C. antidiscrimination and Ingram Family campaigns initiated by the Civil Rights Congress. Terrell chaired both campaigns because she had long cared deeply about the principles at stake, including desegregation, equal protection under the law, and the protection of African American women and their children from violence at the hands of white men and the criminal justice system.

Black activist women's studied silences have made it difficult for subsequent generations to learn their motives, what drove them to prioritize certain reforms, as well as who kept them going and helped uplift their spirits. Terrell wrote a memoir from the late 1920s until 1940, ultimately self-publishing it as *A Colored Woman in a White World*, but she told an incomplete and choppy story. While mentioning the "rocky road" faced by African American women, she emphasized public accomplishments and left out aspects of her personal life. By listening past and through the silences that have hindered the study of prominent black women, *Unceasing Militant* provides a comprehensive account of Terrell's multidimensional life.[4]

This biography is based on many years of deep research in Mary Church Terrell's voluminous papers. According to Terrell's wishes, after her death most of her papers were donated to the Library of Congress and Howard University. I have mined all the public collections of Church and Terrell family papers at the University of Memphis archive, the Library of Congress, and Howard University's Moorland-Spingarn Research Center, among others. My Mississippi State University colleague Stephen Middleton, who was researching Mollie Terrell's husband, Municipal Court Judge Robert H. Terrell, introduced me to Terrell's family members Raymond and Jean Langston. The Langstons kindly invited us to review their private holdings at their home, Mollie Terrell's former summer cottage in Highland Beach, Maryland. Raymond Langston, Terrell's stepgrandson (the stepson of her daughter, Phyllis Terrell Langston), has been the devoted caretaker of her former home, papers, and legacy. The family shared the papers they still held in their collection, including love letters between Mollie Church and Robert H. Terrell, which greatly enrich our understanding of this remarkable woman, her courtship, and the Terrells' marriage (the Langstons have since generously donated their papers to the Oberlin College Archives). Access to her family's collection has helped me tell a new, more complete history of Mollie Church Terrell.

Unceasing Militant presents a sustained analysis of the connections between Terrell's long public career as a civil rights activist and her private experiences. Exploring her family history, intimate relationships, illnesses, finances, and other personal concerns deepens our understanding of her as an individual and amplifies her ideas—her antiracism, feminism, and militancy. Insisting upon African American women's full humanity and equality, Terrell's feminism and suffrage activism were based on her understanding that race and gender are inseparable factors in black women's lives and oppression. Linking her public, activist career to her private life reveals Terrell not only as a prominent clubwoman, educator, and civil rights advocate but also as a daughter, wife, mother, and lover.[5]

This biography of Mollie Church Terrell connects the broader study of the black freedom struggle and the movement for women's equality with an analysis of how movements shape and are shaped by the experiences of individuals within them. It demonstrates how race, gender, intimacy, economics, and illness intersected in one black woman's life. Activism in the civil rights struggle took a serious toll on African American women movement leaders like Terrell, who worked under the oppressive systems of racism and sexism. Exploring the turbulent private experiences of Terrell's life provides a more complete account of her public role and shows her activism as rooted in the ongoing conjunction of experience, determination, and resilience, the outgrowth of circumstance and the development of purpose.

1

The Roots of Activism

Mary "Mollie" Eliza Church Terrell, born in Memphis, Tennessee, on September 23, 1863, had a childhood defined by love and nurturing but also by discrimination and violence. Racism and the precarity fostered by systematic marginalization shaped Mollie's understanding of herself and her world and made her determined to assert her own value as a human being through activism. Her parents, Louisa Ayres and Robert Reed Church, were the children of their white slaveholders and enslaved women, and neither was freed until the end of the Civil War. Remarkably, both became thriving business owners in the Reconstruction era, which gave Mollie an optimistic sense of what African Americans could achieve in spite of terrible odds. This chapter provides a fuller picture of Mollie Church's family history, which has not been clearly established until now.[1]

"My Grandfather Bought Your Grandmother"

When he was an adult, at the turn of the twentieth century, Mollie's father learned much of his family history from letters he received from his white former enslavers that offered their own self-serving versions of the past. Family lore of his white enslavers held that Robert Church's grandmother Lucy, a seamstress and caregiver to her master's children, had regaled them with stories about being a "Malay princess." Her owners found this plausible since she was "a bright red with very long straight black haired young girl" who, to them, did not look African.[2] They described her as a beautiful French-speaking girl brought to the United States between 1805 and 1810 on a slave ship from the French colony of Saint-Domingue. One letter to Robert recounted how his grandmother had been sold to a rich tobacco merchant after a fierce bidding war. She had "attracted a great deal of attention by her beauty and the jewelry she wore, and consequently brought a *fancy price*." Slaveholding men's interest in an enslaved woman's beauty was not a compliment. Being a "fancy girl" typically meant that she was purchased to be sexually available to her white enslaver and for her reproductive capacity, against her free agency to choose. It condemned an enslaved girl or woman to the terror of regular sexual violence. Indeed, while enslaved on the tobacco merchant's plantation, Lucy gave birth to a biracial daughter, Emmeline (ca. 1820–1851).[3]

Lucy's second owner, a white Virginian, Dr. Patrick Phillip Burton (ca. 1786–1875), had participated in the first auction but finally managed to acquire her around 1825.[4] A white Burton descendant later wrote to Robert Church, explaining that Lucy's first owner, the "tobacco merchant at Norfolk failed." Subsequently, as he put it, "my grandfather bought your grandmother, Lucy, who at the time had a most beautiful young daughter that she named Emeline [*sic*]. This Emeline is your mother." He then casually revealed, "My Grandfather made my mother who was then his baby, a present of this girl Emeline for her maid." Emmeline was barely older than her young mistress. Robert Church knew that his mother's biological father had been a white man. Robert was so fair-skinned that he looked white; he pointedly described his enslaved mother as looking "as white as I am." Although clearly of mixed race, the "one drop" rule made them "black" and kept them enslaved until the end of the Civil War.[5]

In their letters, written long after the war and Reconstruction, the Burton family insisted to Robert Church that his grandmother and mother were their beautiful, prized slaves who "never did any menial work." Although it was true that they did no agricultural labor, they worked from very young ages as seamstresses, personal maids, and caretakers of the Burton children. Most heinously, the Burtons sold Lucy away from her child, Emmeline. A Burton descendant described this cruel separation of mother and daughter as a simple economic calculus: "In the changing scenes of commercial life, Grandfather became surety on a Treasury bond and was forced to send 100 negroes at one time from Virginia to Mississippi to be sold to pay this debt. Among the number was your grandmother Lucy. She was bought by a very rich planter near Natchez, Miss. named Sam Davis who gave her the same liberty of action our family had and she became the seamstress of the family. *Never in life was she treated as a slave.* This event separated your mother and grandmother."[6]

Without empathy or irony, the Burton relative could not see that this forced separation was a searing illustration of the Burtons' treatment of and control over Lucy and Emmeline as enslaved women. Robert Church shared this 1901 letter with his daughter, Mollie, by then a mother herself. She was haunted by this matter-of-fact recounting.[7] Mollie recognized this uprooting as representative of the devastating familial destruction experienced by all enslaved people sold away from families and friends. In her writings and speeches, she used this example from her own family's history to condemn white southerners for their hypocritical nostalgia for the days of slavery. She rejected their self-serving fictional descriptions of a world of whites and blacks living contentedly as one plantation "family," headed by an ostensibly benevolent white patriarch.[8]

After the death of his first wife in 1827, Dr. Burton remarried a wealthy woman and prospered on his vast Virginia plantations until he again faced financial problems in the mid-1830s. The downturn in his financial status led Burton to move his family and remaining enslaved people to Holly Springs, Mississippi. There, twenty-four-year-old Emmeline gave birth to Robert Reed Church on June 18, 1839. Robert's biological father was a white slaveholding friend of Dr. Burton, Captain Charles B. Church, also of Holly Springs, who owned a fleet of luxury steamboats that transported passengers, mail, and goods on the Mississippi River.[9]

Whenever any white man forced an enslaved woman to have sex, any resulting offspring belonged to her owner. Since these offspring increased the enslaver's wealth, owners sometimes forced the women they enslaved to submit to sex with their friends, thereby normalizing sexual assault. White men cemented their ties by "sharing" enslaved women. In a ritualization of rape culture, enslavers also often brought their sons to their slave quarters when the boys came of age, inviting them to choose any enslaved woman to have sex with. This rite of sexual initiation highlighted their white supremacy as well as a manhood imbued with violence. Dr. Burton gave Captain Church free and open access to the enslaved Emmeline.[10] The Burton family never acknowledged to Robert that they had sanctioned and participated in a system that allowed and encouraged the impregnation of both his grandmother and mother by white men.

Despite his white descendants' insistent characterizations of Dr. Burton as a benevolent patriarch, he was not a kind man. White contemporaries described him as "autocratic and self-assertive." He was infamous among his peers for his vile temper and propensity for violence. Burton frequently challenged men of his own social class to duels, physically assaulted an elderly white minister, and savagely beat a neighbor with his cane. He also accused another white man, Dr. Trent C. Aikin, of malpractice for an ostensible misdiagnosis of an enslaved woman on a local planation in Batesville, Arkansas, the town where the two doctors both lived in 1841. This malpractice dispute developed into a vicious blood feud, leading to the shocking murders of one of Dr. Burton's sons and of Dr. Aikin. Burton's violence is not an aberration. Violence was endemic to the very enterprise of enslavement, giving the lie to his family's descriptions of him as a benevolent man who never treated Robert or his family members "as a slave."[11]

After Robert Church's mother, Emmeline, died in 1851, Burton sold the

FIGURE 1.1. The white enslaver and riverboat captain Charles B. Church (May 15, 1812–August 4, 1879) was the father of Robert Reed Church. Fearing a possible lawsuit by the white Church family, the Ransdell Corporation publishers asked Mollie in 1940 to cut her mention of Church as her grandfather from her memoir. Mollie's solution was to emphasize the striking physical resemblance between the two men, mentioning their almost identical photographs dressed in full regalia as Knights Templar Masons. (Courtesy University of Memphis Special Collections)

twelve-year-old Robert to the child's biological father, Captain Church. From then on, Robert no longer lived on a plantation. Captain Church resided in Memphis with his wife, Mary, and their two children; however, he chose not to bring Robert, who looked like him, into their home. He kept Robert out of his wife's sight by putting him to work in a series of unpaid menial jobs, including dish washer and knife shiner, on his steamboats on the Mississippi River, though the boy was allowed to earn tips. When he became an older teenager, Robert gained more responsible positions, such as steward. In 1891, Dr. Burton's daughter offered to Robert her justification of how and why he was sold. Captain Church had "promised [Emmeline] . . . he would buy you and emancipate you and put you in school in Cincinnati." But Robert's father/owner never followed through on his promise to the dying Emmeline, who hoped against hope that her son would become a free and literate young man. Like Burton, Church was not the great paternalist slave owner he imagined himself to be—an inherently problematic and self-serving idea. Tellingly, in the 1850s, Church enslaved ten individuals, and three of them (ages two, twenty-two, and twenty-eight) died under his "care."[12]

Just after the Civil War, Robert Church was unclear about who had owned his mother when he was a young boy. He believed that both he and his mother had been enslaved by his father, Captain Church. At that point, he does not appear to have realized that the Burton family had owned him and his mother before 1851. Robert did know that after his mother died, he had lived with and worked directly for his father/master and had obtained some privileges not usually extended to enslaved people. He had more freedom of movement than most other bondspeople, not only because of the captain's permission but also because he was so light-skinned that he easily passed for white.[13]

Whereas Mollie later took pride in the fact that her formerly enslaved mother and father achieved so much after the Civil War, other Church family members coped differently with the painful history of enslavement and oppression. Robert Church's daughter from his third marriage, Annette Church, wrote a book with his granddaughter Roberta Church, in which they tried to distance their family patriarch from the shame they associated with having been enslaved. They wrongly suggested that after his mother's death, at least, Robert was free and working voluntarily on the steamboats with his white father.[14]

Before the Civil War, in 1857, an eighteen-year-old and still-enslaved Robert R. Church married Margaret Pico in an informal ceremony. No legal marriage was possible for an enslaved couple. The two had met due to the riverboat's runs between Memphis and New Orleans, when Captain Church visited his friends the Picos, regularly docking his boat there for a short time before returning to Memphis. A later court document noted that the wedding took place "according to the custom of slave marriages, and with the consent of his [Robert's] master, as well as the consent of the master of Margaret Pico." Residing in different states, the Church couple never lived together but did have a daughter, Laura.[15]

After the start of the Civil War, the Confederacy seized Captain Church's boats and crews to use as troop transports and to send goods between Memphis and New Orleans. Because their route remained unchanged, Robert might periodically have seen his wife and daughter. But the first Battle of Memphis on June 6, 1862, effectively ended their marriage. Captain Church's boat was raided and captured by Union forces. Robert legally remained enslaved by his father, as later records attest: "Soon after the birth of Laura, Capt. Church ceased to run the river, and Robert Church was retained permanently by him in Memphis, thereby entirely separating him from his slave wife, which by the custom and laws of the times produced a divorce."[16]

To escape from arrest or capture by federal troops, Robert jumped ship during the 1862 battle. Some have characterized this moment as Robert Church's successful escape from slavery. The reality appears murkier. Even after the Confederacy lost the Battle of Memphis, enslaved individuals in the city were not free. Robert does not appear in Memphis directories until 1865, suggesting that he gained his freedom at the end of the war.[17]

Under the federal occupation of the city, Robert Church could have been classified as a fugitive slave, if he had tried to claim his freedom. Some enslaved individuals freed themselves by enlisting in the Union Army. Others escaped to contraband camps, where they hoped to be protected by federal troops. Still others who ran away were caught and returned to those enslavers who claimed to be loyalists or Union sympathizers. Among these were Charles Church and Treadwell Smith ("T. S.") Ayres. Both men made their claims of loyalty after the Battle of Memphis, when it became convenient to do so. The Emancipation Proclamation of January 1, 1863, did not apply to enslaved people in Memphis because the federal government agreed to consider the war over in Tennessee and thus to return the state to loyal union status. The proclamation applied only to states in rebellion, so Tennessee whites could keep their slaves, although many found their authority undermined as enslaved people emancipated themselves.[18]

"I Did Not Have to Go through Life as a Slave"

Once Robert Church's time on the Mississippi River ended, he apparently viewed his marriage to Margaret as over. About twenty-three years old, he courted a young Memphian he had known and admired for years, the beautiful and talented eighteen-year-old Louisa Ayres, the enslaved daughter of the

FIGURE 1.2. (*Left*) Robert Reed Church (June 18, 1839–August 29, 1912) as a dapper young man in his early thirties. This young saloon owner aspired to expand his business and move into purchasing and developing real estate and did so in the coming years. The cartes de visite of Robert and figure 1.3 of Louisa Ayres Church were taken between 1872 and 1874 when the prestigious Bingham photo studio in Memphis was called Bingham & Craver Studio. (Courtesy University of Memphis Special Collections)

FIGURE 1.3. (*Right*) Louisa Ayres Church (1844–August 27, 1911) in her late twenties, wearing an elegant, beautifully designed dress with sumptuous fabric and fashionable details. Her lace collar and jewelry further mark her good taste and elite status as a prosperous Memphis hair shop owner. (Courtesy University of Memphis Special Collections)

white Memphis attorney T. S. Ayres. Robert and Louisa wed in December 1862. Robert's first wife, Margaret Pico Church, also remarried before the end of the Civil War.[19]

During the Civil War, Robert Church and his good friend Henry Ayres were both enslaved "body servants" for their white masters in Memphis. Robert frequently visited Henry at the Ayres household and had known his sister, Louisa, before the war. T. S. Ayres also had a white daughter, Laura Ayres Parker, who was Louisa's half sister/mistress. Laura later described Louisa as "my maid and daily and hourly companion" who was also "a belle among her set, on account of her superior attainments," referring to her ability to speak

French and to style hair and wigs into elegant fashions, among other things. Laura recalled that Robert and Louisa had long been known as sweethearts, "For years before they were married . . . everybody knew they would be married at the proper time." Laura was unaware that Robert had already married Margaret Pico in New Orleans, but Charles Church had witnessed it and had probably informed his friend T. S. Ayres. As the young couple's courtship intensified during the Civil War, we do not know if Louisa knew of Robert's earlier marriage or that he already had a young daughter.[20]

Louisa Ayres and Robert Church married in December 1862 before a gathering of white and black guests in the Ayres's back parlor. Although Mollie had heard some of the details of the wedding from her mother, she later learned more from Laura Ayres Parker: "Captain Church and his wife and family were all present for Bob (your father) had been his faithful body servant, as they called them in that day." T. S. Ayres and Captain Church stood as the two witnesses to their enslaved children's marriage. Ayres had given Laura money for Louisa's "wedding dress, of white silk, made at my own dress makers. . . . We were exactly the same figure and the dress was fitted on me." Another gift, bedroom furnishings, came from Louisa's enslaved brother, Henry, "in consideration of the love and affection which he has for his sister."[21]

Within the inherently repressive system of enslavement, Mollie's parents experienced rare advantages because of their white fathers' interest in them. Mollie explained, "When I questioned her [her mother, Louisa] about it, she would usually say that her master had not only taught her to read and write but had also given her lessons in French." In fact, it was her half sister/mistress, Laura, who had taught Louisa. Louisa and her brother, Henry Ayres (who may have been the son of T. S. Ayres), were exceptional in that they had access to material property of some value. In 1866, the county registrar recorded an indenture, or a quit claim deed, originally made on December 1, 1862, by which Henry Ayres gave his sister, Louisa, "2 rocking chairs, 2 bedsteads, mattress, pillows, and bed clothing, 1 bureau, 1 wardrobe, 1 wash stand, 1 bowl and pitcher, 2 three ply carpets . . . 1 marble top table and 1 set of Bohemian glass." This deed initially seems to suggest that Henry and Louisa Ayres were free in 1862. Otherwise, they could not have given or inherited property, but it was recorded in 1866 and may reflect an informal gift given to Louisa that was formalized after the war ended. A later court record points toward their enslavement, describing Louisa Ayres and Robert Church's marriage as being between an enslaved couple witnessed by their masters. The Church couple lived in Louisa's bedroom in the Ayres home until Mollie was born, while Louisa worked as the nursemaid of Laura's baby. Thus far, we have no definitive proof, such as emancipation papers, to confirm whether Louisa and Robert were free or enslaved during the Civil War. Their status was likely a fluid and contradictory mix of free and unfree.[22]

Laura Ayres Parker's information was neither fully accurate nor sensitive to views beyond those of her own white family. In 1913, Mollie Church Terrell had written Parker after the death of her father, Robert Church, when his first daughter, Laura Church Napier, contested his will. Responding to Mollie's question about whether she had known anything about Robert's marriage to Margaret Pico or his first daughter, Parker replied, "Capt. Church would not have allowed a second marriage to have taken place if he had known of another or a previous one. It is absurd and unreasonable." Captain Church served as a witness at both weddings, so this is not accurate.[23]

Reflecting the nostalgic affection white families often had for those they had enslaved, Laura Ayres Parker insisted upon her closeness to Mollie's grandmother Eliza and to her mother, Louisa: "Your grandmother, 'Mammy Eliza,' your mother's own mother, had been raised in our family and nursed my mother's two children and we were all devotedly attached to her. . . . She was present when my first child was born and would almost have given her life for . . . my brother and myself and my own son." In her writings and speeches, Mollie rejected her grandmother's supposed willingness to "almost" die for her white charges. It was a classic claim of white enslavers to suggest that they knew their bondspeople well, in a relationship of mutual devotion. Parker incorrectly asserted: "There is not the faintest possibility of there being any other marriage previous to the one to your mother." She also informed Mollie, "I am sure you were born about a year after your father and mother's marriage. . . . I know you were born after my Charlie McCormick, for your mother continued to nurse him and trundle him around in his carriage before her own marriage. Charlie was born in March 1861. You must have been born in the fall of 63 I believe, for Mammy Eliza went to New York with us during the summer season when Charlie was toddling around in short dresses and Pa sent her back to Memphis to be with your mother to take care of her and be with her at the time of your birth." Parker was right, for Mollie was born on September 23, 1863.[24]

Louisa Ayres Church's life was less carefree than her white owners remembered. In fact, a pregnant Louisa had tried to kill herself a few months before giving birth to Mollie. Her daughter recounted: "By a miracle she was saved, and I finally arrived on scheduled time none the worse for the prenatal experience which might have proved decidedly disagreeable, if not fatal, to my future." Mollie left no clues about the context or cause of her mother's desperation and mentioned it only one other time, in unpublished notes that listed her own self-perceived flaws: "Faults—procrastination. Easily hurt. Magnify little things. Worry. My mother attempted to commit suicide while pregnant . . .

indifference to my own interests. Wouldn't write an account of myself." Mollie associated her mother's suicide attempt to her own lifelong struggles with depression. To her, writing her memoir was an act of self-affirmation. Louisa's attempted suicide was connected to Mollie's sense of urgency to create a life full of meaning—a life worthy of an autobiography.[25]

Getting married did not immediately change Louisa's status as an enslaved servant in the Ayres family home. Parker recalled that "Louise and Bob remained at our house, (for Lou had her own room), until after you were born, when they removed to a little white frame cottage just in the rear of our house on Madison Street." These facts all suggest that Mollie was legally born enslaved. She later reflected, "The fates were kind to me in one particular at least. I was born at a time when I did not have to go through life as a slave." Speaking to the editor of the *Washington Evening Star*, Mollie noted, "I would have been a slave ... if slavery had not been abolished." She was referring to the end of the Civil War in 1865 rather than the Emancipation Proclamation, which did not cover Memphis.[26]

Whereas Parker's memories were all about the devotion of her former slaves, Mollie's maternal grandmother Eliza provided a firsthand perspective of slavery's miseries.

> Grandmother told me tales of brutality perpetrated upon slaves who belonged to cruel masters. But they affected her and me so deeply she was rarely able to finish what she began. I tried to keep the tears back and the sobs suppressed, so that Grandmother would carry the story to the bitter end, but I seldom succeeded. Then she would stop abruptly and refuse to go on. . . . It nearly killed me to think that my dear grandmother, whom I loved so devotedly, had once been a slave. . . . "Never mind, honey," she used to say to comfort me, "Gramma ain't a slave no more."

Although her white grandfathers had offered her parents some protections, more so than most enslaved people, Mollie knew both her parents had been conceived via coercion and that neither father had emancipated his enslaved child.[27]

Grandmother Eliza, an expert healer who doctored blacks and whites alike, told Mollie stories highlighting the vulnerability of enslaved women to violence and sexual assault at the hands of white men: "One day she went into the field on an errand and the overseer challenged her about something. She resented what he said and he threatened to whip her. 'I dared him to tech me,' she said. 'Then he started toward me raising his whip. I took out and run jes' as fast as ever I could and he right after me. When I got to the kitchen door I picked up a chair and said, ef you come a step nearer, I'll knock your brains out with this here chair. An' he never come a step nearer, neither.'"[28]

Yet, like the enslaved women on Mollie's father's side, Eliza was later unable to thwart a white man's lustful advances; her owner, T. S. Ayres, forced himself on Eliza. Mollie described her maternal grandmother as "very dark brown, almost black," but she gave birth to a fair-skinned daughter, Louisa Ayres, whose complexion revealed her father's race. In her mother's and grandmothers' lives, Mollie saw dramatic examples of the power imbalances and cruelties of the system of enslavement and how women were at the mercy of their masters and other white men. In speeches to white audiences, Mollie condemned white men for raping and assaulting vulnerable black women under their control. She also vehemently condemned white women for not seeing themselves in solidarity with enslaved black women and offering protection. In a gesture of affirmation, Louisa Ayres gave her daughter, Mollie, her own mother's name, Eliza, as her middle name.[29]

When slavery was abolished throughout the nation at the end of the Civil War, Louisa and Robert Church and their toddler daughter, Mollie, were free people. The Thirteenth Amendment was ratified on December 18, 1865. Robert and Louisa continued to live together in Memphis after the war ended while raising Mollie and her younger brother, Thomas Ayres Church (b. 1867). Because the couple lived together, their marriage was recognized as legally valid by the state of Tennessee. In contrast, the earlier marriage between Robert Church and Margaret Pico took place between enslaved people from different states and never involved any cohabitation. It was thus considered null and void by Tennessee courts after the Civil War.[30]

Soon after the war ended, T. S. Ayres helped his formerly enslaved daughter, Louisa, set up a hair store that sold human hair extensions and wigs to upper-class white women. Louisa's store was located at a prime location on Court Square, the most elite section of downtown Memphis. Her white Ayres relatives lived and worked nearby.[31] Upending traditional gender expectations, it was Louisa Ayres Church who brought her family into real financial stability. Mollie explained that her mother "was considered an artist, and her reputation as a hairdresser spread far and wide. . . . To her husband Mother was a helpmeet indeed, for it was she who bought the first home and the first carriage we had." Mollie described her mother as "the most generous human being. . . . But, alas, she had less conception of the value of money or the necessity of saving it than anybody I have ever known. She lavished money on my brother and myself." Mollie's perennial concerns about whether she had enough money and whether she was managing her money well seem to have been a response to the anxiety and instability engendered by her mother's spendthrift ways.[32]

Like his wife, Robert Church strove to be a successful entrepreneur but had a rockier start. He used connections with prominent white men he had met on his father's luxury steamboats to obtain loans to open a saloon and billiard hall in Memphis. In mid-April 1865, immediately after the war's end, he applied for a billiard license, but a county bureaucrat denied him one on the grounds of his race. Church defiantly set up shop anyway, but by summer 1865, police arrested him for operating without a license. They brought the charges under the local black codes, one of a set of laws that had been instituted throughout the South to curb the rights of the newly freed. Church's case went to trial just days after Congress passed the federal Civil Rights Bill of 1866, which over-turned the codes, and he won his case, *Church v. State of Tennessee* (1866), in a historic decision.[33]

As a business entrepreneur who had successfully defied the local regula-tions meant to constrain African Americans, Robert Church personified the threat to white supremacy that emancipation and Reconstruction represented. That made him a target for white violence. On May 1, 1866, just days after the court decision, the Memphis Massacre began as tensions over Reconstruction increased and as conflicts between white police officers and African Ameri-can veterans of the Union Army turned violent. The mainly Irish police force spearheaded the Memphis riot. Whites killed forty-six black citizens, raped at least five black women, and burned many African Americans' churches and schools to the ground. Louisa and Mollie huddled inside their home during the riot, but Robert ventured out to protect his saloon. He was shot by rioting police officers, as Mollie recounted, "in the back of his head at his place of busi-ness and left there for dead. He had been warned by friends that he was one of the colored men to be shot. They and my mother begged him not to leave his home that day. But he went to work as usual in spite of the peril he knew he faced. He would undoubtedly have been shot to death if the rioters had not believed they had finished him when he fell to the ground."[34] Although he had a bullet lodged in his head, Church survived.

After the massacre, Robert Church took another great risk by joining other Memphis African Americans in testifying before a congressional committee investigating the massacre. The riot had started on May 1, and the testimony of 170 witnesses was published by Congress only weeks later, on July 25, 1866. All Memphians would have known the contents of Church's testimony. Some of his testimony was incontrovertible. Black men did not have the right to vote until July 1866, when Tennessee ratified the Fourteenth Amendment, so when the committee asked Church, "Are you a registered voter?" his reply was neces-sarily, "No, sir." Church provided a vivid account of the rioting: "On the first of May [Tuesday], between five and six o'clock, as I was standing in front of my house, with fifteen or twenty other persons, some policemen came along with pistols in their hands . . . an old colored man was knocked down, and he was beaten badly." In addition to the first day of violence, he testified, "On Wednesday evening [May 2], about nine o'clock, a [white] crowd came by me, when they got hold of a colored man and beat him unmercifully; they ordered me to shut up my house; they fired at me and struck me in the neck; another ball glanced past me, and another ball struck me; in all they shot twelve to fifteen shots at me." Although wounded, Church managed to make it the few blocks to his business, but the white mob "broke into the saloon, drank all the whiskey, broke open the money drawers; they took out two hundred and forty dollars in big bills and about fifty dollars in small change, making two hundred and ninety dollars in all." This was over $4,600 in today's terms, a huge amount of money for a formerly enslaved man to have access to just a year after the end of the war, highlighting working-class white resentments against prosperous freedpeople in their community.[35]

The committee asked Robert Church to identify those who had shot him. He put his life on the line again by openly identifying a white officer: "One of the policemen who shot at me was Dave Roach. . . . He is [still] lounging about the streets. . . . Most of them were policemen that came into my place. The men that committed the robbery were all policemen." Before the massacre, Roach was already notorious for arresting anyone engaged in interracial socializing and charging them with disorderly conduct. Roach publicly expressed his fears that the end of the war and the rise of the Republican Party were going to lead to miscegenation.[36]

Members of the congressional committee also asked Robert Church directly about his race and status as a formerly enslaved person: "How much of a colored man are you?" He replied, "I do not know—very little; my father is a white man; my mother is as white as I am. Captain Church is my father. . . . My father owned my mother [Robert was unaware that, in fact, Dr. Burton was Emmeline's enslaver]." Asked directly, "Were you a slave?" Church replied, "Yes, sir; but my father always gave me everything I wanted, although he does not openly recognize me." No longer willing to go along with the charade that identified him only as Church's former slave, Robert publicly identified him as his father in sworn testimony that was subsequently published by Congress.[37]

In spite of tensions over public recognition of the nature of their relationship, Robert R. Church and Charles B. Church were close; the son regularly visited his father after the war. On Sundays, Robert brought his young daughter, Mollie, with him to visit her grandfather at his elegant home. Captain Church died in August 1879, when Mollie was fifteen years old. Just as he had not emancipated Robert during the antebellum era, so Charles Church did not make him an heir or mention him in his will.[38]

After the Memphis Massacre, Robert Church had to rebuild his severely injured body, business, and temperament. The couple began to have marital difficulties. Louisa could provide for the family, but she was unable to heal her husband, who was a changed man. The bullet lodged in his head made him desperately moody. Mollie learned firsthand the dangers of virulent racism, describing her father as having "the most violent temper of any human being with whom I have come in contact. In a fit of anger, he seemed completely to lose control of himself, and he might have done anything desperate in a rage." His wife and children feared his newly fierce disposition. Robert suffered from severe migraine headaches for the rest of his life. Mollie recalled: "Sometimes the pain was so great he threatened to take his life." From that point forward, her father regularly used opium and morphine to help him function. Remarkably, despite the persistent pain, he thrived, amassing a fortune through shrewd property purchases and making important political connections in Memphis that cemented his status as a leader in the black community and in Tennessee's Republican Party.[39]

Even after it was recast by the radical Republicans in 1867, Reconstruction carried dangers for black Americans. Robert Church knew this too well and decided to carry a gun for self-protection. Mollie remembered at least two incidents when her father brandished it in front of her. In one, a white conductor called her a "little nigger" and tried to force young Mollie into a train car for African Americans until her father menaced him with the gun. This show of determination, along with Robert's white complexion, enabled Mollie to remain in her seat. She did not understand what she had done wrong, reporting to her mother that she was well dressed and behaving appropriately. She never forgot this first of many times she was treated harshly by train conductors. Thinking back to the tears in her mother's eyes as she tried to offer comfort, Mollie reflected, "Seeing their children touched and seared and wounded by race prejudice is one of the heaviest crosses which colored women have to bear." In another incident, Mollie recalled her father flaunting his family's prosperity, thereby defying white Memphians' jealousies and resentment. He chose to ride his "beautiful sleigh" down the streets of Memphis during a rare winter snowstorm. When a crowd of white men threw snowballs with large rocks in them at him, Robert shot into the crowd. Mollie noted with amazement, "It is a great wonder he was not torn limb from limb, even though he was shooting in self-defense." Her personal experiences with racism and discrimination inspired her later work as a civil rights activist.[40]

Robert Church continued to suffer from white violence during Reconstruction. Not long after the Memphis Massacre, in 1867, a police officer harassing African Americans on the sidewalk near Church's saloon grabbed him. In self-defense, Church fired a warning shot. The officer hit him hard on the head with his pistol, likely worsening his migraines. The officer was not disciplined. Instead, Church was charged with firing his gun but was acquitted. Perhaps

FIGURE 1.4. Mollie Church, about five years old, wears a spotless white dress with a bonnet and bows in her hair. This outfit is similar to what she described wearing when she was accosted by the train conductor who tried to force her into a Jim Crow car. A distressed and mystified Mollie promised her mother that her outfit had been neat and clean and that she had been sitting quietly in her seat. (Courtesy Langston Family)

because of the 1866 police attack on him, the jurors concluded that Church would reasonably have seen the police officer as a threat to his safety.[41]

Robert Church's political and personal militancy, including his blunt congressional testimony, earned him enemies. Over the following decade, Memphis whites made sure to mention his testimony whenever they complained about him and his saloon. After a shooting outside of Church's bar, "the secessionist *Ledger*" derogatorily identified him as "one of the swift witnesses of the Congressional Committee on the Memphis Riots" and described his saloon as "frequented by a crowd of negro loafers . . . all of whom are Radicals of the deepest die." The latter was not entirely untrue; Robert Church did in fact invite the radical Republican county commissioner, a black barkeeper named Ed Shaw, to hold political meetings in his saloon.[42]

Over a decade after the Memphis Massacre, in 1878, Robert Church was again injured by a gunshot to his head, this time while trying to protect a black woman from harassment by a violent white sheriff. The *Memphis Commercial Appeal* reported that the Beale Street "neighborhood was electrified by the news that Church had been shot by Sheriff Furbush of Lee County" and that "Mr. Church was shot in the head and neck but may recover."[43] But the media response and legal outcome both changed from a decade earlier. Robert Church had moved beyond owning just one saloon. He had become a substantial property owner and developer of what became the famous Beale Street, the home of the blues. Only the sheriff was arrested and taken to the stationhouse. As one reporter saw it, Church was now "an influential and prosperous member of his race in this city." His altered financial status clearly changed his reputation. Church had invested in Memphis real estate when prices plummeted dramatically during the yellow fever epidemic of 1878, building the neighborhood around Beale Street into the core of what became his real estate empire. He owned saloons and brothels housing white prostitutes; Mollie was unaware until much later in life that her father had owned houses of prostitution.[44]

Church's increasing wealth, ties to prominent whites, and strategic charitable donations all offered him greater protection, an important consideration as Reconstruction ended and the period that southern whites referred to as the Redemption began. Still trying to manage his hair-trigger temper, Robert Church attempted to change his negative press coverage, publicizing his business ties with prominent white men such as the popular Confederate John Overton Jr., who owned the building Church was leasing. It worked— the press backed off, not wanting to disturb the former rebel, whose father was considered a major booster and developer of Memphis. To emphasize his goodwill and ties to white city founders, Church carefully planned his financial donations, helping rebuild the city of Memphis after the yellow fever epidemics. In a calculated attempt to shelter himself and his increasingly prosperous saloons, gambling halls, and houses of prostitution, he gained white friends by publicly donating substantial sums of money to associations for white Confederate veterans and otherwise unlikely causes. Yet despite his ties to whites, including former Confederates, all presumably Democrats, Church remained true to the party that had passed the Reconstruction Amendments.

During Reconstruction, Robert Church had become an important Republican powerbroker in Memphis, for "it was through his efforts and courage that the separate street car system was abolished in Memphis." Church also "played a major role in negotiations with the Memphis Board of Education to hire Colored teachers in the City school system" after the Civil War. The end of Reconstruction reversed his civil rights successes; state-level segregation laws were enacted in 1881. But even after most black voters in Memphis were disfranchised in 1889, Robert Church became "a delegate to the 1900 Republican Party Convention." Furthermore, his "properties became the nucleus of a neighborhood offering black Memphians public space and relative freedom."[45]

Rewarded for his work on the GOP's behalf, in 1900, Robert Church was elected as a delegate to the Republican National Convention, where he was among those who nominated Theodore Roosevelt for president. Mollie's husband wrote his father-in-law: "I heartily congratulate you. . . . It is a very high compliment to receive an election. . . . I hope I shall be able to run over to Philadelphia the day on which the vote is taken and see you rise in all your dignity and majesty and vote for your man."[46]

Mollie shared her father's political loyalties. Just after the 1888 presidential election, she wrote to her father while she was studying abroad in Lausanne, Switzerland: "You were guided by your guardian angel when you put your confidence in Harrison it appears, for from the papers I can see that he has been elected without a shadow of a doubt." Trying to follow American politics from afar, she hazarded her own observation: "It remains to be seen what schemes for the better or the worse he and Blaine will hatch up. Blaine is really president, after all, I believe. Perhaps I am mistaken. Are any gentlemen of color elected to congress? I presume not."[47]

"I Lift Up My Heart in Gratitude to My Dear Mother"

The long-held assumption has been that Robert Church "divorced from Louisa Ayres (later Martell) and upon their divorce in 1867 the children, Mary Eliza Church and Thomas Ayres Church, lived with their mother." This is an inaccurate timeline. The couple more likely separated in 1870, when Mollie lived briefly with her mother before being sent north for her education the following year. Louisa dared to flout social convention among middle-class blacks and whites by formally filing for divorce in 1874, "alleging harsh and cruel treatment and inconsistency." Mollie knew that her father's volatile temper was the cause of her parents' separation. She empathized with her injured father but also with her mother, for she was aware, even as a young girl, that her mother suffered from his rages yet would be perceived as having failed to keep him happy. (The 1870 census lists Louisa and Robert Church as still living together as husband and wife, although they might have been separated and unwilling to identify as such to the census enumerator. Robert is listed as the head of household, but his occupation was left blank—he was just months away from opening a new saloon and billiard hall—whereas Louisa was identified as a hairdresser. It listed Mollie, age six, and other Church relatives living in the home but neglected to list their son, Thomas, who had been born in 1867.)[48]

After the divorce, Mollie and her little brother lived with their mother. Outside the South, judges had begun following the "tender years" doctrine by the 1870s, which granted mothers custody of children younger than six or seven. That would have put Thomas, then about three, in his mother's care. In the South, however, judges often continued to follow the common law tradition of granting custody to fathers. Mollie explained in her memoir:

> My mother and father separated when I was quite young. This pained and embarrassed me very much. In those days, divorces were not so common as they are now, and no matter what caused the separation of a couple, the woman was usually blamed. The court gave my brother, who was four years my junior, and myself into the custody of my mother. My little brother had been living with my father, and Father wanted to keep him, but the court refused to grant his request. I remember very distinctly the day the "hack" drove up to Mother's house on Court Street, a block below her hair store, and deposited my little brother, bag and baggage on the sidewalk in front of our home. My joy knew no bounds.

Robert's public violence, the fact that he ran a saloon, and Louisa's testimony of problems with his temper at home probably played a role in the court's decision. Mollie and Thomas were very close, seeing each other as best friends and allies in their unstable family. If this happened in 1874, when the papers announced the Church divorce and the courts presumably weighed in, Thomas would have been seven and Mollie would already have been living away, with only holiday visits.[49]

Louisa Ayres Church's business selling hairpieces to fashionable white women boomed in the 1870s. She had enlarged her store and regularly advertised in the papers. In 1876, her advertisement appeared frequently in the *Public Ledger* as the Mardi Gras season approached: "Lou Church at 86 Monroe Street, begs leave to inform her numerous patrons that she is prepared to rent wigs and dress hair in latest styles for the approaching Mardi Gras Carnival. Prices reduced to suit the times." Two years later, in February 1878, while running the same ad, she was targeted for doing business without a license. Perhaps she saw this harassment as a sign that she should make a change, or perhaps Louisa wished to lead a life independent of the power and influence of her increasingly wealthy and prominent ex-husband. By March, she had left Memphis for good. Mollie noted, "Mother finally sold her store in Memphis and moved to New York City, where she established another on Sixth Avenue which she managed with brilliant success."[50]

Just before Mollie's eighth birthday, in the fall of 1871, her parents sent her away to be educated in the North. Their daughter was an exceptionally smart child and a quick learner, and Memphis offered only a single inadequate school for black children. Louisa made the final decisions about where Mollie would go. Initially, she was the primary funder of her daughter's education, using proceeds from her hair shop. To give her daughter the best education possible, Louisa chose the Model School affiliated with Antioch College (developed by the educator Horace Mann) in Yellow Springs, Ohio. For the rest of her youth, Mollie never lived full time with any member of her family. She loved both parents deeply and found their separation and divorce difficult. Her sense of the fragility of family connections deepened when Louisa sent her to Yellow Springs. Although not unscathed, Mollie was a resilient and often joyful child who generally rebounded from the separation.[51]

Friends who had given Louisa excellent recommendations about the school also identified an ideal family to board her daughter for her four years in Yellow Springs. Mollie lived with one of the three middle-class black families in town, a couple she called "Ma" and "Pa" Hunster and their four nearly grown children, with whom she developed a close bond. "Ma" Hunster ran a hotel (the Union House Hotel) and candy store in their big house. Louisa had made a good decision: "Fate surely smiled upon me when she influenced my mother to send me to . . . a school for children connected with Antioch College. . . . When I contrast what my educational foundation would have been if I had remained in Memphis and been sent to the school for colored children, poorly equipped as those schools were then, with what it was in this model school, I lift up my heart in gratitude to my dear mother for her foresight and for the sacrifice she made in my behalf."[52] Mollie's father furnished her rooms beautifully and gave her a generous allowance of $5 a month, so she was able to buy all the sweets she desired. Mollie appreciated her "Ambitious Mother," who paid an Antioch College student to tutor her in German. Louisa had learned some French in her youth from her mistress and half sister, Laura Ayres, and "believed that children should learn at least two foreign languages."[53]

Although Mollie enjoyed her schooling and had many friends among the white students, she was not immune to racist barbs. Once, her white classmates denied that she could be both black and pretty. Mollie could not shake the memory of their taunting: "I could hear the voice of ridicule crying out, 'Your face is pretty black.'" Such experiences led her to develop strong empathy for others treated badly on the basis of race: "Whenever a Chinaman passed by and children, black as well as white, sang out derisively, 'Ching, Ching Chinaman, do you eat rats?' I invariably reminded the colored children that just as they made fun of Chinese people, many people made fun of us."[54]

Mollie began to fight for her beliefs. She recognized that racial difference marked Chinese and African Americans as *others* in a predominantly white society. Choosing to confront white students about their prejudice led Mollie into playground fights: "I would run up to white children and declare with too much emphasis and feeling, perhaps, that I liked the Chinaman's pretty yellow complexion better than I did their pale, white one. Of course, there were always consequences of various kinds after such a speech, which were often decidedly unpleasant. But I made up my mind to stand them, whatever they were." Echoing her father's fearless determination to push back against discrimination, Mollie was unafraid of incurring the wrath of her white classmates, even if it meant being punished by a teacher or getting into a fight she might lose. At the same time, she tried to convince her black classmates that prejudice against others would only come back to hurt them.[55]

Being the target of racist taunts and remembering the terrors of slavery from her grandmother Eliza, Mollie vowed to prove through her own academic achievements that African Americans could overcome their history of slavery and subjection and be recognized as full citizens. She did so well academically that her parents, expecting she would one day attend Oberlin College, moved her from Yellow Springs to Oberlin, Ohio, in 1875, when she was twelve. Mollie attended Oberlin public school from the eighth grade through high school. In the spring of 1879, Louisa attended fifteen-year-old Mollie's high school graduation. Mollie later regretted that her parents did not attend her college graduation and remembered a time when she had to "go to Cleveland to see Father who wouldn't come to see me." Her sense of abandonment was counteracted to some degree by the fact that, as her father got wealthier, he paid for her higher education. Mollie was especially grateful that he made it possible for her to travel and study abroad in Europe for more than two years after she graduated in the late 1880s.[56]

In spite of studying diligently, Mollie enjoyed herself and her friends. As she described it, "While I studied hard at Oberlin College and availed myself of all the opportunities afforded, I did not deprive myself of any pleasure I could rightfully enjoy." She especially loved doing silly "pranks" and "dancing" with her white and black friends there. Her dear (white) friend of seventy-five years, Janet "Nettie" McKelvey Swift, told of first seeing Mollie during the social hour after dinner. Nettie was "attracted by pleasant voices and laughter . . . fascinated by the central figure. . . . She was evidently the admiration of her group of men and women students, whom she was entertaining in the inimitable way which throughout her life was the great gift of 'Mollie Church.'"[57]

Neither of Mollie's parents belonged to a dominant southern black denomination, such as Baptist or Methodist. Her mother was Catholic, and her father's mother had converted to Episcopalianism. Perhaps because she had not had time to absorb either religion, being only eight years old when she moved north alone to be educated, Mollie did not adopt the religion of either parent or of the evangelical South. Instead, she joined the First Congregational Church in Oberlin in 1879, when she was sixteen. Mollie's teenage choice to join a denomination that believed that Christians must try to improve the world they lived in grew from her liberal principles and desire for a like-minded community. Conscience and freedom could create social justice in the world.[58]

As a teenager, Mollie found herself troubled by sections of the Bible that seemed to stand in the way of Christianity as an engine of social change. An Oberlin College Bible course allowed her

> to ask questions about the passages in the Scriptures which troubled me. And no verse came nearer shaking my faith in the justice of God than that one which states, "I the Lord thy God am a jealous God, visiting the iniquity of the fathers upon the children unto the third and fourth generation of them that hate me, and showing mercy unto thousands of them that love me and keep my commandments." I could not understand why a just and loving father should make children suffer for the sins committed by their forefathers. The injustice of the law of heredity stunned me.

Mollie found it difficult to reconcile the Old Testament's forbidding God, punishing and punitive, with her cherished Christian principles of forgiveness and love. Mollie's faith was tied to her need to believe that her Lord was essentially just.[59]

A congregant's words to her at an Oberlin dormitory prayer meeting affected Mollie deeply: "For a long time I led the singing in a Sunday evening prayer meeting in Ladies Hall." Offering a modest public confession, she "stated that, although I tried to be a Christian, I sometimes did things which

I knew a good Christian should not do. 'For instance,' I said, 'I sometimes whisper in a class. . . . I fear also that I giggle and laugh too much and am not serious enough.' And then I expressed the hope that the Christians present would pray for me that I might change my giddy ways and become more quiet and sedate."[60]

After she spoke, "a tall, pale, very thin woman, heavily swathed in black, leaned forward from the back seat, fastened her sad eyes upon me . . . and said most impressively, 'Young woman, laugh and be merry while you can. . . . Some day when you grow older, when the cares and sorrows of life press hard upon you, you'll want to laugh and can't.'" This gloomy warning confused Mollie, but the words took on a deeper meaning a week later when "this woman committed suicide. . . . Both her husband and her young daughter had died . . . and she could not become reconciled to their loss. She had come to study in the college, hoping to divert her mind from grief, but she did not succeed." Mollie later reflected, "Many a time since that Sunday evening prayer meeting, I have tried to laugh when the sorrows and cares of life have pressed hard upon me and couldn't."[61]

While a college student in the early 1880s, Mollie applied for summer jobs in New York City, where her mother lived but, despite securing interviews, was turned down for every position. Whites admitted she was qualified but openly said that they would not hire her because she was black. This was, in her words, her "first bitter experience of inability to secure employment on account of my race."[62]

Determined to graduate from college with a Bachelor of Arts degree, Mollie took the classical four-year "gentlemen's course" at Oberlin rather than the two-year ladies' course. She was often the only woman at Oberlin, black or white, enrolled in fields of study considered exclusively for men. Her friends pointed out that Latin and Greek were hard and that it was unnecessary, if not positively unwomanly, for girls to study an "'old, dead language' anyhow. . . . Worst of all, it might ruin my chances of getting a husband, since men were notoriously shy of women who knew too much." Mollie wanted to marry and had to ignore the common belief that higher education damaged women and made them unmarriageable. She worried that the naysayers could be right, but she chose to take that risk and defy convention. Enjoying her gift for languages, she refused to restrict her studies on the basis of sex, just as she resisted racist proscriptions throughout her life. Mollie pointed out that the "world laughed at [female students] or scolded them according to its mood, then read the riot act to them and tried to deal a death blow to this new departure by warning young women that they would never be able to get a husband if they insisted upon taking a college course." Mollie happily noted, "Lo and behold, it was discovered that women who have studied the higher mathematics, philosophy and Greek, make affectionate wives, fond and devoted mothers, safe, sane and conservative cooks."[63]

"I Could Not Lead a Purposeless Existence"

When Mollie Church received her B.A. (1884) and M.A. (1888), she became one of only a few black women in the United States to have earned both bachelor's and master's degrees. Yet having obtained a first-rate education did not assuage her sense of having been abandoned by her parents. Their financial generosity could not erase her hurt that "neither one of my parents came to see me graduate from college." Her mother sent her a beautiful dress, but "while the gift was greatly appreciated, it did not compensate me for her absence on an occasion to which I had looked forward with such anticipation of pleasure for so many years."[64]

When Mollie graduated, her father announced that he expected her to return to Memphis to live with him. She complied. After she arrived, she learned that her father was planning to marry his third wife on January 1, 1885. Anna Wright Church (1856–1928) was only seven years older than Mollie and had "been a school teacher in Memphis for many years, performed brilliantly on the piano, was one of the most popular young women in the city, and was generally beloved." Mollie later explained that Anna's mother, Lucy Jane Wright, "and my mother had been intimate friends from my earliest recollection." Louisa had even hired Anna "one summer, when I was home on a vacation . . . to give me music lessons. I was well acquainted with her, therefore, and was very fond of her." At the time of the marriage, Anna was principal at a school for African American children. Mollie acknowledged, "If my own mother had been pained or provoked at my father's . . . marriage, perhaps I, too, might have been annoyed or aggrieved. But she had known Anna many years and had always liked her, so she felt my father had made a very wise choice indeed." In subsequent years, Louisa entertained her ex-husband and his new family at her home in New York City and visited with them once she moved to Mollie's home in Washington, D.C.[65]

In his handling of the new family structure, however, Robert Church was needlessly cruel. Shortly after his wedding, her father went to her bedroom, Mollie remembered, and "showed me his will, in which he had originally bequeathed all his property to my brother and myself. He then tore it up, saying as he did so, 'You know I'll have to change my will now.'" Mollie tried hard not to take it personally, insisting that "even then I did not feel the slightest resentment toward him or toward his wife. I felt that he had made his money

FIGURE 1.5. Mollie Church wore fashionable, tasteful
clothes and jewelry while at Oberlin College, shipped to
her by her mother from New York City, where Louisa had
relocated in 1879 and opened another successful hair shop.
(Courtesy Oberlin College Archives)

at the cost of much energy and many sacrifices and that he had a perfect right
to dispose of it as he pleased." But tearing up the will so dramatically suggests
that his struggle with intemperate behavior was not over.[66]

Mollie rejected her father's expectation that she would live a life of leisure
with him and his new wife until she married: "I made up my mind definitely
that, since he no longer needed me, it was wrong for me to remain idle there. I
could not be happy leading a purposeless existence." She wanted to put her college education to "good use," but her father refused to let her "engage actively
in any kind of work outside of the home." This view stemmed in part from his
concern that she would be taking the salary of a young woman who needed the
income to survive. But he also wanted to show off his wealth and play the role

of the generous patriarch, just as wealthy white men did for their daughters and wives: "Naturally, my father was the product of his environment. In the South for nearly three hundred years 'real ladies' did not work, and my father was thoroughly imbued with that idea. He wanted his daughter to be a 'lady.'" But Mollie maintained that she "had been reared among Yankees and . . . had imbibed the Yankee's respect for work." She stayed in Memphis for about six months after her father's wedding and then moved to New York, where she lived with her mother while applying for teaching positions. At twenty-two, she accepted a job at Wilberforce University in Ohio in the fall of 1885.[67]

Knowing her father "was unalterably opposed to my teaching anywhere," Mollie took a calculated risk by taking the position at Wilberforce. She did not tell him about her new appointment until after she had moved there. He responded with one very angry letter and then refused to communicate with her for the entire academic year: "For a few seconds after I read Father's letter . . . I was literally stunned with grief. . . . He reprimanded me severely for disregarding his wishes and disobeying his commands. His reproaches stung me to the quick." But, Mollie explained, "my conscience was clear and I knew I had done right to use my training in behalf of my race." Still, she did what she could "to appease his wrath," including writing to him regularly, even though she received no response, and sending presents to him and his new family.[68]

During the summer after her first year at Wilberforce, Mollie decided to return to Memphis uninvited. Before she got on the train, she sent her father a telegram letting him know when she would arrive. She pointed to the irony that as "some girls run away from home to marry the man of their choice and thus brook their father's displeasure, so I left home and ran the risk of permanently alienating my father from myself to engage in the work which his money had prepared me to do." His fury had ended: "There on the platform waiting to greet me was my dearly beloved father, who literally received me with open arms. So ended the most serious breach between my father and myself which had ever occurred."[69]

After Mollie's second year at Wilberforce, a wealthy white woman invited Mollie to accompany her to Europe during the summer of 1887, an opportunity she was eager to pursue. Her father agreed to pay for the trip, but then Mollie received an offer to teach in the Latin Department of the Preparatory Colored High School (M Street High School) in Washington, D.C. She was torn between her strong professional ambitions and her desire for adventure. To reassure Mollie, her "father promised that if I waited till the following summer, he would go abroad with me himself." Although she believed him and it did, indeed, happen, Mollie feared that something unexpected might foreclose that possibility. "After a nerve-racking period of indecision and torture," she accepted the job, a move that advanced her career and led her to the man she eventually married and with whom she started her own family, Robert Heberton Terrell.[70]

———————

In the end, father and daughter were much alike. Her father recognized that Mollie's tenacious determination to do what she saw as her duty was "simply proving that I was a 'chip off the old block.'" Also like her father, Mollie could become angry and blow up at family, friends, and associates, sometimes over trivial issues. They were both stubborn, focused on their goals, and determined to be successful. As an adult, Mollie was unwilling to give up her civil rights activism even when others begged her to moderate her public stances on controversial issues.

Her mother was also a significant influence on her life and personality. From Louisa, Mollie learned that women could be successful entrepreneurs and could create rich, independent lives with or without male partners. Louisa also taught her about generosity, spontaneity, and fun, for she was a creative free spirit who would throw herself enthusiastically into a new hobby, such as painting. She loved giving gifts and spending money on others. She also gave of herself and her time. This is particularly true when she nursed an adult Mollie back to health after several health crises and when she moved into the Terrells' home in D.C. to take care of her granddaughter so that Mollie could continue her activism. Mollie recognized and appreciated her mother's love and attention and treasured their time together during the last fifteen years of Louisa's life.

From her enslaved grandmothers on both sides, Mollie learned about the terrors of enslavement but also about her grandmothers' capacity to love and to hope for better lives for themselves, their children, and their grandchildren. From her white grandfathers, she learned the moral complexities of a thoroughly evil system. She knew that Captain Church had treated his son, Robert, kindly but also that he had never educated or emancipated him. Similarly, T. S. Ayres was content to provide his enslaved daughter, Louisa, with an elegant wedding in his home but also expected her to continue living there as the enslaved nursemaid, or "Mammy," to the baby of his white daughter, Laura. As a civil rights activist, Mollie drew on her own family history to critique whites' nostalgia for the system of enslavement, a nostalgia that never acknowledged the real harm done to enslaved family members who were separated, humiliated, and treated as less than fully human.

Love and Partnership

Mollie Church found her equal in Robert ("Berto") Heberton Terrell (1857–1925). Theirs was a remarkable love story and partnership that lasted almost forty years, one that is revealed in her diaries and their letters, especially in love letters between the two.[1] Mollie Church was immediately drawn to Berto Terrell's charm, good looks, and brilliance. They supported each other intellectually, emotionally, and professionally for decades. After beginning their lives enslaved, this extraordinarily well educated couple achieved professional, social, and political prominence—independently and together.

Obituaries written after his death in 1925 at sixty-eight highlight Berto's most admired traits and suggest why Mollie found him to be so appealing. One, by W. E. B. Du Bois in the NAACP's journal, *The Crisis*, captured Berto's personality: "The death of Robert Heberton Terrell leaves a void. Terrell was a good fellow: tall and healthy to look at; a lover of men, of his social glass, of a good story with a Lincoln tang to it. His great hearty laugh warmed your heart and his handshake was a benediction." Berto's warmth and intelligence made those around him feel at ease. He was a popular member and leader of many black fraternal organizations, including the Prince Hall Masons and the Boulé, as well as educational and literary societies like the Mu-So-Lit Club (the Music, Social, and Literary Club).[2] A lawyer, journalist, and leader in the D.C. branch of the NAACP, L. M. Hershaw, observed of his friend: "He was a man of abounding good nature and of superabundant kindness and sympathy for all with whom he came in contact." Implicitly contrasting his own and Mollie's personality types to Berto's, Du Bois concluded his obituary: "We shall miss Terrell—we who are strenuous and worried and hurried and given to 'settling' things. We need more of that humanly lovable and good-natured type, those who are just living and enjoying both sunshine and rain and the gift of friends." These were the very characteristics that Mollie cherished in Berto, as she relied on him for emotional support and stability.[3]

FIGURE 2.1. Berto Terrell's graduation photo from Lawrence Academy in Groton, Massachusetts, shows him as a handsome bearded young man in his early twenties. Decked out in his cap and gown, he proudly holds his diploma, ready to enter Harvard College, where he graduated as one of seven magna cum laude scholars in 1884, the same year Mollie graduated from Oberlin College. (Courtesy Oberlin College Archives)

FIGURE 2.2. A beautiful young woman in her twenties, Mollie Church continued to dress in fine clothes; her delicate teardrop earrings enhance her elegant appearance. (Courtesy University of Memphis Special Collections)

Although very different, Mollie Church and Berto Terrell were well matched. She was the more "strenuous and worried" of the two and relied on his "lovable and good-natured" disposition to give her happiness and peace of mind. Berto was attracted to the brilliant, beautiful, intense, and driven Mollie, who radiated high energy and elegance. Within the security of their marriage, he enabled her to thrive and become more confident as a public activist striving to change the racist and sexist world in which they lived. They loved dancing together and did so regularly throughout the decades.

"Splendid Company on General Principles"

When they met in 1886, Mollie and Berto were instantly attracted to each other. Mollie described herself as excited and flustered at first seeing Berto when he came to visit the family of Dr. John Francis—a prominent black obstetrician and gynecologist—with whom she was boarding. He and his wife, Bettie, both served on the school board at various points—in fact, it was Dr. Francis who had recruited twenty-three-year-old Mollie and her Oberlin classmates, Ida B. Gibbs and Anna Julia Cooper, to teach at the Preparatory M Street High School. The Francis family had already told her of Berto, the brilliant twenty-nine-year-old bachelor who headed the Greek and Latin Department in which she would be teaching: "He was described to me as being tall, very good-looking, a fine dancer, and splendid company on general principles. He was also a great favorite among young women, of course." She observed, "Never since the dawn of creation did two teachers of the same subject get along more harmoniously and with less friction."[4]

Berto Terrell was already a celebrity among Washington African Americans. He had started his life enslaved, attended the segregated schools of the District, and in 1884 became the third African American to graduate from Harvard University and the first to do so cum laude. Mollie wrote later that "after one of his friends heard him deliver his oration on Commencement day, he declared 'Ten years ago Robert Terrell entered one end of Memorial Hall as a menial [before he attended Harvard, he worked as a waiter in the dining hall], but today he goes out the other end crowned with the highest honor Harvard can bestow.'" Mollie celebrated that "this colored man who had been born a slave was 1 of 7 to achieve this distinction [of giving a graduation speech] in a class of more than 200 young men belonging to a group whose advantages had been far superior to his."[5]

Mollie was averse to revealing too much about her private life in any public format. In her autobiography (published in 1940), she cautiously limited her discussion of their courtship, saying only that their students noted the chemistry between the two and made lighthearted jokes about it. The prospect of being publicly viewed as sexual beings, even as merely romantic beings in the context of an engagement and marriage, caused anxiety since black women were subjected to constant slurs about their supposed hypersexuality. Talk of courtship might lead minds to wander—something that prominent black activists studiously avoided in reference to themselves.[6]

In more private spaces, such as her diaries and discussions with her best friends in high school and college, the younger Mollie had expressed her interest in several suitors. Later, in abbreviated notes for her autobiography, material she deleted from the published version, she jotted down "my beaux. [Friends said:] Mollie always had a boy tied to her apron strings. Said I'll die for him." She also remembered a time at Oberlin when "Father sees Milton Lee's picture on my dresser and demands to see Mrs. Hatch, who told him I got along nicely in school." Since her love interest had not distracted her from her studies, her father did nothing to end either her schooling or a teenage romance so far from parental supervision.[7]

At Oberlin she had had a romance with the handsome and talented John Hanks Alexander (b. 1864), who started as a freshman and attended for two years before being accepted by the United States Military Academy at West Point in 1883. She later treasured a piece of jewelry because it combined a gift from her father and one from her beau. On special occasions, she "wore my chain Father gave me when I was 16 with the button from John Alexander's coat which he gave me while he was in West Point having it washed with gold and my initials engraved." In 1887, Alexander became the second African American to graduate from West Point. He then joined the Buffalo Soldiers fighting in the American West before teaching at Wilberforce University. The gift of his military coat button was a romantic gesture that they both saw as having a larger symbolic meaning about the history and progress of African Americans.[8]

Mollie did not keep this earlier romance secret from Berto, referring to John Alexander as "a man who was very fond of me when I was a mere child [sixteen] and had asked me to marry him later on. He graduated from West Point and served as a Lieutenant in the Army for quite a while. Then he was appointed to drill the students in a college for colored youth. . . . This man and I had been fond of each other from childhood and remained the best of friends till the end." She also noted, "His relations with my husband were most cordial. Whenever he came to Washington, he was a welcome guest in our home after we married." The two men even joked about how he had lost out to Berto. John Alexander "told Mr. Terrell that the reason he had chosen a feather fan for my wedding present was because he wanted to give me something he could not use. Everybody considered this a good joke and my husband complimented him upon being clever enough to select something which really shut him out."⁹

Berto Terrell was a rare man not to feel threatened by Mollie Church's intellectual abilities. She was a college-educated woman who found love "in spite of" her accomplishments. Her Oberlin classmate Anna Julia Cooper knew how rare that was. In 1892, Cooper explained: "The question is not now with the woman 'How shall I so cramp, stunt, simplify and nullify myself so as to make me eligible to the honor of being swallowed up into some little man?' but the problem . . . now rests with the man as to how he can . . . reach the ideal of a generation of women who demand the noblest, grandest, and best achievements of which he is capable. . . . If it makes them [men] work, all the better for them."¹⁰

Despite their budding romance, or perhaps because she feared it might push her toward the bonds of matrimony before she was ready, Mollie decided to do as planned and take a leave of absence from her teaching job. Her father fulfilled his promise to accompany her to Europe and generously funded her studies abroad. Wishing to increase her fluency in French, German, and Italian and aiming to complete her education with a grand European tour, Mollie left for Europe in July 1888. Father and daughter had a three-month tour of Europe together. When it was time for him to leave her there, "although he rarely showed how deeply moved he was about anything, his eyes filled when he kissed me good-bye and left me alone in Paris. Not a tear was in my eye, however. . . . I was the happiest girl on earth. . . . Not a care in the world, bubbling over with enthusiasm and youth!"¹¹

Mollie and Berto's romance continued haltingly via letters as she spent more than two years studying and traveling abroad. The two corresponded regularly, but Mollie was not yet ready to identify Berto as her sole beau. She did register interest in him in her diaries, which she wrote in French and German to help her practice both languages. She noted when she received letters from him, what he wrote, and when she sent her replies. One diary entry revealed some doubt about whether or how much she should encourage his affection: "Today I received a letter from R. H. T. He asked me to take a photograph of myself and send it to him. What should I do?" She did send him the portrait, though, and made sure it was a flattering one; when she received a proof that displeased her, she returned to the photo studio to try again.¹²

As Berto courted her, he encouraged Mollie's talents and bolstered her self-esteem. At twenty-five, she had great ambitions to be a published writer but also suffered from self-doubt about her writing abilities—self-doubt that plagued her throughout her life. She confided to her diary: "I want to write. I must write. Everything seems to be telling me this is my calling, my sacred duty almost." Mollie then revealed that the "everything" urging her to write

FIGURE 2.3. This portrait of Mollie, Thomas, and Louisa Church might have been made when the three of them were living in New York City when Mollie spent her summers there while teaching at Wilberforce University. It could also have been taken a couple of years later during her study abroad experience in the late 1880s, when Louisa and Thomas were able to join Mollie for an extravagant European tour, funded by a winning lottery ticket purchased by Louisa. (Courtesy Oberlin College Archives)

included Berto: "R. H. T. told me that I write such interesting letters and so much better than all the other women he knows that he was surprised that I did not aspire to write for the press." Over time, she came to realize that his affirmation was just what she wanted and needed.[13]

Mollie's 1888 French diary provides an image of Berto as cautious, self-conscious, and genteel, not overtly expressing his feelings or pressuring Mollie about hers. Gently encouraging her to return, Berto reminded her of her duties to her students and to her race more generally. When she recorded that "R. H. T. assured me that the Latin classes miss me a lot," Mollie surely knew he was speaking for himself, as well. He sent her as a Christmas gift, a new best-selling book by Mrs. Humphry Ward. Mollie noted that she received from "M. Terrell, a very interesting *Robert Elsmere* book, well-written, denying the divinity of Jesus Christ and suggesting the establishment of a new church, or well, of a new order." The selection indicated to Mollie his respect for her as an intellectual and an activist. It was also a subtle reminder that her skills were needed at home, for the book called on those who could to assist the impoverished and uneducated. Mollie was not quite ready to join Berto in this challenge, however. In the same diary entry, she mentioned having received two letters from a suitor named Aleck.[14]

Berto Terrell showed some interest in and was pursued by other women while Mollie was abroad. It is unclear whether he seriously considered them as possible mates or referred to them in his letters as a way to pique Mollie's interest and jealousy. He explicitly mentioned one whom Mollie likely saw as a credible threat: her college classmate Anna Julia Cooper, a brilliant and beautiful young widow who was born into slavery in 1858 and attended Oberlin after her husband's early death. While Mollie was away, Anna was teaching at the high school where Mollie and Berto still taught. In a letter to him written in March 1889, Mollie began by requesting information about the recent presidential inaugural festivities, asking him to tell her all "about the young women who figured most conspicuously from the standpoint of mental caliber, beauty and style. . . . Don't let me pine away here in ignorance of all this, I beg of you. To be sure you are very busy with teaching and studying [in law school] but you will still be able to spare a moment . . . to gratify the curiosity of a . . . co-laborer." She continued, "Your last letter informed me that you were profiting by Mrs. Cooper's words of wisdom and enjoying her most agreeable society. I congratulate you, for you could find no one better fitted than she to throw light into a great many dark places. That isn't half I might say and should like to say but you yourself will supplement the above." In the same letter, she sent "much love to Mrs. Cooper" even as she indirectly criticized her potential rival by explaining, "I shall write to her soon. Her letter just reached me a short while before leaving Lausanne. She had put a two-cent stamp on it by mistake and had directed it to Paris where it remained for a long time on account of the postage. They are so stupid sometimes about little things."[15]

By her second year in Europe, suitors were pursing the beautiful and brilliant Mollie Church and a few white European and American men proposed. In brief notes for her autobiography, she jotted down: "First trip abroad with father. Americans want to marry me. Fred Welmar . . . kissed." In 1940, as she was about to publish her memoir, she fretted: "I am worried about [revealing] the engagement record I had. Still, it was an important part of my life and I told it for a purpose to show that some colored people don't want to marry white folks." She emphasized that she had turned down marriage proposals from three well-off white men, hoping that this would squelch whites' persistent fears that blacks' demands for social and political equality were simply a subterfuge for their supposed desire to marry whites.[16]

Only one suitor posed a threat to Berto. A young German Jewish lawyer, Baron Otto von Devoltz, courted Mollie in Berlin in 1889 and early 1890, tempting her with a vision of life as an expatriate, away from the overt racism of the United States. She enjoyed his company and attention. He had graduated from Heidelberg University and worked as an attorney, and they went "sightseeing, sometimes taking long walks together." Mollie was much affronted by the baron's decision to write directly to her father in February 1890 asking for her hand in marriage without consulting her: "At that time he had not told me how serious his intentions were, and I upbraided him for having written to my father before getting my views on the subject. But he said no gentleman would pay serious attention to a young woman without first getting her father's consent. Since I had been reared in the United States and had always seen young men win the girl before they consulted her parents in the matter, I was not exactly prepared for this explanation and reply."[17]

Her own reluctance to marry a white man was reinforced by her father's adamant rejection of the baron's proposal: "Nothing could induce [me] to give my consent to her marrying and living in Europe." Her father opposed interracial marriages on the ground that they usually led to the erasure and denial of the black spouse's heritage and family. In this case, Mollie feared that her father might overreact to Devoltz's proposal and insist that she return home immediately. Her father did not mention the issue of race to her white suitor but rather focused on his paternalistic notion that "every daughter, married or single, when she has a father needs his protection. . . . Consequently, I want her to marry in America where I could look after her interests." Robert Church did concede that Mollie "has always been an obedient, affectionate daughter" and "writes of you in the very highest terms and I have no doubt as to your worthiness in every respect."[18]

The end of her romance with the baron led Mollie back to the increasingly appealing prospect of creating an equal relationship with the handsome, kind, and accomplished Berto Terrell. Like Mollie, he was a light-skinned African American committed to affirming black heritage and promoting racial equality. She returned to the United States to embrace an engagement, marriage, and partnership that would allow her to launch a career of social and political activism on behalf of her race: "I knew I would be much happier trying to promote the welfare of my race in my native land, working under certain hard conditions, than I would be living in a foreign land where I could enjoy freedom from prejudice, but where I would make no effort to do the work which I then believed it was my duty to do. I doubted that I could respect myself."[19]

"Loving Each Other as We Do"

Upon her return and at Berto's urging, Mollie took up her job at M Street High School and reaffirmed their romance. During her absence he had become a lawyer and gained a job as chief of division in the Treasury Department in President Benjamin Harrison's Republican administration. Mollie later remembered that he "regretted resigning his position as teacher in the High School, but he needed the money." He wanted to have a stable income and a respectable job when he asked Mollie to marry him. (In notes for her autobiography, Mollie later recalled "Berto's love for me. . . . Knew Mr. T the minute I saw him. How he proposed to me." Discretion ultimately got the best of her, however, for she left the latter information out of the final published memoir.)[20]

In a January 6, 1891, letter to Mollie's father written on Treasury Department letterhead, used to show that he was gainfully employed, Berto described "a sacred relationship between your daughter and myself." In contrast to the German baron, Berto made a point of telling his future father-in-law that it was "with Miss Mollie's full consent and approval I write to ask of you her hand in marriage. On our part this is no hasty step. We feel that we know each other thoroughly well and loving each other as we do, it is only natural that we should look forward to a union which we are confident will be one of contentment and happiness." After referring to their mutual love and five-year courtship, Berto got practical. He felt that it was his "duty" to reveal his "material" status: "My accumulations amount to about two thousand dollars and my present position pays me two thousand a year. . . . I am not wholly dependent on political office for a living if the Administration should change in 1893, from Republican to Democratic, I have the profession of law on which to fall back." (Two thousand dollars a year in the 1890s gave Berto a very comfortable purchasing power of about $51,000 a year in our terms. This is remarkable given that the average 1900 U.S. Census salary for all workers was $499. For African American workers, male and female, it was closer to about $165 a year.)[21]

Berto Terrell's declarations of love for Mollie, in addition to his academic and professional accomplishments and fine temperament, all impressed and pleased Robert Church, who might have seen something of himself in Mollie's ambitious and accomplished suitor. They had each been born a mixed-race slave who, after emancipation, overcame the odds to become successful. Yet Robert Church had taught himself to read, although not to write, whereas the younger man had been educated at Harvard College and Howard University School of Law. Church dictated his letter, readily giving the couple his blessings and generously offering his elegant Memphis home as the site for a lavish wedding. He later wrote his new son-in-law that he was "very proud of Mollie. She is a noble and deserving woman and I see no reason why her future life should not be one of supreme happiness." After their marriage, Mollie's brother Thomas asked her to "tell [Berto], dear soul, that I don't blame the girls for being after him and am sincerely glad they didn't capture him; for he is a loveable, dear, kind, affectionate brother in law."[22]

Marriage affected their careers quite differently. Whereas Berto Terrell was, by virtue of his gender, able to pursue a career and marriage without compromising either, Mollie could not pursue both simultaneously. Educated women with teaching careers lost their jobs once they married. Moreover, marriage into the Church family increased Berto's respectability and elite professional status. By the 1890s, Mollie's father was a real estate developer and a well-respected community and political leader in Tennessee whose wealth and prominence would help Berto and his new wife in any number of ways.

Although Mollie was ready to sacrifice her teaching career to marry Berto, she had not anticipated that a better position and career path would come her way. But after the wedding invitations had gone out, just that happened: "Several months before the summer vacation began, I received a letter ... inviting me to become registrar of Oberlin College. . . . Although I had promised definitely to marry the following October, it was a great temptation to postpone my wedding and go to Oberlin as a registrar." She so desired to accept this prestigious appointment that she described her decision as one made with "mature deliberation plus much agony of soul," for she seriously considered postponing or even canceling her wedding in order to take the job, even if just for a year or two.[23]

Mollie's attempt to postpone their wedding greatly upset Berto. He had waited patiently for her to complete over two years of study abroad, but this was too much. When he indicated how unhappy he was that she was considering delaying their wedding to take the job at Oberlin, Mollie impulsively offered to cancel their engagement, and that led to a crisis.

My darling Robert,
Whatever you tell me to do, I shall do. If possible, I want to make you happy. I have tried because I love you. I shall still try if you want me to. My very heart has been wrung at hearing you tell how miserable you are, and seeing it, in spite of everything I have tried in my feeble power to soothe you.

Don't feel bad anymore. I am heartbroken to think of making you feel worse. I thought perhaps release from your engagement might be a relief to your mind and I did it because I thought it cruelty to you not to, and because my love for you is even equal to leaving you if you say so. I am yours forever and ever if you so will it. . . .

Sleep well. I love you with all my heart and soul. I only did what I thought was what you wanted me to do. Forever and ever yours with all my heart, Mollie.

And so, they continued with their wedding as planned, although she always regretted not being able to marry the man she loved while simultaneously developing a prestigious career. Years later, while organizing their papers, Mollie wrote "Reconciled" on the envelope.[24]

Older than most couples at the time, Mollie Church, then twenty-eight, and Berto Terrell, thirty-four, were married on October 28, 1891, at Robert R. Church's grand home in Memphis. Although Mollie's mother, Louisa Ayers Church, maintained a cordial relationship with her former husband and his wife, she did not feel comfortable attending her daughter's wedding at their home. Mollie recounted a poignant moment that Louisa told her about, when she "dressed herself exactly as she would have done if she had actually attended the wedding, and at the hour she knew her daughter was being married she imagined she was listening to the ceremony and was taking part in it." Louisa soon celebrated with them in person, for the newlyweds traveled to New York City to see her for their honeymoon.[25]

"No Ecstasy of Bliss for Me Separated from You"

Their joy was cut short just eight months after the ceremony by a miscarriage. Throughout their marriage, Mollie experienced health problems that critically affected her physical and mental well-being and helped determine how she approached her reform work. At the time, she kept her own body's problems hidden as much as possible, but her public stance on such issues as African American women's access to health care and the care and education of their children were deeply informed by her private experiences. Personal grief, modesty regarding intimate issues of sexual reproduction, and her legitimate fears about the racism directed toward black women and their bodies reinforced her desire for secrecy about her reproductive health even as it added weight to her concerns about the well-being of black women.[26] She wished to keep her problems private, yet they were painful public ones. That she carried one pregnancy into the third trimester and two others to term meant friends and strangers knew that she had been pregnant and lost the infants.[27]

In her autobiography, she only elliptically mentioned the first health crisis that almost took her life: "The summer after my marriage I was desperately ill and my life was despaired of. My recovery was nothing short of a miracle and my case is recorded in medical history." Mollie's miscarriage in June 1892 was brought on by a severe case of kidney disease (acute nephritis), caused by her pregnancy. It almost killed her just eight months after their wedding. After she miscarried, Mollie's condition was so perilous her mother rushed to her side from New York and her father immediately took the train from Memphis to Washington, fearing he might not see his daughter alive again.[28]

In subsequent health crises, Mollie insisted that Berto not inform their wider network of friends or the public. During the first, however, she was in no condition to know what was going on, let alone to direct communications about it. Berto asked Wyatt Archer, his friend and colleague in the Treasury Department and a Howard University–trained pharmacist, to write letters informing their friends of her serious illness. Within two days, Berto began receiving letters from friends across the country expressing deep concern over the news. Many were shocked, since they had just recently enjoyed reading letters from the couple contentedly discussing Mollie's pregnancy and their marital bliss. Once it appeared that Mollie would recover, friends reassured Berto that he and his wife would still be able to have a child. One wrote, "Doctors do not know everything. Your wife is young and then there may be hope while life lasts."[29]

During the emergency, Mollie's parents and family members grew to love and appreciate Berto even more. As her brother Thomas wrote her, "Bob has risen a hundred percent in Mother's estimation—not so much from the affectionate husband that he is as the glorious and paternal deed he has done." It is unclear what Thomas was referring to, but Berto likely helped bury their unborn infant. Mollie went to New York City to receive the full-time care of her mother and a nurse, and then traveled to Saratoga Springs, New York, to rest and recover. Mollie reported to Berto that her mother sang "your praises constantly and thinks you are the best husband in the world."[30]

The love letters between Mollie and Berto during the first year of their marriage are permeated with passionate sexual and romantic desire, longing, and sadness. Although invested in a public image of propriety and respectability, the couple's enforced separation inspired their daily correspondence, and their missives reveal that Mollie did not deny herself sexual pleasure and play in her intimate life. Mollie admitted to Berto that although "Mama is so good and attentive and I am so sure of her great love for me. . . . There is always an aching void and there will be until I'm folded in your strong and loving embrace. . . . With a heart full of love and a burning thirst for your kisses, I am your affectionate wife, Mollie." Her unabashed sexual desire for Berto's physical presence was a recurring theme in her letters while she was recuperating. Though they longed for each other's embrace, the two were able to comfort and provide sustenance to each other from afar. The traumatic experience brought them closer, even as it necessarily produced serious emotional strains that increased over the next six long and painful years as they experienced additional unsuccessful attempts to have a baby.[31]

Just as when she was studying abroad, Berto's praise of her writing meant a great deal to Mollie. During the first year of their marriage, they were still sometimes self-conscious, writing letters designed to impress each other with their erudition—much the way they had written during their courtship and engagement. While she was away recuperating, Mollie thanked her "precious Husband" for writing letters that "are models from a literary standpoint, to say nothing about their other virtues." When he responded in kind, she sent him "many thanks for the compliment to my 'good sense' and 'excellent taste' as exhibited in my admiration and praise of American scenery." She appreciated his support: "Your letter complimenting my feeble efforts of the past Sabbath has been received, and I thank you very much for the kind words of encouragement. It has always been a dream of mine to do something worthy of commendation in the literary line, but for the present, at least, it must rest only a dream."[32]

Formal and stilted passages of the newlyweds' letters are interspersed with unambiguous and unreserved expressions of sexual passion and love. Responding to a letter from Berto, Mollie wrote: "Like you I feel there is no real deep peace, no genuine happiness, no ecstasy of bliss for me separated from you to whom I have given my whole self unreservedly and irrevocably." Mollie did not hold back in describing her physical pleasure, enthusing: "It will not be long before I can kiss you to my heart's content, and feel that indescribable thrill with which your kisses and embraces are always attended." As she anticipated her return to Washington, she asked Berto to "be patient until I can throw my arms around you and lavish so much love upon you that you will forget about our long separation. . . . With dozens of kisses and oceans of love." Letters of sexual longing were intermingled with playful sexual innuendoes and references to "naughtiness." When Berto sent Mollie a letter from his friend Jack Durham, for instance, she answered: "Mr. Durham's letter was thoroughly enjoyed while his note was enough to make a more proper and prudish soul than myself roar with laughter for its very naughtiness and positive wickedness." At another point, she wrote suggestively, "You have always fulfilled your promises—with just one exception which modesty forbids my citing in this letter. If you can't recall this broken promise, dear, I'll refresh your memory when I see you."[33]

The Terrell's uninhibited delight in the physical pleasures of sex as well as their erotic playfulness and passion could not pull their attention from Mollie's health crisis, which precipitated unanticipated kinds of intimacy between the newlyweds. She had had a miscarriage and both of them desperately wanted children. Mollie's letters gave him in-depth (although still somewhat discreet) reports about her reproductive health, including updates about when she was suffering from premenstrual cramps or was menstruating again, all good signs that they could try to have a child: "I feel better since the visitor [her period], so welcome tho' so painful, came to see me, and think her departure will leave me much stronger and fresher in every way, even tho' I'm somewhat languid and ailing while she's with me." Mollie then stopped herself: "Here I am telling my hubby everything, but whom does my condition physical and mental interest more than my good loving husband? You don't think it improper in me to tell you everything about myself, do you, darling?" Mollie also reported on her visits to doctors in New York. A prominent physician assured her that her "kidney affliction is not organic . . . but was brought on by pregnancy. . . . [He] encouraged me by asserting that women who have suffered just as I did have in many cases given birth to children without any trouble." When disturbing symptoms such as diarrhea and vomiting continued for months, Mollie consulted a different physician who gave her medicine to alleviate them and "best of all gave me so much encouragement. He doesn't believe that there is any serious trouble at all and declares that he knows a young girl who before marriage had such an aggravated case of Bright's [kidney] disease that she could hardly sit up not to mention walking but who was completely cured and is now the mother of several children."[34]

Stories about women who had had miscarriages but later delivered healthy babies took on a new, heightened interest for Mollie. While recovering at Saratoga Springs, she spent time with a friend who "teases me about my penchant for hearing about difficult accouchements and says all that is necessary to get my ear and very closest attention is to relate an interesting 'case.'" On a visit with an Oberlin College friend Nettie McKelvey Swift, Mollie learned that

Nettie had had two miscarriages before her oldest daughter was born and that she was now pregnant again. Mollie was thrilled to hear that despite doctors having advised Nettie "not to allow herself to become enceinte [pregnant]," they had been wrong. She confidently concluded that "the physicians mean well, but they don't know it all, I'm thankful to state."[35]

"Hope, Apprehension, and Abject Fear"

In spite of their mutual attempts to focus on the positive, Mollie and Berto found themselves writing to each other on the same day, two months after her miscarriage, mourning their lost baby, who would have been born that month. In a state of what she identified as a deep "depression," Mollie confided, "This is the month in which our fond dream of a sweet little angel from heaven was to be realized. That my heart almost breaks when the cruel reality of the present overcomes me with its crushing disappointment is no sign or argument that I am not grateful for what was a miraculous deliverance from death." Mollie took solace in her husband's sharing her profound sorrow: "Your letter . . . shows that you, too, share in this feeling of irrepressible sadness. I weep for the loss of our little one." She worried, however, that she was not doing enough to pull herself out of her depression and that she might be straining Berto's emotional state: "But, my darling. . . . I am so inexpressibly happy in your love that it seems almost wicked to say anything that will sadden or worry you. I think as little of our bitter disappointment as I can, my Sweetheart, but now and then . . . I must weep the loss of the little baby which had crept into my heart as a happy living reality to be fondly cherished and tenderly loved. The Lord knows best, and I pray almost hourly for a spirit of resignation."[36]

Their loss and enforced separation impelled the newlyweds to reflect seriously on the nature of their relationship. Mollie's deep depression so early in their marriage made her aware of her growing emotional and psychological dependence upon Berto. It was impossible for her not to think of her own mother's suicide attempt. Mollie never seems to have plunged to that depth, but she confessed to Berto that she was experiencing alternating feelings of "hope, apprehension, and abject fear" about whether they would ever be able to have children. In one of her lower moments, she lamented, "My hopes have shriveled up to mere nothingness." She tried to rally, however, vowing: "But I shall from this day forth take a hopeful view of things, Berto, for your dear sake. You are right (as you always are) in chastising me for looking at the world through smoked glasses and with your help . . . I shall try to ignore the shadows altogether."[37]

Just before Mollie's miscarriage, she had been traumatized by the news that her good friend shopkeeper Thomas Moss and two of his friends and business associates had been lynched in her hometown of Memphis. Ida B. Wells was also close with Moss, and his brutal murder inspired her antilynching career. Ida Wells was a direct contemporary of Mollie's, having been born enslaved in Holly Springs, Mississippi, in 1862. Like Mollie, she gained her freedom at the end of the Civil War. In the 1880s and 1890s, Wells, a schoolteacher, requested loans from Mollie's father, Robert R. Church, who had also been born enslaved in Holly Springs. Without having met her, Robert Church generously gave Wells the money and refused to let her repay it. After the 1892 Memphis lynchings, Mollie's father pointedly contributed $10,000 to the Central Oklahoma Emigration Society, helping thousands of black Memphians, or Exodusters, leave for Oklahoma, as Wells urged them to do. Wells soon left for the North, never to return, but in the meantime, she bought a pistol and prepared to defend herself from a mob.[38]

Mollie experienced such profound distress after learning of her friend's death that she feared she had injured her own body, mind, and soul so deeply that it could have permanently harmed her infant, had it survived. This perspective became a means by which she tried to cope with her miscarriage: "The more I thought how my depression which was caused by the lynching of Tom Moss and the horror of this awful crime might have injuriously affected my unborn child, if he had lived, the more I became reconciled to what had at first seemed a cruel fate."[39]

Mollie Terrell intuitively reached for what many epigeneticists now understand—that the trauma of racism and racist violence can have a negative effect on the mental and physical development of black women's unborn children.[40]

> As I was grieving over the loss of my baby boy one day, it occurred to me that under the circumstances it might be a blessed dispensation of Providence that his precious life was not spared. The horror and resentment felt by the mother, coupled with the bitterness which filled her soul, might have seriously affected the unborn child. Who can tell how many desperadoes and murderers have been born to colored mothers who had been shocked and distracted before the birth of their babies by the news that some relative or friend had been burned alive or shot to death by a mob?

Her concerns about the pernicious role of racism in threatening the health and welfare of African American families were bolstered by hereditarian ideas popular at the turn of the century. Blacks and whites held beliefs ranging from the notion that "rakish fathers" could bequeath a negative "moral legacy" to their children to "euthenics," which argued that home surroundings could influence babies' health and welfare.[41]

Rearing black children in a racist society was fraught with conflicting emotions ranging from joy and hopeful anticipation to fear. For African American parents, then as now, high aspirations for their children were always counterbalanced by the painful knowledge that, regardless of class or accomplishment, they confronted hurdles and dangers that white children did not have to face. Soon after her late-term miscarriage in 1892, Mollie remembered, "I was greatly impressed by a statement made by one of my white friends who met me on the street one day shortly after I was bereaved." The two discussed the rise of lynching and segregation in American society as well as the recent murder of Tom Moss. Her white friend said, "I do not see . . . how any colored woman can make up her mind to become a mother under existing conditions in the United States. . . . I should think a colored woman would feel that she was perpetrating a great injustice upon any helpless infant she would bring into the world." Taken aback, Mollie revealed, "I had never heard that point of view so frankly and strongly expressed before, and while I could not agree with it entirely, it caused me much serious reflection." Black women had to wrestle with the burdens of white racism, even in the otherwise conventional decision of a married woman to have a baby.[42]

To move beyond sorrow and loss, Mollie needed a larger sense of purpose. Returning home from Saratoga Springs, she involved herself in antilynching activism. On October 31, 1892, she was honored to introduce Ida B. Wells, the journalist and new antilynching activist, whom she had previously met in Memphis. When Berto went to Boston to give a speech in November 1892, Mollie reported to him that she had been elected secretary of "a Committee . . . to arrange for a repetition of Miss Wells' lecture. Mr. [Frederick] Douglass encourages me so much." Antilynching activism and collaboration with civil rights and women's rights activists like Douglass and Wells helped Mollie work for civil rights goals and provided a focus for her energy and sorrow. When Ida B. Wells returned to Washington in 1893 to discuss her pamphlet *Southern Horrors: Lynch Law in All Its Phases*, Mollie again introduced her: "We admire Miss Wells for her undaunted courage . . . [and for her] recital of the wrongs heaped upon her oppressed people in the South." Well on her way to being a public speaker in her own right, Mollie declared, "When men whose only crime is the color of their skin are denied even the farce of a trial, are forcibly torn from jails of the largest and wealthiest cities of the South and foully murdered, it is time for a persistent and systematic agitation of the subject of Southern Mob Rule. . . . Surely no one can charge us with exaggerating our woes and magnifying the indignities heaped upon us, when the murder of colored men is of almost daily occurrence in the south."[43]

Berto supported Mollie's public work, including her teaching and advocacy on behalf of the race. A couple of years into their marriage, he endorsed the school district's decision to allow Mollie to teach as a substitute for an extended period, even though married women were not usually allowed to do so. The married Mollie Terrell was hired to substitute because she "was the only colored woman college graduate" available. Mollie earned welcome money and found a larger purpose outside the domestic sphere. Significantly, she used her earnings to buy property in Charles Douglass's new African American beach resort in Highland Beach, Maryland. Mollie recognized and appreciated Berto's attempts to advance her recovery, continue her career as an educator, and support their lifestyle.[44]

Years later, she recalled to her sister-in-law, Laura Terrell Jones, that Berto had "forced me to accept an invitation extended by the Whittier Historical Society of Memphis, Tenn., which requested me to deliver an address on Harriet Beecher Stowe. I had just lost a baby, and I did not feel equal to writing an address which would require so much research and study—first, to get the material and then to weave it into an interesting speech." Mollie remembered this speech as a pivotal moment in their early marriage: "When I finished writing my address on Harriet Beecher Stowe, I was thoroughly disgusted with it and discouraged. I told my husband how rotten it was and he asked me to read it to him. . . . I read it to him with fear and trembling. I always had the greatest respect for his judgment and opinion on literary matters. . . . When I finished reading the manuscript to him I was almost on the verge of tears. . . . I wanted my husband to put an estimate on the speech and tell the truth about it, and yet I hated to hear it." Revealing her persistent insecurities as well as how Berto bolstered her spirits and sense of self, Mollie later recounted, "But my husband praised it enthusiastically and declared it was one of the finest biographical speeches he had ever heard. . . . He insisted . . . that he would not make his wife believe a speech she had to deliver in public was good if it was not." Berto persuaded her that he genuinely wanted her to succeed as a public speaker and would never put her work and reputation at risk. Beyond his immediate concerns for bolstering her psychological well-being, he believed that he and Mollie must both participate in the project of racial uplift, which he perceived as the duty of all educated African Americans.[45]

White and black audiences enthusiastically shared Berto's approval of Mollie's speech, increasing her confidence in her husband and herself. Although she might have been nervous, her audiences probably never knew it. Friends remembered her as always having a "deep, compelling voice" and a commanding stage presence. As she revealed to her sister-in-law: "Your brother's estimate of the Harriet Beecher Stowe address was correct. Whenever I delivered it before the big Chautauquas in the West or before highbrow women's clubs in the East [both white audiences], I was always overwhelmed with compliments. No address I ever delivered (and I have delivered many a one as you know) received more or finer press notices than the one on Harriet Beecher Stowe."[46]

"We Had Anticipated Having a Living Child . . .
to Add to Our Happiness"

When Mollie finally became pregnant for the second time, in 1895, things did not go well. She wrote in her diary, "Nearly two months have elapsed since I have penned a line. But a vast amount of happenings has [*sic*] filled up this space. . . . If my hopes are realized, my prayers will be answered about the first week in October." Mollie was doing everything she could to fortify her health and prevent another tragedy: "I have already commenced to diet, am living on milk alone now and intend to eschew meat and everything else which will be injurious to my health. After my dreadful almost fatal experience of the summer of 92, one would think I could hardly look forward with any anticipation of pleasure to a situation or condition which might possibly entail the same consequences. But I have no fear." This might have been a diet she thought would help her avoid developing kidney disease again. Adopting a determinedly philosophical perspective, even in her private diary, she wrote, "If after doing everything in my power to ward off the dreaded possibility, matters terminate disastrously, I can conclude it was intended and that it is my fate. I believe in Fate, but this belief does not make me take a gloomy view of life. On the contrary, it makes me more cheerful." (This is an example of a time when Mollie used the word "cheerful" when she did not mean it.) The second pregnancy ended in a stillbirth.[47]

Recalling it forty years later, Mollie noted that her leadership roles became her salvation: "But like other mothers who have passed through this Gethsemane, I pulled myself together as best I could and went on with my work. I had to go on with it." Referring to her historic appointment as the first black woman on the District's board of education, she explained, "The teachers, the parents of children and others who wanted to talk with the only colored woman who was a member of the board insisted on seeing me and presenting their respective cases, anything my nurse might say to the contrary notwithstanding. And they rendered me a great service for which I am grateful today. Obliged to be interested in the troubles and trials of others, I had little time to think of my own aching heart."[48]

Appointed in 1895, Mollie served on the school board until 1901 and then again from 1906 to 1911. Evaluating her own performance on the board, she said, "It is a great comfort to reflect that with three exceptions I never cast a vote to remove a colored teacher from the public schools. . . . Over and over

FIGURE 2.4. Mollie Church Terrell in a fashionable lace dress in
the 1890s, during the early years of her marriage, pregnancies, and
career as a public figure. This formal portrait was taken in a photography studio, but Mollie owned a chair nearly identical to the
elaborately carved mahogany one in which she is sitting. It is still
in her family's possession in Highland Beach, Maryland, and she
is sitting in it in figure 13.1. (Courtesy Library of Congress)

again I fought desperately to save a teacher against whom charges were preferred, if I believed he or she was innocent." She was also proud of instituting, in 1897, Frederick Douglass Day on February 14 in the colored schools of
the district, suggesting, "Perhaps Douglass Day inspired Dr. Carter Woodson to establish Negro History Week many years afterward." Indeed, she later
worked closely with Woodson to plan annual meetings of the Association for
the Study of Negro Life and History. Mollie considered her most important
contribution to the board to be her introduction of a measure to eliminate oral

exams for high school students who wanted to enter the normal school to pursue a career in teaching and advance their own educations. The exam was seen as particularly biased and kept many African American students out. "When, therefore, my resolution to allow all graduates from the high school to enter the normal school was passed, there was great rejoicing. . . . Everybody had a chance to make a good teacher." Throughout, Mollie did not give up on having a family.[49]

During Mollie's third pregnancy, in 1896, Berto kept his father-in-law regularly informed of her progress, reassuring him that "Mollie is getting along nicely, thank you, and there are at present no indications of anything alarming. Of course, we are both apprehensive and anxious in view of our previous experiences and cannot be expected to be contented until the confinement is over." Berto was proactive: "I have engaged two excellent physicians to be present with her. I have done this in case some emergency should arise at the last minute. I shall take every precaution to bring things out all right. Mollie's mother arrived last Friday. We are expecting things to come to a head about the first week in November."[50]

In spite of their many precautions, their living baby died in the hospital. A few weeks later, Berto reported to his father-in-law: "Mollie . . . became despondent at the Sanatorium and I thought it best to indulge her spirits by moving her home. . . . It is very, very hard on Mollie to lose this baby after bringing it into the world all right. No one can appreciate her condition but one who is with her constantly. . . . We had anticipated having a living child with us to add to our happiness. You can readily see what the disappointment must be to Mollie." She later recalled, "I was expecting a little stranger who would [soon] arrive. . . . He came but did not tarry long with me. It was a bitter, grievous disappointment to Mr. Terrell and myself." Much later, she remembered that she had "worried terribly about losing babies." Each time she went shopping downtown, she recalled that "every young thing stabbed my heart." She confessed, too, that she had suffered from episodes of deep depression: "When my third baby died two days after birth, I literally sank down into the very depths of despair. For months I could not divert my thoughts from the tragedy, however hard I tried." Her desire to have children, she explained, was deep, "The maternal instinct was always abnormally developed in me. As far back as I can remember I have always been very fond of children. I cannot recall that I have ever seen a baby, no matter what its class, color, or condition in life . . . that did not seem dear and cunning to me."[51]

The loss of three infants in a row challenged Mollie's sense of her maternal abilities and identity and profoundly disturbed her sense of self, especially in light of contemporary racist rhetoric that maligned African American women as being incapable of bearing "well-born" babies. Mollie's distress was increased

by the racism that she believed had put her infants at greater risk. Discrimination and segregation were rampant, and even those hospitals that allowed
black patients did not give them equal care or access to sophisticated medical
equipment.[52] She knew from personal experience that racism directly endangered the health and survival of all black mothers and their babies, and she
attributed her third infant's death in part to inadequate hospital care: "Right
after its birth the baby had been placed in an improvised incubator and I was
tormented by the thought that if the genuine article had been used, its little
life might have been spared. I could not help feeling that some of the methods
employed in caring for my baby had caused its untimely end." Inadequate and
segregated health care, what Harriet Washington calls "medical apartheid,"
contributed to higher rates of infant mortality for black infants. These glaring
disparities persist in the twenty-first century.[53]

A trip to see her mother pulled Mollie out of her depression.

> Acting upon my physician's advice, my husband insisted upon my leav-
> ing home, where everything reminded me of my sorrow, and I went to
> visit my dear, sunny mother in New York. She would not allow me to
> talk about my baby's death and scouted the idea that its life might have
> been saved. This short visit to my mother with her cheerful disposition
> and her infectious laugh did much for me physically, mentally, and spiri-
> tually. Many a human being has lost his reason because he has brooded
> over his trouble indefinitely, when a slight change of scene and compan-
> ionship might have saved it. I do not like to think what might have hap-
> pened to me if I had not left home and gone to see my mother at that
> crucial time in my life.

The woman who had tried to commit suicide when pregnant had successfully
alleviated her daughter's depression.[54]

In 1896, the year Mollie became president of the National Association of
Colored Women, she and Berto helped found a progressive black Congregational church in their living room. She later remembered, "It was in this house,
soon after we lost our second baby at birth, that University Park Temple was
organized."[55] Searching for solace in activism and faith, they hoped to create a
church that would pursue "race development" as a central part of its religious
mission. The church would be a means of living what they believed. Speaking to the congregation four years after its founding, Berto asserted, "University Park Temple stands for . . . character, for honor, for race development—
all elements that must enter into the work of the Christian Church." He
also praised its women's league for organizing popular evening studies at the
YMCA. These included Mollie's continuing education course on "German

and English Literature three evenings in the week" for public school teachers. Providing teachers an opportunity to increase their knowledge of a foreign language and literature enabled them to better prepare their students for college. Mollie's race development work in the church also allowed her to keep teaching on a volunteer basis despite her being married.[56]

Public work on behalf of African Americans and women provided Mollie Church Terrell a necessary sense of mission and purpose. Just months after recovering from another near-death illness and operation in 1897, she became pregnant for the fourth time. To distract herself from worry, she spent the Christmas holiday with her family in Memphis (the baby was due in early April 1898). Mollie wrote Berto reassuringly, "This time next year you will have a little one of our own for whom to buy presents and have a Christmas jollification. Mark my words." In a reversal of roles, Berto had become less sanguine and Mollie had to be the positive one: "I enjoyed your letter so much with one exception. I don't like to think of you as being soured on life and as having cast aside all hopes and ambitions of having children in our home. We shall be happy yet."[57]

Her health troubles and the couple's collective fears about the outcome of this pregnancy did not mark a moment of retreat for Mollie, who continued her high-profile public activism.[58] Determined to promote social justice, the visibly pregnant Terrell gave a major speech at the National American Woman Suffrage Association (NAWSA) convention, on February 18, 1898, less than two months before her due date. Before the event, Berto informed her father: "She is the only Colored woman invited to speak. The other speakers will be such women as Susan B. Anthony, Elizabeth Cady Stanton, and Frances Willard." Later, bursting with pride, Berto reported to Robert Church, "Mollie immortalized herself last night before the Woman's Suffrage Convention. She made a magnificent address in admirable style. The Columbia Theatre was filled with the best men and women of the country and their reception of Mollie's speech amounted to an ovation." Berto also described how "several white women went so far as to hug and kiss her when the meeting closed. White and colored people mounted the stage and fairly took her off her feet. It was indeed the greatest triumph of her life. . . . When white women publicly embrace a colored woman you know the reason for it must be strong." This speech and its reception was an empowering, uplifting moment that allowed Mollie and Berto to focus on her successful public work and on their mutual support for woman suffrage.[59]

Even in northern integrated hospitals, "discriminatory policies" and unequal treatment remained prevalent, yet as her due date approached, the couple believed that the then-thirty-five-year-old Mollie had no choice but to leave Washington to find better health care and deliver a healthy baby. Their much-cherished and only surviving child, Phyllis, was born in Philadelphia on April 3, 1898. Two long weeks later, Mollie finally allowed Berto to confirm to her father the good news that he was a grandfather.

> I have just received a letter from Mollie saying that she had informed you of the birth of our daughter. I am very glad of it because I have wanted to write a line and inquire about your health for the last two weeks but couldn't do so on account of Mollie's superstition that letters and tele-grams from me to you were dead bad luck where her babies are concerned. . . . I have been dying to let you and Mrs. Church know about the daugh-ter. I was with Mollie about a week and left her and baby doing nicely. The baby is beautiful, if she is mine. The resemblance between this baby and our last one is very striking. She seems healthy and strong.[60]

Once they knew the baby had survived, Berto revealed more about the de-cisions they had made during the last stages of Mollie's pregnancy. He told his father-in-law, "I was advised by a Washington physician not to let my wife be confined here again where these doctors would be telling her about the loss of our other children and the great danger attending the birth of this one. A change of scene and physicians would be the best thing in the world for her. And so it has proved." The couple decided not to have Mollie go to New York City because her mother's high anxiety would have increased her daughter's. Berto continued, "I suppose Mollie will be able to travel in about two weeks from now when I shall go after her and daughter. Then I suppose my trials will begin, walking the floor at night as I shall have to do. Mollie writes me that baby has a high temper and makes folks stand around." Berto chose the sym-bolically significant and empowering name of a famous black woman poet for their daughter: "I am insisting that Mollie name the baby Phyllis Wheatley since she won't name her after herself." Mollie and Berto had likely already named one of their other babies "Mary." Often superstitious, Mollie probably wished to avoid a name that seemed to be bad luck.[61]

Louisa Ayres Church moved in with the Terrells to help raise Phyllis, who was thriving. Her support allowed Mollie to continue and increase her public work. Praised for her "dignity," "rich and resounding voice," and "sparkling dark eyes," Mollie joined a speakers' bureau in 1900 and began traveling widely on extended lecture tours to white and black audiences, advocating for wom-en's rights and full citizenship rights for black Americans. Away on her first big trip, Mollie wrote to her husband, "I never was so homesick in all my life. It seems that I have been away a year. Kiss Mother's darling [Phyllis], love to Mother, a million hugs and kisses for yourself." When she unexpectedly had to miss Thanksgiving at home, she lamented: "I want to see you so badly, my

FIGURE 2.5. A contented Mollie holds close her toddler daughter, Phyllis (ca. 1899). Taking a cue from the Church family's portrait of Mollie as a child, mother and daughter wear impeccable white dresses with lace and high collars. Later, Mollie dressed Phyllis and her niece and adopted daughter, Mary, in similar white dresses (see figure 4.1). (Courtesy Langston Family)

darling. It seems an age since I have been in your dear arms. I am getting more and more dependent upon you as I grow older." Trying to see their brief times apart as having some benefit, she suggested, "But perhaps this separation, only casual and, as a rule, very short, will work out for both of us as a more exceeding and abundant joy."[62]

Throughout the Terrell couple's marriage, their continued emotional attraction and sexual desire helped sustain them. Their passion was vital to the health of their relationship, for even after the birth of Phyllis, they faced other significant challenges, including financial setbacks that threatened Berto's professional reputation and opportunities for career advancement. Aiming to represent their race as models of achievement, they shared high expectations that Phyllis and, later, their adopted daughter, Mary, would achieve even greater academic and professional successes than they had.[63]

Leading the National Association
of Colored Women

I n the early 1890s, middle-class and elite black women believed they had a
responsibility to show what black women could be, do, and achieve. In
1896, they formed the National Association of Colored Women with Mollie Church Terrell as its first president, hoping it would give them a voice
on the national stage to promote the well-being of all African Americans. The
NACW was the first national secular black organization, not just the first one
for women, and the foundation of black political activism in the late nineteenth century.[1]

Creating a national organization was messy and complicated. The most important extant groups and leading clubwomen from several regions competed
for the highest positions. Black clubwomen's power struggles at that time did
not clearly represent ideological divisions between accommodationism and a
more assertive civil rights activism, divisions that had not yet fully jelled. Starting with the first election to choose a president of the NACW, Mollie Terrell
beat out the competition three times in a row. This significant achievement
formed a strong foundation for her many accomplishments, giving her legitimacy as a national leader and spokeswoman. When her final term ended in
1901, she was named honorary president for life with full voting rights on the
executive board. Thus, Terrell could legitimately claim to be representing the
NACW at any event or when lobbying.

But Mollie Terrell's preeminence and determination to serve for three two-
year terms also contributed to lingering resentments and competition between
her and others who also wanted the NACW presidency in a world that offered
limited opportunities for black female leadership. Terrell's grace, elegance, and
vibrant enthusiasm combined with an unbending will and competitive personality. Her graciousness and fierceness complicated her relations with other

FIGURE 3.1. A stunning Mollie Church Terrell, attired in a satin dress with intricate beadwork, sequins, and fringe, posed for this portrait when she was coming into her own as a leader, with key roles on the D.C. board of education and as president of the National Association of Colored Women. Radiating refinement and sophistication, Terrell's pointed words made a powerful impression, especially when coming in the form of a public speech in her deep, resonant voice. (Courtesy Library of Congress)

prominent women (often equally determined, talented, and competitive), including Ida B. Wells-Barnett, Fannie Barrier Williams, Anna Julia Cooper, Margaret Murray Washington, Josephine St. Pierre Ruffin, and Mary McLeod Bethune. These relationships shifted between moments of genuine friendship and mutual appreciation to private and public feuds.[2]

"Enabling Us to Work Out Our Own Salvation"

In 1892, Helen A. Cook established the Colored Woman's League in Washington, D.C., and Terrell, Charlotte Forten Grimké, Josephine Bruce, Mary Jane Patterson, Sarah Iredell Fleetwood, and Anna Julia Cooper were among the nine founding members. The group called for "forming a National League," making it the first club organized with the intention of uniting black women across the country. The Colored Woman's League initiated significant local projects, including "kindergartens, sewing schools, day nurseries, night schools, and penny savings banks right among the people who need this kind of service." Its kindergartens served as models and training schools, inspiring the District of Columbia to open its own. The league trained "seven of the eight teachers appointed." It also ran "a Day Nursery to provide a place where poor mothers who work out may leave their little ones during the day, knowing that they will be kindly cared for."[3] Inspired by the growing political influence of the suffrage movement, due to its recent unification into one main organization, the National American Woman Suffrage Association, Terrell and her compatriots hoped to create a similar association that would give black women a platform from which to advocate racial and sexual equality. African American women also felt forced to organize because most white women's clubs excluded them and declined to support their specific reform goals, such as the repeal of Jim Crow laws or the passage of federal antilynching legislation.[4]

The Colored Woman's League's founders wrote to other clubs soliciting their affiliation into a national organization and using the model of a correspondence committee to expand. Anna Julia Cooper, Terrell's former Oberlin classmate, colleague, and neighbor, explained: "Within the first year of its existence vigorous Leagues had entered the union in Colorado, Missouri, Virginia, West Virginia, Pennsylvania and elsewhere . . . looking forward to a national organization of all constituent clubs." The black women who joined "for all sorts of progressive endeavor," were, Cooper noted, at most "one generation removed from slavery."[5]

In 1893, Terrell published "What the Colored Women's League Will Do" in *Ringwood's Afro-American Journal of Fashion*. She wrote: "The Colored Woman's League recently organized in Washington has cordially invited women in all parts of the country to unite with it, so that we may have a national organization," and noted that the Women's League of Kansas City, led by Josephine Silone Yates, was one of those already affiliated (Yates later became the second NACW president). Terrell concluded, "Others will soon emulate this worthy example and the League will be an established fact, enabling us to work out our own salvation in that effective and successful manner possible only to earnest, zealous women." Responding to her article, black women representing clubs in several states affiliated with the league.[6]

In 1894, the white women's organization the National Council of Women invited the Colored Woman's League to send "fraternal delegates," a status short of full membership, if it could prove itself a national group. Otherwise, the black women could not participate in the white council's conventions, even in a limited capacity. The league saw this as an opportune moment to formalize its national organization. It contacted its existing affiliates in about a dozen states, asking them to vote by mail to create the National League of Colored Women (NLCW). The member clubs did so, electing national officers and fifteen convention delegates. In late 1894, the NLCW reached out to other black women's clubs, inviting them to send delegates to the National Council of Women's meeting.[7]

When the NLCW approached the Woman's Era Club of Boston, organized a year after the league, in 1893, by Josephine St. Pierre Ruffin, it found a chillier reception. Ruffin, already a member of predominantly white organizations like the New England Press Club and the Massachusetts Federation of Women's Clubs, feared that black women would remain subsidiary partners in white groups. She also intended her Woman's Era Club, whose members represented Boston's black elite, to be the foundation for a national club with her as its leader. She had launched the *Woman's Era* in 1890 as a local paper and as a national newspaper in March 1894. Ruffin invited leading clubwomen from key regions across the country to join the editorial board and serve as contributors to the magazine. Its contributing editors included two women affiliated with the NLCW, Mary Church Terrell and Josephine Silone Yates.[8]

When the *Woman's Era* published a statement about the NLCW's invitation to send delegates to the National Council of Women's national convention, it reported: "A majority of the members of the Woman's Era Club of Boston did not see the advantages of being represented, and voted not to send a delegate." Despite Ruffin's rebuff, the NLCW promised to "ably represent the race" at the predominantly white convention. Its 1895 annual report reiterated its claim to preeminence: "The idea of national organization has been embodied in the Woman's League of Washington from its formation. It . . . has national union for its central thought, its inspiring motive, its avowed purpose—its very reason for being."[9]

Although histories written by NLCW members like Cooper and Terrell emphasized its status as the first national African American women's organization, Chicago's Fannie Barrier Williams wrote histories arguing that Ruffin's came first. She did so by counting Ruffin's national convention as the start of it all. Calling Ruffin as "a woman of rare force of character, mental alertness and of generous impulses," Williams identified the Woman's Era Club as the association best known nationally. Although acknowledging that the league held tenaciously to its "claim as the originator of the idea" of a national association of black women, Williams pointed out that "its claim has always been challenged with more or less spirit by some of the" others.[10] Whereas Cooper and her NLCW allies declared that the *Woman's Era* had, indeed, announced a conference but had not specifically mentioned its plan to create a national organization, Williams emphasized: "The *Woman's Era* journal of Boston began to agitate the matter [of organization] in the summer of 1894" and convened, in July 1895, "the first National convention of colored women ever held in America."[11]

Ruffin's July 1895 Boston convention gave African American women a forum to "discuss and take measures to refute certain accusations against colored women published by a western editor," John W. Jacks, president of the Missouri Press Association. Jacks had written to Florence Balgarnie, the secretary of the Anti-Lynching Committee of London, defaming African American women as "prostitutes and . . . natural liars and thieves." He denigrated all black women, in large part to refute the credibility of Ida B. Wells-Barnett, who had recently toured England, spreading her persuasive antilynching message. Balgarnie forwarded the letter to Ruffin, who sent copies to African American women's clubs, appealing that they gather in a national conference to defend their honor and organize resistance. Facing the persistent racist stereotype of black women as impure and overly sexualized, they challenged this image and also condemned white men's sexual assaults on black women.[12]

In addition to condemning Jacks and defending black womanhood, delegates at the Boston convention addressed other serious issues of concern for African American women. They sought to improve the homes and work opportunities for black women and their families. Further, Selena Sloan Butler, who began the first black parent-teacher association in Georgia, described the convict lease labor system, inspiring the group's Committee on Resolutions to condemn "the Georgia state convict system and the recent Florida educational law [which closed some black schools], and lynching in general." African American women were at the vanguard of the battle against the forces of white supremacy and race hatred.[13]

Mollie Terrell did not attend the Boston convention. She was pregnant for the first time since her late miscarriage in 1892 and was due in October. Although she tried to protect her pregnancy, it ended in stillbirth. Helen A. Cook did attend, representing the NLCW at the meeting. Cook pointed out she was already the leader of an existing national organization and invited the assembled women to join the league. But the Boston leaders and others wanted a new association. The delegates chose to give themselves a new name: the National Federation of Afro-American Women. Cook worried that NLCW members might be forced into subordinate roles within a merged group and declined to join the newly created federation. She explained that she had not asked for or received permission from her member organizations to take such an action. Both groups agreed to negotiate a future merger.[14]

The new National Federation of Afro-American Women elected Margaret Murray Washington, wife of Booker T. Washington, as president. Her election does not indicate that black clubwomen were choosing to align ideologically with her husband. It was two months before Washington's controversial "Atlanta Compromise" speech, and opposition to him was relatively weak. Even those, like W. E. B. Du Bois and Mollie Terrell, who supported higher education for African Americans, appreciated Washington's creation of a strong vocational training program at Tuskegee Institute. Margaret Washington's election was, rather, a way to defuse the regional competition between the District of Columbia and Boston by picking a prominent leader of the largest black women's club in the South, the Tuskegee Women's Club, the section of the country in which most African Americans lived.[15]

Two months later, at the Atlanta Cotton States Exhibition of 1895, Margaret Washington, Helen Cook, and a joint committee had trouble reaching a merger agreement. From the league's perspective, Ruffin's dedication to her own group made the merger more difficult and set the tone for subsequent leadership contests. Ruffin's *Woman's Era* announced, as Terrell described it, "that many were disappointed because the President of the Woman's Era Club [Ruffin], who called the meeting had not been elected president." At this delicate moment, the *Woman's Era* also issued a backhanded compliment: "The Woman's League of Washington . . . in order to meet an emergency and grasp an opportunity to make a creditable showing for themselves, their race, and the cause they were invited to represent, had been obliged to call themselves 'national,' to be eligible to membership in the [National Council of Women]. . . . This action had been taken hurriedly and nothing but praise is due the Washington League for . . . using any measure to make the most of it." The *Woman's Era* then insisted that the Boston conference was "the only legitimate source from which a national organization could spring." NLCW members, Terrell later noted, "were greatly shocked that their organization had been accused of calling itself national before it had actually acquired nationality and an unfortunate misunderstanding between the two groups ensued."[16]

"The Outcome of the Convention Is Mrs. Terrell's Triumph"

Refusing to back down on its claim to national leadership, the NLCW planned its own convention for July 1896 in Washington with 150 delegates from nine states and the District of Columbia. It invited representatives from the National Federation of Afro-American Women "to enter into further conference on union." Agreeing that black women must focus their energies through one group, the federation agreed to hold its own convention in D.C. immediately afterward. With this concession, federation leaders expected to be rewarded with prominent positions in the new group's leadership.[17]

The two conventions of the national African American women's clubs received remarkably respectful and extensive coverage from mainstream white newspapers like the *Washington Post* and the *Chicago Tribune*. The *Post* praised the NLCW, which had its roots in D.C.'s elite black community, accepting its claim to be "the first national association of colored women organized in the United States." It referred to Terrell with respect, as a woman of authority and status—"Mrs. Mary Church Terrell, trustee of the public schools of this city." The *Post* noted: "Since the organization of the National League of Colored Women four years ago [1892], good progress has been made toward the . . . advancement of the Interests of the Negro race throughout the United States."[18] At the league's convention, the Reverend Francis Grimké (who was later active in the Niagara Movement and joined Terrell and Wells-Barnett in founding the NAACP), perhaps inadvertently stoked the competition by praising the D.C. women as race leaders and by inaccurately calling "especial attention to the fact that this convention is the first national convention of colored women ever held in the history of the world." This 1896 meeting was held in the influential Nineteenth Street Baptist Church, which had more than two thousand congregants, including Nannie Helen Burroughs. The league delegates were from Missouri, Colorado, Massachusetts, Rhode Island, Maryland, Pennsylvania, Virginia, West Virginia, Minnesota, and the District.[19]

The NLCW had an ambitious reform agenda. Unlike white women, who had the benefit of a wide variety of national clubs to take up different concerns, black women tried to fulfill many goals through one national organization. At the convention, the league vowed "to assist in the erection of an orphan home and industrial school . . . in memory of John Brown, hero of Harper's Ferry." It "denounced lynchings and recommended the passage of laws requiring counties to pay large fines to the State and full indemnity to the family of the persons lynched." In addition, the league "favored the work of the Atlanta University [led by Du Bois] in collecting statistics in relation to the sanitary and social conditions . . . of colored people living in large cities . . . to relieve alley and tenement-house life from attendant dangers." One resolution promoted higher education for black women "to encourage their entry into professions, especially those of nurse and physician." Another supported black economic nationalism: "We pledge our patronage to the members of our race who prove themselves efficient and reliable in their respective pursuits." These reform goals touched the lives of a wide variety of African Americans, including those living in poverty in the rural South or in cities.[20]

When the National Federation of Afro-American Women met at the same location immediately afterward, Terrell and other women from the league attended. At the federation's meeting, Terrell represented a club from her hometown of Memphis and was also there in her role as a contributing editor to the *Woman's Era*. The lines of separation between the competing women's clubs, even at the leadership level, were not so distinct. District of Columbia leaders, including Mary Jane Patterson, Terrell, and Cooper, had graduated from Oberlin College; Ruffin had been educated at a private school and was part of Boston's black elite, even though she had not earned a college degree.[21]

At the federation's convention, delegates discussed similar topics to those covered at the NLCW convention. The *Washington Post* reported: "Mrs. Victoria Earle Matthews said . . . the work on which the Federation was engaged was on mission, rescue, philanthropic, domestic, and educational lines." Terrell and Ida Wells-Barnett were both chosen to be on the federation's Committee on Resolutions, which subsequently endorsed "higher and more truly practical education," denounced the "separate car law," condemned the convict lease system and lynching, supported Justice John Marshall Harlan's recent dissent in *Plessy v. Ferguson*, advocated "fair trial by law for life and liberty," and proposed a fund to build a John Brown Memorial.[22]

While the white press focused on black women's remarkable organizational efforts, a black paper, the *Washington Bee*, began its coverage of the two 1896 conventions by criticizing the women for competing with each other for leadership positions: "Afro-American women are like men. They cannot agree. Two separate conventions have met in this city and both are for the same purpose. It looks like it was a question of leadership. Women like men, are ambitious for fame and notoriety. The best way to improve the condition of our women is talk less and do more." They were certainly competing for leadership, but all this "talking" was, in fact, part of African American women's intellectual framing of the issues as they attempted to shape and influence legal, political, and social reform in the United States.[23]

On the federation convention's first day, Terrell was chosen to be on its committee to negotiate a merger with the league. With seven members from each organization, the joint group's first task was to choose a chair. That honor and responsibility went to Terrell, who had friends and supporters in both groups and was the only woman on the joint committee representing both sides simultaneously, a sign of the respect she had earned as a highly educated woman who was sitting on the board of education in the nation's capital.[24]

Meeting in a daylong session, Terrell's joint committee began by discussing the most appropriate name for the new organization. As a means of reconcilia-tion, the words "League" and "Federation" were both dropped in favor of "Na-tional Association." Terrell strongly favored *Colored* over *Afro-American* or *Negro*, and on this point she prevailed. It was not an attempt to deny her own or black women's African heritage. While in Europe, she recalled, "Somebody would say, 'You are rather dark to be an American, aren't you?' Yes, I would explain, 'I am dark, because some of my ancestors were Africans.' I was proud of having the continent of Africa as part of my ancestral background. I am an African American." But, she argued, the words "Negro" or "Afro-American" were more limited and implied the color black. She wanted to make the politi-cal and social point that people of her race in the United States had many dif-ferent shades of skin color, ranging "from deep black to the fairest white." The word "colored," Terrell insisted, better represented the wide range of skin col-ors among those of African descent, including light-skinned women like her-self. It highlighted the harsh reality of those with African heritage in Amer-ica—that black women had been raped by white men. For Terrell, the word "colored" was an important reminder of black women's lack of control over their own bodies and autonomy. Such powerlessness had, of course, attended her own grandmothers, both of whom bore white men's children.[25]

The task of choosing a president was not easy. Terrell later recalled that many prominent African American women, including all the members of the joint committee, were nominated for the position, but the vote repeatedly split 7 to 7: "Finally, I was nominated the second time, the deadline was broken, I received the majority of the votes cast and was elected the first president of the National Association of Colored Women. It was nearly six o'clock in the evening when this occurred. . . . Each and every one of us was worn to a fraz-zle. . . . It was the hardest day's work I have ever done." Terrell's unique status as a founding member of the league who nonetheless represented the federa-tion on the joint committee played a role in her single-vote margin of victory. She then endorsed a structure of seven vice-presidents, based on geographic representation, to include all regions in leadership. Terrell's rivals, including Josephine Ruffin, were among the seven vice-presidents.[26]

A "great crowd" had waited into the evening to hear the announcement of the officers and the name of the new organization. The *Post* reported, "It was with deep interest that the audience listened to the committee's conclusions, which were final, because each committee had been delegated the power to act." After the announcement of her election as president, Terrell spoke briefly and "in accepting the office expressed her thanks for the confidence that had been reposed in her, and declared that she would do all in her power to make the new union accomplish what it aims to do."[27]

After the committee's report to the assembled delegates, Terrell assumed that the most difficult work of the day was behind her. But her ascension to the presidency of the NACW did not sit well with Ruffin and her supporters. Rather than accept the joint committee's decision, "there was a disposition on the part of a few of the ladies to attack the honesty and integrity of the committee." Owing to the proportional system of choosing the officers, some federation partisans disputed the league's assertion that it represented a larger number of affiliated clubs. These dissenters demanded, according to the *Bee*, "that the League should be made to show up the great membership claimed." Hoping their numbers might give them the edge, some New England delegates argued that there should be a floor vote despite the previously established rules.[28]

At that tense moment, Terrell spoke, appealing for harmony and cooperation while also threatening to resign as joint committee chair if the delegates would not accept the committee's decisions. She persuaded the assembly that unity was of utmost importance, for black women needed to have one national organization to achieve their shared goals. The *Bee* reported: "In language as classic as the vestal goddesses and with the eloquence of the sirens, she defied anyone to attack the honesty and integrity of the committee. . . . Does this, said Mrs. Terrell, show a Christian spirit? Does this look like you want harmony? Away! With such pretentions and hypocrisy."[29]

Terrell's oratory shifted the mood: "At the conclusion of Mrs. Terrell's speech, the applause was vociferous and enthusiastic all over the church. . . . It was a masterly effort and demonstrated the honesty and integrity in a grand woman. . . . The outcome of the convention is Mrs. Terrell's triumph." The women united behind Terrell.[30] Ida B. Wells-Barnett later acknowledged the logic of the choice: "Mrs. Terrell, a graduate of Oberlin College who had been a teacher in Washington High School for a number of years, herself being the wife of a prominent attorney in Washington and believed to be the most highly educated woman we had in the race, was chosen president of the consolidated organization."[31] Terrell's status as a highly educated African American woman teacher and school board member, with a mastery of several foreign languages and a master's degree, was key to her ascendancy.

Terrell rallied the delegates behind the new NACW and her leadership, but rival leaders, especially those representing other regions, wanted to take the reins of the only secular national African American women's organization as soon as possible.[32] Chicago's Fannie Barrier William and her ally Josephine Ruffin both had strong NACW presidential ambitions. Williams so disapproved of Terrell's dominance that her histories of the club movement, written a few years later, when rivalries between the regional leaders were even more fractious, avoided mentioning Terrell at all. Williams's ultimate act of dismissal was to erase Terrell by omitting her as the first NACW president.

Rather than start her history with the official merger in 1896, Williams began with the 1895 Boston convention and called Margaret Washington the first president, although she was, in fact, the first and only president of the short-lived National Federation of Afro-American Women. When Williams was writing her club histories in the first decade of the twentieth century, she and her husband were very close to Booker T. Washington at a point when Mollie Terrell was aligning herself with the Constitution League, Du Bois, and the NAACP. This may have contributed to her negative perceptions of Terrell.[33]

"To Regain My Health"

Terrell's own well-being continued to be an issue, as she faced tragic losses surrounding reproduction. At the time of her impressive 1896 convention performance, she was pregnant for the third time. Throughout the meeting, she silently coped with the stress and anticipation surrounding her pregnancy, which ended with the birth of a living infant who died within days. Then, during her first term as NACW president, Terrell's life was again in peril. On May 17, 1897, Berto wrote his father-in-law, "Mollie is in New York with her mother. Her condition is not at all encouraging and she is having consultations with the leading physicians in New York. I am afraid that she is losing ground." She received an experimental treatment, electrotherapeutics, designed to address "non-malignant pelvic disease," such as an endometriotic cyst, without resorting to surgery. Berto continued: "I leave . . . tomorrow to see Mollie who writes me that her condition is very serious and that she feels herself failing every day. . . . I confess that I am greatly alarmed."[34]

FIGURE 3.2. (*Facing page*) In 1896, some of the key women who formed the new National Association of Colored Women posed for a group photo in Washington, D.C. Tentative identifications of most of the women—including information on what each of these early NACW leading members was doing in, or had done by, 1896—are as follows.

Back row, left to right: Georgia Washington was educated at the Hampton Institute and in 1893 became the founder and principal of the People's Village School in Mt. Meigs, Alabama; Mrs. A. L. Davis, president of the Phyllis Wheatley Club of Chicago; Mary C. Jackson (McCrorey) attended Atlanta University and in 1896 became associate principal at Haines Normal and Industrial Institute in Augusta, Georgia, founded by Lucy Craft Laney; Victoria Earle Matthews, a journalist and cofounder of the Women's Loyal Union of New York and Brooklyn that supported Ida B. Wells's antilynching crusade; Alice Ruth Moore (Dunbar Nelson), an educator and newly published young poet and short-story writer (she is holding Ida B. Wells-Barnett's baby, Charles Barnett); unknown.

Middle row, seated: NACW president Mollie Church Terrell, with a fan and a striking hat with feathers and fruit (she was pregnant at the time with another baby she would lose); Lucy Thurman of Jackson, Michigan, the only black cofounder of the Woman's Christian Temperance Union in 1874 and national superintendent of colored work of the WCTU since 1893; Fanny Jackson Coppin graduated from Oberlin College in 1860, became the first black teacher at the Oberlin Academy, and then served as principal of Philadelphia's Institute for Colored Youth; Maggie Lena Walker, a leader of an African American benevolent organization, the Independent Order of St. Luke's in Richmond, Virginia, that aided the elderly and ill; Josephine Beall Wilson Bruce, educator and wife of Reconstruction–era African American U.S. senator Blanche Kelso Bruce of Mississippi, who lived in D.C. and became vice president of the National Association for the Relief of Destitute Colored Women and Children in 1882 and a charter member of the Colored Woman's League of Washington, D.C., in 1892; Mrs. Amanda Lyles of St. Paul, Minnesota, the national president of the John Brown Monument Association, WCTU member, owner of a hair salon, and wife of Thomas H. Lyles, an undertaker and editor of the local African American newspaper the *Western Appeal*.

Seated on the ground: unknown; Ida B. Wells-Barnett, educator, journalist, antilynching advocate, and new mother; Selina Butler, an educator who advocated for day nurseries and kindergartens for African American children and founded a kindergarten in her Atlanta, Georgia, home (married to Dr. Henry Rutherford Butler).

The photographer was Luke C. Dillon, who had been a photographer for the Army of the Potomac during the Civil War; the official photographer at Mt. Vernon, George Washington's home; and then a photographer in the District of Columbia. (Courtesy Oberlin College Archives; thanks to Cecilia Robinson and Ida E. Jones for their help in identifying the women)

When the treatment failed, Mollie underwent an operation. Afterward, her gynecological surgeon reassured Berto, "Your wife is improving daily. . . . The abscess is still discharging a little but . . . the cavity is healing up. . . . I think now it will be possible in the near future to remove the [illegible] and leave the womb." The doctor reassured him they might still be able to have a child. Berto reported to his father-in-law, "Mollie is improving very rapidly now. . . . You will not know until I can tell you how near-death Mollie was. . . . We have had a narrow escape."[35] From Mollie's perspective, this operation was her last chance to have a healthy, living child: "I was very ill a few years after my marriage. . . . The surgeon told me frankly that I was taking a chance, and he could not tell what the result of the operation would be. Neither my husband nor my mother wanted me to run the risk. But I felt I would rather die trying to regain my health than drag out a weary, useless existence as an invalid."[36]

As she was recovering from surgery and trying to get pregnant again, Terrell poured her heart and energy into her role as NACW's first president. A few months after her operation, on September 15, 1897, she gave her first formal presidential speech at the NACW convention in Nashville, Tennessee, urging the delegates to establish free kindergartens as the best way to help African American women. She pointed out that black women of all classes experienced institutional and daily racism, including obstructed access to education and employment, rape, health disparities, and disproportionate infant mortality. She knew of the latter danger from personal experience and highlighted disturbing race-based disparities: "The health of our race is becoming a matter of deep concern to many who are alarmed by statistics showing how great is the death rate among us as compared with that of the Whites."[37] Her encouragement of young black women to enter nursing and medical schools reflected her recognition that African Americans needed high-quality health care from well-trained professionals who had a vested interest in their survival and ability to thrive. Terrell's maternalist focus and appropriation of the rhetoric of domesticity and purity was inherently subversive since black women were perceived by most whites as either unsexed laborers or as oversexualized and impure, not as caring, concerned mothers.[38]

To raise fit and thriving children, Terrell argued, African American mothers needed assistance, training, and institutional support like day care programs and kindergartens. Focusing on the needs of black working-class women and their children, she maintained: "Establishing day nurseries is clearly a practical charity . . . for the infants of working women." It "would not only save the life, and preserve the health of many a little one, but it would speak eloquently of our interest in our sisters, whose lot is harder than our own, but to whom we should give unmistakable proof of our regard, our sympathy, and our willingness to render any assistance in our power."[39] Urging the women to raise more money for institution building, she took the initiative and established a fund to build kindergartens and day nurseries. Terrell raised money for the fund by publishing a pamphlet containing her speech on "The Progress of Colored Women," which was sold at NACW and NAWSA conventions.[40]

While working to establish day nurseries, kindergartens, and mothers' clubs, Terrell also advocated the NACW fight for African Americans' civil rights more broadly. She particularly encouraged members to advocate enforcement of the Reconstruction era amendments to the Constitution and for woman suffrage: "In public questions affecting our legal status, let us engage intelligently and continuously, whenever and wherever it is possible to strike a blow for equality and right. Against atrocities like the Convict Lease System whose barbarity no tongue can utter, whose brutality no pen can portray, let us wage ceaseless war."[41]

Using the motto "Lifting as we climb," Terrell appealed to notions of duty and uplift to encourage NACW members to support progressive social and political reform goals.[42] Referring to poor and working-class black women, she spoke frankly to elite clubwomen: "Even though we wish to shun them and hold ourselves entirely aloof from them, we cannot escape the consequences of their acts." The depth and breadth of racism in the United States was so entrenched that all African Americans were maligned by whites as their inferiors. Whites did not bother with distinctions of class, education, or skin tone among African Americans; one "drop" defined a person socially and legally as "black." One black person accused of theft, for example, would reflect badly on all African Americans. Thus, Terrell argued, racial uplift would work only if clubwomen strove for the collective good of all African Americans.[43]

———

During the NACW's 1897 convention, Mollie Terrell, Josephine Bruce, Lucy Thurman, and Margaret Washington were all nominated for president. Terrell was decisively reelected on the first ballot. In a gesture of harmony, Thurman and Bruce moved to make the vote for Terrell unanimous. This seamless process demonstrated widespread satisfaction with and confidence in Terrell's leadership. Focusing on antilynching activism and her own child rearing, Ida Wells-Barnett had declined risking a return to Tennessee, where she had been driven out in 1892, and so was absent from the Nashville convention. While in Nashville, the delegates chose Wells-Barnett's adopted home of Chicago as the site for their next gathering. After holding national meetings in Washington, Nashville, and Boston (in 1895), the delegates chose the Midwest. Pledging to take care of local arrangements, the Illinois women created a coalition of seven clubs led by Fannie Barrier Williams. Terrell gladly accepted the offer of help and was pleased with the selection of a prime midwestern location.[44]

After her reelection, Terrell reviewed the NACW's early accomplishments in an 1898 article. She celebrated the eighty-six affiliated clubs in twenty-six states, organized by "our women, from whom shackles have but yesterday fallen." The young organization was, she noted, the "union of two large organizations both of which had done much to show our women the advantage gained by concerted action." Terrell pointed to initial progress, such as the establishment of old age homes, schools, and kindergartens in cities and towns around the nation. And she reiterated: "Questions affecting our legal status as a race are constantly agitated by our women," who were fighting "to repeal the obnoxious Jim Crow laws."[45]

"An Unseemly Scramble for Office"

In the lead up to the 1899 convention, Terrell published an article in the *National Association Notes* attempting to quash a controversy about who would be running for president and under what terms. Albert B. George, a recent graduate of Northwestern University's Law School and a former student of Terrell's at the M Street Colored High School, charged in the *Colored American* that Chicago was chosen as the convention venue to ensure that Terrell's good friend and ally, Josephine Bruce, would be elected as president. Terrell denied that it was part of what George called "an unseemly scramble for office."[46]

Preparing for each national convention was a huge task. Terrell arranged the program, negotiated reduced train fares, and coordinated the meeting logistics with state and local committee members. This included finding boarding for the delegates. To secure the number of travelers needed to get reduced train fares, Terrell had asked the National Afro-American Council, of which she was a member, if it would hold its convention in Chicago the same week. It agreed, enabling NACW delegates to attend both meetings. Terrell spoke at each, advocating racial uplift while protesting lynching, segregation, and disfranchisement.[47]

In response to George, Terrell stated, "I see no reason why anyone should be ashamed to acknowledge that she wants Mrs. Bruce to be our next president. She is a well-educated, broad-minded, large-hearted woman, with a spotless reputation. I publicly plead guilty to the charge of wanting just such a woman as our next president, and I also promise to oppose any woman who does not represent all this." Since Josephine Ruffin did not have a college degree, this also served as a dig at her and a signal of Terrell's opposition to Ruffin's candidacy. Although Terrell supported Bruce, she insisted that she had not been campaigning for her "either publicly or privately. . . . I do not believe, moreover, that Mrs. Washington has done so." Recently widowed, Bruce had been appointed as "lady principal" at Tuskegee Institute; she and Margaret Washington worked together and were close allies. Along with Terrell, the three were referred to as the "triumvirate."[48]

When her daughter, Phyllis, was born in 1898, Mollie Terrell was serving her second term as NACW president, and she expressed the aspirations and anxieties of new motherhood, counseling black mothers of all economic and educational backgrounds to carefully instill race pride in their offspring. Without it, they would be endangered: "Let a child hear constantly that he belongs to a race vicious, ignorant and with but few redeeming traits and it is impossible to develop in him that self-respect which is both an incentive to effort and a safeguard against wrong-doing." Optimistically believing in the power of nurture, she asserted parents could make a significant difference in the lives and progress of their children: "If the vices of the race were cited less and its virtues discussed more, many false accusations could be easily removed and a higher estimate of its worth be incontrovertibly established." By raising children with a consistent moral standard, black mothers could help fight the sexual double standard and the racist disrespect facing all black youths.[49]

Terrell's husband and father both wanted to protect the new mother's health and well-being and so implored her not to follow through on a desire she initially confided only to her family members—to run for a third term as NACW president at the 1899 Chicago convention. She explained: "Before I left home my father came from Memphis to Washington to urge me not to accept the presidency again under any circumstances. And my husband's opposition to it was as strong as my father's. For this reason, I felt I dared not take the office again and thus turn a deaf ear to the advice and requests of the men in my family."[50]

When Terrell arrived at the 1899 convention, she felt torn about being reelected but believed that she had succeeded in growing the new organization into a powerful force and foundation for putting black women on the national stage. Relying on substantial support from her mother, Louisa, she believed that she could simultaneously run the NACW, serve on the D.C. board of education, and raise her daughter. Her desire to improve the lives of black mothers and their children melded with her personal ambition, and she wanted to hold onto her prestigious position as the national leader of black women.

That the election took place the year after she had given birth to her only living child expands our understanding of Terrell's decision to retain the presidency. Her motivations were rooted in her courage and pain as a new mother, as well as in ambition and pride. Her supporters did not dispute the NACW's constitution, which allowed only two consecutive terms. Instead, they counted the number of her consecutive terms from the date the constitution was ratified in 1897 rather than her first election in 1896. Terrell had left open the possibility of her own candidacy by referring to the NACW's 1897 Nashville convention as the organization's "first," which paved the way for her to run for a constitutionally allowable second term.[51] Although she denied any interest in continuing as president, she craved the delegates' affirmation.[52]

Before the convention, Terrell hoped to harness the influence of the clergy in support of the NACW, suggesting: "If our ministers, all over the country, would preach at least one sermon on the work the National Association of Colored Women has done and is trying to do, it would aid materially in making our convention a success." Since "our women bear the heaviest burdens of the church work," she held, "the pastors should come to our assistance." Clergy of the most prominent African American churches in Chicago allowed Terrell, Fannie Barrier Williams, Josephine Bruce, and Josephine Silone Yates to speak to large audiences on the Sunday before the convention.[53]

But even before NACW delegates arrived in Chicago, trouble was brewing. Fannie Barrier Williams, who led the Chicago delegation, was upset about Ida Wells-Barnett's critiques of Booker T. Washington, a close ally of Williams and her husband. Williams desired to replace Wells-Barnett as the preeminent black woman in Chicago and even hoped to be NACW president herself. If she were not to be nominated, she planned to support Josephine Ruffin, whom she admired greatly. Williams did not want Wells-Barnett to run against her or Ruffin or initiate politicized disputes at the meeting.[54]

Hence, Williams's coalition of black women's clubs in charge of local organizing made an unexpected demand of Terrell, insisting that she keep Wells-Barnett out of the public aspects of the convention, with no formal role or welcome in her adopted hometown. A surprised Terrell pragmatically decided that she needed the Illinois women's help more than she needed Wells-Barnett, who could be disruptive and oppositional. Wells-Barnett called it "a staggering blow" and angrily blamed Terrell, not realizing that the Chicago women had initiated it. When Wells-Barnett discovered that even the Ida B. Wells Club had joined in blocking her, she condemned the Chicago contingent as "narrow-minded." Nonetheless, she continued to direct most of her anger at Terrell, suggesting that she had acceded to preserve her own hold on the presidency. Wells-Barnett did not represent much of a threat, since she did not even have the support of the Illinois women. Trying to mollify her, Terrell pointed out that Wells-Barnett was going to be absorbed that week in her work as co-chair of the Afro-American Council's convention.[55] Rifts continued because some NACW delegates failed to bring their credentials. Terrell decided to enforce the rules strictly in order to set a good precedent for the young organization. Although she insisted that she was simply following parliamentary law,

Terrell's decisions seemed punitive, especially when she ruled Josephine Ruffin out of order on the grounds that she, too, lacked proper credentials.

Trying to secure another term for Terrell, her allies attempted to reelect the entire slate of current officers. After that failed, Terrell declared in executive session that she "had reconsidered her determination not to run" for another term. Initially, she had stated that she needed unanimous approval to accept the position, but then she decided that two-thirds of the vote would be an adequate show of support. Throughout, some continued to oppose Terrell's third reelection on constitutional grounds.[56]

On the floor of the convention, an outraged Ruffin accused Terrell of "treachery, duplicity, and unfaithfulness," but the delegates loudly hissed, showering Ruffin with "torrents of consuming scorn and chastisement." The New Englanders, "who were especially antagonistic to her [Terrell's] reelection, insisted that she resign the chair" during the vote. Lucy Thurman, the second vice-president, oversaw the voting. Ruffin hoped that transparency would somehow help her win, so she moved that each delegate should "come forward and deposit her ballot on a table in front of the pulpit in the presence of the whole convention." This tactic failed to change the outcome. Ruffin, Washington, Wells-Barnett, Williams, and Thurman split 39 votes between them, whereas Terrell received 106 ballots. Getting the endorsement of the majority of NACW delegates was uplifting for Terrell: "Such a spontaneous outburst of confidence in me more than repaid me for all the strenuous efforts I had exerted to make the Association as a whole and the convention in particular a success."[57]

Terrell's reelection proved her continued popularity and the dominance of the D.C. contingent, but it was immediately followed by regional competition for the other top offices. Ruffin was determined to win the first vice-presidency but lost on the second vote to Josephine Bruce. At that point, the New England delegation threatened to leave the convention in protest. It held out hope, however, that a New Englander would be elected as recording secretary. Chicago delegate Connie A. Curl received eighty-one votes but did not win outright. Curl's chief rival was Ruffin's niece, Elizabeth E. Carter, of New Bedford, Massachusetts, who secured fifty-nine votes. The *Chicago Daily Tribune* reported on the chaos that ensued when Carter "announced her determination to leave the association, saying she had been instructed by the Northeastern Federation of Women's Clubs to announce its withdrawal in case it did not secure representation among the officers." Terrell attempted to keep the New England contingent happy by proposing that Curl step aside, leading the Chicago women to threaten to withdraw. Terrell's solution was to allow for more than one recording secretary, including Curl and Carter, thereby managing to keep both regions in the fold. The jockeying for power left all factions dissatisfied, except perhaps Terrell's mid-Atlantic section. Although "she regretted the trouble," Terrell was satisfied with the compromise.[58]

After her contested election, Terrell wrote to her close friend Fannie Settle, of Memphis, explaining, "Although I really did not want the presidency again for many good and sufficient reasons, chief of which is that I have all the work to do . . . still it was one of the greatest triumphs a woman would possibly have." She continued: "In the first place our 'Virtuous Friend' had done all in her evil power to prejudice the minds of the Illinois delegates against me, and when I reached Chicago, I found them hating me with a zeal worthy of a better cause." It seems likely that Williams was the "Virtuous Friend" who had become upset and spoken out upon realizing that Terrell or one of her allies would win the presidency again. Terrell had calculated that she needed to win over almost all the fifty or so Illinois delegates to be elected. After her powerful presidential address on the first evening, "they came to me in droves and openly declared they would vote for no one else as president. . . . I insisted again and again that I would not take a reelection under any circumstances, but they were just as bent that I should." Her reelection upset "Fannie [Williams] and Mrs. Ruffin, who came . . . for the express purpose of getting the presidency by fair means if possible and foul, if necessary."[59]

The NACW leadership struggle went public when Williams and Ruffin introduced themselves to an Associated Press reporter as fellow journalists (which they were) and, according to Terrell, "told him that I had been reelected only after a long struggle and with great opposition. . . . He had no idea of their diabolical scheme of 'getting even with me' for being elected and thus lessening their chances (which by the way were nil)." Thus, he "sent that false report over the wires."[60]

Berto Terrell read the AP report and was upset that his wife had seemingly fought for another term, thereby betraying her promise not to do so. He hastily sent her a letter, which a shocked Mollie told him read as a "sermon on my duty to you." She replied, "You know as well as I do, that I have always discharged my duty to you as a wife." Further, she insisted, "I did not want the presidency of the Association and said so a thousand times. Those women did not want anybody else . . . and simply overwhelmed me. I could not resist them." Mollie reminded Berto that he consistently strove for recognition for himself and his wife, and would have been thrilled to see how, after the vote, the "women wept, threw up their handkerchiefs, rushed to the platform, took me in their arms and covered me with kisses."[61] His letter increased her sense of being under siege, but Berto soon reconciled himself to his wife's reelection.

Once home, Mollie Terrell managed to have her version of events printed in the *Washington Evening Star*; she also convinced the *Washington Post* to retract its original stories. The new slate of NACW officers published its own "Refutation," a point-by-point critique of an article by Ruffin and her allies in the *New York Age* and *National Notes*. Mollie concluded her letter to Fannie Settle, "I did not engage in any disgraceful scramble for an office that I feel that I have held long enough. It was really impossible for me to get out of taking it again. . . . I feel that I came off unscathed. . . . The women who tried to stab me in the back were so badly snowed under that you couldn't even see the tips of their toes."[62]

Fortunately for Terrell and the NACW, the mainstream and black presses did not focus on disunity and were generally positive in their coverage of the 1899 convention. The *Bee* ultimately conceded: "It looks as if Mrs. Terrell, being a better 'wire-puller' and politician than the others, she carried her point."[63] Terrell was proud of being a modern politician, but she also believed that she was criticized for her ambition more than a man would have been.

In the years to come, NACW presidential elections continued to be contentious. In 1901, it appeared that Margaret Washington or Josephine Bruce would win the presidency, but questions about whether they were overly interested in cultivating alliances with white women's groups led delegates to vote instead for Josephine Silone Yates. Yates had been a leader of a large Kansas City club affiliated from 1893 on with the Colored Women's League, had been present at the Boston convention, was from the Midwest, and had darker skin. The latter two factors especially appealed to the delegates. In 1906, at the NACW's Detroit convention, skin color became an explicit issue. Two of the top three candidates, Josephine Bruce and, once again, Mollie Terrell, were light skinned. The third was Lucy Thurman, a midwesterner and a WCTU leader with a darker hue. By 1906, the NACW had gained more members and represented a broader cross section of the African American population. Its members elected Thurman, whose achievements could not be attributed by whites to her mixed-race status. Terrell was friendly with Thurman and stayed with her whenever she visited Michigan, but she likely resented being deemed not black enough, since she saw that all Americans with any black ancestry were deemed black in the eyes of white Americans.[64]

Believing Terrell had blocked her from taking a leadership role in the Chicago convention, Wells-Barnett later wrote that the 1899 election fight had "killed" Terrell's reputation and highlighted her "selfish ambition." Williams, too, thought that Terrell was the most guilty of a charge she also leveled against other NACW leaders—that they had "unworthy ambitions, jealousies, envies, spitefulness, piques, tale-bearing, suspicions, affectations and many other little sins peculiar to human nature generally, and to femininity in particular." In brief notes for her autobiography, Terrell insisted she had "never schemed and

FIGURE 3.3. African American women persisted in their activism, forming the International Council of Women of the Darker Races in 1920 to address colonialism and a more global perspective on race, gender, politics, and activism. This photograph was taken in Washington, D.C., in approximately 1924.

Back row, left to right: Lucy Diggs Slowe, educator and first dean of women at Howard University; Mollie Church Terrell; Nannie Helen Burroughs, leader of the Baptist Woman's Convention and founder of the National Training School for Women and Girls in Washington, D.C.

Front row: Mary C. Jackson McCrorey, educator and chair of the Phyllis Wheatley Branch of the Young Women's Christian Association in Charlotte, North Carolina; Mary McLeod Bethune, educator and founder in 1904 of the Daytona Normal and Industrial Institute for Negro Girls (became Bethune-Cookman College in 1931) in Daytona Beach, Florida, and won the presidency of the National Association of Colored Women in 1924; and Margaret Murray Washington (d. 1925), leading clubwoman, lady principal of Tuskegee Normal and Industrial Institute in Alabama, widow of Booker T. Washington, and founder of the International Council of Women of the Darker Races. (Courtesy Oberlin College Archives) manipulated [or] asked women to vote for me. . . . Laid my cards on the table. Won by being open."[65] But Williams viewed Terrell's ambition as unseemly, repeatedly condemning as "exceedingly offensive" the "ambitions for place and power of some women." Terrell insisted she "didn't do enough of it. [Was] called a politician." Women, she regretted, were held to a different standard of appropriate political behavior than men.[66]

Most NACW clubwomen did not criticize their first president. They saw her as having helped the NACW become a stable and growing national organization. After her last term ended, Terrell was voted honorary president for life. She remained a favorite among the black clubwomen who for decades invited her to speak at their national, state, and local conventions. She was admired by the broader population of African American women joining the association. They appreciated her eloquent speeches calling them to reform activism, and they admired her ability to represent black women not only with elegance and grace but also with power and determination.[67]

4

The Black Elite

FINANCES, MILITANCY, AND FAMILY

Mollie and Berto Terrell were part of the black elite, a status riddled with paradoxes in the decades after the Civil War. What constitutes social grouping is often relative. In the context of the postbellum African American community, the black elite encompassed former slaves and their immediate descendants, like the Churches and Terrells, who secured educations and achieved professional success. Other factors that might designate someone a member of the elite included finances, employment, family lineage, skin complexion, and working for racial justice. Financial success was measured differently for African Americans and whites. Although there were members of the white upper classes who might be considered shabby gentility, the gap between high status and real wealth was often greater among upper-echelon African Americans. The level of financial wherewithal for the white elite was generally far more substantial. White elites held significant savings, property, and/or wealth in stocks and bonds and, if they worked, held prestigious positions in law, politics, finance, and business. Job opportunities were so limited for African American men in the decades after the Civil War that those who earned stable paychecks as postal workers or barbers were middle class, at best, but often considered elites.[1]

In the early 1900s, a scarcity of professional positions available to African Americans inspired Booker T. Washington to develop the District of Columbia as a stronghold for black professional men. White Republicans trusted him to recommend well-qualified, uncontroversial black candidates for the few but coveted government appointments given to them under the system of political patronage.[2]

At the turn of the twentieth century, the Terrells were in an awkward position, caught between their desire for Berto to gain high-status professional positions, which involved political compromises, and Mollie's commitment to being a leading civil rights advocate. She argued that all African Americans should be allowed to thrive as citizens without facing prejudice, segregation, or other forms of discrimination. Confronting roadblocks and prejudice in a context of increasing segregation nationwide, Mollie grew ever more determined to resist the kinds of concessions Booker Washington deemed necessary to conciliate whites. Ultimately unwilling to accommodate the status quo, she affiliated with the "anti-Bookerites," who called for immediate political and social equality for African Americans, focusing on an end to segregation, lynching, disenfranchisement, and discrimination in employment and education.[3]

African Americans who enjoyed some measure of success believed they must work for *racial uplift* through a variety of means, including politics, education, and economic nationalism. W. E. B. Du Bois promoted the idea that a "Talented Tenth" of elite African American intellectuals and professionals could use their achievements to combat racism. The Terrells embraced their role as representatives, demonstrating to prejudiced whites what all African Americans could accomplish, given the opportunity. After they became parents, the Terrells, like other members of the Talented Tenth, provided their daughter, Phyllis, and their adopted daughter, Mollie's niece, Mary, with the resources they expected would make their children even more accomplished and successful than themselves. The rise and spread of segregation made it harder for the rising generation to live up to their parents' expectations even as it spurred the parents into greater activism against Jim Crow.[4]

"The Bank Wrecked Us"

Although at the pinnacle of the black elite social and political world in Washington, D.C., Mollie and Berto Terrell struggled to achieve and maintain markers of wealth and respectability. They earned far more money than most African Americans but still worried about their financial status. These concerns began early in their marriage when Berto, a loyal party of Lincoln Republican, lost his job in the Treasury Department after Democrat Grover Cleveland entered the White House in 1893, the same year that a severe economic downturn began. He was not entirely at a loss, however, for while working during the day, Berto had taken classes at night and had completed a master's degree at Howard University's law school. He joined forces with one of the most prominent black men of the Reconstruction era, John Roy Lynch, the former Republican U.S. representative from Mississippi, under whom he had worked in the Treasury Department. Together, they set up "Lynch & Terrell, Attorneys at Law and Claim Agents," specializing in cases heard by government departments and the U.S. Court of Claims. The firm also facilitated many real estate transactions in the District for Berto's wealthy father-in-law, Robert Church.[5]

The long economic downturn during the 1890s made it a difficult time to start a new business, especially one based on real estate and loans. The idealistic law partners were black nationalists who believed in supporting and promoting black-owned businesses and property ownership. But Lynch and Terrell put themselves at financial risk by signing off on loans for a broad range of African Americans who could not get credit at mainstream white financial institutions but wanted to buy houses and start businesses. Within a few years, Mollie's father had to step in with a loan to try to prevent his son-in-law's insolvency. Berto explained to him, "I am carrying several thousand dollars in paper of other people that I cannot now find any market for." Although Berto made good money, about $2,000 a year, he and Mollie lived from this point on with high anxiety about finances, for he now had more than twice his salary in debt, and things only got worse. Berto knew that he could fail disastrously if the economy and the real estate market did not improve. Yet, he reassured his father-in-law, "I will have no trouble in negotiating this paper when Washington City takes up the task of business reconstruction. . . . You know that real estate is the last thing to fall in value and the last thing to pick up after a panic." Berto's optimism was not matched by reality.[6]

Upheavals in the couple's personal life compounded Berto's business difficulties. In 1897, they had already lost three babies, and Mollie found herself near death for the second time in five years when she underwent surgery in New York City. Berto confessed to Robert Church, "My anxiety almost totally unfits me for business." When Mollie recovered and soon became pregnant for the fourth time, Berto continued focusing on his wife's well-being. Once their daughter was born in 1898, he needed a reliable salaried position to support his family, which now included not only his baby daughter but also his mother-in-law, who had moved from New York to do vital work for her family by helping to take care of her granddaughter. Although Louisa had been a successful entrepreneur, by this point she had no financial resources to bring into the Terrell household. Berto returned to M Street Colored High School, where he and Mollie first met. He worked briefly as a teacher before being appointed principal.[7]

Berto's professional career and elite status soon took a significant turn for the better. Booker T. Washington recommended to President Theodore Roosevelt that Berto be appointed as the first African American justice of the peace in the District of Columbia. He began this position in 1901, one year before the worst financial crisis of his career, which plunged his family into economic instability and plagued him for the rest of his life.[8]

The problems for Berto began in 1887, before his marriage, when he and other investors established the first full-service black-owned commercial bank, the Capital Savings Bank. This was a black nationalist effort to foster entrepreneurialism within the African American community. The bank survived the Panic of 1893 with the help of a wealthy black businessman, but as the businesses it supported continued to fail in subsequent panics, it finally closed its doors. Its directors, including Berto, had mismanaged the bank not only by granting overly risky loans but by borrowing money themselves and not paying it back. A 1902 news article publicizing a lawsuit against them started a run on the bank by customers who feared its insolvency.[9]

Informing his father-in-law that the Capital Savings Bank was about to fail, Berto explained: "Several of the directors owe the bank considerable sums. I am one of them, unfortunately, partly on my own account but largely through business deals in the old firm of Lynch and Terrell which panned out badly but for which we are personally responsible. If our doors should close ... there is no telling what would be said of the directors who had borrowed its funds." Subject to public nominations and Senate votes, he noted, "I hold a judicial position and any criticism of that nature might be a very serious thing for me. ... I must be above suspicion and ugly rumors." Berto admitted that he and the other directors had misappropriated funds and estimated it would "take about $2000 to straighten me out in that institution." Devastated by the symbolism of the bank's imminent failure, he predicted: "To have this institution go under will be a positive calamity to the Colored people of the Country. It has always been pointed to as an evidence of Negro capacity to do business." Berto's ideological commitment to African Americans' economic self-sufficiency made its demise and his failures of judgment even more painful.[10]

Berto's plan to save himself and his family involved Mollie and her wealthy father. He prefaced his request with an apology to his father-in-law: "I dislike very much to broach the subject ... for you have ... done so much for me already." Then, Berto made the bold proposal that Church deed one of his several D.C. properties "to Mollie and then let me raise the loan here. I will proceed to pay it off at once by monthly payments, and when that is completed the property will be reconveyed to you." Church generously agreed to the proposal and gave his daughter the deed, thereby salvaging the couple's finances and elite lifestyle. This allowed Berto to claim he had resolved any outstanding debts to the bank *before* it failed. Mollie's father, a savvy businessperson, later wrote his will to protect his daughter's inheritance from her husband's debts.[11]

After Berto repaid his debt to his father-in-law and returned the property in 1909, Robert Church took a big step toward ensuring his daughter's financial security. During a time when few African Americans owned their own homes, he gave Mollie the house in which the Terrell family was already residing. She recorded: "Papa showed me the deed to the house in which we now live which he has just given me. I am very grateful to him indeed for it gives one a feeling of security to know that he owns property, particularly his own home." The deed ensured that the home was Mollie's alone and could not be seized for her husband's debts. Church further assisted his daughter and son-in-law by letting Berto continue to handle his D.C. property transactions as a side job while he served on the bench.[12]

Thinking of her father as having wealth without limits, Mollie jeopardized her relationship with him by making a further financial request. She did not appear to fully consider how much her father had already done. The Terrell couple had benefited doubly from the deed/loan arrangement. Berto got the $2,000 loan, and she received a monthly rental income from it for seven years. After the property was reconveyed to her father, she asked that she still be allowed to keep the rent, as she had done when the house was technically hers. Berto worried that this request would anger her father, but Mollie persisted.

> Mr. Terrell told me that you want the rent from 1938 4th St. sent to you. I felt that he must have mistaken you, for . . . the rent means a great deal to me. If you decide that I cannot have it any longer, it means that both the children and I must do without things which we should like to have. . . . However, I don't want to be unreasonable. . . . You have done a great deal, as it is, and I cannot find words to express my gratitude to you for your generosity. I sincerely hope you will not get angry about the matter, for I should rather part with a great deal more than the rent than cause you to get provoked. . . . With lots of love and kisses, I am your affectionate daughter, Mollie.[13]

Mollie wanted extra spending money for herself and her daughters in order to maintain the markers of an elite lifestyle, including vacations and fine clothes.

Mollie's request did provoke her father. Exasperated by his daughter's temerity, Church shared his frustration with Berto. His generosity, he feared, was going unrecognized: "I was surprised to receive such a letter from her after I had just given her that house on T St. in which she had lived for years. If Mollie will stop to consider . . . she will see that I have done a father's part by her. She never called on me before nor since her marriage that I have not always responded promptly, it made no difference for what purpose. I have never stopped doing for her since she has been in the world." Mollie apologized: "My dear Father . . . . I am very sorry I wrote that letter asking you to let me have the rent from that house, for it was unreasonable for me to do so."[14]

Berto also irritated his father-in-law by asking to be reimbursed $40 for repairs he had made to the property before he gave back the deed. Responding to Church's anger, Berto protested he had just wanted his father-in-law to know he had been maintaining the house before he returned it: "I believe I have said to you a hundred times that you had been overkind to me, and when Mollie wrote you about retaining the rents from this particular house the act was over my protest. I am glad she reconsidered the matter."[15]

Just months before his death in 1912, Robert Church sent letters to Berto and his real estate partner, Whitefield McKinlay, angrily insisting that they turn over "all my property in Washington" to a different firm. He demanded, "Now I want those leases turned over . . . immediately, or I shall be forced to take other steps to have it done." Church complained to Berto that McKinlay "said . . . you had ordered him to do all the repairing and spend all of the money that he has. It is simply outrageous, and I have asked you both not to do any repairing without first consulting me." Robert Church's resistance to maintaining his properties saved him money in the short term, but his family would soon discover that his tightfistedness left them with a devalued inheritance because many of his properties were in serious disrepair.[16]

As her father's health was failing, Mollie wrote to her husband alluding to their strained relations with the Churches: "To discuss the Memphis situation a minute. I have just written a short letter to Papa inquiring about his health, one to Anna [his wife]. . . . I told her I could not bear to think of Father's passing away without seeing him again. On the other hand, I did not want to excite him and cause him to grow worse by coming. . . . We are powerless to change matters now. . . . A combination of circumstances over which I had absolutely no control has been working against me for ten years." Berto's financial debacle of a decade earlier, as well as a simmering rivalry between the two sets of Church half siblings, had caused a rift. After traveling to Memphis to see her ailing father, Mollie was saddened by his condition though glad to be of some small service: "Yesterday Papa was very willing to let me minister to him. He sat with his feet in my lap a long time, while I fanned the mosquitos off. It is very pathetic to see his desperate fight for life."[17]

Mollie and her brother Thomas , the offspring of their father's earlier marriage to Louisa Ayres, had anticipated an inheritance that would alleviate any financial concerns. Mollie wanted to devote herself to writing, and Thomas dreamed of investing in business. But upon Robert R. Church's death on August 29, 1912, the siblings discovered that his will gave them less of a windfall than they had expected. His wife, Anna Wright Church, inherited the great bulk of the estate, including a farm, the beautiful, large home in which she lived with the couple's two adult children, and many other prominent Beale Street properties. Robert and Annette would become quite wealthy when they received their mother's portion after her death. Church's will included a clause that all sales of his properties should be "for the purpose of reinvesting the proceeds in other real estate," making it more difficult to sell the properties for cash. Inheriting jointly, Mollie and Thomas also had to agree to the sale of any particular lot but rarely did so. Robert Church continued his patriarchal control after his death, for he stipulated that any of his children who contested his will would be automatically disinherited, as if he or she "had died."[18]

Real estate was an important avenue for economic security for African Americans striving to be in or stay in the middle or upper classes. Some black government workers, for instance, bolstered their steady but modest paychecks by collecting monthly rent. Mollie and Thomas inherited a set of dilapidated properties needing significant repair before they could rent them at profitable rates. Although they did not want or intend to become slum landlords, they fell into that role. The siblings were dismayed to learn that many of the buildings they inherited lacked plumbing. Thomas admitted to Mollie, "I know that there is a great deal of plumbing we need in those houses but we will have to do it by degrees." Robert Church had left virtually no cash money, and neither sibling had the necessary cash on hand. They were unable to repair most of the housing units, which were in bad condition. This was not uncommon; well into the twentieth century, many black Memphians "lived in small . . . houses, with communal outdoor toilets or pit privies."[19]

Mollie and Thomas found that their problems with maintaining and renting their properties were compounded by the bad reputation and deteriorating conditions of the poor, segregated neighborhood in Memphis in which their buildings were located. Until the Great Depression, the siblings sometimes realized good monthly returns, allowing them to live comfortably, but they found it stressful and challenging to manage and maintain the rentals, especially from a distance. Relying on agents to handle and improve the units, Mollie and Thomas never got adequate help and feared that they were being swindled.[20]

Berto Terrell's finances had remained unstable since the 1890s. In 1915, a few years after his father-in-law's death, Berto finally had to declare bankruptcy, "listing $13,491.58 in debts and only $62.50 in assets above legal exemptions." The monies he owed comprised more than four times his yearly salary of about $3,000 a year as a judge. (This is the equivalent today of earning about $70,000 a year but owing $330,000. The Terrells were clearly not poor or even middle class, but they lived under a cloud of economic instability that contributed to Mollie's perennial anxieties about money and stability.) Under titles such as "Judge Terrell a Bankrupt" and "Judge Terrell Makes Satisfactory Arrangements," the black press announced his financial crisis. One characterized Berto as "manly" for attempting to pay the depositors who had lost money in the bank's failure so many years before, and another deemed him "practically . . . an 'innocent bystander'" rather than uniquely responsible for its collapse. One article said, "It is an open secret that the Judge, as a matter of pride and conscience, has for years been paying off debts which should have been shared by others, and that the major portion of his earnings has gone this way." Because of his high public profile, Berto seems to have paid a heavier price for the bank's failure than the other officers.[21]

From the moment Lynch & Terrell had begun to falter in the mid-1890s, Mollie tried to find ways to earn an income, including working as a substitute teacher and getting paid as a journalist for her newspaper and magazine articles. Whereas high-status white women often served as unpaid, volunteer social reformers, many more high-status African American women, both single and married, needed to work for wages. To mask her elite family's fiscal concerns, Terrell described her wage-earning work as simply a byproduct of her reform work. Some have taken her statements at face value and mischaracterized her as a woman who did not need an income.[22]

Not coincidentally, Mollie launched her speaking career in 1901, precisely when Berto's Capital Savings Bank disaster was unfolding. Her formidable speaking skills had earned her an invitation to go on the lecture circuit. A speakers' bureau managed her tours, which became her major source of independent income in the first decades of the twentieth century. Mollie could make anywhere from $10 to $50 dollars for a lecture, bringing in as much as $100 dollars (about $2,700 in today's terms) in just a few weeks on the lecture circuit. Berto's conservative associates vociferously criticized him for "allowing" Mollie to go on the lecture circuit, just as they had when Mollie had joined the D.C. board of education and become president of the NACW. They objected to his sanctioning Mollie's decision to take a job that would remove her from her children and husband for weeks at a time: "When . . . my husband consented to let me go on the lecture platform, some of his friends were so shocked and horrified that words simply failed them as they attempted to express their disapprobation and to show him what an irreparable mistake he was making." They tried to convince him that, as Mollie put it, "when a woman became deeply interested in civic affairs and started on a public career . . . a happy home was impossible." Fortunately, she declared, "He was not influenced . . . by the dire predictions made by the prophets of evil who tried to persuade him to confine me within the four walls of our home." Being on the lecture circuit appeared radical because Mollie would be traveling across the nation alone while her mother (and husband) stayed at home, responsible for childcare.[23]

Mollie Terrell pushed back against gendered strictures. She was ambitious and civic minded, and she yearned for a high-profile public role. She also knew that Berto's finances were in shambles. After the bank's failure, she undertook three-week lecture tours approximately once or twice a year, declaring,

"It would seem almost reckless in people of our circumstances to deliberately throw one hundred dollars into the fire when it can be made in three weeks very easily." While away speaking to white Chautauqua audiences, she wrote Berto that she missed him, Phyllis, and her mother but also admitted: "I enjoy very much doing this kind of work because I really feel that I am putting the colored woman in a favorable light . . . every time I address an audience of white people, and every little bit [of money] helps."[24]

"Action on His Wife's Part Would Alienate Dr. Washington"

The constraints imposed by the black elites' emphasis on respectability and the pressure to be loyal followers of Booker T. Washington kept Berto and Mollie Terrell on edge in the first decade of the new century. Conservative Bookerites, African Americans who approved of Washington's views and often wanted the benefits of his patronage and connections, curried favor by eschewing political activism in order to secure or retain their positions. Mollie and Berto lived with divided loyalties, understanding that they had to work with Washington in order to move Berto's career forward even as Mollie expanded her militant activism.

For the sake of her husband's career and to secure their status as an elite black family, Mollie cultivated Washington's good graces. The year after Washington secured Berto's 1901 nomination as justice of the peace, Mollie and her young daughter visited him and his family in South Weymouth, Massachusetts. Writing to Berto on Tuskegee Institute stationery, she reveled in her connection to a real powerbroker: "Behold me sitting at the great Booker T's desk in his magnificent summer house! The great man welcomed me himself . . . and we have had a few words together." Revealing her class aspirations, she wrote, "I wish you were here. It is very fine to be a great man, when you can have a summer home like this." Her personal rapport with Washington enabled Mollie to later describe their relationship as a warm one: "He had a heart full of generous impulses and enjoyed giving pleasure to his friends." This generosity also ensured loyalty among those he favored. Yet Mollie conceded they did not see eye to eye: "He knew full well that I did not agree with some of his views, although I admired him greatly for the work he was doing in his effort to educate and uplift those representatives of his race who had so few and such meagre opportunities to develop themselves."[25]

At W. E. B. Du Bois's invitation, Mollie Terrell spoke at the 1903 graduation ceremony of Atlanta University, which offered a classical higher education to its African American students. Hearing that she was in Atlanta at his rival's institution, Washington seized the opportunity to invite her to speak at the

Tuskegee Institute's graduation, too. Even those black activists who disagreed with Washington's accommodationism and narrow focus on vocational education came away from their visits to Tuskegee impressed by the accomplishments of its students. Terrell declared, "I had never seen a Commencement like Tuskegee's before. On the stage before our very eyes students actually performed the work which they had learned to do in school. . . . They showed us how to build houses, how to paint them, how to estimate the cost of the necessary material. . . . I was completely taken off my feet. . . . Here was a school giving just the kind of instruction that the majority attending it needed." However, she affirmed, "in my heart I was a stickler for higher education."[26]

Returning home, Terrell wrote an article for the *Washington Post* in which she positively described both institutions and their graduations. To her regret, the white editor published only her praise of Tuskegee. Supporters of higher education, including Du Bois, were upset by what they perceived as her betrayal. The *Post* editor did her a disservice by misrepresenting her views. She valued the classical educations that she and her husband had acquired at Oberlin and Harvard and consistently argued that African Americans must have equal access to the full range of educational and professional opportunities available to whites. Mollie also disliked Washington's willingness to denigrate and mock African Americans to pacify whites. After hearing him speak at a National Child Welfare Conference, she wrote in her diary: "I was bitterly disappointed in B. T. W.'s address last night. He did not seize the splendid opportunity he had to plead for the thousands of poor neglected colored children all thru the South." Instead, he had employed racist stereotypes, "implying that all black men were thieves." Washington led "his audience to believe that many colored people who establish orphan asylums do it simply to help themselves—to get some occupation." He thereby denigrated all black reformers, including National Association of Colored Women members who worked so hard at institution building, from founding orphanages and homes for the elderly to establishing kindergartens and day nurseries. "Instead of urging the charitable and good to help the poor neglected children of his race," Mollie regretted that "he said the very thing . . . which would relieve [whites] of responsibility in the matter and justify them in tightening their purse strings when other colored people ask for aid."[27]

In spite of the Terrells' mutual interest in cultivating Washington, beginning in the 1890s, Mollie Terrell took on leadership roles in several new civil rights organizations, including the NACW, the Afro-American League (later the National Afro-American Council, or AAC), and the Constitution League. Committed to ending lynching and segregation and to promoting civil rights, these groups and others, including the National Equal Rights League and the

Niagara Movement, created an activist organizational framework that led to the 1909 formation of the National Association for the Advancement of Colored People.[28]

In the year of her marriage, 1891, Mollie had publicly identified herself as a supporter of the black freedom struggle by writing a letter, published in the *New York Age*, praising the Afro-American League's initiation of lawsuits challenging racial discrimination and segregation. The group had been founded in 1887 by journalist and racial justice advocate T. Thomas Fortune. Its first iteration did not last long, but Fortune and Bishop Alexander Walters revived it in 1898 as the National Afro-American Council. Mollie joined immediately. At that time, she was also serving as NACW president and ensured that the next annual conventions of both organizations would be held consecutively in Chicago in 1899 so that delegates could attend both. Mollie spoke at each meeting, advocating racial uplift and protesting lynching, segregation, and disfranchisement.[29]

Developing an increasingly high profile as an outspoken critic of white supremacy, she implicated all whites in the crime of lynching. Terrell argued that "reputable, law-abiding negroes should protest against the tortures and cruelties inflicted by mobs" and condemned lynchings as "wild and diabolical carnival[s] of blood." Her 1904 essay, "Lynching from a Negro's Point of View," published in the *North American Review*, predicted that white Americans' lawlessness would ruin the nation's high standing in the "civilized world." Inverting common assumptions of black lawlessness, she charged whites with disregarding the laws against murder. All American citizens accused of committing a crime deserved due process, she insisted, including the right to a fair trial. "It is to the credit . . . of the negro," Terrell concluded, "that he tries to uphold the sacred majesty of the law, which is often . . . trampled underfoot by white mobs."[30]

White Christians must do more to combat racial hatred, Terrell argued. White ministers condoned the lynching of black men and women through silence and apathy, she charged: "It is a source of deep regret and sorrow to many good Christians in this country that the church puts forth so few and such feeble protests against lynching." When one orator lionized the United States, claiming that "'a living and practical Christianity is characteristic of its people,'" Terrell countered that such self-satisfied claims could seem plausible only if whites remained willfully "ignorant of the many barbarities and the fiendish atrocities visited by the Southern Whites upon the defenseless and persecuted Blacks."[31]

Her vocal stance against lynching contributed to Mollie Terrell's gaining leadership positions in the Afro-American Council. At the AAC's 1905 Detroit convention, she was reelected as one of its nine vice-presidents. At its 1906 convention, she spoke on "Lynching and Its Remedy." Her speech was, she re-membered, "loudly applauded. Placed me at head of Anti-Lynching Bureau." The other black leaders lauded her as a modern-day heroine—"called me Joan of Arc." As the head of the AAC's antilynching division, she carefully moni-tored debates in Congress. Listening from the visitors' gallery, she heard Sena-tor Benjamin Tillman's "disgusting tirade against N——'s." Outraged by Till-man's racism, including his unapologetic advocacy of lynching, Terrell further "volunteer[ed] to keep accurate account of lynchings . . . for Afro-American Council."[32]

Terrell's searing articles and speeches against segregation, lynching, and the convict lease labor system, as well as her international activism, brought her to the attention of the wealthy white reformer, inventor, businessman and journalist John Milholland, whom she first met in London in 1904. Two years later, she joined Milholland and Du Bois in creating an interracial anti-discrimination group, the Constitution League, to monitor violations of citi-zens' constitutional rights and call for full enforcement of the Constitution by federal authorities. Mollie proudly noted in her diary, "Am first of five charter members to sign papers incorporating Constitution League." The Constitu-tion League disbanded in 1909 to become part of the new NAACP. (In the NAACP, Milholland served as a vice-president, Du Bois as director of pub-licity and research, and Terrell as a member of the executive board.) At the league's inaugural meeting in February 1906, Mollie gave a strong and well-received speech against lynching but was upset by what she perceived as a sex-ist slight. John Milholland opened the assembly, W. E. B. Du Bois spoke as a representative of the Niagara Movement, and Kelly Miller and Archibald Grimké spoke as representatives of Booker T. Washington's Committee of Twelve. The men had gone over their time without being stopped. Only she was asked to shorten her ten-minute speech to make up for their verbal ex-cesses. Nonetheless, the insult was tempered by the fact she "carried my audi-ence by storm."[33]

Even as she increased her militant activism, Mollie tried to be as diplomatic as possible with Booker T. Washington in order to preserve her husband's ac-cess to patronage. While in New York for the Constitution League meeting, she was glad he invited her to lunch, although she could not go. Mollie con-fided to her husband that she had written, "telling him how sorry I was not to lunch with him, for fear he might think it was an evidence of unfriendliness, etc. One has to be so particular to those who wield great power."[34]

Mollie Terrell moved from national to transatlantic visibility as a civil rights leader when she attended and lectured at an international women's conference in Berlin in 1904 (speaking in German and French), as well as published two articles in the British journal *Nineteenth Century and After*. One, in 1906, made the case against segregation in the United States. The next year, her fierce article, "Peonage in the United States: The Convict Lease System and the Chain Gangs," exposed the worst aspects of America's institutional racism to U.S. allies. Describing the victims of the convict lease system as poor, exploited, southern African American men and women, Terrell documented how they were often charged with minor misdemeanors, such as spitting on the sidewalk, only to find themselves facing long jail terms or heavy fines. If they could not pay, they were given over to the custody of white farmers, factory owners, or others who paid their fines while forcing them to work indefinitely at hard labor under inhumane, even deadly conditions. But when she pitched a follow-up article to the *Chicago Tribune's* publisher, he dismissed her with sexist paternalism: "he said I was 'too good a woman to investigate the Convict Lease System.' 'No woman's too good to do such work as that,' I replied." Yet, she was unable to find a publisher to sponsor this project.[35]

As part of her argument regarding the progress and achievements of African Americans, Mollie Terrell strove to create an image of genteel respectability. Yet she was unwilling to play the subordinate, conciliatory role that Booker T. Washington and his followers demanded. When personally confronted by racist insults and segregation in cafeterias and on trains and streetcars, she sometimes even physically resisted being pushed around or mistreated. Like her father, she had a scrappy willingness to fight hard for what she believed. A June 27, 1908, diary entry describes how Terrell was so determined to defend her right to a seat on a streetcar that she hit a white man: "Last night on the little streetcar . . . I had a very disagreeable experience. I had my dress suit case, my old hammock, and a tennis racket in my hand. There was plenty of room for me to have a seat by a white man who refused to move. I asked him to make room for me, but when he did not do so, I simply sat down."[36]

Terrell not only insisted on sitting down next to a hostile white man, she did so while holding leisure items that announced her elite class status, such as a hammock and a tennis racket. This was likely galling to the seated man and his friend who stood nearby, both of whom were of a lower socioeconomic class. After she took her seat, a dangerous exchange followed.

> He said something to me, and I replied, "When I tell you to move, you move." "I won't be sassed by a nigger," he growled. Before I knew it, I hit him in the face, not very hard to be sure, for I tried to restrain my hand and I partially succeeded, but I had slapped him just the same. A tall poor white fellow whose clothes almost hung off him rose and said, "Jim you are not going to let a nigger hit you are you?" "You had better not try to protect him," I replied. Then the white man sitting next to me began to

brandish his umbrella threatening to strike me. "Hit me," I said, "Just hit me, if you think best." But he didn't strike me.

She had violated social norms by slapping a white man, but Terrell was more distressed that no one was willing to protect her, a respectable woman, from the white man who threatened to use his umbrella as a weapon: "Not a white man in the car nor a white woman said a word to dissuade the man from striking me. I don't believe a hand would have been lifted in my defense if the man had struck me." Only a black woman came to her defense: "Mrs. Dyson . . . jumped up when the man brandished the umbrella and said 'Oh, don't let him hit you, Mrs. Terrell.' The lame, lanky, dilapidated white man stood near me while Mrs. Dyson and I were talking trying to intimidate me but I stared at him a second and turned my back on him." Terrell and Dyson survived this encounter unscathed, but both risked physical retribution. The situation could have spun out of control, resulting in violence or their arrest, although the white men would not have been arrested. The scene is reminiscent of her father's bold example of defiance when Mollie was a young girl on the train.[37]

Washington and the Bookerites remained a problem for the Terrells. Mollie's uncompromising attitude and activism disturbed the conservatives, who proclaimed themselves concerned about her "brutally frank" speeches to white audiences. Despite Berto's desire to retain Washington's favor, he supported his wife's activism. Their marriage was based on partnership, not subordination. In fact, despite his efforts to conciliate Washington, Berto was not as narrowly loyal as has been assumed. Throughout his career, he spoke out against disfranchisement, lynching, and other limitations on black Americans' full citizenship. Further, certain values, especially self-help and race pride, were associated with Washington's loyalists as well as with the militants, although the two factions interpreted these values differently.[38]

In 1909, Congress created a municipal court for the District of Columbia. When Republican president William Taft nominated Berto to the new judgeship, Washington again maneuvered behind the scenes to help him secure it. In part, Washington wanted to show he had not lost his power and influence, in spite of the rise of radicals like Mollie Terrell who were challenging his accommodationist approach.[39]

With Berto now a municipal court judge, the Terrell couple reached the peak of African American high society and public prominence. Proud of her husband's appointment as the first black federal judge, Mollie was dismayed to find his appointment being greeted with hostility by white southerners, who vilified the couple by identifying them as radical supporters of social and political equality. She noted in her February 1909 diary, "Papa sent me a paper, the

[Tennessee] *Commercial Appeal*, containing an article headed 'Bob Church's Son-in-Law Made a Judge.'" The article "stated that the appointment was very offensive to the white people not only of Washington but everywhere else. That the Terrell family were great agitators and stood for equal rights with white people. Terrell's wife . . . ." Mollie's sentence trailed off; she did not write down the inflammatory comments about her.[40]

Booker T. Washington's dissatisfaction with Mollie Terrell reached a critical point over her participation in two consecutive annual conferences that led to the formation of the new interracial civil rights organization the National Association for the Advancement of Colored People. On Abraham Lincoln's birthday, February 12, 1909, the grandson of abolitionist William Lloyd Garrison, Oswald Garrison Villard, called for a National Negro Conference to end racism in the United States. Among the "sixty leading social reformers" who signed the call, eight were African Americans and only two of those were women: Mollie Church Terrell and Ida B. Wells-Barnett.[41] Du Bois, Milholland, Wells-Barnett, and Terrell became members of the Committee of Forty on Permanent Organization that created the NAACP. Years later, at an NAACP conference, Mollie recalled its founding as a breakthrough: "I saw a way had been opened whereby we ourselves could take the initiative in working out our own salvation instead of waiting expectantly, hopefully for somebody else to come to our relief. I assure you that the occasion on which the National Association for the Advancement of Colored People blossomed into a full-grown reality and an active functioning certainty was a red letter day in my life."[42]

Mollie's militancy finally provoked Booker T. Washington to contact Berto directly in 1910 to express his displeasure with Mollie's role in the upcoming National Negro Conference: "To have Mrs. Terrell's name appear on a program where the opposition is in charge naturally makes it harder for your friends to help you when the time comes." As Mollie put it, Washington warned Berto that his wife's participation in the conference that was about to establish the NAACP would lead to his "political ruin." This was no idle threat; after an anti-Bookerite riot in Boston in 1903, Washington retaliated by getting several in the radical opposition fired from their jobs. Although undoubtedly concerned about losing the support of such an important power broker, Berto gave his full consent to Mollie's decision to be a principal speaker at the conference, encouraging her to follow her conscience.[43]

"She Is Always Capable of Stirring Up Trouble"

Although deeply involved with and committed to the NAACP from its inception, a savvy and strategic Mollie Church Terrell remained keenly aware of the value of Booker T. Washington's patronage for her husband. In December 1910, she tried to play both sides, offering to tell Washington something about what was going on in the radical movement. In part, she seems to have calculated that if approaching Washington could also smooth over tensions and secure his continued support for her husband, then all the better. Terrell was capable of manipulating and maneuvering behind the scenes if it kept her and her husband at peace with Washington—especially if it could buy her time and space to continue her work in support of civil rights with his tacit consent.

While in New York City giving speeches for the new NAACP, Terrell wrote to Washington asking to meet with him. Referring to the white NAACP leader Oswald Garrison Villard, she reported: "Mr. Villard told me something yesterday which has pained me not a little and that is why I want very much to see you." She approached Washington offering information about an internal NAACP dispute in 1910 to keep herself and her husband in his good graces but also because she was genuinely upset that Du Bois and his male allies were engaging in a public character assault on Washington, a fellow national black leader. She had her own complaints about Washington's pandering to white racism but wrote them in her diary rather than in an open letter. Rather than directly attacking him, she made her politics known simply by choosing to organize and be part of the NAACP, with its overtly political goals and methods for achieving civil rights.[44]

Booker T. Washington eagerly agreed to see her. Their meeting provided him with fodder in his dispute with the NAACP about a circular written by Du Bois and signed by thirty-two African American men entitled, "Appeal to the People of Great Britain and Europe." The document criticized Washington's refusal to acknowledge the breadth of white resistance and violence against black Americans. It was distributed on the stationery of the National Negro Committee, the previous name of what had recently become the NAACP, implying that the new organization was officially condemning Washington. This deeply angered him, and he hoped to destroy the new group by dividing the white leaders and other black NAACP members, including Mollie Terrell, from the black men who had signed the circular. Using her information, Washington wrote Villard: "I have just had a long talk with Mrs. Terrell . . . and she tells me that your committee did not send out that circular." Washington also wrote to his chief ally in the nation's capital, Emmett Scott, giving him a full report: "She says . . . that Villard, a white woman [likely Mary Ovington], and all the lead people are disgusted . . . that such a circular should have been sent out presumably under the guise of the committee. . . . At any rate they seem to be in a pretty big row among themselves. . . . Mrs. Terrell appears to be pretty much disgusted with the whole affair, and I think she will make matters pretty lively from now on." This put Villard in the awkward position of having to claim that he was "on the point of writing to tell you what Mrs. Terrell has already conveyed to you" and saying that the whole incident was simply caused by a secretary's error.[45] Washington concluded to Scott, "I am gradually coming around to the opinion that it is a valuable thing to have Mrs. Terrell connected with that committee [the NAACP].... One of her values is [that] ... she gets on the inside of things and is always capable of stirring up trouble in any organization that she has a part of." He correctly recognized Terrell's willingness to be combative and take on anyone, even allies.[46]

Although Washington hoped so, Mollie Terrell had not become a traitor working against a cause she held dear. Washington's biographer concludes that "there is no evidence that Mary Church Terrell extended beyond this instance her career as a double agent. She continued to lecture for the NAACP.... She was a member of a committee that presented President Taft the NAACP resolutions on lynching. She gave every evidence of complete commitment to the NAACP. ... In 1912, after the incorporation of the NAACP, she became a member of its first board of directors."[47]

Quickly moving away from this exceptional communication with Washington, Mollie focused on her role as one of only a handful of NAACP board members residing in the nation's capital (most lived in New York City, where the organization was headquartered). Active in the local capital branch from its inception, she regularly lobbied senators and representatives to pass antilynching and other antidiscrimination laws. As an NAACP public lecturer, she spoke against disfranchisement, lynching, and segregation to white and black audiences.[48]

―――――――

Mollie Terrell had been honest when she told Washington, as he put it, "that she and Du Bois have absolutely nothing to do with each other; they scarcely speak, and she did not see him during her stay in New York." In fact, Terrell had never felt entirely comfortable with Du Bois. He seemed dismissive of her, and she was aware of his indifference or even disdain. Du Bois might not have liked the fact that she was a woman who did not fawn over him, as so many others did. Perhaps even less acceptable to this man with a large ego was the fact that she wanted to be a legitimate civil rights leader in her own right. In 1905, when Terrell saw him at the train station on their way to a meeting in New York, she reported: Du Bois "asked me if I was going to take a seat in the parlor car, to which I responded 'No, I am not.'" At that, he turned around, walked away, and never came back to talk with her. She concluded that "this very distinguished and most haughty Big Gun" did not approve that she, a "lady," was not riding in the parlor car. She contented herself with sitting next to and chatting with a politician she might want to lobby someday, Republican congressman Alexander White of Pennsylvania.[49]

Many years later, after her husband died in December 1925, Mollie's brother Thomas asked if she might be able to secure a paid position with the NAACP to help support herself. She responded: "I am well acquainted with [NAACP leader Joel] Spingarn and have been for years. I have very little hope of breaking into the N.A.A.C.P., although I was one of the Charter members and helped to put Du Bois into his present position in spite of determined opposition." She had lobbied white NAACP leaders for Du Bois to become editor of *The Crisis* and had long sympathized with his militancy in the black freedom struggle, if not always with his tactics. She concluded, "Du Bois doesn't hate me and he certainly doesn't *love* me. But I'll try everything that is even a remote possibility." Mollie took heart, she confided to her brother, from the news that Georgia Douglas Johnson, "The widow of Henry Lincoln Johnson has just been appointed in the Labor Bureau at a salary of $1800."[50]

Berto Terrell had not directly participated in the founding of the NAACP and was initially more cautious about directly affiliating with it.[51] But in 1913, two years before Booker T. Washington's death, Berto and many other black D.C. elites joined the NAACP's capital branch in order to protest against the new Democratic president Woodrow Wilson's implementation of segregation throughout the federal government and the district. Berto proudly reported to Mollie that his men's social club, the Mu-So-Lit Club, which typically sponsored literary lectures for its highly educated members, had moved into overt civil rights activism: "The [NAACP's] collection for the evening was over $300 cash. Of this sum the Mu-So-Lits gave $102." His club, composed of black professionals, including government workers, had stepped into the political fray by raising a substantial sum to fund the NAACP's work against segregation.[52]

Berto's financial support of the NAACP and attendance at its mass meetings in 1913 indicates that he was not simply cowering in submission to Booker T. Washington. Nor was Berto deterred by the new Democratic administration that would soon be deciding his fate in his upcoming renomination battle. He reported to Mollie about the NAACP's huge D.C. protest meeting of October 27, 1913, featuring Oswald Garrison Villard: "The meeting last night was the most remarkable one ever held by colored people in this country. By seven o'clock twenty-five hundred people had crowded themselves into the Metropolitan Church and by 7:30 there were two thousand others on the outside." Berto praised the "eloquent speeches" and was particularly pleased by the performance of "Archibald Grimke, the president of the branch . . . [who] made the best speech of his life." Mollie was glad that her husband had taken her lead and was now openly supporting the NAACP.[53]

In later years, it was important to Mollie Terrell that the prominent men who had worked with her in the civil rights movement respected and publicly acknowledged her role as a founder. At a 1921 NAACP meeting in the District, Terrell was up on the platform when John Milholland spoke. She noted in her diary, "He said 'Mrs. Terrell, Du Bois and I formed the Constitutional League in Cooper Union in New York City in 1906, 15 years ago.' . . . He said he was prouder of the NAACP than of any organization that had grown out of that meeting." In 1949, trying to secure formal credit for her role in creating the NAACP, Terrell "wrote to Du Bois thanking him for his letter saying my name is given as a member of the General Committee in the first report of the NAACP. 'Doesn't that make me one of the founders?' I asked." A month later, she wrote again: "Letter to Du Bois thanking him for showing I was one of the Founders of the N.A.A.C.P., one to Ray Wilkins asking him to name me as one of the founders of the NAACP." Women were often overlooked or forgotten by the men who were telling the organization's history; Terrell tried to ensure a more accurate, inclusive account that wrote her into the history.[54]

"The Parents Have All the Pride and Aspiration"

Committed to creating a better world for their own and all black children, the Terrells believed that education would build pride in black youths and fend off racism, allowing the next generation to survive and prosper in what Mollie characterized as an unrelentingly "white world." Mollie and Berto provided their children with a highly cultured, intellectually stimulating elite environment, hoping that they could equal or surpass their parents' achievements. Reflecting their cultural and class aspirations, middle-class and elite African American parents like the Terrells measured their own status by the progress and achievements of their offspring. Talented Tenth parents expected their children to be fully invested in their own intellectual and moral development and took it for granted that their progeny would follow their examples. Some were genuinely surprised and disappointed to find that their children did not always share their abilities or drive. The second generation sometimes rejected their parents' project of racial uplift, declining to take on the burden of being exemplars of success in the face of white racism and hostility.[55]

In 1905, Mollie and Berto suddenly became the parents of a second daughter. They had always wished that Phyllis could have a sibling, but the doctors had determined that the risk for Mollie of enduring a fifth pregnancy was far too great. Fortunately, on December 13, 1905, when speaking in Providence, Rhode Island, Mollie met her eleven-year-old niece and namesake, Mary Louise Church (b. 1894), the daughter of her brother Thomas. Thomas's wife had died when Mary was only three. At the time, Thomas had arranged for his daughter to be raised by a female caretaker.

Mollie seized this unexpected opportunity to provide Phyllis, her now seven-year-old daughter, with an adopted older sister. In her diary, she wrote, "little 'Mary Church' . . . is 11 years old, beautiful child who resembles Phyllis. Mrs. Williams said she would have to put her into a boarding school soon as she could not take care of her." Mollie stopped in New York City on her way home from her lecture tour to consult with her brother about his plans for his daughter. After consulting with her brother, husband, and mother, in just over a week, on Christmas Eve, 1905, Mollie recorded: "We all Berto, P[hyllis] and I went to the train station to meet Mary. . . . She is a pretty, sweet child and I hope we shall be able to rear her properly so that she shall become a fine specimen of good, pure, intelligent womanhood. Phyllis and she became fast friends immediately. They played all day." Mollie and Berto now had the same high hopes for Mary as they had for Phyllis—that both daughters would grow up to positively represent their race and sex.[56]

Regretting the gap between their high expectations and reality, Mollie and Berto privately struggled with their disappointment that their children were not particularly ambitious or gifted. They loved, enjoyed, and appreciated their daughters but also expected more from them than either was capable of or interested in achieving. Mollie remarked in a letter to Berto that Phyllis "has real talent in music. I wish she had not. The absence of talent altogether is far preferable to the possession of it without the energy and pride to develop it." Concerned and confused about their daughters' lack of industriousness and intellectual prowess, the Terrells struggled to remedy the problem, mostly by having Mollie dedicate herself to tutoring both girls in academics and music. In a summer 1909 letter to Berto, Mollie expressed her deep love for Phyllis, as well as her frustration and disappointment. She began by describing their eleven-year-old daughter's fondness for horses and her sweet disposition and then reported: "I try to be as calm as I can when I give her her reading lesson, but she is enough to try the patience of Job. I feel certain that no child in Washington passed to the 7th grade knows so little about reading as Phyllis. Bless her dear little heart! She is the sweetest piece of humanity that ever lived." Here, Mollie confided her uncertainty over whether Phyllis deserved to have graduated from elementary school.[57]

Except when she was on tour, Mollie was the hands-on parent for the majority of each year. Berto was a loving father who shared his wife's goals and values, but he played a less active role as a tutor or disciplinarian due to his

FIGURE 4.1. Mary Louise Church Terrell (1894–1966) and Phyllis Terrell (April 2, 1898–August 21, 1989). The Terrell couple embraced Mollie's niece, Mary, as their daughter and a sister for Phyllis. Eleven-year-old Mary is seated and seven-year-old Phyllis is standing. Mollie rightly noted how much the two girls resembled each other and was thrilled that they settled quickly into their new role as sisters. For this portrait, taken soon after Mary entered the family, Mollie chose to dress her daughters in all-white dresses with large white bows in their hair. Both girls had light skin that reflected their biracial heritage. They also had wavy hair often prized by African American women who were ridiculed and mocked in mainstream popular culture for their tightly curled hair. Mary's long hair is displayed falling gently over her front shoulder. Later, Mollie was so impressed by teenaged Phyllis's long, wavy hair that she took snapshots of Phyllis from behind in order to show her hair going all the way down her back. (Courtesy Langston Family)

demanding schedule as a judge. Mollie noted to Berto that she had "tried to use as little force as possible because I feared it would make her hate the sight of a book if I compelled her to read against her will. But now I see she dislikes to read because she actually doesn't know how and doesn't have the remotest idea how to spell out a word so that she can pronounce it." Phyllis may have had an undiagnosed learning disability, since she still had trouble reading, spelling and writing at eleven. But she may simply have lacked the drive, focus, motivation, or intelligence to follow her parents' path.[58]

Mary was not a strong student either and did not apply herself to her studies. Mollie highlighted the following sentences in her diary: "Have been helping Mary with her Latin, which she hasn't studied at all. . . . I am greatly disappointed to think she had no more pride." Mollie was convinced that her daughter could do better if only she tried. The root problem—Mary's lack of pride—seemed to be a character flaw. It was particularly difficult for Mollie to see her daughter refuse to apply herself to her language studies. After all, one of her proudest moments at Oberlin College involved reciting Greek in front of an impressed Matthew Arnold, the visiting English writer, who openly declared that he had not believed anyone "of African descent" could correctly pronounce Greek. Although stung by his racist presumptions, Mollie was gratified to have proved him wrong and to have represented her race well. Berto Terrell, of course, was also an accomplished linguist.[59]

Other talented black parents shared the Terrells' problems. On a visit to Memphis, after a conversation with a childhood friend about her sons, Mollie reported to Berto, "My darling Husband . . . . Fannie came over and talked several hours about the utter worthlessness of her two boys. It is really pathetic to see how utterly good for nothing children of well-to-do, ambitious parents are. The parents have all the pride and aspiration while the children have practically none." Mollie then declared, "If Mary does not improve, if she continues to show such a lack of interest and pride in her High School course as she has manifested up to date, I am going to use heroic measures for a short while, at least."[60]

As it became clear that their daughters seemed unlikely to shine academically, Mollie and Berto decided to cultivate their musical talents. The desire to foster their daughters' musical abilities derived in part from the valuable social and performative aspects of playing music as a form of cultural capital and status. They expected each daughter to become an accomplished musician who could play at least one instrument and sing well. Mollie began to find practice sessions more rewarding: "P[hyllis] is improving so much on the piano. . . . She is such a comfort to me now. She seems to be taking pride in her work." Genuine dedication, whether academic or musical, were precisely what Mollie was yearning for from her children. She was thrilled, therefore, when friends who dropped in on them at home one evening "said we presented a beautiful family scene as we sang together." Phyllis later chose music as her career path; in her late twenties, she finally received a bachelor's degree in music from Howard University and went on to teach music in the D.C. public schools.[61]

As an adult, Phyllis wrote to her mother about her own limitations. "Only wish I had inherited some of your ability. I certainly am an off number, a throw-back, to such parents as you and Dad. Maybe someday I'll have a little more gray-matter but I'll never set the world afire." From Phyllis's perspective, it was difficult to have such high-achieving and accomplished parents who expected so much from their daughters. Even when Mollie's daughters had the opportunity to follow in their mother's footsteps at Oberlin Preparatory High School and Oberlin College, they declined to push themselves academically. Perhaps this was their rebellion from the pressure of such high parental expectations and Talented Tenth ambitions.[62]

As Mollie and Berto worked to shore up their finances, build their careers, and raise their daughters, they encountered a series of unexpected difficulties but also managed to live their lives on their own terms. The family enjoyed walks in the parks near their home, sang together, and laughed at Berto's funny jokes and stories. Mollie moved more decisively into a career as a public speaker, motivated not only by financial need but by an ever-increasing determination that she must participate in achieving the change she hoped to see in America. Ultimately undaunted by the threats of Booker T. Washington and his allies to moderate her stances, she found her voice as a militant civil rights activist. With Berto having achieved the pinnacle of his professional success as a municipal court judge, the couple hoped for more stability going forward. If only they could overcome the challenges presented by Woodrow Wilson's ascendancy to the White House and by their own daughter's rebellious teenage years.

5

The Invasion of Jim Crow, 1913–1914

T he expansion of segregation throughout the U.S. capital and the nation during the early years of the Wilson administration invaded and destabilized the Terrell family's personal and professional lives. Raising children as members of the Talented Tenth (and being such children) was a major challenge in the era of Jim Crow. Mollie Terrell decided to accompany nineteen-year-old Mary and fifteen-year-old Phyllis to Oberlin for the fall semester in 1913, where they encountered racism and segregation. Although Mollie and Berto dealt well with short separations when she went on speaking tours or took their daughters on summer vacations, five months apart stressed them both, especially since her departure coincided with Berto's most difficult fight to maintain his judgeship. Oberlin disappointed Mollie, leading to painful confrontations with administrators over their endorsement of segregation. This experience affirmed and strengthened her conviction that African Americans must organize and fight on all fronts to gain the rights of full citizenship they were denied by white America.

"Fine Specimen[s] of Good, Pure, Intelligent Womanhood"

Although Mollie's primary reason for accompanying their daughters to Oberlin was her concern about them as maturing young women, she also went because of her continued sorrow at living in the D.C. home where her beloved mother had died. She explained: "So many things constantly reminded me of her I felt a change of scene would do me good." Mollie knew that Berto would be upset by this proposal, for they had not lived apart since their marriage more than two decades earlier. The couple's communication was usually open. In her state of depression, however, Mollie did not communicate directly with him: "When I decided the time had come to take the girls away I did not have the courage to broach the matter to my husband, but delegated the girls to break the news to him to see what his reaction would be." She later claimed that Berto "cheerfully consented" to her departure; in reality, he felt abandoned by his wife at a moment when he was under political siege.[1]

Her grief at the loss of her mother was tied into her conviction that she and other black women shouldered a particular responsibility to raise daughters whose morals could not be assailed. As her teenage daughters became interested in boys, she worried about ensuring their conduct and reputations. Aware that black youths' sexuality was freighted with extra risk, given the disapprobation of white America, she viewed their chaste presentation and behavior as an important survival strategy.[2]

Whenever Terrell spoke at the white-dominated social purity conferences that were popular for decades at the turn of the twentieth century, her anxiety increased as she heard other speakers detailing the dangers facing young women. She worried about being away from her daughters. Writing home from one such meeting in 1911, she fretted to Berto: "I do wish I were home tonight. I am dreadfully worried about the girls. I shall never leave them without an elderly woman again. . . . You will do the best you can, but you are a man and you are not at home when they return from school." Her mother had died earlier that year, so the girls were deprived of a protective and caring guardian, and the entire caretaking responsibility fell to their busy parents. Mollie weighed anew the costs and benefits of leaving home to give lectures but soon received a reassuring letter from Berto and replied, "I am glad you are taking such good care of the girls. You cannot be too watchful." He tried his best to alleviate her anxiety, but he, too, remained vigilant about guarding their daughters' reputations.[3]

The Terrells were particularly concerned about Phyllis's romantic relationships with boys. Mollie had seen "the tendency P[hyllis] exhibited for years." By the ninth grade, Phyllis had at least two rival beaux, both from prominent black families and seniors at the M Street High School. One, Earl Hyman, ignored his schoolwork, engaged in pranks, showed too much interest in girls, and generally failed to meet the expectations of social propriety upheld by the black elite. Mollie and Berto, who already saw Phyllis as an indifferent and lazy student, thought that Earl was a bad influence on her. Moreover, Phyllis violated propriety by dating two boys, Earl and one nicknamed Mask, at the same time. Phyllis accepted a ring from Mask, which implied that she was dating only him. Her parents were distraught when she gave Mask's ring to Earl as a sign that she cared more for him. They believed that she should not have accepted the ring from Mask in the first place and certainly should not have given it to Earl. To remove Phyllis from this situation, they sent her to Oberlin's preparatory high school that fall of 1913, when Mary entered the college, a face-saving move no one in their close-knit community would question.[4]

After Mollie and their daughters left for Oberlin, Berto engaged in the awkward mission of retrieving the ring from Earl to return it to Mask. Both young men were then freshmen at Howard University. It took Berto several trips to the drugstore where Earl worked to "catch" him, he wrote to Mollie, referring to the young man as "that little skunk" and "that little scoundrel." When he finally did, the "store was so crowded" that he "didn't have a chance to deliver the strong message which I shall give him." The saga continued when Berto met with Mask to return the ring, which actually belonged to the young man's mother: "My dear Wife: I rather fell down in the ring matter with young Mask tonight. . . . With a great show of interest and virtue I told him that you and I thought that Phyllis should not keep his ring because she might lose it and his mother would be greatly distressed if such a thing should happen." But Mask revealed that he knew that Phyllis had given the ring to Earl and had even seen him wearing it. The Terrells considered the ring exchange and Phyllis's behavior with the two young men as a sign of their daughter's personal failures, including a lack of feminine propriety and of race pride.[5]

At Oberlin, no new boy problems appeared, yet Mollie continued to worry, writing to Berto, "So far as P[hyllis] is concerned, I am very much upset. . . . The germ of evil is there, I fear." Dwelling on their daughter's problematic romantic liaisons, she declared, "That devil [Earl] has exerted such a baneful influence upon her . . . that she can never entirely recover from it, I fear. I shall keep her away from Washington as long as I can, if I am never able to live there again myself in order to carry out this plan. You have no idea how I suffer. I feel like [the] saying from Dante—'Here is a woman who has been through hell.'" Although Mollie identified herself as the sufferer, she upset her husband by holding out the prospect that she might not return to Washington because both Earl and Mask were at Howard, just blocks away from the Terrell home. Her parents' attempt to protect Phyllis, a project in which they were both deeply invested, threatened to keep them apart far longer than they wanted.[6]

"They Shall Not Be Jim Crowed"

Once at Oberlin, Mollie found the racial environment so troubling that she challenged it. She had accompanied her daughters to help ease their transition from the all-black world of their segregated District of Columbia public schools to the predominantly white college. She had hoped that Mary and Phyllis would be treated as equals. Instead, she found Jim Crow had invaded an institution, founded by abolitionists, that had admitted black and female students before the Civil War, served as a stop on the Underground Railroad, and resisted the Fugitive Slave Act. Unfortunately, the Terrell daughters belonged to a rising generation of black students in the 1910s and 1920s who encountered increasingly overt prejudice at predominantly white colleges, even

Oberlin. Phyllis's and Mary's experiences of racial prejudice there were personal and private, but their mother moved quickly from the realm of personal outrage to political activism. Terrell expanded her advocacy of civil rights to include standing up for black students' equal access to all social and educational experiences at integrated but predominantly white colleges. She alerted NAACP national headquarters that Jim Crow had even infested a college with abolitionist bona fides, revealing that administrators, professors, and students alike had abandoned Oberlin's historic legacy.[7]

Not just an immediate response to Phyllis's behavior, Mollie had always wanted to send the girls to Oberlin for she had fond memories of attending it in the late 1870s and early 1880s. She anticipated that her daughters would have similarly enriching experiences. Moreover, Mollie and Berto believed in the benefits of interracial education, including the possibilities for cordial social interactions and the development of real friendships between black and white students. Just as Berto still maintained good relations with his fellow white students from the Lawrence Academy and Harvard College, so Mollie had made lifelong friends across the color line while attending high school and college in Oberlin, Ohio.[8]

Terrell believed that segregated schools and neighborhoods increased race hatred and misunderstandings, whereas social contact could break down racist stereotypes. Referring to a white high school friend with whom she was still close, she argued, "No matter how strongly representatives of the dominant race might insist that certain vices and defects were common to all colored people alike, she would know from intimate association with at least one colored girl that those blanket charges proffered against the whole race were not true." In addition, social contact undermined prejudice in both directions: "A colored girl who has enjoyed the friendship of a white girl knows . . . there are some white people in the United States too broad of mind and generous of heart to put the color of a human being's skin above every other consideration." Mollie's friendships with white students had also allowed her to feel comfortable among whites. Her ability to excel at an elite college built her confidence in her own intellectual and social equality. Later, that self-confidence facilitated her participation in predominantly white reform organizations such as the National American Woman Suffrage Association and the Women's International League for Peace and Freedom, as well as in such integrated groups as the National Association for the Advancement of Colored People.[9]

Although Mollie treasured her memories of Oberlin, she was not unaware of the state of race relations in the country and at her alma mater in the early 1900s. Her father's third wife, Anna Wright Church, had accompanied her son and daughter (Mollie's half siblings) to Oberlin over a decade earlier. At the time, Anna told her of the prejudice they encountered. Mollie remembered this after she visited Oberlin while on a speaking tour in the spring of 1913. She wrote Anna, exclaiming, "But Oberlin itself!! What can I say of the awful change in sentiment that has taken place in my lifetime. All you said about it—a great deal more than you said is true, although it was difficult if not impossible for me to comprehend it when you first made the report." Mollie explained: "I went to Oberlin to make arrangements for the girls next fall. It is a very difficult proposition, I am sorry to say. They shall not be Jim Crowed. I am determined on that point and told Dean Fitch so in no uncertain language." Florence Fitch, the dean of college women, disliked the prospect of having the civil rights activist bring her daughters to Oberlin but conceded that Terrell was a prominent alumna who needed to be treated with respect. Fitch invited her to stay in her old dorm but tarnished Mollie's memories by telling her that she "was the first and only Colored woman who had ever lived there." As Mollie declared to Anna, "It is no credit to Baldwin Cottage if it has never [since] sheltered a Colored woman." Her realization that segregation had taken hold at Oberlin influenced her decision to accompany the girls there. Even before they arrived, Terrell was ready to fight for them.[10]

In an eloquent thirteen-page letter in which Terrell took on many aspects of racism and segregation at Oberlin even before she and her daughters arrived, she informed Dean Fitch that she hoped to secure a room in a dormitory or college-run "cottage" for her daughters. Alternatively, she wondered if they could board with a faculty family, a common practice when she attended. She was disappointed to find that black students were no longer welcome to live in faculty homes, although doing so remained an option for white students. Fitch suggested that Mary and Phyllis might find a place to live where they could do "domestic help" as "maids" in return for board but warned that even this might be difficult to secure. It is unclear whether Terrell perceived this to be a racist slight or a reasonable suggestion of a way to help pay for their educations; either way, she did not respond.[11]

Fitch stated flatly that, as underclass students, the sisters would not be able to live on campus. In fact, Oberlin College officials maintained an informal quota of no more than two black women in any dormitory. They did so by claiming that black applicants had applied too late, which is exactly what Fitch did when she informed Terrell that "Talcott Hall will be out of the question for next year as we have so long a list of applicants and the places have already all been assigned." In a private letter to her staff, Fitch wrote acerbically, "Her daughters may not be as delightful and talented as herself." Fitch's bigger concerns focused on how Terrell might respond to the now-pervasive prejudice on the campus.[12]

Fitch and Terrell clashed over the costs and benefits of accommodating African American students who wanted to live in the dorms and had few other housing options available. Fitch asserted: "As to the other matter of making some special concession to your daughters and giving them places in advance. . . . I do not believe we should be furthering at all the cause of the colored people if it was felt that they were given special favors." Terrell challenged this logic: "When the strong and the weak are placed side by side in any kind of competition, consideration is usually and should always be shown the weak. In games, if one individual has any kind of advantage over the others who are to participate, he is handicapped in some way, so that the weaker may have an equal chance." African Americans should be given special consideration after centuries of oppression and continued racism. Anticipating resistance, she provided a neutral, economic analogy: "No one would think of objecting to this handicap as an injustice. In this country we have had for years a protective tariff, so as to protect the infant industries in their competition with the strong." Taking on Fitch's ostensible concern about wanting to be fair to the white students, Terrell argued that living off campus "would not work a great hardship upon any two white girls . . . [for] there are a number of excellent boarding houses . . . to which white girls are cordially welcomed." It was altogether different, she insisted, for black students to be forced to live separately from whites merely because of their race.[13]

As a result of her persistence, the Terrell daughters were able to live in a campus dormitory in their first academic year. Mollie resided nearby to ensure that the administration kept its promises. She intended to help her daughters navigate the prejudices of Oberlin and to supervise Phyllis's behavior. After the issue was settled for their first year, Terrell and Fitch launched into a debate about the girls' housing for the following one. Terrell insisted that Fitch had agreed that her daughters would be able to reside in Talcott Hall their second year but was told that they must move after their first year to a segregated off-campus boardinghouse for black students. She protested vociferously: "I do not believe in segregation of any group of students on account of race or color or anything else for which they are not responsible. I do not want my daughters segregated in Oberlin College."[14]

Arguing that black students must not be "shut out from the many phases of college life," Terrell insisted that the "segregation of colored students is a badge of inferiority placed upon them." Paying close attention to the concerns of Oberlin's current administration, Terrell noted that she had read that the school was struggling to manage overenrollment. Noting its radical history not only as an integrated but a coeducational college, she provocatively proposed to Fitch that the college should expel overtly racist white students: "It would be better for Oberlin College with its matchless, incomparable record of breadth, justice and Christian charity to an oppressed race and a handicapped sex to lose a few hundred prejudice-ridden students." The administration ignored her suggestion.[15]

Concluding another long letter to Fitch, Terrell exclaimed: "Many a time the memory of the strong and indissoluble bond of union which existed between my white college mates and myself has saved me from utter disbelief in the white man's ability either to live up to the principles laid down in the Declaration of Independence or to be true followers of the Lord Jesus Christ." Fitch did not respond to any of Terrell's deeper questions about current college policies. Instead, she replied narrowly to the question of second-year housing: "I am very certain I was not so unwise as to promise a place at Talcott Hall for next year."[16]

Mary and Phyllis arrived at Oberlin as racial bias was worsening across the country, including on college campuses. Woodrow Wilson's Democratic administration implemented segregation in the federal government and helped normalize the growing racism and segregation found throughout the nation. Mollie despaired to Berto: "I see no reason in the world why a colored boy or girl should come to Oberlin College, if he wished to secure the advantages which came from social contact with cultivated people—one of the most priceless and precious things which a college life can bestow. They are . . . completely shut out from the real life of the college." White students had advantages, including the ability to network, that the offspring of black elites were denied. Oberlin no longer fostered interracial collegiality.[17]

Overt racism at Oberlin meant that social events on campus were difficult for the Terrell sisters, who had no chance to flourish as members of the community. Mary, for instance, narrowly avoided the disadvantages of being the only freshman girl without a senior-class mentor. She finally got one only because one senior's mother, Nettie McKelvey Swift, was an old friend of Mollie's, and her daughter, committed to upholding Oberlin's progressive past, volunteered.[18]

White students' fears about coed interracial social interactions hurt Mary, too. Oberlin tradition dictated that each male senior invite several first-year girls to a reception. A white senior boy invited Mary to join his group of about four white girls, but one of them soon objected to his having invited "a colored girl." Mary got all dressed up and was ready to go when the senior phoned to say that he had recruited a black graduate of Fisk University, who happened to be taking one class at Oberlin, to accompany her separately. Mollie informed her husband that Mary "told me about it and said she didn't want to go." When the young Fisk man arrived at the door, Mollie opened it and said, "You are acquainted with nobody in either class and neither is she, so it will be embarrassing for both." He agreed right away, Mollie wrote to Berto, saying that she thought "he was greatly relieved." Berto, enraged, wrote back: "How my blood boils about that Mary incident and the Senior reception! If that [white] fellow had only had the courage to have done the right thing his action would have gone far towards setting that problem." Mollie took her daughter to the movies while the girls in Mary's dormitory attended the event without her.[19]

The dynamic at Oberlin between Mollie and her daughters was complicated. On the one hand, she wanted to protect them from racism. On the other, she was so protective that it was hard for them to have their own experiences and learn how to deal with challenges.[20] Mollie confided to Berto that "I am still working for them. I stay in their pretty room all day and remain with them till they retire. Maybe I am not doing them any good by helping them so much, but I want to give them a good start. I love to be with them, too." A doting mother, Mollie found it difficult to stop infantilizing her daughters, which may be why they were often angry with her. Mollie lamented to Berto: "Mary is upright and dependable, I think, but I fear she is the incarnation of the basest ingratitude."[21]

"Her Wretched, Inexcusable Showing as a Student"

It was almost inconceivable to the brilliant and accomplished couple that their daughters were struggling to pass their courses. With a combination of denial and hope, they had imagined that the girls could turn things around and thrive academically at Oberlin. But, Berto noted, "Our girls did not learn to study at the high school and they are, therefore, in the crudest kind of a condition for work at Oberlin." Openly envious of the accomplishments of their friends' children, Berto reported to Mollie about "an event at the school the other day that was a very knife to my heart. . . . Some white ladies happened to be visiting the school . . . and they went into raptures over the bright and capable boys and girls who recited." Berto was chagrined that "several of the children of our friends, such as . . . [dean and professor at Howard University] Kelly Miller's daughter, . . . were marvels in their school work. . . . When I thought of all your hours of agony and travail with our girls and what they are in comparison with such pupils do you wonder that I did not feel lifted up?" The situation was particularly unacceptable, the Terrells believed, because the girls had received so many material and educational advantages.[22]

In the first semester, Phyllis passed all her classes, but Mary's report card shocked her father. After venting his considerable anger, Berto bitterly summed up the couple's face-saving approach to their daughters' academic failures: "As for me, I presume that I shall have to go on lying day after day and tell people that my children are doing nicely at school."[23] At the end of the 1914 spring semester, the Terrell daughters left Oberlin with no intention of returning the following year. Mary's abysmal grades were certainly a factor, as was Oberlin's refusal to provide integrated housing or a hospitable social environment to African American students.[24]

"It Is Well to Discuss Difficult Situations to See if Things Cannot Be Improved"

A racial justice advocate to the core, Mollie Church Terrell could never have focused only on injustices done to her own daughters. While at Oberlin, she had repeatedly called attention to and tried to mitigate the broader problem of racism at the school, including that expressed by its president, Henry Churchill King (1902–27). As a prominent Oberlin alumna, she engaged in a dialogue with the administration and fought King's attempts to justify segregation and racism on campus. In conversations and letters throughout the school year, Terrell and defensive Oberlin administrators debated prejudice, race relations, and segregation on college campuses. In a long letter of protest written to President King in January 1914, Terrell cataloged several disheartening changes since her graduation thirty years earlier.

She was disturbed that college officials catered to the overt racism of the white students by strongly encouraging black students to create separate organizations, something new to Oberlin. Black students had come to perceive the prestigious campus literary societies as automatically barring them, so few even applied. Terrell asserted that it was "very disheartening to me to see that some of the Colored students have been really persuaded to believe that by flocking together all the time and never mingling with the white students, they are exhibiting a tremendous amount of 'self-respect.' I have often observed that when our enemies want the Colored man to pursue a course of conduct in deference to race prejudice, they cunningly devise some phrase which will convince him" to accept segregation.[25]

Terrell complained to King that the prejudiced ideas and behavior of current Oberlin administrators, including the college secretary, George M. Jones, made her "almost speechless when he expressed himself so strongly against allowing them [black students] to board in any of the college dormitories and thus be brought into social contact with white students." King defended Jones: "He believes that the College can do a very valuable work for a limited number of colored students; that if that number were unduly increased, it would make it more difficult to do the best for the colored students themselves and increase the sense of friction all along the line. . . . I think he is handling his office in an entirely unprejudiced way."[26]

President King saw Terrell as disruptive. Concerned that she had been stirring up trouble at Oberlin ever since her arrival with her daughters, he remonstrated, "The problem is a difficult one, and I should be sorry to have it made more difficult in any way." Terrell replied that she had "kept away from the Colored students, so that I should not say or do anything which would make their already difficult position any harder." She pointed out that she had not spoken to a "young man who was refused admission into one of the societies, until after he had decided upon the course he intended to pursue." Once the student decided to contest his exclusion, however, she supported him. Terrell pointedly rejected King's assertion that discussing the problem of racism and how to rectify it would only stir up trouble: "Sometimes, however, it is well to discuss difficult situations to see if things cannot be improved."[27]

While striving to enlighten King about how prejudice worked, Terrell also gave suggestions as to how the college could mitigate it. Noting his complaint that black students "monopolized the pool tables," Terrell pointed out to King that "what one Colored person does is laid at the door of the whole race, if it is silly or criminal, whereas the good deeds done by thousands of reputable, sensible, reliable Colored people are forgotten. What a blessing that other races are not judged in this way." King did not seem to grasp the distinction, for he reiterated in a subsequent letter, "I cannot guarantee that, with the large numbers [of white students] coming to us without any special training on this subject [of racial tolerance and social equality], there will not be examples of lack of consideration. And it is just on this account that I want to have the colored students as careful as possible not to give needless offense." Here, King shifted the burden of preventing racist thoughts and behavior onto the African American students, who needed to work harder not to offend the white students.[28]

Telling Terrell that her earlier experience of social equality on campus was not an appropriate model for the current students, President King regretted her unrealistic expectation that her daughters would be able to interact socially with white students. Terrell replied, "You thought that perhaps I had associated so much with the white girls that I might not have gained the right point of view, while I was a student here." She countered: "When I began to review my record, I discovered I had so many close friends among the Colored girls that it was strange that I found time enough to associate with white girls at all." She then detailed for King each of her black roommates and friends.[29]

As a strategic concession to King, Terrell admitted that race relations had not been entirely idyllic at Oberlin College in the 1870s and 1880s. She mentioned three instances when she had encountered prejudice as an Oberlin student. First, she was certain that race was the primary factor in a closely contended election that resulted in an undistinguished white male student winning the position of class poet over her in their junior year. In addition, she had regretted that the town of Oberlin had a separate "Colored church," but she had succumbed to segregation and attended and taught in its Sunday school. Third, she had turned down an invitation to attend "a social func-tion" with a white male classmate because she was afraid that her black friend and classmate, Ida Gibbs [Hunt], would have been left without a companion. Without romanticizing the past, Terrell insisted that Oberlin's inclusive atti-tudes toward African Americans had significantly deteriorated.[30]

Dismissing Terrell's concerns about her daughters living in a segregated boardinghouse the following year, King noted that she had done the same when she was a student. Terrell conceded that she had "boarded with Colored families" for several of her nine years at Oberlin's public high school, prepa-ratory school, and college, yet pointed out that she had never been forced by the college's administration to associate only with students of her own race. Responding to King's suggestion that white students would not want any so-cial interactions with black students, she stated, "I am sure, on the other hand, that no white girl with whom I associated ever accused me of 'forcing' myself upon her. The mother of one of my friends, Mrs. Hayford . . . secured permis-sion for me to spend every afternoon at her house for a whole term. The atmo-sphere must have been entirely different then from what it is now, because it was quite possible to conceive of a white girl's having a genuine friendship with a Colored girl." In a searing critique, Terrell admitted to King, "Altho I try to be optimistic in this wicked and cruel country, in which everything is done to crush the pride, wound the sensibilities, embitter the life and break the heart of my unfortunate race, nothing has come so near forcing me to give up hope, and resigning myself to the cruel fate which many people are certain awaits us, than the heart-breaking back-sliding of Oberlin College."[31] Ignoring the real-ity of her charges, President King denied that the college was no longer living up to its progressive history.[32]

Another administrator, probably without recognizing his own cruelty, asked Terrell why she had not saved everyone the trouble by simply sending her daughters to a good "colored school." In response, she explained that Mary and Phyllis had thus far spent their entire lives within a segregated public school system. She wanted them to be able to interact as equals with white students as she herself had done in a comparatively prejudice-free experience at Oberlin.[33]

Disturbed by the spread of racial discrimination at Oberlin, by the end of the fall semester, Terrell wrote to her NAACP colleague Oswald Garrison Vil-lard asking for help in fighting its policies and attitude. Responding that her re-port was "horribly discouraging," Villard requested a copy of an Oberlin Col-lege catalog with the names of administrators and faculty so that the NAACP might consider contacting them privately. He explained the organization's strategy: "We have just successfully overcome race prejudice at Smith College, and we may be able to help. . . . We found at Smith that quiet work without publicity, but the threat of it, was the best way of tackling the problem."[34]

In the 1910s and 1920s, although a few more black students were admitted to predominantly white colleges, they were, as Terrell put it, "Jim Crowed." A few of the Seven Sisters women's colleges, including Smith, had begun accepting miniscule numbers of African American women at the turn of the century, yet those students were not allowed to live on campus. In 1913, the NAACP became involved when Carrie Lee, from New Bedford, Massachusetts, became the first black woman admitted to Smith College who tried to live in the dorms. Lee's white roommate, who was from Tennessee, immediately protested. Smith College administrators forced Lee to vacate the room, offering her a room in the servants' quarters instead. Lee refused, and her mother considered pulling her from the college until a white female professor stepped in and invited Lee to live at her home. The Lees contacted the NAACP, which wrote letters to members of the board and to Smith College president Marion LeRoy Burton. By the end of her first semester, Lee was allowed to move back into a dormitory, but she experienced several public incidents of racial hatred from white students during her four years at Smith.[35]

A decade later, in 1923, black students and their parents continued to encounter similar problems at other colleges. Harvard alumnus Roscoe Conkling Bruce tried unsuccessfully to get his son placed in a dormitory. He was told by its president that "in the Freshman Halls, where residence is compulsory, we have felt . . . the necessity of not including colored men. . . . I am sure you understand why, from the beginning, we have not thought it possible to compel men of different races to reside together." Bruce rejected this logic and made the correspondence public, triggering protests about the segregation from African Americans and liberal whites. Then, W. E. B. Du Bois published "Negroes in College" in the *The Nation* (1926), which included a "stark narration of exclusion from white institutions," including other "Seven Sisters" schools. Vassar College resisted admitting black students on the grounds that it had enrolled many southern white students and wanted to keep them content.[36]

"It Is Too Bad That We Are . . . So Far Apart from Each Other"

At a moment when no aspect of their lives was free from the deleterious effects of racism and Jim Crow, the Terrells struggled to keep their family and professional lives intact. Berto's life was in chaos; his family had left town at the very moment he was trying to win reappointment from a new Democratic regime that was openly hostile to African Americans. Woodrow Wilson's administration implemented segregation in the federal government, and it spread throughout the capital and the nation. At the same time, Democratic senators, now in the majority, unleashed vile attacks on all black officeholders, including the respected municipal court judge Robert H. Terrell.

When the Terrell couple described themselves as "breaking up a home" or "breaking up housekeeping," they referred to downsizing from a house with a cook or servant to living more modestly—without any help—because of their lack of financial wherewithal.[37] Their motivation to break up housekeeping was multifaceted. Of course, Mollie mourned her mother, but another primary concern was financial. Her relatively modest inheritance from her recently deceased father coincided with Mollie's stark realization that Berto's deep financial problems from the earlier Capital Savings Bank failure were ongoing. Reeling from the gravity of their situation, Mollie concluded that the cost of maintaining their relatively large house and a servant would be too expensive when their daughters were no longer living at home. To economize, the family moved out of their house and put their belongings in storage so they could rent it out. In the meantime, Berto moved into a boardinghouse, where he felt lonely and abandoned. Mollie imagined that his expenses would be significantly less than those for herself and their daughters. A hurt Berto replied with some sarcasm to her proposed budget: "I shall send you the $50 a month. . . . I am very much amused, however, when you tell me that I can live on thirty-five dollars a month. . . . You simply have no idea what it costs to live."[38]

In spite of her disappointment with her inheritance, Mollie had often benefited from her father's largesse during his lifetime; even at this point, she was using money from the sale of property she had previously received as a gift from her father to pay for her daughters' education at Oberlin. The couple's high expectations for their daughters were compounded by the fact that, in addition to all the extra resources that had been given them, Mollie had even sold property to put her children through Oberlin.[39]

During the five months Mollie was away, Berto was destabilized by changes in his family life that came as his professional career was in real peril due to the rise of Jim Crow in national politics. He perceived his wife's move to be harder on him than on her, since she was able to be with their daughters while he was left alone when he most needed her support. After she departed, Berto reflected, "My dear, dear Wife: I am delighted to get your letter. . . . I am so sorry that things were in such a turmoil the last few days . . . that we could not hold a family council behind closed doors for several hours so that the children might get some idea of what it means to break up a home." Feeling the heavy consequences of the decision, two days later he reiterated his sense of alienation and distance: "You can't imagine how much I miss you. This movement is not like going away on a trip for a lecture, you know. . . . Lovingly, Berto." Mollie replied tenderly, confessing that her decision had exacted a significant toll on her, too: "You say you will miss me and I am very glad to hear that. It is music to my ear and balm to my soul. I surely miss you. I knew I would and I did not decide to take such an important step lightly." Her fundamental love for her husband remained clear and strong. She reminded him of a key reason behind her move—their shared desire to remove Phyllis from Washington, D.C.: "I hope these influences of culture and refinement here will have the desired effect upon our girls, particularly upon P[hyllis]."[40]

Wistful and resentful that they would be apart on their twenty-second anniversary in October 1913, Berto wrote, "It is too bad that we are to be so far apart from each other on our anniversary day, which is Tuesday if you don't happen to recall it." His mood changed dramatically for the better, however, when he interrupted his letter to declare: "Your special has just come. . . . I do thank you so much for it. It is so interesting in every line." Mollie's long letter reassured Berto of her love and reminded him of the strength of their romantic and intellectual connections. She shared with him her pleasure in having read in Oberlin's library two thick volumes of "those delicious love letters" of the poets Robert Browning and Elizabeth Barrett. She breathlessly recounted the drama of their courtship, including Barrett's father's refusal to sanction the marriage: "What a tyrant the old villain was! But Browning's great devotion after their marriage made up for the loss of . . . everything else." Berto basked in Mollie's enthusiasm about this other romance and marriage.[41]

On the day of their wedding anniversary, Berto was reflective but hopeful: "It was twenty-two years ago tonight that we started on our marital journey. During the period we have had sunshine and shadows, and I fancy that our career has been similar to that of others who started with us. Let us hope that the rest of the journey will be nothing but happiness and sunshine. In the reckoning, we are on the other grade now. We are on the side of experience and mature thought and surely ought to make more of the life to come. . . . May the good spirits direct us!" The "shadows" on the first two decades of their married life were many, including the unsuccessful pregnancies and infant deaths, Mollie's health problems, their disappointments over their daughters' accomplishments, Berto's financial difficulties, and the current battle over his reappointment.[42]

Mollie shared with Berto that she was not only reading voraciously but was informally auditing classes. Always intellectually alive and interested in gaining new knowledge, she enthusiastically told her husband: "In the morning I sometimes go to a class in literature which meets at nine o'clock. It is intensely interesting. Just at present Professor Wager is lecturing on Carlyle." In contrast, a U.S. history class was far more problematic for it revealed how white supremacist ideas had permeated the college curriculum. By the 1910s, revised American history textbooks emphasized Reconstruction's failures and justified the spread of segregation across the nation. She told Berto: "Twice I have attended a class in American History which is studying the Reconstruction

Period. It makes my blood boil to hear the cold-blooded manner in which the teacher (one of my own former teachers, by the way) criticizes Charles Sumner and Thaddeus Stevens for their 'narrowness' . . . because they did not talk with Southerners to get their point of view." Influenced by the work of new revisionist historians who disparaged Reconstruction as a failure, Mollie's former professor was now teaching a blatantly racist version of American history: "Oh, we have fallen upon grave times indeed, when such a history as the one used here, written by a Massachusetts man [James Ford Rhodes], too, is studied by the rising generation of Northern white people." Mollie explained she had "intended to get one. I borrowed one for a few minutes the other day and after reading a few paragraphs, one of which was [on Louis] Agassiz's *scientific* estimate of the Negro's capacity, and a very low one it is, I tell you, I became so faint and heartsick that I returned it at once." These revisionist texts were popular and respected; Rhodes won a Pulitzer Prize for his *History of the Civil War* in 1918. The teaching of American history, Mollie realized, was being used as a political tool to justify whites' unwillingness to socialize or mix with African Americans in an ever-expanding set of circumstances. Poor scholarship was itself exacerbating changes in social norms. Rightly seeing it as a harbinger of the rise of racism nationally, Mollie glumly noted, "The tide has certainly turned against us."[43]

Fully sympathizing with her concerns, Berto eagerly provided Mollie with a historical counternarrative with which to refute Rhodes's inaccurate and biased *History*. This would help their daughters understand the true history of Reconstruction and serve as material for Mollie's speeches and articles: "The distortionists of facts nowadays never give Stevens and Sumner credit for saving the Negro from a new slavery by giving him the ballot. The black laws of the South made immediately after the War were more diabolical than any slave laws had been. . . . Under the 'Black Codes' the ex-slave was completely at the mercy of his bitterest enemy, the poor white man, and he had no master to protect him." Berto concluded with a recommendation for further reading. Their letters highlighted their many shared political and intellectual interests.[44]

"It Is a Terrible Crime to Be a Negro in This Clime"

Berto Terrell's hopes to be renominated and confirmed in 1913 coincided ominously with President Wilson's implementation of segregation in the nation's capital. Wilson was also battling with the NAACP, of which Berto and Mollie were both members. Judge Terrell's prospects looked less promising than usual. His presence that year at NAACP rallies and open fundraising for the organization exemplifies his courage and determination to fight against discrimination even when he knew he was about to face the most difficult renomination

FIGURE 5.1. (*Left*) A pensive and determined Mollie remained remarkably unchanged in her middle age. (Courtesy Langston Family)

FIGURE 5.2. (*Right*) This formal portrait of a middle-aged Berto nicely captures the dignity and self-possession he projected as municipal court judge. (Courtesy Langston Family)

and confirmation battle of his career. Berto had always encountered resistance to his reappointments, Mollie explained, from southern Democrats who "held out stoutly against his confirmation solely on account of his race."[45] Ever since his first nomination by President Theodore Roosevelt, Berto's reappointments had occurred under Republican presidents. This time, he had to be nominated by a Democratic president and approved by a Democratic-dominated Senate. In the past, he had relied upon the premise that GOP presidents would try to garner support from black voters by appointing a few African Americans to symbolically significant federal positions. Black Republicans always hoped for more profound results from their party, such as antilynching legislation and civil rights enforcement, but often found themselves looking more narrowly at the risk of losing the few patronage positions they had been allocated. As Mollie recalled: "When a Democratic president, Woodrow Wilson, was elected everybody believed the colored judge would lose his job."[46]

Berto Terrell's fiercest congressional opponent was a Democratic senator from Mississippi, James K. Vardaman, a virulent white supremacist who had publicly proclaimed in 1907: "If it is necessary every Negro in the state will be lynched, it will be done to maintain white supremacy." Vardaman met privately with Wilson and threatened to filibuster Berto's nomination. During the meeting, the senator said, "while he was 'not against the Negro as an individual,' he would work against allowing 'the negro and the white man' to 'live together on terms of political equality.'" Going beyond white racists' more typical condemnations of "social equality"—which raised the dreaded prospect of interracial marriage and "miscegenation"—the Mississippi senator openly opposed basic political equality for African Americans.[47]

Senator Vardaman's virulent hostility worried the typically unflappable Berto. Wilson's hesitations meant, as he confided to his wife, that he was "still sitting high on the anxious bench. Our President has not yet made any appointments in this Court. The situation is most extraordinary." In the meantime, Vardaman capitalized on media attention to spew his racism. Berto lamented, "It is really a race case because Vardaman's attack is not on me but on the race, as you will see [from newspaper clippings]. I am now simply a humble factor in the equation." He could not help but worry: "I have so much to contend with—color, political bias and before a Southern Senate! Who can tell what the harvest will be? It is a terrible crime to be a Negro in this clime. But let us hope. Things may turn out all right." Reappointments were always an exhausting and humiliating ordeal for Berto, who was viciously caricatured in editorials and political cartoons by hateful whites who drew him with exaggerated "African" features and defamed him as an illiterate brute, susceptible to bribes and other forms of corruption, meting out injustice. This time, during the Wilson administration's implementation of Jim Crow throughout the capital, was the worst.[48]

Fortunately, Berto had strong backing from whites and blacks in D.C. and around the country. The president and senators received many letters urging his reappointment. To Mollie, he tried to take solace from there never having been "such support given a man as has been given me by business men, the bar, and the press. I am proud of their loyalty." African Americans in both parties united in endorsing him; they all recognized that if Judge Terrell lost his position on the municipal court, President Wilson would choose a white nominee instead. Retaining their very few federal government appointments was an important goal for black professionals.[49]

By the advent of the Wilson administration, Booker T. Washington's political capital had decreased, in part because of militant challenges to his leadership and also because of the rise of the Democratic Party. Nonetheless, Washington still wielded some influence behind the scenes. Berto informed his wife: "A most peculiar situation has developed in my case. At the suggestion of Booker Washington, Bishop Walters came to see the President by appointment on Thursday and brought with him Editorials from the big New York dailies giving the President a drubbing for allowing Vardaman to interfere

FIGURE 5.3. In striking contrast to the dignified image of Berto in figure 5.2, this racist political cartoon depicts Judge Terrell as a caricature of a dark-skinned man with big lips and eyes. Belying his Harvard College and Howard University pedigree, Berto is caricatured making an illiterate pronouncement: "Dis Cote, come to order, you white folks stan' up and receive yo' sentence." Perhaps as a reflection of their own terrible record of meting out "justice" to African American defendants in the criminal justice system, whites' anxieties are on full display here, suggesting that an African American judge could not be fair to white defendants. The Terrells saved this vicious cartoon as a testament to what Berto had suffered and overcome. (Courtesy Langston Family)

with him in appointing me." Booker Washington had asked Bishop Alexander Walters, president of the National Colored Democratic League, to be the face of black support for Terrell, hoping that Wilson might be somewhat more responsive to a leading representative of those African Americans who had voted for him in 1912. Walters strategically ignored the judge's Republican Party affiliation and emphasized instead his qualifications and widespread support. Berto took heart from Wilson's response: the "President said that I was the best endorsed man that had come before his administration and that it was his intention to appoint me, but he had some fears about the attack of Vardaman and his kind. Walters told him that we would look after the confirmation if he sent the name to the Senate; that he had assurances from powerful Democratic Senators that they would put the matter through."[50]

Before Wilson sent his formal nomination to the Senate, Walters worked the Senate floor with Berto, who recounted to Mollie, "The Bishop and I spent the day at the Senate talking with Democratic Senators, and everyone we approached said he would vote for me if the President sent my name in. We only talked with one Southern Senator—Overman of North Carolina, and he was most gracious. He promised to control Vardaman. I doubt if he can do this." The pair focused on Democratic senators from northern states who had black voters in their districts to whom they would be accountable. Berto demurred when Walters suggested that he personally approach his most vicious opponent: "Bishop wanted me to talk with Vardaman and [the Democratic senator from Georgia] Hoke Smith. I refused to approach them for fear of meeting an insult for my temerity." He did meet with Attorney General Thomas Watt Gregory, reporting: "Walters and I had a very pleasant talk with the Attorney General. . . . He told me that I should be proud of the tribute paid me by the citizens of the District." After a productive lobbying day, he optimistically concluded: "I don't see how I can be beaten if the Republicans are on hand and do their duty. Now it is up to the President to do his duty and respond to the request of the community and put me back on the bench."[51]

Mollie returned to D.C. from Oberlin in February 1914 and wholeheartedly joined the fight for her husband's reappointment. She frequently visited senators in the Capitol Building to lobby on his behalf, meeting with Republican Theodore E. Burton of Ohio, for instance, and thanking him for his willingness to support her husband. She cut to the chase, declaring, "The fight against my husband is solely on account of his race." The Terrells mutually despaired because Berto's excellent record as a judge seemed to be of so little consequence in the nation's capital. It was particularly painful and disconcerting to Mollie that Berto was not being evaluated on his record as a judge but was instead subjected to vicious racism. To Senator Burton, she highlighted the irrationality of racial prejudice: "He is being reviled and persecuted for nothing that he himself has done, but solely because he happens remotely to be identified with an oppressed and persecuted race." In lobbying, Mollie took a personal approach as Berto's wife, revealing: "Although my husband is bearing up under the trying ordeal as bravely as any man could, I fear that he is gradually breaking under this fierce and bitter attack upon him." She knew firsthand the psychological toll of these racist attacks, which were contributing to his (and her) feelings of emotional instability.[52]

Mollie later noted that she usually had a harder time withstanding her husband's confirmation battles than he did: "To tell the truth, I suffered much more than my husband, for . . . he was an optimist from the crown of his head to the soles of his feet. I have never seen a more wonderful exhibition of calm, cool-headed courage, of a faith that . . . justice would prevail in the end than that displayed by Judge Terrell." Her tendency to fall into deep depressions and her more nervous disposition usually made these battles harder for Mollie. Although she mostly appreciated and had even relied upon his cheerful equanimity during his earlier such battles, she sometimes resented it. Mollie admitted that she occasionally begrudged Berto's unflappability: "It provoked me to see him so cheerful, cool and calm. . . . I wanted him to suffer a little as I did, and not be so sure he would eventually be confirmed." Mollie remembered, "As for myself, I literally descended into the very depths of despair every time Judge Terrell was the victim of race prejudice." She wanted her husband to acknowledge the pain of racism even as she always wanted him to overcome his critics.[53]

In one of his few actions in office that favored African Americans in any way, President Wilson finally submitted Judge Robert Terrell's name to the Senate. At that point, Booker T. Washington intervened openly, writing to the president and key senators, noting that he had first suggested Terrell's name to President Roosevelt in 1901 and that "it has been a great satisfaction to know that he has lived up to the recommendation." Enduring all the racist invective against him, Berto was confirmed by a vote of 39 to 24; "African Americans nationwide celebrated the victory, thinking of Terrell as 'a larger-than-life hero.'" At that point, Judge Terrell became famous and, like his wife, in demand as a national speaker. African American organizations across the country invited him to give addresses and feted him at banquets held in his honor.[54]

Berto's reappointment crisis and the Terrell daughters' move to Oberlin were made far more difficult by the invasion of increasing prejudice into the couple's private and public lives. The tensions in their marriage were heightened by the racism the family faced in so many ways. The separation marked the lowest point in their marriage, but they healed their wounds, reaffirmed their commitment to each other, and never again lived apart until his untimely death in 1925. Throughout it all, Mollie remained a strong feminist and civil rights activist, providing a framework of political thought for generations of African American women.

Black Feminism

CONTESTING STEREOTYPES AND
ASSERTING EQUALITY

The daily humiliations of racism that crystalized so painfully in 1913–14 were part of a broader problem of inequality in the United States that served as a driving force in Mollie Church Terrell's activism. She wanted to provide all black women, including herself and, later, her daughters, with a new American society based on gender and racial equality, a country in which young black women could grow up expecting to vote and be full citizens, to be free from sexual assaults or constant aspersions on their sexual purity, as well as to be free of the equally pernicious stereotype of black women as asexual mammies. Terrell and other African American women intellectuals in the decades around the turn of the twentieth century—a group that included Frances Watkins Harper, Anna Julia Cooper, Mary B. Talbert, and Fannie Barrier Williams—created a modern intersectional black feminism to help envision this new world and make it a reality.

Terrell's black feminist voice was insistent, clear, and powerful. She identified herself as "a colored woman in a white world" who experienced both racism and sexism throughout her life: "A white woman has only one handicap to overcome—that of sex. I have two—both sex and race. I belong to the only group in the country which has two such huge obstacles to surmount. Colored men have only one—that of race."[1] Articulating the interconnected nature of African American women's lived experience, Terrell built onto a framework of black feminist thought that stretched back to Phillis Wheatley's early abolitionist poetry to New Negro womanhood and, later, to Alice Walker's womanism and Kimberlé Crenshaw's theory of intersectionality.[2]

Three areas of advocacy best reveal Mollie Church Terrell's piercing analyses of the intersections of race and gender in African American women's lives. A discussion of these three separate but interrelated areas of her black feminist thought requires consideration of her youth, her adult years, her family's history of enslavement, and back again. First, Terrell repeatedly asserted black women's full citizenship and right to vote. From her teenage years, she supported women's and African Americans' voting rights. She later insisted on black women's participation in the 1913 national suffrage parade and then fought continuously against the disenfranchisement of African American voters before and after the passage of the Nineteenth Amendment. Second, from the late 1890s through the 1910s, Terrell's speeches against the myth of white women's purity versus black women's alleged impurity became more high stakes and personal as she raised two African American daughters who were necessarily subjected to the dominant culture's conflicting negative stereotypes of black women as either impure and oversexualized or as asexual "mammies." And third, thinking of the histories of her own enslaved grandmothers and mother, Terrell rejected the spread of revisionist histories that maligned Reconstruction while enshrining the antebellum era as a better, more harmonious time. Skewering whites' nostalgia for their mammies, she attacked the U.S. Senate's 1923 passage of a bill to build a national "Monument to the Faithful Colored Mammies of the South."[3]

"The Ballot . . . Is Denied Simply Because of Prejudice of Sex"

Mollie Church started thinking about women's voting rights in 1879, during her college preparatory year at the Oberlin Academy, when she was sixteen. Tackling an assigned question: "Should an Amendment to the Constitution Allowing Women the Ballot Be Adopted?" she had not considered the issue before and was initially unsure. She concluded firmly in favor of women's enfranchisement: "Representation by the ballot . . . is denied simply because of prejudice of sex. [The American woman] is a citizen, is subject to laws, is imprisoned, and has been hung. She is a citizen for says the Constitution, 'All persons born or naturalized in the U.S. and subject to the jurisdiction thereof are citizens.'" Rejecting men's narrow conception of military service, she pointed out that women served their country during wars in multiple ways. Mollie concluded: "Men have such an exalted opinion of themselves that they with assumed superiority and unbounded audacity have come to think that they alone can carry forward the nation's work, and that women are *too something* to be allowed to help in the task." Her early outrage at the injustice of men's opposition to woman suffrage and her mother's example as an independent business entrepreneur inspired Mollie's lifelong commitment to advocacy for women's voting rights and their full participation in public life.[4]

Mollie Church formally entered the woman suffrage movement in February 1891 at the first National Council of Women convention. She approached her public support for women's voting rights with some trepidation; she did not consider it to have fully entered the mainstream.

> The first large suffrage meeting which I attended was . . . in Washington at which women who were interested in the subject were present from all over the world. Among the women sitting on the platform . . . were Elizabeth Cady Stanton . . . [and] Miss Anthony. . . . The presiding officer requested all those to rise who believed that women should have the franchise. Although the theater was well filled at the time, comparatively few rose. . . . I forced myself to stand up, although it was hard for me to do so. In the early 1890s it required a great deal of courage for a woman publicly to acknowledge . . . she believed in suffrage for her sex when she knew the majority did not.[5]

When Mollie told Berto, then her fiancé, "that I had stood up in Albaugh's Theatre and had publicly taken a stand for woman suffrage, he laughingly replied that I had ruined my chances for getting a husband. I told him that I would never be silly enough to marry a man who did not believe a woman had the right to help administer the affairs of the Government under which she lived." Fortunately, "Mr. Terrell . . . believed ardently in woman suffrage when few men took that stance." Countering the arguments of those who claimed that only a few "disgruntled" women wanted suffrage and that most "were perfectly satisfied with their lot," Mollie contended that more "secretly rebelled against their disfranchisement than the world will ever know." She described herself and other suffragists as having "understood fully the masculine motives underlying the embargo placed upon the female brain . . . [and who] chafed against the unnecessary and unreasonable restraints imposed upon them by custom and . . . felt degraded because they were disfranchised by law."[6]

The African American women's club movement came of age on the national scene in the 1890s, during the post-Reconstruction push to secure Jim Crow and disfranchise black men throughout the South. As a leader in the Colored Woman's League in 1892, Terrell protested the flouting of the Fourteenth and Fifteenth Amendments. Voting rights for black women were inseparable from questions of black men's disfranchisement and the broader freedom struggle. She and her fellow clubwomen recognized that the struggle for the vote must include extending full citizenship rights to all African Americans.[7]

Having attended a convention of the newly merged National American Woman Suffrage Association, Terrell later recalled:

> When the members of the Association were registering their protest against a certain injustice, I arose and said, "As a colored woman, I hope this Association will include in the resolution the injustices of various

kinds of which colored people are the victims." "Are you a member of this Association?" Miss Susan B. Anthony asked. "No, I am not," I replied, "but I thought you might be willing to listen to a plea for justice by an outsider." Then Miss Anthony invited me to come forward, write out the resolution which I wished incorporated with the others, and hand it to the Committee on Resolutions. And thus began a delightful, helpful friendship.

Anthony subsequently invited Terrell to speak in Rochester, New York, to the Political Equality Club and, acting on her social equality principles, hosted her as a guest in her home.[8]

Terrell appreciated the personal warmth but recognized by the turn of the century that Anthony was increasingly ignoring the concerns of African Americans as she led a narrowing of NAWSA's focus from a broader women's rights platform toward the sole goal of gaining (white) woman suffrage at the national level, even if it meant accepting restrictions on African Americans' voting rights. Anthony and white suffragists also disrespected others seeking to expand black suffrage. In 1897, when Adella Hunt Logan, the accomplished *lady principal* of Tuskegee Institute, asked Anthony if she could "speak at a NAWSA convention as a black woman on behalf of black women," Anthony replied, "I would not on any account bring on our platform a woman who had a ten-thousandth part of a drop of African blood in her veins who should prove an inferior speaker . . . because it would militate so against the colored race." Ignoring Logan's accomplishments, Anthony assumed that having "an ex-slave'" at the podium would be a humiliating disaster.[9]

Forced apart, NACW leaders created their own brand of suffragism that prioritized racial justice. At the St. Louis convention in 1904, the delegates formally resolved to support woman suffrage. When NACW leaders, including Terrell, petitioned Congress in 1908 for a constitutional amendment to extend the vote to women, they also demanded a federal suffrage bill to protect the voting rights of black men, the enforcement mechanism the Fifteenth Amendment had left to some unknown future.[10] Participating in public discussions about suffrage, Terrell calibrated her tone and approach based on the race and gender of her audiences.

Since the vast majority of black women already supported woman suffrage, Terrell's 1906 article about Susan B. Anthony in the *Voice of the Negro* addressed black male readers who were less sympathetic to extending voting rights to women. She began by acknowledging Anthony's disappointing move away from advocating African Americans' rights after the Civil War. She contextualized this decision by reminding her readers of the Republican Party's rejection of universal suffrage. That, she said, had constituted a betrayal of all women: "Having worked with such genuine, devoted loyalty . . . to help free an oppressed race, it is no wonder that Miss Anthony was wounded to the heart's core, when the men whom she had rendered such invaluable assistance in this cause, coolly advised her to wait for a more convenient season . . . when she implored them to help her secure justice and equality before the law for her own disfranchised sex."[11] Prodding African American men to see the connections between racism and sexism, Terrell insisted that they should be women's best allies in the fight for full citizenship at the federal and state levels since they were equally vulnerable to attempts to keep them from the polls.[12]

Frustrated by African American men's conservativism when it came to women's rights, Terrell and an activist friend discussed why they believed that African American women must take the lead: "Mrs. [Carrie] Clifford and I agree that colored men talk too much about faults of race [and] have too little courage. Colored women have to do the fighting." Referring to their friend, the black clubwoman and suffragist Addie Hunton, Terrell noted, "Mr. Hunton does not want his wife to fight white people." A committed activist, Addie Hunton did not follow her husband's proscription.[13]

When speaking to white suffragists, Terrell implored them to try to understand women's voting rights from a broader perspective. She pointed to racist actions and laws, including lynching, segregation, poll taxes, literacy tests, and the convict lease system that kept African American men terrorized and disfranchised, especially in the South. Throughout her life, when in white social spaces, Terrell tried to be the voice of African American women. Whenever she could, she took on the uncomfortable responsibility of opening dialogue with white suffragists.[14]

White suffragists accepted the elegant Terrell into their ranks, which gave her entry to otherwise segregated spaces, but often they did not act on her appeals. She wrote in her 1910 diary of hearing Ida Husted Harper, the white suffragist and biographer of Susan B. Anthony, "lecture on 'The Evolution of the Woman Suffrage Movement' in Mrs. [Fanny] Villard's elegant apartments. Wealthy women were present." At this formal gathering of elite white women, she was disappointed when Harper "criticized colored men for opposing woman suffrage." Terrell immediately interrupted: "White men do the same. After women of the American Revolution helped free white men from England's tyranny, these same men placed a yoke upon their necks." The Founding Fathers, she noted, had unfairly subjected white women to "taxation without representation." Later in the evening, "Mrs. Harper asked me if I felt bad" about her critique of black men. Terrell diplomatically "told her I did not."[15]

In spite of these tensions, Terrell found inspiration in the transatlantic white suffrage movement's daring tactics. She attended addresses by a variety of activist women, including one by "Mrs. Pankhurst, the 'Militant Suffrag-ette.'" Mollie noted in her diary that she had "enjoyed her address immensely." Impressed by the radical protest tactics of the British suffrage movement, she hoped to participate in direct action in the United States.[16]

The opportunity came on March 3, 1913, only months before she took her daughters to Oberlin, when Terrell proudly marched with other African American suffragists in the first woman suffrage parade held in the nation's capital. It gained much media attention for it was planned for the day before Woodrow Wilson's inauguration, which had drawn reporters from all over the nation and world.

The 1913 march, a seminal event in the history of the campaign for women's voting rights, is well known for being marred by the attempts of white suf-frage leaders to block African American women's equal participation. Alice Paul, a young, white, college-educated Quaker, organized the march for the National American Woman Suffrage Association. Hoping to curry the favor and participation of white southern women, Paul first planned on excluding black suffragists and then hoped to segregate them at the very end of the pa-rade. Many historical and popular culture accounts still wrongly assume that Paul achieved her goal. They describe Ida B. Wells-Barnett's defiant insertion of herself in the Illinois delegation as the exception to black women's capitula-tion to forced segregation. Some even assert that Terrell capitulated and agreed to be segregated.[17]

In fact, African American suffragists, including Terrell, marched through-out the parade. Some marched together and some in primarily white delega-tions organized by occupations or interests. Those who joined state delega-tions were, indeed, at the back, but only because organizers had a carefully choreographed chart for the parade and planned for all the states to assemble there. The black Chicago paper the *Broad Ax* captured the scene that day: "The Equal Suffrage Parade Was Viewed by Many Thousand People from All Parts of the United States. No Color Line Existed in Any Part of It. Afro-American Women Proudly Marched Right by the Side of the White Sisters."[18]

Mollie Church Terrell, the "face of the African American women's suf-frage activism," served as a mentor to Howard University's new Delta Sigma Theta Sorority, whose members organized themselves in order to take an ac-tive role in politics and reform movements, starting with their participation in the march. Terrell, who wrote the oath for the Deltas and became an honor-ary lifetime member, negotiated with Alice Paul on their behalf.[19] The How-ard University students wanted to march together, so the key question was whether they would be able to march alongside the other contingents of col-lege women. A wire from the NAWSA to Alice Paul on the day of the parade insisted that black suffragists be allowed to march without restrictions. The twenty-five Deltas took their rightful place as a contingent from Howard University alongside the other college delegations, dressed in their caps and gowns.[20] Terrell described the last-minute negotiations: "When some of the suffragists objected to having the colored girls of Howard University march in the parade, it was Inez Milholland who insisted that they be given a place with the pupils of the other schools." (Terrell had first met reformer John Milholland and his family in London in 1904 and was particularly struck with Milholland's intelligent eighteen-year-old daughter, Inez. By 1913, the two women were working together for suffrage.) [21]

Mary Beard, the progressive white feminist historian, invited Terrell and other NACW members "to stride alongside the New York City Woman Suffrage Party," which they did. Furthermore, African American women were given the honor of carrying the state banners for New York and Michigan. Black suffragists marched as artists, homemakers, trained nurses, teachers, doctors, writers, clubwomen, college graduates, college women, and musicians. Terrell's friend Carrie Clifford recounted in *The Crisis* that a formerly enslaved "old mammy" from Delaware proudly marched for black women's voting rights, too.[22] An article in the *Philadelphia Inquirer* noted: "Seldom has there been witnessed anywhere a more beautiful spectacle than the pageant of suffragettes.... There were young girls of sixteen and old women of eighty.... There were girls from all the colleges. 'Votes for negro women,' received recognition in the presence of a large delegation of dusky suffragettes from West Virginia." A group of white schoolboys marched, too, saying, "We want our teachers to vote."[23]

An April 1913 editorial by W. E. B. Du Bois described the politics surrounding the participation of African American suffragists: "The woman's suffrage party had a hard time settling the status of Negroes in the Washington parade.... Finally an order went out to segregate them in the parade, but *telegrams and protests poured in* and eventually the colored women marched according to their State and occupation without let or hindrance." Du Bois captured the fluidity and chaos of the situation as well as the resolve of the black women who organized, protested, and won the capitulation of NAWSA and Alice Paul. It is not surprising that historians and stories in popular culture have gravitated to a simplistic story with a clear narrative arc and one heroine—the story that only Ida B. Wells-Barnett defied the segregation strictures while all others capitulated—but it is not accurate.[24] When they took their rightful places throughout the parade, Terrell and the other African American suffragists acted with assurance, pride, and determination.

Despite their differences, Terrell admired Alice Paul's use of militant direct action, from parading to picketing. During World War I, Mollie and Phyllis, then in her late teens and living at home again, joined the *silent sentinels*, peacefully picketing in front of the White House. Braving physical discomforts, mother and daughter sometimes stood on heated bricks to keep warm. Carrying banners with the NWP, Terrell and her daughter willingly risked arrest and violent attacks. Terrell became a lifetime member of the NWP, persistently calling on Paul to collaborate with black suffragists to resist all violations of voting rights. In the decades after the march, Terrell continued to challenge Paul and other members of the National Woman's Party (NWP), asking them to listen and respond to African American women's perspectives and experiences.[25]

In spite of Terrell's efforts, Paul consistently refused to take African American women suffragists' concerns seriously. In March 1919, the NAACP's Walter White wrote to Terrell that she would "probably be interested in a telephone conversation which I had with your good friend, Miss Alice Paul a few days ago. She called me up and was very much surprised (or pretended to be) at anyone taking exception to the statement she made about colored women voting in South Carolina. . . . Just as you say, all of them [white suffragists] are mortally afraid of the South and if they could get the Suffrage Amendment through without enfranchising colored women, they would do it in a moment."[26] A few days later, Terrell heard from Ida Husted Harper, whom she had already confronted regarding her prejudiced comments a decade earlier. In order to pacify southern white women, Harper wanted help convincing the Northeastern Federation of Women's Clubs, an NACW affiliate, to temporarily withdraw its application to join NAWSA. Instead, Terrell warned Elizabeth Carter, who led the Northeastern Federation, of Harper's attempted maneuver.[27]

In August 1920, Tennessee voted for the Nineteenth Amendment, thereby becoming the last state needed to ratify it. The Terrell couple looked forward to seeing its impact. Berto wrote to Mollie: "It looks as if your old state has put the climax on the Woman's Suffrage movement. . . . I am glad the fight is over and the women have won. Twenty-seven million additional voters mean something to the country. No one can reckon the full import of the situation produced by the change until after the big election in November." Mollie also keenly anticipated the effect of women at the polls, especially the potential for reform represented by African American women's votes.[28]

The passage of the Nineteenth Amendment did not diminish the gulf

FIGURE 6.1. This image of Mollie and Phyllis is likely from the early 1920s, when Mollie would have been in her late fifties and Phyllis in her early twenties. Just a few years earlier, mother and daughter had displayed similar solidarity, vigor, and enthusiasm when picketing the White House with the National Woman's Party for votes for all American women. (Courtesy Langston Family)

between white and black suffragists. Paul continued to ignore black women's demands that the NWP work to secure African Americans' voting rights, particularly in the South. When Paul initiated a new campaign for women's equality in 1921, she tolerated only token participation by African American women. She rejected a proposal by Mary Ovington, the white feminist and NAACP cofounder, to invite Mary B. Talbert to speak from the podium as the official NACW representative. Ignoring the vital intersections of gender and race, Paul incorrectly claimed the NACW was not a feminist group but a "racial one" and so banned it from formal participation.[29]

In the weeks before the NWP's 1921 national convention, Terrell participated in a series of meetings between leading African American women suffragists and a white ally, NWP member Ella R. Murray, to try to bring black women's concerns to the attention of the delegates. They planned to introduce a resolution from the convention floor, "urging Congress to appoint a committee to investigate the disfranchisement of colored women." Terrell "discussed the advisability of asking Miss Paul to help colored women get the suffrage. Daisy Glenn said I had picketed, and I said my daughter had done so too." Terrell and her compatriots hoped that their having taken part in direct action would give them more influence. But Ella Murray confirmed their suspicion that, even after having achieved ratification of the Nineteenth Amendment, "Miss Paul did not want to inject the race problem into her suffrage work." In order not to be "double-crossed by Miss Paul" during the convention, the women decided to ask her in advance to endorse their resolution demanding a congressional investigation into violations of African American women's voting rights.[30]

Mollie Terrell and her friend Addie Hunton, representing the NAACP and NACW, joined other black suffragists at NWP headquarters, where Terrell read their statement to Paul. Despite the clarity of their request, Paul asked, "What do you women want me to do?" Terrell replied, "I want you to tell us whether you endorse the enforcement of the 19th Amendment for all women." But to the African American women's disgust, Paul refused to say that she did.

The impasse led to more meetings; after Murray repeatedly phoned her NWP colleagues at headquarters, Terrell was finally invited to bring her delegation to talk with two NWP leaders who "assured us of their sympathy. I told them Alice Paul had displayed the most painful lack of tact I had ever seen." Upon leaving, they regrouped at the YWCA, where Terrell was selected to represent them at the convention, if she were permitted.[31] A few African American women, including Terrell, won the concession that they could participate in the NWP convention as individuals who could speak from the floor. Terrell also "addressed the Resolutions Committee asking for a Congressional Investigation. I said colored women need the ballot to protect themselves because their men cannot protect them since the 14th and 15th Amendments are null and void. They are lynched and are victims of the Jim Crow Car Laws, the Convict Lease System, and other evils."[32]

Trying to make the interconnected issues of black women's disfranchisement and violence against them seem real to the disinterested and distant NWP members, Terrell described the terrifying gendered brutality experienced by African American women. She gave the specific example of the pregnant Mary Turner, who was lynched in Valdosta, Georgia, in 1918 for protesting the lynching of her husband: "A colored woman, two months before she was to become a mother, had her baby torn from her body." Her heart sank upon hearing white feminists' cruel and insensitive comments about the brutal murder: "'What did she do?' one asked. Another said, 'She did something, of course.'" Terrell had wrongly assumed that her white female audience would empathize and find the incident as deeply disturbing as she did. NWP members' interest in protecting women's equality and their bodily integrity did not extend to those who were black.[33]

Terrell later admitted that her feelings had been "lacerated" and her "heart so wounded" by racism. She suffered not only from racism in her daily life but also from what she encountered on the front lines of her work for equality. She had to face the cruel remarks of white women who did not value black lives. She also faced the truth that their resolution had no chance. Nonetheless, Murray presented it on the convention floor, where it was voted down by the white NWP delegates. During this difficult confrontation, Mollie and Phyllis Terrell proudly asserted their rightful place in movement history. With the white NWP picketers, mother and daughter "went to the Hotel Washington to get our Distinguished Service medals for picketing the White House. We all carried banners and marched in. The pins are in the shape of banners."[34]

At their postconvention debriefing, some disheartened black activists floated the idea of picketing the NWP, thereby using its own flamboyant strategy against it. A pragmatic Terrell advised against doing so, noting that Alice Paul's intransigent position was similar to that of Susan B. Anthony's in the late nineteenth century. Both leaders chose to focus as narrowly as possible on one issue: Anthony on gaining (white) woman's suffrage and Paul on ensuring (white) women's equality through an Equal Rights Amendment to the Constitution. Both insisted that all other issues were extraneous. Thus, when Paul rejected what Terrell described as "Crystal Eastman's splendid program including Birth Control and the most advanced reforms," Terrell understood that the African American women were outmaneuvered.[35]

However disheartening and frustrating, Terrell believed that African American women, a relatively small percentage of the U.S. population (about 10 percent), must continue their attempts at interracial dialogue with the majority group, white women, in order to achieve their goals.[36] However, black women always persisted in advocating their own goals and agendas.

"Colored Women Have Been Regarded as the Rightful Prey of Every White Man"

As she pursued voting rights, Terrell simultaneously engaged in a related effort to achieve equality by dismantling racist and sexist stereotypes about black women as sexually impure. The National Association of Colored Women had formed in 1896 in part to provide black women with a national platform from which to defend themselves against scurrilous slander by hostile whites. Such slander had become an excuse for dismissing concerns about sexual violence against black women.[37]

Determined to protect her own and all African American daughters from these racially prejudiced and gendered stereotypes as they grew into young womanhood, Terrell wrote and spoke explicitly about sexual purity. Her public speeches offered cogent critiques of racist caricatures that demonized black girls and women as impure, a stereotype that put them at increased risk of harm. White and black audiences and the newspapers reacted strongly to Terrell's piercing analyses of how sexism and racism affected the lives of all African American girls and women who had to live and survive in a culture that assumed their racial and sexual impurity.[38]

When the white National Purity Association first invited Terrell to give a talk on "Purity and the Negro" in 1905, she noted in her diary that it "is not a subject one can treat easily, altho' there is a great deal to be said."[39] Her first purity talk comprehensively laid out her fundamental black feminist ideas about the intersections of gender, race, and purity—ideas that shaped and were shaped by her experience of raising two African American daughters in a hostile, racist society. Terrell used her time at the lectern to dispute whites' assumption that African Americans were innately more immoral and impure.[40] Completely rejecting that premise, she began by criticizing whites for their racial bias: "Those who insist that colored people are brutes with respect to their sexual natures, as is often asserted by the enemies and traducers of the race, either ignore or maliciously misrepresent the facts." Adroitly shifting the blame to white men, Terrell defended the honor of black women, reminding her audience that "during slavery it was impossible for bond-women to protect themselves from the lust of their masters, the sons of their masters or their masters' friends."[41] Highlighting the vulnerability of black women to rape by white men, she charged that even in the twentieth century, "colored women have been regarded as the rightful prey of every white man . . . and they have been protected from the wiles and lechery of their destroyers neither by public sentiment nor by law."[42]

Crimes against African American women must be taken as seriously as those against white women, Terrell insisted. She reiterated that white male violence undermined the sanctified categories of home and womanhood: "In the South, the negro's home is not considered sacred by the superior race. White men are neither punished for invading it, nor lynched for violating colored women and girls." Condemning a double standard of sexual purity, she contended that until the day when rape was a crime no matter the race of the victim, black women would not be recognized as legitimate victims or full human beings. White men would continue to claim superiority while acting with impunity, whereas black men would be unfairly accused and even murdered for rapes they did not commit.[43]

Daring to shift the terms of the debate, Terrell moved from accusing white men to publicly charging white women with responsibility for perpetuating the problem of assaults against black girls and women. White women must openly protest the rape of black women by white men, she said, for only their voices could "arouse the conscience of the public toward the open and shameless debauchery of colored women by [white women's] husbands, fathers and sons." Instead of forming a sisterhood based on women's collective resistance to sexual violence, Terrell pointed out that "the white women of the South who discuss the subject in the public print . . . seem to delight in exposing the weakness of colored women. . . . In several articles . . . in one of the best magazines . . . southern white women have declared . . . that there is no such thing as a virtuous colored woman in the United States." White female authors used their access to national media to denigrate and further endanger black women by increasing race hatred, whereas most black writers did not have access to mainstream media.[44]

It was white women who had inherited immorality, Terrell countered, because of their callous indifference toward the rape of African American women: "Descended from generations of [white] mothers who were accustomed to look upon the wholesale debauchery of colored women without a protest and without the shock to their moral natures which they would be expected to receive, their daughters have inherited this indifference to the degradation of colored women by the men of the present day." She bluntly told her white audience, "Morally speaking, slavery was a weapon which shot both ways, wounding those who fired as well as those who were hit. . . . Surely [white women] must know that so long as men may despoil the women of any race with impunity, this prevailing standard of morality must necessarily be very low."[45]

Turning to the supposed impurity of African American women, Terrell challenged statistics that seemed to show their proportionately higher number of out-of-wedlock births. She pointed out that private hospitals and special homes for pregnant white women deliberately concealed such cases, whereas black women gave birth in government-funded hospitals that kept careful and public records. Statistics were inaccurately skewed by race and class.[46]

A comprehensive and powerful defense of African American womanhood was at the core of all of Terrell's speeches at white purity conventions. Every time she spoke honestly to white audiences, she took a significant risk. Although her 1905 talk was well received, just a few years later, in 1907, Terrell met resistance. A negative article in the *Cleveland Plain Dealer*, "Colored Woman Raps the South," was picked up by other papers. When she spoke a week later "On the Condition of the Colored Woman" at the National Purity Conference in Battle Creek, Michigan, the press was ready to pounce. The *Battle Creek Enquirer* reported, "Negro Speaker Assails White Women of South." The Associated Press, in a widely reprinted story, denounced Terrell's "furious invective" and charged her with claiming that no black woman was safe working as a servant in a white household. This particularly alarmed the white press and its readers, who feared losing their cheap labor supply if African American women declined to do this work. Although Terrell's speech contained virtually the same message as her earlier talk, this time it hit a nerve. The backlash was so severe that she tried to take some heat off herself by issuing a letter strategically stating that the press had exaggerated her concerns about contemporary black domestic servants' safety.[47]

Invited to speak at the 1911 World's Purity Congress, in Columbus, Ohio, Terrell had not forgotten the backlash but decided to take the same hard-hitting approach. Afterward, she reported to Berto: "My darling Husband: . . . You should have heard that vociferous prolonged applause when I finished my address! . . . I tell you white people like to hear the disagreeable truth, if one has tact and good taste enough to present it forcibly but politely. I am amazed myself at the quantity of hard pummeling they are willing to stand from me." She had again "poured it on to white women good and hard and strong."[48]

Continuing her 1911 lecture tour, Terrell inspired African American audiences, too, with her blunt message about how racism had created distorted notions of purity. Her refusal to accept the fiction of black women's innate impurity resonated with African Americans, who donated money for "Rescue Homes for Colored Girls" within their communities. In Cincinnati, she proudly reported to Berto: "The meeting was so enthusiastic that the Colored folks pledged $150 for the Home for Colored Girls and ninety dollars in cold hard cash was collected." Terrell raised money in each locale as she spoke out for unwed black mothers, asking that they be allowed "morally to face the world again and begin a new life," just as white unwed mothers could.[49]

Terrell also supported other young African American women caught up in the racist criminal justice system. When she arrived at the NACW's 1912 convention in Hampton, Virginia, for example, she helped to draw up a petition asking for clemency for sixteen-year-old Virginia Christian, who was awaiting execution for murdering her abusive white employer, Ida Belote. According to Christian's account as reported in the press, she washed clothes for Belote, a wealthy widowed mother of eight, who falsely accused her of stealing a piece of jewelry and threatened, "I'm going to put you in jail." They argued until Belote threw a spittoon that hit Christian, and the two began to fight physically. Christian told a reporter, "I never meant to kill her. When I lef' she was groanin'." Some middle-class African Americans in Hampton distanced themselves from the poor and poorly educated black girl, but Terrell and the NACW came to her defense and rejected the use of the death penalty for the teenager. Terrell was chosen to chair a small contingent bringing a petition signed by three hundred NACW delegates to Virginia governor William Hodges Mann. The petition asked the governor to commute Christian's sentence to life in prison, given the "extreme youth of this girl, the lack of training during her childhood, and the neglect for which she was not responsible [her mother was paralyzed and could not work to take care of her] are extenuating circumstances to show a merciful clemency to the unfortunate girl." The governor listened to Terrell and granted the women a visit with Christian. He also granted the teen a ten-day stay of execution so that civil rights activists could find more exculpatory evidence but indicated that he had no intention of commuting her sentence. Upon returning to the convention, Terrell's committee issued a pessimistic report. In a show of appreciation for their efforts, NACW member and businesswoman Madam C. J. Walker paid for their travel expenses. The NAACP hired investigators to help, and five hundred northern blacks and whites who opposed capital punishment wrote letters to the governor, but the death of a white woman could not go unpunished. Virginia Christian was electrocuted on August 16, 1912, the first African American teenage girl to be killed by the electric chair.[50]

"The Black Mammy Was the Victim of the Passion and Power of Her Master"

Just two years after her disheartening debate with Alice Paul over whether the National Woman's Party would endorse laws to enforce African Americans' voting rights, Mollie Terrell jumped at the opportunity to expose whites' racism in a different context. This time, it was through a searing critique of the black mammy myth. Just as she continuously challenged the stereotype impugning African American women's sexual purity, so Terrell contested the different but equally damaging stereotype of black women as asexual caretakers of white women's children. Whites' sentimental affection for their black mammies repackaged slavery as a benign institution. It was an erasure of the violence and pain experienced by enslaved women and their families, Terrell charged, and was part of an effort to perpetuate African American women's subordination.

The impetus for her critique was the 1923 passage in the Senate of a bill authorizing the building of a "Monument to the Faithful Colored Mammies of the South" in Washington. Whereas white women had sought to keep black women out of D.C.'s national suffrage parade in 1913, a decade later they tried to fix them permanently in a subordinate, though celebrated, position on a statue in the nation's capital.

The national black mammy monument was the brainchild of southern white women in the United Daughters of the Confederacy (UDC). Founded in 1894, the UDC raised funds and built Confederate memorials and, not coincidentally, often placed "loyal slave" plaques nearby. The UDC's most successful memorialization of slavery at the national level coincided with the presidency of segregationist Woodrow Wilson, when, in 1914, it erected the Confederate Monument at Arlington National Cemetery. Panels on the monument depicted "loyal" slaves, including a mammy figure embracing a white child. Reconfiguring forced labor as a form of maternal love while commemorating slaves' fidelity allowed the UDC to affirm Jim Crow and deny racial equality. During Wilson's administration, prosegregationists mobilized the nostalgic black mammy myth to confound critics of their racist policies.[51]

By the early 1920s, segregation had hardened and spread across the nation. Rising nativism against immigrants, non-Protestants, and people of color resulted in the rebirth of the Ku Klux Klan, which enjoyed a huge surge in its popularity and membership. White revisionist stories about slavery—as well as depictions of Reconstruction as a disastrous failure—had become the dominant national narrative.[52]

Mollie Terrell recognized these myths as attempts to justify slavery and further institutionalize white supremacy. She also had personal reasons to oppose the black mammy monument and whites' nostalgia for slavery. Those reasons are rooted in her and her husband's family histories, as well as in their interactions with the white families that had owned them and/or their ancestors. Mollie and Berto were both intimately aware that southern whites had been cultivating nostalgic stereotypes about loving mammies on plantations with happy extended families, made up of enslaved black people and their white masters.

In 1922, the Terrells were directly confronted by white southerners' idealized views of their enslaved mammies. Berto received a letter from Mrs. J. Douglas Chaney, née Terrell, of Virginia after the death of her ninety-two-year-old father Oliver H. P. Terrell, Berto's former slave owner. Like other whites, Chaney thought nothing of waxing nostalgic to her "dear Old Mammy's" biological son about how much his mother loved her white charges. She believed her mammy to have been the best, least threatening, black person. Chaney referred to Berto's mother, Louisa Ann Coleman Terrell, as "Aunt 'Luisann'" and "my dear Old Mammy, whom I loved as well as I did my dear Mamma. . . . She was a dear old soul, and she did love us children so dearly."[53]

The popular myth of the contented plantation slave was supported by whites' conviction that enslaved people had no aspirations for their own children. If they did, they were not taken seriously. Thus, Chaney mocked Louisa Ann's pride in her son, telling him: "Mammy was always so proud of 'Robert.' She would put on extra airs with her mouth when she would talk about you." Chaney thought it amusing that Louisa Ann called her son by his full name rather than a diminutive. African Americans could be the objects of affection of white slave-owning families and their descendants only if they remained subordinate. Missing from Chaney's caricature is the fact that Louisa Ann Coleman Terrell was a woman of aspirations who knew who her heroes were and what ideals she held dear.

Berto's younger sister, Laura Terrell Jones, told a story about their mother that conveyed her full humanity. Inspired by reading her sister-in-law Mollie's article, "I Remember Frederick Douglass," Laura recalled: "Mamma and I were coming along . . . and she saw the Honorable Frederick Douglass and stopped him, told him of her admiration for him and that she had named a son for him (Fred D. Henry) and that she wanted me to be able to say that I had shaken hands with him. He raised his silk hat as she spoke to him and he shook hands with me with a courteousness that I have never forgotten." Berto's mother valued education for her children but had been forbidden to read or write as a slave. After Emancipation, she never learned to write and may not have been able to read. Laura recalled "the dictation I used to take down from Ma's lips when writing for her." Berto certainly lived up to his mother's hopes, for he learned Latin and Greek and gained a higher education, just like the Terrell men who had owned him. His mother had asserted her autonomy, race pride, and clear expectation that her children, less than a generation removed from slavery, could achieve great things and contribute to advancing the status of African Americans.[54]

Mollie, too, had had contact with those who owned her mother and grandmother. She had been glad to hear the memories of the white Ayres family about her deceased maternal grandmother.[55] But her grandmother's stories about the horrors of slavery ensured that Mollie would never romanticize it. She was haunted, too, by the experiences of her enslaved relatives on her father's side: "Many a time I have lived over that parting scene when Emmeline, my grandmother, who was then only a small child, was sold from her mother never to see her again. Often have I suffered the anguish which I know that poor slave mother felt, when her little girl was torn from her arms forever." Pivoting from this memory of her own family's history to white Americans' nostalgia for slavery in the early twentieth century, she continued, "When slavery is discussed and somebody rhapsodizes upon the goodness and kindness of masters and mistresses toward their slaves in extenuation of the cruel system, it is hard for me to conceal my disgust. There is no doubt that some slaveholders were kind to their slaves. Captain Church was one of them, and this daughter of a slave father is glad thus publicly to express her gratitude to him. But the anguish of one slave mother from whom her baby was snatched away outweighs all the kindness and goodness which were occasionally shown a fortunate, favored slave." Highlighting the hypocrisy of whites who professed to love their mammies, Terrell recounted a piece of her family history to white audiences: "Both my grandfathers were white. Charlie McCormick, grandson of my grandmother's master rushed to see and kiss my grandmother before he went and when he returned from school. . . . He hugged and kissed her saying 'Oh Mammy, Mammy, I'm so glad to see you.'" In spite of their great shows of affection, Terrell observed, neither of her white grandfathers nor their families ever made any move to liberate their slaves: "I would be a slave if emancipation had been delayed till the South voluntarily freed the slaves."[56]

———

Mollie Church Terrell's scathing critique of the planned monument to the myth of the loyal black mammy received widespread attention. Her 1923 letter to the editor, entitled "The Black Mammy Monument," was published in the mainstream white newspaper, the *Washington Evening Star*. Terrell was horrified that the "Monument to the Faithful Colored Mammies of the South" bill passed just weeks after another devastating defeat of the Dyer Anti-Lynching Bill and a year after the Lincoln Memorial was dedicated in front of a segregated audience.[57]

Her defiant 1923 editorial condemned the *Evening Star*'s recent endorsement of the proposed monument. Terrell deeply resented the cruel ironies of white revisionist histories of slavery and Reconstruction and fought back against southern whites who redefined and reappropriated the mothers of black children into their own devoted mammies. She struck a nerve; her editorial was widely reprinted in black and white newspapers, with its largest circulation via the *Literary Digest*, which had almost one million readers (although it reprinted her words without attributing authorship). Terrell was not alone; other leading African American clubwomen, including the president of the National Association of Colored Women, Hallie Quinn Brown, also wrote outraged editorials.[58]

In stark contrast, the African American male leaders of the NAACP's District of Columbia branch declined to fight against the erection of the monument. When contacted by national NAACP leadership from New York to see how they wanted to fight the monument, these out-of-touch men replied that they did not want to alienate poor southern black migrants in the District by, as they put it, seeming to "mock" the statue in an overly "high browed" way. Fundamentally misjudging the situation, local elite black men in the NAACP feared that formerly enslaved women who had served as caretakers for white children might be upset if the civil rights group objected to this tribute.

African American women of all classes had no similar doubts. Many of their own enslaved grandmothers and mothers had been forced to work as caretakers for other women's children. Terrell's editorial cut right to the heart of the myth of the unproblematic love whites imagined they had given and received from enslaved women: "Colored women all over the United States stand aghast at the idea of erecting a Black Mammy Monument in the Capital of the United States. The condition of the slave woman was so pitiably, hopelessly helpless that it is difficult to see how any woman, whether white or black, could take any pleasure in a marble statue to perpetuate her memory." Being forced to care for white children came at a price: "The Black Mammy was often faithful in the service of her mistress's children while her heart bled over her own little babies who were deprived of their mother's ministrations and tender care which the white children received." Although she conceded they did their jobs as caretakers well, Terrell insisted that her readers see enslaved black women as three-dimensional human beings who were psychologically tormented by their enslavement: "The anguish suffered by one Black Mammy whose children were snatched from her embrace and sold away from her forever outweighed in the balance all the kindness bestowed upon all the slave women fortunate enough to receive it." She refused to romanticize, normalize, or excuse a cruel imbalance of power. Knowing that white southerners were actively rewriting the history of enslavement, Terrell observed: "Surely in their zeal to pay tribute to the faithful services rendered by the Black Mammy, the descendants of slaveholding ancestors have forgotten the atrocities and cruelties incident to the institution of slavery itself."[59]

Calling attention to other sins of white slaveholders, Terrell noted that the

light skin color of many African Americans was not happenstance. Throughout her life, she insisted on using *colored* rather than *black* or *Negro* to describe
African Americans. Terrell believed that it highlighted how and why so many
African Americans were light skinned.[60] It was, for her, a political term. African Americans' varied complexions had a history: "The black mammy had
no home life. . . . Legal marriage was impossible for her. If she went through a
farce ceremony with a slave man, he could be sold away from her at any time, or
she might be sold from him and be taken as a concubine by her master, his son,
the overseer or any other white man on the place who might desire her." After
her grandmother was torn from her mother, Emmeline's new master allowed
another white man, Charles Church, to act on his desire for her. In addition,
her father's first slave marriage to Margaret Pico had no legal validity. Thinking of her own white grandfathers, Terrell noted, "It frequently happened that
on the same plantation with the children of his white wife little bronze images
of the master might be seen who sometimes resembled their white father more
than his legitimate offspring did."[61]

White men were not solely responsible for the sexual abuse of African
American women; Terrell again indicted southern white women for their
complicity in the crimes committed by their husbands and sons. Hoping to
shame white women into abandoning their support for the Black Mammy
Monument, she took the same approach as she had done in her speeches at
social purity conferences: "When one considers the extent to which the Black
Mammy was the victim of the passion and power of her master or any other
white man who might look with lustful eyes upon her it is hard to understand
how . . . the wives, mothers and sisters of slave owners could have submitted
without frequent and vigorous protests to such degradation of the womanhood of any race. And it is harder to understand why their descendants should
want to behold a perpetual reminder of the heart-rending conditions under
which Black Mammies were obliged to live."[62]

Asserting the authority of the African American community to define and
value itself, Terrell turned acerbic: "If the Black Mammy statue is ever erected,
which the dear Lord forbid, there are thousands of colored men and women
who will fervently pray that on some stormy night the lightning will strike it
and the heavenly elements will send it crashing to the ground so that the descendants of Black Mammies will not be forever reminded of the anguish of
heart and the physical suffering which their mothers and grandmothers of the
race endured." Terrell's condemnation of the myth of the black mammy enabled African American women to be proud of their past and their present.[63]

In response to her editorial, Terrell received grateful letters from people
around the country. William L. Reed of Boston wrote, "Please permit me to
express my appreciation for your splendid letter . . . which appeared in the

Boston Herald of today. It is calm, dignified and convincing, and a stinging in-dictment of the hypocritical element representing the movement. One might well be pardoned for rejoicing over the occasion which inspired such a classic from a woman of the Race." NACW and NAACP leader Mary B. Talbert, of Buffalo, New York, who graduated from Oberlin just two years after Mollie, asked for typed copies of several of Terrell's articles, including "the one about the black mammy monument. A friend showed me this last denouncement of yours and I laughed until I held my sides when I read that last statement of yours where you said that you hoped lightening would strike it, if it were erected. I said O, Lord, if the white people ever read this article they will be afraid to erect that monument in Washington. I want to reproduce each of these articles in *Woman's Voice.*" White people did take notice. The Senate's passage of the bill led to so many protests that it never got out of committee in the House.[64]

Denying an easy or universal sisterhood based on gender throughout her ac-tivist career, Terrell insisted that white and black women's experiences could not be conflated. Describing white American racism as a form of "assault and battery committed on a human being's soul," she called attention to the dif-ference race made in black women's lives. Terrell bluntly told white women reformers: "I assure you that nowhere in the United States have my feelings been so lacerated, my spirit so crushed, my heart so wounded, nowhere have I been so humiliated and handicapped on account of my sex as I have been on account of my race."[65]

Rather than letting humiliation stop her, Mollie Church Terrell created a distinctive black feminist voice that centered the protection of African Amer-ican women, offered them hope, and even used humor as a way to achieve equality. She imagined more for her race and her gender and articulated that vision as she battled the forces of intolerance. Similarly, in the political arena, Terrell championed democracy and condemned white supremacy at home and abroad. She supported the rights of the "darker races" of the world and insisted on a place for black women like herself in reaping the rewards of the partisan system of political patronage.

Civil Rights and Partisan Politics,
1890–1932

The Republican Party's legacy as the party of Abraham Lincoln and its leadership in securing the Thirteenth, Fourteenth, and Fifteenth Amendments that secured citizenship rights to African Americans and voting rights to all black men guaranteed that Mollie Church Terrell would be a member of the GOP throughout her life. This progressive legacy outweighed the party's failure to enforce the amendments, a responsibility their wording gave to Congress, as well as its unwillingness to pass federal antilynching legislation. Despite Republicans' increasing apathy and inaction on issues of race, Terrell could not forgive the Democratic Party's role as the party of secession or its continued embrace of segregation and white supremacy.[1]

Robert Church had played a key role in shaping his daughter as a lifelong Republican. He had facilitated her first meeting with Frederick Douglass when Mollie, then in her first year at Oberlin College, attended Republican James Garfield's 1880 presidential inauguration at the invitation of Church family friends, the black Mississippi senator Blanch K. Bruce and his wife Josephine W. Bruce. In the early 1890s, once she moved to D.C., Mollie often collaborated with Douglass. Her work with Douglass, a leading Republican, had included organizing Ida B. Wells's antilynching speeches in the nation's capital. They also visited the White House together to ask President Benjamin Harrison to take a strong public stand against lynching.[2]

Terrell saw herself as Douglass's protégé and intellectual compatriot, someone who could carry his legacy into the next generation. Long before Carter G. Woodson's 1926 promotion of Negro History Week, Terrell used her position on D.C.'s board of education to persuade its members to institute in 1897 a "Frederick Douglass Day" in the district's African American schools. To promote an appreciation of African American history and women's voting rights, teachers taught students about Douglass as an abolitionist and a supporter of woman suffrage at the 1848 Seneca Falls woman's rights convention.[3]

At the turn of the twentieth century, Terrell pushed back against the rise of a national white reconciliation that blurred the difference between the two main political parties. She repeatedly insisted that civil rights must remain an important aspect of the GOP's identity. Speaking at the Republican Club of New York City, for instance, Terrell implored white Republicans to end "the persecution and the constant degradation" of African Americans. Conceding that white voters could disagree about economic policy, she insisted that they could not do so when it came to civil rights: "Let me also remind our friends in the North that they may be . . . neutral or differ widely in their opinions on the tariff, on the statehood bills or even concerning the way we should dig the Panama Canal, but I insist that neutrality on the wholesale disfranchisement of Colored men is nothing less than treason."[4]

Trying to keep the party true to its roots, Mollie Terrell argued that the GOP's international and domestic policy agendas must prioritize racial equality. Doing so would help distinguish the Republicans from the Democrats in the eyes of African American voters. On the foreign policy front, she favored self-determination of nations and became an anticolonialist, criticizing Woodrow Wilson's insincere espousal of these ideas. Focusing on the status of what she termed the "darker races of the world," Terrell approached race and equality from a transnational perspective.[5]

The Republican Party meant two important but different things to her— first, it was more likely to pursue advances in civil rights, and second, she and Berto relied on it for patronage appointments. Mollie believed African Americans must be full citizens, able to participate in all aspects of civic life, including partisan politics. Partisanship also provided benefits for its most loyal supporters, including jobs for her husband, whose judicial position had first come from Theodore Roosevelt. Once women won the right to vote with the ratification of the Nineteenth Amendment in 1920, Mollie's involvement in GOP campaigns intensified as she secured paid campaign work in presidential elections and in at least two Illinois senate races.

"I Could Never Respect and Admire Him as I Did Before"

In 1901, President Theodore Roosevelt earned Mollie and Berto Terrell's respect and gratitude with two bold public acts that riled segregationists. He invited Booker T. Washington to dine with his family at the White House and appointed Berto as a D.C. justice of the peace.[6] Yet for the Terrells, the president's apparent fair-mindedness was upended by his punishment of black soldiers at Fort Brown, near Brownsville, Texas. The crisis began in August 1906, when a white man was killed and a white police officer wounded in a shooting. The African American soldiers blamed for the crime denied knowledge of the shootings. Refusing to consider the possibility of their innocence, Roosevelt charged that they were all engaging in a "conspiracy of silence."[7]

Summoning Booker T. Washington to the White House, Roosevelt informed him that he was going to order all 167 black soldiers in three companies of the Twenty-Fifth U.S. Infantry be dishonorably discharged. He ignored Washington's pleas to refrain. He did cynically wait to announce his decision, however, until the day after the November elections to keep African American voters in the Republican fold.[8]

Fearful of losing his personal influence with Roosevelt, Washington chose not to fight this racial injustice publicly. His silence came just weeks after the brutal Atlanta Riot of September 1906 had generated criticism of his accommodationist stance. Instead, militant activists, including Mollie Terrell, became the public voice of moral outrage, condemning the president's decision as racist and arguing that he would have treated white soldiers differently.[9]

As a founding member of the Constitution League, Mollie was ready to intervene. President Roosevelt was out of the country, so John Milholland requested that she, as the only Constitution League founder living in D.C., go meet with Secretary of War William Howard Taft. She recorded in her November 1906 diary: "The first time my phone rings after it has been installed, Mr. Milholland from NY asks me to see Secretary of War for colored soldiers who have been dismissed." Terrell went to Taft's office immediately and waited all day to speak with him. Though she had no appointment, her persistence paid off, enabling her to request that he put the president's order on hold until Roosevelt returned, so that the president might reconsider the evidence. She told Taft: "As colored people we take great pride in our soldiers. They have always had an unblemished record and they have fought bravely in every war this country has waged. It seems more than we can bear to have three companies of our soldiers summarily dismissed without honor, at least until a thorough investigation has been made." Listening thoughtfully, Taft agreed to Terrell's request, sending a telegram informing President Roosevelt that he had temporarily suspended his order.[10]

Terrell then traveled to New York City to meet the directors of the Constitution League, who had sent the lawyer Gilchrist Stewart to Fort Brown to interview the soldiers before they were disbanded. Terrell and Stewart then met with President Roosevelt, hoping to persuade him to review the soldiers' testimony and restore their good honor. He firmly declined, telling Secretary Taft, "'I care nothing whatever for the yelling of either the politicians or the sentimentalists.'" For years, Terrell and others demanded the reversal of the dishonorable discharges. She repeatedly returned to the Capitol, supporting efforts to expose and remedy the injustice done to the men.[11] (In 1972, the conclusions of a formal investigation led President Richard Nixon to posthumously pardon and restore the good military records of all the discharged soldiers.)[12]

Secretary Taft's willingness to treat her request seriously meant so much to Terrell that she exempted him from her overall condemnation of the administration's treatment of the Brownsville soldiers. Yet he cared less than she surmised. In January 1908, she recorded, "Went to see Secy. Taft today and waited for nearly two hours. Had a few words with him. He complained because Colored people charge him with being unfair to them and unfriendly. . . . I told him we were very grateful to him for what he had done but I was sorry the soldiers had been dismissed without honor. 'They surely have had a hearing now,' he said." Rather than seeing himself as responsible, as secretary of war, for securing fair treatment for the dishonored soldiers, Taft felt aggrieved that his initial gesture had not absolved him of further responsibility.[13]

When Taft ran for president in 1908, Terrell believed that black voters could trust him and campaigned on his behalf. She hoped she might have continued access to him if he became president. Republican National Committee official Judith Ellen Foster recommended Terrell as a GOP speaker as a way to build support for Taft among black voters. Mollie was eager to take the work on.[14]

Most other black militants had been angered by Secretary Taft's quick capitulation to President Roosevelt, especially the War Department's 1907 report formally accepting the president's assessment that the black soldiers were to blame. During the 1908 presidential election, the Afro-American Council publicly challenged him. Once Taft won the presidency, the AAC continued to confront him on his inaction on civil rights, his failure as president to push through an antilynching bill, and his appointment of far fewer African Americans to office than Roosevelt had. Worse still, he often replaced African Americans in government with hostile southern whites.[15]

During the campaign, Terrell disagreed with the Afro-American Council, of which she was a member, as well as with any criticism by African Americans of the new president. She viewed them as being opposed to her personally, not just to her support of Taft. Feeling alienated and frustrated, she continued to pursue her civil rights goals as she saw fit. Mollie wrote heatedly to her husband that she would not allow Taft's critics to "deter me from doing something to help remove the awful conditions which injure you and me and all the rest of us. . . . They shall not stand between me and the principles in which I believe with all my heart and for which I am willing to suffer, if need be, and work."[16]

Ignoring Taft's flaws, Terrell instead relished her personal connection to a president of the United States. At the District's high school graduation ceremony in June 1909, she and Taft sat together, and he told the audience that "he had come to the Commencement at the invitation of Mrs. Terrell 'who had great influence at the White House.'" She celebrated the occasion as "one of the red letter days of my life." Terrell considered Taft's public acknowledgment of her a moment of triumph—a recognition of her as a political powerbroker like her male peers W. E. B. Du Bois and Booker T. Washington.[17]

When Teddy Roosevelt decided to challenge Taft for the presidency with his new Progressive Party in 1912, Terrell was unwilling to abandon Taft or the GOP, explaining, "Theodore Roosevelt had been one of my idols.... He seemed really to love his fellow man, whether he was white or black, high or low, rich or poor. I was personally acquainted with him and he knew my brother [Thomas Church] in New York City well.... But after he had meted out such terrible punishment upon many innocent men over whom he had the power of life and death ... I could never respect and admire him as I did before."[18]

The Progressive Party's program at the 1912 convention in Chicago ensured that Terrell could not support it. Roosevelt chose to make his party national in scope by courting southern whites and agreeing to a "lily white" southern policy, allowing states to pick their own delegations. Delegates voted down such platform planks as legislative solutions to disfranchisement and lynching. Roosevelt also summarily excluded all black southern delegates on the dubious grounds that seating them would amount to catering to corrupt interest-group politics.[19] Black delegations from southern states appeared at the Chicago convention and asked to be seated, only to be publicly turned away. Liberal whites in the new party, including Jane Addams and the NAACP's Joel Spingarn, objected, Spingarn offering a resolution in favor of making the Progressive Party "a big humanitarian movement for the rights of all, irrespective of race, color, or creed." Their protests were ignored, and the resolution was tabled. Under pressure, Roosevelt agreed to seat only some northern black delegates.[20]

Terrell's 1912 article "The Progressive Party and the Negro" condemned Roosevelt's catering to white southern racism and praised African Americans who remained loyal Republicans: "The Negro voters of the North ... have declared that there is no need for another National Jim-Crow party, the Democratic Party having exercised that function for nearly fifty years." Terrell insisted: "A party that attempts to be Progressive in the North [but] reactionary in the South on the Negro question ... shall not receive the support of the Negro voters."[21]

Disillusioned by Taft's apathy and Roosevelt's antipathy, some African

Americans decided to risk endorsing a Democratic candidate for the first time. Terrell questioned the wisdom of diluting the power of African American votes, yet a few key leaders, including bishop Alexander Walters, W. E. B. Du Bois, and Monroe Trotter took the chance. Disregarding Wilson's southern heritage, they placed their hopes on his seemingly sincere but vague promise to act with "justice" toward all. With the majority of the nation's votes split between the Republican and Progressive Parties, the Democrats won the election. Wilson quickly betrayed his black supporters by instituting segregation throughout the federal government. Several of his African American backers soon let it be known that they regretted their choice of candidate. Terrell berated those who had broken ranks to support the predictably prosegregationist Democrats.[22]

"The White Man's Treatment of the Darker Races Is Devilish"

The U.S. entry into World War I created a moral dilemma for Mollie, who was a member of the Woman's Peace Party. She did not abandon pacifism, believing that all countries should avoid the horrors of war. But she did take heart in Wilson's expansive rhetoric, including his promise to "fight . . . for the cause of human liberty." Her hopes were raised, she explained, because "we as a nation were going to help in the great world struggle for liberty." Hence, she made a pragmatic appeal to African Americans to support the war effort. She and other black activists, including Du Bois and Alice Dunbar-Nelson, gambled that African Americans could leverage Wilson's rhetoric to gain liberty at home as well as for people of color around the globe. Patriotic support of the war could lead to better wage-earning work and full political citizenship for African Americans. Initially, the activists' strategic calculus seemed to pay off when industry opened to black workers, whereas "a few months before nobody would have dreamed they would ever secure" such good jobs. At the end of the war, however, African Americans were the first to lose these better-paying, higher-status jobs, and black soldiers returned home to segregation and lynchings.[23]

Nor did the Wilson administration improve its domestic policies or attitudes toward African Americans. Pointing to the widespread and terrifying white-on-black 1919 riots and the failure of the federal government to act in the face of lynchings that had targeted returning African American veterans and their families, Terrell lamented that hundreds of thousands of black veterans had been forced to ask: "'Was it for this treatment our race is receiving . . . that we fought these battles in France? Was it for this cruel denial of our rights . . . this deliberate attempt to destroy the manhood and the womanhood of the race that many of us . . . have returned home crippled and maimed and some have sacrificed their lives?'" The Wilson administration's dismal record confirmed Terrell's conviction that the Democratic party must be removed from power.[24]

In May 1919, Terrell, along with prominent white activists like Jane Addams and Jeannette Rankin, traveled to Zurich, Switzerland, as a member of the American delegation of the International Committee of Women for Permanent Peace. There, she joined the newly formed Women's International League for Peace and Freedom (WILPF). Yet when she arrived at the conference of the International Congress of Women, Terrell found that she "was the only woman taking part . . . who had a drop of African blood in her veins." She was the sole representative of "the women of all the non-white countries of the world." Painfully aware that her solitary status derived from the exclusion of all others deemed nonwhite, Terrell wrote a resolution against racial discrimination: "We believe no human being should be deprived of an education, prevented from earning a living, debarred from any legitimate pursuit in which he wishes to engage or be subjected to humiliations of various kinds on account of race, color, or creed." It was a bold move. The other Americans agreed to support the resolution, and then the entire conference agreed. Terrell achieved her goal of ensuring the promotion of racial justice, equality, and full citizenship as an explicit part of the worldwide peace movement.[25]

Terrell differed with other African American leaders about the League of Nations. Some, although sorely disappointed with Wilson on the domestic front, believed that the Paris Peace Conference and the League of Nations might guarantee the self-determination of African nations. They also anticipated using the league to promote equality and human rights in the United States and around the globe. Yet Terrell opposed it because the idea had come from Wilson, who led a segregationist party. Viewing foreign affairs through the lens of racial inequality at home, she could not imagine it as a viable organization for the extension of human rights to people of color. She saw the Democratic Party's support of the league as a ruse to capture black votes on false pretenses: "We are told also there is nothing so small, or so unimportant that the members of the negro race cannot bring to the council of the [League of] Nations." But, "How can we believe that we would be able to induce Democrats who might represent this country on the council to consider anything" of importance to African Americans. "Can we plead with them to respect the Constitution of the United States? . . . What . . . could be more vital to human beings than the right to protect themselves by ballot at the polls?"[26]

Terrell was disturbed, too, when Wilson blocked Japan's determined attempts to include a resolution asserting the universal principle of racial equality. As chair of the League of Nations Commission, he bluntly refused to honor the majority vote of nations to approve it. Terrell accurately anticipated that the league would not significantly affect international colonialism or domestic racism. Republican Warren G. Harding's opposition to joining the league confirmed her support for him in the 1920 presidential election.[27]

"Suffrage Is Going to Help Us Mightily"

The ratification of the Nineteenth Amendment in 1920 raised the stakes for African American Republican women, who hoped that having the right to vote would advance their civil rights goals, especially the passage of an anti-lynching bill. They expected that white politicians would have to pay attention to black women as voters and be compelled to create better policies and offer more political patronage.

Terrell and some of her Washington allies formed the Woman's Republican League and set about creating a black women's national organization that could be officially sanctioned and, they hoped, financed by the RNC. Terrell's group ran into a problem in the fall of 1920, when it appeared that African American women were as divided as was the Republican Party. Another group of African American women, led by Monen L. Gray, was also trying to form a national organization. More troubling, Terrell's group was formally affiliated with the local white Harding and Coolidge Club, but she had also accepted the invitation of the Harding and Coolidge Republican League, No. 1, to join its executive committee and, having been assured it "would be splendidly financed," to become the chair of its women's auxiliary. She was surprised to receive a rebuke from a white Republican, Virginia White Speel, of the Harding and Coolidge Club, demanding that she resign immediately from the club run by "members of the opposition." Terrell apologized to Speel but noted, "It does look queer to have Republicans referred to as the 'opposition.'" She understood her reproof to be evidence of a lack of trust and poor communication across the racial divide (as well as among whites): "White people do not confide in colored people, so that it frequently happens we do not know how bitter one faction is to another."[28]

In addition to doing volunteer campaign work, Terrell lobbied for a paid position. The RNC recognized the significance of American women's first national election and made a concerted effort to mobilize the newly enfranchised women of both races for the upcoming presidential election. The African American RNC leader Henry Lincoln Johnson promised her an appointment, but no official notification arrived. Terrell decided to send her half brother Robert Church Jr., also a prominent RNC leader, two telegrams in one day asking for his help. One read: "I hope you will secure the appointment. You told me everything would be all right when I talked with you in New York so

I put myself wholly in your hands and asked nobody else to help me. You have the power so I know I will be appointed." She had, in fact, asked others for assistance but wished to make her point clear.[29]

Having secured the backing of Henry Lincoln Johnson, Robert Church, and Charles W. Cottrill, the three most powerful black Republican men, Terrell was appointed director of Work among Colored Women of the East. She arrived in New York City to begin her work and sent her husband a delighted description of her new office at RNC headquarters. Berto replied, "I was mighty glad to get your special this morning and to learn that you had gotten down to work with your Secretary." His sense of celebratory triumph was not just for his wife alone. Berto predicted, "Woman Suffrage is going to help us mightily.... Our women are well-educated and they are inclined to go forward in movements."[30]

Mollie worried that the leading black male GOP operative, Henry Lincoln Johnson, did not believe that he had been given adequate credit in the press for securing her prestigious appointment. She wrote to Johnson that she was disappointed that a news article "failed to give you credit for it. You were the first and only person to suggest that I be made Director of the East. I thank you for it from the depths of my very heart." When she shared her concerns with Berto, he replied, "If necessary we can send a statement to the press that will give Johnson all the credit. Who cares as long as you are 'Mrs. Director.' ... I am glad you wrote him as you did since he feels so deeply on the subject. There is nothing like having everybody happy."[31]

On the campaign trail, Mollie Terrell told black women they had a responsibility to use the Nineteenth Amendment as "a weapon of defense" in upholding African Americans' constitutional rights. For the suffrage amendment to have real results, black women had to educate themselves as voters: "Colored women should certainly watch carefully what the legislatures of their respective states are doing and keep posted on the bills which vitally affect us as a race." Seeing the NACW as playing a vital role in voter education, Terrell urged that each "state chairman on legislation should keep the women of the various states well informed on the measures ... which will help or hinder our race.... Colored women should send letters to their state or national representatives, urging them to take a stand for or against measures in which they are especially interested."[32]

Although heartened by Harding's speech accepting his nomination, in which he acknowledged African Americans' "full measure of citizenship," black women were discouraged when the party allowed "for the first time, the seating of lily-white delegations" at the same convention. Referring to Robert Church's successful fight to be seated in an integrated, or "black and tan," delegation from Tennessee, Berto told Mollie he was glad that her brother "and Link Johnson have won at Chicago. I hate a lily white republican. Would rather vote for Vardaman than one of them."[33]

As the RNC's director of Work among Colored Women of the East, Terrell traveled up and down the East Coast giving talks to black voters. On October 13, 1920, the veteran lecturer experienced a shocking run-in with a white railroad ticket agent when she arrived in Dover, Delaware, to give a speech. Mollie described what happened to NAACP president Moorfield Storey: "I consider myself the first woman victim after the Ratification of the Nineteenth Amendment north of the Mason & Dixon Line. I was arrested in Dover, Delaware, by the ticket agent five minutes after I reached the city, because I asked him if he knew a certain colored man who had been arranging meetings for the Republicans [she could not find his name in the phone directory]. He became angered and charged me with 'disorderly conduct.' I was not actually arrested and taken to jail." When railroad agents arrived at her GOP meeting they waited until she finished her eloquent speech and then decided not to present her with the warrant for her arrest. In her official "repudiation of the charges," she stated: "Howard West . . . stormed, raged at me, and threatened me with arrest because . . . he saw standing before him the representative of a race which he probably would like to see in slavery today, and he is determined to keep in its place." Terrell did not shrink from the controversy that ensued, explaining, "It sometimes happens that a woman has . . . to live up to her highest ideals even if she knows that by doing so she may be a victim of unpleasant notoriety . . . for resenting *the insult not only to myself, but through me to the womanhood of the whole race*, than to lose my self-respect, because I was too cowardly in a crisis to do what I know to be right."[34]

She was untroubled by the possibility of being charged: "Personally, I should not have been worried much if I had actually been arrested. . . . It would have been a good thing. It would have shocked white and black alike if I had been sent to jail on a charge of disorderly conduct." She was surprised to find that the black men she consulted took a paternalistic approach, worrying about her respectability. They were far less comfortable than she was with the prospect of her being taken to jail: "The men especially appeared horror-stricken at the thought of my being placed under arrest . . . and assured me that such a disgraceful experience would have ruined me for life."[35]

After Terrell's appointment, other African American women turned to her in hopes of securing positions in her office or in the field as a speaker. Terrell had limited authority to hire, since recommendations for speakers had to be sent in from each state. But perception was as important as the reality, and when some black Republican women did not get the jobs they hoped for, they blamed Terrell. One disgruntled woman was Hallie Quinn Brown, the prominent educator, activist, Republican partisan, and NACW president

(1920–24). She wrote to Terrell expressing her disappointment that she had not received the top RNC position available to a black woman, national director of Colored Women's Work. Terrell responded that her executive committee had sanctioned and forwarded her name, but "for some reason, Mr. Kealing's department did not forward the request to the colored bureau." Brown had sent letters of reference to bolster her case, but Terrell wrote back to say they were unnecessary: "I have known you for years . . . and I know of your official position and your general standing." Referring to Brown's experience as a professor of elocution at Wilberforce University, Terrell advised that she apply to be a speaker, which she suggested would be far less "tedious" than the kinds of office work she was facing. There is no chance, however, that Terrell herself would have preferred to be a speaker rather than director.[36]

Correspondence between Terrell and Lethia Cousins Fleming, who secured the position Brown had hoped for, reveals some of Terrell's best traits and most significant weaknesses as a friend and collaborator. These two smart, dynamic women developed a close bond but found it hard to sustain the pleasure of their friendship. Fleming, over a decade younger, was Terrell's high-energy kindred spirit. They were both educators, suffragists, and members of the NAACP, as well as Republican partisans. Fleming visited Terrell's office in early October 1920. They clicked immediately, bonding over their shared exhilaration at their high-powered positions and enjoying their time together exploring the city. On her return to national RNC headquarters in Chicago, Fleming wrote an affectionate, playful letter to Terrell, who could be great fun to be with: "My dear 'Lady' Mary. . . . Let me know how many times you have been lost since I left and how you are amused, and also how many pie ala modes you eat." Terrell's response began, "My dear Lady Bug. . . . The more I read, the more I grinned." But a later, generally friendly letter from Terrell hinted at brewing tension: "Have just received your telegram notifying me not to touch West Virginia." Fleming was the national director, so Terrell, one of two regional directors, resented the instructions she nonetheless had to follow.[37]

Their friendship began to unravel after their successful campaigning helped put Harding in the White House. Most of the problems stemmed from the fact that the Terrells were moving into a new home, so Mollie did not receive Fleming's letters and telegrams. Fleming, who was counting on Terrell to help her plan a conference in Washington to build a new national black women's Republican organization, was frustrated by what she misunderstood as Terrell's completely ignoring her. By her fifth letter, Fleming was panicking because another group seemed to be making progress with a similar plan. Fleming insisted that theirs must be the only officially RNC-sanctioned national organization: "We must show Hallie [Quinn Brown] and her gang that we carry no white feathers in our head gear." Competitive and unwilling to surrender, Fleming was, indeed, Terrell's kindred spirit. The road ahead, however, was rocky.[38]

After being out of touch for at least two months due to the disruptions of her move, Terrell finally received one of Fleming's letters expressing stress and anxiety at not hearing from her. Terrell responded defensively, especially to Fleming's decision to go around her to get the names of the state leaders in the eastern district in order to invite them to this organizing conference. Fleming responded, "As you say, it is your district. However we are both responsible. . . . I am sure you can see why I took the above action, and will agree that I have not . . . failed in my effort to work in absolute harmony."[39]

Fleming and Terrell disagreed on organizational strategy because Terrell had a tendency to conflate forming an organization in the nation's capital with having a national organization. She was less dedicated to building organizations from the states up, which led some to see her as undemocratic. Not living in a state, not having the right to vote in D.C., and living at the center of the federal government reinforced Terrell's indifference to this issue. Fleming tried to remind her about process: "The organizations have first got to be in the State and then the representatives from the various States, forming the National body, that is the only legitimate organization." Fleming also sent what she thought was good news—that the three highest-ranking black male Republicans, Charles Cottrill, Henry Lincoln Johnson, and Robert R. Church Jr., would be speaking at their meeting—giving their planned organization the imprimatur of legitimacy.[40]

In the end, the men successfully deflected the women from creating their own organization. They hijacked the 1921 conference by endorsing the creation of a female director at the black Republican headquarters in Washington and then demanded that the women raise the funds for this appointment. This forestalled the creation of a permanent black women's national Republican organization until 1924. But at the time, the women felt celebratory—they had played a significant role in a national election, helped to elect Harding, and had the prospect of a female director at the black RNC headquarters. Division between the two groups of Republican African American women did not help—their jockeying for power and recognition made it harder to reject the men's more limited plan for a women's directorship rather than a separate organization.

Wanting to be the new female director the men had proposed hiring, Terrell visited Henry Lincoln Johnson "to tell him how the women feel about Mrs. [Monen L.] Gray's gaining the ascendancy." Although no national organization had been formed, the existence of a second, rival group trying to form one still rankled. She complained to Johnson about Fleming as well, saying she did not deserve to be called the "big chief," which he had done. Johnson chided her for her seeming lack of gratitude regarding her own significant RNC campaign appointment: "'Let's think of the nice things we have done for you, Mrs. T.'"[41]

Terrell still expected to be rewarded for her strong campaign performance. If she could not become director, she had other ideas. Visiting RNC headquarters in New York City, she asked "for an appointment on the Human Welfare Bureau" but was advised to wait until after Harding's inauguration to apply. When she told her brother Robert that she "would like to have something in the Human Welfare or Educational Department," he dismissed her political work as irrelevant and undeserving of patronage appointments: "He said he would help me but this Woman's Division to which I belong amounts to nothing." Whether this was a sexist dismissal of political organizing by black women, a desire to keep patronage appointments in the hands of black men, or an endorsement of her rivals is unclear. A persistent Terrell also went to the White House to see President Harding's secretary, framing her request for a position as part of a larger goal: "I asked him whether Colored people would receive any recognition" for their campaign work and votes. After visiting the offices of various RNC officials, she finally asked RNC chair Postmaster General Will Hays: "Are colored women to be recognized, Mr. Hays?" His response was cagey, "'Not as Colored women. There are neither men nor women, black or white in the Republican Party. But,'" he assured her, "'their color will not be against them.'"[42]

Once in office, Harding briefly raised African Americans' hopes for civil rights and patronage in an October 1921 speech in Birmingham, Alabama, when he "stunned the [southern white] crowd by declaring that 'the negro is entitled to full economic and political rights as an American citizen.'" Yet Harding soon reversed course by saying that he believed in "natural segregations." Most disappointing, he failed to follow through on his initial endorsement of an antilynching bill. As one of his white federal appointees put it, "Everyone was trying to poison the President's mind against honest people. Terrible propaganda against colored man."[43]

"Colored People . . . Felt That They Had Been Stabbed in the House of a Friend"

Lobbying for a government appointment did not keep Terrell from weighing in on a 1921 international controversy. She was disturbed by sensational charges that black soldiers stationed under French command in occupied German territory were raping German women. Terrell was even more troubled by the decision of the Women's International League for Peace and Freedom to distribute a petition to its executive committee for signatures demanding the

removal of those troops. The only African American on the executive committee, Terrell refused to sign and instead offered her resignation. She wrote to
WILPF president Jane Addams, "I cannot sign the petition . . . because I believe it is a direct appeal to race prejudice."[44] She reminded Addams of the long
and terrible history of lynching in America and the numerous false charges of
rape to which black men had been and were still being subjected. Noting that
the suffragist and pacifist Carrie Chapman Catt had found no truth to the
charges when she investigated from Geneva, Switzerland, Terrell suggested
that they were motivated by racial prejudice. She also pointed to the hypocrisy of whites, who rarely perceived African American women—frequent victims of assault—as needing protection: "The most terrible crimes are said to
be committed by these black troops against the German women. I belong to
a race whose women have been the victims of assaults committed upon them
by white men and men of all other races. As a rule, these men have ruined and
wrecked the women of my race with impunity." Although she sympathized
with any women who were the victims of violence, Terrell reiterated that she
had "been informed that the charges proffered against the black troops are not
all founded in fact."[45]

In reply, Jane Addams conceded that the goal of the WILPF, a propeace and
proarbitration organization, should be to demand the removal of all troops—
not just black troops—occupying another country. Acknowledging the evidence supporting Terrell's position and perhaps realizing that the petition
was racist, Addams withdrew the appeal and declined to accept Terrell's resignation. Staying on the WILPF board, Terrell tried to persuade her white
colleagues that they must see imperialism and colonization as antithetical to
peace. The board's minutes summarized her argument: "No permanent peace
could be achieved until the 'dark Peoples' of the world were allowed to develop
without exploitation by the white races." In addition, she implored the league
to protest "any attempt of the Powers to exploit China." The board did not,
however, take any specific action.[46]

When WILPF headquarters moved to Washington, D.C., in November
1921, Terrell recruited some black friends to attend a luncheon and consider
joining the organization. She hoped to make it interracial, if only locally. Ten
of the twelve she invited accepted. One who declined: "Had asked 'Do they
(the white women) want me?'" Terrell's response was deliberately ambiguous:
"I told her they wanted me as much as they did her." Her black friends and
colleagues justifiably feared that they were not truly welcome, especially in the
more racially charged social setting of a luncheon rather than a formal business meeting.[47]

Terrell was not reelected to the WILPF's executive board in 1923. Perhaps
her protest against the petition or her attempts to integrate the organization

hurt her. Some, too, objected to Terrell's celebration of the Civil War as having liberated her people, which they viewed as a betrayal of the organization's strict pacifist stance. Terrell's pacifist, antiwar position was too nuanced for most white WILPF members to accept. Even as she advocated peace and reconciliation, Terrell praised the patriotic war work of African American soldiers, emphasizing their legitimate claims to full citizenship. WILPF members criticized the "purity" of her convictions.[48]

African American women campaigning for Harding had expected real improvements after the backsliding of the Wilson years. They soon became concerned, however, because, "the few political plums which colored men had been in the habit of receiving from the Republican party in the good old days had not been shaken down from the tree to them by Mr. Harding." Yet Terrell noted that Republican partisans tried to "swallow their disappointment" and focus on their most important goal: "Having been helpless victims of violence for so long, a large number of colored people worked for the passage of the Dyer Anti-Lynching Bill with all their heart, soul, mind and strength. But the Republican Congress allowed a few Southern Democrats to filibuster this bill to death."[49]

Congressional inaction generated ill-will among African American voters toward the GOP. Terrell declared that it "was literally the last straw that broke the camel's back. Many colored people believed that they had been duped by the Republican Party, that it had never had the slightest intention of passing the bill to prevent lynching and they felt that they had been stabbed in the house of a friend." Republicans failed to enact any significant legislation to advance civil rights during the 1920s, when three Republicans occupied the White House and while the GOP controlled Congress, leading more black voters to consider abandoning their longtime loyalty.[50]

The failure of the Dyer Anti-Lynching Bill spurred prominent African American Republican women to create a new, independent, national organization just before the election of 1924. Unlike in 1920, the National League of Republican Colored Women (NLRCW) was intentionally established as outside the RNC's control. NLRCW activists, including Terrell, sought a means for advancing black women's legislative and reform priorities. She became treasurer of the new organization.[51]

Two months later, Terrell traveled to RNC headquarters in Chicago, trying to secure a job in the upcoming 1924 presidential campaign. Berto's health had entered into a serious decline starting around 1921, when he had the first of a series of terrible strokes. From that point on, he experienced numerous health setbacks with only partial recoveries. As Berto's health deteriorated, he was mostly unable to work, but he still earned his salary as a judge because of his many years of service. Mollie and Berto both worried about the prospect of her having to support herself if he died. They agreed that she should continue taking short-term jobs even while he was ill. Fearing the economic as well as emotional costs of losing her husband, Mollie realized that she needed to prepare to support herself. She secured RNC campaign work in Calvin Coolidge's 1924 presidential campaign.

Fortunately, the Terrells had help from a young woman, Eula Edwards, who had boarded with them while attending school but had then left briefly to work elsewhere. When she found herself pregnant in 1922, Edwards had feared that her chances for an education were over. She was attending Howard University but felt she could not do so as a single mother with a child to raise. At that point, Mollie and Berto had invited her back into their home, sheltering Edwards while she was pregnant and supporting her through an adoption process, earning her real devotion. As Berto's health deteriorated, Mollie was able to rely on Eula, whom she employed to help care for him.[52]

In 1924, while working on Coolidge's campaign, Mollie wrote Berto: "I am so glad you are getting along so nicely during my absence from home. *I think about you constantly.* I know Eula is doing everything for you she can." After receiving a detailed update from Eula, she confessed, "It relieved my mind to know that everything was going smoothly at home. Keep improving." In spite of his dire situation, Mollie continued to hope that her husband would make a full recovery.[53]

In the 1924 campaign, Mollie tried to persuade African American voters to remain in the GOP, insisting that the Democrats were still a southern-dominated party of white supremacists. The Democratic Party's nominee, John W. Davis of West Virginia, had been a member of the House of Representatives, served as U.S. solicitor general, and been an ambassador under President Wilson. His racist record and conservative social, economic, and foreign policies gave African American Republicans like Terrell ammunition. His conservativism also forced a split in the Democratic Party, with Robert La Follette of Wisconsin running as the Progressive Party candidate. Terrell pointed to Davis's service as Wilson's ambassador to Britain and his support of U.S. membership in the League of Nations as indications of his willingness to increase entanglements abroad. Expressing her anti-imperialist, pan-African perspective, she worried that his election would mean that "our brothers, husbands and sons might be sent to India to help Great Britain to place the iron heel of oppression still harder on the brown necks of that cruelly oppressed dark race, or we colored women might have to send our sons to help Great Britain subdue completely the brown and black Egyptians."[54]

The 1924 election was marred by the open participation in mainstream politics by the increasingly popular and powerful Ku Klux Klan. La Follette and Davis condemned it, with Davis's public denunciation satisfying a few prominent black former Republicans, such as Alice Dunbar-Nelson, who was so disillusioned when the Republicans did not pass the Dyer Anti-Lynching Bill that she endorsed the Democrats.[55] Trying to halt more defections, Terrell quoted Davis's earlier racist resolution against black voting rights in the West Virginia legislature, as well as his successful championing of a resolution in favor of segregated railroad cars.[56] Terrell pointedly shared Davis's shameful record with African American women: "Let us vote against the man who tried to subject colored women to inconvenience, to discomforts, to physical suffering and to actual danger by forcing them to ride in Jim Crow cars." In her 1924 talk "Some Facts for Colored Women to Think About," she reminded her audiences that the Democrats controlled the South and were responsible for having imposed segregation and the convict lease labor system.[57]

In the 1920s, Terrell also became a leader in the International Council of Women of the Darker Races (ICWDR), founded by Margaret Murray Washington, the widow of Booker T. Washington. The group was intentionally small, composed of about twenty prominent NACW members devoted to developing and promoting pan-Africanism and cross-ethnic racial understanding.[58] The ICWDR constructed a more expansive definition of race, placing the "Negro problem" in a dynamic national and global context. An international organization for women of color was necessary, they argued, since the white-dominated International Council of Women was not addressing the concerns of the world's "darker races" and was not inclusive.[59]

Terrell's late 1920s "Up to Date" column in the most influential black newspaper in the nation, the *Chicago Defender*, featured critiques of European colonization. Sharing her political and social views on contemporary news and cultural events, she praised the nonviolent teachings of Mahatma Gandhi, predicting that Indians would ultimately achieve home rule, since they had managed to get Britain to withdraw a tax increase they did not want to pay. Terrell touted this as "a wonderful illustration of what an oppressed people can do who organize against injustice perpetrated upon them by the rich and powerful. The farmers are boycotting British goods.... They are spinning and weaving their own cloth." In South Africa, she predicted, "as the natives of that wonderful country, which has been pilfered and plundered and partitioned among the great powers of the earth, become more enlightened they will grow more and more restless and dissatisfied with the terrible conditions imposed upon them by the white oppressors." Responding to condemnations by ruling white South African officials against the entry of the Communist Party into South Africa, she approved the party's goal of putting "the iron into the black man's soul and teach[ing] him to throw off the yoke of oppression."[60]

Mollie Church had learned Republican politics from her father during Reconstruction. She and Berto both entered their 1891 marriage devoted to the party of Lincoln, even as they consistently pushed it to actively defend African Americans' civil rights. Berto's career was shaped by GOP patronage, including his appointments to government posts by presidents from Harrison to Coolidge. Trying to prioritize civil rights in the domestic and international arenas, Terrell's politics were driven by her commitment to racial justice and equality. By the end of the 1920s, Mollie remained a Republican partisan and benefited from RNC campaign appointments, but it became more difficult for her and other black women to generate real enthusiasm for Republican presidential candidates. At the end of the decade, she finally had the opportunity to work for a Republican candidate who truly inspired her, a progressive white woman, Representative Ruth Hanna McCormick, who was running in Illinois for a seat in the U.S. Senate.

8

Ruth Hanna McCormick's Senate Campaign

I n May 1929, Terrell had the opportunity to put her Republican Party partisanship to great use when she joined the senate campaign of the new freshman Republican congresswoman-at-large from Illinois, Ruth Hanna McCormick, supporting her bid to be the first woman elected to the upper house. McCormick had to begin by challenging incumbent Illinois senator Charles S. Deneen in the GOP primary in April 1930. McCormick's history of support for woman suffrage and her historic run captured Mollie's imagination. Thrilled by the prospect of helping elect a progressive Republican woman who stood for equal justice and had a good record of antisegregation stances, Terrell enthused that Illinois voters could "blaze a new trail . . . by sending a woman to the Senate."[1]

A full ten years after women secured the franchise, suffrage activist Mollie Church Terrell had not yet had the opportunity to vote; she was a resident of Washington, D.C., which was administered by Congress and had no representation on Capitol Hill. That changed in 1930, when Mollie wrote excitedly to Phyllis back in D.C. that she had registered in Illinois using the Chicago address of her other daughter, Mary: "I have worked for suffrage all my life and the first vote I shall be able to cast will be for the first woman who has had the courage to run for the United States Senate. That certainly gives me a kick."[2]

Although her entry into McCormick's campaign was exciting and seemed promising, Terrell's temperament, need for employment, loyalty to the GOP, and desire for a leadership position all converged into a volatile conflict with African American women in Illinois. It started promisingly enough until Terrell faced unexpectedly fierce competition for political patronage and influence from black Illinois Republican women seeking campaign positions. They vocally opposed her, for they had expected paid employment for themselves and their family members. The outcome of the campaign, too, was a blow to Terrell, for although McCormick won the Republican primary, she was defeated in the general election by a Democrat. McCormick's loss was an early signal of a political realignment of the Democratic and Republican Parties that would prove costly to Terrell in the next decades.[3]

"Blaze a New Trail"

Ruth Hanna McCormick was the daughter of former senator Mark Hanna of Cleveland, a major fundraiser and kingmaker for the Republican Party. African Americans appreciated him as a politician who had openly advocated, as Terrell put it, "justice and fair play on their behalf." Terrell hoped to build interest in McCormick's campaign by emphasizing to black voters that she was Senator Hanna's daughter. She also pointed to McCormick's work as a progressive reformer and lobbyist. During the first two decades of the new century, McCormick had been active in such reform organizations as the Women's Trade Union League and the National Child Welfare Bureau. Terrell credited McCormick's leadership with helping secure passage of the Nineteenth Amendment, which made "women bona fide citizens of the United States." McCormick had fought for and achieved much-needed protective labor legislation in Illinois that "reduced the working hours for women from ten to eight hours a day. . . . Mrs. McCormick has been trying for years to improve the condition of all working women, black as well as white."[4]

In the 1924 primary, her husband, Senator Medill McCormick, was defeated by a GOP challenger, Governor Charles S. Deneen. McCormick committed suicide just before his term ended in February 1925. Rebuilding her life and her husband's legacy, Ruth Hanna McCormick first ran for a seat in the House of Representatives in 1928. Almost immediately, she also announced her intention to run for Senator Deneen's seat, hoping to bring her own and her husband's priorities—and their name—back to the Senate.[5]

McCormick dramatically increased her credibility among black voters on April 15, 1929, the day House members were sworn in, by acting behind the scenes to ensure that her fellow Illinois Republican, Representative Oscar Stanton DePriest, would be able to take the oath of office. He was the first African American to be elected to Congress in the twentieth century and the first ever from the North. McCormick convinced House Speaker Nicholas Longworth of Ohio to arrange for a mass swearing-in ceremony, which avoided the possibility that DePriest's enemies could dispute his being seated. Terrell praised "the manner in which Mrs. McCormick had worked to save embarrassment to the whole race. . . . Her strategy thwarted the deep laden plans of prejudiced southerners." McCormick's plan, Terrell emphasized, "required courage and a right attitude toward us."[6]

Once Representative DePriest moved to Washington, Terrell saw him often at social and political events, and they built a friendship based on their shared interest in politics and civil rights.[7] Their alliance helped Terrell, a seasoned Republican campaigner with a great track record of her own, move into a prominent position in McCormick's Senate campaign. Soon after the Illinois representatives took up their new jobs in Congress, DePriest wrote to McCormick, recommending that she hire Terrell for her upcoming campaign: "It is indeed with a great deal of personal interest that I introduce to you the bearer . . . Mrs. Mary Church Terrell of Washington, D.C." He explained, "Mrs. Terrell would be of inestimable value." DePriest assured his colleague that Terrell "has had extended experience in matters of publicity and is an able, intelligent, capable and sincere advocate of the forward progress of mankind. . . . Mrs. Terrell is a power on the platform and is thoroughly acquainted with matters in connection with the business of the nation at the capitol here and public affairs in the United States generally." Terrell secured the position, telling her brother Thomas, "At last I have found a job. . . . I am glad to be earning a little money. It has been a year since we received anything from the [Memphis] property and my exchequer was getting lower and lower every day in every way. Thank God I can recuperate a little financially." Terrell would only be working for a few months, but each week she would be earning a substantial $75 a week ($300 a month, or about $4,400 in today's money).[8]

Initially, although she remembered earlier troubles over the NACW presidency, Terrell's collaboration with black Illinois Republican women seemed unproblematic. A number of prominent black women Republicans, including Terrell, had joined together in Chicago in 1924 to create the National League of Republican Colored Women. (Black women had also created their own Colored Women's Republican Clubs of Illinois, led by Irene Goins, since their influence was rapidly increasing in Chicago politics owing to the Great Migration's swelling of its black population.) In addition, Terrell had been welcomed in Illinois in 1926 when she worked on GOP senator William McKinley's reelection campaign. Black women supported McKinley because he undertook the politically unpopular task of reintroducing a version of the Dyer Anti-Lynching Bill in the Senate.[9]

"I Am Not Here to . . . Usurp Any Power"

The *Chicago Defender* provided Terrell with extensive and sympathetic coverage. The paper had recently carried Terrell's weekly column, "Up to Date: A Brief Survey of Current Happenings," for approximately a year, paying her a substantial $50 a month. A few weeks after she arrived for the McCormick campaign, in September 1929, the *Defender* published her photo alongside a feature article entitled, "Mrs. Terrell Here to Head Senate Drive." Terrell was friends with the *Defender's* publisher and its general counsel, and the paper trumpeted her arrival: "Mrs. Terrell is one of the best known women in public life in the country. She is a writer, lecturer and scholar and has the distinction of having been the first woman of her race to be placed upon a board of education in any city in the world." Terrell said, "This is the greatest political opportunity that our women have ever enjoyed. Mrs. McCormick's cause is our cause."[10]

In the *Defender* interview, Terrell remembered past rivalries and tried to soothe any tensions: "I am not here to . . . usurp any power. Neither am I here to dictate or high-hat anybody. . . . I hope there will be no confusion regarding my position. Mrs. McCormick's campaign is not confined to the narrow limits of state and I am not here as a state woman, but as a national woman." She pointed out that Representative McCormick had brought in "national women of the other race" to lead her campaign among white women, so her position was no different.[11]

As the NACW's national chair on legislation in 1926, Terrell had insisted that she must lobby Congress rather than go out and canvass for state-level laws. She wrote to NACW president Mary McLeod Bethune: "Even if I had had the money to go into the various states, I would have been obliged to exercise very great discretion indeed" because of women's animosity to "having 'outsiders' come into a State and 'dictate' to the women. I was the first colored woman asked by the Republican Party to take charge of the Eastern Division in the Harding-Coolidge Campaign . . . and I know how the women in the States feel. . . . I have too much experience in such things and too much common sense, I hope, to do any such stupid thing as that."[12]

Terrell recognized that she was moving into a campaign attended by disagreements among black women: "Today our women have small influence because they have permitted party bickerings and petty personalities to divide their forces. . . . I may be classed as an outsider insofar as connection with sets or diverging factions are concerned. It is for that reason possibly that I was chosen. . . . My viewpoint is entirely impersonal." Black women in Illinois Republican politics rejected her characterization of them as "petty," "bickering" women. Whether their lack of influence was caused or exacerbated by such disagreements or was a function of sexism, the women did compete with one another.[13]

The new president of the Colored Women's Republican Clubs of Illinois, Irene M. Gaines, three decades younger than the sixty-six-year-old Terrell, had expected to head the campaign's Colored Division. Disappointed that McCormick had not appointed her, Gaines initially chose to be gracious and welcoming. At a beautiful reception for Terrell with more than two hundred

FIGURE 8.1. Mollie Terrell at age sixty-four is dressed in a sophisticated black lace and silk dress. This 1927 portrait was made just
a couple of years before she joined Representative Ruth Hanna
McCormick's campaign for a seat in the U.S. Senate. The photograph was taken at the prominent Harris & Ewing Photo-
graphic Studio in Washington, D.C. (Courtesy Oberlin College
Archives)

women in attendance, "Mrs. Gaines . . . said that, whereas Mrs. Terrell has for
many years made her home in Washington, D.C., because of her great service
to the women (and men) of the country, she belongs to all the states."[14]

Despite her excellent qualifications and the positive press reports, Terrell
encountered serious difficulties. Black Illinois women soon demanded leadership of the campaign. Three *Defender* articles revealed tensions that had been
simmering since Terrell's arrival. The first continued the positive coverage of
McCormick and Terrell, featuring a flattering photo of McCormick with
eight prominent black women and men who were working on her campaign:

"In one suite of four rooms was installed a busy staff who will be in charge of Mrs. McCormick's campaign among the Colored people. Those include Mrs. Mary Church Terrell, brought to Chicago . . . as an expert organizer." Unaware of the jealousies and competition for the top job in her campaign, McCormick continued trying to capitalize on her decision to hire Terrell: "Mrs. McCormick told the *Defender* reporter that she was delighted to be able to induce Mrs. Terrell to remain in Illinois and assist the colored women of Chicago and the state in organizing for the campaign." The reporter concluded, "Mrs. Terrell is a woman of charming personality and of intense enthusiasm. Modesty is apparently one of her chief virtues and Mrs. McCormick's success in the present campaign is her one absorbing interest." Terrell's dynamic personality won over the reporter, but those who wanted their share of the limelight did not similarly appreciate her "modesty."[15]

But the same issue also included "Women Voters Oust *Defender* Reporter." It detailed a meeting of black women from several Illinois and Chicago-based Republican clubs who had "been exceedingly antagonistic toward one another" but had come to unite with "a common grievance" over the selection of a non-Illinois woman to head McCormick's campaign. They "sought to make it clear that there was no fight against Mrs. Terrell, nor were the women . . . seeking to injure Mrs. McCormick's chances of winning." They simply wanted one of their own appointed to the key leadership post. One woman had hosted a major testimonial luncheon for Ruth Hanna McCormick in 1925, for example, and expected to be recognized and rewarded for her early support. The principal speaker was Ida B. Wells-Barnett, who began: "Anyone who knows me knows well that I would be among the first to protest against the bringing of another woman from another state to lead the women of Illinois in a political campaign. I have made protests before but have found it difficult to get other women to stand with me." Wells-Barnett was eager to capitalize on this moment of unity, especially since Terrell's appointment stirred up personal and regional rivalries that had played out in the early battles for the presidency of the National Association of Colored Women. A prominent and respected reformer and politico, Wells-Barnett had a contentious relationship with her adopted city because of her insistence on fighting for whatever she believed was right, no matter the consequences. Anticipating that the *Defender* reporter would not provide them with positive coverage, Wells-Barnett motioned that "he be asked to withdraw."[16]

If it were not yet clear to *Defender* readers that a crisis was brewing in McCormick's campaign, a third article, "Apology Demanded from Mrs. Barnett," made it clear. It featured a letter by McCormick's campaign manager for the Colored Division, LeRoy M. Hardin, demanding an apology and a retraction from Wells-Barnett for publicly stating that Hardin "occupied the position of 'spittoon cleaner'" in McCormick's office. This racially tinged denigration of Hardin, a black man in a position of authority in a white woman's political campaign, was not only cruel but did not accurately reflect Hardin's four years of work as a clerk and then manager in McCormick's office. Hardin openly objected to Wells-Barnett: "Whatever your grievance is against Mrs. McCormick for having Mrs. Terrell here to handle her campaign among the women, it has no bearing as to why you should attack me."[17]

Representative McCormick had hoped that her appointment of Terrell would solidify support for her among black voters. Instead, disputes among prominent African American Republicans about the top campaign position were airing publicly. The *Defender* issue of October 19, 1929, revealed more rifts. "Women Open War on Mrs. Ruth McCormick" reported that a meeting of "50 key women representing six Republican women's organizations in Illinois," chaired by Wells-Barnett, delivered an open letter to McCormick stating: "Whereas, the Negro women who have loyally supported Mrs. McCormick every time she has asked their vote, and who thus *had the right to expect political recognition for themselves and their daughters*, which they have not received at her hands, regret that she could find no Negro woman in the state . . . to head her campaign; therefore be it Resolved that we hereby serve notice . . . that we resent the slight."[18]

McCormick had personal wealth and was willing to finance her campaigns generously, so the Illinois women believed she should pay back her supporters by hiring them for her next run or by finding government jobs for them or their family members. Black Illinois women were especially insistent on gaining patronage from McCormick because their decision to endorse her when she first ran the House in 1927 was not straightforward. African American Republican women had feared then that McCormick did not support their priorities. They were especially concerned about her ambiguous stance on the repeal of prohibition, which most black women opposed. The repeal of any constitutional amendment, they feared, would put at risk the Fourteenth and Fifteenth. Their refusal to endorse repeal also derived from a long-held belief that alcohol threatened the safety and sanctity of family life by encouraging spousal abuse and increased rates of destitution. Most African American women insisted on better enforcement of the Eighteenth Amendment, not its abandonment. Although McCormick was dry and recognized the amendment as the law of the land, she had also said that the federal government "either ought to enforce it or repeal it," and that appeared to some as waffling.[19]

Ultimately, black women in Illinois had decided that McCormick deserved their support for her run as congresswoman-at-large. They were impressed by her clear record of personal resistance to Jim Crow laws and other restrictions of black life. Most symbolically important was the day she had walked side by side with two companies of black women in a huge 1914 Illinois suffrage parade. The black women of her state appreciated this gesture, especially in light of Alice Paul's attempt to block African American women, including most famously, Chicagoan Ida B. Wells-Barnett, from participating as equals in the national suffrage march just one year earlier.[20]

After having worked so hard to cultivate good ties with African American women Republicans in Illinois, a surprised McCormick was put on the defensive by their angry resolutions. The "first time Mrs. McCormick spoke to a group of colored people after these resolutions were forwarded to her," she said, "Mrs. Terrell is my friend. All her life she has worked for black women and she has worked for white women, too. She has lived at the seat of Government and has been interested in politics for years. She knows better than some of you why a woman is needed in the Senate. I am prouder of having brought Mrs. Terrell to Illinois than anything I have ever done in my life."[21]

Several months later, Irene Gaines, who had initially acquiesced to Terrell's appointment, wrote to Hallie Quinn Brown, the prominent African American Republican activist and past president of the NACW: "To begin with, I am told, and reliably so, that Mrs. Mary Church Terrell approached our Congressman DePriest and asked that he give her a letter to Mrs. McCormick saying nice things about her ability." Although that was correct, Gaines incorrectly speculated: "This was done with the advice from our Congressman that if she was engaged for the campaign, she must stay in the background. (Behind the Illinois women leaders). I heard him remind her of this in Mrs. McCormick's office at headquarters." Gaines wrote months after Terrell's entry into the campaign and after the protests from the Illinois women. DePriest had only cautioned Terrell in light of those tensions. Gaines then spelled out her own qualifications: "I have known Mrs. McCormick for twelve or more years; served on her Woman's Committee twelve years ago; worked in her office in her last campaign for Congressman-at-large, etc., and last April I was elected to succeed our beloved Irene Goins as President of our State organization. Shortly after that Mrs. McCormick said I was to be in her office for this campaign."[22]

As Gaines pointed out, she was not the only dissatisfied Illinois woman: "Mr. DePriest had also requested her [McCormick] to use Miss Jennie E. Lawrence, his most outstanding woman worker in the Third Ward." Gaines surmised that "this information Mrs. McCormick evidently gave to Mrs. Terrell, so that when she came to Chicago and settled herself, she immediately got in touch with me and later with Miss Lawrence, and 'confided' to us the fact that Mrs. McCormick had chosen her to be chairman of the Executive Committee (colored), and that upon inquiry in the community she had found that we were so valuable and so experienced in Illinois affairs, that she just had to have us working with her, etc." Terrell might have been informed by DePriest rather than McCormick, but either way, veteran Illinois politicos did not appreciate being "discovered" by an outsider.[23]

Unhappy with Terrell's appointment but supportive of Representative McCormick and in need of paid campaign work, the two women grudgingly accepted the situation. As Gaines explained, Terrell "asked if I would consent to come into the office and assist her. I consented and about one month later Miss Lawrence also came on the staff. Both of us had previous knowledge of the fact that Mrs. McCormick was to have us at headquarters. However, Lady Terrell did not know that we had been so informed and persists in saying even now that we were her selections and that she was responsible for our appointments." A tone-deaf Terrell was so happy to be holding this position that she congratulated herself on her excellent choices and expected gratitude, while they saw her as a haughty "Lady" putting on airs. Even if they had expected to join the staff, Terrell could still, of course, have rediscovered and brought them on independently.[24]

Terrell's superb organizational outreach skills made things worse, as she launched into her work by writing two sets of letters. The first were to women in nearby states asking for "the names of women who will make good workers in the State of Illinois." Illinois women did not appreciate her seeking such information from outside the state. Far more problematic was a letter Terrell sent to about a thousand black Illinois Republican women in early October. The letter offended many simply by informing them that she was in charge of McCormick's campaign: "Headquarters have been opened for the women of our group. . . . Mrs. Irene M. Gaines, a state woman, and I a national representative, are trying to reach and interest every colored woman voter in Mrs. McCormick's Candidacy. . . . Yours very sincerely, Mary Church Terrell, Chrm. of Executive Comm."[25] Gaines described what happened next: "As soon as the Illinois women learned that Mrs. Terrell was here and had sent out one thousand letters to them over her signature signed as Chairman of the Executive Committee, a great protest was made, and I was called down by many as President of the Colored Women's State Republican Organization for allowing myself to be used as her assistant." Once the Illinois women realized that an outsider had taken the primary leadership role, Gaines reported that "indignation meetings were held, letters of protest came and finally a petition with nearly a thousand signers was sent to Mrs. McCormick protesting the leadership of a woman who did not even have a vote in her own town, etc."[26]

Digging in, Terrell mobilized support to retain her position. She asked Robert Nelson, editor of the African American paper the *Washington Eagle*, for his paper's backing. Nelson responded, "I sympathize with you . . . and am taking care of the matter in the best way I can—namely, by an editorial . . .

calling attention to the fact that you were the first colored woman to head up a National campaign . . . the Harding campaign in 1920. . . . The further fact that Mrs. McCormick is a candidate for a National office should certainly obviate any criticism of you." Nonetheless, the protests forced a staff meeting at McCormick's headquarters to resolve the crisis. It was convened by a man, Representative DePriest, whom the Illinois women believed best able to protect their interests. Needing Illinois black women's votes, McCormick agreed to reorganize her staff. Gaines became chair of state work, known as head of the "Colored Women's Division," and Terrell became a "state speaker." As Gaines described the resolution: "Congressman DePriest came in and had a conference with members of our staff and with Mrs. McCormick, with the result that the Executive Committee was done away with . . . and Lady Terrell was taken out of the office and sent through the down State counties as a speaker." The Illinois women got what they wanted and were glad about De-Priest's intervention. They may not have recognized that his mediation also helped Terrell remain on staff. To sweeten her demotion and take her out of the office at campaign headquarters now used by Gaines and the other disgruntled women, Terrell was moved to a beautiful space with new office furniture. She delightedly wrote to Phyllis: "I have been given a nice new Mahogany desk with three drawers on each side, brass handles, and a swivel chair to match. The desk is between the two windows in that large area where the typists are. It's gorgeous!"[27]

McCormick and DePriest hoped to resolve the problem by getting Terrell onto the campaign trail. While still at the Chicago headquarters, as Gaines described it, "Mrs. Terrell became most violent and abusive to each of us and to Mrs. Joan Snowden, who had frankly told her that the women of Illinois would welcome her coming in to help them . . . but that they would not stand for an outsider to come as the head of the Woman's Division as long as there are so many capable women leaders in Illinois, etc." Snowden insisted that the Illinois women's grievances were not based on personal objections to Terrell herself. But, Gaines reported, "Mrs. Terrell accused us on the staff of agreeing with Mrs. Snowden and . . . she was especially nasty to me, saying that I could have prevented and stopped the women in their protest if I had wanted to; that I must have wanted her job for myself." Gaines admitted to Brown that she had resented Terrell's appointment from the start.[28]

Perceptively observing the contradictions in Terrell's personality, character, and reputation, Gaines concluded her narrative of events at McCormick headquarters by asking Brown, "Did you have any idea that she is like this? I have always thought her to be so cultured and refined." Terrell was, indeed, cultured, refined, and elegant. She also had a strong ego and great determination to succeed at whatever she did. She could be condescending, arrogant, and combative when she felt underappreciated or under siege or if a source of income was threatened.[29]

The extent of the negative reaction to her appointment made Terrell defensive and defiant: "I belong to the Illinois family. Some of you claim I am not a legitimate child. . . . I am not going to let anybody kick me out of my Illinois family. I am going to contend for my rights—especially my political rights—to the very last ditch."[30] McCormick might have recognized something of herself in Terrell's response, for she too had been attacked for her political ambitions and gender nonconforming behavior. Indeed, after an earlier fight within the National American Woman Suffrage Association over how best to achieve the vote for women, McCormick admitted to a reporter, "I don't deny that I slammed doors and pounded desks and possibly shook my fist. . . . I was excited and I was angry." A white woman running against McCormick charged her with "personal ambition for power. . . . She is Mark Hanna's daughter, with his desire to be boss." McCormick did not fire Terrell, who was arguably doing a thorough job.[31]

"I Have Had Marvelous Success All over the State"

As she moved into her new speaking role, Terrell felt vulnerable and tried to protect and promote herself by forwarding letters of support, some of which she solicited, to McCormick. Frank B. Jackson of the Illinois Boosters Club wrote from Carbondale to tout Terrell's unique skills, especially her ability, as a resident of the nation's capital, to inform audiences of McCormick's work there. He explained that Terrell had added substantively to what they already knew of McCormick's state-level work. Pointing out that "although in the minority, we [black voters] have the balancing power," Jackson believed that Terrell could secure "at least 90% of the Colored vote" if she were to speak across the state, a broader field of operations than she had been given. He concluded by noting Terrell's ability to appeal across class divides: "Irrespective of the social standing of various individuals, they are treated alike by Mrs. Terrell."[32]

Drawing on personal experiences, Terrell believed that her perspective was valuable: "I cite specific cases which have come under my own observation, or in which either my husband or myself have figured to show that if colored people do not vote and do not cast their ballots for representatives and senators who will give them a square deal in the national Congress, our status in the country will grow rapidly worse than it is today. . . . I find that giving examples to prove this point makes a deep impression upon our group and often converts dissenters to my point of view."[33]

Once Terrell began working for McCormick, she had greater access to Representative DePriest. He had protected her as best he could during the dispute and then readily complied with her requests for information to use in her speeches. Viewing DePriest as a political comrade, Terrell thanked him for best wishes for her work on McCormick's campaign. Then, using the inclusive words *we* and *our*, she wrote: "We all need them [best wishes] in our business." Their mutual identification as Republican politicos drew them closer. Wanting DePriest to see her appointment as working out well in the end, she enthused: "I have had marvelous success all over the State. The women not only have worked 'with me,' but they have received me with open arms everywhere I have spoken. The men have too, for that matter. The women have given me receptions on several occasions and said lots of nice things about me." Some of this was defensive self-promotion, but it also conveys Terrell's genuine delight in stumping for McCormick. Terrell concluded with: "My daughters say they will have to send me to a sanitarium if Mrs. McCormick is defeated. I trust she will win." DePriest knew her daughters, and this reference revealed Terrell's personal and humorous side.[34]

Terrell enjoyed and excelled at public speaking, and some Illinoisans gladly worked with her on McCormick's campaign. In January 1930, she told Phyllis she was meeting with large crowds and "a Ruth Hanna McCormick Club was formed right then and there." She happily concluded, "So you see I am meeting with pronounced success. I am working hard to elect Mrs. McCormick." Terrell was thus surprised and disappointed when McCormick's campaign manager for black voters, LeRoy Hardin, wrote a short, harsh letter saying: "Long distance complaints coming in from Peoria say that you are organizing places where you have been, and it is unsatisfactory to the people in these communities. This cannot go on, as I thought that you understood that you were simply to make speeches . . . and not to form any organizations. I am writing Mrs. McCormick regarding this, as it is simply causing me more trouble and work."[35]

Terrell took Hardin's criticism as a direct threat to her employment and reputation. Mounting a robust defense, she sent back a strongly worded telegram. Backpedaling, Hardin replied that he would hold off contacting McCormick but would visit Peoria to assess the situation. In a more conciliatory follow-up, he wrote that it was "certainly pleasing to know that you are meeting with such wonderful success. . . . I have pasted your [news] clippings from Peoria and Quincy on the bulletin board." Yet he reemphasized the division of labor: "I suppose you understand that I am not making speeches, only when requested, but I am getting the organizations into working order" and reminded Terrell she must do the opposite—speak but not organize—a job that should be left to him.[36]

Class differences exacerbated tensions over Terrell's role in the campaign. Replying to her questions about the specific source and nature of the complaints about her, Hardin complied. Only one man, an African American attorney named Frank Summers, had complained that Terrell was "trying to appoint people there to lead the organizations who had no political standing, and who were only of the so called 'silk stocking' class." Summers charged that Terrell had wrongly put a female leader of a social service (rather than a political) club as leader of Peoria's McCormick club, thereby stirring up the "women's petty jealousies." His complaint about Terrell catering to the "'silk stocking' class" contradicted praise she had received earlier about her ability to reach a wide variety of people, "irrespective of . . . social standing."[37]

Hardin's critique was gendered; as head of the Men's Division of Colored Work, he pontificated: "I think it would be wise for you to understand that this is not solely a woman's campaign, and many of our men will not follow women's leadership. Therefore it is not expedient to try to name leaders just among the women." Hardin asserted that black men could not accept and would "not follow" black women, whose dominance in the campaign had already led him to complain to McCormick about funding disparities. McCormick had not changed course, insisting that this uneven division of funds reflected the real organized strength of African American women voters in the state.[38]

Immediately after receiving Hardin's note regarding "complaints" against her, Terrell responded forcefully with a four-page single-spaced letter. He expressed shock at what he considered the excessive length of Terrell's response to his short critique: "It would not be well for me to express to you some of the things that I really think, but I will say that your letter reminds me of the prattle of a child." His dismissive characterization further alienated her. Hardin threatened to share their communications with Representative McCormick. Concluding that he could no longer work with her, he wrote, "I think that you are too important in your own mind to even consider my cooperation. I would like to add that we want to advertise Mrs. McCormick through the newspapers and not so much the activities of Mrs. Terrell. We are not running the campaign to keep anyone in the limelight other than Mrs. McCormick." Hardin continued: "I am not only insulted over receiving such a letter as you have written to me, but it depresses me to think that one of our so-called leading colored women would even write about some of the things you mentioned in your communication."[39]

But Terrell was not limiting her addresses to the social elite, and she was promoting the candidate. Facing Hardin's chauvinism and hostility, she struggled with how to respond. An undated draft of a telegram to Hardin suggests that she did not back down: "I always obey instructions. If any trouble is made in Peoria, you will make it yourself. I made none. I am not easily frightened by anybody. Mary Church Terrell." She did, however, fear that Hardin could cost her the job.[40]

She immediately wrote to McCormick's general (white) campaign manager, James Snyder: "I am obeying instructions given me at headquarters to the letter." To refute the "silk stockings" charge, Terrell drew on a part of her childhood she usually kept under wraps to show that she was comfortable venturing into places that might be considered difficult for an elegant woman. She told him of her early exposure to her father's saloons and the nightlife on Beale Street in Memphis and pointed out she had not hesitated to reach out to gamblers or prostitutes while soliciting votes for McCormick. Pointing to her comfort interacting with many kinds of voters in a variety of settings, Terrell told of visiting "John Brown's place," a saloon in Peoria not frequented by respectable elites. She noted that the "men were playing cards (maybe they were gambling, but that was none of my business) and I talked to them about Mrs. McCormick. Some women were also present (maybe they were not saints. I didn't stop to inquire.) But they all listened to me attentively and respectfully. I invited them to come to my meeting the following Sunday afternoon. They applauded me loudly."[41]

The heated exchange between Hardin and Terrell initiated another set of letters about class, this time between Terrell and a black Republican, Joseph H. Conway, who was running for local office in Peoria. Conway reassured Terrell of her appeal to all classes: "I again referred to and called your name to an underworld meeting on Friday . . . that you would return again in March to address them. They like to have torn the roof of the house cheering and clapping their hands, hollering McCormick, McCormick,—hurrah for Mrs. McCormick." Terrell could not have asked for better evidence that Summers's charges were false. She was particularly delighted with the way Conway closed his letter, assuring her that "you stand as well with the underworld as with the silk stockings. Read this letter to Hardin, Snyder, and Mrs. McCormick," which she promptly did. Terrell replied, "I am very glad that the underworld enjoyed the news that I am to return to Peoria. I shall be glad when they send me back."[42]

Social class played a role in elections, but not as pundits and politicos might have expected. Just after the local ballot in Peoria, Terrell wrote Conway with condolences, "I am very sorry you were defeated in the recent election. But when you think that you lost by only 221 votes with a registration of over 30,000 votes, of which only 2,000 were Negroes, it really seems more like a victory for you than a defeat. Nevertheless, I wish with all my heart you had won." She then addressed a comment he had made about how class had affected the results. Carefully distancing herself from the black elite, she referred to "the silk stockings" as "they" while again playing up her own ability to connect to the lower classes: "I am glad the underworld treated you right. It is a pity the silk stockings make such a poor showing when it is up to them to discharge the duties and obligations which citizenship imposes. They are usually 'weighed in the balance and found wanting' in that emergency. I hope you will have better luck next time."[43]

"A Thrilling Experience"

Out on the campaign trail, Terrell was in her element. She took her first plane ride to travel from one speaking venue to another. A huge fan of Charles Lindbergh, she was delighted that the route was the same one Lindy, as she referred to him, had used when he delivered mail from St. Louis to Chicago. Reveling in defying gender stereotypes, she told Phyllis, "It was a thrilling experience, I tell you. I was the only woman in the plane with ten men. . . . It made some . . . sick, *but not your mother*!"[44]

To provide a thorough account of Representative McCormick's work in the House, Terrell's campaign speeches drew from pamphlets, records of investigative hearings, the *Congressional Record*, and newspaper articles. She pointedly contrasted McCormick's record to that of her opponent, incumbent GOP senator Charles S. Deneen. Terrell critiqued Deneen's long career, including his time from 1896 to 1904 as state attorney of Cook County. While in office, he had collected almost a quarter-million dollars above his salary of $56,000 by pursing convictions for petty misdemeanors in a system that paid him for every guilty verdict. Deneen said it was up to state legislature to change the law.[45]

Terrell combed the *Congressional Record* for any mention of Deneen since he had become a senator in 1925. She provided a detailed description of every time he spoke on the floor during the previous five years to highlight just how little he had said and done. And what he had done was objectionable, she charged. Deneen's first speech on the Senate floor, in March 1926, for instance, was in opposition to a fellow Republican's bill designed to protect farmers from high charges on railroads for short hauls. Terrell reported that "Mr. Deneen took up the cause of the railroads and the bill ultimately was defeated. Organized labor in Illinois has severely condemned Mr. Deneen's position."[46]

Of great interest to African American voters was whether the two Republican primary candidates believed in enforcing the Fourteenth and Fifteenth Amendments. A *Chicago Tribune* questionnaire asked just that. Deneen did not reply, leading Terrell to charge that he "has refused to put himself on record as favoring enforcement of the two amendments of the Constitution which confer suffrage upon colored people." In contrast, McCormick had followed through on her House campaign promise to enforce the law, voting for an amendment to the Census and Reapportionment Bill that, had it been enacted, would have enfranchised African American voters.[47]

Terrell also celebrated McCormick's willingness to challenge the color line in the strictly segregated capital. She told African American voters that "Mrs. McCormick is big and broad enough to treat everybody with courtesy and justice without regard to race or creed. The courtesy which she has uniformly accorded Oscar DePriest since he entered the National House of Representatives is one of many proofs of this quality in her character. She treats Mr. DePriest as she does other members of Congress." Terrell reminded voters of a national news story that told how she saw him in the House restaurant "entertaining at lunch some of his colored friends from Chicago with whom she herself was acquainted. The gentlemen invited [McCormick] to take a seat.... She accepted the invitation, sat down and chatted with them as she would have done with other acquaintances from her State." A white woman sitting to chat with black men was a bold, even radical act. McCormick's civil behavior toward African Americans made some furious whites cry out against "social equality." At that time, some other members of Congress chose to eat at the Senate restaurant "to avoid 'the embarrassment' of lunching in the same room" as Representative DePriest.[48]

In stark contrast, Deneen not only accepted segregation but did nothing after southern senators insulted Mrs. DePriest when First Lady Lou Hoover continued the tradition of inviting all the wives of representatives to a White House tea. To limit controversy, she held four separate teas and invited Jessie DePriest to the last, with just a few carefully chosen congressional wives. Democratic South Carolina senator Cole Blease viciously attacked the Hoovers and DePriests on the floor of the Senate by reading a poem offensively entitled "Niggers in the White House." Terrell responded, "Many present expected Senator Deneen to say a few words in defense of the colored Congressman from his own State. But he sat as silent as a wooden post, absolutely unmoved." She insisted that Deneen did not deserve to be sent back to Washington with the help of any African American voters.[49]

Thriving on the campaign trail, Terrell wrote to her sister-in-law, Laura Terrell Jones, "I am getting along famously now. The opposition to me which consisted of about six or eight catty, envious, jealous women has quieted down now. . . . It will break my heart if Mrs. McCormick is not elected. . . . She is a wonderful woman. I love her both for herself and for her attainments." Terrell shared in the joy of McCormick's success when she won the primary by 175,000 votes. Strong support among African American voters indicates that the early firestorm over Terrell's appointment had not permanently cost McCormick.[50]

The campaign results thrilled Terrell's family, who celebrated her skills as a campaigner and lecturer. Her sister-in-law recalled:

In the fall [1929] when the campaign had just opened there were some visitors here [at Tuskegee, where she taught] from Chicago and after their departure I was saying to one of the men here that my Sister was handling the colored voters' end. This man quoting one of the visitors said "Oh, pshaw! Mrs. McCormick hasn't the ghost of a chance etc." For just a second it upset me and then I rallied and said "Well [all] I have got to say is that my Sister Mollie can put over any job and I think she'll do this one jam up." When I read of the victory I ran to the phone and called this man up.[51]

Envisioning a reprise of her role as a campaign speaker the following fall when McCormick faced her Democratic challenger, James Hamilton Lewis, Terrell returned to Chicago in early September 1930 to secure a paid position. By that point, McCormick faced new and more serious challenges. Most important, Lewis took the popular stance of favoring the repeal of the Eighteenth Amendment on the grounds that it was not working and that the mob was profiting from the illegal sale and distribution of alcohol. His position appealed to Chicago's large population of immigrant voters and other anti-prohibitionists. McCormick also carried the disadvantage of economic privilege. She opened her campaign in the spring of 1930, just months after the stock market crash of October 1929 but, like many Republicans, remained unconvinced that Americans were facing more than a temporary economic downturn. Out of touch with the needs of her constituency, McCormick accused Democrats of "calamity howling." These insensitive remarks were compounded by President Herbert Hoover's inadequate response to the crash. Voters in Chicago and the rest of the state were suffering, and wanting solutions, they were ready to turn to the Democrats. This was the beginning of a political change that ultimately marginalized Terrell in terms of her role in partisan political campaigns. She put a great deal of effort into gaining other jobs in forthcoming GOP campaigns but found her party less and less interested in courting African American voters, who, in turn, were ready to consider the Democrats.[52]

McCormick's progressive reputation, moreover, was damaged by the Nye Commission's inquiry into her primary campaign spending. In September 1930, Senator Gerald Nye of North Dakota, a young, ambitious Republican eager to make a name for himself, investigated McCormick's high campaign expenditures. Holding his first hearings in Chicago in July, he hoped that the publicity would lead to the enactment of his bill placing limits on campaign spending. Thus, he aggressively pursued McCormick, even though she was member of his own party. Initially, she cooperated with Nye and declared that she would support campaign spending limits if they became law. McCormick pointed out that she had not been given the money by lobbyists or corrupt politicians trying to buy her vote. Instead, the money came from her family's wealth and was therefore clean. Nye and others thought that it was inadvisable, if not illegal, for her to have spent so much money. McCormick was unapologetic, arguing that she needed to spend more than her opponents to be taken seriously as a female candidate facing an RNC-backed incumbent senator. But it did not help to emphasize her personal wealth at a time when most voters were concerned about how to sustain themselves at the most basic level.[53]

The Nye Commission hearing exposed McCormick to a great deal of negative publicity immediately before the election. Her opponent was able to caricature her as being unaware of the problems facing ordinary Chicagoans. Terrell exclaimed to Phyllis, "What I would like to do with Nye is nobody's business!" Attending the hearing, Terrell greeted Representative McCormick, reporting to Phyllis: "I told her I had come to bring her good luck. . . . After Court adjourned she said she would see to having my name put on the Speakers Bureau. So that seems to be settled. That means earning some money and I'm glad of it." Terrell again traveled the state giving speeches for McCormick. Because she was not appointed to a leadership role at headquarters, there was no controversy surrounding her appointment.[54]

In the short general election campaign, McCormick also struggled with whether to accept or reject affiliation with the powerful but corrupt Republican Chicago political machine run by Mayor Bill Thompson. Her disavowals of any connection angered the mayor, so just days before the election he circulated a pamphlet charging her husband, Medill McCormick, with racial prejudice. Thompson's tactic failed because African American politicians such as Oscar DePriest came to McCormick's defense. McCormick retained the support of black voters on election day. In fact, the predominantly black wards of Chicago were the only ones McCormick carried. In a Democratic landslide that presaged the shift in national politics, McCormick lost to Lewis by 744,000 votes.[55]

Before Representative McCormick left the capital to return to Illinois, Terrell visited to request a formal letter of commendation for the upcoming 1932 presidential campaign. McCormick complied, expressing her "grateful acknowledgement" of Terrell's "many services" as an organizer and speaker: "Your work required the greatest industry, tact, judgment, and loyalty, and you generously filled all those requirements." On McCormick's campaign, Terrell had secured income, prestige, and an exhilarating sense of purpose. In the short term, Terrell's connections to the Republican Party remained strong.

The McCormick campaign served as a launching pad to a position for Terrell in Herbert Hoover's 1932 reelection campaign at RNC headquarters in New York City. Writing Phyllis, she reported, "I have fairly started on my duties here and I enjoy the work very much, as I knew I would."[56]

For African American women activists like Terrell, Gaines, and Wells-Barnett, partisan politics enabled them to promote their reform agendas while earning good wages. Partisan politics allowed women, who had only had the right to vote at the national level for a decade, to exercise political power and influence. The bitter competition at McCormick headquarters points to the continued limited opportunities available to black women to earn good money and gain prestigious appointments.

Representative McCormick's loss to a Democrat in the 1930 midterm election was just the beginning of a long downturn for the Republican Party, which had an increasingly hard time holding onto both power and African American voters. Terrell remained a loyal Republican until 1952, yet she found that other African Americans were losing faith in the party of Lincoln and turning to Franklin Delano Roosevelt and the Democrats. The 1930s were in many ways a decade of crisis and transition for her, but her developing friendship with Representative Oscar DePriest made her feel less alone in the shifting politics of the New Deal.

Attraction and Politics in the Great Depression

REPRESENTATIVE OSCAR STANTON DEPRIEST

After his long illness, Berto Terrell had died on December 20, 1925, leaving his widow bereft and emotionally drained from helplessly witnessing his deterioration. Mollie and Berto had a strong, loving relationship based on their complementary personalities as well as their shared desire to achieve full citizenship for all Americans. In her 1940 autobiography, she rued what she and the world had lost with her husband's passing: "In the midst of a brilliant career my husband was suddenly stricken and remained an invalid for four years. After a union of thirty years we were finally separated by death. Since then I have been carrying on alone. Throughout his illness he was a philosopher. No man ever bore a similar affliction more cheerfully than he did." Berto had been a true partner in all aspects of her private life and public activism. Mollie reflected, "I did not realize until he passed away how dependent upon him I was for information of every kind. About matters pertaining to the Government, to politics and to every phase of the Race Problem he was a veritable encyclopedia. Now that he is gone it is very gratifying to see the estimate placed upon him by those among whom he lived and labored."[1] Her sense of a strong love and connection to Berto continued to the end of her life. As late as 1949, Berto still meant so much to the octogenarian Mollie that she took a long bus ride and walk to Lincoln Cemetery to bring him long-stemmed red roses: "I was happy to put flowers on Berto's grave," she wrote in her diary.[2]

Widowed in her early sixties, Mollie was still a vibrant woman and prominent civil rights activist. She had received marriage proposals after Berto died but rejected them. Valuing her autonomy, she seems to have intentionally maintained her independence. In 1931, when she was sixty-seven, Mollie Church Terrell chose to begin a love affair with a married man.[3]

In a letter to Phyllis the previous year, Terrell had described herself as having enjoyed a Memphis party given by the Boulé, an elite organization for black professional men to which her husband had belonged. The party featured a large whist card game with thirty players and a dance. She wrote with joie de vivre, "I enjoyed myself very much because I didn't miss a single dance. You know your young mother had a gorgeous time under those circumstances!" Terrell had loved dancing with Berto at clubs and balls throughout their marriage. Always energetic, she still adored dressing up, dancing, and having a good time. If the right man appeared, she was ready to add some romance to her life.[4]

Not just any man could be a good partner for her. It had to be someone who could weather comparisons to Berto Terrell—a man of high professional status, with charisma, intelligence, and good looks. Republican representative from Illinois Oscar Stanton DePriest (1871–1951) fit the bill. Their affair began in 1931, when both of their lives centered around the heady politics of the nation's capital. Their relationship has been missed by most chroniclers of Terrell's life. She tried to be discreet about it in her diaries, so it has, quite simply, been hard to see.[5] Furthermore, less attention has been paid to Terrell's life and activism in the 1920s, 1930s, and 1940s, with historians reentering her story in the mid- to late 1940s to chart her late-life activism. Yet the 1930s mark a crucial time of transition for Terrell, when her personal and partisan dramas converged. She underwent major transitions, including a new relationship, financial pressures, health problems, and the stress of party realignments that threatened her lucrative employment in GOP campaigns as well as her political worldview.

———————

In 1931, identifying with the Grand Old Party still seemed to be a logical choice for two politicos who were committed to rallying African American voters to achieve their civil rights goals. Republican partisanship was part of the bond between Terrell and DePriest, especially as they both found themselves more marginalized as black activists and voters increasingly moved toward Franklin Delano Roosevelt and the Democratic Party. In 1934, Terrell and DePriest's relationship unraveled at the same time that he was replaced by the first African American Democratic Representative elected to Congress. Similarly, Terrell found fewer opportunities for employment in GOP campaigns or in the federal government, where being a Democrat facilitated greater access to jobs in the expanding New Deal bureaucracy.

FIGURE 9.1. A tall, imposing man in his late fifties, Oscar Stanton DePriest, in the light suit (*right*), stands in front of the office of one of the most prominent African American Republican Party politicos, Mollie Church Terrell's half brother, Robert Reed Church Jr., in Memphis, Tennessee, in the months just before or after winning his historic 1928 election as the first African American from the North in the U.S. House of Representatives. (Courtesy University of Memphis Special Collections)

When it began, Terrell welcomed a relationship with DePriest as an opportunity for her to create another collaborative political and civil rights romantic partnership such as she had had with her husband. DePriest and Terrell sent each other newspaper clippings by or about themselves or each other. They gave speeches and wrote statements in support of each other's political, reform, and activist projects, especially their shared civil rights goals. Terrell also volunteered in DePriest's Capitol Hill office, responding to queries he received about African American history and politics. She could talk politics with DePriest to her heart's content.[6]

The comparable political and social standing of Terrell and DePriest was an important part of their mutual attraction. Elegant, well-educated, and cultured, she offered him access to Washington's black elite and the opportunity to be associated with one of the most famous African American women in America. Being linked to Terrell, the activist who had helped found the NACW and the NAACP, accorded DePriest some of her respectability and prominence in civil rights circles. In turn, he offered her a chance to be at the center of African American national political power with one of the most prominent black men in the United States. A powerful and prosperous politician, DePriest could open doors for her in Republican Party circles and further increase her social capital. Both ambitious, Terrell and DePriest relished their standing as leaders who did what was necessary to promote their civil rights goals and themselves. As compatible fighting spirits, neither tolerated prejudice and discrimination without a struggle.[7]

As a male politician, DePriest could leverage his democratic populist persona into political power in a way that Terrell as a woman could not. Terrell claimed her leadership based on her education and respectability as a member of the Talented Tenth, whereas DePriest claimed his authority as an authentic member of the "common herd." He operated comfortably in the arenas of hardball machine politics and urban vice. Because his formal education was limited and because he was determined to be an accessible politician, DePriest proudly and defiantly emphasized his working-class background and speech.[8]

Despite their presenting different public personae, Terrell and DePriest shared childhood traumas of racial violence that led to their championing civil rights. Oscar DePriest was born in 1871 to former slaves in Florence, Alabama. By the end of Reconstruction, African Americans in rural Alabama faced escalating anti-Republican and racist attacks. In 1878, a white lynch mob had come to the DePriest home to find a black Republican politician his father was hiding; shortly after, young Oscar "discovered the blood stains" of three white Republicans who had been murdered outside their home. The DePriests soon joined the first wave of African Americans migrating west to Kansas to escape racial terrorism. These horrible experiences stayed with him and not only made him determined to fight injustice against African Americans but also seem to have left him lonely and in need of attention, even when he was married, famous, and surrounded by an adoring public that viewed him as its champion. Mollie Church Terrell, too, had been traumatized by the results of the violent assault on her father during the Memphis Massacre when she was three, as well as by the 1892 lynching of her childhood friend Tom Moss. Despite her more privileged childhood, she could never forget the brutal violence waged against her family and friends simply because they were successful, politically active black entrepreneurs.[9]

DePriest and Terrell each had something to lose in terms of reputation and respectability if their affair (which was, by definition, scandalous) became public. As a politician, DePriest had been repeatedly accused of immoral behavior regarding campaign contributions and police protection of vice in his district. The discovery of an extramarital affair could have been another way for his enemies to attack his morals. As an African American woman, Terrell, too, had much to lose if their affair were to be exposed.[10]

Terrell knew that African American women's sexuality was always subject to scrutiny and slander. As an activist and a mother, she had spent much of her adult life combatting the stereotype of the immoral, sexually overcharged black female. At national purity conferences, Terrell had demanded that African American girls and women be equally protected against rape and sexual harassment. Aware that her respectability was automatically questionable to hostile whites, she was not one to enter into an affair lightly. If Terrell moved forward with an extramarital relationship, she had to do so carefully.

An older woman whose public identification was as Mrs. Mary Church Terrell, the respectable widow of municipal court judge Robert H. Terrell, she seems to have hoped that her position could provide a shield of respectability to deflect unwanted public attention from her intimate life. Ultimately, the power of their attraction and her excitement about being at the center of American politics seems to have short-circuited Mollie's long-standing commitment to the politics of respectability.

Even after her own affair began, she remained concerned about her daughters' respectability. Phyllis's first marriage had failed, with a years-long separation and later a divorce. Perhaps because Phyllis was young enough to remarry and have children, Terrell perceived Phyllis's behavior and reputation as a bigger problem than her own. It disturbed her that her daughter had begun dating school principal F. E. Parks before she divorced her first husband, Billie Goines. When the divorce was finalized in the early 1930s, her mother thought that Phyllis waited too long to remarry. When Phyllis did so, in 1934, Terrell yearned for an announcement to appear in the society pages of the black news-papers so that she would no longer face rumors and questions regarding her daughter's marital status.[11]

Only a few months after Terrell and DePriest began their affair, she was horrified to find that her other daughter, Mary Terrell Tancil, had been un-faithful to her husband, who was threatening her with divorce. Mary had jeop-ardized her marriage to a kind and loving man, Dr. Leon Tancil, of whom her mother was very fond. To Mollie's great relief, they reconciled. That Mary and Phyllis both violated their wedding vows disturbed their mother. It seemed less problematic to her that she, an older widow, was having an affair several years after her husband's death rather than while she was still married. De-Priest, of course, was married.[12]

Although sharing her secret does seem to have brought Terrell closer to Phyllis, who helped her arrange her rendezvous with DePriest, her daughters might have found it hypocritical or ironic that their mother was willing to enter into a morally compromised situation while condemning their behav-ior so unconditionally. Phyllis lived with Terrell and had to manage the stress caused by her mother's unfulfilled expectations. She may have thought she should receive less criticism than she did since her mother was behaving in a similarly compromised way. Yet Terrell continued to worry more about her daughters' reputations than her own.[13]

DePriest and Terrell socialized at the same D.C. parties, banquets, and con-ventions. He had been married to Jessie L. Williams DePriest for over thirty years and showed no willingness to change his marital status, although he and his wife did not appear close. As a member of his family remembered: "Repre-sentative DePriest and his wife had a 'don't bother me and I won't bother you' relationship. He did not have much to say to her." Terrell seems to have known and accepted the fact that, for political considerations alone, he would never leave his wife. Prominent men like DePriest, as well as W. E. B. Du Bois, re-mained married but had many affairs and were thus conveniently unavailable for a permanent attachment to any other woman.[14]

"He Was Most Cordial"

The nature of the relationship between Terrell and DePriest shifted in Febru-ary 1931. From the start, DePriest seemed energized by taking risks. He began paying her visits at her home, a private setting that allowed them to be alone. One Sunday, she noted in her diary that "DePriest came to see me this morn-ing. He was most cordial." His initial visit itself was not particularly remark-able, since male friends regularly came to see her at home—both before and after her husband's death. She noted those visits in her diary simply to record

the various political and reform topics discussed. Yet Terrell recorded no specific purpose for DePriest's first visit and focused on his personal behavior—
"he was most cordial." Her first mention of his friendly behavior was buried
in her diary in a long list of other events in her typically busy day, including
attending a lecture about Soviet antiracism and having talked with a friend
who suggested that she could solve some of her financial problems by convert-
ing her elegant three-story home in the Gold Coast neighborhood, which she
and Berto had purchased in 1920, into three separate apartments.[15]

Pleased by DePriest's attention and hoping to see him again, Terrell attended a session of Congress the next day. Soon, a diary entry with the word
"Alpha" at the top, read: "Went to Congressman DePriest's office. . . . Talked
with Miss Armistead." When Terrell recognized that DePriest and his staff
were treating her as a special person, she became more guarded in her diary,
making a feeble attempt to obscure which representative had given her a reserved seat: "A Congressman gave me a ticket to the gallery of the House. A
Reserved Seat." Although the evidence in Terrell's diary is easy to overlook,
exciting days soon followed. Trying to be discreet, she attempted to obscure
their deepening relationship. After her visit to his office, the next day's entry
does not mention his name. For a short while, Terrell referred to DePriest in
her diary as "my friend," "my friends," and even as "she," but slipped so often
that she eventually gave up the subterfuge and simply referred to him as "De-
Priest," "DP," or "the Congressman." She did not typically refer to anyone else
as "my friend"; she was far more likely to refer to even close friends by their
formal names, as in "Mrs. Caliver came to see me today."[16]

Representative DePriest's visits to her alone at her home marked her move
away from being emotionally self-identified as the wife and widow of Judge
Robert H. Terrell. There is no evidence she had entertained the idea of having
an affair while her husband was alive and did not seem to consider seriously
the marriage proposals she received after his death. Her March 5, 1931, entry
is therefore notable. She put two check marks by the date and then another
check mark by the words "I had company this morning." Then, she highlighted
the following sentence: "I have been so moved today by an unprecedent[ed]
occurrence I have done little." Terrell's entry characterized their encounter as
"unprecedented," suggesting that she and DePriest acknowledged the strength
of their physical, emotional, and intellectual attraction and acted on it in some
way. The next day, she continued to be distracted: "I can think of nothing but
my visit yesterday morning." There is no mention at all of Representative De-
Priest for a month afterward. It is likely that he was out of town on a speaking
tour, but she may also have realized the significance and danger of the shift
in their relationship. Her strong investment in the politics of respectability
suggests that an affair with a married man was not an easy choice. When she

left Washington, D.C., to speak at the fiftieth anniversary celebration of the Tuskegee Institute, she had the time and distance to consider the situation.[17]

DePriest had no such hesitations. Within a few months of his taking the oath of office, black newspapers were enthusiastically celebrating Representative DePriest, calling him "the outstanding man of the race" and a "National Idol." The *Chicago Defender* described crowds receiving him "rapturously" as he traveled the country. From 1929 through the early 1930s, his speeches were often attended by hundreds and even thousands of adoring supporters, giving him numerous opportunities to initiate intimate relations with women he met. DePriest regularly behaved recklessly.

Newly discovered love letters written to him by younger women residing in different states show that he juggled several extramarital affairs during his time in Congress.[18] By all accounts, women were attracted to Oscar DePriest's dynamic and imposing physical presence, energy, and political power. After meeting him in California, one wrote, "It is wonderful for a nice big Congressman like [you] to be thinking of me when he is so far away and to know that he likes me a *little bit*. . . . I never dreamed when I met you at dinner that Sunday that I would feel as I do today about you. . . . Lots and lots of love, Mamie." DePriest had seduced Mamie at a dinner in his honor hosted by local black Republicans, finding time to be alone with her after the formal event was over. DePriest's affairs were generally with African American women in their twenties and thirties, ardent Republicans who had attended his rallies or dinners in his honor. In general, however, the love letters to DePriest from women other than Terrell contain little mention of politics or civil rights.[19]

Some of his lovers emphasized the difference in their status. One woman in her midthirties flippantly signed her letter, "Getting dumb. Heaps of everything. . . . Just Me." She had just met the congressman and described herself to him after their weekend of sex: "Please don't know me better, as I have no great amount of intelligence. . . . Born in 1895 in Chicago, surname Reid, high school education. Spoiled and erratic and willful. Is that enough?" Their connection had been primarily sexual; she alluded to the size of his private parts in her letter, saying, "This is my dream day honestly I can't contain myself. Darn—wish today wasn't here—that is, was still the memorable 5" + 6" [triple underlined]. Lost in reverie."[20]

DePriest kept in touch with his lovers by phone, postcards, and letters and tried to see them each time he passed through their cities. One enterprising young dancer fantasized about moving to Chicago to be near him: "I do wish I were where you are then I should prove to you *how much I love* and *adore* you. . . . Perhaps I can get a job dancing there in one of the Night Clubs." Then, she gave him her resume: "I do Spanish and Oriental dancing and also High Kick Waltzes. Wouldn't that be divine?" She understood that their relationship was illicit and had to remain private, and gave him instructions he already knew well: "Write on *plain* paper and sign no name. I'll do the *same*. I shall *always protect you* because . . . I adore you with *all* the *fire* of my *gypsy soul.*" With a bold confidence that he would be forgiven, DePriest often left women waiting "until 1 a.m." or deeply "disappointed" when he failed to appear.[21]

DePriest seems to have relied on the male-dominated press to keep his sexual indiscretions out of the public eye. News of an affair might have cut into his support among the majority of African American women voters who backed him but also prioritized their hard-won respectability. Black society, however, seems to have expected great men like DePriest and Du Bois to have insatiable sexual appetites and room for more than one woman in their intimate lives. These men relied on a code of complicit silence to engage in their affairs.[22]

Upon returning from Tuskegee, Terrell found that her attraction to DePriest had not abated. She was pleased when he visited her again and their relationship intensified. Writing self-consciously and cryptically, she noted that she was traveling to West Virginia to speak to students in Harpers Ferry and then highlighted the words: "One of my friends rushed to see me just before I started for train and took me to station." Two days later, in April 1931, Terrell circled the date twice and wrote, "Had an imperative call to go to Congress this afternoon and had a very interesting interview with a friend. At 9 I visited a house whose surroundings and happenings I can never forget. . . . It was truly a red letter day in my life. A treasure [a piece of jewelry] was left by mistake but I phoned about it and was assured it wd. be recovered." Under normal circumstances, Terrell would not have been at a married man's house in the evening without his wife there to greet her. Nor would she have taken off any of her valuable jewelry and, distracted, left it behind.[23]

That day marked the beginning of her first sexual and romantic relationship since becoming a widow. The house she had visited was the large and gracious home of Oscar and Jessie DePriest, who lived in her old LeDroit neighborhood where she and Berto had lived for over two decades. The next day, Terrell recorded: "The pin was brot to me about noon. A friend came to call and staid an hour." And so began a series of secret meetings and separations necessitated by their full and complicated public schedules as well as his obligations as a married man who was, unbeknown to Terrell, also juggling several affairs at the same time. At least initially, Terrell assumed she was the only other woman having an extramarital relationship with this attractive man with a big ego and sense of his own place in history and politics.[24]

Terrell was no fawning younger woman. Then sixty-seven years old—his senior by seven years—she had a commanding presence that captured the attention of those who met her. She impressed her audiences with her poise, eloquence, and a deep, resonant voice, as well as with her strong civil rights agenda. Terrell and DePriest engaged in long discussions about politics. Collaborating to advance civil rights and the Republican Party, they united their political and personal interests. Since their political partnership had begun before their affair, they could be together in a number of public contexts without necessarily raising suspicions about the changed nature of their relationship.

Mutual interests and attraction drew them together, but DePriest's marriage, his other affairs, and his busy schedule in Congress and on the road meant that they struggled to find times to meet. Soon after their "red letter day," DePriest was already preparing to leave on a speaking tour. Although she hoped to see him and waited for him, a disappointed Terrell wrote, "The friend who was to leave did not have time to call." She was distracted from her loneliness by the publication of her article in the *Washington Evening Star* about the fiftieth anniversary celebration at Tuskegee Institute. She wrote in her diary, "O joy, O rapture. My article on Tuskegee appeared in the Sunday *Star* today. 2 columns and a half.... Sent paper to Mr. D. P. who asked me to forward it to Providence, KY where he speaks April 30." Terrell was an activist and author with an agenda and voice of her own, but just as when her husband was alive, she had a special confidant whom she knew would be pleased for her. They often celebrated each other's accomplishments. As she tracked DePriest's travel plans in her diary, she recorded that he had "phoned tonight he would come to call tomorrow, 'I am all alone in the World,' he said." The ego-driven DePriest claimed to feel emotionally alone even though he was surrounded by admirers, was engaging in several affairs, and had been married for over three decades. Mollie Terrell was thrilled to find a new partner, even if it meant that she had to accept the problematic statement of a married man that he, too, was "all alone in the World." For the meantime, she willed herself to believe it.[25]

"Bitter Disappointment"

Serious health problems almost immediately threatened Terrell's new happiness, starting with a case of Bell's palsy that she feared might jeopardize her new love affair by keeping her in pain and making her less attractive, even if likely temporarily, at a point when she wanted to look her best. The episode began within a week of their affair. While promoting education for black children, she found herself "stricken. Thursday is my doomsday. One week ago tonight I had an experience which I can never forget. This afternoon at 4 while I was talking to Miss Mulholland sent by Dr. Anson Phelps Stokes I began to feel difficulty in speaking. . . . The left eye could not be moved and my mouth twisted to the side. I had a case of facial paralysis." At the start of a new romance, when her attractiveness was so important to her sense of self, Terrell did all she could to heal herself quickly while hiding her condition. As she went from one doctor to another, she avoided some of her regular friends and meetings so fewer people would see her. Only DePriest could sometimes break through her insecurities: "Had a call tonight about 8:30 as I was about to go to bed." She and DePriest talked about Republican politics, including who would be his campaign manager and how much to pay him. Then, DePriest convinced her to let him come to her house. She consented and reported dreamily, "I had a soulful time this evening. The young woman who won the Pulitzer Prize says Love makes time pass and Time makes love pass. I wonder."[26]

Another health crisis hit soon after; Terrell had to have all of her teeth removed and a set of dentures made. Her diaries reveal much but also leave much unspoken. An entry from June 1931 reads, "Had 8 teeth removed on upper jaw— a terrible ordeal." Her painful experience was reduced to ten unadorned words. Yet it affected her greatly. The process of extracting her teeth and building a plate of false teeth kept Terrell in excruciating pain for most of that year, but she tried not to dwell on it. The dental work also damaged her public face and affected her speech. It could not have helped that contemporary American culture increasingly prioritized youth and beauty, putting pressure on all women as they aged. Invested in projecting a public image of respectability and elegance at a point when black women were still assumed by most whites to have neither, Terrell remained concerned about her physical appearance. She struggled with whether she should hide herself away or continue to participate in her full rounds of meetings, conferences, luncheons, and more. Terrell either had to cancel speaking engagements or risk presenting herself in a way that conflicted with her goal of always appearing an elegant and eloquent spokesperson for African American women.[27]

When DePriest came back into town and saw her a few weeks later, he charmingly reassured Terrell that their shared connection was not based solely on physical attraction. Terrell circled the date in her diary: "This morning a stranger called me up. I reported I was a wreck." Dismissing the importance of her appearance, DePriest insisted that his attraction to and feelings for her were based on far more: "The friend said 'I love you just the same. It is not how you look but what you are.'" Those kind words reassured her their bond was deep. His open and clear avowal of his love for her—indeed, the fact that he used the word—made Terrell feel so confident that he convinced her to accompany him that evening to an intimate social gathering: "I attended some exercises which began about 8 and remained till 11. I enjoyed them at a private residence as it was much more cozy and comfortable with only a few on such a hot night." As the months went by, a larger circle of their friends learned of their affair. Friends, Terrell's family members, and his office staff knew and even joked with her, making playful innuendoes. A diary entry from December 1931 read, "Blanche Washington said a gentleman [DePriest] who had called on Bishop [E. D. W.] Jones [on] Sunday could not be persuaded to remain longer because he had started out to call on Mrs. Terrell." Terrell seems to have appreciated these coded acknowledgments of her special connection to the representative.[28]

During the Great Depression, Terrell tried to maintain an elite image when she appeared in public by discretely taking old gloves and dresses to be repaired at a discount at a nearby vocational school.[29] A devastating blow came when Terrell and her brother Thomas realized that they could no longer rely on their Memphis properties for income. They first understood this when they received a monthly statement from their rental agent accompanied by a check for only $15. Mollie was a writer and an activist, not a businessperson, and she had hoped that her brother, with his legal training, might be able to monitor their rental agent's accounting system. But he was also unable to do so, especially from afar. According to the 1931 report, their many properties were yielding no returns, and quite a few were in such bad shape that they were scheduled for demolition by the city. Terrell implored the Memphis chief of police "to prevent houses from being wrecked."[30]

Terrell was far more fortunate than those who lost their homes during the Depression, but she did experience a blow to her sense of class respectability and stability. To ensure herself an income, she had to downsize, turning her three-story home into three separate apartments. When the renovations were done, she was "about $500 in debt" but hoped to recoup it with rental income. Drawing up plans, it became clear that "Phyllis cannot have a room to herself. Bitter disappointment to both of us." Terrell and her thirty-three-year-old divorced daughter would have little privacy in the modified house. They moved into the first-floor apartment, a much smaller space than before, and had to give up some markers of elite status as they cleaned "out the garage . . . to make room for the dining room furniture." The lack of privacy in the apartment made things harder not only for Terrell and DePriest but also for Phyllis and her beau, F. E. Parks. In 1934, when Phyllis and F. E. wed, they rented the second-floor apartment despite the couple's many conflicts with Terrell, who perceived her new son-in-law as having weakness similar to her daughter's, including a lackluster work ethic and an overappreciation of drinking, socializing, and playing cards with friends.[31]

A week after Terrell began planning the structural changes to her home, she recorded that "Congressman DePriest came to tell me good bye. He looked at the changes to be made at the house and approved of them." This was a relief, since up to that point much of their affair had been conducted in the privacy of her large home. When DePriest returned from his southern speaking tour, the apartment was finished, and she was pleased by "a phone call this morning saying a friend arrived yesterday. We had a conference about the political situation from 8 till 12. Heard many interesting things. The apartment was praised as having plenty of room for P and myself." The couple still managed to achieve some privacy. On a Sunday morning in December 1931, Terrell recorded in her diary that she had received a "phone call this morning. I was asked to go the office to see the papers on the Bipartisan conference but I did not understand. About 9 I got a phone call asking what was the matter." His elliptical way of indicating that he wanted to see her had been too cryptic. When he discovered the misunderstanding, DePriest told her, "'I'll call this afternoon between 2 and 6.'" Although she waited for him all afternoon, he did not make it to her house until early that evening, when Phyllis had already returned home. As Terrell described it, "Phyllis came, closed the door between the two rooms, turned on the radio and made out her marks [Phyllis taught music in a D.C. school]. My companion and I enjoyed ourselves as usual."[32]

When he was out of town, DePriest and Terrell relied on his staff to stay in touch. He authorized members of his staff to give her his itinerary. With this information, she was able to have a letter or telegram waiting for him at each stop along the way. As they did for the various women he met on his speaking tours, DePriest's staff sent her photos, books, and articles. He managed some of his own correspondence, too, sending a "postcard from San Antonio. Having a good time." Corresponding about his political prospects, Terrell noted that DePriest mailed a "letter asking me to send clippings and saying he expects to win the election 2 to 1. I hope so." She affirmed, "He richly deserves recognition and success," things she deemed important in her own life, as well. Terrell finished her diary entry with: "Went to get my teeth [dentures]. Not ready. Tomorrow afternoon. A friend [D. P.] will arrive Aug. 29th or 30th—Joy!" DePriest sent a letter from Chicago noting, "Yours . . . received and read with a great deal of interest." He also responded to her worries about critics who claimed he was spending too much time giving speeches across the country and too little time in Congress. "My speeches have been a source of great value and an inspiration," he reassured her, "I never worry about what people say about me. It is the votes of the people of my district here in Chicago that counts."[33]

Sometimes Phyllis's and F. E. Parks's friendship with DePriest made Terrell painfully aware of social events she was not invited to. Once, after she had waited all day for a call from him, she "found P getting ready to go to F. E.'s for a little affair for the DePs." On other occasions, however, the three of them "talked a long time about DeP," since they were all invested in his agenda and political prospects. Sometimes, her daughter's connection to F. E. Parks enabled Terrell to join small social gatherings that included DePriest and his wife. In November 1931, DePriest had facilitated an invitation for her to attend a dinner party at F. E.'s mother's home, even though he was bringing his wife. DePriest put his desire to see Terrell over the emotional comfort of his wife, Jessie DePriest, who must have known about her husband's affairs. Eager to spend as much time with him as possible, Terrell willingly put herself in an awkward intimate setting with his wife. Having both women in the same space did not lead him to become reticent. Enjoying the thrill of risk taking, DePriest was the life of the party.[34]

"The Republican Party . . . Must Mean What It Says"

The relationship between Terrell and DePriest was the product of a complex mix of attraction and politics. Both were Republicans who insisted that the Democratic Party could never live down its history as the party of racism, secession, and white supremacy. Yet DePriest had always been more flexible in his partisanship than Terrell; he willingly supported politicians of any party to achieve his policy goals, remain in office, or increase his political influence. This frustrated more steadfast Republican Party loyalists, including Terrell.[35]

DePriest organized a major three-day Non-Partisan Conference for early December 1931. Revealing a tension between their political positions, Terrell used the term "bi-partisan" when referring to it. She did not believe that true nonpartisanship was possible. Their word choices reflect different positions, with Terrell still focusing on the GOP as the only viable option for African Americans, whereas DePriest challenged Republicans to earn the loyalty of black voters. He later explained his dissatisfaction bluntly: "It is difficult to sell the Republican Party as long as its leaders in Congress preach Republicanism by day and are locked arms with race-baiting bourbon Democrats of the south by night, defeating measures that are beneficial to Negroes and other minorities. This is the one thing that makes Negro Americans and other minorities reluctant to trust Republican leadership."[36] DePriest managed to convince Terrell that the conference could help African Americans increase their pressure on the Republican Party to add substantive civil rights goals to its platform. As he told a crowd of 2,500 African Americans in Boston, they could wield significantly more political power: "If the Negro were organized even in communities where they constituted just one-fifth of the population and voted intelligently they could demand recognition."[37]

DePriest timed his Non-Partisan Conference for just before the 1932 presidential election cycle, when Republican president Herbert Hoover would be running for reelection against Democrat Franklin Delano Roosevelt. Almost two hundred delegates from twenty-five states, including "many nationally influential black leaders," attended. They rebuked the Republicans for their inaction on civil rights in a resolution: "The difference between the two major parties was quickly 'dwindling to the point of indistinction.'" DePriest counted on Terrell's prominent participation. The conference was organized around disfranchisement, lynching, civil service, distribution of federal educational funds, economic opportunities, religion and politics, and women in public life. It was for this last session that DePriest invited Terrell to speak.[38]

At first, Terrell chose not to, writing in her diary that "De P was much provoked because I had declined to speak at the Bi-Partisan Conference. I said I thot I was not wanted." His program committee, not he, had extended the invitation, and she told him: "I feared I was not wanted at the conference because nothing had been said to me about it." DePriest replied that she was "'too sensitive'" and insisted, "'I shall put your name down for the afternoon of the 4th at 3 o'clock. The program has not been printed yet.'" But only when he declared to her, "'The man was 'nutty about the woman,'" did Terrell agree to participate. Terrell later called the conference "a good meeting. While I was eating lunch I felt somebody's hand on my face and it was my friend behind me. 'I thought you would holler.'" Although they usually tried to hide their affair from those outside their immediate circle, DePriest pushed boundaries of propriety by boldly touching the face of a woman who was not his wife. His gesture was that of a husband or a lover, not a political compatriot. Terrell knew it was out of bounds but was flattered by his open attention. Despite having been worried he did not want her there, she found instead that he was signaling their physical and emotional closeness.[39]

Received at the meeting as both an elegant woman and an eloquent one, Terrell was pleased not only that her talk was well received but that she was repeatedly complimented on her looks. This mattered to her, especially given her affair, age, recent struggle with facial paralysis, and the ordeal of getting dentures. Her diary entry read: "I spoke this afternoon.... Charlotte Hawkins Brown introduced me in a most complimentary fashion. 'Mrs. T is cultured and refined not as a colored woman but she stands out among women of the world.' The audience arose in respect or reverence. DeP was sitting on the front seat and he arose too. Last night when I attend the reception everybody said I looked like a million dollars. DeP said so himself." Later, she noted, "My friend said last night that he was satisfied because I was properly introduced. He liked the dress and the woman in it." Terrell was gratified to hear that she was still eloquent and elegant and "looked like a million dollars."[40]

Throughout their first year together, even during the many times when De-Priest could not make time to see her, Terrell found their intimate connection a source of solace: "At 11 I was informed that some of my friends [DePriest] were too busy getting ready to leave to call. Sorry. . . . Lonesome but happy. A new interest in life!" Just as he had counted on Terrell to deliver a speech at his Non-Partisan Conference, so she relied on DePriest when she was working on a cause of importance to her. An advocate for world peace since before World War I, Terrell believed that people of color would be better off in a world without battles for colonization and empire. In 1932, she wrote a pamphlet for the Women's International League for Peace and Freedom linking world peace to progress toward the achievement of human rights more broadly. She showcased quotations from prominent black men, securing statements from Du Bois and DePriest and adding an earlier one from Frederick Douglass. DePriest declared: "It is a sad commentary on the inhabitants of the world when disputes have to be settled by force of arms. All . . . civilized people . . . should settle their differences either through arbitration or at a round table conference."[41]

Sometimes, DePriest's and Terrell's busy schedules allowed them to attend the same events separately. As the widow of Judge Robert Terrell, as well as a leading civil rights activist in her own right, she attended a banquet given for East Coast judges. "I was an honor[ed] guest," she wrote, and her introducer "referred to my accomplishments and said when I spoke in three languages in Berlin I attracted the attention of the civilized world." DePriest attended as the only African American member of Congress. "When he arose to speak, he was given an ovation and made an appropriate short talk. . . . Some men took us in their taxi. Had phone call about 2am." Both were celebrated as public figures and enjoyed sharing these experiences. The physical proximity of their houses had permitted them to share a taxi with other attendees.[42]

In other instances, their busy schedules made it harder to connect: "The lady [DePriest] with whom I was to attend a conference phoned. She could not keep the engagement as some friends were coming to her house that night. I was disappointed of course." Another time, Terrell received a call and said, somewhat petulantly, "'I am glad you haven't forgotten me.' DePriest responded, "That would be impossible. Will you be at home tomorrow night?" She explained that she would be at a party and a banquet but that he could arrive at 10 p.m. He agreed to meet her then.[43]

Terrell's final diary entry for 1931 stands out as one of the most expansive and self-revelatory from any year. She concluded that although the year had

FIGURE 9.2. Mollie, in her late sixties, stands for a full-length portrait, resplendent in a gorgeous velvet dress. She is in the living room at her home at 1615 S Street N.W. The Terrells bought the home in 1920 and were among the first to integrate this upscale neighborhood on Sixteenth Street that was eventually nicknamed the "Gold Coast" by African American Washingtonians because those with wealth and African heritage aspired to live in the neighborhood. Even after Mollie had to turn it into three apartments during the Great Depression, it still had a grand living room in which she entertained many visitors, with the fireplace mantel and mirror with its gold gilt frame as the centerpiece. Mollie lived in the home for thirty-four years, from 1920 to 1954; the same fireplace is visible in figure 13.1, taken in the last year of her life. (Courtesy Oberlin College Archives)

been one of her worst in terms of her health and finances, it had been made immeasurably better by her romance with DePriest.

> This year has been good and bad to me. I have converted my house into apartments, 3 of them. I live on the first floor and the second floor is rented, third vacant. I am about $500 in debt $250 due in February. I was stricken at 4pm Thursday April 30 and while I am on the road to recovery, I am far from well. My . . . taste is terrible all the time. I hope for complete recovery. April 23 Thursday 9pm was a red letter day in my life, the week before I was stricken. Something like a miracle has been wrought. I am enjoying a wonderful friendship and I pray earnestly that it may continue. Life without it wd. be dreary indeed. I shall do everything I can to preserve it. Here's hoping 1932 will be at least as kind to me as 1931—I love 1931 for the great gift of friendship which it brought me—I hope it will wax bigger and better in 1932![44]

"I Won't Be a Door Mat!"

Yet their affair became stormier and more painful for her in 1932 and beyond. Terrell grew concerned that DePriest was lying to her about whom he was spending time with and whether he was in the capital or away on business. Until just a few days before she expressed her hope that the new year would be still better, she seems to have naively believed that DePriest was deceiving only his wife. It had not occurred to her that he might be having more than one affair. Her first intimation of this possibility came when F. E. Parks caught DePriest in a lie. On Christmas Day, Terrell noted, "P[hyllis] told me DP was still here. He had phoned F. E. I could not believe it. He told me he was leaving for Chicago Thursday."[45] Terrell's diary entry from Wednesday, December 23, 1931, had noted: "Had a pleasant visit today. My friend told me he was 'just crazy' about a friend he had met here. He leaves tomorrow [Thursday] night for the West. . . . He will distribute more than 1200 baskets to the Chicago poor."[46] Perhaps he wished to avoid having to sneak out to see her on Christmas Eve or Day, holidays when he would be expected to be fully present for and with his own family. Or he might have had plans with another woman. An outraged Terrell was determined to confirm this information. The following day, she engaged DePriest's congressional assistant in a casual phone conversation: "I referred to the nice itinerary DP had and asked when he would leave. 'He will leave tonight' said Lewis. I am shocked at the duplicity practiced. I want to sign off completely. Here and did not even greet me [on] Christmas. Actions speak louder than words. I won't be a door mat!" She deeply resented DePriest's duplicity toward her, even though she had accepted it whenever he lied to his wife and others in order to see her. Considering it betrayal, she saw it as threatening their "wonderful friendship" by making her suspicious and jealous. DePriest and Terrell carried on their affair for two more years, although increasingly tempestuously, even as unhappiness with the new Democratic administration gave them a new focus for conversation and connection.[47]

———

During the 1932 election season, DePriest wrote her from Chicago, "I am lonesome in not seeing you." He reported that the Republican National Committee had assigned him the unenviable job of following the itinerary of the Democratic presidential candidate, Franklin D. Roosevelt. Once FDR finished his speech and left town, DePriest would come to the same place to stump for President Hoover and "talk about the economic conditions confronting this government." Acknowledging the "rather difficult task" of defending Hoover's inadequate response to the Depression, DePriest said, "In the midst of my tasks and responsibilities I carry the thought of you and your interest in me as an *inspiration* and for that reason will always do the best I can, thinking of what you would say in my stead." *Inspiration* had become his nickname for her. A member of DePriest's staff wrote to Terrell on DePriest's official letterhead using the same language: "Dear 'Inspiration,' I suggested to the Congressman that you might appreciate a 'session' pass and he was so happy to have me send it on to you. Hope you're well today. Always Lovingly, Blanche." Just after his reelection to Congress in 1932, DePriest wrote to Terrell thanking her for her "kind words of congratulation, to which you have added words of a closer and more personal interest in my public activities. Your telegram was received and I was happy to realize that your hopes for my future were not blasted by the terrific landslide that swept so many republicans out of office."[48]

Once Franklin Roosevelt won office and the Democrats continued to gain popularity, DePriest and Terrell shared their disappointment in the new president. They were especially distressed by FDR's indifference to issues of racism and violence against African Americans. Representative DePriest confronted the president directly on the issue of white terrorism after introducing an anti-lynching bill in the House in 1933. It passed there but then faced a filibuster in the Senate, which DePriest tried to avoid. He requested and received a private meeting with FDR. Given Democratic majorities in both houses of Congress, he believed that Roosevelt could save the bill if he openly supported it, explaining, "So you see, Mr. President, this much needed bill will erase the strains that the atrocious lynchings have placed on America." FDR replied, "I quite agree with you, Congressman, and I shall do my utmost to have it passed. However, at this moment, I am very busy." When DePriest replied caustically, "Well, I'm

from Missouri, Sir," the president asked, "Don't you believe me? Are you calling me a liar?" DePriest answered, "You can interpret my statement in any way
you choose." Unmoved, the president sent the representative out of his office,
and the bill again went down to defeat. Roosevelt never publicly supported a
federal antilynching bill, guaranteeing that neither DePriest nor Terrell could
change their partisan affiliation from the Republican to the Democratic Party.
They could not forgive this Democratic president or his party for its many failures to protect African Americans, even though the little the administration
did for them was more than any had done previously.[49]

The second and third years of their affair are considerably harder to document
because Terrell's 1932 and 1933 diaries are missing. Over the next two years,
DePriest arranged for Terrell to work as an unpaid staffer in his congressional
office. Thus, he saw her easily when he was in D.C. This arrangement allowed
Terrell to facilitate the political agenda of a man whom she greatly admired
and whose goals she shared. In some ways, it was a satisfying position, for she
enjoyed being at the heart of Washington politics and had already spent many
hours over the years inside the Congressional Office Building, lobbying representatives and their staffs. Her work for DePriest involved doing research
and answering questions from colleagues and constituents on matters relating to African American history. Representative Thomas A. Jenkins of Ohio,
for instance, wrote to his black congressional colleague asking for "material
on the 'Achievements of the Negro.'" At the bottom of the letter, DePriest assigned the task: "Have Mrs. Terrell look this up. DePriest." One J. A. Shelton
of the American Legion of West Virginia wanted to know more about the history of African Americans' service in the U.S. military. Terrell had published
several articles on the subject, so DePriest gave Terrell the letter to answer.
She was pleased to have her political and intellectual skills acknowledged, yet
the arrangement exploited her as an unpaid assistant. Typically, Terrell would
not have agreed to work in any office for free. It also made her available—
professionally, emotionally, and intimately—at DePriest's beck and call. Over
time, Terrell resented DePriest for having taken advantage of her. Her presence in his office also made her painfully aware of his many other affairs, for
he routinely had staff field his lovers' phone calls and requests for photos.[50]

On the first day of 1934, Terrell wrote about their relationship in the past
tense: "I am glad the end has come. There is no pleasure in a so-called friendship with anybody who violates all the laws of friendship, who betrays yr. confidence, tattles to a man [and] has him listen in to his conversations with you.

It is a test!" Proud of his many conquests, DePriest had bragged about their affair. Far worse, he had verified it to an incredulous male acquaintance who could not imagine the respectable Mollie Church Terrell in this role. Sophomoric and insensitive, DePriest invited his friend to eavesdrop on intimate phone conversations. As their relationship unraveled, Terrell was more hurt by his philandering and the cruel eavesdropping incident than by his remaining married.[51]

By early 1934, Terrell and DePriest were testy and ill at ease with each other. Witnessing the increasing popularity of Roosevelt's Democratic Party among African American voters, they correctly feared that DePriest, and the Republican Party more broadly, might lose seats in the upcoming midterm election. This added a sense of pointlessness to their continued association. Two weeks after the entry describing the eavesdropping, Terrell noted a phone conversation with DePriest that showed her trying to resist conversing with him and him knowing how to draw her right back in: "Call tonight. [DP:] 'How are you?' [MCT:] 'Who is this?' [DP:] 'You know.' [MCT:] 'No, I don't. Who is it?' [DP:] 'You know damn well who it is.' [MCT:] 'Of course, I do now.' [DP:] 'Hear your daughter is going to get married.' [MCT:] 'I don't know anything about it.' And soon a lot of talk about F. E." DePriest pulled her into a conversation about her daughter's marital prospects. When he stated he had "just got back from Chicago yesterday," she replied jealously, "I don't know when you go or come any more. You phone other people." She knew of his other affairs, but DePriest tried to reassure her and answered, "You are the only one I've phoned. We'll go to the Night School some time you and I together." When Terrell asked, "Did you go to the reception (President's) last night?" he smoothly replied, "Yes, I would have been happy if I'd have been there with you." DePriest continued his overtures, but she finally decided that she had had enough of playing second, or even third, fiddle. DePriest provoked Terrell by revealing that he had tried to call at her house with his wife. As she wrote in her diary, "D. P. called me up. I told him I didn't want to see him. He said he and his wife had called to see me but I wasn't at home." If she had been home, she would have had to host their visit graciously. Their affair was clearly over, but either he could not let go or chose to taunt her.[52]

DePriest continued to value his connection to Terrell because of her social prominence. By the election of 1934, the political ground had shifted on DePriest and caught him unprepared for the increasing realignment of black and immigrant voters to the Democratic Party. After he lost his reelection bid to the black Democrat Arthur Mitchell in the fall of 1934, DePriest was determined to have Terrell be the "toastmistress" at a huge farewell testimonial dinner being given in his honor as he left Congress, for she was an eloquent and entertaining public speaker. He lobbied her incessantly and enlisted Phyllis and F. E. to persuade her to do it. Terrell steadfastly refused to be put in the awkward position of praising him publicly when she felt betrayed. She fumed: "He has treated me brutally. I worked in his office gratuitously for nearly 2 yrs off and on and he refused to let me use his machine when I wanted to type a manuscript." By the time it ended, their relationship had shifted far from the ground of mutual compatibility and respect which she had presumed when it began.[53]

More than his lies or the end of their affair, DePriest's refusal to let her use his office typewriter became the focus of her resentment. His denial of her attempt to work on her autobiography, her claim to a place in history, hurt the most. She had already spent over a decade writing and revising it for publication. She had made trips to see publishers in New York and elsewhere but was repeatedly rebuffed. Her inability to find a publisher created a sense of failure. It salted the wound for DePriest to reject her request, especially after she had given her labor for free. She found herself a supplicant, with a level of dependence she found deeply uncomfortable. She had initially anticipated that her high-profile partner would help make her voice heard in public. Instead, he slowed her efforts to share her life story.[54]

In a dramatically changing political landscape, DePriest and Terrell had steadfastly remained Republicans. Vehemently opposed to large federal deficits, they could not let go of their objections to the big-spending federal relief programs of the New Deal. They both found themselves on the defensive, trying to justify their political positions and respond to the dominance and popularity of the Democrats and their New Deal. The new political climate was not good for African American Republicans, and they paid for their unwillingness to move into the Democratic Party. DePriest finished his final term in January 1935 and returned to Chicago. There is no evidence of continued communications between them after he left the capital.[55]

While it lasted, their affair had provided Terrell with excitement, a passionate political compatriot, and a satisfying intellectual connection with an equally powerful and compelling personality. For a time, these benefits made it worth the risk and the effort. When the affair finally ended in 1934, Terrell, then seventy, was left feeling alone and vulnerable at a point when continued financial pressures compelled her to find full-time employment in, ironically, a New Deal agency.

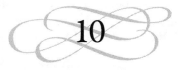

Discrimination and Partisan Politics
in New Deal Agencies

I n a material and political bind in the mid-1930s, Terrell experienced several stresses as she tried to find paid employment. Not only had her relationship with DePriest soured, but a seventy-year-old Terrell struggled
against intersecting prejudices regarding her race, gender, age, and partisan affiliation. All converged to create a difficult employment environment
for her.

Once in office, President Franklin D. Roosevelt declined to move substantively away from the Democratic Party's longtime endorsement of segregation
and discrimination. In the expanding New Deal bureaucracy, racial prejudice
led supervisors to reject Terrell's applications, despite her strong qualifications.
Even when she did secure employment in low-level jobs, she encountered racism in government offices. The indignities Terrell received while employed in
the federal government expose pervasive racism within New Deal agencies.
Segregation and prejudice in state-level administrations and in the distribution of New Deal programs is well documented, but there are fewer accounts
of how black employees experienced discrimination in government agencies
in the nation's capital. Terrell's seven-month sojourn there in 1934 illuminates
one black woman's personal perspective on her New Deal work experience.
Her interpersonal encounters in the federal workplace highlight her acts of
defiance on behalf of African American wage earners.[1]

Terrell was not just searching for a job to pay her bills; she sought a prestigious position that would help her maintain her hard-earned reputation as
a well-known civil rights activist, journalist, and community leader. But she
encountered the wrong side of patronage politics with the triumphant ascen-
dency of FDR's Democratic Party. Her public loyalty to the Republican Party
made it nearly impossible for her to find a high-profile position in the federal
government.

Once she secured employment, Terrell risked her job by openly protesting workplace racial discrimination in the federal government. Furthermore, she continued her civil rights activism, including working with the NAACP and the Communist Party's International Labor Defense on behalf of the Scottsboro Nine.

"If I Were More in the Limelight"

The Great Depression and subsequent New Deal did not represent the first significant moment when African Americans tried to gain greater access to federal employment. During World War I, Terrell and her daughters, both young adults, joined other hopeful black applicants who applied for a variety of jobs, hoping that the wartime expansion of the federal workforce could get them in doors usually shut to them. Like most educated African American women, they lacked career options beyond teaching (and this profession was closed to Mollie Terrell as a married woman). In spite of wartime need and their qualifications, the Terrell women were denied most jobs on the basis of race. When they did get employed, they invariably encountered prejudice. In 1917, for instance, Mollie Terrell was hired but then fired from the War Risk Insurance Bureau because whites expressed discomfort about working with her. She then found a new job at the Census Bureau but quit in protest over the forced segregation of the women's restrooms.[2]

Disturbed by the discriminatory employment environment for black workers during World War I, Terrell helped create the Woman Wage Earners' Association of Washington, D.C., in 1917. African American women were generally excluded from unions; this group encouraged them to organize, unionize, and demand protections. Terrell formed the group with leading NACW members Julia F. Coleman and Jeanette Carter, arguing: "Our women wage-earners are a large factor in the life of the race. They are becoming more so every day as the business interests of the race expand and the demand for intelligent workers grows with expansion." After the war, Nannie Helen Burroughs and Mary McLeod Bethune expanded the group into the National Women Wage-Earners Association, which affiliated with the NACW and lasted from 1920 into 1926. Even after the GOP regained the presidency and Congress in the 1920s, black men and women faced increasing hostility from white government coworkers as well as systematic segregation.[3]

The Great Depression and the presidential election of 1932 offered yet another opportunity for black Republicans to engage their party in a serious discussion about employment discrimination in the federal and private sectors. The head of the Tuskegee Institute, Robert Moton, tried unsuccessfully to help President Hoover see that African Americans were suffering under "regulations and practices enforced against colored employees that subject them to inconveniences and indignities purely because of their racial identity." Hoover and the GOP ignored him and other loyal African American Republicans.[4]

———————

When her work for Representative Ruth Hanna McCormick had ended in the fall of 1930, Terrell again looked for paid employment. She pieced together a living by writing for newspapers, giving lectures, campaigning for the RNC, and collecting rent from her property in Washington, D.C., while applying for work in governmental agencies. As a public intellectual and activist, she needed a high-profile position to continue securing income as a writer, speaker, and political campaigner. This tension expressed itself in a mainstream white publisher's mid-1930s rejection of her autobiography. As Terrell summarized it, "They would publish it if I were more in the limelight."[5]

Terrell's least realized but most deeply held ambition was to be a professional fiction writer who could make a decent living solely from her writing. She wanted recognition, like Frances Watkins Harper, Pauline Hopkins, or Jessie Fauset, as an author of short stories and novels. Containing heavy-handed messages about racial equality and progress for African Americans, her stories were not her best work. Still, Terrell credibly identified herself as an author (if not a fiction writer) because she regularly published in journals and newspapers. Over a few years in the early 1930s, Terrell published an occasional article in the *Washington Star*, a leading white newspaper in the nation's capital, for example, earning from $10 to $25 each (about $160 to $390 in today's dollars). Terrell's sister-in-law congratulated her, noting, "To command that much space in a big daily like the 'Star' is to my mind an achievement."[6]

Serving on boards and committees also allowed Terrell to engage in social activism while enhancing her public prominence and credibility as a writer and speaker. She lobbied hard to get these prestigious unpaid positions and was pleased in 1931 when the progressive white New Jersey minister Buell Gallagher appointed her to a subcommittee on race relations of the National Council of Churches. She also pressed behind the scenes for an honorary degree from Oberlin College. Terrell was not alone in using this approach. Other prominent black women, including Alice Dunbar Nelson and Georgia Douglas Johnson, also experienced financial and employment difficulties as they grew older. In 1944, at sixty-four, Johnson wrote letters to friends to see if she could secure "some kind of a degree (honorary) tacked on to me so that I can get work or something that will not keep me to the grindstone as this job does."[7]

Terrell had long been aware of ageism. Several months before the stock market crash, she had advocated pensions for older Americans, explaining, "It is becoming more and more common for corporations and employers to discharge men and women at the age of 50 or less, under the pretense that their efficiency is on the wane." She wrote approvingly of states that realized that "an effort must be made to provide old age pensions." Indeed, ageism had long been a serious problem in the U.S. labor market due to mandatory retirement rules. During the Depression, older workers were pressured to give up their jobs; politicians and employers alike argued that their positions should be given to younger people. Terrell was seventy when she looked for and found work in the federal government at a time when the life expectancy of American women was seventy-five.[8] American business culture preferred youth, conventional beauty, and whiteness. Only about 7.5 percent of white female clerical workers were above forty in the 1930s. Black women held "only .5 percent of all female office jobs in 1930."[9]

Viewing herself as exceptionally fit and vigorous, so much so that when she was in her seventies, Terrell visited Mordecai Wyatt Johnson, the first black president of Howard University, and offered to become dean of women after the death of the long-time incumbent, Lucy Slowe: "Went to see Mordecai Johnson to tell him he is one of God's Favored Sons. I had thought prayerfully about this and the thought had come straight from Heaven. I told him Howard University should celebrate the 100th anniversary of Coeducation and then I said, 'I should like to be Dean' and left my record." Aware that her age might be held against her, she asserted: 'I am younger than either one of my daughters, I can walk farther and faster and have greater powers of endurance.' 'You are wonderful,' he said. Maybe nothing will come of it, but I was guided to say it." Nothing did come of it. It was likely painful for a proud woman like Terrell to think that people might be viewing her as elderly.[10]

"The Most Flagrant Discrimination"

The election of Democrat Franklin Roosevelt had not led to immediate or sweeping changes in hiring or to improved conditions in government jobs for African Americans, despite their hopes that it would. Secretary of the Interior Harold Ickes had ended segregation in restrooms and cafeterias in his department in 1933, but his support of integration did not encourage others to do the same. Although merit requirements had helped African Americans gain and retain jobs based on performance alone, Roosevelt tried to curry favor with southern whites by ending merit requirements, meaning that African Americans could be arbitrarily barred or removed from jobs on the basis of race.[11]

Terrell and the local District of Columbia chapter of the NAACP had launched letter-writing and telegram campaigns against employment discrimination but achieved few improvements. As a prominent branch member, Terrell frequently received accounts of discrimination in federal employment from African Americans asking for her help. Just before she began her own search for a government job in December 1933, Harriet Lee wrote to tell her about her son, Milton A. Lee, who had been offered three jobs, only to be dismissed when his race became apparent: "The most startling of all occurred Tuesday when at 10 minutes to three p.m. he was called over the telephone to report for duty at the Munitions Building at once. He was there at 4 o'clock and when they saw that he was colored the clerk informed him that the place had been filled." His mother worked in a government office and believed herself "powerless to fight this to the bitter end for I must retain my position." Instead, she asked Terrell to call for change because she was already openly "fighting for the civil rights of our race and against segregation and the most flagrant discrimination . . . in making appointments of clerks."[12] Terrell and her fellow activists opened doors for more black workers and took important steps toward racial equality, but not until 1941, as the nation mobilized for another world war, did the number of African Americans hired into civil service positions improve significantly.[13]

The institutional culture in the district and federal administrations did not honor Terrell's qualifications and experiences and generally expected her to show the subservience and invisibility assumed of lower-ranking employees. Racial discrimination pervaded administration agencies at all levels of government. Terrell repeatedly found herself the only African American hired. Her white coworkers often resented her presence, and she was also the first employee to be fired.[14]

On a cold day in January 1934, Terrell began her search for a job by walking from one office to another to meet with officials who might employ her. By the end of the day, she had entered five or six different offices and talked to at least seven managers. She found a position with the Public Schools of the District of Columbia at the "Francis Junior High School section to work up Community Center there." She had previous experience with this kind of work. During World War I, the War Camp Community Service had hired her to set up community centers for African Americans throughout the country. Her Depression era job involved going door to door for six hours at a time, visiting poor and working-class black families on D.C.'s west side, a trek from her home. These families became the nucleus of a new neighborhood community center.[15]

Despite her greater education and social class, Terrell was personable and sympathetic, so people told her their stories. She wrote: "Heard two tragedies in my rounds—a man shot another 3 times in S. C. on account of his attention to his wife and a woman told me her husband was a gambler in Atlantic City and was shot and killed instantly." Although she was good at the job, after only five days, she asked for a better one. Commuting across the District, walking in the cold, hearing the stories of terrible tragedies in the lives of the people she was meeting, and Terrell's conviction that she was being underused and underpaid all inspired her to seek something less burdensome.[16]

Her request was honored when she was offered a position as "Drama Leader and Lecturer" for the school district, a job that appeared well suited to her talents. Terrell had informed her employers that she had written pageants on black history, such as one on the life of the poet Phillis Wheatley, that had been performed in the D.C. schools. But she hesitated to take the post once she heard that she would "have to work 6 hours a day 3 to 5 and 7 to 11pm. I told her I wasn't sure I'd accept. She was peeved and spoke curtly to me. She said she can't be changing jobs." Terrell's confidence in her own value as an employee might have seemed like pushiness or arrogance, especially if her employer believed that she was doing an older African American woman a favor.[17]

Terrell did not take the position, for the hours meant that she would "never get home before midnight" and would have to walk and take public transportation at an unsafe hour. She worried that the schedule "would nearly kill me. . . . I would be a perfect slave." In addition to being physically exhausting, the job threatened to interfere with her ability to do what mattered most to her—civil rights activism. The late schedule would have kept her from attending her many evening meetings. So, Terrell reversed course, making a point of telling her immediate supervisor: "I love going from house to house meeting people." She was good at it. Sympathetic to people's plights, she successfully elicited their stories and proved to be an excellent organizer. Still, she continued to search for something that would allow her to have fewer financial worries without making her "a perfect slave" to her job.[18]

A couple of weeks later, Terrell wrote in her diary: "The Washington Branch of the Oberlin Alumnae voted unanimously to ask Oberlin to confer an honorary degree upon me for the service I have rendered my race and for my efforts at bringing about a better understanding between the two races." She hoped the honor of being nominated would increase her prominence, thereby allowing her to secure a better position in the federal government. But her hopes went unrealized. In her government jobs over the next several months, most of the whites she worked with remained oblivious to her accomplishments or felt threatened by them.[19]

Determined to find a position that would be a better fit, Terrell approached the secretary of the director of the Board of Public Welfare, asking for an appointment to see a Mr. Reed. Hoping to discourage her, his assistant forced her to wait all day. But Terrell remained in the waiting room, unintimidated and undeterred. Terrell's persistence again paid off; when Reed finally did see her, he offered her a better job in a government office with daytime hours.[20]

Terrell's new job would be interviewing applicants for emergency relief, a key component of the safety net offered by the New Deal. Ironically, two years later, during the 1936 campaign, in keeping with Republican Party positions, she strongly criticized federal relief programs and the New Deal more generally. In 1934, however, she focused on more immediate concerns. Reed assured her that she "would get $15 the first week and then he would reclassify" her. During the Depression, $15 a week was considerably better than what domestic servants made in 1935 New York City ($3 a week) but was about what garment industry workers were earning ($12–$15 a week). When he did not follow through on his promise to raise her salary, Terrell waited for several weeks and approached Leroy Halbert, director of the Division of Emergency Relief, but it made no difference.[21]

Entering the workplace, Terrell was painfully aware that federal offices were highly segregated spaces and that Washington remained a segregated southern city. Fifteen years after having worked for the government during World War I, she found that African Americans were still not welcome in federal agencies. White women frequently protested working with black women, reflecting prejudice and fears that their own purity and respectability, sexual and racial, might be diminished by proximity to black women in integrated workrooms, restrooms, and cafeterias. During the New Deal, only a few African Americans obtained government jobs outside of a limited number of divisions, such as the U.S. Postal Service. Moderately sympathetic white reformers who entered the New Deal's federal bureaucracy did not manage to change the culture. During World War II, white women still wanted "to maintain social distance" and not work alongside black women. In fact, from the nineteenth century through World War II, white women workers walked out on strike and/or protested working alongside black women, especially objecting to sharing bathrooms and cafeterias.[22]

When Terrell initially asked to change from community organizing to an office job, she was acting in line with her practical concerns as an activist who wanted time to attend meetings and as an older woman worried about late work hours and the amount of time she was expected to be walking outside in the winter. Yet the community organizer position had the advantage of allowing her to work independently while visiting African American families in their homes and apartments. The question of racism in the workplace did not arise. Once she began office work, Terrell recognized the behavior of her white coworkers and supervisors as racially motivated attempts to undermine her in a variety of ways. When she first went to get paid, for example, "Nobody told me what to do or how the thing was done." The white workers in her office watched her struggle to figure out how to get her paycheck, making it harder for her than it needed to be.[23]

Terrell was sure her white coworkers were keeping their distance while hoping she would fail. Given the history of petty and pervasive racial discrimination against African Americans in federal jobs, she was probably right. It may be that her less well educated white coworkers resented not only her race but also her more educated, elegant, and perhaps even superior or condescending demeanor. Terrell certainly resented their unwelcoming silence, writing in her diary: "It is most unpleasant to work with cheap ignorant white people."[24]

Wishing to avoid playing into racist stereotypes that supervisors and coworkers could use against her, she worried about being late or doing anything that could be seen as lazy. Many black workers were fired for less. She recorded nervously that "Mrs. Neilson referred to people seen on the street at 11 o'clock in the morning. I went to see about my lost check at the Treasury Annex about that time." Months later, she "rushed to the bank at noon. Bot [sic] milk when I returned and went down into the basement to drink it. Just as I finished, I turned around and saw Mr. Whitsey. I wish he had not seen me at that hour although I do not take recess either in the morning or in the afternoon. I work overtime." Terrell was certain that her work ethic and behavior had to be perfect for her to have a chance of keeping her job.[25]

Terrell also encountered explicit racism. On her first day on the job, she interviewed those of both races. At least one white coworker found it inappropriate for her to interview white people seeking assistance. The prospect of their revealing their financial problems to a gainfully employed black woman was too much for the white woman, who expressed her disapproval directly to Terrell. White clients came up to the fair-skinned Terrell in a room full of white employees, probably assuming that she, too, was white. This misperception upset her coworkers.[26]

Within two months, a supervisor openly told Terrell that she was reassigning her to a different floor where she would no longer be interviewing white people but would "make out the records for the interviewers." In spite of her disappointment about the racially motivated transfer, Terrell expressed some relief at getting out of a difficult workroom. She had stubbornly persisted in interviewing any whites who came to her, ignoring the objections of her white coworkers and supervisors. As she started her new job, she reflected, "I shall like the work. It will be better than being embarrassed making out applications and instructed not to make them for white people. Of course, I did make them for white people when they sat in my chair." It took an emotional toll to resist the pressure to interview only black applicants.[27]

Transferred to yet another position later that year, Terrell found her white coworkers trying to segregate her within her first few days on the job: "This morning when I reached my work, I found 2 newly appointed white men in my place. They were seated next to the little funny-looking specimen by whom I had sat Friday. I simply put my purse and hat right on the table in front of my place, climbed over the bench and sat down! They had planned to put me down at the end of the table and segregate me. I just wouldn't stand for it." She remained determined to fight back, even if it meant squeezing in next to whites whom she did not respect.[28]

Terrell also witnessed her white coworkers harass and humiliate African Americans who applied for relief. One "morning a poor colored girl cried because she needed help and her husband was ill. A bad snowstorm raged outside. Cosman told her to go home and get papers to prove she had lived here one year." Terrell would not have sent the young woman back into the snow and resented gatekeeping white bureaucrats like Cosman, who did what they could to make it difficult for African Americans to get emergency relief.[29]

She also found herself subjected to a common tactic used to harass black government workers—the refusal of supervisors and coworkers to give black employees any work to do, making them sit idly and so implying that they were not needed. When Terrell and several other employees were reassigned to a new office closer to her home, she arrived promptly, only to sit "all day reading without being assigned any work. It is harder to be idle than it is to work. . . . I am greatly disappointed." The reassigned whites, she noted, were immediately put to work.[30]

In response, Terrell spent days going from office to office trying to keep her job while encountering people who were "curt," "very nasty," and "too busy to see" her. After again waiting hours to see Mr. Reed, she "followed him down the steps talking to him." Exasperated, his secretary asked, "Now what's the trouble?" Because white clerks were quickly reassigned whenever work dried up, Terrell not only persisted but was incredulous of claims that no positions were available. In the meantime, she continued to go to the new office, where she sat idle. Finally, someone relented and gave her something to do: "I worked hard all day writing messages for the people who complain and want to say something to their case worker. I was alone for at least 1 ½ hours. A young [white] woman met me on the street as I was going and said she wanted to change places with me to write messages. She was posting, she said, and she heard me say I like to post. We went to Mrs. Dodson's. When she saw me she said 'Is this the Mrs. Terrell you meant? You'll have to see Mr. Swelzer.' He refused to make any changes." The idea had come from Terrell's white coworker, and Dodson had orally approved it; all seemed fine until Terrell's race became an unmentioned but undeniable issue. Within a week, Swelzer fired her.[31]

"Mrs. T., They Say You Belong to the NAACP"

In early May 1934, Terrell went to see Leroy Halbert, the director of the Division of Emergency Relief, to protest her firing. She "told him frankly about Miss Neilson [a supervisor] who said I was critical." Halbert's response reveals how Terrell's presence raised the hackles of white employers, supervisors, and coworkers: "Mrs. T, they say you belong to the NAACP, that you write for colored newspapers and that you are critical." All three complaints had nothing to do with the quality of her work but focused on race and what they had begun to learn about Terrell's prominence within the African American community as a reformer, activist, and writer.[32]

Activism was not a valid reason for firing her. Terrell was not a civil service employee, but even if she had been, the rule of such employment forbade only active election campaigning while on the job. Advocating reform, even if with a political agenda, was not against the law. Yet other African American civil service employees were wrongly fired simply for being members of activist civil rights groups like the NAACP.[33]

Terrell knew all this but remained undeterred. Leroy Halbert's charge, however unfair and irrelevant, was accurate. She remained involved with the local and national NAACP in the 1930s and beyond; she also worked with the Communist Party–affiliated International Labor Defense to help free the Scottsboro Nine.[34] During her time as a government employee, she served as chair of the Committee on Charities for the NAACP's D.C. branch, became secretary of its Committee on Finance, and was a member of its Committee on Education. She had also agreed to be listed as an NAACP branch speaker to fill impromptu requests for lecturers who could discuss any pressing civil rights issue. In addition, she served as a member and treasurer of the local NAACP's Inter-Racial Committee, which focused on "discrimination in the schools of the District," one of her longtime concerns.[35]

Terrell remained active with other organizations, as well. While an employee of the federal government, she was also secretary of the Committee on Race Relations of the Washington Federation of Churches, attending meetings and preparing the minutes. In 1934, the group undertook several key projects, including improving the condition of housing for African Americans in the District, exploring the question of how "to prevent race riots," and protesting the lynching of George Armwood, a black Maryland man, through a letter-writing campaign and by having its members attend House committee hearings on antilynching legislation.[36]

The committee's biggest undertaking in 1934 was its support of Representative DePriest's attempt to allow black members of the public to eat in the House cafeteria. Terrell's personal and political relationship with DePriest and her own longtime resistance to segregation in federal cafeterias and restaurants meant that she eagerly participated in this campaign. As she had with the National Woman's Party during World War I, Terrell joined direct action protests. Participating in cross-class collaborations with the New Negro Alliance, she picketed stores in the Don't Buy Where You Can't Work campaign. These protests successfully pressured stores that profited from black customers to hire black workers. Her participation is reminiscent of her work during the Great War, when Terrell had organized black women workers to improve their conditions. She was also an active member of the League of Women Shoppers, left-feminist consumers who supported the labor movement by organizing under the slogan "Use your buying power for justice." The league supported strikes and boycotts and pressured store owners to provide better pay and safer working conditions for laborers. She continued to support working-class African Americans during the Great Depression.[37]

Terrell also joined the Committee on Citizenship of the National Conference on Fundamental Problems in the Education of Negroes. The conference was sponsored by the Secretary of the Interior Harold Ickes's Office of Education, where a Terrell family friend, Ambrose Caliver, worked as a senior specialist. Terrell agreed to collaborate and proposed that she focus on "The Part that Woman Plays in Promoting Citizenship." Even as she worked full-time as an unrecognized clerk in a federal agency, she engaged in significant, sustained, and visible civil rights activism.[38]

Yet Terrell refused to let Halbert dictate the terms of their conversation by forcing her to defend her activities outside work. She ignored his mention of the NAACP and flatly denied that she published newspaper articles, based on the technicality that she had not published anything while she worked full-time for the government. She reported in her diary: "[I] told him I did not write for colored or white newspapers and that I simply tried to get the proper material with which to work." Focusing on the obstructions she encountered at work, Terrell redirected Halbert's attention to her need for the "proper material" and support to do her job.[39]

On the issue of being critical, Terrell pointed out that she was blocked on the job and was critical only of being harassed and not being given what she needed to do her best work. She ignored the larger meaning of the word, which included both her public activism and her willingness to oppose her working conditions, her low pay, and the discriminatory segregation and racist slights she experienced from coworkers and supervisors alike.

Not sure how to respond to Terrell's emphatic self-defense, Halbert tried to deter her from seeking redress by stalling, telling her to remain in his office: "'Stick around,' he said. So I sat there nearly all day. It was hard." Refusing to be intimidated or shoved out of a job, she stayed outside his office door for hours. She returned the next day, only to be told that he was too busy. From there, she went to see several other Roosevelt administration officials in order to find a job. When she went back to Halbert's office for the third time, "he sent word at 4:35 to report for work at Mr. Whitsey's tomorrow morning! Am I glad!" Terrell's persistence and assertion of her rights had again paid off.[40]

Terrell was thrilled with her new appointment in a section of the Emergency Relief Division under the supervision of Charles Whitsey, who was somewhat more open-minded on issues of race than her previous white supervisors. Showing both sympathy and distance, Whitsey told her that he felt connected to African Americans because his aunt had taught black students at Tougaloo College and Oberlin and that he had met some of them when he visited her home. Terrell shared her background and accomplishments, hoping that he would treat her with respect. He did, but it did not translate to better working conditions; she again faced immediate hostility from her white co-workers who did not know, or care to know, who she was. On her second day there, Terrell recorded, "I bought a bottle of milk at a little luncheonette next to John Marshall Place. I sat down at a table to drink it. After a while I realized the woman in front of me was not there. She had left her sandwich to complain that I was sitting at her table, I am sure. Lo and behold it was the white woman and her friend in the department in which I work. Trouble ahead!"[41]

Her academic excellence, qualifications, and experiences made her certain that she could and should find work and be treated with respect. Terrell reflected, "It seems a shame that a woman who has had the training, the experience and the success that I have had should be unable to find anything to do to earn a living." In her refusal to accept segregation at the office worktable or in the lunchroom, Mollie followed the example of her father, who never backed down when faced with discrimination. He had used the 1866 Civil Rights Act to challenge his arrest for operating a pool hall despite a state law granting billiard licenses only to whites. The judge agreed and dismissed the charge against him. As her sister-in-law saw it, "You surely are Bob Church's daughter for I have thought so often of the things you have told me of his bravery." Fiercely determined, Mollie refused to give up even in the face of dispiriting and humiliating rejection.[42]

Terrell had showed courage in 1930, too, when she was hosting the prominent black educator Fannie C. Williams of New Orleans and another friend. Her visitors were in D.C. attending President Hoover's Child Welfare Conference. When they were hungry and there were no dining options for African Americans anywhere nearby, they had entered the Interior Department restaurant. Terrell had warned them that it was segregated and thought that they were ready to confront white hostility. But when the white cafeteria manager showed open antagonism, her guests left the restaurant so quickly that they did not even tell her they were leaving. She tried to convince them to go back, but they refused.[43]

Determined not to be intimidated, she returned to eat alone. But, she wrote later, "Just as I was finishing my meal . . . I saw a policeman. . . . 'Why did you come in here, Mr. Officer?' I inquired. 'Oh, I just came in to see what was going on,' he replied. 'No, I beg your pardon,' I said, 'you came in here to intimidate me. . . . I haven't broken any law, but you came in here for me just the same.'" As she walked out of the restaurant with the officer, a crowd of white restaurant workers and patrons gathered to watch, anticipating her arrest. But there was none. When the conference ended, she "went to the Secretary of President Hoover and to the Secretary of the Interior, Dr. Ray Lyman Wilbur, and related the story to them. But . . . I was advised against instituting a law suit for damages in this case, as I was in another [the incident with the Delaware ticket agent]." Having no viable legal recourse was frustrating. (Terrell finally got her chance to challenge a restaurant for racial discrimination when she filed a successful lawsuit against a segregated eatery in 1950. The Supreme Court's 1953 ruling in her case dismantled segregation in D.C.'s restaurants and stores.)[44]

Given her white coworkers' hostility at the lunch table, Terrell knew there would be yet more racism and resistance in the office. When she described the rest of her day, which involved "making out blanks showing how much is given to recipients of relief," she noted with some concern that "Mr. Lee, Mr. Whitsey's Ass't pointed out several mistakes." She reflected, "It isn't hard work, but one has to learn it." Terrell reasonably feared that even trivial errors by a new worker could be used by disgruntled whites as an excuse to fire her. Another time, anticipating the worst, she asked a supervisor "if any complaints were made about me to tell me, so I could defend myself."[45]

A week after Halbert challenged her activism, Terrell became involved in a left-wing protest on behalf of the Scottsboro Nine, Alabama teenagers (only one had reached twenty) who, in 1931, had been falsely accused of rape and sentenced to death. Their plight remained a priority for civil rights activists in 1934. The NAACP had declined to represent them; it generally avoided defending black men accused of raping white women. But the Communist Party's International Labor Defense took up their cases. In 1934, the Communist International, or Comintern, began to emphasize fighting fascism and working with noncommunist allies through its popular front strategy, rather than focusing on the immediate overthrow of capitalism. From the 1930s through the 1950s, the communist left used the rhetoric of domesticity, familialism, and a "valorization of black motherhood" to support the black freedom struggle in the United States.[46]

The Communist Party's International Labor Defense gained the goodwill of African Americans by championing poor black defendants like the

Scottsboro Nine. It collaborated with prominent African American allies, including Mollie Church Terrell. In spite of Halbert's comment, she refused to be intimidated and let go of her activism. Terrell accepted the invitation of William L. Patterson, an African American attorney and Communist Party leader of the International Labor Defense, to join a delegation of women accompanying "five Scottsboro Mothers" to the White House on Mother's Day, asking Roosevelt "to intervene, to exercise his moral power to put an end to the machinations of the legal lynchers of the South." Terrell had earlier written editorials and speeches against the unjust convictions. An indifferent Roosevelt declined to meet them or send a high-ranking official in his stead. Terrell shared Patterson's assessment: "The failure on the part of the President to meet with these grief-stricken mothers . . . [gives] moral support to the lynchers." Like the International Labor Defense, Terrell pointed to racial discrimination and disfranchisement in the South as strikes against the Democratic Party. Her collaborations with the American Communist Party were not unusual during the Great Depression and World War II, when a fair number of prominent noncommunist African American activists participated in popular front protests.[47]

In her conversation with Halbert a month earlier, Terrell had pointedly ignored his description of her as a prominent activist, but she brought her prominence to bear when it might help. In early June 1934, a white community leader named Elwood Street became the new director of Public Welfare after having headed the Community Chest organization. He and his wife knew Terrell personally because as the longtime president of the Southwest Community House, she was an ex officio member of the Community Chest's board of trustees. In January 1929, Terrell had appeared on the radio urging African Americans to contribute "liberally," explaining that "as a colored woman the Community Chest appeals strongly to me personally because it enables people of all races and religions to help each other without thinking how they may differ in color or creed." Because the Community Chest pooled its donations, black organizations benefited from funds donated by whites as well as by African Americans. Terrell had also recently interacted with Street in another capacity, for in early 1934 he had been nominated to be a member of the Washington Federation of Churches' Race Relations Committee, of which Terrell was the secretary.[48]

When Street and Alice Hill, the new director of emergency relief, met Terrell coming out of her office, she reported that he "presented me to her with great flourish of trumpets. 'Mrs. T is one of Oberlin's most distinguished alumnae,' he said. 'She was recommended for a degree of doctor of philosophy.' That seems providential. I hope it will mean something substantial to me." Terrell was thinking of a better, well-paying job.[49]

Within a month of Street's arrival, Terrell was asked to speak at a program honoring Leroy Halbert when he left his position as director of the Division of Emergency Relief. It appears that Street's familiarity with Terrell's background played a role. His support also led Miss Meister, Halbert's usually officious secretary, to treat Terrell with more respect. Meister invited her to give one of three tributes. Later, Terrell wrote: "I was selected to pay a tribute . . . from all the many capable, highly educated white people in the organization. I was not asked to represent colored people but I was asked to pay a tribute to him for the whole organization. I was loudly applauded."[50]

Once back in the office, Terrell's supervisor, Whitsey, said, "I want to congratulate you upon doing a fine job. Your speech was perfect. I would not change a word of it." Some white coworkers also complimented her: "This morning as I sat at work, I heard someone say 'Is your name Terrell?' I looked up and said 'Yes.' 'Well I want to tell you you made a wonderful speech Saturday. It was very fine.' Mrs. Clawson who sits opposite me asked, 'Were you the only speaker?' 'They asked me to pay a tribute to Mr. Halbert.' 'Have you written your speech? I should like to read it.' I told her Mr. Whitsey was going to have it mimeographed and give it to people who want it. 'I would like to have it,' she said." Her white coworkers, who had rarely spoken to her before and had not known her name, had become interested in finding out a bit more about her and even said a few words to her. Having gained some respect, Terrell hoped to build upon it.[51]

"The Same Bitter Dose of Race Prejudice"

A few weeks later, knowing that she was still being underused as an office clerk, Terrell "saw Miss Hill, Director of Emergency Relief and told her to give me a good job. She remembered me and said Mr. Street told her who I am." But Terrell's assertive approach did not produce results. At the end of July, she wrote in her diary that Whitsey's "force is to be reduced and I shall have to go." Writing later in her autobiography, she clarified: "I was the only colored woman working on the files at that time and I was the only woman dismissed. And then, in trying to get employment elsewhere I had to swallow the same bitter dose of race prejudice in my old days that I did in my youth." Although Terrell acknowledged her age, she considered race the bigger obstacle. When Whitsey tried to help place her in other divisions, the men he called indicated that they needed workers and readily agreed to consider her until she appeared for an interview and they realized she was an African American.[52]

Knowing how difficult it was to be hired in all-white government divisions, Terrell predicted that she would not be hired when, in one case, she "had to walk down a very long room full of clerks, all of whom were white and most of them women. To me that was painfully significant." When the man doing the hiring saw her, he suddenly realized that he did not need another clerk after all. Terrell put it clearly: "Colored people are the last to be hired and the first to be fired." She wrote that Whitsey, who had suggested her for the job, "praised my poise and bearing and appearance but Mr. Sterner would not give me a job." Whitsey's recommendation had focused on her external appearance, rather than her competence, which suggests that he was trying to convince Sterner that this particular light-skinned, well-educated African American woman would not visually or otherwise disturb her white coworkers. On July 26, 1934, Terrell succinctly recorded: "Mr. Turndale, one of the men working with me on the master files got a job today. He is white. I didn't [get a new job]."[53]

Just before her seventy-first birthday, after months of trying to secure and keep a position, Terrell wrote, "Without a job. I felt very bad this morning both physically and mentally. I have lost my job." Her departure from that position proved bittersweet. Some of her white colleagues had begun treating her with respect and indicated that they liked the quality of her work, but she was forced out before she could develop truly collegial relationships with them. On her final day there, she recorded: "I went back to the office to get some papers about 7 and found Mrs. Baine there. . . . She said 'Mrs. Terrell, you have been so nice to everybody.' She said she wanted to keep my boards for herself. Mr. Whitsey said he enjoyed his association with me more than with the other clerks."[54]

Still holding out hope, she wrote to the one person she thought might best understand her worth, the director of public welfare, Elwood Street, explaining that she would like a job with him. Street replied neutrally "I appreciate very much your thought that you would like to work with me. I wish there were some opening, but unfortunately the Emergency Relief Division is cutting down on their staff rather than adding to it." Terrell's work in federal agencies had come to an end.[55]

As Terrell's public role as an activist had become more visible, her employers and potential employers also became more aware of her continued connection to the Republican Party. This visibility added political party to race and age as another significant problem in her search for a job in the heart of the New Deal. Other African Americans had begun switching to the Democratic Party. Although still second-class citizens under the New Deal, they did receive relief and, sometimes, employment, albeit at lower levels and less pay than whites. As the incumbent party, the Democrats had patronage jobs to offer, and partisanship became an important qualification, or disqualification, for employment. On her last day of work, Terrell wrote, "I called up Miss Meister to tell her I had lost my job and she said everything is in politics now. One must have political backing."[56]

The following year, Terrell helped organize a Conference on the Betterment of Race Relations in Washington, D.C. The gathering issued a report in 1935 that included stark statistics. Of the more than thirty-five thousand people working in federal jobs in Washington, fewer than two hundred were black. "The government has taken no interest in the economic recovery of the Negro," it averred. In her own evaluation of the Roosevelt administration's hiring record, Terrell concluded: "It is exceedingly difficult for a colored woman to secure employment, no matter what her fitness may be, what service she may have rendered her community or her country and no matter how great her need."[57]

Based on her experience as the only black woman in the various New Deal offices in which she had worked, Terrell was certain that her race was her greatest burden: "I am well aware that the inability to secure employment for its citizens without regard to race, religion, or sex is a vexatious problem. . . . But the average broad-minded citizen in this country . . . does not realize that for every difficulty experienced by a white woman or a white man seeking a way to earn his or her daily bread, at least 50 times that many confront his brothers and sisters of a darker hue." Despite the difficulties and indignities endured by Terrell and other African Americans, she and her fellow activists opened doors and took important steps toward racial equality. At the same time, finding ways to protest and address discriminatory workplace practices gave her a larger sense of purpose and maintained her fighting spirit.[58]

Her many personal struggles against racial discrimination in New Deal agencies reaffirmed Terrell's refusal to switch parties; she simply could not see the Democratic Party as the more inclusive and racially progressive one. Her experiences also highlight the limitations of the racial politics of the New Deal. African Americans who voted for Roosevelt did so as a way to register their support for New Deal programs, but many refrained from formally changing their party affiliation until the late 1940s. Terrell believed that black voters could be wooed back to the GOP if it would only take steps toward civil rights and job patronage.[59]

It got more difficult to defend her party loyalties with the rise of the New Deal Democrats, the shift of many African American voters out of the Republican Party, and a growing disinterest on the GOP's part to try to keep or win back black voters. Once the party abandoned its courtship of African Americans, Terrell found paid campaign work harder to come by.[60]

11

Remaining Republican during the Rise of the New Deal Democrats

The upheavals in Terrell's personal life in the early to mid-1930s, including the end of her affair with DePriest, experiences with discrimination while working for the government, and continued financial vulnerability combined to heighten her anxieties about the destabilizing changes occurring in partisan politics. Terrell remained in the Republican Party in the 1930s and 1940s, when the great majority of African American voters were beginning a long, uneven, but decisive partisan realignment to the Democratic Party. Terrell's personal discomfort over this shift mirrors larger political dilemmas facing African American voters during this tumultuous time.

In 1932, the Democratic candidate for president, Franklin Delano Roosevelt, won the election without significant support from African American voters, who remained loyal to (if increasingly ambivalent about) the party of Lincoln. After FDR's victory, Terrell tried to make sense of the changing political landscape. In 1933, she even asked friends in New York City to help get her daughter Phyllis hired by any party in the city's mayoral campaign.

Quite a few prominent African American Republicans made the leap to the Democratic party as New Deal legislation helped all Americans to varying degrees. Yet, during FDR's presidency, southern Democrats continued to wield much power in Congress. Roosevelt often acceded to conservative demands to maintain the racial status quo in exchange for their support for his fiscal and regulatory policies. His refusal to support antilynching legislation in the Senate confirmed for Terrell that she simply could not campaign or vote for him or his party.

In this rapidly shifting political climate, Terrell uncharacteristically and cynically pondered unconventional approaches to defeating Roosevelt. Feeling politically unmoored, she briefly considered a fringe proposal to encourage a third-party coalition between the GOP and anti–New Deal Democrats (including southern racists) in a last-ditch effort to deny Roosevelt a second term by drawing Democratic votes from him. On a practical level, in 1936, Terrell needed a job. The Republican National Committee had been her most reliable employer since the enactment of the Nineteenth Amendment. For the first time since 1920, Terrell did not gain a paid campaign position, and she realized in the campaign's last days that the party was virtually giving up on winning back African American voters.[1]

"In Defense of the Republican Ticket"

Stepping back to look at the 1932 campaign to help reelect President Herbert Hoover, we find Terrell moving from her work for Ruth Hanna McCormick to becoming Assistant Adviser to Colored Women in the RNC's eastern campaign headquarters in New York City. This prestigious position provided an influx of much-needed cash.

Given that the economy had not improved under Hoover, Terrell and other African American Republican women faced skepticism among black voters. Perhaps that is why the white director of the RNC's Women's Division, Lenna Yost, who had played a role in securing Terrell's position on the National Planning Board for Colored Voters, wrote of her concern that Terrell's official statement of support for the Republican Party mentioned Hoover only once. Yost correctly suspected that it signaled Terrell's ambivalence about the candidate.[2]

Terrell had reached out, as she had in the past, to secure endorsements from prominent African American Republican women. Mary McLeod Bethune endorsed Hoover, although by the next presidential election she had become the best-known black woman associated with the Roosevelts, the Democrats, and the New Deal. Also responding to Terrell's request was Nettie Langston Napier, president of the Frederick Douglass Memorial and Historical Association and a leading Republican woman in Tennessee: "We women are working with complete faith in the reelection of Herbert Hoover and with deep and sincere loyalty to the party to which we owe our advancement." After Hoover's defeat, Napier wrote to Terrell, her good friend, with a more blunt assessment: "As our advocate or friend Hoover was *never that*. Our hope was in him *only* because he represented our party." Hoover's most dedicated black women supporters were barely that.[3]

Some of those Terrell had contacted reported that many African American voters they spoke to were "bitterly opposed to the President." For one thing, Hoover had not appointed African Americans to federal jobs. One black campaigner explained that voters were also unhappy about Hoover's nomination of the segregationist North Carolinian Judge John J. Parker to the Supreme

Court. Terrell had actively opposed Parker's confirmation. Representative De-Priest had fought vehemently and successfully to block the appointment in the Senate. Yet while in the employment of the RNC, she hedged: "The President did not know [Parker's] views regarding our racial group" when he nominated him, Terrell said. She remained concerned about whether this excuse was viable, as a question she asked a coworker reveals: "Tell me what the reaction was when you presented these facts to the women."[4]

Unlike the enthusiastic speeches she had given for Ruth Hanna McCormick, Terrell's speeches for Hoover fell flat. One, "In Defense of the Republican Ticket," illustrates how difficult her task had become. Terrell found herself awkwardly defending prejudice in the Hoover administration. Most African Americans had been deeply offended when white and black Gold Star Mothers were booked on segregated trips to visit the European sites where their sons had fallen during World War I. Again, Terrell had also opposed that decision but felt compelled to defend it on the campaign trail. She did so with the weak argument that the accommodations and treatment the mothers received, although different, were substantively "the same." In short, she used a version of the separate-but-equal argument from the 1896 *Plessy v. Ferguson* decision she loathed. She insisted, "Whatever your criticism *and mine* of divisions in the classes of our citizenry, it cannot be leveled at the Republican Party. Nor can the Democratic Party, responsible as it is for all manner of segregation, and grossly unfair and unequal segregation at that, hope to win votes by raising this type of false issue." Terrell was still waving the bloody shirt when it came to domestic policy choices.[5]

Terrell tried to deflect criticism of Hoover's earlier work overseeing relief in the South after the great 1927 Mississippi River flood, when some African Americans sheltering in relief camps were impressed into labor while others received less aid and fewer jobs than whites during rebuilding. She complained that black critics of the GOP "seek to place on the Republican Administration all the burdens for prejudice and injustice in the Democratic South." The repressive conditions and unequal distribution of resources and work, she insisted, had been directed at the local level.[6]

Terrell had two responses to the question of economic recovery. First, she claimed that the "wild extravagances of the [Democratic] Wilson Administration during the World War is the cause of the unfortunate financial condition of the country more than any other one thing. Millions of dollars were spent for equipment which was not needed and which had to be destroyed when the armistice was signed." She further reasoned the Republicans could not be held "responsible for the hard times" because of the global scope of the economic collapse.[7]

Moving away from her uncomfortable defense of the GOP, Terrell found it far easier to find fault with the Democrats. A strong proponent of peace, U.S. neutrality, the self-determination of all nations, and anticolonialism, Terrell castigated the Democrats for their policies on Haiti: "Under President Wilson's administration the United States marines seized Haiti in the name of the American Government and occupied it, although Haiti had been an independent government for more than one hundred years, was a member of the League of Nations and signed the Treaty of Versailles as such." Haiti was relevant to the 1932 election because Franklin Roosevelt had been assistant secretary of the U.S. Navy when the marines moved in. He proudly touted his writing of Haiti's new constitution, but Terrell saw him as having "snatched from that small and helpless country every right which it had previously enjoyed as a sovereign nation and made the people of Haiti vassals of the United States."[8]

Roosevelt's decision to cater to the white South on the issue of race, including his choice of white Texan John Nance Garner as his 1932 running mate, had made it impossible for Terrell and many other African Americans to consider abandoning the Republican Party. She believed that it was genuinely unsafe for black Americans to vote for the Democratic ticket. In 1901, Garner had endorsed white supremacy and supported disfranchising African American voters with a Texas poll tax. She contended that in spite of its attempts to repackage itself, "the South *is* the Democratic Party." As Terrell pointed out, even after the Supreme Court had ruled in *Nixon v. Herndon* (1927) that African Americans had the right to vote in Democratic primaries, several southern states, including Texas, had resisted the decision and vowed to "circumvent the highest law in the land." Suggesting that the Democratic Party's unofficial slogan in Texas was still, "This is a white man's party. . . . No Blacks need apply," Terrell reminded audiences, "If anything should happen to Roosevelt, Garner would be president of the United States."[9]

But in 1932, Terrell's confidence in her party was shakier than ever before. She publicly conceded that not all Democrats were inherently bad: "There are broad-minded, justice-loving Democrats in the North as well as in the South, who stand for a square deal and fair play, it is true." She also admitted that her own party's approach was flawed: "Even though one grants for the sake of argument that the Republican Party might have done more to promote the welfare of colored people than it has done. . . . Of whatever sins of omission or commission the Republican Party may be accused, the fact remains that colored people are indebted to it for the only rights and privileges which they enjoy as citizens in the United States today." That the GOP had its own sins was not a strong argument.[10]

Yet most African American voters in 1932 agreed with Terrell and with the Republican campaign's slogan, "Who but Hoover." They could not overcome their concerns about the Democrats, including FDR's unwillingness to fight states' rights, which guaranteed the continued entrenchment of segregation and inequality. Hoover ran from 70 percent to 80 percent ahead in those urban districts that were largely African American. The only exception was in New York City, which turned out to be a harbinger of the national political realignment to come. There, just 46 percent of African Americans voted for Hoover; 50 percent voted for FDR.[11]

Headquartered in New York City during the 1932 presidential campaign, Terrell had recognized that African Americans there were joining the Democratic Party. In a private letter, she wrote: "There are a great many colored people in New York who are Democrats and who I fear will vote the Democratic ticket." She continued, "However, I am very hopeful . . . Hoover will be elected and we shall be spared the horrible possibility of having Garner the Texan in the White House." Immediately after Hoover's defeat, Phyllis wrote her mother, "Needless to tell you how I feel about the election. There was a landslide. It is a shame. But you did all you could so you musn't feel bad. . . . The people just wanted a change."[12]

"Under the New Deal the Daughter Is a Loyal Democrat"

In 1933, Terrell had tried to get Phyllis a job in New York City's mayoral campaign and had drawn on her political and professional networks for help. Phyllis was at the time engaged to Krishna Sobrian, originally from Trinidad, who lived in New York City.[13] Terrell's desire to see her daughter married to a man who promised to be a good husband trumped her partisanship. She was thrilled with Phyllis's kind and attentive beau, who spoke of marriage and treated his potential mother-in-law with love and respect. So, early in October 1933, Terrell mobilized her connections to try to get Phyllis a job as soon as possible, hoping it would induce her to leave her life in Washington, especially her other beau, F. E. Parks, behind.[14]

Elite African Americans could not typically exercise direct favoritism because they were not the ones giving out jobs. Rather, they relied on a reciprocal system of favors to assist others in their circles to obtain work. In this instance, Terrell called on her friends Roscoe and Clara (Carrie) Burrill Bruce, who had been key members of Washington's black elite before they moved to New York, where they seemed well placed to help Phyllis. Roscoe Bruce, the Harvard-educated former assistant superintendent of black schools in the District, was the son of Blanche Bruce, the senator from Mississippi during Reconstruction, and his wife, Josephine Beall Wilson Bruce, who were longtime friends of the Church family and of Mollie. In New York, Roscoe and Carrie Bruce were managing the Paul Laurence Dunbar Apartments and publishing a paper, the *Dunbar News*. The Bruces had become Democrats and tried to get Phyllis a job in the mayoral campaign, but that year's complicated election made it difficult.[15]

Realizing that the city was already on its way to becoming an African American Democratic stronghold, Mollie and her friends made some strategic political maneuvers. In 1933, Phyllis Terrell Goines became a New York resident by listing her uncle Thomas A. Church's address as her own. She then registered as a member of the Democratic Party with her mother's approval. This remarkable move could have threatened Mollie's continued access to RNC patronage, but her interest in finding her daughter a job in New York outweighed such concerns.[16]

New York City's 1933 mayoral campaign was a messy three-way race in which independent parties played a key role.[17] Following the money, Mollie's friends tried to predict which would pay for campaign work and which would win. Bruce apparently did not approach the Tammany Hall Democrats. Introducing "Miss Phyllis Terrell" (rather than Mrs. Phyllis Goines in order to avoid discussion of her divorce and to emphasize her ties to the Terrell family), Bruce began by writing to the Reverend Adam Clayton Powell Jr., a prominent African American serving as campaign manager for the Recovery Party's mayoral candidate. Bruce stated: "Her father and mother are nationally known as Republicans but under the New Deal the daughter is a loyal Democrat." Although there was a Democrat running on the major party ticket, Franklin Delano Roosevelt was quietly supporting Joseph V. McKee, the Recovery candidate, in a private effort to create a group of loyalists there.[18]

The decision to have Phyllis register as a Democrat turned out to be a mistake. Fiorello La Guardia, the City Fusion/Republican candidate, won the election, dealing a blow to Tammany Hall and its old-school Democratic bosses. After the election, an undeterred Bruce wrote optimistically to Mollie, "We have friends in the LaGuardia administration. . . . They will gladly help Phyllis." However, he could not find her a job.[19]

Had Phyllis quickly obtained work, she might have moved to New York and married Krishna Sobrian. Without it, however, Phyllis began to pull away from her suitor. She may very well have resented her mother's heavy-handed interference in her love life. Still living in her mother's home and working in the District, she continued to see F. E. Parks and ultimately married him.[20]

This time of partisan flux created other acrobatics on the part of formerly Republican African Americans, some of whom attempted to rewrite history. The editors of the *Pittsburgh Courier* informed Terrell that, "under the leadership of Hon. Robert Vann, we have changed our politics." The editors asked her for a photo of her deceased husband, whom they incorrectly wished to highlight as "among the early colored Democrats." Mollie did not agree to this request to misrepresent Berto.[21]

"Mrs. Roosevelt . . . Insisted on Equality"

From the start of his first term, President Roosevelt had been unreceptive to requests that he pay greater heed to the concerns of African Americans. Instead, the First Lady was evolving into a champion of civil rights. Eleanor Roosevelt's intellectual and moral growth as an antiracist was encouraged in the mid-1930s by her developing friendships with African American activists, especially educator and activist Mary McLeod Bethune and Walter White, the executive secretary of the NAACP. In the first year of the Roosevelt administration, Terrell had asked to meet with the First Lady, but her request had been declined.[22]

Terrell may have been hoping to provide the kind of friendship and guidance that, during FDR's second term, became Bethune's role as her friendship with Eleanor Roosevelt grew. Bethune was well positioned to press the First Lady, whom she had first met in 1927, on issues of racial justice. She was the president of Bethune-Cookman College, a former president of the NACW, and founder and head of the new National Council of Negro Women (NCNW), and she had become a registered Democrat.[23]

Terrell saw herself as Bethune's mentor as well as her friend. They had regularly visited and corresponded with each other and worked closely when Bethune headed the NACW from 1924 to 1928. At a Founder's Day celebration of Bethune's National Council of Negro Women, in 1940, Terrell gave a speech recalling the first time she met Bethune, who was a dozen years her junior, at an NACW convention. Bethune "waited to speak and president wouldn't let her. I urged the president to give her five minutes. She did. I was sorry when she stopped, told her she had qualifications and characteristics which NA of CW needed, hoped I would live long enough to see her president."[24]

During the New Deal era, they continued to collaborate. Along with Jane Spaulding and Carter G. Woodson, for instance, Terrell and Bethune advocated federal funding for the proposed National Exposition of Negro Progress and Achievement. Spaulding, president of the West Virginia State Federation of Women's Clubs, enlisted Terrell to lobby Congress for such funding and to speak at a 1936 Senate Appropriations Committee meeting. Terrell's initial report of her work in the halls of Congress inspired Spaulding to write, "I knew that you were the best qualified person in our group to act as lobbyist. . . . You may rest assured that should the bill pass, a position on the staff will be yours." After visiting D.C. to assist Terrell's lobbying efforts, Spaulding wrote: "I enjoyed being with you; it is a great pleasure and privilege to work with you. I think that I have caught some of that indomitable spirit that radiates from you; it makes me very happy to know that I have your help in this work." Terrell, Bethune, Spaulding, Woodson, and a few others spoke before the Senate committee. Terrell noted, "I conducted the meeting and read the statement about the N. A. of C. W. and the plan for the Exposition." They successfully gained congressional support for an American Negro Exposition to be held in Chicago in 1940, under the sponsorship of a variety of New Deal programs.[25]

During the Great Depression, a time of heightened class tensions among poor, working-class, and middle-class women, Bethune had come to view the NACW as exclusive and out of touch with politics and with black working women's concerns. Indeed, at its 1930 convention, the NACW had dramatically narrowed its expansive agenda by cutting its thirty-eight departments to two: Mother, Home, and Child and Negro Women in Industry. Bethune was frustrated, too, that black women's voices were subordinated within the white-dominated National Council of Women, which had only one national black women's organization, the NACW, among its thirty-plus member groups. Bethune founded the National Council of Negro Women in 1935 as an independent national political organization to allow black women to speak for themselves on all critical political and legislative issues and to be able to join the predominantly white National Council of Women. Although concerned about diluting the power of the NACW, Terrell agreed to join Bethune's new association as the NCNW's first vice president.[26]

In July 1935, Terrell was probably unaware that Mary McLeod Bethune was about to be appointed to an advisory committee of the National Youth Administration (NYA). Busy trying to get a position there herself, Terrell wrote to Josephine Roche, assistant secretary of the Treasury, offering to work on behalf of African American youth and proposing that she be hired to conduct fieldwork for the NYA. Roche's assistant replied: "I have told her of your interest in the problems of the colored younger generation which, I am sure, are just that much more acute than the other half of the world, and as you know, we both have your problems very much at heart."[27]

A month earlier, Josephine Roche had been invited to present Bethune with the NAACP's prestigious Spingarn Medal for her work promoting social justice. Roche was so impressed with Bethune's list of accomplishments and her speech at the awards ceremony that she recommended to Eleanor Roosevelt that Bethune be placed on the NYA's National Advisory Committee (which she soon was). Then, in June 1936, Bethune was appointed to head the new Division of Negro Affairs of the National Youth Administration, which made her the highest-ranked African American woman in the federal government.[28]

It was not out of the ordinary for Terrell to record a visit from Bethune in her diary, but the reason for the visit was extraordinary: "Mrs. Bethune came to see me tonight. . . . She told me she had been appointed Supervisor of the Youth Administration and will get $5,200 a year [at a time when average annual income was about $1,360]. Her office will be in Wash." Bethune wondered: "'What will Nannie Burroughs say?' . . . and then smiled significantly." Burroughs, the founder of the National Training School for Girls and Women and head of the Women's Auxiliary of the National Baptist Convention, would also have been eager for the job.[29]

These three strong African American women had worked together for years in the National League of Republican Colored Women and held leadership roles in the NACW. During the New Deal, each sought a well-paid and important government position like the one Bethune secured. They had all been loyal Republicans, but it helped Bethune that she had become a Democrat. Terrell did not register any jealousy in her diary and even recorded with equanimity a grandiose statement Bethune made later that year: "Went to NACW Headquarters. Mrs. Bethune talked about Youth Administration and told of the wonderful things she was doing. 'I am Esther. I want you women to help me,' she said." By comparing herself to the biblical queen who saved her people from destruction, Bethune was saying that she aimed to save her race from the worst of the Great Depression and invited black clubwomen to assist. Bethune's sense of her own importance extended even to small issues. In 1946, when she and Terrell were both going to New York City to attend the National Council of Women, Mollie wrote: "Bethune called up early. She wants to room with me at Waldorf Astoria. Was angry when I said Vivian Mason had assigned me to Mrs. Bryant. 'I room with anybody I choose,' said Bethune." And Terrell complied.[30]

––––––––––

As Terrell sought out opportunities to meet Eleanor Roosevelt at national conferences and frequently heard her speak, the First Lady's increasingly progressive stance regarding race gained her admiration. Terrell and other African American women appreciated her unpretentious disregard of racial hierarchies and growing interest in advancing racial justice. At the same time, Mrs. Roosevelt was making some white women uncomfortable, especially conservative southern Democrats who did not like how the party was changing. When Terrell went to hear the First Lady speak at the U.S. Chamber of Commerce in March 1935, she was pleased that Roosevelt acknowledged her with a smile and a nod from the podium. Terrell grew upset, however, when a white southern woman who sat down next to her and, assuming she was white, "criticized Mrs. Roosevelt saying she showed poor taste in running around so much, that she was like her Uncle Teddy, that her husband could do nothing with her, etc." When the woman asked Terrell her name, she physically recoiled and "moved away from me and sat at the end of her seat!"[31]

As the First Lady became more vocal in her advocacy of civil rights for African Americans, Terrell's enthusiasm increased. In April 1935, for instance, she heard Roosevelt speak at the Metropolitan A.M.E. Church, reaching out to those who were ready to hear her most progressive ideas. Terrell exclaimed that the First Lady "was wonderful. She insisted on Equality of all kinds, educational, employment, etc. She urged colored people to get what they want through politics. It was the most courageous thing she ever did. She is truly a good, useful, and noble woman! I love her."[32]

Yet Terrell's now-ardent support for Eleanor Roosevelt did not translate into an appreciation of her husband. Nor did it lead her to switch to the Democratic Party. Terrell's short diary entry from about a week later says it all: "Heard President Roosevelt's Fireside Chat. He said nothing about Lynching." During his first term, Eleanor's progressive ideas had not changed her husband's stance on the basic racial justice priorities many black voters considered a litmus test. Terrell believed that given his Democratic majorities in Congress, President Roosevelt could have exerted the necessary pressure to get an antilynching bill passed in both houses of Congress. His inaction made it impossible for her to change parties.[33]

During her husband's first term, Eleanor Roosevelt fought hard against his inner circle's reluctance to press forward with civil rights policy. A 1935 conference on "The Position of the Negro in the Present Economic Crisis," sponsored by Ralph Bunche of Howard University, "agreed that the New Deal 'has utterly failed to relieve the exploitation' of Afro-Americans . . . and that 'the government has looked on in silence and at times with approval'" to their economic disfranchisement. Terrell was not alone; quite a few prominent African American business, religious, and civil rights leaders remained loyal to the Republican Party.[34]

When speaking to black voters, however, Terrell had to admit: "Some of my friends laugh at me, when I review the benefits of the Republican Party. 'That's handkerchief-headed stuff,' they ridicule," referring to the fact that it was the freed slaves and not their descendants who were most indebted to the party of Lincoln. Terrell continued, "But I don't see how it is possible to . . . FORGET THE PAST." This history, she insisted, still affected their lives in the present: "In practically every state of that section controlled by the Democratic Party, the constitutional amendments created by the Republican Party to confer citizenship upon colored people have by trickery, fraud and violence been openly and flagrantly violated for years. And today the Democratic Party is making a special effort in several states to disfranchise the women of the race. How can our women in the North, East and West vote for a party which deals with her sisters in such a lawless, cruel way?" The prominent African American historian Carter G. Woodson also refused to support FDR in 1936, chastising prominent black Americans who did so as having been "appointed to 'Jim Crow' federal positions set aside to reward Negro politicians."[35]

"I Doubt That I Can Work under the Conditions Prescribed"

By the presidential election of 1936, the ambitious legislative initiatives of President Roosevelt finally began to meet the immediate relief needs of a broader number of Americans. As New Deal programs began benefiting African Americans, even to a limited degree, they started voting for the Democrats. In the 1936 presidential election, 76 percent of northern African Americans voted for FDR. Yet even then they remained unsure of the Democratic Party's long-term intentions; only half of African American voters formally switched their party affiliation before 1940. The GOP did nothing to win back these voters, even when FDR bowed to the demands of southern whites on lynching and segregation.[36]

Entering her seventy-third year, Terrell still needed paid employment. Ever tenacious, she lobbied her many RNC contacts for yet another campaign position. Making the rounds on Capitol Hill in January 1936, Terrell informed Senator Daniel Hastings, a Republican from Delaware, "I'd like to take part in [the] coming campaign." Hastings was receptive, telling her that he had "heard a colored woman make the most wonderful speech he ever heard in Wilmington. He thinks it was I. He says I'm interested in you. Write a speech. I'll send you out to speak."[37]

Over the next few months, Terrell also tried to get campaign work through a wealthy white Republican, Julia Grant Cantacuzene, the granddaughter of Ulysses S. Grant.

From Terrell's perspective, their first meeting did not go as well as she had hoped. She wrote in her diary, "I doubt that I can work under the conditions prescribed. She wants me to give my services." Cantacuzene requested that Terrell send her a detailed letter outlining how she could serve the RNC. Terrell proposed giving speeches to African American women, a task that would be easy for her "because I am the first president of the National Association of Colored Women, have been attending their Biennials for years and am well known to my group throughout the country." Alternatively, Terrell suggested she could mail material to black women criticizing New Deal policies, including by "showing them how disastrously they have been affected by the NRA [National Recovery Administration]."[38]

Telling Cantacuzene that she viewed the speaking tour as more feasible than the writing, Terrell uncharacteristically confessed to some age-related problems: it "would be very difficult for me to function efficiently without assistance. I have no helper in my own home. Answering the door bell, the telephone, and doing my own work would greatly interfere with the duties which I should discharge. . . . Letters must be written and answered." If hired to write and send campaign literature, she hoped to be assigned a secretary.

In contrast to the physical constraints she foresaw in a letter-writing and literature-distribution campaign, Terrell was confident that she "could accomplish a great deal by speaking in some of the Eastern and Western States where the colored population is large" by "creating public sentiment among [African American women], influencing them by our point of view and arousing them to action." She suggested that this "could be done much more easily and quickly by coming into direct contact." Public speaking was Terrell's forte, and she could still inspire and motivate her audiences. Clear about what her travel expenses would be, Terrell promised that she could "arrange that the cost of room and board would never exceed three dollars per day." She explained to Cantacuzene that she needed a salary: "Like many others I have been seriously affected by the unfortunate conditions prevailing in this country today. My income is so small that I feel I would not be justified in giving my services gratuitously, however much I might desire to do so."[39]

After receiving Terrell's proposal, Cantacuzene interviewed several people, black and white, who all attested to Terrell's character and prominence in the African American community. Having confirmed Terrell's account of her accomplishments and capabilities, Cantacuzene visited RNC headquarters in New York City and met with its general counsel. A follow-up letter to the counsel emphasized that she had asked around and found that "they all love and respect her [Terrell] and revere the memory of her husband. . . . Mrs. Terrell's brother, whose name I have forgotten [Robert Church Jr.], is the best Boss among the men of his race in this country."[40]

Everything pointed to the RNC's quick reemployment of Terrell. In the end, it was not Terrell's age, infirmities, or questions about her prominence or competence that blocked her hire. Instead, national white GOP leaders took a hard look at the shift of African American voters to the Democratic Party in the 1934 midterm elections and calculated that they had little to gain from wooing black voters. Abandoning most attempts to claim the mantle of Abraham Lincoln, a shortsighted Republican Party began to view black voters as a virtually lost demographic.[41]

Cantacuzene tried anyway. First, she explained she had spoken with a GOP leader who "felt it desirable to make an effort to capture what we could of it [the African American vote]." Then, she mentioned "the fact that everybody whom I have consulted feels that Mrs. Terrell is a very outstanding person." Those combined factors, she noted, "gives me courage to" recommend her. Cantacuzene proposed two different possibilities: "I would like . . . to see Mrs. Terrell attached in some capacity to the organization of the Republican National Committee." Anticipating resistance, she offered an alternative. If it were "desirable for her to work . . . on the side for a time, I shall be happy to take up the matter with her, make some plan of activities for her to be submitted to you, and to finance her efforts until the money given me by Mrs. Archbold is exhausted." Cantacuzene asked for assurances that the RNC "has a definite intention of using her when this small sum is exhausted." In the 1936 election, the GOP had plenty of money from dissatisfied conservatives who opposed New Deal regulations but chose not to use it to recapture the African American vote.[42]

Cantacuzene had bad news for Terrell. There would not be any work for her before the Republican National Convention in early June, and she should re-apply later. Perhaps to avoid having to admit the RNC's disinterest in seeking black support, Cantacuzene tried to blame Terrell for not being hired. Terrell recorded: "Saw Mme. Cantacuzene today. She said I had failed to give her an outline of what I could do. If I could make engagements to speak before the Republican Convention, she could get $500 for me. She had never told me that before. She seemed impatient because I had done nothing . . . [but] she [had] said nothing about my making speeches." This substantial sum (worth about $8,300 today) would have eased Terrell's financial insecurities. The next day, Cantacuzene requested her "not to make engagements until I submitted every-thing to Rep[ublican National Committee] in writing. She would then send my statements to Mrs. Archbold."[43] Terrell heard nothing for weeks but laid the groundwork for a possible speaking tour by sending letters to key African American Republican women inquiring whether they might wish to invite a speaker to their state and inquiring about the party affiliation of black voters in their states. She did not mention her own availability.[44]

Her prospects appeared better in April when "Mrs. Archbold phoned me about 3pm to say that she had seen the plan for me to address Conventions of the Elks and that we could now start something! Oh Joy, Oh Rapture! . . . She will send her car to take me to her house! It looks like something good is going to happen!" Terrell's visit to the grand home of Archbold, a GOP patron with Standard Oil wealth, quickly tempered her optimism. She found Archbold's class status defined by racial hierarchies; she was discomfited to find that not only was the chauffeur who came to pick her up "a colored man" but "so is the maid and a man servant." When Archbold asked about the salary, Terrell re-quested $50 a week while noting that "Mrs. McCormick paid me $75." Arch-bold promptly "canceled the engagements in Florida, Alabama, and Georgia." Willing to pay low wages to African American men and women to work as her servants, Archbold was unwilling to pay a competitive wage to an African American woman to campaign for the GOP.[45]

Since she was not to be paid, Terrell chose not to deliver any formal speeches for the Republicans before the Republican National Convention of June 1936. Then, in July, Terrell went directly to RNC headquarters in New York and spoke to George Akerson, who had been Hoover's press secretary and "was very cordial." The next day, she again tried to see Natalie Couch, the RNC's director of the Eastern Women's Division, but was stonewalled: "Mr. Akerson said nothing would be done for a week and advised me to go home." He assured her, "'You have many friends at Court,'" and claimed that Couch was not trying to avoid her since she "had seen nobody yesterday."[46]

In August, the RNC finally appointed a black woman, Maude B. Coleman, of Harrisburg, Pennsylvania, as the women's director of the Colored Eastern Division but still did not hire Terrell as a speaker. Only days before the 1936 election, Terrell recorded in her diary that "Mrs. Maud[e] Coleman called up to ask me to broadcast [on the radio] for the Rep. Party. I said I would think about it. They hadn't needed me before and it is rather late now. . . . I don't know whether I have done right or wrong!" Recognizing with some bitterness that African American voters were just an afterthought for the RNC, Terrell still worried about whether she should have swallowed her pride and done the unpaid broadcasts.[47]

In the end, the RNC was content to have Terrell speak, but only for free. Unwilling to do political work without compensation, she had held out for gainful employment, finally realizing just before the election that none would be forthcoming. Throughout the 1936 campaign, the RNC leadership debated internally about whether and how much to woo African American voters. It ultimately decided that they were not worth much effort. Terrell was a direct casualty of that decision. The GOP's abandonment of African Americans became part of its crisis of identity during the New Deal and beyond.[48]

"Wicked, Wasteful, Wanton"

The tone and content of a handwritten eleven-page draft speech Terrell prepared on the New Deal are different from her other surviving political talks and articles, but they fit the mood and approach of other prominent Republicans during the 1936 campaign. The draft reveals the intellectual and ideological stresses Republicans faced. Some criticized Roosevelt's New Deal so intemperately in 1936 that they may have added to FDR's landslide victory. At a time when economic orthodoxy held that governments should balance their budgets during downturns, Terrell and her fellow Republicans were deeply concerned about deficit spending. Even Roosevelt did not disagree. He had allowed red ink only because he would not watch people starve but promised a balanced budget in his second term.[49]

Accusing New Dealers of "bankrupting the country," Terrell argued that deficit spending and higher taxes hurt all Americans. She predicted that the country would be ruined "unless the wicked, wasteful, wanton spending stops." She did not see New Deal spending as providing poor and working-class people with real relief. Terrell believed that deficit spending ultimately hurt the working classes because the "dollar will become worth less and less, capital will invest less and less, [un]employment will mount more and more. The rich will pull through but the wage-earner, the salaried man on a fixed income will be hit harder and harder as time goes on." Her understanding of fiscal policy was shared by others who gave angry, bitter speeches at the GOP convention.[50]

Given the uncharismatic Republican nominee, Alf Landon, Terrell acknowledged that the president's personal dynamism presented a problem. She warned voters against being beguiled by Roosevelt's charming personality: "We must forget the mellow voice, the heavenly smile, and remember what has been done to us. The New Deal has not worked and is on the rocks." Voters were drawn to FDR's dangerous fantasies about how he and the Democrats could end the Depression, she claimed, without thinking about whether the ideas were workable.[51]

Terrell recognized that Republicans had no chance of winning the election unless they did one of three things: allied with anti–New Deal Democrats in a new party, convinced dissatisfied Democrats to vote for the GOP, or implored them to sit the election out. None of these reflected her fundamental values before or after 1936. She had never wanted any group of Americans not to vote: her mission was to increase all citizens' access to the polls. But she hoped that a third party might split Democrats' votes enough to let the Republican Party regain the White House. She was heartened by the fact that an anti–New Deal Democrat, Henry Breckinridge of New York, had decided to challenge the popular incumbent FDR for the Democratic nomination, thereby giving "Democrats who oppose New Deal & Republicans a chance to register a protest vote. . . . Breckinridge might head 3rd party." Acknowledging that he would not win the Democratic primary, Terrell looked forward to his creating a party to siphon off votes from Roosevelt. A year later, mainly in response to Roosevelt's court-packing proposal, Republicans and anti–New Deal Democrats did attempt to form a coalition. Southern Democrats grew more receptive as they became increasingly worried about the infusion of northern African Americans into the party. They also feared that packing the court would change its political balance and lead it to sanction more of the New Deal programs they opposed.[52]

Terrell's endorsement of a possible coalition of Republicans with anti–New Deal Democrats can perhaps be squared with her fierce Republican partisanship. But it was antithetical to her lifelong civil rights priorities. In this one speech, she seized on a desperate strategy for winning in November 1936— aligning with the very people she had resented and distrusted for so many decades. She thought the GOP could not win the election: "Unless Antis help . . . [Democratic Virginia senator] Carter Glass [and] Governor Albert Richie of

Md., most respected leader in Democratic party said the New Deal is not only a mistake it is a disgrace to the nation." Her speech berated southern senators for being afraid to abandon the Democratic Party, although she understood that despite their disagreements with him, views presumably shared by their constituents, they hoped to win reelection on Roosevelt's long coattails as he pulled those same voters to his side. In fact, FDR won more votes in their districts than southern Democratic senators did, but they received enough to retain their seats.[53]

Going beyond her 1932 attempts to downplay evidence of discrimination in the Hoover administration, Terrell took a position she had always decried and would never take again: she defended states' rights. She quoted Albert Ritchie and Carter Glass without any overt irony as "respected" Democratic leaders. Both were strong states' rights proponents. Glass was also an avowed white supremacist who trumpeted segregation, disfranchisement, and the subordination of black workers as the three keys to peaceful race relations in the American South. As Glass put it in what became his most infamous statement: "Discrimination! Why that is precisely what we propose. . . . To discriminate to the very extremity of permissible action under the limitations of the Federal Constitution, with a view to the elimination of every negro voter." Terrell was always dedicated to exposing the racism of southern white politicians, including John W. Davis in the 1924 presidential election and John Nance Garner as the vice-presidential nominee in 1932. She knew that Glass had a hate-filled record. Ritchie and Glass condemned New Deal legislation for violating state autonomy, a complaint that always led back to the white South's insistence on its right to segregate and discriminate against African Americans. The many changes and insecurities in Terrell's life seem to have left her briefly unmoored and ready to adopt an ideological position otherwise abhorrent to her.[54]

During the New Deal, other African American leaders sometimes compromised their strongly held beliefs in order to achieve other goals, but not to such a drastic extent as Terrell did in this instance. When Mary McLeod Bethune became head of the new Division of Negro Affairs of the National Youth Administration in 1936, she decided to compromise her antisegregation principles. To gain limited access to jobs, training, and relief for young African Americans, Bethune accepted access via separate facilities and programs. This was not as big a break with her principles as Terrell's contemplated alliance with white southern Democrats, but it does suggest that pragmatic African American reformers and leaders in both parties sometimes compromised their ideals to achieve other goals.[55]

Terrell's views in 1936 were echoed by some Progressives, including NAACP leader Oswald Garrison Villard, who criticized the New Deal for putting too much power in the hands of the chief executive. In the fall of 1936, at least

"60 anti–New Deal progressives produced a running conservative commentary which, although not without its bleak stretches of unrestrained hysteria, makes it clear that the New Deal affronted the progressive spirit."[56]

Her 1936 draft speech also expressed Terrell's concerns about FDR's court-packing plan. The president, she accused, was feeling thwarted by a series of Supreme Court decisions finding his New Deal legislation unconstitutional. The Court had "hammered nails into personal platform of [a] President trying to maintain powers he sees slipping out of hands of Federal Government. [FDR] Wants Federal control over Industry. . . . Speaking for general welfare does not give [him the] right to invade reserved rights of states and could destroy balance fixed by the Constitution." This is an unusual critique for Terrell, who usually viewed a strong federal government as the only way to protect African Americans, who had no basic rights of citizenship or protection in southern states. Even though the Supreme Court's record on civil rights was weak, she had always hoped that it would, at some point, uphold the Fourteenth and Fifteenth Amendments.[57]

Terrell's erstwhile ally Oscar DePriest had different objections to an expanded court. He feared that it might undo recent decisions that had, in fact, been beneficial for African Americans: "Twice the United States Supreme Court has intervened to save the lives of the Negro defendants in the Scottsboro cases," by finding that they had been denied representation and by determining that African Americans had been wrongly systematically excluded from the juries. DePriest quoted a 1936 *Chicago Tribune* editorial warning of Roosevelt's court-packing plan: "If ever the power of the Supreme Court to uphold the constitution is restricted, the findings of the local courts in these cases will be final." From DePriest's perspective, states' rights would likely be bolstered by a transformed Supreme Court, so he preferred the status quo.[58]

Terrell's draft speech begs the question of why she opposed the New Deal and the Democratic Party so much that she would accept a coalition with its most conservative members to defeat Roosevelt in 1936. No subsequent speeches by Terrell reveal similar states' rights ideas, so it did not represent the beginning of a shift in her views. Instead it seems to have marked a temporary and unusual disruption. Many prominent white Republicans shared Terrell's sense of crisis, but her intemperate draft raises questions about how she was coping emotionally and spiritually with the disruption and dislocation brought on by the combined forces of the Great Depression and the party realignment symbolized by FDR and the New Deal.

Not coincidentally, Terrell experienced a spiritual crisis at the same time that she was trying and, at least temporarily, failing to make sense of a changing political landscape in which she felt marginalized as an older African American Republican woman.

Religion

PERSONAL PEACE AND SOCIAL JUSTICE

During most of Mollie Terrell's life, there is little indication in her surviving diaries or letters that questions of faith preoccupied her or were a source of inner struggle. Christian faith provided her a respectable religious identity and the necessary religious bona fides to move easily within African American social and cultural spaces. A Congregationalist, Terrell saw religion and Christian churches as a natural part of her social life and reform activism from which she could advance her social justice causes. In the 1890s, in an effort to enlist their coreligionists in racial justice work, she and Berto had created their own Congregationalist church. Ever since, Mollie maintained an ecumenical, progressive, and racial and social justice–oriented outlook. Religion gave her access to large numbers of like-minded women in pursuit of social justice. Theologically and socially liberal, Terrell embraced the ecumenical goal of unity and cooperation among all denominations and hoped for a racially integrated and activist militant church. She taught Sunday school in Congregational churches throughout her life but made a point of attending church services, dinners, and women's events at a wide range of African American Christian denominations in Washington, D.C., and across the nation. Receiving numerous invitations from black ministers to speak to their congregations on secular reform topics, she developed close working relationships across and between churches and denominations.[1]

In the mid-1930s, on a superficial level, Mollie's basic life patterns, reform activities, and interests remained the same, yet under the surface, in this time of partisan, economic, and family turmoil, things seemed not quite right. In the past, she had periodically slipped into depression, most notably during the 1890s, when she struggled to bear a healthy baby, and again in the early 1910s, when her mother and father had both died and she worried about safely and successfully raising her teenage daughters. Decades later, she found herself falling into another depression. In 1936, at age seventy-three, she appears to have been less able to cope than when she had stronger support systems. Her husband had died over a decade before, and her relationship with DePriest was over. In her own home, she was alienated from Phyllis's second husband, F. E. Parks, and argued bitterly with him. As a result, she saw far less of her daughter, even though the couple rented her second-floor apartment. Likewise, she engaged in heated disputes about repair and maintenance bills with her third-floor renters in her D.C. home and was not earning income from her dilapidated Memphis properties. The stressful months leading up to the presidential election also revealed Mollie's marginalization from the Republican National Committee. Feeling generally unmoored, she wrote her exceptional draft political speech but then realized that the Republican Party would no longer be a reliable income booster during upcoming elections.[2]

Amid this change and uncertainty, an unsettled Mollie briefly entered into a new spiritual journey that brought her closer to an evangelical approach to her faith than she had ever had before. She was surrounded by whites who were not, in the end, as progressive as she was, nor were they as racially inclusive or as committed to racial justice as she had hoped. This period of spiritual uncertainty soon passed. Mollie's overriding faith in the power of Christianity as a force for positive social change remained strong.

After World War II, Mollie grew more and more satisfied with the institution of the Christian Church as more ministers stepped up to the call and became leaders, along with their congregations, of the Civil Rights Movement. Having advocated that Christianity be a force for racial justice and equality for many decades, she was thrilled to be a part of and a witness to this sea change.

"I Have Deliberately Grieved the Spirit"

Just as her 1936 draft political speech was atypical, so was Mollie's diary from that year. The first signs of her spiritual journey appear in a seemingly mundane but, for her, unusual act. Unlike in any of her other previous diaries, she copied a prayer into the first page of her 1936 diary. It read: "God my Heavenly Father . . . teach me how to pray / Drive the gloomy thoughts away / And make the good ones stay." Eager to find spiritual help in combatting her anxiety and depression, Mollie yearned to achieve an inner peace and optimism that would give her the strength to sustain her writing and activism.[3]

In no other surviving diary did Mollie agonize over the nature of her belief in God, but in 1936, it was a consistent theme. Her spiritual crisis is revealed in a diary entry that started with her episodic lament about not being able to find the time and energy to write. This time, however, Mollie understood the problem differently from her usual dissatisfaction about the discrepancy between her ambitions and self-perceived limitations. In this case, she did not refer to having let down herself or her race. Instead, she noted, "It is hard for me to write. I have deliberately grieved the spirit." Worried about having willfully disappointed the Holy Spirit of God, she referred to Ephesians 4:30, the biblical passage that implores the faithful not to bring sorrow to the Savior by the way they live. The passage goes on to say, "Get rid of all bitterness, rage and anger." Mollie struggled with that directive. Her anger at injustice fueled her battles against worldly injustice and helped her thrive as an activist. Yet it also contributed to her depressions and to her difficulty maintaining an even temperament with friends, family, and coworkers in the black freedom struggle.[4]

At this vulnerable moment, Mollie was proselytized by members of the predominantly white Oxford Group, a nondenominational evangelical religious movement founded after World War I by Frank Buchman, a Lutheran minister and missionary. In 1936, the Oxford Group was at the peak of its popularity, having gained recruits through its process of securing prominent converts, convincing them to hold large house parties, thereby drawing in other influential converts, and then spreading the movement throughout the community. The Oxford Group held its First National Assembly in 1936, attracting almost ten thousand people, including Mollie, to Stockbridge, Massachusetts. It is uncertain exactly when or how she met the white women affiliated with the movement, but for several months, she became immersed in it.[5]

It may be that Terrell knew that the Oxford Group leaders shared her opposition to the Democrats. Frank Buchman was "very cool indeed towards Roosevelt's" policies and programs. If she was aware of this, it might have added to the group's appeal, but her diary and writings never refer to the politics of the Oxford Group.[6] Buchman was not just unsympathetic to the Democrats. He was also strongly opposed to the Communist Party at a moment when Terrell was involved with its Labor Defense Fund. She supported its efforts to exonerate the Scottsboro Nine as well as its other popular front civil rights campaigns. In the wake of the Scottsboro case, sympathy for organizations aligned with Communists was ubiquitous in the African American community. Even as Terrell was working with black communist leaders like William Patterson, Buchman was taking a much different approach. He so objected to communism as a godless, atheistic ideology that in 1936 he gave an interview predicting "heaven for a man like Adolf Hitler, who built a front line of defence against the anti-Christ of Communism." Just over a decade later, during the post–World War II Red Scare, in contrast, Terrell increased her involvement with and leadership roles in the leftist Civil Rights Congress (condemned by anticommunists as a communist front organization), even when that support came with greater risks.[7]

The Oxford Group's emphasis on the necessity for pushing for societal change in this world, not just in heaven, as well as its encouragement of personal reflection, drew Mollie to it. She appreciated its promotion of an outward-looking spirituality that prioritized earthly reform goals. The Oxford Group encouraged social activism by asking participants "to look *at the needs of others and the world* from the Holy Spirit's perspective." One of its innovations was daily meetings in which participants talked about their problems. The focus on fixing personal and world problems through purity and self-improvement helped drive the movement's growth. The Oxford Group promised converts that publicly confessing their sins and reaffirming their faith would make their worries disappear. Finding a way out of anxiety strongly appealed to Mollie. She hoped to achieve the peace and inner calm that eluded her. Yet she soon turned away, discouraged by racial prejudice and segregation within the movement.[8]

————————

Mollie's intensive interactions with the Oxford Group started when a white missionary, Aura Jones, began visiting her at home, trying to convert her. The Oxford Group's method had been to convert and network with influential white men. Movement leaders seem to have been willing to experiment with a similar approach in African American elite circles. If an influential black woman like Mollie Church Terrell became a convert, she might be convinced to hold a recruitment house party for African American women. Pursuing the movement's one-on-one conversion technique, Jones visited Mollie repeatedly while urging her to convert so that she could attend meetings. Although the context of how Jones initiated her initial visit is uncertain, she brought Mollie hope.

Jones promised Mollie if she experienced a conversion she would be freed from anxiety. In early March 1936, Mollie recorded, "Mrs. Jones of Oxford Group came at 3. She knows God cares for everything connected with her life. She worries about nothing! She is guided in everything." After another visit, Mollie reported, "Mrs. Jones came to see me today to tell me more about the Oxford Group. I am eager to join. I am willing to surrender everything so far as I know. I really want to please God. He will help me I know."[9]

With Jones imploring her to surrender herself to God, Mollie began interpreting all happenings though a lens of faith. When the wealthy GOP donor Mrs. Archbold expressed interest in her as a speaker for the Republican Party, Mollie echoed Jones's language, writing in her diary, "I thank God for this.

He certainly protects and helps me. I should be ashamed not to trust him completely. He really gives his angels charge concerning me!" Similarly, she found the hand of God at work when she was permitted to speak at an African Methodist Episcopal (AME) conference. She had been promised time at the lectern, but when she asked for her turn, she found that her insistent GOP partisanship had made AME leader Dr. John R. Hawkins reconsider, seeing her as an overly divisive presence. Reflecting a broader church reluctance to introduce partisan politics, especially at a moment when so many African Americans were shifting out of the Republican Party, he told her that she "must not inject politics [into a religious meeting] and was by no means cordial." Mollie believed that her feminism was also a problem for the AME leadership, noting, "A woman asking that women be ordained was howled down by the Conference."[10]

On the conference's second day, a persistent Mollie managed to be seated on the platform and got her promised opportunity to speak after all. She took Hawkins's warning to heart and did not discuss the upcoming 1936 election. Instead, she focused on civil rights, highlighting the need for the United States to uphold the Constitution's granting of citizenship to African Americans. Although her determination to speak was in keeping with her lifelong approach to asserting herself as a vocal leader, she attributed being able to do so entirely to her newfound faith. Certain that her faith "meant everything," she concluded, "God helped me."[11]

Visiting repeatedly, Aura Jones stayed for hours. Mollie reported, "She wants me to 'surrender' so that I may attend a meeting." Interested and compelled by the force of Jones's enthusiasm, she converted. By May 1936, Mollie attended "the big meeting of the Oxford Group at the Y.W.C.A. and was called upon to say a few words. I was not satisfied with what I said." While there, she met some Oxford Group leaders, including one who "talked about the National Assembly meeting. . . . He is genuine and a good talker. He invited me to the assembly. I'd like to go."[12]

Her increasing faith was yielding results. One day, Mollie noted, "Three remarkable things . . . happened today. 1. I lost a letter, didn't worry and found it later. 2. Saw Mrs. Parks visiting F. E., ran and got a taxi for her when she couldn't get one in front of the house. 3. Typed my article for the *Star* in 2 hours." Mollie believed her new faith had inspired her not to worry, to be more helpful, and to work diligently. It removed much of the anxiety that kept her miserable and let her see quotidian achievements as "remarkable."[13]

The teachings of the Oxford Group also helped Mollie allay her insecurities about writing. Anxious that she could no longer write a good, publishable article, she feared: "I have lost the art of writing. I long to write but I am too lazy, too discouraged to do so. 'It won't be accepted.' I haven't the heart to try."

Reminding herself of her newfound faith, she contacted Theodore Noyes, the editor-in-chief of the *Washington Evening Star*, proposing to write an article on "the celebration of the hundredth anniversary of Asbury [Methodist Episcopal] Church." Noyes replied affirmatively. She noted, "I wrote the article on the A.M.E. Church Wednesday after 12 . . . [saw] Mrs. Aura Jones at night, typed it after 2 o'clock Thursday and finished it this morning. Quick work. It shows what I can do when I try." Looking for the article in print, she opened "Section B of the *Sunday Star* expecting to find my article on the A.M.E. Church. I was cruelly disappointed. It was not there. I asked God to keep me from being depressed and He did. As I was reading the news in Section A on page 6, I saw my article! I could scarcely believe my eyes. I was glad I had not allowed myself to be depressed."[14]

A letter of invitation from Aura Jones to attend the mass meeting in Stockbridge became for Mollie a "wonderful . . . sign" that she must attend. This huge event gained nationwide media attention. Phyllis wrote her mother that she had seen a newsreel about it: "We tried to find you among the crowds. . . . 'Twas most interesting."[15]

"Disappointed Because There Is No Fellowship"

Arriving at the weeklong assembly, Mollie immediately became self-conscious at this almost entirely white event. African Americans who stayed in predominantly white hotels or ate in hotel dining rooms in the United States, including in the North, embodied whites' greatest fears of social equality. They often faced snubs and were seated separately or asked to eat in their rooms. Mollie felt uncomfortable in the hotel dining rooms: "Disappointed because there is no fellowship in the hotel." Hoping that her distant and disinterested dining companions might come to accept or even respect her, she shared a printed list of her accomplishments with the whites who sat next to her. As one of the few African American participants, Mollie noted, "I was hurt because the Washington women did not invite me to stay at Stockbridge for a chat. Then when I thot about it and prayed over it I saw how silly I was and asked God to forgive me. I am improving."[16]

Trying to focus on religious reflection and self-criticism, Mollie attempted not to notice or react to slights, even those that might have been intentionally exclusionary and racist. Yet two southern white women with whom she was seated at breakfast one morning were impossible to ignore. One woman's reactionary criticism of Franklin and Eleanor Roosevelt put Mollie off. The woman "from Florida who says she is related to Pres. Roosevelt by marriage" charged "that he is a 'spoiled boy' and nobody expected him to hold such a responsible position. She was shocked when I said I admired Mrs. Roosevelt."

Mollie also noticed "a [white] woman at the table from Kentucky who was not pleased at my presence." Each incident was relatively small but created discomfort and raised questions for Mollie about whether the Oxford Group was the best expression of her Christianity.[17]

Terrell spoke publicly at least once a day during the Stockbridge meeting. She expressed a tenet of the movement that resonated most with her core beliefs—her "desire to change other people's lives and determination to do it." Each individual, she claimed, was his or her own "most Valuable Equipment" for the job of world transformation. Terrell wanted religion and spirituality to lead people to focus on social justice and outlined her hope for the development of a "militant" Christianity. Most of her own reform work had been secular in its orientation, she admitted, so she "didn't like to throw brick bats at the church" for its inaction in the face of racial injustice. Rather, she saw herself as not having done enough to try to shift the orientation of institutional religion.[18]

Even though she regularly spoke at the meetings, Terrell felt marginalized and insecure and was frequently reminded of her racial difference. In one awkward encounter, she introduced herself to Oxford leader "Frank Buchman just before afternoon meeting but he was very cold." Mollie blamed herself: "It was my fault. I was indiscreet to approach him at that time." But she must have known that much of what she encountered there was racial prejudice. Mollie met another African American woman who was dismayed by the racism of the group's white women: "Talked with Mrs. Walker and she thinks we must have a separate organization in the Oxford Group . . . thinks a separate black affiliate might be the best way." Viewing segregation as antithetical to fellowship and to racial equality, Mollie disagreed.[19]

Other African Americans were aware of and some participated in the Oxford Group, but despite a few notable adherents, the movement never caught on in the black community. One African American, Gordon B. Hancock, a professor, Baptist pastor, and Urban League leader in Richmond, Virginia, wrote an article describing his positive encounter with the Oxford Group when he was living in England in 1937. After a chance encounter, he attended an Oxford Group world conference with "more than seven thousand delegates from 26 nations." Hancock was "the only Negro in that vast assemblage." Nonetheless, he was pleased to be asked to speak. Impressed by the Oxford Group's hospitality and by its ideas, he described it as having "more promise therein for Negroes" than Marxism or other radical ideas: "The Oxford Group is committed to one general proposition and that is this world needs a revolution and that the principles of Jesus Christ are sufficient to bring this revolution if practiced in the lives of men." This is certainly what attracted Terrell to the movement. In 1938, Buchman transformed the Oxford Group into a virulently anticommunist organization, Moral Re-Armament (MRA), that nonetheless promised to "re-arm" people with fundamental principles of hope and forgiveness in order to achieve world peace. In Mary McLeod Bethune's last years, in the early 1950s, she became an ardent MRA supporter, seeing it as a way to achieve global racial reconciliation.[20]

As the New Year approached, Mollie's interest in and commitment to the Oxford Group was waning. Perhaps it had served its purpose by helping her find renewed faith and calm. More likely, issues of race and racism within the movement were becoming increasingly problematic for her. Some white women members approached Mollie with a suggestion that might have been their objective all along—that she hold a segregated house party. She had rejected Mrs. Walker's idea of a separate affiliate as a solution to the lack of fellowship from white women, but when the white women asked her if they could use her apartment for the segregated meeting, she reluctantly agreed. Her diary entry from December 1, 1936, noted, "Mrs. Aura Jones and Mrs. S. J. Wilkern [visited]. . . . They want to hold a meeting in my house for people interested in the Oxford Group. I cheerfully consent." Mollie often used "cheerfully" in a way that implied forced good humor as she complied with what she saw as a duty. In fact, she was ambivalent, at best: "I'll see what happens."[21]

During a planning meeting for the event, Jones and Wilkern managed to make Mollie feel uncomfortable in her own home. Wilkern noted that she disliked *Green Pastures*, a popular Broadway show (and a 1936 film) with an all–African American cast, including a black actor playing God. African Americans were split in their views of the play and movie. Three years earlier, Terrell had helped organize protests against African Americans' exclusion from the National Theater audience for the play, so she was among those who saw it as an important opportunity for black actors to work in a major theater (and movie) production. Thus, she did not welcome Wilkern's comments. Worse yet, Aura Jones, who had spent so much time with her, "said something about 'little darkies.' I told her colored people resented that." Despite Mollie's appreciation of the Oxford Group's moral guidance and its help in lessening her anxiety, she was ultimately put off by group members' racism. Her involvement with the Oxford Group did not last through the end of the month.[22]

Before ending her connection with the Oxford Group, Mollie held the separate recruitment meeting for African American women as promised. She fit it into a busy day of writing an article about her friend the poet Paul Laurence Dunbar and shopping for Christmas presents. She then went "home after dinner to clean the house for the Oxford Group at 7:30. I had to rush as I never did before." She did not say if the meeting was successful. After ten months of intensive interactions with Aura Jones and the Oxford Group, Mollie did not mention the evangelist or the movement at all in the next two years of diary entries. She did so only once in her 1939 journal, when she noted, "Three people invited me to an Oxford Group meeting tonight, but I shall not go."[23]

"Surely There Is a Role for the Church Militant to Play"

Mollie Terrell's disillusionment with the Oxford Group did not change her basic Christian faith. She continued to speak in churches, participate in religious conferences, and attend interfaith and interchurch meetings and dinners. In fact, soon after she left the Oxford Group, Mollie was invited to speak at the 1937 World Fellowship of Faiths meeting in London. Traveling abroad was not an easy decision since she was perennially concerned about her finances. Her brother Thomas Church's death in January 1937 had initially increased her expenses, for she had hired a lawyer to help her win her (successful) battle with her younger half brother, Robert Church, over the care of their young nephew, Thomas A. Church Jr. But her brother Thomas's death also allowed her to sell some of their Memphis properties, since she and her sibling no longer had to agree upon what and when to sell. Thus, later that year, Mollie felt financially secure enough to splurge on international travel.[24]

This was the first time Terrell participated in a multiracial international conference. In contrast to her experiences in 1904 and 1919 at otherwise all-white women's international conferences, she was overjoyed not to be the sole representative of people of color at an international conference. Writing of her interactions with World Fellowship of Faith delegates from India and Africa in glowing terms, Mollie celebrated being with so many Christians from around the world, especially those representing its "darker races."[25]

Throughout her life, Mollie had a vision of Christian militants—activist, progressive, and reform-oriented Christians—working together for racial justice. They would transform churches as institutions and advance social change. Back in 1901, for instance, Mollie had been appointed by the congregation she and Berto had created, University Park Temple, to approach the more established Lincoln Memorial Congregational Church requesting a merger. She offered her vision of a merged church that could "become a tower of righteousness . . . and a bulwark of strength." Yet this new Congregational church, with an activist agenda looking beyond its walls to needs in the wider African American community, was only a start. The "church militant," she believed, must include whites as well as African Americans.[26]

White Christians had been and could be relevant and praiseworthy, Terrell held, when they were social justice activists, such as when radical ante-bellum era Quakers and Christian perfectionists had taken up the cause of abolishing slavery. In contrast, antebellum-era mainstream white Protestant churches had condoned and perpetuated slavery. The issue of the role of religion in the struggle for human rights continued to concern Terrell. In 1946, she took part in a discussion about this in a predominantly white space, an annual meeting of the National Council of Women in New York City. When another African American attendee, Christine Smith, stated that the "Church had failed in its responsibility" to fight for human rights, Terrell followed up by mentioning her discussions with questioning young African Americans: "I said students in college asked how I . . . could be a Christian when people who called themselves Christians had been so unkind to their race and ministers in South throughout slavery had been paid salaries with money from sale of slave mothers torn from their children and sold." After she spoke so bluntly to the mostly white audience, Mollie mused in her diary: "I am sure I got myself disliked. Should I have done that?" (These concerns did not stop her, however, for the next day she again confronted the NCW members by asking them to endorse the controversial Equal Rights Amendment.)[27]

As Terrell toured the country giving lectures throughout the first half of the twentieth century, black high school and college students continually questioned her about the hypocrisy of the white Christian church. As she summarized it, students said: "'I don't see how you, as an intelligent woman, can have any faith in religion or the church.'" She understood their point. Trying to separate the sinful behavior of "those who administer the affairs of the church" from faith itself, Mollie admitted, "I fear the youth of the race may lose their faith in religion unless the [white] church takes a more active part in trying to bring about a better understanding between the racial groups and is itself more careful to avoid discrimination against colored people." White American churches were enforcing segregation by setting African Americans apart in the pews or outright excluding them. They were also mostly indifferent about civil rights. Agreeing with the questioning students, Mollie noted in her diary, "It is a wonder that any intelligent colored person who reads History can have any faith in the so-called Christianity of A[merica]. I hope it will not make us a race of infidels." Continually marveling at the piety of African Americans and their forebears, enslaved Africans who had been converted to Christianity in inhumane circumstances, she commended the "colored man's loyalty to the Christian religion in spite of the outrages and crimes perpetrated upon him by people who call themselves Christians [as] one of the most striking and beautiful exhibitions of faith."[28]

Arguing that Christianity should form the basis for a new racial justice movement in the United States, Terrell provided her own version of what would later be termed liberation theology: "In the face of so much lawlessness to-day, surely there is a role for the church militant to play." Her vision of an activist, antiracist church did not come into being before the 1950s. Only late in her life did black churches, ministers, and congregations begin to take prominent leadership roles in the Civil Rights Movement.[29]

Just before and during World War I, Terrell had joined several new pacifist groups, including the Woman's Peace Party, the Women's International League for Peace and Freedom, and the Fellowship of Reconciliation. By the 1920s, the Fellowship of Reconciliation had committed itself to Gandhian nonviolence to promote civil rights. During World War II, the fellowship's offshoot, the Congress of Racial Equality (CORE), came into being and embraced activism for racial justice through nonviolent civil disobedience against segregation. In 1947, Terrell attended interfaith interracial workshops and meetings sponsored by the interracial Fellowship of Reconciliation and CORE to support a Journey of Reconciliation bus trip though the South, on which an interracial group was about to embark. A forerunner to the early 1960s Freedom Rides, its purpose was to test the Supreme Court's recent ruling in *Morgan v. Virginia* (1946), which prohibited segregation on interstate travel.[30]

These developments made Terrell more hopeful about the possibility of a militant Christian church playing a role in reforming the United States. Speaking at age eighty-four to the assembled activists, Terrell referred to Jesus Christ's tolerance and love: "Being a member of the Fellowship Group has . . . renewed my hope and increased my faith in the Church's desire and determination to call the attention of its members . . . to follow the principles laid down by Jesus Christ, especially the one which tells them Thou shall love thy neighbor as thyself."[31]

Terrell was particularly pleased that the Fellowship of Reconciliation was fostering interracial social interactions: "The fact that the Fellowship Group has defied tradition and custom . . . [to] engage in friendly conversation with each other and to break bread together," she said, "has greatly increased my faith." She stated, "I believe if Jesus Christ were here tonight, he would say 'You must love your neighbors as yourself, even if your neighbor's complexion is a few shades darker than your own.'"[32] Envisioning an interracial path to a more humane and just future, Terrell remarked, "I believe if there were a chain of Fellowship Groups throughout the U.S. like this one, particularly in that section where discrimination against the minority group is strongest and where its representatives are often the victims of murderous mobs, the Fellowship Groups would be powerful factors in spreading the Kingdom of God and making our beloved country a Democracy in fact as well as in name, where all human beings without regard to race would be free."[33]

For most of Terrell's life, Christianity gave her a social structure, a reform network, a community, and a set of ideals by which she aspired to live. Her liberal theology focused on freedom in this world as much as in the next. Terrell's encounter with the Oxford Group movement during a difficult time had introduced her to a more evangelical engagement with religion. She had hoped that her renewed faith might lead her to inner peace as well as to achieving more of her civil rights goals. But the Oxford Group could not become ballast for her because its members did not treat her as an equal. In the late 1940s, Terrell finally felt optimistic when the Fellowship of Reconciliation began bringing blacks and whites together to practice a Christianity based on love, freedom, and social justice. This sense of optimism and, as important, determination extended to all aspects of Mollie's life, as she undertook new challenges to sexism and racism in the United States.

13

Fighting for Equality

INTEGRATION AND ANTICOMMUNISM

Through her seventies and eighties, Terrell continued her remarkably varied activism. The advent of World War II in Europe inspired her to issue more critiques of European colonialism as well as of American racism. As the U.S. economy geared up for wartime production, she worked with A. Phillip Randolph to broaden employment opportunities for African Americans. During the war, although Russia was an ally, anticommunism was playing a role in the U.S. government's increasing intolerance of free speech and social activism at home. Civil rights crusaders, Terrell complained, were finding it "more and more dangerous to protest against injustices. . . . Those who call attention to them are looked upon with suspicion and they are likely to be called communists and are accused of being engaged in subversive activities." In this jingoistic, ultrapatriotic environment, she observed, "a really good colored citizen is expected . . . to keep his mouth shut about things to which he is entitled as a citizen but cannot get." Proponents of racial justice and equality met with character assassination, government harassment, and firings.[1]

After the war ended, in spite of African Americans' overwhelming support of U.S. war efforts at home and abroad, segregation and discrimination remained part of the fabric of American laws and culture. On the social level, white women continued to resist racial equality by maintaining segregated organizations. In 1946, Mollie decided to join one of her closest white Oberlin College friends, Janet ("Nettie") McKelvey Swift, in a fight to integrate the D.C. branch of the American Association of University Women (AAUW). Neither woman expected to set off a three-and-a-half-year battle. Once she agreed to be the test case for AAUW desegregation, Mollie faced repeated rejection and humiliations but ultimately triumphed. Through it all, she worked to communicate her personal experience of racism to her friend and ally, Nettie. The three-plus years of trying to integrate the AAUW tested their friendship but also deepened it.

As she fought to desegregate the conventionally liberal and thus anticommunist AAUW, Red Scare hysteria threatened her eclectic activism. Mollie faced intense pressure from her AAUW allies to disavow her associations with left-wing groups, but she chose to continue listening to, learning from, and working with a wide range of left-leaning activists.[2]

"We Must Cultivate Moral Courage"

As World War II began to unfold in Europe, Terrell publicly cautioned that the brutal history of European colonization could undermine African Americans' enthusiasm for possible U.S. intervention in the hostilities. In "The Race Problem and the War," a speech she gave repeatedly, she decried Hitler's racism and anti-Semitism but pointedly warned that it could be hard to convince African Americans and other people of color to sympathize with England and France, given their record of colonization in India and Africa: "England has been both unjust and cruel to her African subjects. . . . Her hands are stained with blood. She and France have held in their vice-like grip the most beautiful, fertile, and valuable sections of Africa, sections full of diamonds and gold."[3]

Refusing to accept American propaganda portraying the Allies as completely virtuous defenders of democracy, Terrell noted the Allies' glaring failures to ensure self-governance for those under their rule. This made them, she argued, less than ideal partners to protect and expand human freedoms worldwide. Whereas Britain's repression of India went against democratic values, Gandhi's movement for social change inspired and upheld these values. Terrell condemned the British for trying to use "every way to intimidate and silence the leaders of the Indian Congress who have been working hard to force England to let their country govern itself. She [Britain] has recently sentenced men to long terms in prison whose only crime was the effort they made to get India a little taste of that democracy for which England claims to be fighting today." Nonetheless, from the start, Terrell readily identified Nazism as the more immediate and greater evil that must be overcome.[4]

As President Franklin D. Roosevelt's administration contemplated U.S. entry into the war, Terrell joined labor leader A. Phillip Randolph's March on Washington Movement, which threatened a mass demonstration in the nation's capital unless Roosevelt made steps to desegregate the military and end discrimination in hiring.[5] The movement highlighted the discrepancy between the embarrassing reality of African Americans' second-class citizenship and the international reputation of the United States as a bastion of democracy. Hoping to avoid massive protests and unwelcome international attention to U.S. racial inequality, in 1941, President Roosevelt issued Executive Order 8802 to create the Fair Employment Practices Committee. Keeping pressure on the administration to deliver on its promises and enforce the order, Terrell helped Randolph plan a massive rally to celebrate and publicize the president's policy. The order and protests produced results, for as she noted, "colored men and women are now being employed in all kinds of jobs."[6]

Once the United States formally entered the war in December 1941, Terrell, though still an anti-imperialist pacifist, strategically decided to celebrate the contributions of African American workers to the war effort, just as she had during World War I. Juxtaposing the soaring rhetoric of the wartime government with the racial injustice still endemic in the United States, she argued that the federal government must live up to its rhetoric about freedom by passing an antiracism legislative agenda that would model real democracy for the rest of the world.[7]

Randolph, Terrell, and other African American leaders initiated what the *Pittsburgh Courier* dubbed a Double Victory campaign, calling for justice and democracy on the home front as well as abroad. Black activists exposed the nation's hypocrisy in fighting a war against prejudice while maintaining segregation and discrimination in the United States.[8] Terrell condemned, for example, discrimination in the military: "There is a constant call for recruits in all branches of the service, in Army, Navy, Marines, and in the Air. But when a colored man presents himself at a recruiting station he is generally cold-bloodedly and often insultingly turned down." Those seeking civilian work faced similar problems. Government officials claimed to want to help African Americans find jobs, but, in the face of white employers' and employees' resistance, "offered no plan by which colored workers could be employed in defense" plants that directly profited from government spending on the weapons of war.[9]

African Americans' patriotism and sacrifices on the military and home fronts did not bring full citizenship rights or lead to a reduction in violence against them.[10] Terrell called attention to "colored soldiers sent to southern camps" being "deprived of proper recreational facilities . . . refused transportation on buses . . . [and] beaten and murdered by bus drivers, civilians, and M.P.'s." No real peace or democracy could be achieved, she insisted, without an end to riots, lynching, and all other forms of violence and racial discrimination.[11]

"If a Woman Is Qualified She Should Be Admitted"

Seeing the horrific consequences of the racist ideologies of the Nazis during World War II, some progressive white American women began questioning

racial discrimination in their own social clubs and lives. Some members of
the American Association of University Women, for instance, became critical
of the discriminatory practices followed at most AAUW branches, including
the denial of otherwise qualified African American women from membership.
Prejudice against African Americans, they recognized, challenged the veracity
of white Americans' patriotic trumpeting of the United States as the world's
greatest democracy. Nettie Swift had moved to Washington, D.C., in 1939 and
joined the local AAUW. Nettie and other progressive white women sometimes invited their college-educated black friends (including Mollie) to dine
with them at the AAUW clubhouse, which was also the site of the national
headquarters. Conservative branch members pushed back by trying to change
the rules so that only whites could eat in the dining room. Nettie, along with
a minority group of local branch members, responded by trying to integrate
not just the dining room but also the D.C. chapter.[12]

The AAUW had been established in 1882 to provide white college-educated
women with a social network and to promote academic and professional opportunities for women. The national organization had tried for years to avoid
confronting the problems of segregation and racism in the local branches by
offering eligible African American women national membership without
branch affiliation. In 1946, the AAUW had over ninety thousand members
and a thousand local chapters, of which only seven were even nominally integrated. Several hundred African American women were general members in
the national organization.[13]

By virtue of having graduated from the predominantly white Oberlin College (which was on the AAUW's list of approved colleges and universities),
a young Mollie Church had automatically received a membership invitation
to the AAUW and joined after she settled in Washington. Sometime after
1906, she had let her membership lapse, perhaps because few African American women were welcomed into the District of Columbia branch.[14]

As more black women began earning bachelor's degrees, the national
AAUW kept most of them out by barring all graduates of black colleges and
universities. In response, Mollie had invited twelve other African American
women to gather at her home in 1910 to found the College Alumnae Club, a
national professional networking and advocacy association open to all black
female college graduates. In addition to providing networking opportunities,
the club aimed to improve access to high-quality higher education for African
American female students.[15]

Nettie first proposed that Mollie reapply for membership in the D.C.
branch in May 1946, when the two women were both in their eighties, telling Mollie that she would sponsor her application to rejoin the AAUW. Both
knew that Mollie's attempt to rejoin the AAUW would be painful for her

were she to be rejected by white women who were her peers in terms of their educational and professional attainments. At a branch meeting, Nettie tested the waters by bringing up the possibility of integration. Mollie described the outcome of this test as a "Race Problem flare up re: admitting colored women. It will ruin Club, etc." Hearing that so many white members opposed her, Mollie "told her to let it alone," but she reluctantly promised Nettie that she would think about it. The issue lay dormant for several months.[16]

White women had persistently resisted integration, prioritizing whites-only social networking and repeatedly spurning and humiliating African American women who hoped to join their associations. Mollie herself had regularly encountered racism in mainstream American women's professional, social, and reform organizations. In 1900, Mollie had attended the General Federation of Women's Clubs (GFWC) as the president of the NACW but "was denied even the courtesy of being allowed to bring official greetings from her association to the convention, as several southern white members of the GFWC objected and threatened to resign." She was one in a long list of African American women who were publicly denigrated. In 1920, the educator and women's club leader Charlotte Hawkins Brown was forcibly removed by several white men from a Pullman car and put in the segregated coach. White southern women on their way to the women's conference of the Commission on Interracial Co-operation, where Hawkins Brown was to be a featured speaker, watched passively as she was assaulted. NACW president Mary McLeod Bethune and other black women attended the 1925 International Council of Women convention only to find themselves unexpectedly forced into separate seating.[17]

Segregation in the AAUW's D.C. branch remained the status quo until October 1946, when Nettie again encouraged Mollie to apply. Terrell went to the AAUW for lunch with a white friend, Anna Wiley of the National Woman's Party and the Consumers' League. After Wiley left, Terrell stayed in the clubhouse and "decided to make out an application to become a member. Answering 'Yes' to 'Have you ever been a member?' 'Long Ago.' Mrs. Swornstedt who was a member then testified I had once been a member. I paid $25.20 and was given a receipt." Mollie assumed it was enough that she had once belonged.

Thinking she had broken the race barrier on the easy technicality of prior membership, Mollie celebrated. Nettie soon informed her, though, that the local leadership had unanimously turned down her application. Mollie summarized the rejection: "I must have a card to show I once was a member," she noted, "Nobody's word saying I was a member will be taken. . . . But of course my card will never be found." Unbeknown to her, her lunch companion and fellow NWP activist Anna Wiley had joined the majority of local members who vowed to maintain an all-white AAUW, explicitly basing her objections on the grounds of "race purity."[18]

Blocked by the local branch, Mollie and Nettie regrouped. Their first steps were to have Mollie join the national organization and draft a letter of protest to the national AAUW. Nettie and a few other local branch members formally contested the local's decision. For years, Mollie had worked closely with branch members in various capacities and made a list for Nettie of those who might be sympathetic to desegregating the AAUW. Three of those she mentioned included the president of the D.C. board of education, a member of the "Minority Group" of the League of Women Voters (through which white members investigated the needs and concerns of underrepresented minority voters), and a wealthy philanthropist whose husband was the publisher of the *Washington Post*. Mollie wanted Nettie to assure them that she had not begun the initiative: "Urged Nettie to tell people I did not beg her to act as sponsor for me, saying I don't want to socialize with those who spurned me. I have too much self-respect and pride." Although she wanted to desegregate the AAUW, begging hostile white women for social equality was not high on her to-do list.[19]

Disconcerted by her swift rejection, Mollie momentarily reconsidered serving as the test case, even though she understood the larger civil rights implications: "Said I would not go to any trouble for myself but for colored women in the future." Although the branch stated that she could not use oral or written testimony of current or former AAUW members to prove her prior membership, Mollie pursued that strategy. She called Otelia Cromwell, the first black graduate of Smith College, and told her: "I thought I had joined the AAUW soon after I came [to D.C.] but did not know the date. . . . She said she graduated in 1900. The college sent her card to the AAUW. She joined, saw me 'dressed gorgeously.'" The AAUW board would not have taken testimony from another black woman as proof, but it helped Mollie corroborate her account when she was feeling under siege.[20]

After an incident at a meeting of the American Friends Service Committee, Mollie fully embraced her fight to desegregate the AAUW as part of the larger civil rights movement against racial discrimination. She had traveled to Europe in 1919 as the only black member of the American women's peace delegation and had been on the board of directors of the Women's International League for Peace and Freedom. She was thus unprepared for hostile comments in what should have been the comparatively safe space of a Quaker meetinghouse. She found herself immediately accosted: "Mrs. Hummel saw me enter. . . . She marveled I thought I could be admitted. . . . She told me no white woman's organization here would admit me and challenged me to tell her one that did."

These aggressive comments pushed Mollie into a public struggle to integrate the AAUW.[21]

Next, it was Nettie's turn to get cold feet. Nettie had consulted with Fay Bentley, a judge of the Juvenile Court of D.C., who "said the AAUW could be sued. If a woman is qualified, she should be admitted. Nettie doesn't know how she feels." Although she had initiated the process, Nettie hesitated when it came to suing an organization she loved.[22]

Together, however, the two friends decided to persevere. To gain supporters, Nettie and her allies distributed copies of Mollie's record of accomplishments and phoned members, explaining that she fit all objective criteria for membership in the club. Their next step was to ask members "if they favored [accepting] colored women." Sympathetic white members, identified by Mollie as "Nettie and her group," did make headway: "Some at the meeting to consider admitting me and other colored women were enthusiastic and talked about resorting to legal action." Mollie was buoyed by letters of support from "members of the AAUW who approved admitting colored women. All were fine and most of them referred in a most complimentary way to me."[23]

The internal AAUW controversy became a public civil rights issue when it moved into the press and then the courts. Unlike Mollie, Nettie had spent her adult life in the private sphere, as a mother and the respectable wife of a Congregational minister, the Reverend Clarence F. Swift. She had no experience with talking to reporters and was unprepared for the publicity. Mollie, in contrast, was a journalist herself. She was pleased when "Nettie called me up and told me a reporter from the *Afro-American* was there to get the facts about the AAUW." Mabel Alston interviewed the two women in detail. Anticipating a feature story, the next day Mollie bought two copies of the paper for herself and Nettie. The large headline read: "Mrs. Terrell to be Voted on by White College Alumnae." Nettie blamed the reporter because "she promised to keep it out of the paper." Slightly annoyed, Mollie explained how journalism works: "Phoned Nettie that Mable Alston was not to blame for the *Afro* article. . . . Alston thought an intelligent woman would know that the Managing Editor and not a reporter decided what was to appear in the paper."[24]

Soon, the local AAUW members voted 364 to 250 against admitting Terrell. Reflecting on the whirlwind, Mollie mused, "I wish it had been possible for me to stay out of this mess without being a coward. But when Nettie asked me whether I was willing to apply for reinstatement I was literally 'on the spot.' I would have been a coward if I had not consented." Like her father, Mollie believed nothing could be worse than seeming to shirk from fighting for what was right. Once the desegregation battle started, she threw herself into it with her customary determination.[25]

After losing the vote to reinstate her membership at the local level, the white members who supported integration appealed to the national AAUW board, which declared that local branches must follow its membership policy of admitting all eligible women from the accepted list of colleges, so "there can be no authorization for any discrimination on racial, religious, or political grounds." Mollie was jubilant: "Nettie phoned . . . that the [national] AAUW had unanimously voted to admit qualified colored women. Dorothy Swift [Nellie's adult daughter] came right over, hugged and kissed me at the front door and I embraced her." Nettie's daughter Dorothy, who did much of the practical behind-the-scenes organizing work for her elderly mother and her friend in their desegregation campaign, embraced Mollie in public but also at her home—a clear sign of her belief in social equality. Fully expecting to be accepted by the local branch, Mollie immediately reapplied. But the branch resisted the national board's directive.[26]

The next stages in the drawn-out fight took a physical and psychological toll on Mollie. More than a year in, the Washington branch mandated that its membership requirements be determined by its local board of directors rather than the national board. Mollie admitted that she "was disgusted with the slow methods pursued." In this context, she read an article in the *Washington Post* headlined: "Doctor Says Fit of Anger May Lead to Cold in Head." Convinced she had found the reason that she was not feeling well, Mollie called Nettie to declare "that my feelings about AAUW had given me a cold and caused my nose to run."[27]

As they worked to integrate the AAUW, the two friends tried to bridge the racial divide. Swift sometimes found it difficult to hear Terrell's anger over the hypocrisy inherent in an American democracy that upheld segregation. She also resented Mollie's repeated criticisms of Althea K. Hottel, who was elected president of the national AAUW in 1947. Hottel held a Ph.D. in sociology from the University of Pennsylvania, where she had become a professor and dean of women and had integrated the AAUW's Philadelphia branch. Nettie saw her as an important ally and wished to cultivate good relations with her, whereas Mollie focused on Hottel's backsliding after becoming AAUW president: "I criticized the AAUW for not living up to their statement that all women graduated from accredited colleges are eligible for membership." Nettie responded: "Her convictions are all right and she thinks you are a wonderful woman." Refusing to let this become an issue of whether Hottel liked her, Mollie replied, "The AAUW has to decide whether it will live up to its avowed principles of Democracy. The women in the West don't want the Japanese. New England AAUW doesn't want the Jews, etc. I told her the AAUW was [not] worth saving if it discriminated against races and I wouldn't want to be a member of it. I said instead of being a Democracy that was a case of Hypocrisy."[28]

Seeing Althea Hottel during the AAUW's 1947 convention in Philadelphia, Terrell "told her there was only one thing for the National AAUW to discuss. Will they abide by the [AAUW] Constitution which admits all qualified women, or will they change it so that the Branches can exclude women on account of race or religion. Colored women, Japanese, or Jews." To Terrell's dismay, Hottel backed away from her support of integration. As the new national president, "she said 'All I want to do is keep the AAUW together.'" Terrell tried to assure Hottel that the AAUW would survive a mandate from the national organization to integrate the branches. She shared a personal example: the President of the Washington, D.C., Board of Commissioners, John Wesley Ross, had dared to appoint her to the board of education in 1895, "although the dominant group threatened him and said no self-respecting white woman would serve on a Board with a colored woman. But Com. Ross did the right thing and there was no trouble." She assured the AAUW president, "I served 11 years and several white women were appointed during the time I served." Terrell's advice to ignore the voices of doom and resistance failed to convince her. In a letter to Swift, Hottel suggested that "forcing people to do things was not the best solution to any problem." Without leadership from the top, Terrell accurately predicted, the branches would vote to continue denying black women.[29]

Nettie's discomfort with Mollie's assessments of the current state of American democracy led her to some unexpected questions. She asked, "Why do you stay here?" Mollie understood the question as implying otherness—that Nettie did not see her black friend as truly American. Too shocked and flummoxed to immediately reply, when she did, she tapped into a long and honorable tradition of critical patriotism: "I stay here as William Lloyd Garrison did." Garrison, the white radical abolitionist, had publicly burned a copy of the Constitution, insisting he was a true American patriot who condemned its compromise to allow slavery in the new republic as a violation of the core principles of both the Bill of Rights and the Declaration of Independence. Mollie stayed in the country of her birth because she understood true patriotism as requiring outrage over the nation's betrayal of its core principles. Nettie followed up her first question with "Where could you go?" Mollie replied, "I could go to Norway, to Sweden, to England, altho' soldiers of the U.S.A. have poisoned the mind of Europeans against us." Mollie's and Nettie's interracial partnership pushed both to new understandings as they confronted what it meant to criticize the country one loves, especially if one was not a white American.[30]

Invoking the words of the NAACP civil rights leader Walter White, Nettie challenged Mollie's discontent. "Nettie called me," she reported, "and told me there is an article ... quoting Walter White and other colored people as saying we have many advantages and blessings here. We don't talk enough about them and talk too much about discrimination and segregation. I told her Walter White . . . is practically a white man [who] goes where he pleases all through the South. Colored people who suffer and are persecuted because of their race would not agree with that point of view. I told her I would rather be a pauper in London where I would not be discriminated against on account of my race than a millionaire in Washington." Their conversations helped them confront and sometimes surmount the barriers of racial difference.[31]

"My Indignation at the Damnable Injustice and Hypocrisy of the Women Who Rejected Me"

The stress of the friends' struggle to integrate the AAUW led them sometimes to take their frustrations out on each other. During a visit with Nettie, Mollie criticized Hottel's comment about keeping the AAUW branches together: "If the [white] college-bred women set such an example of injustice as that, the outlook for peace and the practice of the vaunted Democracy is very gloomy." But "Nettie called my strong denunciation of the violation of the AAUW Constitution 'scolding' her. I told her I was not 'scolding' her but expressing my indignation at the damnable injustice and hypocrisy of the women who rejected me." This long and contentious process was upsetting, and Mollie used strong language. Nettie had initiated the challenge to the AAUW but then defended it from Mollie's withering criticism. Mollie's righteous indignation made Nettie feel as if she personally was under attack.[32]

Difficult and uncomfortable questions about race, racism, class, and social equality continued to arise as the friends spent more time together. When Mollie visited one day, she recorded, "Saw Nettie. . . . She was less cordial than usual. I talked a great deal. The girl was ironing but I didn't know it. Perhaps I appear to be too independent and not subservient enough. I don't want to make her dislike me." It is unclear if Nettie's domestic servant was white or black, but either way, Mollie noticed Nettie's coolness. Replaying their conversation, Mollie recalled that she had "ridiculed the idea of not doing anything 'provocative.' If I should go to the dinner there [the clubhouse], that would provoke the 'ladies' who object to having a colored person dine there. Disgusting." Even with a friend of almost seventy years, Mollie wondered about the racial dynamics of their interactions: Was Nettie made uncomfortable by their social equality in her home and within earshot of a domestic servant?[33]

Swift continued to make comments that took Terrell off guard. After one visit, Mollie recorded: "She asked me whether I could prevent [Howard

University's president Mordecai Johnson] from asking to have colored colleges accredited. I told her I could not." Nettie wanted Mollie to help ensure that AAUW membership would not extend to the significantly larger number of African American women who graduated from predominantly black colleges and universities rather than the few who graduated from predominantly white ones. Dismayed, Mollie refused. She also fumed when Nettie "said the word 'eligible' in the constitution of the AAUW could exclude colored women." Although Nettie might have been merely reporting this to her, Mollie "exploded and called the women claiming that hypocrites dodging behind a smoke screen. . . . The National organization had admitted me, showing that the word eligible makes it possible to admit colored women. I used 'damnable' many times. I told Nettie I am disgusted, have no faith in them."[34]

Fed up, Mollie considered taking legal action on her own. She consulted with the leaders of a new group, Americans for Democratic Action (ADA), about suing over discrimination in the AAUW's branches. Founded by Reinhold Niebuhr and Eleanor Roosevelt in January 1947, Americans for Democratic Action advocated an expansion of the New Deal, proposed civil rights reforms, and opposed communism. On her eighty-fourth birthday, Mollie again visited ADA offices, explaining that she wished to pursue a legal option because it was "my nature to fight." Ultimately, she did not have to sue because the local branch sued the national organization to maintain its right to discriminate.[35]

In May 1948, Mollie joined Nettie and Dorothy Swift in federal district court to hear the oral arguments in the AAUW case. She recorded: "*Star* Photographer takes picture of Nettie and Me. Real Red Letter Day! . . . Met . . . lawyer for Washington Branch 'I hear you are a very fine person,' he said." She reported that "Mrs. Rhoads resented" the attorney's hypocrisy for complimenting Terrell even as he was trying to exclude her and all other African American women from branch membership. Putting the AAUW's general director, Kathryn McHale, on the stand, the lawyer for the branch posed questions designed to stir up anxieties in the Cold War climate. Never mentioning race, he provocatively asked if the branches must accept all "eligible" women, even if that meant accepting "10,000 Communists" or "a woman who openly and notoriously advocated the overthrow of the United States by force and violence."[36]

Seeing AAUW president Hottel in the courtroom, Mollie approached her and said, "I never thought I would live to see the day when I would be in a Washington Court trying to get into an organization from which I was excluded. That it was disgraceful educated women had done such a thing, that the National Board should have enforced the Constitution." Hottel deflected the criticism, saying, "She was not a member at the time." She then congratulated Terrell on the honorary doctorate she was about to receive from Oberlin College. At lunch during a court recess, in front of several white supporters, Mollie again criticized Hottel for prioritizing retaining the segregated branches in the AAUW. "That angered Nettie," reported Mollie, who then "said her head hurt her and was wheeled in a chair by policemen and then by a nurse." When Nettie's daughter Dorothy acted coldly to her, Mollie worried: "Maybe she thinks my criticism of Dean Hottel yesterday caused her [Nettie] to nearly collapse." Terrell did not want to lose her progressive white friends and allies but refused to suppress her views.[37]

During oral arguments, Mollie sensed that the chief justice of the U.S. District Court for the District of Columbia, Bolitha Laws, favored the lawyer for the Washington branch. Perceiving racist intolerance, Mollie disagreed with her compatriots, who saw the judge as trying to "get points in our favor" for an appeal. She wrote, "I hope so. I fear he has not. He cast a look upon me when he saw me in Court the first time which bodes me no good." Judge Laws ruled for the local branch in July 1948, determining that the national AAUW's longtime acceptance of segregation at the branch level would mean that revising its bylaws was the only way to bring the locals into line.[38]

Even as the national AAUW appealed the decision, it also moved forward with a convention vote on new bylaws rules, identified by the judge as the only path to integration. President Hottel wrote to the AAUW's general director, "'I'm fighting mad now and between you and me Judge Laws will have his bylaws changed if I have to stump the country,'" which she did. But Hottel also strategically shifted the focus of the debate, framing it as an issue of national control rather than a moral crisis over racial justice and integration. A three-judge panel of Washington's federal court of appeals upheld the right of the local branch to discriminate on June 13, 1949. Mollie wrote tersely, "The U.S. Court of Appeals has rendered a decision allowing the Washington Branch to bar colored women. I am not surprised." The national AAUW moved forward with bringing its bylaws revisions to a vote at its convention in Seattle later that month. The prosegregationist Washington branch members preemptively withdrew from the AAUW before the convention met.[39]

Private correspondence between two white D.C. members illustrates the virulent racism that drove resistance to integration. In public, these women described their fight as being about branch autonomy; in private, they expressed fears of "social equality." Mollie had known Anna Kelton Wiley for years as a fellow member of the National Woman's Party. She did not know that Wiley was vehemently opposed to letting her join the AAUW. Despite referring to her as "a very fine woman," Wiley framed the vote to leave the AAUW in overtly racist terms: "Segregation is the only method we have of protection from intermarriage of the races." Wiley asked another white AAUW member, "How would you like to have a Negro grandchild?" Opposition to social equality once again rested on fear of miscegenation. Wiley signed her letter, "Yours for race purity." Mollie did not imagine that this woman she considered a friendly colleague was expressing overt racism behind her back.[40]

On June 22, 1949, the national AAUW voted overwhelmingly to open membership to all women who met the educational requirements. This included African Americans, Jews, and those of Asian descent who were variously excluded by local branches. Mollie celebrated, "I have won my fight! . . . This is indeed a great day! After fighting nearly 3 years, the AAUW 'took a step today to prevent a branch group from ever again barring a Negro woman college graduate from membership.' I read this in *N Y Times* . . . on way to train to Washington. . . . I am the first to notify Nettie! . . . Go out, get . . . 2 *Washington Posts*." Mollie received a "Telegram from Dorothy Swift: 'We win—Revised ByLaws Passed by Overwhelming Majority.' The vote was 2,168 against barring colored women, with only 68 opposing votes." Mollie's white New York City supporters wired, "We all rejoice tonight in gratitude to our Convention and in thanksgiving for upholding you of whom we are proud." And Nettie wired, "Glory, Glory Hallelujah. Her Truth is Marching On. Your Pal." In the midst of her celebrations, Mollie observed, "No telegram has come from a colored woman. I thank God for this victory." African American women may not have telegrammed her, but a significant number eagerly joined the newly integrated branches. It may be that some black college graduates in the National Association of College Women, which Mollie had helped found, worried about the fate of their own organization. But both groups remained strong and collaborated on joint programs; the black women's organization continued to play an important role by prioritizing equal access to higher education.[41]

Nettie wrote an article about their AAUW integration fight for the Oberlin College alumni magazine. Satisfied, Mollie concluded, "It is very good and sets forth clearly the prominent part she played in the AAUW affair. Mentioning me, she says 'in all honesty . . . patience is not her crowning virtue, nor is it my own.' Also, 'Molly Church's mastery of the English language is phenomenal and at times during the long period of suspense, I often wondered that our telephone equipment did not collapse under the torrents of impatient eloquence which assailed the wires. It was a long, trying strain nervously and spiritually.'" Nettie captured their dynamic and the intense stress of the struggle while praising her friend's public demeanor: "Through it all, Mary Church

Terrell presented a calm, dignified front.... Dr. Terrell victoriously upheld her Oberlin training and the honor of the Oberlin Doctorate conferred upon her in 1948." Mollie concluded contentedly, "I enjoy that praise!"[42]

The change to the AAUW was far greater than the token integration that might have ensued had Mollie been allowed to renew her lapsed membership. Nettie and Dorothy Swift and their local allies formed a new integrated AAUW branch in Washington. Fifty college-educated African American women, including Mollie, joined. Mollie gladly reported: "Many colored women attend meeting. Most interesting meeting of AAUW." Again, she noted, "Not one [black woman] congratulates or praises me." Just a few months later, however, in October 1949, she received the recognition she desired when the National Association of Colored Women organized a huge banquet in her honor.[43]

Just before Terrell's eighty-sixth birthday, the new Washington AAUW branch met to elect officers. Mollie had missed Nettie, who had moved to New York to live with another daughter, noting, "Nettie and I embraced when we saw each other." This was a historic and special moment for the two old friends. After Nettie spoke to the assembled crowd, Mollie "congratulated and thanked the Minority Group for the fine work they had done to make that meeting possible, said they had worked to make women all over the world beneficiaries of their struggles and battles." Putting their fight for equality into a global context, she reminded AAUW members about how this victory would look during Cold War debates about the relative virtues of democracy and communism. Framing the successful desegregation of the AAUW as part of the broader struggle to make the United States live up to its founding ideals, Mollie elaborated: "They would cause colored people all over the world to believe the U.S.A. is a Democracy and some day that would help to pursue peace. I was loudly applauded. Many members spoke to me and shook hands with me after the meeting."[44]

Terrell and Swift (whenever she was in D.C.) tried to create an AAUW chapter that represented their priorities: "Nettie moved not to have Style [fashion] Show.... I seconded the motion ... saying ... we criticized old Branch for too many social affairs. They will laugh at us if we start that way." The friends preferred to engage the chapter in substantive causes, such as ensuring women's equal access to graduate education, as well as promoting the hiring of women in educational and other professions.[45]

"Bringing the Branch into Disrepute"

Nettie's daughter Dorothy Swift, who had been instrumental in the integration campaign, became a leader of the new AAUW branch. Uncomfortable with Mollie's more progressive views, Dorothy argued that her work with left-leaning groups could place the new AAUW branch in a bad light. Mollie, she insisted, must remember she now represented the AAUW and must tone down her speech and activism. Although Mollie was grateful for Dorothy's support and wanted to maintain strong ties with the white AAUW women who had endorsed integration, she refused to abandon her broader fight for equality.[46]

Ever since Alice Paul and the National Woman's Party had proposed the Equal Rights Amendment in 1923, reform-oriented women had disagreed about it. The National Association of Colored Women supported the ERA. Having witnessed the partial opening of the job market during both World Wars, NACW members wished to secure as much access as possible to previously restricted jobs. In contrast, Mary McLeod Bethune's National Council of Negro Women opposed it, concerned that it would dismantle hard-won protective labor laws for women. Mollie, an active NWP member, had long lobbied Congress for the ERA.[47]

Testifying before the House Judiciary Committee in 1948, Mollie Terrell supported the ERA and called on the United States to live up to its claim of being more democratic than other countries.[48] American women must be able to pursue equal educations and work opportunities to make substantive contributions to their nation, she argued: "Thousands of women are obliged to support themselves and their families entirely or help to do so." She asked Congress to recognize black and white American women as "loyal citizens" and reminded the representatives that during World War II, "women proved they were both capable and willing to render service to their Government as satisfactory as that performed by men." But women deserved more than just the opportunity to work. The ERA would allow some women "to make a brilliant record for themselves along certain lines of human endeavor and at the same time to make valuable contributions to their country of which it is now deprived." The nation was disadvantaged, she insisted, when women could not make substantive contributions to society.[49]

Despite her commitment to the Equal Rights Amendment, Mollie could not persuade Dorothy Swift or the AAUW to support it. She reported an incident at the "Washington Branch AAUW. Dorothy Swift, Mrs. Fairbanks, Nettie Swift and I . . . talked about Equal Rights Amendment. I talked too 'positive.' Dorothy asked us to stop serious discussion." As in so many areas, Mollie was an outlier, and Dorothy did not want her to stir up controversies within the group. (The AAUW did not endorse the ERA until 1971.)[50] In turn, Mollie was troubled by Dorothy's positions on a range of questions:

FIGURE 13.1. This portrait of Mollie was taken by Ollie Atkins, Washington photographer for the *Saturday Evening Post*, in January 1954. She is seated in her mahogany chair in front of her ornate fireplace mantle. Above her head is a painting of Mollie that is leaning on the mantel in front of the gold gilt mirror visible in figure 9.2. Also visible on the mantel are the photograph with her mother and brother (figure 2.3) and of her husband (figure 5.2). (In 1946, Mollie sat for a different formal portrait, painted by the artist Betsy Graves Reyneau for the National Woman's Party. During Mollie's lifetime, it was displayed in NWP's Washington, D.C., headquarters as well as on tour. It is now in the collection of the National Portrait Gallery, Smithsonian Institution.) (Courtesy Oberlin College Archives)

"Talked with Dorothy who ardently agrees with Hottel. I may have talked too strong and too much. Am disgusted & angry." Mollie's anger was a driving force in her activism, but it sometimes alienated close allies.[51]

During the early years of the Cold War, anticommunism became an increasingly disruptive force within white liberal groups and black civil rights organizations. Growing anticommunism was sowing suspicion and dissention within black women's organizations and in predominantly white ones like the AAUW. Members of the National Council of Negro Women, for example, split on whether they should work with members who had also joined anticommunist loyalty review boards.[52]

Terrell continued championing peace, human rights, national self-determination, and a full and meaningful citizenship for all, irrespective of gender, religion, and race. At a 1946 meeting of the International Alliance of Women, a women's rights advocacy organization, the chair asked Mollie to share her views in a discussion of a book on the USSR. Challenging the white women in attendance, she "said Russia is the only country in the world where the Brotherhood of man is really practiced. . . . A woman doubted that. I cited Paul Robeson taking his son there to escape prejudice."[53]

During her AAUW battle, Mollie served as a voting board member of the Council on African Affairs (founded 1937) of which Paul Robeson was chair, W. E. B. Du Bois the vice chair, and Max Yergan executive director. The group supported anticolonialism and Pan-Africanism but began to face serious internal divisions over the question of communism. In 1948, the organization was in the full throes of a struggle for control. Since Mollie was not planning on attending the council's board meeting in New York City, she gave her proxy vote to Paul Robeson, whom she knew and admired. The solidly anticommunist Mary McLeod Bethune and Max Yergan visited, trying to convince her to rescind her proxy, but she refused. Mollie told Yergan, "I am not a Communist but I am grateful to people who believe we should have equality of opportunity and all our rights." She observed: "Both the political parties here have promised us our rights and have lied to us. Maybe the Communists would do exactly what the Republicans and Democrats have done" but, she implied, not worse. The next day, Mollie attended and supported Paul Robeson at a fundraiser by the left-leaning Civil Rights Congress, where he sang to raise money for striking D.C. cafeteria workers, whose cause Terrell had been championing. The CRC organized mass political actions and provided legal assistance for black defendants and civil rights advocates charged with communism. Meanwhile, the struggle in the Council of African Affairs over communist influence resulted in Yergan's removal by the board, which Mollie supported. This did not make the AAUW more comfortable with her politics.[54]

Boldly testifying at a Justice Department hearing, Mollie defended her friend Louis Rothschild Mehlinger, who was being subjected to an internal loyalty review purge. Mollie knew him in several capacities. After World War I, he had become a Justice Department lawyer and cofounded both the Washington bar association for black lawyers and the Robert H. Terrell Law School in her husband's name. In the mid-1940s, Mehlinger joined the National Lawyers Guild (NLG), which was defending individual African Americans and civil rights organizations against the House Un-American Activities Committee (HUAC). When the loyalty review board accused Mehlinger of being a member of subversive organizations, Mollie spoke on his behalf, even though testifying in favor of a suspected federal employee, in addition to having membership in a variety of civil rights organizations, could become grounds for charges of communism against her.[55]

Speaking at a March 1949 meeting of the CRC, Mollie reminded the audience that "the colored people of the National Capital need your ministrations and efforts" to "eliminate disfranchisement, segregation and discrimination" just as much as did those in the Deep South. She continued, "It was suggested that I would run a great risk if I attended this meeting, because some communists might be here. But I am not easily scared, and, moreover, I should think that a human being in this country would have as much a right to be a Communist as I have to be a Republican." In her diary, she second-guessed herself, wondering, as she often did, if she had gone too far: "Spoke at Night Meeting of Civil Rights Congress. Audience stood up and cheered me so long I was embarrassed. Sorry I referred to Communism."[56]

Throughout the AAUW desegregation struggle, Mollie faced rumors that she was a communist or fellow traveler. Invited to be a delegate at the World Peace Congress in Paris in April 1949, she initially accepted. Nettie and Dorothy Swift argued vehemently that she should not go: "Nettie tells me World Peace Congress is Communist. I'll be smeared. Long argument with Dorothy who blasts Communism. 'Every[one] in Russia a slave.' I say an English Clergyman's book praises Russia." Terrell was uncertain what to do after the *Washington Star* denounced the conference as being communist-sponsored. She told the assistant chief of the passport division, "People here pretend they fear Communism to keep folks from talking about the shameful manner the U.S.A. is violating the Constitution." When she finally decided not to attend, the *Afro American* covered it as an example of the pressure put on civil rights activists to contain their activism. She was not silenced for long, however.[57]

In the same month, June 1949, when the federal appeals court ruled on the AAUW's desegregation case and the AAUW changed its bylaws, the

executive secretary of the Civil Rights Congress asked Mollie to join an integrated test group to challenge segregation in the capital. She attended the
meetings that created the CRC's new Coordinating Committee for the Enforcement of the D.C. Anti-Discrimination Laws but initially wavered on her
level of involvement. She feared bringing negative attention to the AAUW
because the CRC was on the attorney general's list of subversive organization.
Nonetheless, in October 1949 she agreed to lead the Coordinating Committee
as its chair. Mollie's AAUW desegregation battle had been won, so she could
turn her attention to organizing boycotts and picketing and to initiating a
lawsuit to desegregate D.C. restaurants and department stores. As chair, she
worked closely with workers' unions and other civil rights organizations that
were under attack as potentially subversive. Further defying anticommunist
hysteria, Mollie worked with National Lawyers Guild attorneys, who argued
her case when she initiated the CRC's legal challenge to restaurant segregation in D.C.[58]

Her work with the Civil Rights Congress confirmed for some AAUW
members that Mollie was, indeed, a communist. At a reception for Charles
King, the former president of Liberia and the current Liberian ambassador to
the United States, an AAUW member told her that the local branch had rejected her for being a communist rather than for being an African American.
"I used very strong language denying it," she wrote, "Too strong." When she
asked Nettie about it, her friend said it was untrue and that the racially prejudiced local group had been willing to accept communists as members. If so,
the majority who had opposed Mollie were more willing to admit white communists than a noncommunist African American woman.[59]

In spite of her worries about how her public activism would be perceived
within the AAUW, Mollie did not keep a low profile. She praised the Soviet
Union's commitment to antiracism, which she contrasted to the U.S. government's endorsement of segregation. Terrell often raised these provocative positions at predominantly white meetings, such as one held by the League of
Women Voters and attended by a number of AAUW members. The United
States could not "win the peace," she stated, if it continued spreading prejudice
around the world.[60]

Seizing an opportunity to confront anticommunist hysteria, Terrell replied
in February 1951 to Attorney General J. Howard McGrath, thanking him for
inviting her to the Annual Brotherhood Dinner of the National Conference
of Christians and Jews. She noted: "You say the enemy of the country is Communism. I know very little about communism. . . . But I cannot believe that
any group of human beings outside of an insane asylum could imagine that
they could overthrow the . . . richest and strongest government in the world."
Belittling the claims of those who tried to sow fear, she pointed instead to the

"race problem" facing African Americans: "I wish more of our government officials and good citizens would try to create public sentiment against the atrocities and injustices of which colored people in this country are victims, especially in the South, where they are often murdered with impunity, denied their rights guaranteed them by the Constitution, and are humiliated in every conceivable way." Linking African Americans' civil and human rights to the government's desire to win the Cold War, Mollie pointed to Russia's track record of "assiduously cultivating the friendship of the colored people, especially those in Asia. . . . It grieves me to think that . . . millions of black, brown, and yellow people in other parts of the world hate my country because colored people here have often been the victims of so much injustice."[61]

As Mollie tried to resist the fearmongering that accompanied the intensifying Cold War, she found that any perceived sympathy for communism was increasingly problematic for AAUW leaders. National and local officials were afraid because before World War II, HUAC had opened a file on the organization, alleging that it associated with other potentially "subversive organizations" such as the National Consumers' League and the League of Women Shoppers, which promoted minimum wage, maximum hours, health insurance, and other policies and were eventually designated communist fronts by the federal government. Mollie was an active member of the League of Women Shoppers, which supported local unions.[62]

In the early 1950s, HUAC rattled the already skittish AAUW by opening new loyalty investigations into two of its national leaders. An AAUW leader tried to prove her organization's patriotism by joining the federal Subversive Activities Control Board, whose mission was to root out communists from liberal organizations. Not surprisingly, Dorothy Swift and the local AAUW leadership went on the offensive against Mollie's activism when she became involved in the American Peace Crusade (APC), which formed in 1951. The APC was sponsored by W. E. B. Du Bois and the nuclear physicist Philip Morrison, among others, who were concerned about nuclear war and mass annihilation. Mollie signed APC petitions, letters, and telegrams, but local AAUW branch member Emily Morrison was the wife of APC founder Philip Morrison, who had been a member of the American Communist Party as a student in the 1930s (he soon after renounced it). Although he had done top-secret work on the Manhattan Project, HUAC suspected Morrison of subversion because he had become an advocate for peace after touring Japan and witnessing the devastation of the atomic bombs at Hiroshima and Nagasaki. In 1951, the year the APC was founded, HUAC launched a formal investigation of Philip Morrison for communist subversion.[63]

Dorothy Swift, a longtime anticommunist, hoped to shield the AAUW from further scrutiny by HUAC by convincing Mollie that the APC was a communist organization she should spurn. Mollie wrote: "Dorothy Swift wants me to withdraw my name as a Sponsor of American Peace Crusade so that I won't bring the Washington AAUW into disrepute since it is a communist organization. I told her I called up Attorney General McGrath's office and was told it is not Communistic. From whom did she learn it is Communistic? She had read it in the paper and heard it from some 'Loyalty' organization." Both women were right. The State Department listed the APC as a communist front in 1951, but the Justice Department did not do so for another two years.[64]

Mollie's support for the American Peace Crusade was not only based on her abstract belief in peace and conflict resolution. As she explained, she was glad that the group advocated getting "our soldiers out of Korea. Colored soldiers [are] badly treated, given unjust sentences. 10 years in a trial with hostile surroundings lasting less than one hour. Personal with me. Don't want my nephew Thomas to go as a soldier to Korea." Although President Harry S. Truman had signed Executive Order 9981 desegregating the military in 1948, integration did not begin until the very end of the Korean War. In the meantime, African American soldiers served in segregated units and found themselves "disproportionately subjected to capital sentences and court martial hearings." Prominent civil rights lawyers, including Thurgood Marshall, flew to Korea to help defend them and publicize their plight. Mollie was visited by those who "beg me to continue as a Sponsor to American Peace Crusade. . . . I told them I had worked 3 ½ years to get colored women admitted to the Washington Branch of the AAUW and didn't want to do anything to cause them to criticize me for bringing the branch into disrepute by becoming a Sponsor to a Communist organization." She also feared making it harder for the new African American AAUW members.[65]

Conducting their own loyalty review, AAUW local leaders told Mollie she must meet with the international relations branch representative to discuss her relationship with the American Peace Crusade. Ironically, this was Emily Morrison, the wife of APC founder Philip Morrison. Her formal report held that Terrell had a critical view of race relations in the United States and "consistently implied and sometimes even stated" that no progress had been made on the "Negro problem." Put in the bizarre position of rooting out communist subversion in the AAUW while her husband was under investigation by HUAC, Emily Morrison told Terrell to decide for herself about resigning from the APC. "She was very courteous and kind," Mollie reported. "We discussed everything." Yet Morrison sent the national AAUW a hostile report, possibly to improve her own and her husband's claims of anticommunism. Morrison suspected that Mollie would "forget to take any action." Yet the pressure on her remained intense; Mollie resigned as a sponsor of the APC in

March 1951. Nevertheless, she decided to work with several other targeted organizations during the last years of her life.[66]

HUAC never launched an investigation into Mollie's activities, but it did
release an April 1951 "Report on the Communist 'Peace' Offensive: A Campaign to Disarm and Defeat the United States," in which it decried "a campaign to sabotage American morale and military superiority by undermining
domestic support for nuclear weapons." The report denounced Paul Robeson
as a Communist and named W. E. B. Du Bois, Langston Hughes, and Mollie
Church Terrell as "fellow travelers." The Federal Bureau of Investigation also
developed a file on her and she appeared in several of its investigations into
"subversive" organizations from 1947 on, including as a member of the Council on African Affairs and as a signatory to petitions protesting Congressional
banning of the Communist Party in 1947. Using evidence gathered from articles mentioning her in the Communist Party's *Daily Worker*, the FBI correctly
reported that Mollie supported the American Committee for the Protection
of the Foreign Born, the World Peace Appeal, the Washington Committee
to Defend the Bill of Rights, the National Council of the Arts, Sciences and
Professions, and the Emergency Civil Liberties Committee, among others. In
the end, the FBI came to a similar conclusion as HUAC, characterizing Mollie
as a fellow traveler rather than a full-fledged Communist.[67]

The fight to integrate the AAUW was long and painful but ultimately successful. It signaled that the campaign against segregation and for equality was
progressing. By the time she reached her late eighties, Mollie Terrell was ready
to lead two committees sponsored by the leftist Civil Rights Congress. Her
chairing of the National Committee to Free the Ingram Family and of the Coordinating Committee for the Enforcement of the D.C. Anti-Discrimination
Laws was no accident or aberration. In the last decade of her life, resisting
heightened anticommunism, she gladly took on significant leadership roles in
a revitalized black freedom struggle.

14

The Black Freedom Struggle

Cold War competition between the United States and Soviet Union enabled Mollie Terrell and other civil rights advocates to frame racial justice in a global context. Pointing to the U.S. government's endorsement of white supremacy, Terrell argued that the Soviet Union appealed to nonwhite peoples around the globe: "Even if [Russia] tells nothing but the truth about the lynchings, the disenfranchisement, discrimination, segregation, and prejudice of which colored people are victims, she is continually sowing seeds in the minds and hearts of colored people which will make four-fifths of the population of the world hate the United States." The black freedom struggle grew after the war as longtime activists like Terrell were joined by those who felt they could no longer accept the government's empty platitudes about democracy and equality.[1]

Terrell's refusal to bow to the Red Scare is demonstrated by her leadership roles with communist-affiliated and other left-wing organizations, lawyers, and activists, including her backing of the 1948 strike by the United Cafeteria and Restaurant Workers Local 471. In Cold War America, all activists—communist or not—were charged with subversion simply for advocating civil rights, taking an anti-imperialist stance, or working with communists or leftist activists. In a speech to a peace organization, Terrell supported anticolonial freedom struggles worldwide and condemned the U.S. government for using anticommunism to suppress black Americans' calls for civil rights. The best antidote to communism at home and abroad, she suggested, would be for the government to enforce the Constitution rather than allow its repeated violation. African Americans needed to prepare themselves to lead a postwar fight for equality, Terrell argued: "We ourselves must cultivate moral courage enough to take a definite, firm stand for justice and rights."[2]

Throughout her eighties, Terrell continued to work for justice at a pace that would have overwhelmed many people much younger. She launched a

multifaceted civil rights battle against discrimination in the nation's capital and led another against the inhumane treatment of a black woman in
the criminal justice system. The first involved her chairing the Civil Rights
Congress's Coordinating Committee for the Enforcement of the D.C. Anti-
Discrimination Laws from 1949 until she died in 1954, just months before her
ninety-first birthday. In that campaign she used her years of experience to lead
boycotts, set up picket lines, and sue D.C. stores and restaurants that discriminated against African Americans. During those same years, she headed another CRC committee, the National Committee to Free the Ingram Family,
to push for a pardon and release from prison of the African American Georgia
sharecropper Rosa Lee Ingram and her sons, who had been convicted of the
murder of a white man who was assaulting her. Terrell continued to address
the vulnerability of black women to sexual assault and violence at the hands
of white men acting with impunity.

The last years of Terrell's life represent not only the culmination but also
an intensification of the pace and success of her earlier reform work. With
the D.C. coordinating committee, she experienced the satisfactions of participating in a well-orchestrated and concerted civil rights movement. As the
activists desegregated stores and restaurants, momentum built in their favor.
Terrell was able to be a militant activist at a time when greater numbers of like-
minded people were willing to protest with her, even in the face of a growing
red scare. Undaunted by smears of being a communist sympathizer, Terrell
used familiar direct-action tools of picketing, boycotting, and sit-ins to achieve
social change. She valued her new interracial collaborations in the movement
and began to feel that her talents and leadership capacities were at last appreciated by white and black Americans.

Civil rights organizations, especially the NAACP, had laid the legal
groundwork in the 1930s for the post–World War II movement through a
series of court cases chipping away at the separate but equal doctrine. After
World War II, more African Americans began participating in direct action
protests to defend the principles of equality and justice, joining longtime activists like Terrell in concerted actions to undo segregation. While the Civil
Rights Movement of the mid-1950s and 1960s is identifiable as separate and
distinct from the earlier civil rights struggles, prominent activists like Terrell
(1863–1954) and Du Bois (1868–1963) are an important bridge between these
earlier and later eras, enabling us to take a longer and more continuous view
of a black freedom struggle that culminated in the Civil Rights Movement.[3]

Terrell was not newly radicalized but, rather, found more compatriots and
opportunities to challenge the discriminatory practices and laws that had a
stranglehold on African Americans. The NAACP's membership rose expo-
nentially from 50,000 in 1940 to almost 450,000 in 1946, showing the rapid

change in African Americans' expectations for significant social and political changes in the United States. Terrell's activism is part of a "historical continuity of Black women's experiences of multiple oppressions, the thematic consistency of their activism, and the activist influence from one generation to the next." She lived long enough to see her continuous, persistent activism, and that of others like her, pay off.[4]

"I Felt That I Would Go through Fire and Water"

Terrell's Coordinating Committee for the Enforcement of the D.C. Anti-Discrimination Laws derived from wartime protests that began without her direct involvement. In 1943, an African American student who was to become a civil rights leader in her own right, Pauli Murray, was then one of two women enrolled in Howard University Law School. Murray mentored an undergraduate who joined two other Howard undergrads in a sit-in held to protest having been denied service at a lunch counter. When the students were arrested, Murray helped raise money and planned protests. The following year, fifty-six students, joined by African American soldiers, sat in at Thompson's Restaurant, later the site of Terrell's 1950 antidiscrimination lawsuit. The persistent students and soldiers were eventually served, but their success did not translate into long-term or widespread change. University president Mordecai Johnson demanded that Howard students stop their protests because the university relied so heavily on federal money, and he feared being defunded.[5]

Soon after the protests ended in 1943, Howard Law School's librarian made an important discovery of two District of Columbia antidiscrimination ordinances from 1872 and 1873. Originally written and introduced by Lewis Douglass, a son of Frederick Douglass, the laws made it illegal for Washington's shops, restaurants, and hotels "to refuse to serve any respectable, well-behaved person without regard to race, color or previous condition of servitude." Pauli Murray researched the statutes and discovered they had never been repealed, arguing in a college paper that the "lost laws" were likely still enforceable. But they continued to lie dormant.[6]

In 1948, still in her AAUW desegregation battle, Terrell became a key supporter of a strike by the predominantly African American United Cafeteria and Restaurant Workers Local 471, which communist labor leader Annie Stein had helped organize. The 1947 Taft-Hartley Act, which amended the National Labor Relations Act (NLRA) of 1935, barred members of the Communist Party and even left-leaning activists from holding office in unions. In December 1947, Government Services Incorporated (GSI), the private

employer that ran federal cafeterias, argued that the NLRA no longer applied
if a union did not require its labor leaders to sign a pledge of anticommunism.
But Local 471 of the United Cafeteria and Restaurant Workers and its parent union, the United Public Workers of America (CIO), disagreed, refusing
to make anyone sign. The union risked condemnation for being infiltrated by
communists, even if it was not.[7] The strike began on January 5, 1948, when
about twelve hundred workers walked off the job in protest. The strike lasted
seventy-eight days during a frigid winter. Although the Labor Department
solicitor, William S. Tyson, held that unions that had not secured pledges
could indeed represent the workers, Republican representative Clare Hoffman
began dragging its leaders and workers to testify before his House Education
and Labor Subcommittee. Grilling them about possible communist affilia-
tions, Hoffman tried to force the strikers to capitulate.[8]

Terrell already knew some of the union members and leaders. During the
1948 strike, they requested and received her support. When she wanted to
"cheer the pickets" but could not be there in person, she "sent a telegram to
Richard Bancroft President Cafeteria and Restaurant Workers—Hearty congratulations on stand you have taken. Best wishes for victory over Prejudice
and Bigotry."[9] She also helped recruit speakers for a mass fundraising meeting of the Civil Rights Congress, at which Paul Robeson performed before
an audience of 2,500, raising $7,000 for the strikers. The workers later paid
tribute to Terrell as "most beloved by members of Local 471. When the chips
were down in the 1948 strike she was one of the outstanding champions of the
union's cause. She was not confused by the propaganda in the daily papers but
was clear on the real issue that 1300 Negro workers have a right to a union. Dr.
Terrell spoke out when others were mum and was always present at meetings
held, to encourage us to fight on to save our union." Terrell did all this when
others feared aligning themselves with those whom politicians and businesses
were calling communists.[10]

The Truman administration handed the union a partial victory by insisting that GSI open talks. But it also demanded that the union's leaders sign
the pledges. Its president, Richard A. Bancroft, a World War II Marine Corps
veteran and Howard University graduate, resigned rather than sign the Taft-
Hartley oath renouncing the Communist Party. But eight other officers signed
in order to end the strike. In March 1948, the union won recognition when
GSI agreed that most workers would be rehired and union dues would be de-
ducted from paychecks.[11]

Throughout the postwar era, Terrell regularly listened to oral arguments in
civil rights cases being heard by the Supreme Court. In *Morgan v. Virginia*

(1946), NAACP lawyers William Hastie and Thurgood Marshall successfully challenged a Virginia law mandating segregation on interstate buses as a violation of the Constitution's Interstate Commerce Clause. Terrell recorded in her diary that she "went to Supreme Court hearing of case on Miss Morgan's being forced to ride in Jim Crow car in Virginia. Judges listed attentively to Hastie." She often noted whether the justices seemed to be paying respectful attention to a lawyer, taking it as a sign that he or she might win the case.[12]

Terrell seized on indications that the time might well be right to demand an end to Jim Crow laws in the nation's capital. She learned of the rediscovered antidiscrimination laws from her neighbor, Tomlinson Todd, the director of the *Americans All* radio program, who "often remarked to her: 'The people of Washington should do something about this, Mrs. Terrell.'" In November 1948, the National Committee on Segregation in the Nation's Capital, on which NAACP special counsel Charles H. Houston served, published a pamphlet confirming Pauli Murray's earlier conclusion: the laws had never been overturned. As soon as the report was public, Houston sued two D.C. restaurants for discrimination. In December 1948, Terrell attended a CRC meeting with William Patterson and members of the Truman administration to discuss strategies to desegregate the District's public restaurants and shops. The executive secretary of the CRC, Thomas G. Buchanan Jr., asked Terrell to participate in a test case. She was interested but took time to consider it since she worried about the CRC's being on the attorney general's subversives list. Finally, in May 1949, the National Lawyers Guild also determined the laws were still in effect, concluding that a legal challenge to segregated restaurants and shops in D.C. might succeed. At that point, Terrell and other civil rights activists mounted their full-scale assault on segregation in the nation's capital.[13]

As chair of the Coordinating Committee for the Enforcement of the D.C. Anti-Discrimination Laws, Terrell led a successful campaign to desegregate Washington's restaurants and stores. On June 25, 1949, just two days after the AAUW voted to integrate, an interracial group of about two dozen activists, many of them Terrell's longtime acquaintances, gathered to discuss securing enforcement of the long-ignored antidiscrimination laws. Although Terrell had just recently become chair of the Ingram Committee, she was ready to immerse herself in yet another big fight for equality. After participating in the discussion about dismantling segregation in the capital, labor organizer Annie Stein invited Mollie to chair the committee. Terrell agreed on October 3, 1949, explaining, "I felt that I would go through fire and water, for the time to come for us as colored people not to be treated as animals."[14]

Marvin Caplan, a journalist in charge of the committee's publicity efforts, concluded: "Without someone of Mrs. Terrell's organizational skill and recognized eminence at its head, it is doubtful that so large and heterogeneous a group could have been held together." The committee brought together "more than 100 civic, social, and labor groups" and used such actions as lawsuits, negotiations, sit-ins, boycotts, and picketing to force businesses to desegregate. These were all long-employed tools that became more common in the movement after the 1955 Montgomery, Alabama, bus boycott.[15]

As chair of the coordinating committee, Terrell worked closely with Annie Stein, its executive secretary; they were equally determined and militant. Publicity director Caplan described their "their mutual trust and their affection and high regard for one another" as "one of the Coordinating Committee's great operational strengths." Stein was a master of behind-the-scenes organization, and Terrell served as the voice of the movement. These "two women of different religions, styles, [races,] and generations . . . shared a feisty determination to end Jim Crow. Terrell, at age eighty-six, the grand dame of Washington's civil rights movement, remained a vociferous advocate for racial equality. She embraced her role as chair of the coordinating committee, willing to walk a picket line, testify before public officials, or pigeonhole a reporter to give a piece of her mind." A "scrappy, indefatigable thirty-six-year-old," Stein was "a swirling force of nature. Her husky voice, salty language, and frenetic energy struck a sharp contrast to the stately, dignified Terrell, whom she adored. . . . For nearly four years, the two were the heart and soul of the movement."[16]

Terrell participated fully in the daily campaign. She went often to Stein's home, which served as the unofficial headquarters, to stuff envelopes or "give final approval to a picket sign slogan or a leaflet design. And during some of the fiercer engagements, she came to meet informally with picket captains and map out new plans, rather after the manner of a general weighing the reports from the battle front."[17]

In February 1950, the committee's work began by challenging segregation directly in order to secure a ruling affirming the validity and enforceability of the antidiscrimination statutes. Terrell, "never the person to shrink from a task because of her age or the prospect of public humiliation," helped organize an interracial group of D.C. residents to eat at Thompson's Restaurant. In a later interview, she said, "When I realized what they [the laws] meant . . . that when a restauranter refused a person service . . . he could be fined $100 and lose his license, I felt it would be stupid to just sit and think about it." She asked the Reverend William H. Jernagin of the Mount Carmel Baptist Church and president of the National Sunday School and Baptist Training Union Congress if he would join her for lunch at Thompson's. Jernagin replied that they would not be served, to which she answered, "'I know we won't be served, but let's go anyway.' Then I called Geneva Brown of the Cafeteria Workers, and she said she would go. That was three colored people. A white person ought to go. I couldn't think of anybody but David Scull, of the [American Friends]. I said I did not want to put him on a spot, but three colored people were going to Thompson's Restaurant. He said he would go. That was the Thompson Restaurant case."[18]

After they were refused service, they went, as planned, to the law firm of Joseph Forer and David Rein, two progressive white lawyers with offices next door to the restaurant. The attorneys and their African American colleague Margaret Haywood were members of the National Lawyers Guild, the first racially integrated bar association to take labor and civil rights cases. Forer, Rein, and Haywood had helped write the NLG's report concluding that the lost laws had never been repealed and had sent the report to the D.C. corporation counsel, who adopted a strategy of delay.[19]

The Thompson's Restaurant case was designed to press the District counsel to stop stalling and hold businesses that were discriminating solely on the basis of race to be in violation of the still-valid laws. After Terrell and her compatriots provided sworn affidavits about having been denied service, the District gave in and took up the case. The legal climate had grown more favorable to civil rights challenges than in earlier decades. Charles Houston and other lawyers from the NAACP Legal Defense Fund, founded in 1940 by Houston's law student Thurgood Marshall, had been urging the Supreme Court to take seriously the equal protection and due process clauses of the Fourteenth Amendment. Finally, their arguments were taking hold. After the campaign began, Terrell praised the Supreme Court's decisions in *McLaurin v. Oklahoma* and *Sweatt v. Painter* (June 1950), which opened up institutions of higher education to African Americans on the basis of the Fourteenth Amendment's equal protection clause. Anticipating *Brown v. Board of Education* (1954), she called for these decisions to be extended to elementary and secondary schools, saying it was "unfortunate and embarrassing" that the "Greatest Democracy on earth" continued to deny black children their equal rights.[20]

Finally, too, Terrell saw houses of worship play an important role in the struggle for civil rights. Ministers had long opened the doors of their churches to meetings of the NAACP and other African American and interracial organizations. But this campaign to desegregate D.C. businesses was different because the ministers themselves took part. They picketed and entered restaurants in integrated groups to see how management responded. In doing so, they risked harassment, attack, and arrest.[21]

Terrell's years of work with religious leaders on a wide variety of committees and for so many different causes were paying off. In 1951, she was able to "secure the sponsorship of 20 leading ministers," who sat on the rostrum at a special mass meeting where several spoke and offered prayers. She had attended services at many of their churches over the years, given speeches from their pulpits, and attended many hundreds of congregation dinners. Her appeal to the ministers to join the movement carried weight because of her background as an esteemed, if unusually ecumenical, churchwoman. Her religious liberalism had influenced her politics by making her interested in social justice as a righteous cause. It had also allowed her to cultivate relationships across denominations with other African American civil rights leaders and ministers, most of whom hailed from more evangelical backgrounds.[22]

Terrell publicized her coordinating committee's work at interchurch, interfaith, and interracial fellowship dinners, always asking for support. When "asked if women should not engage in Civic Affairs more than they do," rather than shame them, she simply "told the women to help us in our work." When invited to explain to a group of white women why activists were picketing Kruger's Department Store, she explained: "White women were allowed to sit while eating lunch but colored women were forced to stand up. This was done to humiliate them and to brand them as second-class citizens." Sensitive to the role of dress and conduct in reinforcing whites' views of African Americans as inferior—and noting the antidiscrimination law's guarantee of equal service to all "respectable well-behaved persons"—she and the other protestors made a point of always wearing their Sunday best when meeting, speaking, testing segregated managerial policies, and picketing.[23]

Charming and elegant, tough and relentless, Terrell was an excellent negotiator as she visited restaurant and store managers, pressing them to end their discriminatory policies. She was "eloquent by conviction and practiced in argument from her long years . . . on the lecture platform." Terrell led "delegations impressively sprinkled with ministers and attorneys into the business offices." Sometimes, just one phone call or visit from Terrell did the trick. If not, more intensive discussions, supplemented by threats of boycotts, made a difference.[24]

In addition to protests, the committee used publicity to put economic pressure on businesses to desegregate. To encourage diners to patronize cooperating restaurants, it published a frequently updated survey of establishments that served African Americans without discrimination. The lists became very popular and widely used, increasing the number of people involved beyond those actively protesting. At the same time, the committee's *Adopt a Restaurant* campaign invited organizations and individuals to test and monitor specific eateries. Terrell described one typical day's work: "We saw the Manager and urged him to serve colored people at the Lunch Counter. He will think about it. Went to Woolworth's. The manager is willing to serve colored people. The waitress says she won't serve them." Since simply publicizing unequal treatment quickly affected the bottom line of dime-store chains, several changed their policies immediately, and others did so within eight or ten weeks.[25]

If owners and managers refused to negotiate and change policies, the

FIGURE 14.1. Mollie Church Terrell, chair of the Coordinating Committee for the Enforcement of the D.C. Anti-Discrimination Laws, picketing in 1952. This iconic image displays her pride, determination, and vigor. Although she sometimes held her cane and a picket sign, in this case, she is holding her purse in one hand and a cane in the other. The picketers ranged in age from Terrell, in her late eighties, and middle-aged women and men to the young man next to her. One protestor's sign referenced his military service in the Korean War as part of his claim for full citizenship, and to Terrell's right is her compatriot in the Thompson Restaurant case, William H. Jernagin, whose sign boldly identified himself as taking part of the struggle in his capacity as a reverend. (Courtesy Oberlin College Archives)

committee threatened to boycott their businesses. It planned a boycott of Kann's department store, for instance, after "Mrs. Terrell reported on her visit with Mr. Sol Kann.... After a long discussion with him she secured a commitment from him that he would 'study' the situation further." The committee did not miss a beat; it decided to "send a letter to Mr. Kann suggesting that he change his policy and *then* 'study' the effects of the change." A large interracial delegation and an attorney went to see Kann and also filed a legal complaint against the store. Its ultimate success in achieving desegregation in this and other cases inspired even more people to join the committee's direct-action protests.[26]

Picketing was the final strategy used to force capitulation and was a difficult step for the committee to take. Even after the Kresge department store refused to buckle in the face of a boycott, the group had a contentious debate over whether to picket. Some argued that picketing was "undignified and dangerous." Terrell understood their concerns but argued that it was crucial to do whatever they could to force recalcitrant companies to change. Caplan remembered Terrell's confident defiance: "Turning a deaf ear to last-minute warnings of the impending race riots and violence that would result, she put on her fur coat, wrapped a scarf around her head, and with her cane in one hand and a picket sign in the other, led the first detachments of pickets in a snowstorm."[27] This image of Terrell as an elderly civil rights organizer determinedly leading the charge is inspiring and unsurprising.

In January 1951, after eight weeks of picketing, Kresge's gave in. The coordinating committee planned a victory meeting at the Asbury AME Church. Terrell was pleased that a D.C. resident "said he had been a member of committees working against discrimination since he was a child and we had done more than any other had ever done." Indeed, this success was considerably greater than any Terrell had achieved in a lifetime of fighting for equality.[28]

Throughout the campaign, Terrell took part in many picket lines, sometimes bringing celebrities such as Josephine Baker with her. After six months of picketing at Murphy's, for example, she and Annie Stein joined "three women reporters from the *Afro-American*, the *Pittsburgh Courier*, and the Associated Negro Press" for lunch at the counter. They were served without incident. The reporters' celebratory stories provided national coverage for the campaign.[29]

If she felt that her unique contributions to the movement were ignored, Terrell pointed them out, even when that meant confronting friends and allies. She had been the first to call attention to the Hecht department store's advertisement embracing "bridges of brotherhood" even as it adamantly maintained discriminatory practices. But a news story about the store's hypocrisy did not discuss Terrell. She wanted the press to give her credit for the committee's clever new posters and flyers calling out the store's insincerity: "My name was not mentioned in *Courier* Hecht story, although I was the one asking the question about the 'Brotherhood' Hecht advertised in the *Post* only to be told by Schwartz, one of the Hecht officials, that the Hecht Company only wanted money."[30]

As the activists pressed forward with direct action, the Thompson's Restaurant case made its way through the courts. Municipal Judge Frank Myers ruled in July 1950 that the D.C. Anti-Discrimination Laws were no longer in effect. The committee appealed to the Municipal Court of Appeals, which overturned Myers's decision in May 1951 and affirmed that the 1873 statute still held. Terrell called it a "Great Day! . . . We had won our case! . . . . Court of

Appeals declared . . . because the law is not observed does not mean that it is not valid." Both parties, however, appealed once more. Thompson's Restaurant wanted to be free to discriminate, whereas D.C.'s corporation counsel wanted a more definitive ruling. For its part, the coordinating committee hoped to confirm that the 1872, not just the 1873, antidiscrimination ordinance was also still valid.[31]

Terrell sharply criticized the corporate counsel's decision not to prosecute restaurant owners for violating the antidiscrimination laws until the Supreme Court ruled on the case. Her nephew Thomas Church Jr., a newly minted lawyer, explained that the counsel was not legally obliged to prosecute them. Although he sympathized with his aunt's politics, he worried that she might become a victim of redbaiting. Thomas suggested: "If you attack him [the corporation counsel] too viciously or indorse a plan which borders on violence—for example, inciting Negroes to go to the downtown restaurants en masse—some people may place a vicious interpretation on such acts to your detriment and to the embarrassment of the people you represent."[32] Offering "a few words of caution from your loving nephew," he confessed that he feared "the malicious and wanton mudslinging and 'red washing' (I just coined that term) that is going on today."[33]

While waiting for the next decision, Terrell shared her partial triumph with Nettie Swift, who knew just how long and arduous court cases could be: "Had dinner at 1st Cong. Church with Nettie. Told her about our victory, she was very happy." Terrell also celebrated some good publicity, noting that the *Afro-American* gave a "long account of Victory in Thompson Restaurant Case, my picture with Rev. Elmes and Joan Williams. Very good picture of me. . . . Picture of me picketing also. *Afro* treats me handsomely."[34]

To celebrate, the coordinating committee planned a mass meeting on June 15 and asked Terrell to be the main speaker. She initially refused because, despite her desire to be recognized as a movement leader, she had just spoken elsewhere and had impulsively decided to give up oratory. When asked why, she claimed, "The doctor doesn't want me to make any more public speeches." This was just an excuse, however, because she admitted in her diary: "At the time, I dreaded writing and delivering a speech at that Mass Meeting more than a toothache." By the next day, she had changed her mind, concluding, "It will be a fine chance to express opinions that I couldn't present anywhere else." The coordinating committee was one of the most progressive groups with which Terrell was involved, giving her great latitude when addressing its integrated audiences.[35]

Despite her nephew's caution, Terrell made the issue of prosecuting recalcitrant businesses the subject of her speech: "Great Ovation after my speech on Corporation Council West's refusal to enforce Anti-Discrimination Law pronounced valid by Municipal Court of Appeals. Audience stood up, applauded long and loud. $250 raised to carry on work."[36] The funds generated by her eloquence were much needed. A pleased Annie Stein wanted to print her talk: "Mrs. Stein said my speech was superb. . . . Full of wit and humor." Despite her anger at continued racism and the slow pace of change, Terrell maintained her sense of humor and ability to entertain and inspire audiences.[37]

In February 1952, the committee targeted Murphy's, the last dime store holding out. All the others and forty restaurants in the city were providing African American customers equal access to their lunch counters and dining rooms. Terrell, Stein, and two colleagues planned a Murphy's "sit down" to see if they would be served. Terrell recalled, "We sat there from 6 o'clock until it closed. One of the waitresses tried to serve us. She was a white waitress. One of the oldest waitresses. She said, in a low tone, 'I am very sorry I cannot serve you.'" Terrell appreciated her support.[38]

When Murphy's continued to discriminate against African American customers, the coordinating committee sent picketers to march out front. The elderly Terrell found it physically difficult to participate, so her compatriots staffed the picket line "with Mrs. Terrell watching them from a little canvas chair, like a fond teacher observing a group of her favorite pupils." Each week, different groups, including the NAACP and church organizations, joined individual ministers and members of the committee and the organizations they represented, taking turns on the line. Even when dealing with serious issues, Terrell said, "I can always see something funny" in a situation. Especially fond of pie, she laughed to herself when "Annie Stein and I went up and talked to the manager and told him 'how wicked it was of him not to let me have a piece of custard pie.'" After more than four months of picketing, the manager finally phoned Terrell to capitulate, inviting her and Stein to have coffee and pie as his treat. As Ella Baker later explained to students forming the Student Non-Violent Coordinating Committee (SNCC) in 1960, Terrell knew it was "bigger than a hamburger" or a piece of pie.[39]

The U.S. Court of Appeals finally took up the Thompson's Restaurant case. A friend of the court brief was signed by "prominent Washingtonians," including several ministers, a rabbi, a past president of the National League of Women Voters, and "Miss Dorothy R. Swift, past president, Washington Branch, American Association of University Women." The brief urged that the antidiscrimination laws be recognized as enforceable. But the court decided in January 1953 that the ordinances were no longer valid and, even more implausibly, that segregation was necessary for public order. Terrell responded with outrage: "This moral justification of segregation is in direct conflict with the realities of life. Segregation notoriously promotes tension and racial strife—not peace and good order." The committee vowed to appeal the decision to the U.S. Supreme Court: "The decision of the U.S. Court of Appeals is a disgrace to our country. It is openly racist, and has been compared to the *Dred Scott* decision, which led to the Civil War. It justifies segregation as a way of maintaining peace and order and implies that violence and rioting would follow in our national capital if all citizens were permitted to sit down in restaurants."[40]

Annie Stein moved back to Brooklyn in early 1953, before the case was decided in the Supreme Court. Terrell declared, "It was a tragedy. I didn't see how we could get along without her." In some ways, Stein had become the smart, engaged, activist daughter that Terrell had hoped Phyllis would be, following in her footsteps and taking a leading role in the Civil Rights Movement. After Stein left, the women corresponded. Stein's first letter began, "Dearest Mrs. Terrell, I have been thinking of you and remembering so much and even dreaming about you since I left Washington." Acknowledging their friendship and a reception in tribute to her that Terrell had organized, Stein wrote, "I miss you very much. . . . Let me thank you again for that beautiful reception—it was perfect in every detail and a memory to be cherished. . . . With all my love to you, Yours, Annie."[41]

The two activists soon had something to celebrate. On June 8, 1953, the Supreme Court unanimously issued a ruling, written by Justice William O. Douglas, that the antidiscrimination ordinances were still in effect. Terrell was thrilled: "I will be 90 on the 23rd of September and will die happy that children of my group will not grow up thinking they are inferior because they are deprived of rights which children of other racial groups enjoy." The coordinating committee responded by appealing to African Americans "to make full use of their rights" to ensure that all stores and restaurants complied with the decision. It emphasized that every customer must be given equal access and respect.[42]

To celebrate Terrell's ninetieth birthday, the committee organized a huge banquet. One thousand attendees heard accolades from Walter White of the NAACP and Judge William Hastie, the first black federal judge and former NAACP lawyer. Turning ninety did not mean that Mollie Terrell intended to slow down. She and the committee decided to push for the broadest possible interpretation of the Supreme Court decision by immediately targeting movie theaters. They announced that an integrated group of four friends would accompany Terrell to dinner and a movie on her birthday. Understanding the implications of the ruling and the threat of an impending desegregation campaign, each of the still-segregated D.C. theaters capitulated.[43]

The coordinating committee was never expected to be permanent; it was designed to bring other organizations together to desegregate Washington stores and restaurants. But after the movie theaters desegregated, it immediately launched two new campaigns, one for equal access to District hotels and one for fair employment, working to break the color barriers denying African Americans jobs in bus driving, department stores, and government employment.[44]

The committee's successes, Stein's departure from D.C., and Terrell's death on July 24, 1954, signaled that the group had attained its main goals. Without its leaders, it disbanded. The coordinating committee had rid the nation's capital of overt discrimination in public facilities and proved the value of its direct action tactics combined with a legal assault on discrimination. Subsequent campaigns, including the Montgomery bus boycott that began the year after Terrell's death, used many of the same methods that had proved successful in Washington, D.C. Yet the District fight was unique in the Civil Rights Movement of the 1950s and 1960s because it was officially and jointly run by two women, one African American and one white, rather than by black male ministers.

"Colored Women Have Two High, Hard Handicaps to Hurdle"

While Terrell led the coordinating committee's battle against discrimination, she simultaneously fought for justice for Rosa Lee Ingram and other black women subjected to sexual violence. In November 1947, Ingram, an African American widowed sharecropper and mother of fourteen, with twelve living children, was beaten over the head with a gun by her neighbor, a white male sharecropper, in rural Georgia. In an interview with the *Pittsburgh Courier*, Ingram revealed that her assailant was a predator who had tried to assault her sexually in the past, although the issue was not overtly raised by her lawyers during her trial. Two of Ingram's young sons begged the neighbor to stop beating their mother and ran for help from their sixteen-year-old brother, who took the man's gun and struck him on the head. The assailant died, and Rosa Lee Ingram and two of her teenaged sons were charged, tried, convicted, and condemned to death by electric chair in February 1948, despite their lawyers' argument that they were innocent of murder on the grounds of self-defense.[45]

Once word of the death sentences spread through the Atlanta media to the national African American press, a huge outcry ensued, leading to a grassroots campaign to overturn the unfair sentences. In March 1948, a delegation of women, including Terrell, met with President Truman and Attorney General Tom Clark to plead for their intervention. In an uneasy alliance, the NAACP worked on a legal defense while the Civil Rights Congress focused on developing public support and fundraising appeals to assist the other Ingram children. The NAACP feared getting smeared as communist for working with the CRC. It also worried about the CRC's willingness to use dramatic publicity stunts that might drive up its own membership while ignoring the careful legal strategy the NAACP was pursuing to dismantle Jim Crow. However, by the next month, public attention and pressure led the local judge to commute the Ingrams' sentences to life in prison with the possibility of parole in seven years.[46]

The commutation of the Ingrams' sentences ended the NAACP's legal defense options but opened the door to the CRC's organizing of public protests demanding pardons and/or early parole. Early in March 1949, two black women, Ada Jackson of Church Women United and Maude White Katz, a Communist Party activist and CRC member, met with Mollie Terrell to discuss forming the National Committee to Free the Ingram Family, with Terrell as chair. Since her AAUW fight had not yet been resolved, she knew that she risked disapproval for agreeing to lead a communist-affiliated organization, but sexual violence against African American women and the country's unfair criminal justice system were issues of importance to her, and she eagerly agreed to lead the committee.[47]

Ingram Committee officers Terrell, Katz, and Jackson worked together closely as they planned events in Washington and Georgia. Their first move was to send an interracial delegation of women to meet with the Ingram family, as well as with Georgia's segregationist governor, Herman Talmadge, son of the recently deceased governor Eugene Talmadge. Although the national NAACP shied away from the CRC, some local NAACP branches were more willing to work with them. While in Georgia, the Ingram Committee delegation met with Austin T. Walden of the local NAACP. Walden expressed appreciation of Terrell's high-profile role as chair, for she lent prestige and gravitas to the cause.[48]

Terrell took the lead in planning for a group of women to gather in D.C. to implore President Truman to intervene. She approached the special and administrative assistants to the president—both of whom she had met before. These relatively liberal white men, from whom she expected a courteous, if not warm, response, gave her the runaround. They and their clerks avoided committing themselves, or the president, to a meeting. To escape the bad publicity of rejecting their direct appeals, Truman refused to meet them. Although the delegates had not secured an invitation, Terrell accompanied them to the White House offices, while saying to the press, "It would be a shame to have 50 or 100 women ... come here just to have their picture taken."[49]

Although unsuccessful, their actions brought media attention and pressured officials to consider the case of a poor African American woman punished by the criminal justice system as if she had been the assailant. Terrell's Ingram Committee also held interracial prayer vigils, sent delegations of women to Georgia, mailed thousands of pointed Mother's Day cards to Truman, and collected tens of thousands of signatures on petitions to the United Nations.[50]

The National Committee to Free the Ingram Family held a fundraising reception in New York City in June 1949 and honored Terrell and its executive
secretary, Theresa L. Robinson, national grand directress of the Elks. Terrell
was introduced by a white woman and friend Dr. Gene Weltfish, an anthro-
pologist who taught at Columbia University. Terrell gave her speech, received
"large beautiful bouquets," and then went "to see Dr. Du Bois" to invite him
to write a petition to circulate on behalf of the Ingrams. The Ingram Committee sought his name and talents to lend prestige and publicity to their cause.
Reaching beyond typical petitions to Congress, the committee planned to
take the petition to the United Nations. Du Bois agreed.[51]

The committee gathered an impressive thirty thousand signatures on the
petition to take to the Human Rights Commission of the United Nation's
Economic and Social Council, meeting at Lake Success, New York, on September 19, 1949. Terrell traveled from New York City with Weltfish, "a most
congenial companion. I consider her a dear friend. I am perfectly satisfied with
the manner in which I read the address. Many women complimented and
praised me." Noting their interracial friendship, she recorded, "Dr. Gene Weltfish and I walked arm in arm most of the time."[52]

Although she had been skeptical of the League of Nations after World
War I, Terrell had more faith in the United Nations, viewing it as a serious
response to the horrors of World War II. She believed it to be the best international forum at which African American women could level a formal protest
against legally sanctioned racism in the United States. Speaking before the
U.N. Human Rights Commission at the General Assembly, Terrell formally
presented "a Petition to the United Nations Protesting Discrimination in the
U.S. and the Rosa Ingram Case" to the General Assembly on behalf of "Mrs.
Ingram, individual," and, just as important, "for colored women on general
principles." The petitioners protested gendered, sexualized racism and violence
in the United States, citing the Ingram case as one example.[53]

Terrell's U.N. speech represents the final evolution of her political thought
and concerns in the last years of her life as a militant activist. In it, she protested against the inhumane and unjust treatment of African Americans. She
highlighted the failures of the nation "called 'the Greatest Democracy on
Earth'" to ameliorate "the conditions under which thousands of colored people are forced to live"—conditions she described as being "as unjust, cruel, and
shocking as any which history records." The case of Rosa Lee Ingram was a way
to protest the criminal justice system more broadly. Terrell described Ingram
as a widowed mother who had been "convicted and sentenced to be hanged
in a Georgia court for a crime she did not commit." Ingram and her sons had
acted in self-defense, and Terrell emphasized the racist double standard at

work: "Under similar circumstances it is inconceivable that such an unjust sentence would have been imposed on a white woman and her two sons."[54]

For the first time, Terrell used an international forum to criticize the United States, pushing back sharply against its claims to democracy and freedom, critiquing them as mere Cold War rhetoric with no substantive equality of treatment behind them. Emphasizing the intersectional nature of race and sex discrimination in the United States, Terrell reiterated her long-held claim that African American women encountered "difficulties and disappointments . . . at every turn. The white women of the country have only one handicap to hurdle—that of sex. Colored men have just one handicap to hurdle—that of race. Colored women have two high, hard handicaps to hurdle—both race and sex." Ingram's situation, she insisted, was not an anomaly: "A colored woman who is the victim of a white man's advances or violence has no redress in the courts."[55]

Hoping to be heard sympathetically at an international venue dedicated to human rights, Terrell shared the horrific information that she had presented two decades earlier to the National Woman's Party and to which she had received a hostile, indifferent response. Noting that African American women were unrecognized as lynching victims, she referred to particularly traumatizing cases: "On several occasions, the bodies of colored women have been ripped open, their babies snatched out, and thrown into a river nearby or on the ground." Terrell informed her global audience, when "colored people are lynched in the United States . . . the perpetrators of these crimes are rarely punished."[56]

Condemning pervasive racism and discrimination in the United States, Terrell described unequal, "dilapidated," segregated schools and terrible "living and housing conditions [that exist] . . . because of prejudice against their race." She explained that "well-trained colored people are unable to secure employment, so that they can earn a living and help support their families." She gave specific examples of racial discrimination and segregation in Washington, D.C., arguing: "If colored people living in the national capital are subjected to such injustice and humiliation, one can easily imagine what the status and fate of colored people, especially colored women, must be who live in Georgia or in the other states where slaves were bought and sold for nearly 300 years." Concluding, Terrell asked the Human Rights Commission to "thoroughly investigate" the Ingram case on behalf of African American women in the United States so that Rosa Lee Ingram and her sons could be freed. The United States was not, she maintained, upholding its commitments to its own constitution or as a member of the United Nations.[57]

Satisfied with having had an international platform upon which to indict the United States, Terrell noted that her U.N. speech had been "a thrilling experience." To Phyllis, she wrote, "This has truly been a wonderful day. I have presented a petition on behalf of Mrs. Ingram and I have been overwhelmed with congratulations. I was allowed to read every word of it, although I expected to be allowed to read only a few sentences." In her diary, she described it as "A Great Day—Present petition for Mrs. Ingram and colored women to Mrs. Myrdal. About 70 women present. Only 4 allowed [to speak]. Petition greatly praised." Women there told her, "Some of us had tears in our eyes. All of us had lumps in our throats." (Terrell thought humorous the comment of a woman who mistook her for the mother of civil rights activist Shirley Graham, saying, "Shirley Graham's mother really can talk.")[58]

By the end of summer 1951, the Ingram Committee's pace slowed because its New York leaders found themselves overextended, being called on by the Civil Rights Congress to participate in several other high-profile court death-penalty cases involving black men. Some radical African American women resented this redirection of their attention and organized a separate group in August 1951, the Sojourners for Truth and Justice. A sympathetic Terrell joined the 132 Sojourners who met in Washington, but she also agreed to chair a reorganized and revitalized CRC committee, the Women's Committee for Equal Justice (WCEJ). Because of pressure on the CRC from African American women leaders, the WCEJ operated more independently in order to focus solely on the Ingram case.[59]

The WCEJ continued to send interracial delegations to Georgia, always trying to meet with the Ingrams as well as with Governor Talmadge. In 1953, Talmadge agreed to meet a delegation of sixty women, led by the indomitable Terrell, who asked that he grant the Ingrams clemency. Although he did not change his position, insisting that clemency was the sole purview of the parole board, the women's continuous protests had disquieted him enough to force a meeting with him. Annie Stein, Terrell's compatriot in the D.C. anti-discrimination fight, exclaimed, "You didn't even mention your courageous visit to Georgia to see the Governor. Even I, who knows so well what wonders you are capable of, was astonished by your daring. How I wish I could hear a blow by blow description of that visit from your own lips!"[60]

The intrepid Terrell kept the Ingram case in the public eye into her ninety-first year while also highlighting black women's defense of themselves. She was planning to lead another delegation to Georgia on Mother's Day in May 1954 when she fell ill with heart problems and cancer. That month, she celebrated the Supreme Court's decision in *Brown v. Board of Education* with her daughter, Phyllis, in Highland Beach, Maryland. She died on July 23, 1954, in an Annapolis hospital, just a few months before her ninety-first birthday. Terrell's

FIGURE 14.2. Mollie is with her son-in-law, Lathall DeWitt Langston, whom Phyllis married after the death of her second husband, F. E. Parks. Langston is showing his mother-in-law the *Washington Afro-American* headline announcing the U.S. Supreme Court's *Brown v. Board of Education* May 17, 1954, decision. This landmark ruling deemed segregation laws unconstitutional, providing a ninety-year-old Terrell with a good measure of satisfaction at the progress the black freedom struggle was making. The photograph was likely taken at Mollie's Highland Beach home, which she shared with her daughter and son-in-law. Visible in her hands on her lap is her hearing aid. In her later decades, Mollie sat in the front row or front table at meetings and banquets whenever possible, often using an ear trumpet to try to hear the speakers. (Courtesy Oberlin College Archives)

death left her Women's Committee for Equal Justice without strong leadership just as its parent organization, the CRC, was coming under intensifying attacks as a communist organization. Protests continued at a less intense pace until the Ingrams were finally freed in 1959.[61]

As part of a global community of "women of darker races," Mollie Church Terrell joined African Americans whose international perspectives on human rights, equality, and full citizenship broadened the scope of the Civil Rights Movement. In the Cold War era, they forced the federal government to take civil rights more seriously—as an issue with global, foreign policy ramifications. Terrell's international experiences and perspectives allowed her to approach the fight for civil rights as a broader, linked struggle for all women and people of color around the world.

Conclusion

Born on the cusp of slavery and freedom, Mollie Church Terrell became a foundational figure in the black freedom struggle. Terrell's temperament and bearing embodied what she termed "dignified agitation" and announced her pride in being both an African American and a woman. Asserting her full humanity, Terrell maintained her determined optimism for a better future throughout her long and productive life. Her family history of enslavement as well as her experiences with the daily indignities of racial prejudice, segregation, employment and workplace discrimination, and financial stresses, among others, shaped the range of her activism and her determination to confront and eliminate prejudice and injustice. A passionate advocate for social change, Terrell used her privilege in constructive ways, lobbying in the halls of Congress and meeting with presidents to argue for federal antilynching laws, improved funding for black schools, better jobs and training for African Americans, and an end to segregation.[1]

Although she had been happy and carefree as a girl, even then Mollie had seen in herself the "beginning of temper and rebellion." She had reasons to be angry, as did civil rights leader Ella Baker, who recalled trying "to control my temper. I had a high temper." Societal norms for a more compliant femininity made anger in women, especially black women, seem frighteningly out of control and in need of repression. Yet Terrell, Baker, and other African American women activists turned their outrage at the injustice of racism into a creative, generative, redemptive anger—a powerful motivating force for their involvement in social justice activism.[2]

A leading black clubwoman and civil rights icon, Mollie Church Terrell was a complex, multidimensional woman whose private life helps us understand her reform priorities. Like other prominent African American women, she understandably often hid her personal life from a potentially hostile public gaze. Yet her joys, weaknesses, strengths, and struggles illuminate her motivations and reveal the connections between her personal circumstances and activism.

Born during the liberatory violence of the Civil War, Mollie also saw the brutal white supremacist terrorism of the Reconstruction era that almost killed her father. Her enslaved grandmothers had birthed children who were the product of white men's sexual assaults; the rape of African American women by white men did not stop with the end of slavery. Nor did vicious stereotypes that denied black women the sexual purity and respectability that mainstream American society assumed of white women. It was in part to debunk these attacks that African American women first formed their own national organization, the National Association of Colored Women. Violence against African American women and men is a legacy of slavery that persists today, as evidenced in police shootings, stand-your-ground laws, and mass incarceration.

───────────

To advocate equal rights for African Americans and women, Mollie Terrell sought a national platform. She first gained that platform when she was elected president of the National Association of Colored Women in 1896. Her NACW reform priorities reflect her empathy and compassion, especially her decision to focus on materially improving the lives of African American women and their families. This was not an abstract charity project. Having experienced the reproductive challenges suffered by so many black women as well as having witnessed the traumatic damage caused by white supremacist violence, Mollie chose to transform tragedy into programmatic action.

Aiming to create a safety net to sustain African American families, Terrell linked childcare and maternal health and welfare to a broader civil rights agenda. She encouraged the NACW's institution building, including its establishment of day care facilities, kindergartens, settlement houses, homes for unwed mothers, orphanages, old age homes, and professional nursing schools. Insisting that segregation and convict lease labor programs be dismantled, Terrell also encouraged NACW members to fight for the passage of federal antilynching laws, equal access to education, a full range of employment opportunities, and a woman suffrage amendment.

Mollie Terrell's reproductive experiences reveal another legacy of enslavement. African American women's experience of loss around childbearing was and is devastating. Enslaved women's lack of access to high-quality health care and autonomy over their bodies manifests itself in the ongoing crisis of infant and maternal mortality. Researchers find that "black infants are more than twice as likely to die as white infants, and this rate is still increasing."[3]

In a dominant culture that defined white women as the only victims of rape, Terrell condemned the mistreatment and sexual abuse of African American women at the hands of white men, especially those in vulnerable jobs such as domestic service. Insisting on the full humanity and just treatment of African American girls and women, she pointed out that those caught up in the criminal justice system had little ability to exercise their citizenship rights.

In 1912, Terrell met with the governor of Virginia to defend the life of a poor African American teenaged girl sentenced to death in the electric chair for accidentally killing in self-defense her abusive white woman employer. After the 1919 D.C. riots, too, Terrell approached the prosecutor to defend a black teenage girl against the false charge of murder after her family's home was invaded by gun-wielding whites. And in 1953, Terrell led a delegation to meet with Georgia's governor to advocate for clemency for Rosa Lee Ingram.

Two civil rights icons, Mollie Church Terrell and Rosa Parks, were committed to defending African American women from violence or rape by white men as well as from the institutional violence of the U.S. criminal justice system. A decade before Parks initiated the Montgomery bus boycott, they worked on the same case in 1945. The much younger Parks formed the Committee for Equal Justice for Mrs. Recy Taylor, a rural Alabama woman who had been gang raped by six white men who abducted her as she walked home from church. Parks could not accept that Taylor's assailants were well known in the community but were free, without any investigation of their crime. Terrell joined the national board of advisers of Parks's Committee for Equal Justice, demanding a formal investigation to hold the men accountable for their violent crime.[4]

———

The black freedom struggle necessitated, from Terrell's perspective, a multi-pronged approach, including engaging directly with white women's groups. Her class status, higher education, and light skin tone enabled Terrell to enter otherwise off-limit spaces in which she voiced African American women's distinct priorities, highlighting the links between racial and gender justice. Once in those spaces, she aimed to convince white women in the mainstream suffrage, peace, and feminist movements of the necessity of demanding full equality for all women, regardless of color. Terrell identified black men's unjust disfranchisement as a significant problem in itself and then linked it to black women's struggle for the vote and for equality. Yet access did not always lead to greater understanding; Terrell and other black women persisted for decades but did not successfully break through white women's indifference to achieving and protecting voting rights and equality for all.

That Terrell persisted in bridge-building work even when it subjected her to racist humiliations reveals her stubborn determination, strength of character, and contradictions. Wise enough to know when compromise was life-saving and when it might be the only way to achieve an end, Terrell was periodically forced to do so by the very exigencies of black female life in America, conditions she fought to correct. She was not ideologically pure or consistent. Rather than divorce herself from movements or political parties that offered a less radical position, Terrell worked within them, trying to move them toward an agenda of racial and gender justice. From her perspective, it was worth it to endure prejudice and slights in order to put social justice issues onto other groups' platforms and agendas.

At one level, Terrell was a pragmatist, willing to compromise to achieve substantive, if incremental, change. But she was simultaneously a radical willing to help found interracial civil rights organizations like the Constitution League and the NAACP as well as to work with communist front organizations fighting for workers' rights and racial justice. When the lives of poor African American Americans were on the line, Terrell embraced alliances and coalitions that spanned the class spectrum. She willingly participated, for instance, in communist-led popular front activism on behalf of poor black men's civil rights. The NAACP's initial decision to decline to mount a legal defense for the Scottsboro Nine inspired Terrell to work with the International Labor Defense legal team. She lent her respectability and political voice to defend the rights of these young African Americans, most still legally children, who were unjustly accused of gang rape.

Just as Rosa Parks's activist life was far longer and more complex than the one moment when she sat down on the bus in Montgomery, Alabama, so Mollie Church Terrell cannot be defined by one or two moments, whether it be her presidency of the National Association of Colored Women or her desegregation win in the U.S. Supreme Court. From the 1890s through the 1950s, Terrell had a complicated, multilayered life and approach to activism, pressing continuously for full equality and justice. For decades, she engaged simultaneously in many forms of civil rights advocacy and activism. Writing and speaking were her most important means of promoting social justice, but Terrell used varied other tactics, including direct action to achieve her goals of full citizenship for blacks and women.

The octogenarian Terrell gladly seized the opportunity to lead post–World War II direct-action civil rights protests. Her late-life protests against segregation, discrimination, and the mistreatment of black Americans gratified her because they were part of a vital postwar civil rights movement that was gaining more traction with a wider public than at any earlier time. Remaining optimistic and forward-thinking to the end of her life, on her eighty-sixth birthday, Mollie reflected in her diary with contentment and gratitude: "I can go where I want to, my mind is alert as it was and my capacity for enjoyment is as great as it ever was. . . . I have the respect of everybody so far as I know, the affection of many people and the desire of many to honor me in every way they can."[5]

FIGURE C.I. In February 1954, two different generations of civil rights activists, Mollie Church Terrell and Thurgood Marshall, were presented with the Seagram Vanguard Award by the Utility Club, an African American women's community service organization in New York City. Marshall and a beaming Terrell were recognized for their desegregation work. Her plaque celebrated her successful efforts to desegregate Washington, D.C., restaurants and stores as an "inspiration to people everywhere." (Courtesy Oberlin College Archives)

A deeper, longer perspective on her activism helps us place Mollie Church Terrell more prominently into nearly a century of struggle for African Americans' and women's rights. She was, as Paul Robeson characterized her, an "unceasing militant" struggling "for the full citizenship of her people." Terrell, he proclaimed in his eulogy, "leaves us a rich heritage and a noble example to be followed by us all until full and final victory."[6]

Mollie Church Terrell's life history matters today. It shows us what real activism looks like. Social justice work is often slow, continuous, and undramatic. It requires perseverance and dedication, even when there are no signs of progress. Terrell suffered periodic episodes of depression and self-doubt, but hardly a week went by during her adult life when she did not attend more than one meeting and often several on the same day. She was persistent, attending as many NAACP meetings, for example, in the 1940s as she had in earlier decades of the twentieth century. Terrell realized that social change was slow and uneven, but she never gave up hope. She was sometimes hard to get along with, demanding, and critical of others who were not as ready for persistent action or to take her lead. But by constantly showing up and participating in discussions about reform priorities and tactics, by understanding the way certain issues needed to be elevated at particular historical moments, and by watching and participating in the long arc of activism, Terrell both provided leadership and perspective and encouraged and inspired younger generations.

ACKNOWLEDGMENTS

These acknowledgments start by commemorating two great women, my mother, Joanne Johnson Parker, and my mother-in-law, Carol Lamar Blake. I wish they had been able to read this completed biography of Mary Church Terrell, for they cheered me on and offered ideas and support as I wrote it.

My family history informs my interests and approach to the life of Mary Church Terrell. As a young woman, my mother, Joanne Johnson Parker, was still writing her dissertation in English literature at Northwestern University when she got her first teaching job at the Woman's College of the University of North Carolina, Greensboro. The college had been integrated since 1956, when the first two black students entered the freshman class. By 1962, almost a dozen African American and about eight Jewish students were admitted. More famously, just two years earlier, four college students from the historically black North Carolina A&T State College had nonviolently protested segregation with a sit-in at a downtown Greensboro Woolworth's. My mother and her students organized boycotts and picket lines to try to integrate three establishments adjoining their campus—a coffee shop, a small restaurant, and a movie theater. Their actions were met with fierce resistance from their white neighbors, who spat in their faces, threw beer cans filled with urine at them, shouted racial epithets, and threatened them. All three establishments eventually gave into their demands and integrated.

My mother was the only faculty member who participated in the movement, inviting students to use her office as their headquarters, picketing the local stores, and going with them in integrated groups to desegregate the movie theater. In response, white faculty members wrote "N—— lover" on her door in faculty housing. She did not stay in North Carolina, but she was there long enough to have a transformational experience that gave her a new perspective on civil rights and equality.

Joanne Johnson Parker carried with her the need to pursue social justice, an insistence on racial equality, and a passionate commitment to lifelong organizing for social change. Later, in the wake of the women's liberation movement, she became deeply involved in the struggle for the Equal Rights Amendment and women's reproductive rights. She capped a long teaching career with two decades at Westlake School for Girls, a private college preparatory school in

Los Angeles. By the early 1980s, she had initiated one of the first high school–level women's studies courses in the nation and won outside funding to bring in remarkable women to speak for women's history month, including Alice Walker, Gloria Steinem, Toni Morrison, Shirley Chisholm, Amy Tan, Sally Ride, Pat Schroeder, Judy Chicago, and Bella Abzug.

My mother was my role model and my inspiration. I trace my own commitment to social justice to her fierce and loving insistence that we never accept the status quo if we can envision something better. I hope I have begun to pass on this legacy of empowerment and social justice on to my remarkable daughter, Frances Caroline Parker-Hale. I have all confidence she will make her grandmothers proud.

I give deep thanks and appreciation to my loving and creative sister, Sabrina Parker, who devoted herself to caring for our mother and providing her joy in the last years of her life.

Geoffrey Hale has sustained me emotionally and intellectually throughout our more than thirty years together. He recently agreed to uproot our lives in Rochester, New York, in order to have a new adventure in Philadelphia, as I started a new job. This happy new beginning, including his finding an exciting job, coincided with the untimely deaths of his mother and then mine. Supporting each other through these challenging times has only increased our love for each other.

My sincere thanks go out to my colleague Stephen Middleton, who introduced me to Mollie Church Terrell's family. Raymond Langston, Terrell's stepgrandson, his wife, Jean Langston, and their daughter, Monique, generously shared their private collection of Terrell's papers with me. Thanks, too, to my friends and colleagues at Oberlin College who welcomed the family's gift of Terrell's papers. At Oberlin, Carol Lasser introduced me to President Marvin Krislov and Archivist Ken Grossi, who worked with the Langstons to accept their bequest. Oberlin College Archives has done a wonderful job of preserving Terrell's papers. Many thanks, too, to Cecilia Robinson, digital librarian at Oberlin, who shared with me her extensive research on Louisa Ayres Church.

Librarians and archivists are historians' best allies, helping us access the documents that let our histories come alive. I greatly appreciate the assistance of librarians at the Library of Congress; the librarians at the Moorland-Spingarn Research Center at Howard University, especially Joellen El Bashir, Ida Jones, and Tewodros Abebe; librarian Edwin Frank and Head of Special Collections Gerald Chaudron at the University of Memphis; the librarians at the New York Public Library's Schomburg Center for Research in Black Culture; and the staff at the Chicago History Museum.

Carol Lasser also helped me reach out to Nancy Bercaw, a curator at the

Smithsonian Institute's National Museum of African American History and Culture, to facilitate the Terrell family's gift of several of her important artifacts to the museum. I had the generous assistance of the family of U.S. Representative Oscar Stanton DePriest, too, as I researched Terrell's relationship with him. My understanding of DePriest was enriched by a series of phone interviews I conducted with his relatives. Representative DePriest's great-grandson Philip DePriest generously invited me to come to Chicago to review their private collection of his papers.

I am fortunate to have had several dear friends and colleagues who played key roles in helping me improve my manuscript at various stages. Steve Maizlish is a great friend whom I first had the pleasure to meet while teaching at the University of Texas, Arlington. He generously and heroically read and offered cogent comments on an early draft of the entire manuscript. Always a smart and careful reader, Steve guided me to put my arguments up front while putting the historiography into my endnotes. His enthusiasm for my project uplifted and encouraged me. Other University of Texas at Arlington colleagues who became close friends are Susan Hekman, Wendy Faris, and Joyce Goldberg.

Jenny Lloyd, a friend from the State University of New York, College at Brockport, also played a heroic role toward the end of the project, when she, too, read every chapter and helped me edit for clarity. I deeply appreciated— and gratefully accepted—Jenny's kind offer to help me with the bibliography. Others similarly gave of their time and expertise, reading significant portions of my manuscript at various stages (often more than once). Peter Eisenstadt, one of my most erudite friends, with an encyclopedic knowledge of American history, offered me cogent advice on multiple chapters, helping me to improve them by pointing me to scholarship I might otherwise have missed. Lori Ginzberg, an old friend who is now a new neighbor and walking companion, provided valuable assistance with my introduction and conclusion.

For almost two decades, I had the pleasure of running the Rochester United States History (RUSH) working papers group, which allows Americanists from a variety of universities and colleges to share our work. Some of us have read multiple chapters from more than one book together. These scholars became my lively intellectual community. I am especially grateful for the help and collegiality of RUSH members Tamar Carroll, Susan Goodier, Carol Faulkner, Victoria Wolcott, Rich Newman, Carole Emberton, Timothy Kneeland, Jennifer Lloyd, Peter Eisenstadt, Dorinda Outram, Rachel Remmel, Michael Brown, and Rebecca A. R. Edwards, among others. I am also grateful to my History Department colleagues at the State University of New York, College at Brockport, including Steve Ireland, Meredith Roman, Katherine Clark Walter, Anne Macpherson, and Bruce Leslie. I thank Brockport for granting me Scholarly Incentive awards and the Kutolowski History Department Research Scholar award.

My loving friends have been a source of solace and joy over the years. From the bottom of my heart, I thank Tina Chung, Caterina Falli, Jyothsna Ponnuri, Amy Hsi, Jun Okada, Pilapa Esara Carroll, Sonia Kane, Greta Niu, Valeria Sinclair Chapman, Deepika Bahri, and Roz Gallman for always being there.

I am truly grateful to have been selected to be an Andrew Mellon Advanced Fellow at the James Weldon Johnson Institute for the Study of Race and Difference at Emory University (2017–18). That year gave me the time to write intensively while developing friendships with an amazing cohort of scholars, especially Amrita Chakrabarti Myers, Felipe Hinojosa, Charissa Threat, Ashante Reese, Derek Handley, Justin Hosby, Taina Figueroa, Alexandria Lockett, and the welcoming scholars who ran the program, Kali-Ahset Amen Strayhorn and Andra Gillespie. I also received help from Nicole McCoy as a graduate assistant. An invaluable benefit of the fellowship was a book workshop. I was honored to have some of the best minds in the field, Carol Anderson, Kimberly Wallace-Sanders, Rosetta E. Ross, and Jacqueline A. Rouse, read my manuscript and offer incisive and constructive critiques and encouragement.

Thanks are also due to my editor, Amy E. Davis, who took a real interest in Terrell and helped make this a better (and shorter!) book. In addition, my sincere gratitude is due to the supportive and helpful team at the University of North Carolina Press, including Dylan White, Jay Mazzocchi, Allie Shay, and Anna Faison. From the start, Chuck Grench, executive editor of the Press, recognized the significance of publishing the first scholarly full-length biography of Terrell. I appreciate his faith in me. Chuck and Dylan generously offered a developmental edit before the manuscript went into copy editing, helping to make it a more accessible read. I am also grateful to the anonymous expert readers for the press who offered close readings and excellent suggestions to improve the manuscript. I tried my best to follow their advice.

The unfailing and generous support of three amazing friends and mentors, Ula Taylor, Nancy Hewitt, and Carol Lasser, has made all the difference. Finally, my new colleagues have made my arrival at the University at Delaware such a joy.

NOTES

Abbreviations

CD	*Chicago Defender*
Church Papers	Robert R. Church Family Papers, University of Memphis Libraries, Special Collections
DP	Oscar DePriest private collection, DePriest family, Chicago
HB	Mary Church Terrell private collection, the Langston/Terrell family, Highland Beach, Maryland. Most of these papers are now in the Oberlin College Archives.
MCT	Mary Church Terrell
MCT Collection	Mary Church Terrell Collection, Moorland-Spingarn Research Center, Howard University, Washington, D.C.
MCT Additions	Mary Church Terrell Collection Additions, Moorland-Spingarn Research Center, Howard University, Washington, D.C.
MCT Papers	Mary Church Terrell Papers, Library of Congress
RHT	Robert Heberton Terrell
RHT Papers	Robert Heberton Terrell Papers, Library of Congress
WB	*Washington Bee*
WP	*Washington Post*

Introduction

1. Terrell was born on September 23, 1863, and died on July 24, 1954.

2. Pioneering black women's historians introduced us to Terrell in the 1980s and 1990s, focusing on her turn-of-the twentieth century presidency of the National Association of Colored Women (NACW). While praising the NACW as the first national forum for black women's leadership, they critiqued the NACW's motto, "Lifting as we climb," as showing the class distance and patronizing attitudes of middle- and upper-class black clubwomen toward poor and working-class women. Deborah Gray White, for instance, identified "the promise of protection [from sexual assault and denigrating stereotypes] clubwomen had demanded" and stated that this was a "promise the extended gloved hand of Mary Church Terrell could not fulfill." Sharon Harley similarly concluded: "Despite the progressive views expressed throughout her active public life, Terrell epitomized black upper-middle-class leadership and seldom appeared among the black masses, except in church gatherings . . . her efforts on behalf of the masses were limited largely to an occasional comment about the need for a training school for black domestics and talks on the subject of 'Colored Domestics.'" In the intervening years, scholarship on Terrell has expanded, giving us chapters in books and articles that have

begun filling in the story of Terrell's life and activism. The only full-length studies of Terrell in the past decades are biographies by young adult and children's authors as well as a monograph by Joan Quigley on Terrell's late 1940s and early 1950s antidiscrimination campaign in Washington, D.C. These authors provide a compelling but inaccurate narrative arc, suggesting that Terrell was so concerned with respectability that she was less radical early in her career. They correctly identify her as the daughter of well-off formerly enslaved parents and as the "respectable" leader of the NACW and a strong orator. Then, they jump a few decades ahead to the end of her life. For example, Quigley argues that Terrell was less confrontational earlier in her career and moved to direct action in her old age only because she felt she had less to lose and was frustrated by the lack of progress on her cherished civil rights goals. For the narrative arc, see Robnett, *How Long?*, 51; Jones, *Quest for Equality*; and Quigley, *Just Another Southern Town*. See Fradin and Fradin, *Fight On!*; Lommel, *Mary Church Terrell*; McKissack and McKissack, *Mary Church Terrell*; Swain, *Civil Rights Pioneer*; Sterling, *Black Foremothers*. Several scholars have established Terrell as a significant public figure: Jones, *Quest for Equality*, 1–92; Quigley, *Just Another Southern Town*; Cooper, *Beyond Respectability*; Lindsey, *Colored No More*; Harley, "Mary Church Terrell"; Higginbotham, *Righteous Discontent*; Davis, *Women, Race, and Class*; White, *Too Heavy*; Salem, *To Better Our World*; Terborg-Penn, *African-American Women*; Gatewood, *Aristocrats*; Moore, *Leading the Race*; Shaw, *What a Woman*; Shepperd, *Mary Church Terrell*; Wilks, "French and Swiss Diaries." Other scholars include her in their studies of African American radicals, including Carle, *Defining the Struggle*; Alexander, *Army of Lions*; McDuffie, *Sojourning for Freedom*; Gore, *Radicalism*; and Horne, *Black and Red*. Works that highlight her family history of enslavement are by Jones-Branch, "Mary Church Terrell," and Jenkins, *Race*. Theoharis, *Rebellious Life*, and McGuire, *Dark End of the Street*, discuss how Rosa Parks was similarly misunderstood as one-dimensional.

3. See McDuffie, *Sojourning for Freedom*, 175–76; Gore, *Radicalism*, 85–98; and Quigley, *Just Another Southern Town*.

4. Anastasia Curwood laments that "the inner lives of African Americans" have been hidden. Curwood, *Stormy Weather*, 7; Higginbotham, "African-American Women's History," 266; Hine, "Rape," 915–16; Hammonds, "Black Female," 99; Farr, "Question," 459–60.

5. Higginbotham, "Foreword," ix; Curwood, *Stormy Weather*, 139; duCille, *Coupling Convention*, 46.

Chapter 1

1. Louisa Ayres Church became known as Louise Martell after she moved to New York City in 1878. The New York City directories document her name change and list her as a hair store owner. I have not discovered a record of a second marriage to a Mr. Martell. The 1880 census lists her as M. L. Church, a white female head of household with two children, Thomas and Mary E., who were "at school." The Shelby Country Register of Deeds (https://register.shelby.tn.us) contains the Memphis Directories and Robert and Louisa's real estate transactions. Louisa's gravestone, put up by Mollie in the Lincoln Memorial Cemetery in Prince George's County, Md., reads "Louisa Ayres Church, 1844–1911, Mother of Mary Church Terrell." Louisa is buried beside her son, daughter,

and son-in-law. See the New York City Directories, New York Public Libraries Digital Collection; the 1880 U.S. Federal Census for Memphis, Shelby County, Tenn., https:// archive.org/details/populationschedu1563unit/page/n17; and https://www.findagrave .com/memorial/171865804/louisa-church#view-photo=147994919. Many thanks to Cecilia Robinson, digital librarian at Oberlin College, who shared her extensive research on Louisa Ayres Church.

2. Lucy might have grown up on a Caribbean island, since "Malay" was used to refer to "mixed Indian-African enslaved peoples from the Caribbean. Childs, "Red Clay," 110; Jenkins, *Race*, 159–60; P. P. B. Hynson to Robert R. Church Sr., 1901, HB.

3. Mollie inherited a coral necklace her family believed to have been worn by her great-grandmother when she arrived in the United States. We do not know with certainty the identity of Emmeline's white father. Finley, "'Cash to Corinna,'" 420–22; Green, "Mr. Ballard," 17–40; Clark, *Strange History*, 131, 161; Landau, *Spectacular Wickedness*, 58; Hynson to Church, 1901 (emphasis added).

4. I have been able to identify Dr. Phillip Patrick Burton, for the first time, as the Church family's owner. Jenkins observes that the Burton family letters do not name "their ancestor, the Virginia planter who originally purchased Lucy. He remains anonymous, the protection of the original paternal slave-owner's name making it difficult to determine the identity of the white family." Part of the confusion comes from Captain Church's having purchased his twelve-year-old son Robert; many assume that he had always been Robert's owner. Robert R. Church received a letter from Emily Scott Burton Wilson Byers, a daughter of Dr. Burton, in December 24, 1891. The eighty-one-year-old Byers had read an article about Church in the Memphis *Evening Scimitar* celebrating his many successes and decided to write to him. Later, in 1901, Robert Church also corresponded with Byers's nephew P. P. B. Hynson, whose mother was Rosalie Burton Hynson Archer. Robert Reed Church received at least three letters from Dr. Burton's daughter Mrs. Emily Byers in 1891. Two of these letters survive at the University of Memphis archives. Jenkins, *Race*, 160–61; Church and Church, *Robert R. Churches*, 6; E. S. Byers [Emily Scott Burton Wilson Byers] to R. R. Church and Wife, December 24, 31, 1891, both in Church Papers; "Robert R. Church," *Colored American Magazine*, February 16, 1901, 9.

5. "A former slave . . . noted that white men 'will buy a sprightly, good-looking girl that they think will suit their fancy, and make use of them.'" Elna C. Green notes the "frequency with which white men acknowledged black children, even those who were owned by other white men—something not uncommon given the proximity of many enslaved women to their master's white male associates and friends." Green, *Remember Me*, 18, 72; Robert R. Church, "Congressional Committee Testimony," June 2, 1866, in Fogelson and Rubenstein, *Mass Violence*, 226–27; Hynson to R. R. Church Sr., 1901, HB.

6. Hynson to Church, 1901 (emphasis added).

7. Hynson to Church, 1901.

8. MCT, "The Black Mammy Monument," 1923, MCT Papers, reel 21.

9. Charles B. Church (May 15, 1812–August 4, 1879) lived in Ohio, in Holly Springs, Miss., beginning in the 1830s. By 1850, he moved to Memphis. In an 1873 history of that city, he is listed as a member of the "Old Folks of Shelby County" and as "a prominent Mason and a founding director of Union and Planters' Bank." Keith, *Fever Season*, 198–99; Jenkins, *Race*, 160–61, 163; Davis, *Old Times Papers*.

10. Emily Epstein Landau notes, "Many planters used slaves for sex. This was the prerogative of planters, elaborating the privileges of patriarchy in an immediate and tangible way." Landau, *Spectacular Wickedness*, 56.

11. "Burton-Aikin Feud," *Encyclopedia of Arkansas*, http://www.encyclopediaofarkansas .net/encyclopedia/entry-detail.aspx?entryID=5477; "The Burton-Aikin Feud," *Independence Country Chronicle*, April 1972, 1–31; Lankford, *Surprised*; Byers, *Torn by War*; A. C. McGinnis and W. Jasper Blackburn, "Tragic Events," *Batesville (Ark.) Guard*, February 28, 1883; Hynson Family biography in *Biographical and Historical Memoirs of Fulton County, Arkansas* (Goodspeed, 1889), 289, www.mygenealogyhound.com/arkansas -biographies/ar-fulton-county-biographies-p-p-b-hynson-geneaology-fulton-county -arkansas-mammoth-spring.html. Neill, "Reminiscences of Independence County."

12. Population Schedules of the Seventh Census of the United States, 1850, Shelby County, Tenn., Memphis Ward 6, Charles B. Church and family microform, National Archives.

13. Emily Burton Byers later asked Robert Church: *"What became of you when you was taken from me?* My twin brother who attended to my affairs at that time was under arrest for killing a Dr. Aikin who had murdered a younger brother of ours." Jenkins, *Race*, 161–65; Church and Church, *Robert R. Churches*, 6–9; E. S. Byers to "Friend R. R. Church and Wife," December 24, 31, 1891, Church Papers; Church, "Testimony."

14. Robert Reed Church Sr. and Anna Wright Church had two children: Robert Reed Church Jr. (October 26, 1885–April 17, 1952) and Annette Elaine Church (August 6, 1887–March 19, 1975). Mollie's half sister, Annette, and her niece, Sara Roberta Church (June 5, 1914–July 15, 1995), the daughter of her half brother, Robert Church Jr., self-published a book on Church family history in 1974. Church and Church, *Robert R. Churches*, 5–7; Sigafoos, *Cotton Row*, 42–43; MCT, *Colored Woman*, 1.

15. Robert and his second wife, Louisa, agreed on one important first order of business—that he should provide an education for Laura, his daughter with Margaret Pico: "After the emancipation, probably about 1866, Robert R. Church made a visit to New Orleans . . . and requested of his former slave wife that he be allowed to take their daughter Laura, and care for her and place her in school." Margaret agreed, so Robert visited again around 1867, arranging for Laura to join him in Memphis. Laura did not stay long with the Church family, although she briefly met Louisa, Mollie, and the new baby, Thomas. Young Mollie did not remember this brief encounter with Laura, who might have been introduced to her as a Church relative rather than as her half sister. Schooling for African Americans was so terrible in Memphis that Robert sent Laura to Nashville to be educated as a teacher at Fisk University during the 1868–69 academic year. Laura probably stayed only one year before returning to her mother in New Orleans, where she continued her schooling. In 1878, when Laura was about twenty, she married. She and her father "corresponded occasionally" over the decades. After her father's death, Laura Church Napier sued her father's third wife, Anna Wright Church and her adult children, Robert Reed Church Jr. and Annette Church, hoping to inherit some of her father's estate. The Supreme Court of Tennessee determined that although she was indeed his child, Laura "was never made a member" of his household and was thus illegitimate and had no claim to her father's inheritance. Richardson, *History of Fisk*, 2–15, quotation on 15; *Napier v. Church* 132 Tenn. 111 (1915).

16. Margaret Pico, Robert R. Church, and Laura Church Napier are mentioned in the *Memphis Commercial Appeal*, November 16, 1928; Lauterbach, *Beale Street Dynasty*, 1; Keith, *Fever Season*, 44–45; *Napier v. Church*.

17. Memphis Directories, https://register.shelby.tn.us/index.php; Church and Church, *Robert R. Churches*, chap. 1.

18. Louisa's owner/father, T. S. Ayres, characterized himself as a Union "loyalist" when, during Reconstruction, he repeatedly filed suit to receive "rent" from the U.S. government for use of his building, which had been seized by the quartermaster general in January 1863. Right after the war, his claim was summarily rejected on the grounds that "Memphis was a hostile city captured from the enemy, and it and everything in it became prize of war." By 1874, Congress was more receptive to notions of national white reconciliation. Its Committee on War Claims reported his claim "favorably to the House," which gave Ayres the substantial sum of $5,995 (he had asked for $7,815). Mills, *Southern Loyalists*, 23; Ira Berlin et al., *Slaves No More*, 35, 49, 59, 75; Report of Committee on War Claims, H. Rep. Bill no. 3186 "for the relief of Treadwell S. Ayres," *Cong. Rec.*, vol. 2, part 5, June 5, 1874, 4627–28; Durham, *Nashville*, 233–34, 270–72.

19. *Napier v. Church*.

20. Laura Ayres Parker to MCT, May 25, 1913, HB.

21. Henry Ayres to Louisa Ayres, Indenture Made on December 9, 1862, registered April 28, 1866, Shelby Country Register of Deeds, book 0056, p. 095, https://register .shelby.tn.us/index.php.

22. Church and Church, *Robert R. Churches*, 11; Henry Ayres to Louisa Ayres, Indenture; Parker to MCT, May 25, 1913, HB; *Napier v. Church*.

23. Parker to MCT, May 25, 1913.

24. MCT, *Colored Woman*, 10; Parker to MCT, May 25, 1913.

25. The American novelist Julia Van Rensselaer Cruger first suggested that MCT write her life history in 1905. Cooper, *Beyond Respectability*, 68; MCT Diary, September 9, 1905, quoted in MCT Diary [1916, but is copies of diaries from earlier years] and Notes, 29, HB.

26. Parker to MCT, May 25, 1913; *Napier v. Church*; MCT Diary, December 29, 1947, MCT Additions; MCT, *Colored Woman*, 1.

27. MCT, *Colored Woman*, 11.

28. MCT, *Colored Woman*, 11.

29. Eliza Ayres lived with her former son-in-law Robert Church on Ruth Street in Memphis until she died at sixty on July 7, 1882. For the traumas of slavery, see Painter, "Soul Murder," 127. MCT, *Colored Woman*, 10; "Died," *Memphis Daily Appeal*, July 12, 1882; MCT to Robert R. Church Sr., September 26, 1900, Church Papers.

30. *Napier v. Church* .

31. Jenkins states that Ayres "gave or loaned Louisa $800 for beauty-store products." Commenting on the spread of segregation, Mollie noted, "If she were alive today [1940] I doubt very much whether she or any other colored woman could rent a store in such a prominent business section." Jenkins, *Race*, 151–52; Mills, *Southern Loyalists*, 23; Report of Committee on War Claims, 4627–28; *Taylor-Trotwood Magazine*, 404; "Funeral of Mrs. C[atherine] M. Ayres," *St. Louis Republic*, October 7, 1903.

32. Jones-Branch, "Mary Church Terrell," 71; MCT, *Colored Woman*, 9–10.

33. *Public Ledger* (Memphis), August 2, 1876, as quoted in Lauterbach, *Beale Street Dynasty*, 46–47, and chap. 2; Jenkins, *Race*, 174–75.

34. Church, "Testimony"; Lauterbach, *Beale Street Dynasty*, 16, 28; MCT, *Colored Woman*, 7.

35. Church, "Testimony."

36. Kidada Williams notes that "when African Americans decided to testify about experiencing . . . racial violence, they were not merely giving statements; they were resisting violence discursively." Williams, *They Left*, 6; Lauterbach, *Beale Street Dynasty*, 16; Church, "Testimony."

37. Church, "Testimony."

38. Charles Church did not name his children in his will and appointed his wife, Lizzie, as the executor of the estate, with her and their (white) children getting equal shares. See Shelby County Probate Records, Charles B. Church, Will 1879, case no. 4022 (image 501).

39. Jenkins, *Race*, 151–52; Lauterbach, *Beale Street Dynasty*, 70, 175; MCT, *Colored Woman*, 6–7, 9, 36.

40. Rosen, *Terror*, 61–66; Patler, *Jim Crow*, 29; Fogelson and Rubenstein, *Mass Violence*, 5, 35–36; MCT, *Colored Woman*, 7–8, 15–17.

41. As Preston Lauterbach notes, "His reputation still clung to violence, as he seemed constantly at the center of every Negro shooting affray, cutting incident, and brass knuckle assault from 1866 to 1876." Lauterbach, *Beale Street Dynasty*, 45.

42. *Public Ledger* (Memphis), August 2, 1876, quoted in Lauterbach, *Beale Street Dynasty*, 45–47; Jenkins, *Race*, 181.

43. Even at sixty-four in 1903, Robert R. Church defended himself forcefully and was unwilling to be treated disrespectfully. When two white brothers started "a street fight" with Church "by insulting and provoking" him, they ended up "incarcerated with their heads broken," while Church was described as being in his mansion, "recuperating from a wound on the head and cuts." *Memphis Commercial Appeal*, January 11, 1878, September 20, 1903, quoted in Ingham and Feldman, "Robert R. Church," 137.

44. Jones-Branch, "Mary Church Terrell," 69; Crosby, *American Plague*; Sigafoos, *Cotton Row*, 99; McKee and Chisenhall, *Beale Black and Blue*; Lauterbach, *Beale Street Dynasty*, 32–33, 46–47, 70, 160.

45. Jeanette Keith notes, "The 1880s had been good to Robert Church, but the 1890s saw a decline in freedom for all black people in Memphis. White Memphis politicians succeeded in disfranchising most black male voters in 1889." Keith, *Fever Season*, 200–201; Church and Church, *Robert R. Churches*, 51–53; Lauterbach, *Beale Street Dynasty*, 46–47; MCT, *Colored Woman*, 37–38.

46. RHT to Robert R. Church, March 16, 1900, series 1, box 1, folder 25, Church Papers.

47. Mollie Church to Robert R. Church Sr., November 21, 1888, HB.

48. "Biography," Robert R. Church Family of Memphis Guide to the Papers with Selected Facsimiles of Documents and Photographs, edited by Pamela Palmer, in *Bulletin: An Occasional Publication of the Mississippi Valley Collection* 10 (Memphis, Tenn.: Memphis State University Press, 1979), 9; Jenkins, *Race*, 151; Lauterbach, *Beale Street Dynasty*, 39. Federal Census, Schedule 1, "Inhabitants in the Seventh Ward, Memphis, in

the Country of Shelby, State of Tennessee," 1870, https://archive.org/details/population schedu1563unit/page/n17. "A Church Divorce," *Public Ledger* (Memphis), March 4, 1874.

49. The Shelby County divorce records for that time period are missing, according to the registrar (correspondence with author, October 2018). Kuersten, *Women and the Law*, 88; Bardaglio, *Reconstructing the Household*, 148; MCT, *Colored Woman*, 10.

50. The *Memphis Daily Appeal* announced, "Last night the police station house docket contained the following arrests: Lou Church . . . for doing business without license." Later, the recorder "disposed of the following business . . . Lou Church (colored), doing business without a license, case continued." *Public Ledger* (Memphis), March 8, 1878. On March 10, her name appears in the *Memphis Daily Appeal* among the list of undelivered telegrams remaining at the Western Union telegraph office. Louisa had moved to New York City, and the case remained unresolved. She is listed in the 1879 New York City directory as Church, Martel L., Hair, 421 Sixth Ave. She is also listed in the 1880 Census in New York City as M. L. Church, living at 421 Sixth Ave., as the white female head of household, hair store owner, with two children, Thomas and Mary E., "at school." See *Public Ledger* (Memphis), February issues in 1876 and 1878; Population Schedules of the Tenth Census of the United States, New York, microform, National Archives. Thanks to Cecilia Robinson of Oberlin College for these citations. MCT, *Colored Woman*, 10, 81.

51. Cooper, *Beyond Respectability*, 69–70; MCT, *Colored Woman*, 18–20; MCT Diary and Notes, 36, HB.

52. MCT, *Colored Woman*, 27; MCT Diary and Notes, 33, HB.

53. MCT, *Colored Woman*, 18–19; MCT Diary and Notes, 130, HB; MCT Diary, February 23, 1940, HB.

54. MCT, *Colored Woman*, 23.

55. MCT, *Colored Woman*, 23.

56. MCT Diary and Notes, 130, HB.

57. Janet H. McKelvey Swift, "Mary Church Terrell as I Knew Her," 1954, MCT Additions; MCT, *Colored Woman*, 51.

58. Her father's mother, Emmeline, was the first black person confirmed in the Episcopal church in Arkansas. Mollie regretted having to attend a segregated church in Oberlin, an ostensibly progressive town with a history of abolitionism. The Congregationalists' restrained worship appealed to college-educated black women such as Anna Julia Cooper, who, according to White, "found the emotionalism of black worshippers 'ludicrous,' and Mary Church Terrell [who] found it 'discouraging and shocking to see how some of the women shout, holler and dance' during services. To Cooper and Terrell, such behavior only reinforced the pervasive negative images of black women." Jenkins, *Race*, 160–61; MCT, *Colored Woman*, 31; White, "Cost of Club Work," 261.

59. MCT, *Colored Woman*, 41.

60. MCT, *Colored Woman*, 46.

61. After her encounter with the distraught widow at Oberlin, Terrell was not as comfortable with leading public prayers or participating in testimonials or communion. During a 1911 lecture tour to raise interest and money for homes for pregnant black teens, she was visiting a Cincinnati home for "wayward" white girls and felt awkward about public prayers. She wrote her husband, Berto: "I had to pray at morning prayers Monday morning, a thing I hate to do in public because I don't know how to talk to

the Deity aloud, not being on such familiar terms with him as you are." Despite the tentative and private nature of her faith, she reported, "I got by somehow." In 1894, W. E. B. Du Bois almost lost his job as a professor at Wilberforce University because he refused to lead the students in a public prayer. Marable, *Du Bois*, 22; MCT, *Colored Woman*, 46, 285–86; MCT to RHT, October 31, 1911, MCT Papers, reel 1.

62. MCT, *Colored Woman*, 46–47.

63. Most African American women did not receive any liberal arts degrees but instead earned teaching certification. Evans, *Black Women in the Ivory Tower*, 38, 47, 49; Solomon, *Company of Educated Women*; Gordon, *Gender and Higher Education*; Washington, "Anna Julia Cooper," 264; MCT, *Colored Woman*, 32, 41; Cooper, *Voice from the South*; MCT Diary, February 13, 1909, MCT Papers, reel 1; MCT Diary, April 27, 1907, quoted in MCT Diary and Notes, 227, HB; MCT, Address on Woman Suffrage Delivered to Teachers of the Public Schools of Washington, April 12, 1910, MCT Papers, reel 21.

64. MCT Diary, August 31, 1888, in Wilks, "French and Swiss Diaries," 12, 31; MCT, *Colored Woman*, 48; MCT Diary and Notes, 33, HB.

65. Jenkins, *Race*, 151; Church and Church, *Robert R. Churches*, 27–28, 30, 32n9; MCT, *Colored Woman*, 58–59.

66. MCT, *Colored Woman*, 59.

67. MCT, *Colored Woman*, 59–60.

68. MCT, *Colored Woman*, 62–63.

69. "After that Father never objected to my teaching." MCT, *Colored Woman*, 63.

70. MCT, *Colored Woman*, 63–64.

Chapter 2

1. The couple's love letters, until recently, were privately held by Mollie Church Terrell's family. They are now at the Oberlin College Archives. They help dispel Joan Quigley's mischaracterization of their marriage as always being on the verge of divorce. Quigley, *Just Another Southern Town*, 66–68, 79.

2. Robert Terrell may sometimes have had more than a "social glass." There are some indications in Mollie's letters and diaries that he had trouble controlling his drinking. A popular Berto became grand master of the Prince Hall Masons of the District of Columbia by 1898. According to Audrey Kerr, the Mu-So-Lit Club had "its own clubhouse. . . . W. E. B. Du Bois frequented the club during visits to Washington to engage in friendly debates with his peers." The twenty-five or so members of the Boulé Epsilon chapter in Washington included men with advanced educations, ranging from B.A.s to Ph.D.s, as well as medical and law degrees from prestigious institutions. After Berto's death, Mollie put up a tombstone that read: "Robert Heberton Terrell, 1857–1925, Commencement Orator Harvard Univ. 1884, Judge Municipal Court, D.C. 1902–1925." See the membership list in the *Boulé Journal: The Official Publication of Sigma Pi Phi Fraternity*, September 1920, in RHT Papers, reel 4; Kerr, *Paper Bag Principle*, 59; Moore, *Leading the Race*, 63, 181–82; W. E. B. Du Bois, "Terrell," *The Crisis*, March 1926, 216; and MCT, "Robert Heberton Terrell, a Colored Judge of Washington, D.C.," 2, ca. late 1920s, box 102-1, folder 15, MCT Collection.

3. Robert Terrell's ability to win friends and respect across the color line in the highly

segregated capital is reflected in the attendance at his funeral of white municipal court judges, the U.S. marshal, and the clerk of the court of appeals. Lafayette McKeene ("L. M.") Hershaw, "From the Back Woods of Virginia to Judicial Eminence: A Brief Sketch of the Character and Career of Judge Robert H. Terrell," *Howard Alumnus*, January 15, 1926, 86; "Bench and Bar Pay Highest Tribute to Memory of the Late Judge Robert H. Terrell, Harvard's First Negro Honor Graduate, Appointed Judge of the Municipal Court of the District of Columbia by Presidents Roosevelt, Taft, Wilson and Harding," *Howard Alumnus*, January 15, 1926, 1, RHT Papers, reel 4; Du Bois, "Terrell"; Dr. Alain L. Locke, "Phi Beta Sigma Memorial to William Henry Lee (Zeta Sigma Chapter) and Hon. Robert H. Terrell (Alpha Sigma Chapter)," March 28, 1926, Royal Theatre, Baltimore, RHT Papers, reel 4.

4. MCT, *Colored Woman*, 65–66.

5. W. E. B. Du Bois earned his B.A. from Harvard College in 1890 and became "the first Black graduate to receive the PhD [from Harvard], in 1895." Mollie also appreciated Berto's choice of graduation speech topic: "The Negro Race in America since the Emancipation." As the black lawyer Raymond Pace Alexander described it, this "was certainly a very ambitious subject for a young man belonging to a race which had been free less than twenty years." Writing to her husband from Cambridge, Mass., where she was visiting in 1902, Mollie exclaimed, "I have come to the conclusion that next to being the wife of the president of the United States, being the wife of a Harvard graduate is the greatest honor that a woman could have." MCT to RHT, June 10, 25, 1902, June 10, 27, 30, 1909, MCT Papers, reel 2. Mary M. Meehan (curatorial associate, Harvard University Archives) to Dr. M. Sammy Miller (acting chairman, Department of History and Geography, Bowie State College, Md.), June 23, 1975, HB; MCT, "Robert Heberton Terrell," 1, 4, ca. late 1920s, box 102-1, folder 15, MCT Collection; Raymond Pace Alexander, "National Bar Association Issues Sketch of Judge Terrell's Life," March 17, 1931, MCT Papers, reel 6.

6. Patricia A. Schechter finds Ida B. Wells's autobiography "nearly silent on the emotional dimensions of the courtship not at all surprising given the heavy, negative scrutiny to which Wells-Barnett's sexuality had been subjected as an unmarried public figure." Schechter, *Ida B. Wells-Barnett*, 176; Giddings, "Last Taboo," 441–70; MCT, *Colored Woman*, 64–66.

7. Milton Lee was likely a member of the Lee family of the Memphis black elite. Mollie seems to have stayed in contact with the Lee family, helping a Milton Lee Jr. fight against job discrimination in Washington, D.C., in the 1930s. Noting her own physical desires, Mollie remembered, for instance, the "boy I saw at matinee attracted me." MCT Diary and Notes, 1916, 12, 15, 133, 137, HB.

8. Gatewood, "John Hanks Alexander," 103–28; MCT Diary, February 7, 1946, HB.

9. MCT, *Colored Woman*, 283–84.

10. Cooper, *Voice from the South*, 70–71.

11. MCT, *Colored Woman*, 66–68.

12. Mollie wrote, "You must tell me all about your Law work, the Literary Society, and the school work.... I must not take up so much of your time as I have with so many of my interminable letters." Mollie Church (Berlin) to RHT (D.C.), March 1889, HB; Quigley, *Just Another Southern Town*, 28; Wilks, "French and Swiss Diaries," 14.

13. Mollie became a part-time journalist. She was invited to be a correspondent for

the *Memphis Daily Scimitar* in 1886. By 1893, she was being paid for her contributions in the *Colored American* and writing for other journals. Wilks, "French and Swiss Diaries," 25; G. P. M. Turner to Miss Mary E. Church, December 19, 1866; and Thomas J. Calloway to MCT, April 26, 1893, both in MCT Papers, reel 3; MCT (Paris) to RHT (D.C.), July 1, 1904, HB; MCT Diary, November 10, 25, 1905, MCT Papers, reel 1.

14. Wilks, "French and Swiss Diaries," 26–29.

15. In the following years, there was some tension between the two women; Berto may be one of many reasons for the competitive nature of their relationship. Mollie Terrell told a "Mrs. Hill about Mrs. Cooper's enmity to me that I had never fought her, etc." From July through September 1906, two school board members, Dr. Atwood and J. F. Cook, tried to remove Cooper from her position. Terrell did not aid them, but she seems not to have rallied to Cooper's side. May, *Anna Julia Cooper*; MCT Diary, September 5, 1906, as quoted in MCT Diary and Notes, 200, HB; Mollie Church (Berlin) to RHT (D.C.), March 1889, HB.

16. For a thorough discussion of white Americans' fears of interracial marriage, see Pascoe, *What Comes Naturally*; MCT Diary and Notes, 21, 34, HB; MCT Diary, May 22, 1940, HB.

17. Otto von Devoltz to Miss Mary Church, October 1889 (postcards in Italian), January 7, 1890, MCT Papers, reel 3; MCT, *Colored Woman*, 88, 91–92.

18. Later, in 1940, Mollie mused about what it might have been like for a black woman to have been married to a Jewish man during the rise of the Nazis, suggesting that any dream she might have had of avoiding persecution by living abroad would not have been fulfilled. "Letter from Otto von Devoltz asking Father to let him marry me, February 7, 1890," MCT Diary and Notes 1916, 141, HB; Robert R. Church to Devoltz, February 26, 1890, Church Papers; MCT, *Colored Woman*, 92.

19. Referring to Frances Harper's *Iola Leroy* (1892), Ann duCille argues that "sexual desire is not *displaced* by social purpose but *encoded* in it—regulated, submerged, and insinuated into the much safer realm of political zeal and the valorized venue of holy wedlock." duCille, *Coupling Convention*, 44–45. See also Rudolph, "Victoria Earle Matthews," 119; Du Bois, *Soliloquy*, 86; Lewis, *Du Bois: Biography of a Race*; and MCT, *Colored Woman*, 91–92, 372–82.

20. Frances Watkins Harper "reconfigured the fictional conventions of the marriage plot so as to envision relationships that would satisfy black women's desire for individual development, romantic love, and racial uplift." Field, "Frances E. W. Harper," 113; Parker, *Articulating Rights*, 182–84; MCT Diary and Notes, 27, HB; MCT, "Robert Heberton Terrell," 4.

21. RHT to Robert A. Church, January 6, 1891, MCT Papers, reel 3.

22. Lauterbach, *Beale Street Dynasty*, 99; duCille, *Coupling Convention*, 14. Robert R. Church Sr. to RHT, November 24, 1891; MCT Diary and Notes 1916, 19, 27; and Thomas A. Church Sr. to MCT, June 15, 1892, all in HB.

23. Mollie was offered the job in a letter from Amelia Field Johnston, the dean of women, and Oberlin's first female professor. "Mrs. Mary Churchill [*sic*] Terrell, '84," by G. R., December 26, 1933, Correspondence of President E. H. Wilkins, MCT file, 28-2/7/1, box 75, MCT Collection, Oberlin College Archives; MCT, *Colored Woman*, 103.

24. Higginbotham, *Righteous Discontent*, 42; Neverdon-Morton, *Afro-American Women*, 13; Mollie Church to RHT, October 24, 1890 (Treasury Department, "a 1st

letter, 4am"); and Mollie Church to "Mr. Terrell," undated, 1891, both in HB; MCT, *Colored Woman*, 103.

25. The median age of first marriages by gender (not race) in 1890 was twenty-six for males and twenty-two for females. U.S. Census Bureau, Historical Marital Status Tables, https://www.census.gov/data/tables/time-series/demo/families/marital.html. MCT, *Colored Woman*, 104–5.

26. Darlene Clark Hine identifies "a culture of dissemblance"—of black women's protective silence that "shielded the truth of their inner lives and selves from their oppressors." Hine, "Rape," 912, 915; Wagner-Martin, *Telling Women's Lives*, 11; Gurstein, *Repeal of Reticence*; Dickerson, *Dark Victorians*, 10, 64, 95; Buick, "Ideal Works," 190–207; Gaines, *Uplifting the Race*, intro.; MCT, *Colored Woman*, 106–7.

27. At the turn of the twentieth century "blacks had the greatest birth-rate decline of all," much of it apparently by choice. For information on black women's fertility and birth rates, see Marsh and Ronner, *Empty Cradle*, 92–93, 143; D'Emilio and Freedman, *Intimate Matters*, 246–48; Gordon, *Woman's Body*, 154; Giddings, *When and Where*, 137, 149; Mitchell, *Righteous Propagation*, 91, 233; and Rodrique, "Black Community," 293.

28. I have been unable to locate Terrell's medical records. On dangers of pregnancy, see Leavitt, "Shadow of Maternity," 328–46; Leavitt, "Birthing," 243; and Ulrich, "'Living Mother,'" 27–48. MCT, *Colored Woman*, 106–7; Robert R. Church to RHT, telegram, June 9, 1892; and Thomas A. Church to MCT, June 15, 1892, both in HB.

29. Wyatt Archer was a leader of a D.C. social club for elite black men, the Lotus Club. Kerr, *Paper Bag Principle*, 54. Mollie Durham (Philadelphia) to RHT, June 16, 1892. See letters dated June 11–29, 1892, HB, to Berto from: Marianna Gibbons (Bird in Hand, Pa.); John K. Rector (D.C.); Joseph Lee (proprietor, Woodland Park Hotel, Auburndale, Mass.); Fred (Van Vranken Brothers, Merchant-Tailors, Albany, N.Y.); John E. W. Thompson (NYC); T. Thomas Fortune (*New York Age*, NYC); S. Liang Williams (husband of club woman Fannie Barrier Williams and Chicago law partner of Ferdinand Lee Barnett, who married Ida B. Wells in 1895); Ella L. Smith (Newport, R.I.); Rene Barquet [sp?] (Treasury Department, Office of U.S. Commissioner of Immigration, Port of New York); Harry (Newport, R.I., and Brooklyn, N.Y., addresses); Mollie Durham (Philadelphia); Marianna Gibbons (Bird in Hand, Pa.); Josiah T. Settle (attorney at law, Memphis, Tenn.); Clarence V. Smith (U.S. Courts, Boston); Louise C. Smith (San Francisco); and Alex Powell (NYC).

30. Thomas A. Church Sr. (NYC) to MCT (D.C.), June 15, 1892; and MCT (NYC) to RHT (D.C.), July 22, 1892, both in HB.

31. Abdur-Rahman, *Against the Closet*, 83; Lewis, *Du Bois: Biography of a Race*, 193; Lewis, *Du Bois: Fight for Equality*, 226–27; MCT (NYC) to RHT (D.C.), July 31, 1892, HB.

32. MCT (NYC) to RHT (D.C.), July 25, 1892; and MCT (Saratoga Springs, N.Y.) to RHT (D.C.), August 23, 27, September 7, 1892, all in HB.

33. In other instances, Mollie signed her letters, "With long, lingering kisses." Fortunately, the Terrell couple did not experience the awkward situation faced by a newlywed W. E. B. Du Bois with his wife, Nina. He remembered the awkward start of their marriage in 1896, which contributed to their distant relationship: "My wife's life-long training as a virgin, made it almost impossible for her *ever* to regard sexual intercourse as not fundamentally indecent. It took careful restraint on my part not to make her

unhappy at this most beautiful of human experiences. This was no easy task for a normal and lusty young man." DuBois had assumed his male "sex instinct" would be much higher than that of his "conventional" wife but was disturbed by the level of her aversion to sex, a problem that made him feel justified in having sex with other women to fulfill his desires. Du Bois, *Soliloquy*, 179; duCille, *Coupling Convention*, 109; MCT to RHT, July 25, 26, 27, 30, August 1, 2, 25, September 3, 1892; and RHT to MCT, December 22, 27, 1897, all in HB.

34. In New York City, Mollie was seen by a Dr. Flint and a Dr. McEwen. MCT (NYC) to RHT (D.C.), July 25, 26, 27, 28, September 2, 1892, HB.

35. Her friend, "Miss Shadd," was probably Harriet P. Shadd [Butcher], who taught at M Street High School in the early 1900s. MCT (Saratoga Springs, N.Y.) to RHT (D.C.), September 7, 14, 1892, HB.

36. MCT (NYC) to RHT (D.C.), August 1, 1892, HB.

37. Jones-Branch, "Mary Church Terrell," 69; MCT (NYC) to RHT (D.C.), July 25, 28, August 1, 31, 1892, HB.

38. Mollie's father and Thomas Moss were both members of the Tennessee Rifles black militia, which had prided itself on keeping black Memphians relatively safe from lynchings. Lauterbach, *Beale Street Dynasty*, 100–105; Schechter, *Ida B. Wells-Barnett*, 75–78; Giddings, *Ida*, 175–76; Bay, *To Tell the Truth*, chap. 3; Ida B. Wells correspondence to Robert R. Church, Church Papers.

39. The daily work of putting on "psychological armor" as a strategy of "vigilance," and a cloak of respectability to live and survive "in a racialized and racially stratified" nation, had and has serious psychological and physical costs for black Americans. Rhodes, "Pedagogies of Respectability," 422; Henderson, "Toni Morrison's *Beloved*," 77; Du Bois, "Of the Passing," 102; Lewis, *Du Bois: Biography of a Race*, 226–27; MCT, "The Progress & Problems of Colored Women," ca. 1920, MCT Papers, reel 20; MCT, *Colored Woman*, 105–8.

40. Scientists now recognize the "toxic stress" of racism on maternal health. DiPietro, "Role of Maternal Prenatal Stress," 71–74; Buss et al., "High Pregnancy Anxiety," 141–53; Shonkoff, Boyce, and McEwen, "Neuroscience," 2252–59; Wise, "Anatomy of a Disparity," 341–62; Richardson et al., "Exposure," 2506–17.

41. For concerns about bringing children into a world defined by enslavement, see Jacobs, *Incidents*, 62; Painter, "Soul Murder," 15–39; Williams, "Spirit-Murdering," 229–36; Erevelles and Minear, "Unspeakable Offenses," 127–46; Roberts, *Killing the Black Body*; Lorde, "Uses of Anger," 9; Mitchell, *Righteous Propagation*, 77, 105, 147, 159, 295; Bakare-Yusuf, "Economy of Violence," 311–23; and MCT, *Colored Woman*, 108.

42. MCT, *Colored Woman*, 108.

43. Referring to Wells's pen name, "Exiled," Terrell introduced her as "an exile driven from home, because she dared to raise her voice in defense of her own oppressed and persecuted people." Williams, *They Left*, 128–29; facsimile of an October 1892 announcement of a lecture by Wells from the *Washington Bee*, reprinted in Schechter, "'All the Intensity,'" 48; MCT, "Introduction of Ida B. Wells, to Deliver an Address on Lynching," 1893, MCT Papers, reel 20; MCT (from the D.C. Sanitarium of Dr. John R. Francis) to RHT (Boston), November 8, 1892, HB (Dr. Francis was "the owner of the Francis Sanatorium on Pennsylvania Ave., which specialized in obstetrics, gynecology, and surgery for women"); Chesnutt, *Exemplary Citizen*, 49n2.

44. On black resorts, see Alexander, *Homelands*, 445–50; Lutz, *Chesapeake's Western Shore*, 61–64; and Kahrl, *Land Was Ours*, chap. 3. Gerson, *Harriet Beecher Stowe*; Hedrick, *Harriet Beecher Stowe*, 208; MCT, *Colored Woman*, 158; MCT Diary and Notes, 44, 111, HB; MCT Diary, May 16, 1909, MCT Papers, reel 2; MCT to Laura Terrell Jones, February 20, 1930, MCT Papers, reel 6.

45. MCT to Jones, February 20, 1930.

46. When Mollie initially went on the lecture circuit, she was promoted in the Chautauqua Lecture programs as "the Female Booker T. Washington." Cooper, *Beyond Respectability*, 26; Marvin Caplan, "The Lost Laws Are Found Again," in MCT, *Colored Woman*, 434; Chautauqua Program, Danville, Ill., August 2–16, 1900, Rev. Edward Ellis Carr, Manager, RHT Papers, reel 4; MCT to Jones, February 20, 1930.

47. MCT Diary, March 12, 1895, MCT Collection; RHT to R. R. Church, November 6, 1895, Church Papers.

48. MCT, *Colored Woman*, 127, 151–52.

49. In 1933, Carter Woodson wrote Terrell, "The joy which I experienced in meeting with you from week to week was just as great as that afforded by the conference itself." MCT, *Colored Woman*, 135, 127–42; Woodson to MCT, November 8, 1933, MCT Papers, reel 7.

50. RHT to R. R. Church, October 25, 1896, Church Papers.

51. MCT, *Colored Woman*, 151–52, 106–7; RHT to R. R. Church Sr., November 26, 1896, Church Papers; MCT Diary and Notes, 46, HB.

52. Lewis, *Du Bois: Biography of a Race*, 212, 227–28; Mitchell, *Righteous Propagation*, 10, 133; Thomas, *Deluxe Jim Crow*, 34–36, 74, 206; Beardsley, "Race," 122–31; Rosenberg, *Care of Strangers*, 301. For infant mortality and hospital use among black women, see Dye and Smith, "Mother Love," 102–4; and Carson, "And the Results," 348–50.

53. Laurie A. Wilke argues that "for African-American women, motherhood and activism were not contradictory or mutually exclusive. For women who had been stripped of their mothering rights during enslavement, mothering *was* activism." Wilke, *Archaeology of Mothering*, 82, 180, 211; Washington, *Medical Apartheid*, 189–215; Roberts, *Killing the Black Body*; Kapsalis, *Public Privates*, 41–42; Morton, *Disfigured Images*, 23–24; Engerman, "Changes in Black Fertility," 129–31, 135; Mitchell, *Righteous Propagation*, 82; Thomas, *Deluxe Jim Crow*, 43–44, 80–81; Wertz and Wertz, *Lying-In*, 163, 244; Ross, "African American," 264; Reverby, *Examining Tuskegee*; Jones, *Bad Blood*, 232–33; MCT, *Colored Woman*, 107.

54. MCT, *Colored Woman*, 107.

55. Including the late-term miscarriage, this was her third failed pregnancy.

56. Rosetta E. Ross writes, "An African American religious worldview is the understanding that religious duty includes religious uplift and social responsibility, two foci that derive from, respectively, survival and liberation themes of Black religion." Ross, *Witnessing and Testifying*, 223–24; Alldredge, *Centennial History*, 20–23, 64; Quigley, *Just Another Southern Town*, 32–32; MCT, *Colored Woman*, 114. RHT, "Address to the University Park Temple Church," ca. 1900, RHT Papers, reel 2; MCT, "The Lincoln Memorial Congregational Church," 1901, MCT Papers, reel 22; MCT, "Up to Date," *CD*, November 24, 1928, 2; "Facts about the Establishment of the Lincoln Memorial Congregational Church Told [to] Mary Church Terrell by Mrs. Otwiner Smith," March 10, 1931, MCT Papers, reel 22.

57. See, e.g., RHT to R. R. Church, January 29, February 12, 1898, Church Papers; and MCT (Memphis) to RHT (D.C.), December 23, 29, 1897, HB.

58. For a discussion of how pain and fury similarly motivated Fannie Lou Hamer's activism, see Lee, *For Freedom's Sake*, 38, 181; and McGuire, *Dark End of the Street*, xvii–xxii, 26, 65–66.

59. RHT to R. R. Church, January 29, February 19, 1898, Church Papers.

60. See Carson, "And the Results," 359–62; Bogdan, "Childbirth," 116–19; and Lynaugh, "Institutionalizing Health Care," 251–53. For more on the prevalence of miscarriages, see Gordon, *Woman's Body*, 49; and Marsh and Ronner, *Empty Cradle*, 11. RHT to R. R. Church, April 18, 1898, Church Papers; Dr. Charles J. Jones to RHT, Bill "For Professional Services to Mrs. Mary C. and Baby Terrell," Philadelphia, April 10, 1898, HB.

61. In her diaries, Terrell often noted strange coincidences or times when she had psychic abilities. RHT to R. R. Church, April 18, 1898, series 1, box 1, folder 24, Church Papers; MCT, *Colored Woman*, 283–85.

62. She was thirty-seven. Whenever she was away lecturing, Mollie and Berto corresponded daily, revealing their continued closeness. While in Europe to speak at the International Congress of Women, Mollie wrote Berto, "If I could just feel your big strong arms around me, I'd almost die with joy." Another night she wrote, "I have never before understood what it means to be 'consumed with desire'—I fairly burn with longing to be near you." For the description of Terrell as a speaker, see Janet "Nettie" H. McKelvey Swift, "Mary Church Terrell as I Knew Her," 1954, MCT Additions. Marsh and Ronner, *Empty Cradle*, 107. MCT, *Colored Woman*, 115, 125–26; MCT to RHT, November 24, [n.d.], 1900, July 13, 1902, MCT Papers, reel 2; MCT to RHT, August 2, 1902, MCT Additions; MCT to RHT, July 14, 28, 1904, HB; MCT Diary, December 24–25, 1905, MCT Papers, reel 1.

63. Mollie said: "I could write all night—It's the only way I can be with you all night, alas. . . . Kiss her [Phyllis] and yourself thousands of times for me." When she was away in 1910, she sent Berto "a big, long, soulful kiss for you from your affectionate Wife." MCT (South Weymouth, Mass., written on B. T. Washington's Tuskegee stationery) to RHT (D.C.), July 4, 1902, HB; MCT to RHT, August 2, 1902, MCT Additions; MCT to RHT, June 25, 1902, July 24, 1910, MCT Papers, reel 2.

Chapter 3

1. Its first president, Mollie Church Terrell, addressed regional and national issues from establishing kindergartens to fighting lynching and segregation. A comprehensive history of the NACW is beyond the scope of this biography. Instead, this chapter is a study of Terrell's experience and role in the early history of black women's national club formation. Chapter 6 takes up Terrell's intersectional black feminism. See Parker, *Articulating Rights*, for an analysis of Terrell's political thought. On black women's clubs, see, e.g., Higginbotham, *Righteous Discontent*; Shaw, "Black Club Women"; White, "Cost of Club Work," 249–69; White, *Too Heavy*; Hendricks, *Gender, Race, and Politics*; and Flannagan, *Seeing with Their Hearts*.

2. Deborah White points out that at the turn-of-the-century there were too "few other opportunities for talented black women" to secure positions of power and author-

ity. Furthermore, men with strong egos received less criticism. Lewis concludes that "ego and obdurancy were integral to Du Bois's makeup. . . . Another name for them was vision." White, *Too Heavy*, 64–65; Lewis, *Du Bois: Biography of a Race*, 512. Wells-Barnett, *Crusade for Justice*; Schechter, *Ida B. Wells-Barnett*, 118, 124.

3. Also in 1892, Victoria Earle Matthews founded the Women's Loyal Union in New York City. White, *Too Heavy*, 27–29; MCT, *Colored Woman*, 148–49; "Colored Woman's League Preamble," June 1892, as quoted in MCT, "History of the Club Women's Movement," *Aframerican*, Summer and Fall 1940, 34–37; Anna Julia Cooper, "The National Association of Colored Women," *Southern Workman*, September 1896, 173–74; MCT, "First Presidential Address to the National Association of Colored Women," 1897, MCT Additions, and MCT Papers, reel 22; Fannie Barrier Williams, "The Club Movement among Colored Women of America," in *A New Negro for a New Century: An Accurate and Up-to-Date Record of the Upward Struggles of the Negro Race*, by Norman B. Wood and Booker T. Washington (Chicago: American Publishing House, 1900), 386–87 (hereafter cited as "Colored"); Fannie Barrier Williams, "Club Movement among Negro Women," in *The Colored American, from Slavery to Honorable Citizenship, by J. W. Gibson and Prof. W. H. Crogman; Special Features: National Negro Business League and introd. by Prof. Booker T. Washington; Club Movement among Negro Women, by Fannie Barrier Williams* (Atlanta: Hertel, Jenkins, 1905), 207 (hereafter cited as "Negro"); NACW, "Colored Woman's League," 451.

4. Terrell admired the abolitionists and suffragists Frederick Douglass and Susan B. Anthony, both of whom she knew personally and collaborated with in the early 1890s. Cott, *Grounding of Modern Feminism*, 68; Higginbotham, *Righteous Discontent*, 152; Terborg-Penn, "Discrimination," 17–27; MCT, *Colored Woman*, 148; Salem, *To Better Our World*, 14–27; White, *Too Heavy*, 27–29.

5. "Act of Incorporation, The Colored Woman's League," January 11, 1894, MCT Papers, reel 14; Cooper, "National Association," 173–74.

6. MCT, "What the Colored Woman's League Will Do," *Ringwood's Afro-American Journal of Fashion*, May–June 1893, 1–2, in Early Miscellany, no. 59, Records of NACW, 1895–1992, reel 6.

7. Anna Julia Cooper explained: "Toward the close of 1894, Mrs. Rachel Foster Avery, Corresponding Secretary of the Women's Council, which takes cognizance only of national bodies and comprises upwards of 700,000 women, invited the Colored Women's League to send fraternal delegates to the Triennial Council to be held in February, '95." Cooper, "National Association," 173–74.

8. The contributing editors were Victoria Earle Matthews, of New York; Fannie Barrier Williams, of Chicago; Josephine Silone Yates, of Kansas City; Elizabeth P. Ensley, of Denver; Alice Ruth Moore [Dunbar], of New Orleans; and Mollie Church Terrell, of D.C. (By 1896, Ruffin had to cut the paper to a bimonthly publication schedule because of lack of funds and stopped it entirely in 1897.) Streitmatter, *Raising Her Voice*, 64–69; MCT, "History of the Club Women's Movement," 36.

9. *Woman's Era*, November 1894, quoted in MCT, "History of the Club Women's Movement," 36; Mrs. J. Silone Yates, president, professor of history, in Lincoln Institute, "Report of the National Federation of Colored Women's Clubs to the National Council of Women at Washington," *Colored American Magazine*, May 1905, 263; NACW, "Colored Woman's League," 451; second quotation in Williams, "Colored," 387.

10. "To Form a National Society. Colored Women in Session at Boston Decide upon a Federation," *Chicago Times-Herald*, August 2, 1895, 10; Editorial, *WB*, August 17, 1895, 2; Williams, "Colored," 390, 392; Williams, "Negro," 208–9.

11. "Let Us Confer Together," *Woman's Era*, June 1895, quoted in MCT, "History of the Club Women's Movement," 36; Williams, "Colored," 400.

12. John W. Jacks to Florence Balgarnie, March 19, 1895, reprinted in 'A Timely Call,'" *Indianapolis (Ind.) Freeman*, June 22, 1895, cited in Silkey, "The Right," 171, 175n71. On negative stereotypes of black women, see Collier-Thomas, *Jesus*, 262–64; Herndl, "Invisible (Invalid) Woman," 136; White, *Ar'n't I a Woman?*, 49; Morton, *Disfigured Images*; Brown, "Imaging Lynching," 100–24; Kelley, *Race Rebels*; Rhodes, "Pedagogies of Respectability," 204–5; and Wolcott, *Remaking Respectability*. Sander Gilman argues that nineteenth-century pseudoscience represented black female sexuality as the most "pathological." Gilman, "Black Bodies," 212–13, 216. Cooper, "National Association," 173–74; "To Form a National Society. Colored Women in Session at Boston Decide upon a Federation," *Chicago Times-Herald*, August 2, 1895, 10; Editorial, *WB*, August 17, 1895, 2; Wells-Barnett, *Crusade for Justice*, 242; Williams, "Negro," 208–9; Williams, "Colored," 401–2.

13. Haley, *No Mercy*, 124–25; "Mediates for Miss Willard, Mrs. Lillie B. Anthony Seeks to Set Her Right with Colored Women," *Chicago Times-Herald*, August 1, 1895, 10.

14. Cooper, "National Association," 173–74.

15. Even the New England opposition to Terrell was not clearly ideological or political, since many African Americans in Boston were still debating whether and how much to criticize Booker T. Washington and Mollie Terrell's connection to him was already compromised by her more radical activism (see chapter 4). However, William Monroe Trotter of the *Guardian* was a fierce critic of Washington and his supporters in the Equal Rights League and was connected to some members of Ruffin's Woman's Era Club. Giddings, *Ida*, 419–20; Brown, *Pauline Elizabeth Hopkins*, 178–81; White, *Too Heavy*, 106–9; Salem, *To Better Our World*, 32–36; MCT, *Colored Woman*, 155.

16. "Call to the National Federation of Afro-American Women, Organized in Boston, Mass., July 31, 1895"; Editorial, *Woman's Era*, October 1895, quoted in MCT, "History of the Club Women's Movement," 37.

17. Cooper, "National Association," 173–74.

18. "Conventions of Colored Women: National League and the Afro-American Federation to Meet in July," *WP*, June 28, 1896, 2; "Colored Women's League: An Interesting Program Arranged for the Meeting Tomorrow," *Washington Evening Star*, July 13, 1896, 8.

19. Terrell did concede that the 1895 Boston conference was, as the *Woman's Era* put it, "the First National Conference of the Colored Women in America." Higginbotham, *Righteous Discontent*, 174, 180, 182; "Call to the National Federation of Afro-American Women," in MCT, "History of the Club Women's Movement," 37; "Morality Their Creed: First Session of the Colored Women's Convention. An Address by Mrs. Douglass. She Thinks Justice Could Be Aided by the Placing of Women upon the Police Court Branch—Report of the Credentials Committee Shows Delegates from Many Cities—Appointing of Standing Committees—Progress of Work in Several Branches," *WP*, July 15, 1896, 7.

20. Jones, "Mary Church Terrell," 25; "Mrs. Cook Re-Elected: Officers for a Year

Chosen by Colored Women's League," *WP*, July 17, 1896, 4. For black nationalism, see MCT, "Duty of the National Association of Colored Women," 263.

21. "May Unite Their Forces: Officers of Two Colored Women's Associations to Confer. Second Annual Convention Today of the National Federation, Following Closely upon the Convention of the National League," *WP*, July 20, 1896, 10.

22. "Assisting Their Race: Second Annual Convention of Afro-American Women. Delegates From Many States. The Sessions Presided Over by Mrs. Booker T. Washington, of Alabama—Address of Welcome in the Nineteenth Street Baptist Church by the Rev. Dr. Brooks—Response by Mrs. [Rosetta] Douglass Sprague [Frederick Douglass's daughter]—A Review of Auxiliary Work by Mrs. Brown," *WP*, July 21, 1896, 4; "Are Rivals No Longer: Colored Women's League and Federation Now United. Full Set of Officers Elected. The Last Day of the Federation's Session Taken Up in Christening Its Youngest Member, Master Barnett [Wells-Barnett's baby, Charles Barnett]—Many Speeches and Papers—Resolution Criticizing the Supreme Court for Sustaining the Single Coach Law [*Plessy v. Ferguson*]—Lynching Denounced," *WP*, July 23, 1896, 4. The list of resolution committee members is from "The Afro-American Women. Hon. John W. Ross, District Commissioner Welcomes Them to the National Capital in a Timely Speech. Mrs. Booker Washington, Presided," *WB*, July 25, 1896, 4.

23. "Cannot Agree," *WB*, July 18, 1896, 4; "They Say," *WB*, July 18, 1896, 2.

24. The *Bee* listed Terrell as from Memphis. Editorial, *WB*, July 25, 1896, 4; "MCT, "History of the Club Women's Movement," 37.

25. Streitmatter, "Josephine St. Pierre Ruffin," 149; MCT, "The Black Mammy Monument," 1923, MCT Papers, reel 21.

26. Giddings, *Ida*, 374; MCT, "History of the Club Women's Movement," 38.

27. "Uniting Their Forces: Committees of Colored Women Agree on Details. Officers Will Be Elected Today. The Name of the Consolidated Afro-American Federation and the Women's League Will be the National Association of Colored Women—Convention of the Federation Session All Day—Addresses by Mrs. Booker T. Washington and Many Others," *WP*, July 22, 1896, 4; "Are Rivals No Longer."

28. For the club numbers, see "Assisting Their Race"; and "Mrs. Terrell's Triumph," *WB*, July 25, 1896, 4.

29. The *Bee* concluded that Terrell "displayed more natural sense, logic and eloquence than we have heard for some time." Tepedino, "Founding and Early Years"; "Mrs. Terrell's Triumph."

30. Another section of the paper identified Terrell as "the feminine Demosthenes," praising her oratorical and political skills as well as her beauty. "Mrs. Terrell's Triumph" and "Convention Notes," *WB*, July 25, 1896, 4.

31. On the contested relationship between Wells-Barnett and Terrell, see Schechter, *Ida B. Wells-Barnett*, 116, 144; Paula Giddings, *When and Where*, 106–8; and Wells-Barnett, *Crusade for Justice*, 243, 258–60, 328.

32. On religion in black activist women's lives, see Jones, "'Make Us,' 153; Jones, *All Bound Up*, 201; Collier-Thomas, *Jesus*; and Higginbotham, *Righteous Discontent*, 147–53.

33. Hendricks, *Fannie Barrier Williams*, 142–46; Williams, "Negro," 210.

34. This "electrical treatment" was known as gynecological electrotherapeutics. Giddings mistakenly assumes that Terrell was getting the electroshock therapy that some of her peers, such as Adella Hunt Logan, underwent. Giddings, *Ida*, 416; Massey,

Conservative Gynecology, intro.; combined quotation from letters, RHT to R. R. Church, May 17, 23, 1897, series 1, box 1, folders 23, 25, Church Papers.

35. Goelet, *Technique of Surgical Gynecology*; Augustin H. Goelet, M.D. (NYC), to RHT, June 7, 1897, HB; RHT to R. R. Church, July 13, 14, 1897, series 1, box 1, folder 25, Church Papers.

36. Felstiner, *Out of Joint*, xiii, xv, 16; Longmore and Umansky, "Introduction," 7; MCT, *Colored Woman*, 285.

37. MCT, "President's First Address," September 15, 1897, Nashville, MCT Papers, reel 20; MCT, "Duty of the National Association of Colored Women," 262.

38. Tiyi M. Morris asserts: "Black women's community mothering should be recognized as a cultural practice that celebrates the significance and empowerment of women for the survival of the race." Kevin Gaines suggests that the elite prioritized respectability politics and looked down on the masses. This claim has shaped the historical narrative about the NACW but it is not entirely accurate. Bay, "Battle for Womanhood," 89; Morris, *Womanpower*, 9, 6; Gaines, *Uplifting the Race*. On negative stereotypes of black women, see Herndl, "Invisible (Invalid) Woman,"136; Morton, *Disfigured Images*; Brown, "Imaging Lynching," 100–124; Kelley, *Race Rebels*; Wolcott, *Remaking Respectability*, 4–6; and Rhodes, "Pedagogies of Respectability," 204–5. MCT, "President's First Address"; MCT, "Duty of the National Association of Colored Women," 262.

39. Collins, *Black Feminist Thought*, chap. 8; Higginbotham, *Righteous Discontent*, 17; Shaw, "Black Club Women," 434; Boris, "Power of Motherhood," 221; MCT, "Duty of the National Association of Colored Women," 256–57, 259.

40. The first funds she raised went "to assist the Maggie Murray Kindergarten of Atlanta, Ga., the Alice D. Karey Kindergarten of Charleston, S.C., and the Butler Mission Kindergarten of Chicago." Mrs. Josephine Silone-Yates, "The National Association of Colored Women," *Voice of the Negro*, July 1904, 286.

41. Higginbotham, *Righteous Discontent*, 1; Terborg-Penn, *African-American Women*, 119; Salem, *To Better Our World*, 7–28; Hine and Thompson, *Shining Thread*, 177–83; Cash, *African American Women*, 36–37; MCT Diary, February 13, 1909, MCT Papers, reel 1.

42. Over time, NACW lost some of its earlier sense of cross-class purpose and interests, becoming more insular. Mary McLeod Bethune, a protégé of Terrell's who led the group in the late 1920s, decided that a new black women's organization was needed to focus more expressly on working-class women's concerns and politics. Terrell was concerned about creating a competing organization but became a vice-president of Bethune's new National Council of Negro Women in 1935. Hanson, *Mary McCleod Bethune*, 116–17.

43. MCT, "Service Which Should Be Rendered the South,' *Voice of the Negro*, February, 1905, 182–86; MCT, "A Plea for the White South by a Coloured Woman," *Nineteenth Century and After*, July 1906, 70–84; MCT, "Duty of the National Association of Colored Women," 256–57, 259.

44. Chicago was home to many black women's clubs, including the Ida B. Wells Club, whose president was Agnes Moody. Giddings, *Ida*, 383, 416; Salem, *To Better Our World*, 32–33; Hendricks, *Gender, Race, and Politics*, 21–22; "Minutes of the National Association of Colored Women, Nashville, Tennessee, September 15–18, 1897," MCT Papers, reel 16.

45. Terrell declared: "Against the barbarous Convict Lease System of Georgia, of which Negroes, especially the female prisoners, are the principal victims, the women of the national association are waging a ceaseless war." MCT, "The National Association: The Efforts and Aims of Our Noted Negro Women. A Strong and Beneficial Organization Earnestly Struggling in the Interests of Their Race in the Sacred Dominion of the Home Brings Evidence of Toil," *The Freeman: An Illustrated Colored Paper*, December 24, 1898, MCT Collection.

46. MCT, "The Attack on Mrs. Bruce. A Graceful Defense of a Gracious Woman by a Most Worthy Exemplar of Her Sex," *National Association Notes*, June 1899, 1, MCT Collection.

47. Ida Wells-Barnett was cochair of the Afro-American Council's program committee. In an article published in Timothy Thomas Fortune's *New York Age*, Mollie supported his Afro-American League in 1891 and joined again when he revived it as the Afro-American Council in 1898. The meeting was taking place in Berto's office when Mollie made her request. Fortune upset Republicans by supporting the Democratic Party from 1886 to 1888. On the Afro-American Council, see Elliot, *Color-Blind Justice*, 368n51; Alexander, *Army of Lions*, 120–21; and Marable, *Du Bois*, 56. MCT, "Preparations for Second Convention of NACW," July 15, 1899, MCT Papers, reel 20; MCT, "National Association of Colored Women. Everything Now in Readiness for the Annual Session, August 14, 1899," *National Association Notes*, August 1899, 1, MCT Collection; MCT to Frances Settle, September 5, 1899, MCT Papers, reel 3.

48. In 1924, Albert George became the first black municipal court judge appointed in Chicago. Terrell stated: "No one who has the slightest acquaintance with Mrs. Bruce will believe for one moment the rumor, that Mr. George claims is related with persistency in Chicago, that Mrs. Bruce offered to entertain the delegates at her own expense if the convention were held in that city." Gatewood, *Aristocrats*, 252; Giddings, *Ida*, 416–17; MCT, "Attack on Mrs. Bruce."

49. MCT, "An If or Two," 1898, MCT Papers, reel 20.

50. John Hope, president of Atlanta Baptist College, ridiculed NACW members as "lazy" big-talkers who engaged in empty "clubwoman swagger." Hope also told his wife, Lugenia, that his work and their child should be her top priorities over her work as a reformer and activist. Giddings, *When and Where*, 106–7; Guy-Sheftall, *Daughters of Sorrow*, 150; Rouse, *Lugenia Burns Hope*, 37; White, *Too Heavy*, 81, 67; MCT, *Colored Woman*, 154–55, 194.

51. Carle, *Defining the Struggle*, 160–61; MCT, "Attack on Mrs. Bruce"; MCT, *Colored Woman*, 154–55.

52. Terrell was criticized for running again by other leading women who themselves wished to be president. Several other women who were praised for their vision and accomplishments were nonetheless criticized for, as in the case of Mary McLeod Bethune, "being a power monger, crushing or removing all who opposed her." Evans, *Black Women in the Ivory Tower*, 188; Antler, "Having It All," 111; Carle, *Defining the Struggle*, 160–61; MCT, *Colored Woman*, 154–55; MCT, "Attack on Mrs. Bruce"; MCT Diary, June 4, 1946, HB.

53. MCT, "An Especial Appeal from the President of the Association," *National Association Notes*, June 1899, 2, MCT Collection; "Take Up Negro's Rights: Delegates from Colored Women's Clubs in Local Pulpits. Fanny Barrier Williams at All Souls,'

Decries Prejudice against the Race—Social Conditions in the South—Discourses at Other Churches—Program Arranged for Today—Toasts at the Banquet—Convention of the Afro-American Council," *Chicago Daily Tribune*, August 14, 1899, 9.

54. Hendricks, *Fannie Barrier Williams*, 143–46; Giddings, *Ida*, 412–16; Salem, *To Better Our World*, 32–33.

55. Agnes Moody, the Ida B. Wells Club president, resented Wells-Barnett for not respecting her authority. Terrell and other NACW women were scheduled to be taking part in the Afro-American Council; Wells-Barnett retaliated by giving Terrell, Ruffin, Washington, and Williams the least popular speaking times and chose as their subjects education, morality, and the home, rather than what she perceived to be meatier topics, such as antilynching. Robert Terrell also appeared on the Afro-American Council program. Hendricks, *Fannie Barrier Williams*, 143–44; Giddings, *Ida*, 412–16; Salem, *To Better Our World*, 32–33.

56. "Take Up Negro's Rights," *Chicago Daily Tribune*, August 14, 1899.

57. Quoted in Giddings, *Ida*, 419–20; MCT, *Colored Woman*, 154–55; "May Disrupt the Order: Election in Colored Women's Convention Breeds Trouble. Choice of Mrs. Mary Church Terrell to a Third Term as President Meets Opposition, and Miss Elizabeth E. Carter of Massachusetts, Candidate for Recording Secretary, Announces the Withdrawal of the Northeastern Federation—Results of Balloting," *Chicago Daily Tribune*, August 17, 1899.

58. In 1908, Carter was elected NACW president. "May Disrupt the Order."

59. MCT to Settle, September 5, 1899.

60. MCT to Settle, September 5, 1899.

61. MCT to RHT, August 22, 1899, HB.

62. Alisha Knight suggests that the novelist, journalist, and clubwoman Pauline Hopkins drafted the "resolutions of censure against the association" and, thus, against Terrell. Knight, *Pauline Hopkins*, 73. MCT to Settle, September 5, 1899; "Refutation of the False Charges Made by the Woman's Era Club of Boston, Based upon the Report of Its President, against the Officers and the Delegates to the Last Convention of the National Association of Colored Women," in MCT Collection and MCT Papers, reel 16.

63. "The Women Divided," *WB*, August 19, 1899, 4.

64. Weisenfeld, *African*, 24; Giddings, *Ida*, 431–32; Salem, *To Better Our World*, 35–6.

65. Quoted in Giddings, *When and Where*, 106; Williams, "Negro," 229–30; MCT Diary and Notes, 26, HB.

66. Williams, "Negro," 215–16; Fannie Barrier Williams, "Work Attempted and Missed in Organized Club Work," *Colored American Magazine*, May 1908, 282–83; MCT Diary and Notes, 26, HB.

67. Addie W. Hunton, "Women's Clubs: The National Association of Colored Women," *The Crisis*, May 1911, 18.

Chapter 4

1. Jones-Branch, "Mary Church Terrell," 68, 87; Frazier, *Black Bourgeoisie*, 50–51; Nielson, *Black Ethos*, 56; Moore, *Leading the Race*, 24; Gatewood, *Aristocrats*, 7, 23–24,

27, 63–64; Jones, *Quest for Equality*, 44; Summers, *Manliness*, 6–7; Higginbotham, "Sound of Silence," 59; Sterling, *We Are Your Sisters*, xiii; MCT, *Colored Woman*, 191.

2. Genny Beemyn notes, "By 1900, Washington, D.C., was becoming a popular set-tling place for blacks migrating from the Deep South, and the black population, total-ing 94,000 by 1910—included 1,500 people who were classified as 'professionals.' This professional class included more than 400 colored teachers, 50 qualified physicians, 10 dentists, more than 90 ministers, and some 30 lawyers." Beemyn, *Queer Capital*, 49; Patler, *Jim Crow*, 29; Kerr, *Paper Bag Principle*, 49; Evans, *Black Women in the Ivory Tower*, 61, 122.

3. Perdue, *Race*; James, *Transcending*, 19, 23.

4. Kenneth W. Mack defines *a representative of the race* as "a person who encapsulated the highest aspiration of his [or her] racial or cultural group. . . . The very existence of such persons was a potent argument for inclusion of marginalized peoples in the larger fabric of American life." Mack, *Representing the Race*, 4; Masur, *Example for All*, 264; Shaw, *W. E. B. Du Bois*, 61–67. For characterizations of Terrell as not just an elite but elitist, see Higginbotham, *Righteous Discontent*, 206–07; Harley, "Mary Church Ter-rell," 320; White, *Too Heavy*, 121; Gaines, *Uplifting the Race*, xiv, 2–4; Patler, *Jim Crow*, 29; Wallinger, *Pauline E. Hopkins*, 104; and Lake, *Blue Veins*, 45–46.

5. Berto's admission to the bar gave him the right to practice law in all the courts in the District of Columbia. Berto identified properties for his father-in-law to buy in Washington, D.C., oversaw the local collection of rents, and sent him records, including titles, deeds, and trusts. Dorsey, *We Are All Americans*, 105; Lewis, *Du Bois: Biography of a Race*, 518–19; "Official Certificate of Admission to the Bar of the Supreme Court of the District of Columbia," July 31, 1893, HB; "Decennial Report of the [Harvard] Class Secretary of 1884," no. 4, June 25, 1894, 43, RHT Papers, reel 4; RHT to Rob-ert R. Church, ca. June 16, 1896, series 1, box 1, folder 23, Church Papers; MCT, "Rob-ert Heberton Terrell, a Colored Judge of Washington, D.C.," ca. late 1920s, box 102-1, folder 15, MCT Collection; W. E. B. Du Bois, "Youth and Age at Amenia," *The Crisis*, October 1933, 226–27.

6. RHT to R. R. Church Sr., November 26, 1896, folder 24; RHT to R. R. Church, November 2, 1897, February 12, 1898, folder 23; and Deed of Trust, November 25, 1899, folder 25, all in series 1, box 1, Church Papers.

7. Berto returned to M Street High School in 1898 and was principal by 1899. In the spring of 1900, Berto Terrell and W. E. B. Du Bois both vied for the position of school superintendent of the district's "colored" schools and both hoped for support from Washington (this was before Du Bois earned Washington's enmity by publicly criticizing him in his 1903 *Souls of Black Folk*). Congress unexpectedly eliminated the dual superintendency system for the white and colored schools, so the highest posi-tion that an African American could attain was assistant superintendent. Neither man was appointed to this downgraded post. Moore, *Booker T. Washington*, 65–66; Norrell, *Up from History*, 227–28; Lewis, *Du Bois: Biography of a Race*, 228, 233; RHT to R. R. Church, May 17, 1897, series 1, box 1, folder 25; RHT to R. R. Church, March 16, 1900, Church Papers; "Two Colored Justices," *Cambridge (Mass.) Chronicle*, November 23, 1901, 13.

8. Thomas G. Dyer writes, "Roosevelt's frequent and vociferous claims that he had followed a progressive policy with regard to patronage for blacks did not . . . mask the

fact that the number of black appointments declined during the 1901–1909 period." Anna Julia Cooper became principal of M Street High School after Berto's 1901 appointment as justice of the peace. Dyer, *Theodore Roosevelt*, 105; May, *Anna Julia Cooper*, 24.

9. Eric Yellin notes that the Capital Saving Bank was "the first bank in the country controlled and operated by African Americans. . . . Within five years of opening, the bank had taken in over $300,000 and was paying investors handsomely. The Capital Savings Bank failed in 1902, however, with federal employees its most common clients. . . . Between 1899 and 1905 one out of four black banks failed because of poor commercial investments, speculation by officers, and mismanagement." Leonard C. Bailey was the wealthy black businessman. E. Franklin Frazier found that of twenty-eight black banks, "at the end of 1905 . . . only seven were still in existence." Yellin, *Racism*, 37; Justesen, *George Henry White*, 402; Jaynes, "Banking," 79–81; Meier, *Negro Thought*, 137; Mitchell and Mitchell, *Industrial Bank*, 8–9; Harris, *Negro as Capitalist*, 104; Frazier, *Black Bourgeoisie*, 39, 41; Du Bois, *Soliloquy*, 177; Barksdale-Hall, "Entrepreneurs," 476–77; RHT to R. R. Church Sr., November 26, 1896, series 1, box 1, folder 24, Church Papers.

10. RHT to R. R. Church Sr., April 23, 1902, series 1, box 1, folder 24, Church Papers.

11. In 1903, Berto gained the right to practice law before the Second Circuit Court of Shelby County, Tenn., and in the criminal court to be better able to represent his father-in-law as his lawyer, supervising his purchase of properties in Washington. Robert Reed Church's will protected the property of both of his (legitimate) daughters, Mollie and Annette. For Mollie, the will stated that her inheritance was "free from the debts, contracts, and control of her present husband or any husband she may have." This was fairly standard language but also seemed to acknowledge Berto's financial failures. See letters to and from Booker T. Washington in Washington, *Washington Papers*, 458–65, 472. RHT to R. R. Church Sr., April 23, 1902; R. R. Church, "Last Will and Testament of R. R. Church"; MCT, "Robert Heberton Terrell."

12. In 1900, "Only about one-fifth of African American household heads owned their own home (less than half the percentage among whites)." Thomas N. Maloney, "African Americans in the Twentieth Century," *EH.Net Encyclopedia*, edited by Robert Whaples, January 14, 2002, https://eh.net/encyclopedia/african-americans-in-the-twentieth-century/. RHT to R. R. Church Sr., February 18, March 16 (on stationary that reads "John C. Dancy, Recorder, Office of the Recorder of Deeds, U.S. Court House, Washington, D.C."), 1909, series 1, box 1, folders 1, 23, Church Papers; Deed from Robert R. Church Sr. to MCT, September 7, 1909, HB; MCT Diary, September 7, 1909, MCT Papers, reel 1.

13. MCT to Robert R. Church Sr., ca. November 1, 1909, series 1, box 1, folder 25, Church Papers.

14. MCT to Robert R. Church Sr., November 18, 1909, series 1, box 1, folder 26, Church Papers.

15. Robert R. Church Sr. to RHT, December 1909, series 1, box 22, folder 1; and RHT to R. R. Church Sr., December 13, 1909 (on Municipal Court, D.C., stationery), series 1, box 1, folder 25, both in Church Papers.

16. Robert R. Church Sr. to RHT, May 6, 1912; and Robert R. Church Sr. to Whitfield McKinlay, May 6, 1912, both in series 1, box 22, folder 3, Church Papers; MCT Diary, February 1, 1909, MCT Papers, reel 1.

17. MCT to RHT, ca. August 21, 1911, MCT Papers, reel 1; MCT (Memphis) to RHT (Municipal Court, D.C.), September 11, 1911, HB.

18. Church and Church, *Robert R. Churches*, 20; "Last Will," January 14, 1911, Church Papers.

19. Schweninger, *Black Property Owners*; Freund, *Colored Property*; Lauterbach, *Beale Street Dynasty*, 69; Bond and Sherman, *Images of America*, 21; McKee and Chisenhall, *Beale Black and Blue*, 15; Miller, *Memphis*, 92; Thomas A. Church to MCT, December 1, 1921, MCT Papers, reel 3.

20. In its heyday, Beale Street was a "polyglot street featuring dry goods and clothing stores, pawn shops, real estate and banking offices, saloons, gambling dens, theaters and houses of prostitution." Sigafoos, *Cotton Row*, 117; Bond and Sherman, *Images of America*, 7; Lee, *Beale Street*. On the pervasiveness of saloons in postwar urban areas, north and south, see Mouser, *Black Gambler's World*, 17. RHT to MCT, December 7, 1916, HB; RHT to MCT, February 11, 1915, MCT Additions; Thomas A. Church Sr. to MCT, May 12, 1920, MCT Papers, reel 3.

21. Moore dates Berto Terrell's bankruptcy to 1913, but it occurred in May of 1915. Just before and during World War I, Berto traveled more frequently; the speakers' fees looked more attractive to him as his family tried to cope with their debts and the era's high inflation. His stagnant salary was insufficient to cover their expenses. Moore, *Leading the Race*, 138, 231n16; RHT to T. E. Davis, September 16, 1915, RHT Papers, reel 1; "Judge Terrell a Bankrupt: Seeks to Protect Himself against Depositors in the Old Defunct Capital City Savings Bank," *Afro-American Ledger* (Baltimore), May 29, 1915, 1; "Judge Terrell Makes Satisfactory Arrangements," *Freeman*, June 12, 1915, 1; RHT to MCT, February 21, 1916 (on stationary from the Indiana Association of Colored Men, Indianapolis), RHT Papers, reel 1; RHT to MCT, August 27, 1918, MCT Additions.

22. Stephanie J. Shaw provides a useful discussion of Terrell as a professional woman but writes, "Mary Church Terrell stands out as one who neither needed to earn an income nor had to work within her house," while Willard Gatewood argues that "even Mary Church Terrell, who lectured extensively under the auspices of the Slayton Lyceum Bureau, claimed that she did so not to make money but rather 'to create sentiment in behalf of my race.'" He continues, "Mothers and wives of upper-class black families were mainly 'parlor ladies' who usually did not work outside the home. If they did, they were teachers, lecturers, or writers. Some served as occasional columnists for newspapers." In fact, teaching, lecturing, writing, and being a journalist were among the few respected forms of paid work available to educated women. These professions had the added benefit of allowing them to further their activism. Newspapers and journals often paid for articles, so a black woman reformer like Terrell could spread her civil rights message and help support herself and her family at the same time. Clark-Lewis, "'This Work,'" 197–98; Kessler-Harris, *In Pursuit of Equity*, 28, 43; Shaw, *What a Woman*, 119; Gatewood, *Aristocrats*, 191.

23. MCT, *Colored Woman*, 158.

24. Alice Kessler-Harris notes: "About half of all married African-American women earned wages in 1920, compared to less than a quarter of white women." In 1907, Mollie recorded, "Deposited $340 after month's engagements." She explained to Berto, "I must arrange a [speaking] trip in the Spring which will enable me to make some money, for I have not much left from the amount I made on my Southern tour three years ago. . . .

I need some things so much which I do not want if I cannot earn the money myself."
Kessler-Harris, *In Pursuit of Equity*, 43; MCT, *Colored Woman*, 115, 125–26; MCT to
RHT, August 12, 1900, MCT Papers, reel 2; MCT Diary, February 24, 1907, quoted
in MCT Diary and Notes, 218, HB; MCT Diary, January 14, 1908, MCT Papers, reel 1;
MCT Diary, January 4, December 12, 1909; and MCT to RHT, undated, ca. 1909, all
in MCT Papers, reel 2.

25. Gatewood, *Aristocrats*, 314; MCT, *Colored Woman*, 191; MCT (South Weymouth,
Mass., written on Booker T. Washington's Tuskegee stationery) to RHT (D.C.), July 4,
1902, HB.

26. Gomez-Jefferson, *Sage of Tawawa*, 109; Rich, *Transcending the New Woman*,
86; Morgan, *Women and Patriotism*, 74; Moses, *Golden Age*, 111; Lake, *Blue Veins*, 46;
MCT, *Colored Woman*, 232–33.

27. Mollie reported in dismay that Booker Washington "said nobody had ever heard
of a starving negro—he neither begs nor starves & implying he steals. He also told a
story of a negro who had a turkey filled with shot intended for him." Moses, *Golden
Age*, 111; Bellinger, "Hope of the Race," 7; MCT, *Colored Woman*, 191–93; MCT Diary,
January 26, 1909, MCT Papers, reel 1.

28. Carle, *Defining the Struggle*, 26, 57–63; Alexander, *Army of Lions*, xii, 263, 284–85,
chap. 5; Waldrep, *African Americans*, 64; MCT, Diary and Notes, 179, HB.

29. Mollie and other women were members of the local and state AAC affiliates but
were not present at its first national convention in 1890. Fortune welcomed female activists, but other black male leaders were still debating how much of a public role black
women should play. Some black men objected to the election of Ida B. Wells as financial
secretary to the AAC in 1899. Patricia A. Schechter explains that they "thought her better placed 'in an assignment more in keeping with the popular idea of women's work.'
This was achieved by making Wells head of the newly created Anti-Lynching Bureau."
Perhaps Wells's role as the first prominent antilynching advocate made it seem an appropriate job for a woman. The second conference of the Niagara Movement was open
to women and met in 1906 at Harpers Ferry, W.Va. Terrell likely attended, but I have
not confirmed this. Schechter, "Unsettled Business," 309; Alexander, *Army of Lions*,
26, 120–21; Marable, *Du Bois*, 56; MCT diary, August 30–31, 1905, MCT Papers, reel 1.

30. Marks, *Black Press*; MCT, "Lynching from a Negro's Point of View," *North American Review*, June 1, 1904, 858, 859, 865.

31. Lawyer, orator, and future U.S. senator from New York Chauncey M. Depew
made this claim at the Chicago World's Fair. MCT, "Introducing Ida B. Wells, to Deliver an Address on Lynching," 1893, MCT Papers, reel 20; MCT, "Lynching from a
Negro's Point of View," 866.

32. Mollie was pleased that "Father was there" to hear her give a speech and to hear
her praised as a modern-day heroine. She replaced Wells-Barnett as head of the Anti-
Lynching Bureau. Carle, *Defining the Struggle*, 117, 151, 159; Alexander, *Army of Lions*,
119–21, 252–53, 290; MCT Diary, October 11, 1906, quoted in MCT Diary and Notes,
170, 203; MCT Diary and Notes, January 7, 10, 11, 21, November 17, 1907, 216–18, 250,
all in HB; MCT, 1907 Correspondence file, August–October 1907, MCT Papers, reel 3.

33. Terrell met John Milholland after attending the 1904 International Council of
Women's congress in Berlin. In the Constitution League's first year, 1906, she worked
with it to protest President Teddy Roosevelt's unfair dismissal of black soldiers in

Brownsville, Tex., and to promote antilynching legislation. (See chapter 7 for a discussion of Terrell's protests against the Brownsville dishonorable discharges.) Terrell was appointed to the NAACP's steering committee and its committee on membership and credentials. NAACP organizers, realizing they needed more African Americans on the board, expanded to a Committee of One Hundred and added more black men and black women supporters, including NACW leaders Josephine Yates and Carrie Clifford. Terrell became a member of the general board of the NAACP when it formally incorporated in June 1911. Waldrep, *African Americans*, 64; Carle, *Defining the Struggle*, 265; MCT Diary, February 3, 1906, quoted in MCT Diary and Notes, 179, HB; NAACP Records, Founding Documents, Library of Congress; MCT (NYC) to RHT (D.C.), February 3, 1906, HB.

34. MCT to RHT, February 3, 1906.

35. The publisher was Raymond Patterson. A year before, Mollie published an antisegregation article in the same journal. Salem, *To Better Our World*, 150–51; Booth, "Herculean Task," 26, 33–34. See Mancini, *One Dies*; MCT, *Colored Woman*, 227–31; MCT, "Peonage in the United States: The Convict Lease System and the Chain Gangs," *Nineteenth Century and After*, August 1907, 306–22; MCT, "A Plea for the White South by a Coloured Woman," *Nineteenth Century and After*, July 1906, 70–84; MCT Diary, March 6, 1908, quoted in MCT Diary and Notes, 267, HB.

36. Mollie later admitted she had decided to "sit by [a] hard-looking customer in street car purposely." MCT Diary and Notes, 28, HB.

37. Ida B. Wells physically resisted being forced into a segregated car, biting and scratching the conductor. In her autobiography, Terrell described an incident in a Washington, D.C., streetcar when she entered laden with shopping bags, saw a seat between two white men, asked them to make room for her, and, when they ignored her, sat down anyway. The men became infuriated with her, yelled at her, called her "a nigger woman," and threatened to hit her. Although she did not strike out in self-defense, Terrell persisted in sitting between them. She was saved from physical assault by a black woman who defused the situation by telling the men that they "would get into a lot of trouble" if they hit her. This is likely the same incident presented in a sanitized way that omits her instinctive response of slapping the white man and transforms her elite leisure objects into more neutral shopping bags. DuRocher, *Ida B. Wells*, intro.; MCT, *Colored Woman*, 417. See original entry, MCT Diary, July 27, 1908, MCT Papers, reel 1; and summary in MCT Diary and Notes, 289, HB.

38. Some scholars see Berto as beholden to Washington and only Mollie as independent. Hanna Wallinger describes him as "a loyal follower of Booker T. Washington." Manning Marable states, "Becoming the district's first black judge in 1901, the liberal educator [Robert Terrell] was forced to comply with most of Tuskegee's wishes." Susan D. Carle correctly notes that although he benefited from Washington's support, Berto "sometimes gave public speeches in which he sounded every bit like a civil rights militant." Drake, "Booker T. Washington," 39–40; Marable and Mullings, *Let Nobody Turn Us Around*, 165; Carle, *Defining the Struggle*, 180; Wallinger, *Pauline E. Hopkins*, 74; Marable, *Du Bois*, 58; Smith, *Emancipation*, 137–38; Meier, *Negro Thought*, 166–69; Wintz, *Black Culture*, 40; Moore, *Booker T. Washington*, 81–82; Mack, *Representing the Race*, 31; Miller, "Robert Heberton Terrell," 109–18, 142n89. See RHT speeches, RHT Papers.

39. Smith, *Emancipation*, 138; Moore, *Booker T. Washington*, 81–82.

40. MCT, "Robert Heberton Terrell," 5; MCT Diary, February 24, 1909, MCT Papers, reel 1.

41. The eight were: "Du Bois, Walters, Brooks, Bulkey, Waldron, Wells-Barnett, Francis Grimke, and Mary Church Terrell." Terrell was appointed to the steering committee of the May 1909 conference and gave a speech there. Even as late as World War I, some otherwise progressive African American men still expected women play a secondary role in politics and reform, as well as to be demure and uninterested in advertising their accomplishments. As Willard Gatewood summarizes it, Charles B. Purvis, a founder of Howard University's medical school, wrote a 1918 letter to the civil rights activist and minister, Francis F. Grimké, in which he "was highly critical of Mary Church Terrell for what he considered her aggressiveness and immodesty . . . unbecoming a lady of her social standing. Purvis found especially distasteful the advertisements announcing her lectures, in which she was described as a fluent speaker in several languages." Gatewood, *Aristocrats*, 188; Kerr, *Paper Bag Principle*, 41. For partnering couples, see Higginbotham, *Righteous Discontent*, 49; Diana, "Narrative," 180–81, 187; Scanlon, *Until There Is Justice*, 75; Curwood, *Stormy Weather*, 13–14; Rouse, *Lugenia Burns Hope*, 30–33, 45–46, 55; Schechter, *Ida B. Wells-Barnett*, 174–76, 188–89; Luker, *Social Gospel*, 166; Rauchway, *Refuge of Affections*, 2, 12, 25–26; and Pycior, Slack, and Abir-Am, "Introduction," 34–35. For the NAACP, see Patler, *Jim Crow*, 58; Dorrien, *New Abolition*, 250; Alexander, *Army of Lions*, 294; Kellogg, *NAACP*, 26–27, 36n25; and Luker, *Social Gospel*, 261–62.

42. Again, Terrell and Wells-Barnett were the only black women. MCT, "Address of Welcome to the 38th Annual Conference of the NAACP," June 24, 1947, MCT Papers, reel 22.

43. In the spring of 1912, Mary Ovington explained, "The Board of Directors to which you have been elected is the same thing as the Executive Committee [the Committee of Thirty] only newly named under our articles of incorporation." Ovington to MCT, January 24, 1912, quoted in Carle, *Defining the Struggle*, 1, 261–69, 359n7, 252; Pycior, Slack, and Abir-Am, "Introduction," 34; Harlan, *Washington*, 366; Guy-Sheftall, *Daughters of Sorrow*, 150; Moore, *Booker T. Washington*, 74–75; Sullivan, *Lift Every Voice*, 6–21; Kellogg, *NAACP*, 45–47; Alexander, *Army of Lions*; Jonas, *Freedom's Sword*, 401n12; MCT, *Colored Woman*, 194.

44. Moore, *Booker T. Washington*, 92–94.

45. Harlan, *Washington*, 371–73.

46. Harlan, *Washington*, 371–73.

47. Harlan, *Washington*, 373.

48. Carle, *Defining the Struggle*, 269, 280–81; White, *Too Heavy*, 85; Salem, *To Better Our World*, 156, 171; MCT, *Colored Woman*, 193; MCT to Thomas A. Church, January 10, 1926, MCT Papers, reel 3.

49. Salem, *To Better Our World*, 152, 171; Berg, *"Ticket to Freedom,"* 12–13; Kellogg, *NAACP*, 26–27, 36n25; Marable, *Du Bois*, 72; Harlan, *Washington*, 372–73; MCT, *Colored Woman*, 212; MCT Diary, October 1, 1905, MCT Papers, reel 1.

50. Georgia Douglas Johnson and Du Bois had been having an affair before and after Johnson's husband's death, but it is unclear if Mollie knew this. Lewis, *Du Bois: Fight*

for Equality, 183–85; Carle, *Defining the Struggle*, 269, 280–81; MCT to Thomas A. Church, January 10, 1926.

51. Washington's friends reported Berto's disloyalty in February 1907: "Hearing that Judge Terrell had criticized the dismissal of black troops, he [Charles Anderson] wrote Washington that 'Judge Terrell had better take a stitch in his tongue . . . . He is "a Washington man" when the Doctor is around, and yet he manages to give his approval and support to all of his enemies.'" Harlan, *Washington*, 310–13, 323, 365.

52. Robert and Mollie Terrell believed in the benefits of interracial cooperation and in having high-profile whites in some leadership positions in the NAACP, in part because they commanded the attention of the mainstream media. Mollie also attended equal rights meetings led by Monroe Trotter. Constance Green notes that the NAACP's D.C. branch was formed in 1912 and "within a few months it was one of the largest in the country and counted 143 dues-paying members." Wilson's prosegregationism led to a huge increase of the NAACP's national membership to over 100,000. Green, *The Secret City*, 169; Patler, *Jim Crow*, 59; Sullivan, *Lift Every Voice*, 29–30; Moore, *Leading the Race*, 63; RHT to MCT, October 19, 28, 1913, in MCT Additions; MCT Diary, December 15, 1921, HB.

53. A little over a week after the big NAACP rally in D.C., Berto explained to Mollie his understanding of why there was a split between those like Du Bois (and the Terrells), who supported an integrated leadership team for the NAACP, which included white leaders like Oswald Garrison Villard and Moorfield Storey (NAACP president, 1909–29), versus those like William Monroe Trotter, who demanded that African Americans should hold all the key leadership roles in the organization: "The leaders of it say that the white men in N.A.A.C.P. are trying to get honors that colored men should have in this fight. What a ridiculous attitude to assume! . . . I don't think we would get very far in our protests it if were not for men like Villard and Storey who are helping us—men who can get the attention of the country when they speak." For the conflict between Du Bois, Trotter, and Woodrow Wilson, see Patler, *Jim Crow*; Yellin, *Racism*, 143–69; Carle, *Defining the Struggle*, 280–83; Startt, *Woodrow Wilson*, 89–90, 188–89, 219–20; Schneider, *Boston*; Risjord, *Populists*, 256–58; Fox, *Guardian of Boston*; and Broderick, *W. E. B. Du Bois*, 92–93. For primary source documents from the Trotter/Wilson debate, see Lunardini, "Standing Firm," 244–64. For debates over white leadership of the NAACP, see Jonas, *Freedom's Sword*, 114–15; Kellogg, *NAACP*, 15; Sartain, *Invisible Activists*, 14–19; Carle, *Defining the Struggle*, 259–60; and Sullivan, *Lift Every Voice*, 29–30. RHT to MCT, October 19, 28, November 9, 1913, MCT Additions.

54. MCT Diary, April 10, 1921, October 22, November 30, 1949, in HB.

55. In 1909 Mollie urged Berto to splurge and take the whole family to the twenty-fifth anniversary of his graduation from Harvard to provide Phyllis and Mary the added impetus to excel scholastically. Du Bois also had high expectations of his daughter, although she struggled to pass her classes. Certain that his own progeny would necessarily be smart and talented, a frustrated Du Bois "commanded Yolande to become superlatively educated and emancipated." Moore, *Leading the Race*, 34; duCille, *Coupling Convention*, 62; Rauchway, *Refuge of Affections*, 3; Gatewood, *Aristocrats*, 248; Lewis, *Du Bois: Biography of a Race*, 450–51; Lewis, *Du Bois: Fight for Equality*, 12; MCT Diary, November 8, 1905, MCT Papers, reel 1; MCT to RHT, June 7, 1909, MCT Papers, reel 2.

56. Thomas Ayres Church (1867–1937) graduated from Marietta College in Ohio and from Columbia Law School. After clerking in the law firm of freethinker Robert Ingersoll, he became a clerk in the New York City Magistrates' Courts around 1896, with a decent regular salary. He stayed in that job for four decades. Thomas had been in a common law marriage with Florence White Church, a light-skinned black woman in Newark, N.J. Florence died age twenty-eight, probably in childbirth; their son was born the same year as her death. Their son, Robbie Smith, was raised by Florence's family after her death. Mollie wrote in her diary: "Go to see Mary's Newark Aunt Fannie. . . . Went to see Mary's 9 year old brother 'Robbie Smith.'" MCT Diary, May 4, September 8, December 13, 14, 17, 18, 23, 24, 1905, MCT Papers, reel 1; MCT Diary, November 5, 1906, quoted in MCT Diary and Notes, 206, HB; MCT to Thomas A. Church, July 27, 1927, MCT Papers, reel 3; MCT Diary, December 2, 1937, MCT Collection.

57. Phyllis resented her mother's judgments and interference and idealized her gentler father but lived with her mother her entire life, including with each husband, in her mother's home until her mother died. Curwood, *Stormy Weather*, 15; MCT Diary, May 7, 1909, MCT Papers, reel 1; MCT Diary, May 12, 1907, quoted in MCT Diary and Notes, 231, HB; MCT (Opequon, Va.) to RHT (D.C.), July 29, 1907, HB; MCT to RHT, August 15, 1909, MCT Papers, reel 1; MCT (Oberlin) to RHT (D.C.), October 24, 1913, HB.

58. MCT Diary, January 28, 1909; and MCT to RHT, August 15, 1909, both in MCT Papers, reel 1.

59. MCT, *Colored Woman*, 41; MCT Diary, November 23, 1909, MCT Papers, reel 1.

60. Mollie's friend was Fannie Settle. MCT to RHT, October 15, 1910, MCT Papers, reel 1.

61. MCT Diary, February 19, 20, August 16, September 2, 3, 8, 25, November 25, 1909, MCT Papers, reel 1; MCT Diary, June 15, 1911, MCT Additions; MCT to RHT, October 27, 1912, MCT Papers, reel 2.

62. Just a few years before she died, Mollie was still expressing her disappointment. Her 1949 diary noted, "Phyllis has been moved from the Browne School to the Miller. . . . She has been placed further and further out. She certainly has not made a brilliant record as a teacher." Phyllis Terrell [age ca. 31] to MCT, undated, 1929, MCT Papers, reel 3; MCT Diary, July 14, 1947, September 12, 1949, HB.

Chapter 5

1. See the death and funeral announcement, "Martell," *Washington Evening Star*, August 30, 1911, in which she is identified as "Louise Martell, mother of Mrs. Mary Church Terrell." MCT, *Colored Woman*, 243.

2. MCT Diary, December 24, 1905, MCT Papers, reel 1; MCT to RHT, ca. August 21, 1911, MCT Papers, reel 2; RHT to MCT, January 17, 1914, HB.

3. When Mollie attended the following year's National Purity Conference, she told Berto, "It is a very nerve racking performance this thing of representing my race and trying to please narrow-minded white people, too. Still, I shall try." Shaw, *What a Woman*, 121; MCT to RHT, May 18, 1903, October 31, November 5, 1911, October 27, 1912, MCT Papers, reel 2.

4. The last section of her letter to Berto is missing. MCT to RHT, September 28, 1913, HB; RHT to MCT, January 29, 1914, HB; MCT to RHT, ca. March 21, 1915, MCT Papers, reel 2.

5. Two years later, Berto noted to Mollie that "Sydney Williston took his father's car out Thursday morning, went 'joy riding' with Earl Hyman and Robbie Douglass, speeded down to the high school to show off before the girls, ran over an M Street high boy Senior, broke his leg and an arm and cut him up generally. The injured was probably worth more to the community than all three of those rapscallions put together." These young men were sons of prominent members of the black elite, including Robert Smalls Douglass, the grandson of Frederick Douglass. RHT to MCT, October 6, 1913 (two letters), January 31, 1915, MCT Additions.

6. MCT to RHT, October 24, 1913, HB.

7. For more on President King, the town of Oberlin, and race, see Kornblith and Lasser, *Elusive Utopia*.

8. Out of the 130 black women who had graduated from any college by 1889, 35, including Mollie Church, had graduated from Oberlin. Bellinger points out that "black students usually only made up 4% of the student body at Oberlin." Southern black women typically applied to junior colleges or to Oberlin, which they positively associated with its early acceptance of African Americans and women. When Du Bois was a student at Harvard, he boarded in the home of a black woman off campus and made friends with other black college students at Harvard and in the Boston area: "I sought no friendships among my white fellow students. . . . I was encased in a completely colored world, self-sufficient and provincial. . . . This was self-protective coloration, with perhaps an inferiority complex, but with belief in the ability and future of black folk." Johnson, *Southern Women*, 100; Bellinger, "Hope of the Race," 224–25, 228; Du Bois, *Soliloquy*, 84–85.

9. Mollie was referring to Janey Hayford Packard. For the concept of representing the race, see Mack, *Representing the Race*; MCT, *Colored Woman*, 33, 34.

10. Mollie's half brother, Robert R. Church Jr., graduated in 1904. Mollie noted in 1907: "[Dr.] Glenn says colored students at Oberlin have to sit together at artistic recitals." MCT Diary and Notes, 187, HB; MCT to Anna Wright Church, June 26, 1913, series 6, box 22, folder 25, Church Papers.

11. Soon after Mollie graduated in 1884, "white students would no long board at houses that accepted Black students. As a result, white families would no longer accept Black students resulting in a housing shortage for these students." Referring to black female students at the University of Iowa in 1915, Evans states that "not all . . . could find the usual work as domestic servants in exchange for boarding," suggesting this arrangement was not uncommon. Waite, "Segregation of Black Women," 355; Evans, *Black Women in the Ivory Tower*, 106; Dr. Florence M. Fitch (dean of college women, Oberlin College) to MCT, April 21, 1913, MCT Papers, reel 4.

12. Quoted in Bigglestone, "Oberlin," 209.

13. Fitch revealed her prejudice when describing a "dinner at a colored boarding house as being a 'novel experience,'" saying, "We did not mind our colored companions at all." Quoted in Bigglestone, "Oberlin," 208. Fitch to MCT, April 21, 1913; MCT to Fitch, October 1913, MCT Papers, reel 4.

14. Moore says that Terrell rented a house in Oberlin for her daughters since they could not live in college-run housing. In fact, the girls lived in Tenney Cottage, and she lived on North Professor Street. Moore, *Leading the Race*, 113; MCT to Fitch, October 1913.

15. In arguing the case *Plessy v. Ferguson* (1896), Homer Plessy's lawyers had used the phrase the "badge of inferiority" to describe the negative effect of segregation laws on African Americans. More than a decade after Mollie graduated from Oberlin, the Supreme Court justices dismissed Plessy's claim. Yet the phrase continued to resonate with her as she fought for racial equality. Although Chief Justice Earl Warren did not quote that phrase in *Brown. v. Board of Education* (1954), it continues to be used in Supreme Court decisions about racial and other grounds used to discriminate. MCT to Fitch, October 1913.

16. MCT to Fitch, October 1913; Fitch to MCT, November 4, 1913, MCT Papers, reel 4.

17. MCT to RHT, October 24, 1913, HB.

18. As Mollie reported to Berto: "Helen Swift, the daughter of my dear old college mates, Nettie McKelvey and Clare Swift, told Mary she [had volunteered to be] . . . her Senior Counselor." On the spread of segregation, see Patler, *Jim Crow*; Yellin, *Racism*; and MCT to RHT, October 24, 1913, HB.

19. MCT to RHT, October 24, 1913; RHT to MCT, October 26, 1913, MCT Additions.

20. Du Bois sent his daughter Yolande to a private boarding school "in Great Britain, entrusting the shaping of her impressionable mind and spirit . . . to white teachers. . . . who . . . thought it self-evident that the British Empire was ordained by God working through history to be global custodian of the white man's burden. . . . It had pretty nearly crushed whatever self-confidence might have survived the burden of being her father's daughter." Lewis, *Du Bois: Fight for Equality*, 32.

21. MCT to RHT, September 28,October 24, 1913, HB.

22. Miller's daughter, May Miller, became a well-respected playwright and taught at the Frederick Douglass High School in Baltimore. Perkins and Stephens, "May Miller," 174–75; RHT to MCT, October 26, 1913, MCT Additions.

23. In despair, Berto wrote to Mollie, "My dearest Wife, The more I think of Mary's failure the greater nightmare it becomes. . . . I want her to know from me just how I feel over her wretched, inexcusable showing as a student." Similarly, Du Bois was shocked when his daughter was asked to leave her exclusive English boarding school in 1916 because of her poor showing as a student. The future writer Angelina Weld Grimké tried to please her father, Archibald Grimké, but "he was very demanding, and at times could be quite cruel. . . . Particularly disappointing to him was her lack of commitment to academic pursuits—she ultimately attended three different secondary schools before graduating." Booker T. Washington's daughter, Portia, socially isolated and failing her classes, was forced to leave Wellesley College after her first year. The pressures of being expected to equal and even outshine their remarkably talented parents was challenging for some of the progeny of the Talented Tenth. Lewis, *Du Bois: Fight for Equality*, 464–65; Lewis, *Du Bois: Biography of a Race*, 107, 30–31, 464–65; Johnson, *Southern Women*, 100–102; Beemyn, *Queer Capital*, 69; "Miss Washington Fails: Daughter of Negro Educator Has Left Wellesley College—Her Presence Caused Factional Hatred,"

New York Times, November 2, 1902, sec. 1, 1; RHT to MCT, December 15, 1913, HB; RHT to Phyllis Terrell, December 18, 1913, HB.

24. According to Phyllis Terrell's stepson, Raymond Langston, she regretted not being able to continue her education at Oberlin and blamed her sister Mary's scholastic failures for foreclosing her opportunities. The discrimination they experienced also played a role in her parents' decision to send her to a boarding school in Vermont the following year. Ray and Jean Langston, interviewed by the author at the Oberlin College symposium on Mary Church Terrell, February 26, 2016.

25. For examples of literary societies debating the acceptability of any black students' memberships, see Bigglestone, "Oberlin," 198–219; MCT to King, January 26, 1914, MCT Papers, reel 4.

26. Lewis, *Du Bois: Biography of a Race*, 31, 145; MCT to King, January 26, 1914; King to MCT, February 4, 1914, MCT Papers, reel 4.

27. MCT to King, January 26, 1914.

28. Historian Cary Waite confirms that King "hastened segregation . . . by allowing the prejudice of students and faculty to decide the fate of Black students at Oberlin." Horton concurs that King "believed that even the most stalwart of institutions must accommodate itself to the reality of [white] public opinion." Waite, "Segregation of Black Students," 363; Horton, "Black Education," 491; MCT to King, January 26, 1914; King to MCT, February 4, 1914.

29. MCT to King, January 26, 1914.

30. At one point during the academic year 1882–83, the dining room was segregated and then reintegrated because of protests by some alumni and students. Mollie does not mention this incident. Diepenbrock, "Black Women," 31; MCT to King, January 26, 1914.

31. In another jab at the current administration's policy, she concluded, "I am glad that nobody ever impressed me with the fact that segregating myself or allowing myself to be segregated was evidence of 'self-respect.'" Mollie was referring to Janey Fitch Hayford Packard and her mother, Hannah Vera Hayford. MCT to King, January 26, 1914.

32. In fact, King condoned racial segregation in student housing and in Oberlin neighborhoods, expressing concerns that white property values might otherwise fall. He also suggested in a 1910 speech that African Americans should embrace their difference from whites as more congenial, musical people. Gary Kornblith and Carol Lasser cite a front-page article in the *Cleveland Plain Dealer* from April 20, 1910, that read "Oberlin College Turns on Negro" and described black students' exclusion from literary societies, sports teams, clubs, and housing. Kornblith and Lasser, *Elusive Utopia*, chap. 9; Love, *Henry Churchill King*, 156–57.

33. Perhaps Mary and Phyllis were fortunate that their mother chose private meetings and correspondence as her venue for raising her complaints about racism at Oberlin. Du Bois was invited to give the keynote speech when his daughter was graduating from Fisk University in 1924. He used it as a moment to give a scathing speech condemning Fisk's white president, who was later driven from office. Left unrecorded is how Yolande felt about her father upstaging her and being so critical. By 1910, there were thirty-two black colleges granting full bachelor's degrees. Lewis, *Du Bois: Fight for Equality*, 132–34; Bellinger, "Hope of the Race," 218–19; MCT to King, January 26, 1914.

34. Most of the Seven Sisters (colleges that enrolled only women at that time)

officially barred black applicants. The rest found ways to reject each of them individually. Bellinger, "Hope of the Race," 228–29; Oswald Garrison Villard to MCT, January 13, 1914, MCT Papers, reel 4.

35. Joel Spingarn, New York's NAACP chair, visited with Burton, urging him to find a solution. Carrie Lee became a reporter in D.C. Ovington and Luker, *Black and White*, 106–8; Wall, *Women of the Harlem Renaissance*, 43; Sylvander, *Jessie Redmon Fauset*, 40–41; Harriet A. Lee to MCT, December 7, 1933, MCT Papers, reel 7.

36. In March 1923, Harvard College issued a statement declaring that black men could not be compelled to live outside of the dormitories, but no black student moved into the dorms for decades. Jewish and Asian students were subjected to quotas at many colleges and universities in the 1920s and 1930s, and black Americans were excluded altogether. Wolters notes that in 1926, too, "students at New York University approached the NAACP with requests for legal aid in the fight against discrimination on their campus." Painter, "Memoranda," 628; McDaniel and Julye, *Fit for Freedom*, 320; Lewis, *Du Bois: Biography of a Race*, 31, 145; Johnson, *Southern Women*, 95–105, 320; Wolters, *New Negro*, 320.

37. Joan Quigley mistakenly suggests that this phrase implied that Mollie planned to permanently dissolve the family unit. The term had a different meaning. A white friend from Mollie's Oberlin days, Janey Hayford Packard, had recently had the experience of "breaking up housekeeping" and wrote, "I would certainly stay out of housekeeping for a year. The breaking up is worth a year's rest. One does become tired of the grind and if your girls like Oberlin and stay after this year, it will hardly pay for you to have so much housekeeping machinery as you have had the last fifteen years." Quigley, *Just Another Southern Town*, 71, 76, 79, 101; Janey Hayford Packard (Lewiston, Mont.) to MCT, October 16, 1913, MCT Papers, reel 4; MCT Diary, February 23, 1921, HB.

38. (Average American wages in 1913 were about $108 per month.) Berto declared bankruptcy two years later, in 1915. RHT to MCT, October 6, 1913, MCT Additions; RHT to MCT, November 28, 1913, HB; "Judge Terrell a Bankrupt: Seeks to Protect Himself against Depositors in the Old Defunct Capital City Savings Bank," *Afro-American Ledger* (Baltimore), May 29, 1915, 1; "Judge Terrell Makes Satisfactory Arrangements," *Freeman*, June 12, 1915, 1.

39. MCT to RHT, September 28, 1913, HB.

40. RHT to MCT, September 25, 27, 1913, MCT Papers, reel 2; MCT to RHT, September 28, 1913.

41. RHT to MCT, October 19, 1913, MCT Papers, reel 2; MCT to RHT, October 24, 1913, HB; RHT to MCT, October 26, 1913, MCT Additions.

42. RHT to MCT, October 28, 1913, MCT Additions.

43. The book Terrell referred to was James Ford Rhodes's *History of the United States from the Compromise of 1850 to the Final Restoration of Home Rule at the South in 1877* (New York: MacMillan, 1913). Rhodes and members of the Dunning School believed in "negro incapacity." Morton explains: "The Dunning school of historiography, which emphasized the horrors of 'Black Reconstruction,' seemed to substantiate this Negro decline, while also endorsing its symbolization by the figure of the rapacious 'black brute.... Hence, their inflamed ambitions for equality led to 'the hideous crime against white womanhood.'" This turn is exemplified the release of the nation's first blockbuster

motion picture, *Birth of a Nation*, by D. W. Griffith, in 1915. The film was an adaptation of Thomas Dixon's 1905 virulently racist attack on Reconstruction, the best-selling novel (and later play) *The Clansman: An Historical Romance of the Ku Klux Klan*. See Kendi, *Stamped from the Beginning*, 44–46, 257; Byrd and Clayton, *American Health Dilemma*, 110–12; Foner, *Reconstruction*, xx; Morton, *Disfigured Images*, 19, 27; MCT to RHT, October 24, 1913.

44. RHT to MCT, October 26, 1913.

45. For more information on Berto and the confirmation battle, see Wolgemuth, "Wilson's Appointment Policy," 457–71; Osborn, "Wilson Appoints Terrell," 111–15 (the biographical material on Terrell is incorrect in this article; Osborn assumes that Berto was raised in the "upper-middle class" because he attended Harvard University, e.g., see 481–82); Blumenthal, "Wilson and the Race Question," 1–21; Miller, "Woodrow Wilson," 81–86; Harlan, *Washington*, chap. 17; MCT, "Robert Heberton Terrell, a Colored Judge of Washington, D.C.," 5, ca. late 1920s, box 102-1, folder 15, MCT Additions.

46. This brief period of his career has attracted the most attention from historians. I focus on the private letters he sent to Mollie while she was at Oberlin. Eric Yellin claims that others, including Berto, "saw a chance to bolster their own positions" after President Wilson and black activist William Monroe Trotter clashed in their meeting at the White House. See Wolgemuth, "Wilson's Appointment Policy," 457–71; Miller, "Robert H. Terrell," 209–10; Osborn, "Wilson Appoints Terrell," 111–15; Miller, "Woodrow Wilson," 81–86; Yellin, *Racism*, 168–69; and MCT, "Robert Heberton Terrell."

47. Quoted in Ward, *Hanging Bridge*, 63. McMillen, *Dark Journey*, 224; Belknap, *Federal Law*, 7; Danielson, *Color of Politics*, 43; Finkelman, *African Americans*, 296–303; Tsesis, *We Shall Overcome*, 163.

48. RHT to MCT, January 29, 1914, HB.

49. Many copies of letters of support are in Berto's records: RHT Papers, reels 1–2; RHT to MCT, December 23, 1913, MCT Papers, reel 2; RHT to MCT, January 29, 1914, HB.

50. RHT to MCT, February 7, 1914, HB.

51. RHT to MCT, February 7, 1914.

52. Mollie continued, "After struggling for years to excel in his chosen profession, after receiving indisputable proof of the fact that he has achieved brilliant success, he now feels the ground slipping from under his feet, and sees failure staring him in the face. It is a great wonder that a man in his position does not lose his mind." MCT to Sen. Theodore Burton, March 29, 1914, MCT Papers, reel 4.

53. Later, Mollie had a "prescription for medicine for nerves," which she also called her "prescription for nervousness." MCT, *Colored Woman*, 260–61; RHT to MCT, February 7, 1914, HB; MCT Diary, July 27, 31, 1940, HB.

54. Mollie was pleased that "the Bar Association of Washington composed of Republicans and Democrats, some of whom were Southerners, unanimously endorsed Judge Terrell's reappointment. It was the first time in the history of that organization that it took such a stand in anybody's behalf." The Senate voted on April 24, 1914. Smith, *Emancipation*, 138; Harlan, *Washington*, chap. 17; Patler, *Jim Crow*, 23; RHT to MCT, March 23, 1923, MCT Additions; MCT, "Robert Heberton Terrell."

Chapter 6

1. Most black women at the time identified as colored or as Afro-American, but Margaret Murray Washington suggested the term "The New Negro Woman" in 1895. Rich, *Transcending the New Woman*, 69; MCT, *Colored Woman*.

2. Cooper, *Beyond Respectability*.

3. In 1910 in Athens, Ga., whites incorporated and founded a "Black Mammy Memorial Institute" to provide young black girls and women with "domestic training" to solve the "servant problem." Democratic senator John Sharp Williams of Mississippi introduced S. 4119 in December 1922, and the bill was passed by the Senate on February 28, 1923. Democratic representative Charles Stedman from North Carolina introduced the same bill in the House in January 1923, but it died after the controversy surrounding the Senate's passage. See Patton, "Moonlight," 149–55; McElya, *Clinging to Mammy*, 124–29, 200; and Cox, "Confederate Monument," 158.

4. MCT, "Should an Amendment to the Constitution Allowing Women the Ballot Be Adopted?," November 7, 1879, MCT Papers, reel 20 (emphasis added).

5. See Dinkin, *Before Equal Suffrage*. Also see Wellman, *Road to Seneca Falls*; Brown, "To Catch the Vision," 137; MCT, *Colored Woman*, 144; and MCT Diary and Notes, 44, HB.

6. The National Council of Women meeting was in February, and she married on October 28, 1891. MCT, *Colored Woman*, 144; MCT, "The Justice of Woman Suffrage," 1890s, MCT Papers, reel 23 (although the title is the same, this is not the same article that Terrell published in the *The Crisis* in September 1912).

7. See Salem, *To Better Our World*, 14–27; White, *Too Heavy*, 27–29.

8. Terrell summarized the first months of 1895 in one diary entry: "The [National Women's] Council's second Triennial was a grand success and I enjoyed the meetings I attended very much, although I was in such a wretched physical condition [she was in the midst of a second difficult and ultimately unsuccessful pregnancy]. I became quite well acquainted with Rachel Foster Avery and Susan B. Anthony, learned to admire profoundly May Wright Sewall." MCT, *Colored Woman*, 143, 145; MCT Diary, March 12, 1895, MCT Collection; MCT Diary, February 15, 1940, HB.

9. Carby, *Reconstructing Womanhood*, 119.

10. The 1908 petition read, in part, "We, the members of The Equal Suffrage League, representing the National Association of Colored Women through its Suffrage Department . . . ask to have enacted such legislation as will enforce the 14th and 15th Amendments of the Constitution of our country, the United States of America, throughout all its sections." Dorothy Salem dates the NACW official endorsement of suffrage as having been in 1912, whereas Rosalyn Terborg-Penn puts it in 1916. Quotation from Terborg-Penn, *African-American Women*, 88, 95; Guy-Sheftall, *Daughters of Sorrow*, 107; Salem, *To Better Our World*, 42, 104–5.

11. MCT, "Susan B. Anthony, the Abolitionist," *Voice of the Negro*, June 1906, 411–16.

12. Giddings, *When and Where*, 120; Roediger, *Colored White*, chap. 7; MCT, "The Justice of Woman Suffrage," *The Crisis*, September 1912, 243–45; MCT, "Susan B. Anthony."

13. MCT Diary, November 25, 1907, in MCT Diary and Notes, 252, HB.

14. For a broad overview of the difficulties black women faced in interracial activism,

see Freedman, "Race," 1–14; Terborg-Penn, *African-American Women*, 110–35; Lunardini, *Alice Paul*, 50–52; Gilmore, *Gender and Jim Crow*, 215–17; and MCT Diary, November 12, 1909, MCT Papers, reel 2.

15. Fanny Garrison Villard was the sister of abolitionist William Lloyd Garrison and the mother of Owald Garrison Villard. Terborg-Penn, "Discrimination," 305; MCT Diary, February 18, 1910, in MCT Diary and Notes, 367–68, HB.

16. MCT Diary, November 4, 1909, MCT Papers, reel 1.

17. Mary Walton, Katherine H. Adams and Michael L. Keene, Amelia R. Fry, Susan Ware, and Treva B. Lindsey, for instance, mistakenly accept Alice Paul's "personal recollections" from an oral interview conducted six decades later. Paul's memories are unreliable; she consistently made racist statements and policy decisions throughout her career and then unashamedly denied doing so. Adams and Keene, *Alice Paul*, 87– 88; Lindsey, *Colored No More*, 95, 103, 105–6; Ware, *Why They Marched*, 175; Walton, *Woman's Crusade*, 59, 64, 73, 77; Mary Walton, "The Day the Deltas Marched into History," March 1, 2013, *Washington Post*; Amelia R. Fry, "Conversations with Alice Paul: Woman Suffrage and the Equal Rights Amendment," November 1972, May 1973, Suffragists Oral History Project, University of California, Berkeley.

18. Although the *Broad Ax* journalist claimed not to support woman suffrage, he described Wells-Barnett's participation in the parade and noted "the part taken by the Colored women. They were very much in evidence, were accorded every courtesy and did nothing to reflect discredit on the race. Prominent among the Colored women in the procession were Mrs. Mary Church Terrell, Mrs. Carrie Clifford, Mrs. Daniel Murray, and Miss Gibbs. . . . A feature of the College section was a very pleasing bevy of Colored girls, all looking quite nifty in caps and gowns. They were greeted with hearty applause all along the line." See Julius F. Taylor, "The Equal Suffrage Parade Was Viewed by Many Thousand People from All Parts of the United States. No Color Line Existed in Any Part of It. Afro-American Women Proudly Marched Right by the Side of the White Sisters," *Broad Ax*, March 8, 1913, 1. Paula J. Giddings and Dorothy Salem correctly note black women's wide participation. Giddings, *Ida*, 518; Salem, *To Better Our World*, 128–29. "Illinois Women Feature Parade: Delegation from This State Wins High Praise by Order in Marching. Cheered by Big Crowd. Question of Color Line Threatens for While to Make Trouble in Ranks," *Chicago Daily Tribune*, March 4, 1913; "Order of Organizations in the Processional," National Woman's Party Papers, Library of Congress, reel 2.

19. Early in 1913, before the parade, Howard University undergraduate members of Alpha Kappa Alpha decided to create a new legally chartered national sorority, called Delta Sigma Theta. In response, Howard graduate Nellie Quander recruited other graduates to officially incorporate AKA. Quander was also interested in marching and sent a letter of inquiry to Alice Paul regarding black women's participation. MCT, *Colored Woman*, 426; MCT, "Our Oath," Program of the Ninth Annual Convention, Grand Chapter, Delta Sigma Theta Sorority, Howard University, Washington, D.C., 1919–27; Edna B. Johnson-Morris, Grand Historian, "Queen Delta's Violets: A History of Delta Sigma Theta Sorority, Inc., Manuscript Submitted to the Sixteenth National Convention for approval, change, or rejection, December 26–30, 1941, Detroit Michigan," MCT Papers, reel 14. Lindsey, *Colored No More*, 95.

20. Carrie W. Clifford, "Suffrage Paraders," *The Crisis*, April 1913, 296.

21. Lunardini, *Alice Paul*, 112–32; Ford, "Alice Paul," 174–86; Zahniser and Fry, *Alice Paul*; Lumsden, *Inez*, 25–26, 89; MCT, *Colored Woman*, 212–13; RHT to MCT, October 26, 1913, MCT Additions.

22. Walton, *Woman's Crusade*, 60; Clifford, "Suffrage Paraders."

23. "5000 Women Make Brave Showing in Parade for Vote, Insults of Hoodlums Bring Suffragettes to Tears; Pageant on Streets of Washington Unlike Anything World Has Ever Seen, *Philadelphia Inquirer*, March 4, 1913, 4. For more on Michigan flag bearer Mary McCoy, see Yurgalite and Gidlow, "Mary Eleanora McCoy."

24. W. E. B. Du Bois, "Politics," *The Crisis* 5, no. 6 (April 1913): 267 (emphasis added).

25. NAWSA's leadership also prioritized gaining the support of white southern women over the inclusion of black women and paying attention to their concerns. Green, *Southern Strategies*, 10, 13, 89, 92, 129–32; Materson, *Freedom*, 32, 190; Terborg-Penn, "African American Women"; Hendricks, "Ida B. Wells-Barnett"; Gidlow, "Sequel"; MCT, *Colored Woman*, 316–17; RHT to MCT, August 15 (ca. 1917), MCT Additions.

26. Walter White (assistant secretary, NAACP) to MCT, March 14, 1919, MCT Papers, reel 4.

27. In 1921, Carter and Terrell worked together to protest the unfair murder charges against a black teenager, Clara Johnson, whose home was invaded by a white mob, including plain-clothes police detectives, during the 1919 D.C. race riot. Schneider, *Boston*, 102–3; Terborg-Penn, *African-American Women*, 130. Ida Husted Harper to MCT, March 18, 1919, MCT Papers, reel 4; MCT Diary, January 6, 1921, HB.

28. RHT to MCT, August 25, 1920, MCT Additions; MCT, "An Appeal to Colored Women," 1921, MCT Papers, reel 21.

29. See Cott, "Feminist Politics," 51–54.

30. Terrell was pleased to find that Murray was "deeply interested in colored people." MCT Diary, February 10, 1921, HB.

31. For information on the 1918 lynching of Mary Turner that Terrell referred to, see Armstrong, *Mary Turner*. MCT Diary, February 11, 14, 1921, HB.

32. The current NACW president, Hallie Quinn Brown, also participated. MCT Diary, January 21, February 17, 1921, HB.

33. Armstrong, *Mary Turner*. MCT Diary, February 17, 1921, HB.

34. Darlene Clark Hine suggests that white Americans' racism made them view as "unimaginable the possibility that a Black woman could be raped, sexually exploited, or harassed." Hine, "For Pleasure," 101; Brown, "Imaging Lynching,"169; Crenshaw and Ritchie, *Say*; Feimster, *Southern Horrors*, 158; Cott, "Feminist Politics," 51–54; Southard, *Militant Citizenship*, 181–83; MCT, *Colored Woman*, 316–17; MCT Diary, February 17, 18, 1921, HB; Ella Rush Murray, "The National Woman's Party and the Violation of the Nineteenth Amendment," *The Crisis*, 21, no. 6 (April 1921): 259–61.

35. Terrell believed in a form of reproductive justice that would give black women their full bodily integrity, from being able to bear and raise a thriving infant to being able to decide when they did not want to be pregnant.

36. As late as 1949, Terrell witnessed and complained about NWP women's prejudice against visiting Haitian officials. Mark Schneider mislabels Terrell "conservative" because she declined to picket the NWP. For information on Anthony and Stanton, see Dudden, *Fighting Chance*; and Ginzberg, *Elizabeth Cady Stanton*. Schneider, *Boston*, 102–3; MCT Diary, Friday, February 18, 1921, April 2, 1949, HB.

37. Rudolph, "Victoria Earle Matthews," 106; Guy-Sheftall, *Daughters of Sorrow*, 26–27; Salem, *To Better Our World*, 20–22; Hine and Thompson, *Shining Thread*, 180.

38. Even after her father's death, Mollie remained sensitive about his background as a saloon owner and developer of Beale Street. Berto reassured Mollie: "By all means attend the Social Purity Congress. Nobody is giving your father's life a thought. He atoned for all of his sins by accumulating and leaving a fortune. You are entirely too sensitive about his career." Preston Lauterbach argues that Church's houses of prostitution were protected by white police officers and Memphis officials because he supplied white prostitutes to white men in a protected vice zone. There is no evidence that Mollie knew about this aspect of his business. Lauterbach, *Beale Street Dynasty*, 87, 113; RHT to MCT, November 6, 1913, MCT Additions; MCT, "What the Colored Woman's League Will Do," 155–56; MCT, "Lynching from a Negro's Point of View," *North American Review*, June 1904, 853–68; MCT, "Purity and the Negro," 1905, MCT Papers, reel 2 (published in the *Light*, June 1905, 19–25).

39. In the *Light* (1905), Terrell was described as "one of the principal speakers at the Conference, her message is always in behalf of the colored people. Herself a colored woman, she can plead the cause of this struggling race with deep earnestness and feeling and we prophesy that there will not be a dry eye nor a cold heart in the audience." In advance of the 1927 International Purity Conference, it described her as "probably the most eloquent Negro Woman on the American platform. . . . She is a former member of the school board in Washington and is a high official of the International Council of Women of the Darker Races." That year, Terrell served on a Joint Committee on Delinquency and Crime in Washington, D.C., which noted that "colored girls are arrested and placed in jail more quickly than white girls and an investigation along this line was suggested." "Notes on Meeting, Joint Committee on Delinquency and Crime," 1927 and undated, MCT Papers, reel 15. "National Purity Conference," La Crosse, Wis., October 17–19, 1905; the *Light* gives detailed information about the speakers on the Purity Conference programs as well as National and International Purity Congresses, 1905, 1907, 1913, 1927, and undated, MCT Papers, reel 16; MCT Diary, September 17, 22, 1905, MCT Papers, reel 1.

40. For more on white purity organizations, see Foster, *Moral Reconstruction*, 140–43. For its investigations of prostitution, see Rosen, *Lost Sisterhood*, 14; Satter, *Each Mind*, 208–9.

41. In a 1905 *Voice of the Negro* article, Fannie Barrier Williams similarly pointed out that "the women of other races bask in the clear sunlight of man's chivalry, admiration, and even worship, while the colored woman abides in the shadow of his contempt, mistrust or indifference." Fannie Barrier Williams, "The Colored Girl," *Voice of the Negro*, June 1905, 400–401, quoted in Guy-Sheftall, *Daughters of Sorrow*, 90, n. 167, 195; James, "Shadowboxing," 349; MCT, "Purity and the Negro."

42. Chapman, *Prove It*, 49; MCT, "Purity and the Negro."

43. See Collins, *Black Sexual Politics*, 217; Perkins and Stephens, "Introduction," 5; Hall, *Revolt against Chivalry*; Wells-Barnett, *Southern Horrors*, 49–72; Feimster, *Southern Horrors*, 97–92; Freedman, *Redefining Rape*, 73–88; Rosen, *Terror*, 9–11; White, *Dark Continent*, 33; Kuhl, "Countable Bodies," 133–60; and Terrell, "Lynching from a Negro's Point of View," *North American Review*, June 1904, 853–65.

44. Similarly, in the YWCA, Addie Hunton "and her colleagues sought to persuade

white women that they (white women) had a Christian duty to improve race relations." Robertson, *Christian Sisterhood*, 26; Dunlap, "Reform of Rape Laws," 352–72; Shaw, *What a Woman*, 197, 210; Gilmore, *Gender and Jim Crow*, chap. 6; MCT, "Purity and the Negro."

45. Educator Charlotte Hawkins Brown made a similar point in 1920: "We have begun to feel that you are not, after all, interested in us. . . . The Negro women of the South lay everything that happens to members of her race at the door of the Southern white woman." Brown quoted in Laville, *Organized White Women*, 43; MCT, "Purity and the Negro."

46. Reagan, "Medicine," 389; Kunzel, *Fallen Women*, 69–73, 155–59; Solinger, *Wake Up*; MCT, "Purity and the Negro."

47. Sherie Randolph observes, "The voices of black women . . . had to be protected from hostile responses both within and outside the black community." Randolph, "Not to Rely Completely," 242; Quigley, *Just Another Southern Town*, 62–63.

48. When she spoke to white women in Wilmington, Del., for instance, Terrell challenged them: "Did you ever feel, sisters of Wilmington, that you are to a certain extent responsible for the downfall . . . of these girls[?] . . . .Did it ever occur to you, good people, how many and how great are the temptations to which colored girls are subjected in various sections of the country? They are marked as the legitimate prey for the evil minded of all races and complexions." MCT to RHT, October 27, 1911, MCT Papers, reel 2; MCT, "Address to Raise Funds for a Home for Delinquent Girls" (undated), MCT Papers, reel 23.

49. Odem, *Delinquent Daughters*, 9–11, 118–20; MCT to RHT, October 31, 1911, MCT Papers, reel 2; MCT, "Purity and the Negro"; MCT, "Address to Raise Funds."

50. Brumfield, *Virginia State Penitentiary*, 128–34; Bundles, *On Her Own Ground*, 128–29; William Anthony Aery, "National Association of Colored Women," *Southern Workman*, January–February 1912, 538.

51. MCT, "The Black Mammy Monument" (*Washington Evening Star*, February 10, 1923, widely reprinted), MCT Papers, reel 21; Lula Briggs Logan to MCT, February 20, 1923, MCT Papers, reel 5; McElya, *Clinging to Mammy*, 128–30, 139–41, 146–49; Janney, *Burying the Dead*. On the rise of the second KKK, see Gordon, *Second Coming*; Pegram, *One Hundred Percent American*; Maclean, *Behind the Mask*; Blee, *Women of the Klan*; Yellin, *Racism*, 99. See W. E. B. Du Bois, "The Black Mother," *The Crisis*, December 1912, 78; James Weldon Johnson, "The Black Mammy," *The Crisis*, August 1915, 1176 (Mollie and Berto Terrell and Oscar DePriest all wrote in support of woman suffrage in this issue); and Bellinger, "Hope of the Race," 211–12.

52. Grace Hale notes that a nostalgic "mammy craze swept through the region and indeed the nation between the 1890s and the 1920s. . . . Mammy became the crucial nurturer, protector, and teacher of white children." Furthermore, D. W. Griffith's popular film *Birth of a Nation* (1915) encouraged white Americans, North and South, to identify Reconstruction as an era of chaos and disorder brought about by out-of-control freedmen who wreaked havoc on the lives of white southerners—until white men came to the rescue via a violently heroic Ku Klux Klan. See Hale, *Making Whiteness*, 98; Jewell, *From Mammy to Miss America*.

53. Chaney had been following Berto's post-Emancipation career in the newspapers

and invited him to visit if he was ever in the area. Mrs. J. Douglas Chaney to RHT, April 14, 1922, RHT Papers, reel 2.

54. Berto's mother, Louisa Ann Coleman Terrell, apparently gave birth to her other surviving children, Will, Laura, and Fred D. Henry, after Emancipation. Chaney's brother, Glanville Terrell (1859–1936), just two years younger than Berto, was a professor of Greek at the University of Kentucky. Berto attended Harvard University before Glanville. When Glanville arrived in Cambridge, he tracked the prestigious career of his former playmate and his family's former slave. Berto's sister, Laura, born in the decade after the end of slavery, said to Mollie, "From my earliest recollections I have heard Brother Robert speak of Glanville." Laura Terrell Jones to MCT, February 3, 1908, MCT Papers, reel 2; Masur, *Example for All*, 156. On the priority of education, see Butchart, *Schooling the Freed People*; Litwack, *Been in the Storm*, 472–76; and Schwalm, *Hard Fight for We*, 103–4. Elliot, *Stanford*, 109. James E. Edmunds (of Edmunds and Hamner, Attorneys at Law) to RHT, October 12, 1921, RHT Papers, reel 2; Chaney to RHT, April 14, 1922; "State Educator of Note Dies in Virginia," *Kentucky New Era* (Hopkinsville), October 5, 1936, 6; Chaney to RHT, April 14, 1922; Jones to MCT, April 15, 1928, February 22, 1933, MCT Papers, reel 2.

55. In Mollie's case, there was an extra level of entwinement because both her white grandfathers (the fathers of Robert Church and Louisa Ayres) were also her parents' owners. In 1905, decades after the end of slavery, Mollie met with members of the white Ayers family, whose parents had enslaved Mollie's grandmother Eliza and her mother, Louisa. MCT Diary, October 25, 1905, MCT Papers, reel 1; Laura Ayres McCormick Parker to MCT, May 25, 1913, HB.

56. Her 1904 article "Lynching from a Negro's Point of View" mocked southern "gentlemen" and "gentlewomen" who viciously denigrated all African Americans but could hardly find "words sufficiently ornate enough to express their admiration for a dear old 'mammy,'" whom they had not allowed to care for her own children or to learn to read or write. Quoted in Wallace-Sanders, *Mammy*, 104; MCT, *Colored Woman*, 5; MCT Diary, March 17, 1948, HB.

57. MCT, "Black Mammy."

58. Terrell and others were not paid for letters to the editor or op-eds, just for articles. McElya, *Clinging to Mammy*, 153, 189–91. See "For and against the 'Black Mammy's' Monument," *Literary Digest*, April 28, 1923, 49.

59. W. Fitzhugh Brundage points out that whites "possessed the power to silence parts of the past; they, for instance, reverently erected monuments to 'faithful' slaves but raised no statues of black Civil War soldiers." Brundage, "'Woman's Hand,'" 71. For more on the myth of happy slaves, see Gallagher and Nolan, *Myth of the Lost Cause*, 16; Simon and Stevens, *New*, 35; McElya, *Clinging to Mammy*, 153–59; Rudolph, "Victoria Earle Matthews," 112–13; and MCT, "Black Mammy."

60. For debates about "colored," "Negro," "African," and other terms, see Litwack, *Been in the Storm*, 540–41; Wright, *Black Identity*, 134–35; Moses, *Golden Age*, 127–29; and Banner-Haley, *Fruits of Integration*, xix.

61. Laura, his child from that marriage, was later unable to claim a part of his inheritance. MCT, "Black Mammy."

62. Fox-Genovese, *Plantation Household*; MCT, "Black Mammy."

63. MCT, "Black Mammy."

64. Talbert was the recent past president of NACW and the current national director of the Anti-Lynching Crusaders, which raised funds for the NAACP's continued
attempts to pass the Dyer Anti-Lynching Bill. For information on Talbert, see Williams, "Mary Morris Burnett Talbert," 1137–39; Schneider, *We Return Fighting*, 188;
and Davis, *Women, Race, and Class*, 193. William L. Reed (on stationery from the Commonwealth of Massachusetts, Executive Department) to MCT, February 15, 1923, MCT
Papers, reel 5; Mary B. Talbert to MCT, April 17, 1923, MCT Papers, reel 5.

65. Beverly Guy-Sheftall suggests: "We will continue to distort the intellectual history of African Americans if we fail to include the work of the womenfolk who have
consistently provided some of the most passionate and insightful analyses of what it
means to be black and female in this patriarchal, capitalist, racist culture." Guy-Sheftall,
"Where Are the Black Female Intellectuals?," 225; Terborg-Penn, *African-American
Women*, 65; Guy-Sheftall, *Daughters of Sorrow*, 112; MCT, *Colored Woman*, 423; RHT
to MCT, February 11, 1915, MCT Additions.

Chapter 7

1. African Americans began a slow shift out of the GOP with the 1932 election of
FDR and the rise of the New Deal. In 1936, 71 percent of African Americans voted for
the Democratic presidential nominee, but their Democratic Party identification was
only at 44 percent. Not until 1948 did a majority of black voters, 56 percent, identify
themselves as Democrats. In 1952, at age eighty-nine, Terrell finally endorsed a Democratic candidate, W. Averell Harriman, as the presidential nominee and then shifted
her support to Adlai Stevenson after Harriman lost in the primary. (For a discussion of
African Americans, Terrell, and New Deal politics, see chapter 11.) Fauntroy, *Republicans and the Black Vote*, table 1.1, 5; Lisio, *Hoover, Blacks, and Lily-Whites*; Weiss, *Farewell to the Party of Lincoln*; MCT, "Endorsement of Adlai Stevenson for President," ca.
September 1952; and MCT, "Vote for Harriman and Home Rule," 1952, both in MCT
Papers, reel 23.

2. Terrell and Douglass together visited the 1893 Chicago World's Fair, where there
was much controversy over the segregation and representation of African Americans.
Both also attended the 1895 National Woman's Council's convention. She recalled: "Mr.
Douglass died suddenly one evening at his home after attending a business meeting of
the Woman's Council at which I was present and saw him. He invited me to lunch with
him but unfortunately for myself, I declined, and thus missed the last opportunity I
shall have of listening to his dear voice." She declined because she was in the midst of
a difficult, ultimately failed, pregnancy. MCT, *Colored Woman*, 49-51, 110–11, 133–34;
MCT to RHT (Boston), November 8, 1892, HB; MCT, "Introduction of Ida B. Wells,
to Deliver an Address on Lynching," 1893, MCT Papers, reel 20; MCT, "An Ethnolo-
gist's Injustice or Ignorance," *Ringwood's Afro-American Journal of Fashion*, April 1893,
1, MCT Collection; MCT Diary, March 12, 1895, MCT Collection.

3. Brittney Cooper notes, "Terrell created a new genealogical branch for Black politics and Black leadership, one that proceeds through a range of Black women directly
into the Civil Rights struggle." Pero Galo Dagbovie misses Terrell's contribution. Cooper, *Beyond Respectability*, 86, 60–61; Dagbovie, *Early Black History*; Terborg-Penn,

"Black Male Perspectives," 36; Frederick Douglass to Josephine Sophie White Griffing, September 27, 1868, in Foner, *Frederick Douglass*, 598–600; MCT Diary, February 22, May 20–22, 1908, MCT Papers, reel 1; MCT, "I Remember Frederick Douglass," *Ebony*, October 1953, 72–80.

4. On national white reconciliation, see Blight, *Race and Reunion*; Steedman, *Jim Crow Citizenship*; Sexton, *Amalgamation Schemes*, 229; Blum, *Reforging the White Republic*, 171, 208; Lorini, *Rituals of Race*, xiv; and MCT, "Addressing a Meeting Called to Protest against the Disfranchisement of Colored Men in the South," February 1, 1906, MCT Papers, reel 21.

5. RHT to President William Harrison, October 1892, RHT Papers, reel 2; MCT Diary, October 6, 12, 1908, MCT Papers, reel 1; Thomas L. Jones, President, Charles E. Robinson, Secretary, Francis Wells, Vice President, Coolidge and Dawes Republican League and the Allied Republican Clubs, "Memorial Resolution for Robert H. Terrell," ca. 1926, RHT Papers, reel 4.

6. Davis, *Guest of Honor*.

7. A graduation speech by Roosevelt set the wrong tone, Terrell noted: "President Roosevelt advises N's [Negroes] to put duty before rights at Howard University. We do not need this advice." Smock, *Booker T. Washington*, 188; MCT Diary, June 1, 1906, quoted in MCT Diary and Notes, 191, HB.

8. Weaver, *Senator*.

9. The dismissed included six soldiers who had received the medal of honor. The black divisions of the Twenty-Fifth Infantry had supported Roosevelt's famous charge up San Juan Hill during the Spanish-American War in 1898. Godshalk, *Veiled Visions*; Dorsey, *We Are All Americans*, 34; Harlan, *Washington*, 310–11; Alexander, *Army of Lions*, 292–93; MCT, "The Disbanding of the Colored Soldiers," *Voice of the Negro*, December 1906, 554–58; MCT, "A Sketch of Mingo Saunders: Late First Sergeant Company B. Twenty-Fifth Infantry, United States Army. Dismissed without Honor after Serving Twenty-Six Years," *Voice of the Negro*, March 1907, 129–30 (this article also appeared, unattributed to Terrell, in *WP*, February 12, 1907).

10. Roosevelt was visiting the site of the Panama Canal. Alexander, *Army of Lions*, 284–86; Lumsden, *Inez*, 25–27; Carle, *Defining the Struggle*, 119; Lane, *Brownsville Affair*; Weaver, *Brownsville Raid*; Rucker and Upton, *Encyclopedia of American Race Riots*, 80–81; Emberton, *Beyond Redemption*, 103–9, 130–32; MCT, *Colored Woman*, 270; MCT Diary, November 17, 29, December 2, 1906, quoted in MCT Diary and Notes, 208–10, HB; MCT Diary, June 3, 1908, MCT Papers, reel 1; MCT, "Taft Befriended Disgraced Troops," 1930 [on the death of William Taft], MCT Papers, reel 22.

11. Gould, *Presidency of Theodore Roosevelt*, 239–43, 294; Dorsey, *We Are All Americans*, 114; Sheffer, *Buffalo Soldiers*, 150–52; Wolraich, *Unreasonable Men*, 84–91; Gould, *Republicans*, 123–24; MCT Diary, November 29, December 2, 1906, quoted in MCT Diary and Notes, 209, 210, HB; RHT to Robert R. Church, undated, ca. 1906–7, series 1, box 1, folder 25, Church Papers; MCT Diary, January 17, March 3, April 4, 1907, quoted in MCT Diary and Notes, 217, 220, 224, HB; MCT Diary, January 12, 15, 1909, MCT Papers, reel 1.

12. Only one soldier was still alive. Weaver, *Senator*; and Gould, *Presidency of Theodore Roosevelt*, 236–43, 294.

13. MCT, *Colored Woman*, 277; MCT Diary, January 8, 1908, MCT Papers, reel 1.

14. MCT, *Colored Woman*, 277; MCT Diary, January 8, October 5, 1908, MCT Papers, reel 1; MCT, "Taft Befriended Disgraced Troops."

15. Moore, *Booker T. Washington*, 81.

16. Just as Washington decided not to criticize Teddy Roosevelt publicly, so Mollie Terrell did the same with Taft. Alexander, *Army of Lions*, 292–93; Dansker, "William Howard Taft," 226–28; MCT to RHT, undated, ca. 1909, MCT Papers, reel 2.

17. MCT Diary, June 18, 1909, MCT Papers, reel 1.

18. Roosevelt had been New York City police commissioner in the late 1890s when her brother Thomas was hired as a legal clerk in the police courts. See Jeffers, *Commissioner Roosevelt*; Kohn, *Heir to the Empire City*.

19. The Progressive Party's formal endorsement of woman suffrage could not make up for its discriminatory policies and racism. No political party included any mention of civil rights in its platform that year. Robyn Muncy observes that white progressives "barely noticed racial inequality until the 1930s, and others soft-pedaled opposition to racial injustice in hopes of winning the white South to the new party." Muncy, *Relentless Reformer*, 45; Kazin, Edwards, and Rothman, "Progressive Parties," 606; Gustafson, *Women and the Republican Party*, 126–32; Lewis, *Du Bois: Biography of a Race*, 421; Frymer, *Uneasy Alliances*, 85; MCT, *Colored Woman*, 271.

20. Ali, *In the Balance*, 112–13; Walton, *Invisible Politics*, 148; Link, "Correspondence," 480.

21. Terrell did not usually use the word "Negro," so this was probably a publisher's choice. Church and Church, *Robert R. Churches*, 111–15; MCT, "The Progressive Party and the Negro: Aftermath of the Chicago Convention. Exclusion of Negro Delegates and Adoption of the Lily White Policy by the First National Progressive Convention Causes Sensation in American Politics," 1912, MCT Papers, reel 21.

22. Goethals, *Presidential Leadership*, 140–41; Zhang, *Origins*, 40; Lewis, *Du Bois: Biography*, 277–78, 332; Craig, *Progressives at War*, 119–20; Logan, *Betrayal*, 361–71; MCT, "Lynching," 1923, MCT Papers, reel 21.

23. Terrell was turned down for several government jobs based on her race and was fired from others when her white coworkers objected to her presence. Jordan, "'Damnable Dilemma,'" 1562–83; Jonas, *Freedom's Sword*, 16–17; Edgerton, *Hidden Heroism*, 66–99; Jensen, *Mobilizing Minerva*, 12–13, 24–27; Salem, *To Better Our World*, 201–30; Greenwald, *Women, War, and Work*, 20–27; Hine and Thompson, *Shining Thread*, 225, 264; Cobble, *Other Women's Movement*, 13–16; Tischauser, *Changing Nature*, 123; MCT, "A Doughboy's Fatal Mistake in London," undated, ca. 1919, MCT Papers, reel 23; MCT, "The Racial Worm Turns" or "The Race Problem and the War," 1918–20, MCT Papers, reel 21.

24. At least thirteen African American veterans were lynched, including some in uniform, after World War I. For more on the riots, see Slotkin, *Lost Battalions*, 428–35; Williams, "Vanguards," 347–70; Williams, *Torchbearers*, 9, 237, 260; Parker, *Fighting for Democracy*, 39, 45; MCT, "Racial Worm Turns."

25. The American delegation had not segregated her: "Jeannette Rankin asked to room with me in 1919.... We roomed together at the Continental Hotel in Paris." Under the title "Nationality, Race and Color," the final text of the resolution read: "Holding that no human being on account of his nationality, race, or color should be deprived of education, prevented from earning a living, debarred from any legitimate pursuit he may

wish to follow, or subjected to humiliation, this International Congress of Women resolves to work for the abrogation of laws and changes of customs which lead to such discrimination." Alexander, *Parallel Worlds*, 185; Schott, *Reconstructing Women's Thoughts*, 78–79; Fontaine, "International League," 600–601; Lieberman, "'Another Side," 19–21; Mollin, *Radical Pacifism*, 3; MCT Diary, April 25, 1946, HB; MCT, *Colored Woman*, 204, 332–33; "Extract from the Forthcoming Report of the International Congress of Women, Held at Zurich, May 12–17, 1919, WILPF, International Office, Geneva, International Congress of Women," 1919, MCT Papers, reel 14.

26. Du Bois and Ida Gibbs Hunt, a friend of Mollie's since her Oberlin College days, organized the 1919 Pan-African Congress in Paris to call international attention to the human rights priorities of Africans and those in the African Diaspora. The WILPF supported a League of Nations but was concerned about whether it would be appropriately anti-imperialistic and whether women would be included on key committees (such as the Disarmament Commission). It also opposed the Treaty of Versailles as too harsh on Germany. Rosenberg, *How Far*, 39–70; Salem, *To Better Our World*, 201–30; Tuttle, *Race Riot*; Ellis, *Race, War*; Madigan, *The Burning*, 87–89; Terborg-Penn, *African-American Women*, 96; Rupp, *Worlds of Women*, 30; Howard, *Struggle*, 247; Meyer and Prugl, *Gender Politics*, 110. For discussions of the treatment of black American and French colonial soldiers in France during World War I, see Stovall, *Paris Noir*, 1–24; Stovall, "Love," 309; and MCT, "Black People and Arguments by Democrats in Favor of the League of Nations," Providence, R.I., October 26, 1920, MCT Papers, reel 21.

27. Terrell's interest in the Virgin Islands, including women's voting rights, continued into the 1930s. Gallicchio, *African American Encounter*, 20–25; Lauren, "Human Rights," 271–73; Terborg-Penn, "Enfranchising Women," 51–53; MCT, "In Defense of the Republican Ticket," 1932, MCT Papers, reel 22; Harold L. Ickes (secretary of the interior) to MCT, May 31, 1935, MCT Papers, reel 7; Elise Hill to MCT, December 7, 1935, MCT Papers, reel 7; MCT Diary, November 10, 1936, MCT Papers, reel 2.

28. Gray's group was the Negro Women's Republican League; Terrell's was the Colored Women's Republican League. Daisy F. Welch to MCT, September 4, 1920; Virginia White Speel to MCT, October 6, 1920; and MCT to Speel, October 19, 1920, all in MCT Papers, reel 5.

29. She also wrote to Edward F. Colladay, a white lawyer, civic leader, and RNC operative. Gustafson, *Women and the Republican Party*, 191–93; Colladay (RNC of D.C.) to Will Hays (chairman, RNC, NYC), September 13, 1920, series 1, box 22, folder 6, Church Papers; MCT to R. R. Church Jr., telegrams, September 21, 1920, series 1, box 22, folder 6, Church Papers; MCT, "An Appeal to Colored Women to Vote and Do Their Duty in Politics," 1921, MCT Papers, reel 21; MCT, "Colored College Women in Politics," 1925, MCT Papers, reel 22.

30. MCT to R. R. Church Jr., telegrams, September 21, 1920; Colladay to Hays, September 13, 1920; RHT to MCT, October 6, 10, 1920, MCT Additions.

31. MCT to Henry Lincoln Johnson (RNC headquarters, Chicago), October 7, 1920; and Elizabeth Chase Carter to RHT, October 12, 1920, both in MCT Papers, reel 5; RHT to MCT, October 10, 1920, MCT Additions.

32. MCT, "Appeal to Colored Women"; MCT to prospective black women voters, October 12, 1920, MCT Papers, reel 5.

33. Terborg-Penn, *African-American Women*, 143–44. For more on issues surrounding

Harding's race, see Payne, *Dead Last*, 95–125; Anthony, *Florence Harding*; Murray, *Warren G. Harding*; Yellin, *Racism*, 181–82. RHT (Tampa, Fla.) to MCT (D.C.), June 5, 1920, HB; and MCT, "Campaign Speech Made at Newport, Rhode Island," October 12, 1920, MCT Papers, reel 21.

34. Relishing the fight, Terrell wrote to Lethia C. Fleming, "I had a thrilling experience in Dover, Del. about which you will read in the press. I wish you had been with me. I know I would have enjoyed your few brief remarks to that 'southern gentleman.'" MCT to Fleming, October 20, 1920; MCT to James Hall Anderson, October 23, 1920; and MCT to Moorfield Storey, October 27, 1920, all in MCT Papers, reel 5; MCT, "Statement of the Treatment Received at the Hands of a Ticket Agent at Dover, Delaware, October 13, 1920," MCT Papers, reel 21 (emphasis added).

35. Welke, *Recasting American Liberty*; Kelley, *Right to Ride*, 78; MCT, "Statement of the Treatment Received"; MCT, *Colored Woman*, 315.

36. See Lisa G. Materson's compelling account of these rivalries and of the founding of the National League of Republican Colored Women. Terrell also sent letters of regret to her good friends Mrs. Daisy Welch and Mrs. Willie Layton. Materson, *Freedom*, chap. 3; MCT to Hallie Quinn Brown, September 20, 1920; MCT to Daisy Welch, October 6, 1920; and MCT to Mrs. S. W. ["Willie"] Layton, October 25, 1920, all in MCT Papers, reel 5.

37. They knew each other from Berto and Mollie Terrell's visits with their mutual friends, George and Maude Myers, who were leaders of the Ohio black Republicans; Lethia's husband, Thomas W. Fleming, was a prominent Republican and Cleveland's first black city councilmember. Fleming to MCT and MCT to Fleming, October 19, 20, 1920, MCT Papers, reel 5.

38. Fleming to MCT, December 28, 1920, MCT Papers, reel 5.

39. Skin color did not seem to be as overtly an issue since Brown was also fair-skinned. Fleming to MCT, January 7, 1921, MCT Papers, reel 5.

40. Fleming to MCT, January 7, February 10, 21, 1921; Bertha G. Higgins to MCT, February 23, 1921, all in MCT Papers, reel 5.

41. Lisa G. Materson states that Gray's National Women's Republican League did not last past 1921. Materson, *Freedom*, 117–18, 144; MCT Diary, February 9, March 8, May 16, 1921, HB.

42. When Mollie returned to see him, Robert did not have a job for her, but he told her that "he had been promised" that Phyllis would be "given a job" in the post office. MCT Diary, January 27, 28, March 14, May 14, 18, 26, June 13, September 28, 1921, HB.

43. Earlier, in June 1921, Terrell had gone to see Henry Lincoln Johnson to commiserate "about the Republican Committee's endorsing Lily Whites in Southern States. We are all discouraged that this should be done." Walker, *Presidents*, 59; Francis, *Civil Rights*, 116–19; Glasrud, "Beginning the Trek," 6, 24; Walker, *Presidents*, 59; Lewis, *Fight for Equality*, 55–56; MCT Diary, June 9, November 30, December 7, 1921, HB.

44. Studying at the Library of Congress about the evils of colonialism and the broader struggles of people of color around the world, Terrell "read about the injustice perpetrated upon the East Indians by Great Britain, the Socialists in India, the indignities heaped upon the Indians in South Africa, etc." Her continuing education confirmed her belief that "the white man's treatment of the darker races is devilish. His sun will set soon." Also in 1921, she attended lectures on international affairs, including one

by Chinese students, who presented "China's case against the governments who have despoiled her." Blackwell, *No Peace*, 94–96; Blackwell, "Peace," 255–57; MCT Diary, May 13, December 15, 26, 27, 1921, HB; MCT to Jane Addams, March 18, 1921, in "Mary Church Terrell Protests," 281.

45. Terrell and Addams had developed a good relationship. MCT to RHT, August 6, 1902, HB; MCT Diary, January 19, 1921, HB; MCT to Addams, March 18, 1921, in "Mary Church Terrell Protests," 280–82.

46. Attending a board meeting soon after, Terrell noted the presence of "Mrs. Brown who wanted me to sign the resolution asking for the recall of the African troops." The minutes passively noted: "The sense of the Committee was cordial agreement with Mrs. Terrill's [*sic*] statements" about China. MCT Diary, November 10, 1921, HB; MCT, "Remarks at Mass Meeting on Subject of War," November 15, 1921, MCT Papers, reel 21; "Minutes, Meeting of the Executive Board of the W.I.L.P.F. U.S. Section was held at the New Washington office, 732–17th St., N.W.," November 12, 1921, WILPF, 1919–1921 and undated, MCT Papers, reel 20; Dorothy Baker (Intercollegiate Liberal League) to MCT, December 21, 1921, MCT Papers, reel 5; MCT, "Colored People and World Peace, or Colored Women and World Peace," 1932, MCT Papers, reels 22, 20 (two versions).

47. Ever the interracial bridge builder, Terrell was still attending WILPF dinners in 1951. MCT Diary, November 13, 14, December 15, 1921, HB; MCT Diary, April 28, 29, 1922, quoted in MCT Diary and Notes, 119–20, HB; MCT Diary, April 27, 1951, MCT Papers, reel 2.

48. Melinda Ann Plastas notes that this reflects WILPF members' "inability to understand thoroughly how race, gender and war intersected." Some WILPF leaders later claimed that Terrell had not attended meetings regularly, but the board minutes suggest otherwise. Plastas, *Band of Noble Women*, 22–24; Blackwell-Johnson, "Peace," 257; MCT Diary and Notes, 57, HB; MCT Diary, October 5, 1921, HB.

49. Samuel Krislov argues, "By 1928 the percentage of Negroes in the federal service as a whole was estimated as 9.59, representing almost a doubling from the beginning of the Republican era in 1921." By 1938, "the percentage of Negroes in the service rose only slightly, to 9.85 percent." Krislov, *Negro in Federal Employment*, 22–23; Moore, *Leading the Race*, 152; MCT Diary, April 10, December 15, 1921, HB; MCT Diary, May 7, 1922, quoted in MCT Diary and Notes, 128, HB; MCT, "Lynching," 1923, MCT Papers, reel 21.

50. Mjagkij, "Julia Ward Howe," 254; MCT, "Lynching," 1923; and MCT, "Some Facts for Colored Women to Think About," November 1924, both in MCT Papers, reel 21.

51. In the mid-1920s, Terrell headed the NACW's Legislative Department and used her *National Association Notes* column to alert women to lobby for or against key pieces of legislation of particular interest to African Americans. Harley, "Beyond the Classroom," 264; Materson, *Freedom*, 123–24, 108–28, 185; Higginbotham, "In Politics," 298–99, 303; MCT Diary, November 7, 12, 1921; and MCT to Mary McLeod Bethune, ca. early January 1926, all in HB.

52. April 2, 3, 27, 1922, MCT Diary and Notes, 93–94, HB; MCT to RHT, August 10, 1922, August 13, 1924, MCT Additions.

53. Berto died December 20, 1925. For more, see chapter 9. MCT to RHT, March 11,

1922, HB; MCT to RHT, June 10, 1924, MCT Papers, reel 2; MCT to RHT, August 13, 1924, MCT Additions (emphasis added); Blanche Wright to MCT, October 4, 1924, HB.

54. As Terrell had predicted, the League of Nations did not promote global anti-colonial struggles. Smith, *Emancipation*, 195, 297; Grant, *Way It Was*, 336; Jackson, "Perry Wilbon Howard," 417–18; MCT, "Black People and Arguments by Democrats in Favor of the League of Nations," October 26, 1920; and MCT, "Talk Made during the Coolidge-Dawes Campaign, October 1924," both in MCT Papers, reel 21.

55. Coolidge remained silent and did not actively campaign, after the recent death of his sixteen-year-old son. Tucker, *High Tide*, 50, 180, 186; "John William Davis (1873–1955)," in Biographical Directory of the United States Congress http://bioguide.congress.gov/scripts/biodisplay.pl?index=d000012; Harbaugh, *Lawyer's Lawyer*, 228–30. For more on the rise of the second KKK, see Wade, *Fiery Cross*, 193, 197–201; McVeigh, *Rise of the Ku Klux Klan*; Pegram, *One Hundred Percent American*, 19–20, 209, 213–16; and MacLean, *Behind the Mask*, 16–18.

56. It read: "We declare the Democratic party is in favor of amending the constitution, so as to preserve the purity of the ballot and the electorate of the State from conferring the powers and privileges upon those who are unfitted to appreciate its importance." MCT, "Talk Made during the Coolidge-Dawes"; MCT, "Some Facts for Colored Women."

57. Davis's black supporters were likely fooled by his record as solicitor general because he had argued a few antidiscrimination cases for the U.S. government—cases that did not represent his own beliefs. Materson suggests that Alice Dunbar-Nelson "would not have been aware of this disjuncture between his professional service and personal views." Davis remained a strong segregationist, later serving as lead counsel defending the 'separate but equal' doctrine in *Brown v. Board of Education* (1954). Terrell viewed the relative prosperity of the early 1920s as proof that the Republicans had better economic policies. The dire economic crisis of 1893 and the recession of 1913–14 had both occurred during Democratic administrations. Terrell noted that in "all terrible financial crises it is always the women and children who suffer most. When you go to the polls, my sisters, remember that it is the Democratic party that so mismanages the affairs of this government that it takes bread and butter out of the mouths of women and men." Materson, *Freedom*, 132; MCT, "Talk Made during the Coolidge-Dawes"; MCT, "Some Facts for Colored Women."

58. The ICWDR was founded in 1920. Gerald Horne notes that Madam C. J. Walker founded an International League of Darker Peoples in 1919, but the group did not survive her death later that year. Margaret M. Washington, Mary Church Terrell, Mary Burnett Talbert, Addie Hunton, Mary McLeod Bethune, Nannie Burroughs, Lugenia Burns Hope, and Addie Dickerson were founding members of the ICWDR. Terrell was elected as one of its two vice-presidents. Although the NACW had included speakers on pan-African issues and anticolonialism at its national conventions, its focus was generally more local and national in scope. For a discussion of the NACW's attention to international issues, see Neverdon-Morton, *Afro-American Women*, 198–201. Rief, "Thinking Locally," 214–17; Materson, "African American Women's Global Journeys," 35–42; White, *Too Heavy*, 134–35, 146; Salem, *To Better Our World*, 234–36; Chandler, "Addie," 270–83; Rupp, "Challenging Imperialism," 8–27; Horne "Race from Power," 51; "International Council of Women of the Darker Races Correspondence," 1922–1925,

MCT Collection; Addie W. Dickerson (president, ICWDR) to MCT, December 10, 1934, MCT Papers, reel 7.

59. ICWDR members were particularly interested in the status and condition of women and children in Sierra Leone, Japan, Brazil, Puerto Rico, Haiti, China, Nigeria, the West Indies, and the Philippines. Pan-Africanist black women who participated in the Universal Negro Improvement Association, the Harlem Renaissance, and the new ICWDR, whatever their ideological differences, urged people of color to fight collectively for racial equality worldwide. Terrell's participation in the ICWDR was a natural expansion of her earlier friendships, experiences, and ideas, including with her Oberlin friend Ida Gibbs Hunt. Alexander, *Parallel Worlds*, 24–30, 132; Plummer, *Rising Wind*, 9–21; Dossett, *Bridging Race Divides*, 24–30, 183; Taylor, *Veiled Garvey*, 41, 102; McDuffie, "'[She] Devoted," 219–50; MCT Diary, September 28, 1921, February 14, April 24, 1949, HB.

60. Terrell's "Up to Date: A Brief Survey of Current Happenings" column ran in the *Chicago Defender* from 1928 through March 1929. At this time, the *Defender* had a national circulation of around "225,000 copies sold per week with an estimate total of 1,200,000 readers for each edition." Patricia A. Schechter notes, "Mary Church Terrell's 'Up To Date' column reached hundreds of thousands of *Defender* readers every week, and in 1928 Terrell became the only African American woman to have her name inscribed on a plaque unveiled at a national commemoration of the life of Susan B. Anthony." Schechter, *Ida B. Wells-Barnett*, 237; Reed, *Rise of Chicago's Black Metropolis*, 102; Drake and Cayton, *Black Metropolis*, 400; MCT, "Up to Date," draft for *CD*, 1928–29, MCT Papers, reel 22; MCT, "Up to Date," January 13, February 9, 16, 23, 1929, *CD*, pt. 2, p. 2.

Chapter 8

1. Mollie Church, "Should an Amendment to the Constitution Allowing Women the Ballot Be Adopted," November 7, 1879, MCT Papers, reel 20; MCT, "Campaign Speech for Ruth Hanna McCormick (undated)," MCT Papers, reel 22.

2. MCT to Phyllis Terrell Goines, April 7, 1930, MCT Papers, reel 3.

3. The GOP outreach to African Americans in the 1920s consisted largely of patronage rather than substantive legislative changes to advance civil rights. Yellin, *Racism*. Materson has an excellent account of Illinois black Republican women that tells this story from a state perspective. Materson, *Freedom*, 187.

4. Mark Hanna served in the U.S. Senate from 1897 until his death in 1904; his teenaged daughter Ruth (1880–1944) worked on Capitol Hill as her father's secretary and assistant. Mollie and Berto Terrell had met him through their close friends and GOP partisans, George A. and Maude Stewart Myers, in Cleveland. Terrell noted that Ruth came from "a family of Quakers who have always been noted for their interest in colored people." In 1903, Ruth Hanna married Joseph "Medill" McCormick, whose family owned the *Chicago Tribune*; he also served in the U.S. Senate. Ruth McCormick led a successful 1912 lobbying campaign to gain Illinois women the right to vote for presidential electors and in township elections. From 1913 to 1914, she served as chair of the Congressional Committee, the non-partisan lobbying wing of the National American Woman's Suffrage Association. Medill McCormick was elected to the House of

Representatives (1917–19) and then to the Senate (1919–25). Miller, "McCormick and the Senatorial Election," 192; Miller, *Ruth Hanna McCormick*, 16; "Hanna, Marcus Alonzo ("Mark") (1837–1904), in Biographical Directory of the United States Congress, http://bioguide.congress.gov/scripts/biodisplay.pl?index=H000163. See George A. Myers Papers, 1890–1929, Ohio Historical Society, http://memory.loc.gov/ammem/award97/ohshtml/myers/overview.html; MCT, "McCormick (undated)"; MCT, "Campaign Speech for Ruth Hanna McCormick, (prior to April 8, 1930)," MCT Papers, reel 22.

5. McCormick served as the first elected national committeewoman of the RNC from Illinois from 1924 to 1928. "Ruth Hanna McCormick (1880–1944)," Biographical Directory of the United States Congress, http://bioguide.congress.gov/scripts/biodisplay.pl?index=M000372

6. McCormick used her personal friendship with Alice Roosevelt Longworth, the daughter of Theodore Roosevelt and wife of Speaker Longworth, to persuade him. "Oscar Stanton De Priest," History, Art and Archives, U.S. House of Representatives, http://history.house.gov/People/Detail?id=12155; Materson, *Freedom*, 203; Louis R. Lautier, "De Priest to Face House Precedents: May Meet Snag When Congress Opens," *CD*, November 17, 1928, 2; "De Priest and Dan Jackson to Face Trial," *CD*, December 29, 1928, 1; Evangeline Roberts, "Mrs. Terrell Here to Head Senate Drive," *CD*, September 28, 1929, 8.

7. Terrell wrote Phyllis: "3 cheers for Mr. DePriest! He is seated! The news came yesterday. I shall send him a telegram of congratulation," which she did on behalf of the NACW. DePriest replied, "My dear Mrs. Terrell, I wish to acknowledge receipt of your telegram . . . and to thank you for your words of congratulations and good wishes, in which you include Mrs. DePriest." Terrell saw DePriest frequently through Phyllis, who was dating his friend, F. E. Parks, principal of the Cardozo Vocational School for Boys and then the Armstrong Manual Training High School. Church and Church, *Robert R. Churches*, 159, 184; MCT Diary, June 27, December 31, 1927, MCT Papers, reel 2; MCT to Goines, April 17, 1929, MCT Papers, reel 3; State Senator Adelbert H. Roberts to MCT, March 11, 1929, MCT Papers, reel 6; Oscar DePriest to MCT, April 17, 1929, MCT Papers, reel 6.

8. In 1927, to prepare herself for upcoming campaigns, Terrell obtained a diploma from a School of Politics in Washington, D.C. Her political connections in Chicago ran deep; Aldermen Robert R. Jackson and Louis B. Anderson sent letters to Representative McCormick commending her appointment. Terrell obscured DePriest's role and her own ambitions in her autobiography, implying that she had not sought the position. Writing to her brother Thomas, she was more direct: "Congressman DePriest gave me a letter of introduction to Mrs. McCormick last Spring. The rest was easy. She decided to have me help her right away." Schechter, *Ida B. Wells-Barnett*, 240; Miller, *Ruth Hanna McCormick*, 16; MCT, *Colored Woman*, 355; MCT Diary, March 26, 1927, MCT Papers, reel 2; DePriest to Ruth Hanna McCormick, May 27, 1929, MCT Papers, reel 6; Robert R. Jackson to McCormick, September 18, 1929; McCormick to Louis B. Anderson, September 26, 1929, MCT Papers, reel 6; MCT to Thomas A. Church, September 28, 1929, MCT Papers, reel 3; MCT Diary, April 23, 1936, MCT Papers, reel 2.

9. Wilkerson, *Warmth of Other Suns*, 9; Materson, *Freedom*, 185, 188; MCT, "An Appeal to Colored Women," *National Notes*, November 1925, 1, 5; MCT, Citizenship

Department, "What Colored Women Can and Should Do at the Polls," 1921 and 1926 versions, MCT Papers, reel 21.

10. Fifty dollars a month would be about $734 in today's money. See MCT, "Up to Date: A Brief Survey of Current Happenings," *CD* (microfilm), February 1928–March 1929; N[athan] K[ellog] McGill (attorney-secretary of the *CD*) to MCT, February 15, 1928, MCT Papers, reel 6. Roberts, "Mrs. Terrell Here."

11. Roberts, "Mrs. Terrell Here."

12. MCT to Mary McLeod Bethune, February 16, 1926, MCT Papers, reel 6.

13. MCT to Bethune, February 16, 1926; Roberts, "Mrs. Terrell Here."

14. The event was at the Poro Institute, founded by Terrell's friend Annie Malone. Poro trained saleswomen to sell beauty products. Hill, "Annie Malone," 406; "Mrs. Terrell Honor Guest at Reception; Mrs. Irene M. Gaines Charming Hostess," *CD*, October 5, 1929, 19.

15. Knupfer claims that "tensions developed among clubwomen when the NACW selected Mary Church Terrell . . . to assist in McCormick's campaign," but there is no evidence that it played a role. Knupfer, *Chicago Black Renaissance*, 105; "At Mrs. McCormick's Headquarters."

16. The organizers were Bertha Montgomery and Susie Myers. Materson, *Freedom*, 202–12; Schechter, *Ida B. Wells-Barnett*, 235–36, 241; "Women Voters Oust *Defender* Reporter," *CD*, October 12, 1929, 8.

17. "Apology Demanded from Mrs. Barnett," *CD*, October 12, 1929, 9.

18. Myers denied Terrell's accurate but insensitive claim that McCormick had played a role in obtaining a promotion and a raise for Myers's husband, a post office clerk, after he returned from serving in the U.S. military in France. "Mrs. Meyers [*sic*] Answers Mary Church Terrell," *CD*, October 19, 1929, 5; "Mary Church Terrell Refutes Statement of Mrs. Susie Myers," *CD*, October 26, 1929, 8; "Women Open War on Mrs. Ruth McCormick," *CD*, October 19, 1929, 9 [emphasis added].

19. Some black women appear to have chosen to interpret McCormick's ambiguity as support for their position. Miller, *Ruth Hanna McCormick*, 117, 187, 195; Materson, *Freedom*, 169, 185–86, 195, 208; Parker, *Articulating Rights*, chaps. 3, 4; "Women Open," *CD*, October 19, 1929, 9; Harriet A. Lee to MCT, April 10, 1930; McCormick to Lee, April 16, 1930, MCT Papers, reel 6.

20. Between 1920 and 1950, the number of African Americans living in Chicago "increased from 109,000 to 492,000." Duncan and Duncan, *Negro Population*, 87; Materson, *Freedom*, 190, 194, 200–201; Miller, *Ruth Hanna McCormick*, 92–93, 131; Hendricks, "Ida B. Wells-Barnett," 263–75; Terborg-Penn, *African-American Women*, 121–23.

21. MCT, *Colored Woman*, 356; MCT, "Narrative of Work for Ruth Hanna McCormick," November 1929, MCT Papers, reel 3.

22. Irene M. Gaines to Hallie Quinn Brown, December 14, 1929, box 35, Hallie Quinn Brown Papers, Central State University, DeWine, Ohio.

23. Gaines to Brown, December 14, 1929.

24. Mary McLeod Bethune was similarly accused by men and women of "having an 'ego problem' and of becoming 'more domineering and arrogant as she acquired power and prestige.'" Savage, *Your Spirits*, 134; Gaines to Brown, December 14, 1929.

25. Several of those whom Terrell contacted ran businesses and, as a matter of policy, declined to share their business mailing lists with anyone. F. B. Ransom (attorney and manager, Madam C. J. Walker Mfg.) to MCT, September 26, 1929; Annie M. Malone (Poro College) to MCT, September 26, 1929; MCT to Miss Johnson, October 2, 1929, all in MCT Papers, reel 6.

26. One thousand women did not sign the petition but were represented by the fifty representatives of black women's political clubs. "Women Open War"; Gaines to Brown, December 14, 1929.

27. Materson, *Freedom*, 210–12; Robert J. Nelson to MCT, October 17, 1929, MCT Papers, reel 6; Gaines to Brown, December 14, 1929; MCT to Goines, February 11, 1930, MCT Papers, reel 3.

28. A page is missing from Gaines's letter in the archives, so this sentence and the narrative of the conflict are not complete. Gaines to Brown, December 14, 1929; LeRoy M. Hardin (campaign manager, Colored Division) to MCT, November 14, 1929, MCT Papers, reel 6.

29. In the 1950s, Gaines exhibited a similarly competitive and self-promoting nature when, as Knupfer puts it, she "fought fiercely" for a third term as president of the National Association of Colored Women. Gaines was accused of creating "factionalism" when she "demanded absolute allegiance from clubwomen she had appointed as officers." Knupfer suggests that Gaines engaged in "an abuse of power" when she "asked an NACW member to revise her speech for the 1956 NACW convention so that the Republican Party, not Mary Church Terrell, would be given credit for desegregating restaurants in Washington, D.C." In fact, Terrell had "led a three-year protest against restaurants in Washington, resulting in her victory in the court case, *District of Columbia v. John Thompson* [1953]. Her victory was nationally known and celebrated by blacks (see chapter 14)." Knupfer, *Chicago Black Renaissance*, 113–14; Gaines to Brown, December 14, 1929.

30. It is unclear whether she gave this response. Undated notes from 1929 Correspondence folder in MCT Papers, reel 6.

31. McCormick's rival was Lottie Holman O'Neill. Miller, *Ruth Hanna McCormick*, 92, 197, 223.

32. Frank B. Jackson to McCormick, December 12, 1929, MCT Papers, reel 6.

33. Jackson to McCormick, December 12, 1929; H. Boas Nelson (president, Ruth Hanna McCormick Fifth Ward Republican Organization) to MCT, December 31, 1929; and MCT to Nelson, January 3, 1930, all in MCT Papers, reel 6.

34. Terrell wrote this same line in letters to several other family members, friends, and coworkers. MCT to DePriest, February 26, 1930, MCT Papers, reel 6; MCT to Goines, April 7, 1930 MCT Papers, reel 3.

35. Hardin to MCT, February 1, 1930, MCT Papers, reel 6.

36. See, e.g., B. F. Sayre [Payne?] to MCT, October 26, 1929; Lelah Morris Brown to MCT, November 24, 1929, MCT Papers, reel 6; MCT to Goines, January 20, 1930, MCT Papers, reel 3; Hardin to MCT, February 1, 3 (letter and telegram), 1930, MCT Papers, reel 6; MCT to Mrs. Shepperd, February 12, 1930, MCT Papers, reel 6.

37. Hardin to MCT, February 3, 1930 (second letter); and Jackson to McCormick, December 12, 1929, both in MCT Papers, reel 6.

38. Materson, *Freedom*, 210; Hardin to MCT, February 3, 1930 (second letter); Jackson to McCormick, December 12, 1929, MCT Papers, reel 6.

39. Hardin to MCT, February 4, 1930, MCT Papers, reel 6

40. Hardin to MCT, February 4, 1930; MCT to Hardin, telegram draft (on Western Union form dated 1930), MCT Papers, reel 6.

41. Terrell asked Snyder to "please be kind enough to request him [Hardin] not to threaten to wire Mrs. McCormick every time somebody accuses me of doing something to which he objects." Miller, *Ruth Hanna McCormick*, 211; MCT to James Snyder, February 5, 1930; Louise W. Thomas to MCT, February 5, 22, 1930; and MCT to Thomas, telegram, February 10, 1930, all in MCT Papers, reel 6.

42. Conway to MCT, February 10, 1930; and MCT to Snyder, February 11, 12, 1930, all in MCT Papers, reel 6.

43. MCT to Conway, February 15, 1930.

44. MCT to Goines, February 11, 1930, MCT Papers, reel 3.

45. Charles S. Ruff to McCormick, February 7, 1930; and MCT to H. O. Farr, February 20, 1930, both in MCT Papers, reel 6.

46. Terrell cited a 1904 pamphlet, "Charles S. Deneen versus the Public Schools and Public Peace . . . Being an exposition of the Greatest Fee-Office in the United States. How the prosecutor grows fat while the school children starve." She hoped the title said it all. MCT, "Charles S. Deneen as a State's Attorney," 1929; and MCT, "Charles S. Deneen's Senate Record," speech, ca. October 1929, both in MCT Papers, reel 22.

47. Gosnell, *Negro Politicians*, 188–89 (Cong. Rec., 71st Cong., 1st Sess., vol. 72, June 6, 1929, 2457); "'What about 14th, 15th Amendments?' President Is Asked; Tinkham Asks Mr. Hoover Some Pertinent Questions," *CD*, April 13, 1929, 1; "Census Bill before House for Passage: Dixie States May Lose Seats in House," *CD*, June 8, 1929, 4; "Tinkham Amendment Killed by Southerners: Dixie Solons Still Uphold Vote Fraud; Census Bill Will Not Aid Disfranchised," *CD*, June 15, 1929, 1; Rep. George Holden Tinkham (Committee on Appropriations) to MCT, March 1, 1930, MCT Papers, reel 6; MCT, "McCormick, (prior to April 8, 1930)."

48. Patler, *Jim Crow*, chaps. 2, 8; Rudwick, "Oscar De Priest," 77; MCT, "What It Means to Be Colored in the Capital of the United States," *Independent*, January 24, 1907, 204; MCT, "Report of Speeches Made and Work Done, November 12–24, 1929, inclusive," Ruth Hana McCormick, Illinois Senatorial Campaign, 1929–1930, MCT Papers, reel 15; MCT, "McCormick, (prior to April 8, 1930)"; "At Mrs. McCormick's Headquarters: Mrs. McCormick Has Record of Fairness," *CD*, October 12, 1929, 3.

49. Representative DePriest saw his wife insulted by many white Americans and shunned by the other Representatives and their wives, including northern Republicans. Herskovits, "Race," 1061; "Socially Elite Aim Dart at Mrs. DePriest; Capital Society Up in Air about Mrs. DePriest," *CD*, January 26, 1929, 1; "Women Stir Up Trouble Says Writer; Scores Stand against Mrs. Oscar DePriest," *CD*, February 9, 1929, 2; "Room Next to DePriest Irks Dixie Solon; Orders Aid to Return Office Key," *CD*, April 13, 1929, 2; "DePriest Asks All Republicans in Congress to a Musicale," *New York Times*, June 17, 1929, 17; MCT, "McCormick, (prior to April 8, 1930)"; "White House Tea Starts Senate Stir: Blease Resolution Objecting to Presence of Negro Congressman's Wife Is Expunged. Florida House Protests, Condemns 'Social Policies of the Administration'

by Vote of 71 to 13, after Sharp Debate," *New York Times*, June 18, 1929, 39; "Offers 'Nigger' Poem: Senator Blease Sees It Expunged from the Record," *Providence (R.I.) Evening Tribune*, June 18, 1929, 7; MCT, "McCormick, (prior to April 8, 1930)."

50. Phyllis wrote that she was not surprised certain Chicago women were jealous, "but there isn't anyone that can even touch the hem of your skirt, so to speak. No one can hold a candle to you. I'm proud of you." Miller, *Ruth Hanna McCormick*, 218; Gosnell, *Negro Politicians*, 44; Phyllis Terrell Goines to MCT, undated 1929, MCT Papers, reel 3; MCT to Laura Terrell Jones, February 20, 1930, MCT Papers, reel 6.

51. Jones to MCT, April 10 (telegram), July 23, 1930, March 15, 1931, MCT Papers, reel 2.

52. Miller, "McCormick and the Senatorial Election," 197, 202, 206.

53. Miller, *Ruth Hanna McCormick*, 233; Gosnell, *Negro Politicians*, 44–46.

54. MCT to Goines, September 15, 1930, MCT Papers, reel 3.

55. "Oscar Stanton De Priest," http://history.house.gov/People/Detail?id=12155; Miller, "McCormick and the Senatorial Election," 202, 204–5, 208, 210; LeRoy Hardin to MCT, November 7, 1930, MCT Papers, reel 6.

56. Ruth Hanna McCormick (Simms) to MCT, February 14, 1931, MCT Papers, reel 6; MCT Diary, February 19, 1931, MCT Additions; MCT to Goines, September 29, 1932, MCT Papers, reel 6.

Chapter 9

1. When she said in her 1940 autobiography that she carried on alone, she did not acknowledge her relationship with Oscar DePriest. MCT, *Colored Woman*, 425.

2. This date did not correspond to any particular birthday or anniversary but reflects his continued presence in her thoughts and heart. MCT Diary, April 16, 1949, HB.

3. In 1947 a reporter with the *Afro-American* wrote that Terrell claimed to have received one hundred marriage proposals after Berto died. She proclaimed in her diary, "Even if I had had one hundred proposals, I would not have been so brazen and such a fool as to tell a newspaper woman. I said no such thing." Although she denied having so many proposals, her response suggests that she had at least a few. MCT Diary, November 12, 1909, MCT Papers, reel 1; MCT Diary, September 11, 1931, July 31, 1947, MCT Additions.

4. Brittney Cooper perceptively notes, "Because Terrell is considered one of the foremost proselytizers of respectability, a turn toward her articulation of pleasure politics richly complicates the manner in which we read her as a theorist of racial resistance and gender progressivism." This embodied discourse is articulated by Terrell in her autobiography where she expresses her love of dancing and swimming, even as an older woman who is expected to do neither. Cooper, *Beyond Respectability*, 29–30, 58, 75; MCT to Phyllis Terrell Goines, April 21, 1929, MCT Papers, reel 3.

5. Joan Quigley notes the affair but dismisses it in a short paragraph, describing Terrell as acting "like a much-younger woman afflicted with a crush." Quigley, *Just Another Southern Town*, 116–17.

6. Weiss, *Farewell to the Party of Lincoln*, 84–88; William K. Divers (regional representative, National Housing Agency) to Oscar DePriest, January 7, 1944, DP; "Oscar Stanton De Priest," http://history.house.gov/People/Detail?id=12155.

7. Although DePriest is deserving of one, there is not yet a full-length study of him. The best account is by Harold F. Gosnell, his contemporary. Gosnell, *Negro Politicians*, 192, 181–82; Travis, *Autobiography*, 51; Grimshaw, *Bitter Fruit*, 75; Yellin, *Racism*, 157–58.

8. Gosnell, *Negro Politicians*, 191.

9. Oscar's parents were Martha and Neander DePriest. Oscar's father was a friend of James T. Rapier, a former black Republican U.S. representative from Alabama, whom he rescued from an 1878 kidnapping attempt by hiding him in the woods as the terrified but defiant DePriest family hid in their home and tried to guard it from an armed white mob. DePriest later listed his education as simply "Salina Kansas Public School." Gosnell, *Negro Politicians*, 164–65; Miller, "Oscar Stanton DePriest," 229–30; Hendricks, "'Vote,'" 181; "The DePriest Family Tree," comp. Rosalind DePriest, 1974, Oscar Stanton DePriest Papers, Chicago History Museum; Oscar S. DePriest III, "The Life of Oscar DePriest," December 18, 1946, DP.

10. Divorces were uncommon among elite African Americans. Extramarital affairs were more common, though still not openly socially acceptable. Gatewood, *Aristocrats*, 190.

11. MCT Diary, June 7, 1927, MCT Papers, reel 1; MCT to Laura Terrell Jones, February 20, 1930, MCT Papers, reel 6; MCT Diary, January 10, February 22, 1934, MCT Additions; Jones to MCT, September 25, 1934; and MCT Diary, December 5, 1935, both in MCT Papers, reel 2.

12. MCT Diary, May 13, 1931, MCT Additions.

13. Hine, "Rape," 912–20; White, *Too Heavy*, 23.

14. According to my conversations with family members, the DePriests were greatly affected by the drowning of their promising oldest son and subsequently grew apart emotionally. Philip DePriest, interviews with author, December 8, 2014, March 28, 2015; Betty Blanchette DePriest (she married DePriest's grandson Oscar DePriest III), interview with author, January 15, 2015; Philip DePriest (great-grandson), interview by William B. Bushong, David M. Rubenstein National Center for White House History, Washington, D.C., November 10, 2011, http://www.whitehousehistory.org/presentations/depriest-tea-incident/media/pdfs/depriest-transcript; Virgil Wright, "Descendants Seek Recognition for Pioneering Congressman," *Bay State Banner* (Boston), April 7, 2005, clipping, DP; Lewis, *Fight for Equality*, 187–88.

15. Terrell lived at 1615 S Street in what was called the Gold Coast neighborhood of upper 16th Street near DuPont Circle. "Went to church. Went to Friends Meeting House and heard 'Can Europe and America be Brothers.' I asked whether it would not be a good thing to take a group of American colored people to Russia since the speaker said there was no racial discrimination there. Dr. Taylor advised renting our second floor." From 1928 to 1937, several delegations of African Americans, including Langston Hughes, visited the Soviet Union. Roman, *Opposing Jim Crow*, intro.; Quigley, *Just Another Southern Town*, 116–17; MCT Diary, February 22, 1931, MCT Additions.

16. I have chosen to refer to the couple as "Terrell" and "DePriest" rather than as "Mollie" and "Oscar" because they do not appear to have addressed each other in such a casual and familiar way. The closest DePriest came to having a nickname for her (other than "Mrs. Terrell") was when he began to refer to her as his "Inspiration." MCT Diary, February 23, 25, March 4, 1931, MCT Additions.

17. MCT Diary, March 5, 6, 1931, MCT Additions; Jones to MCT, April 1931, MCT Papers, reel 2.

18. Oscar DePriest's great-grandson Phillip DePriest generously shared his privately held papers with me. Gosnell, *Negro Politicians*, 185, 194–95; *CD*, March 9, 1929, cited in Mann, "Oscar Stanton DePriest," 136.

19. One young clubwoman mentioned her involvement in the local Phyllis Wheatley settlement house. Another knew about the local black Republican organization that hosted his visit. One lover said, "Darling, . . . The box (when candy is demolished) I shall save until it gets frayed, for I know it will be eons before I see you again." In a coy reference to her current youth and beauty, she wrote, "Then who knows I may be an 'old hag' then too. . . . Should I not be satisfied. I'm trying to be but you are still so vivid." She ended self-deprecatingly by saying: "Maybe the picture would not be so good—a constant reminder. Jaber and Jaber [*sic*]. I ramble on and on. Toodle'oo." Unsigned and undated with no salutation [punctuation as in original], DP. One note on a postcard-size paper, begins, "My one request. Please send me a picture." The handwriting is similar to the other letter from —— Reid (born 1895). One photo from his lecture tour in Kentucky is of Representative DePriest arm in arm with several stylish young black women under a caption, written by the sender: "The girls are the grandest in Kentucky," DP. See the photos of Representative DePriest with the young women members of the Bessie Coleman Aero Club of Los Angeles, dated September 30, 1929. There are also photos of him in a two-seat plane and photos of him with the black women pilots. *CD*, April 20, 1929; Clay, *Just Permanent Interests*, 62; Gosnell, *Negro Politicians*, 164, 166, 192; "Mamie" to "My dear Oscar," no punctuation and undated (from California), DP. Eight love letters from other women survive in DePriest's papers, DP.

20. To "My dear [referring to DePriest]," undated, from "Just Me," DP.

21. From "With Love, O.M." to "My dear Mr. DePriest," August 25, 1932, 415 Bayview Ave., Pleasantville, N.J.; and another letter with no salutation but in which the writer addresses DePriest as "Darling"; no signature or date, on a postcard-size piece of paper; Unsigned to "Darling" dated Tuesday, October 4, [1932], all in DP.

22. Some W. E. B. Du Bois admirers expressed themselves similarly; in a 1923 letter, a young Los Angeles woman, Anita Thompson, who still lived with her parents, wrote that his visit "was like a lovely dream from which it has been rather difficult for me to awaken (I haven't known if you were really here and 'adopted' me or if the Chinaman gave me a six-months pipe o' rap. Perhaps? ha ha)." It was more openly tolerated for prominent black men, but some equally prominent black women also engaged in affairs. In the early 1920s, for instance, Alice Dunbar-Nelson was involved with "a very married Emmett Scott, Howard University's self-important treasurer" and a key Booker T. Washington ally. Speaking of a purported 1911 sexual indiscretion by Washington, Du Bois later brushed it off, saying, "Most great men have had an occasional moral lapse. . . . The only surprising thing is that [Washington] had only one come to the surface." Behaving recklessly, DePriest met and spent intimate time with "O.M." in Atlantic City, N.J., in 1932. When he returned to the area a few weeks later, she wrote: "I could not say anything sweet to you over the phone as you asked me because your voice carried to the people in the room—eight in number and they were all querying me about the night before. In the face of them hearing you asking me to meet you in Washington Monday, I don't think it will be discreet for you or me if I should leave so suddenly. . . .

Please don't be angry with me for not coming but I can't help it. You don't know how much I'd love to be there with you." White, *Too Heavy*, 23; Lewis, *Du Bois: Biography of a Race*, 345, 528; Lewis, *Du Bois: Biography*, 287, 524; Lewis, *Du Bois: Fight for Equality*, 104, 185–6, 274, 382; Curwood, *Stormy Weather*, 28–31. From "With Love, O.M." to "My dear Mr. DePriest" August 25, 1932, 415 Bayview Ave., Pleasantville, N.J. Also see from "Yours Friendly, O.M." August 4, 1932, 415 W. Bayview Ave., Pleasantville, N.J. [No salutation], DP.

23. MCT Diary, April 21, 22, 23, 1931, MCT Additions.

24. The DePriests lived at 419 U Street in the LeDroit neighborhood, where Terrell still owned and rented out her home at 326 T Street. There is no evidence that Terrell ever had any other affair. Shelly Stokes-Hammond, "Pathbreakers: Oscar Stanton DePriest and Jessie L. Williams DePriest," House Historical Association, http://www.whitehouse history.org/whha_shows/depriest-tea-incident/african-american-congress.html; MCT Diary, April 24, 1931, MCT Additions.

25. MCT Diary, April 26, 28, 1931, MCT Additions.

26. Canon Anson Phelps Stokes was a leading white supporter of black education through the Phelps-Stokes Fund. The quotation is attributed to Euripides. The connection to a female Pulitzer Prize winner is unclear. MCT Diary, April 30, May 4, 14, 1931, MCT Additions.

27. This troubled Terrell because, as she had written in her *Chicago Defender* column in 1929, "One of the first signs that any human being is 'slipping' is his indifference to his appearance." See Chapman, *Prove It*, 3–19; Marchand, *Advertising*, 186–205; Parker, "'Picture of Health,'" 1–44; MCT to RHT, November 24, 1900, MCT Papers, reel 2; MCT, "Up to Date," *CD*, January 19, 1929, pt. 2, p. 2; and MCT Diary, April 30, June 5, 9, September 11, 1931, November 19, 20, 1934, MCT Additions.

28. MCT Diary, June 22, December 14, 1931, MCT Additions.

29. Mother and daughter saved money by having their dinners prepared at a boardinghouse at a discounted rate: "Phyllis and I started to get our dinners at Mrs. Holmes, 725 Fairmont St. this afternoon. $3.25 each for dinners for a month. I hate to accept such an offer." Even during this renovation, Terrell still had access to new loans. She unsuccessfully tried to get her half brother, Robert Church Jr., to sell her the house next to her T Street rental property—the adjoining half of her duplex. In 1940, she inquired into "how much I could buy 328 T Street for. I would like to buy it and build an apartment out of 326 and 328 combined." MCT Diary, February 19, March 3, October 19, December 31, 1931, MCT Additions; MCT Diary, March 26, 1935, MCT Papers, reel 2; MCT Diary, March 6, 1940, HB.

30. The city of Memphis invoked eminent domain, condemnation, and police powers in order to raze buildings like those owned by Terrell and her brother. In the 1970s, a large swath of land on and near Beale Street was leveled by the Memphis Housing Authority, with "300 substandard buildings" demolished so that "the area resembled a bombed-out Berlin of 1945." A new Beale Street has been rebuilt for tourists. Sigafoos, *Cotton Row*, 277–78; Bond and Sherman, *Images of America*, 112; MCT Diary, February 25, March 14, 1931, MCT Additions; Thomas A. Church to MCT, January 4, 1932, MCT Papers, reel 3.

31. The friend was Dean Andrew Fleming West. Amid negotiations over the work, Terrell noted in her diary that DePriest had not phoned. The illicit nature of their

relationship meant that she had to wait for calls from him, the married man. Terrell recorded that Phyllis bought "a daybed for the library" so that they could have separate sleeping spaces when necessary. Phyllis lived in the same house as her mother until Terrell died in 1954. MCT Diary, June 23, 24, 28, July 24, August 8, October 12, December 31, 1931, MCT Additions.

32. MCT Diary, June 29, August 8, 30, December 13, 1931, MCT Additions.

33. Even after the 1931 takeover of Chicago City Hall by the Democrats, DePriest maintained the support of black Chicagoans and survived one more election. Thurber, *Republicans*, 27. For the Democratic takeover, see Green, "Anton J. Cermak," 99–110; Green, "Mayor Richard J. Daley"; Savage, *Roosevelt*, 57–58; and Guglielmo, *White on Arrival*, chap. 5. MCT Diary, July 25, 27, 28, August 3, 7, 19, 22, 1931, MCT Additions; DePriest to MCT, August 17, 1931, MCT Papers, reel 6.

34. MCT Diary, September 4, November 19, 26, December 3, 6, 1931, MCT Additions.

35. "Mr. DePriest's Methods," *New York World*, as quoted in the "Other Papers Say" section of the *CD*, August 10, 1929, pt. 2, p. 2.

36. "DePriest States His Position," ca. 1945, political pamphlet, DP; Gosnell, *Negro Politicians*, 194.

37. Stokely Carmichael and others said similar things in Lowndes County, Ala., and also about the Mississippi Freedom Democratic Party in 1969. John Kirby criticizes the conference for eschewing the Communist Party as a viable third-party alternative. Jeffries, *Bloody Lowndes*, 45–59, 194–95; Kirby, *Black Americans*, 103; "DePriest, in Boston, Flays Our Leaders: Helps Rush Church Celebrate," Carroll News Service, *CD*, November 30, 1929, 13.

38. Program, "Non-Partisan Conference," December 2–4, 1931, MCT Papers, reel 20.

39. Terrell agreed to be an official member of DePriest's Non-Partisan Committee, which presented its ideas as a memorandum to the Republican National Committee in May 1932. During his visit, DePriest managed to get Terrell to agree to speak at his conference; he also pleased and distracted her so much that she forgot all about her YWCA meeting. Similarly, one of DePriest's other lovers noted that his presence with her "last night" had preoccupied her: "Truly I forgot the formal opening of the Phyllis Wheatley House. . . . I was to pour tea. See what you did." Lisio, *Hoover, Blacks, and Lily-Whites*, 253, 255; To "My Dear" from "Just Me," undated, DP; Bishop E. D. W. Jones to MCT (on Representative DePriest's official stationery), November 4, 1931, MCT Papers, reel 7; MCT Diary, November 18, 20, December 3, 1931, MCT Additions; DePriest to MCT, April 28, 1932, MCT Papers, reel 7.

40. Charlotte Hawkins Brown was a prominent clubwoman and educator who founded the Palmer Memorial Institute for African Americans in North Carolina. Program, "Non-Partisan Conference," December 2–4, 1931; MCT Diary, December 4, 14, 1931, MCT Additions.

41. In the pamphlet, Terrell touted the WILPF's policy work in Haiti and protests against slavery in Liberia. MCT Diary, May 15, 23, 1931, MCT Additions; E. D. W. Jones to MCT (on Representative DePriest's official stationery), November 4, 1931; MCT, "Colored People and World Peace, or Colored Women and World Peace," 1932, MCT Papers, reels 22, 20 (two versions), 3.

42. MCT Diary, December 12, 1931, MCT Additions.

43. MCT Diary, June 28, September 3, December 11, 1931, MCT Additions; Buell

Gordon Gallagher (First Congregational Church, Passaic, N.J.) to MCT, December 9, 1931, MCT Papers, reel 7.

44. MCT Diary, December 31, 1931, MCT Additions.

45. Even if Jessie DePriest knew, her husband still routinely engaged in elaborate subterfuge to keep his affairs "secret." MCT Diary, December 25, 1931, MCT Additions.

46. MCT Diary, December 23, 1931, MCT Additions.

47. During his second term as alderman during World War II, DePriest was still soliciting food donations and cash donations for his Thanksgiving, Christmas, and summertime dinners and picnics (see DP). MCT Diary, December 26, 1931, MCT Additions.

48. There is no way he would have said these things to the woman who signed her letter "Getting dumb" or to the dancer who wrote after just one night together, "I miss you already, you are so *great* and *so dear*, it seems you fill my *entire* life." Blanche was probably Blanche Wright Nelson, who was related to Anna Wright Church, Robert Church's third wife. There is a letter to Terrell much earlier, in September 1919, when Nelson had moved from Memphis to Richmond, Va., in the same handwriting with an identical signature. When Terrell was working for the RNC in New York, DePriest sent her a telegram telling her that he would be in town and wanted to "have letter there informing me where I can reach you." See love letters in the DP collection; Blanche Wright to MCT, September 24, 1919, MCT Papers, reel 4; MCT, "Colored People and World Peace," 1932, for the WILPF, MCT Papers, reels 20, 22; DePriest to MCT, January 12, 1932; Wright (writing for DePriest) to MCT, February 2, 1932; DePriest to MCT, September 17 (emphasis added), October 10 (telegram), and November 14, 1932, all in MCT Papers, reel 7.

49. DePriest III, "The Life of Oscar DePriest," 1946, DP.

50. Harriet A. Lee wrote to Terrell asking her to help her "in placing my son, Dr. C. Dudley Lee as Associate Physician in the Hospital at Tuskegee. I am desirous of having an interview with our Congressman DePriest and the only one whom I am certain could succeed in making an appointment with him for me is your own dear self." Anna D. Borden, president of the Negro Woman's League of Yonkers, wrote Terrell asking her to "secure for us as a speaker the Hon. Oscar DePriest." Terrell replied that Roscoe Simmons was in charge of the Speakers Bureau, but she feared that "even though you wrote to Col. Simmons, you would not be able to get Congressman DePriest. I have heard that his dates are all filled in the West until the election." J. A. Shelton to DePriest, May 19, 1932; Anna D. Borden to MCT, October 10, 1932; MCT to Corrine [*sic*] D. Borden, October 15, 1932; Thomas D. Jenkins to DePriest, November 4, 1932; and Harriet A. Lee to MCT, October 12, November 6, 1933, all in MCT Papers, reel 7; MCT Diary, May 27, 1934, MCT Additions.

51. MCT Diary, January 1, 1934, MCT Additions.

52. His lover O. M. felt a bit ignored by DePriest but did not take their new relationship too seriously: "You're a nice one. A fellow who can forget a friend so soon is guilty of a misdemeanor and shall receive a life sentence. You promised to drop me a line and never a one have I received. I missed you very much after you left, so much so that I sometimes feel like a cancelled postage stamp." O. M. to "My dear Mr. DePriest," August 25, 1932, 415 Bayview Ave., Pleasantville, N.J., DP; [no salutation] from "Yours Friendly, O.M." August 4, 1932, 415 W. Bayview Ave., Pleasantville, N.J., DP; MCT Diary, January 18, February 25, 1934, MCT Additions.

53. Even in 1934, the Democrats, including Mitchell, still "lost heavily in the black precincts" of Chicago. Leah Wright Rigueur notes, "Mitchell narrowly defeated De-Priest. He won by 3,130 votes out of a total 52,810 cast. The returns showed Mitchell with 27,970 to DePriest's 24,840." Mitchell "won handily in the two all-white wards while losing in every all-black ward." Harold F. Gosnell points out that part of the erosion of DePriest's black voting base was caused by infighting among two of his key supporters who had both wanted his support in their contest to become second ward committeeman. Kelly Miller invited Terrell to be a member of the General Committee on Arrangements for the "Nationwide Testimonial to the Hon. Oscar DePriest in recognition of the great service he rendered the Race during his membership in Congress." She declined, but many individuals in cities and states all over the country organized local testimonial dinners; Miller claimed that DePriest's "courage is admired to the point of amazement. He demands for his race—every man, woman and child of them—immediate and unconditional fulfillment of every guaranteed constitutional right." Gosnell, *Negro Politicians*, 90n76, 190; Rigueur, *Loneliness of the Black Republican*, 14; Sitkoff, *New Deal*, 88; Clay, *Just Permanent Interests*, 71; Jenkins to DePriest, November 4, 1932; Shelton to DePriest, May 19, 1932; MCT Diary, May 27, 1934, MCT Additions; Kelly Miller to MCT, December 7, 19, 1934, MCT Papers, reel 7; Kelly Miller, "Oscar DePriest, Commoner," in *Kansas City Plaindealer*, March 5, 1935, clipping, DP.

54. Terrell self-published *A Colored Woman in a White World* in 1940. It was reprinted in 1968 by the National Association of Colored Women. More recently, it has been reprinted by other presses. Jones, *Quest for Equality*, 63; MCT, "Moral Courage," 1945 version (also 1925, 1928, and undated), MCT Papers, reel 21.

55. FDR favored a balanced budget, had only gone into debt to ensure that no one starved, and during the 1936 election publicly committed himself to ending deficit spending. See chapter 11. Telegrams to DePriest, August 22, 23, 1945; and "DePriest States His Position," campaign pamphlet, ca. 1945, all in DP; "DePriest Makes Plea to Place Member of Group on Ballot for Judges," *Chicago Press*, March 30, 1946, Oscar Stanton DePriest Papers, Chicago History Museum.

Chapter 10

1. See Cole, *African-American*; Neubeck and Cazenave, *Welfare Racism*, 46–48; Quadango, *Color of Welfare*, 19–24; and Katznelson, *Fear Itself*, chap. 5.

2. In November 1918, Terrell got a job with the War Camp Community Service until she went to Zurich for the Women's Peace Conference in the spring of 1919. MCT, *Colored Woman*, 250–59, 318–27; J. E. [last name illegible] to MCT, August 9, 1919, MCT Papers, reel 4.

3. Coppens's timeline shows Terrell as having co-organized the Woman Wage Earners' Association (WWEA) in 1917 as "a group that will help organize and protect black female workers. This year, in Norfolk, Virginia, some WWEA members are trying to help local workers organize. Some 600 waitresses, domestic workers, cigar makers, and tobacco stemmers decide to strike, demanding better working conditions. They are arrested by police as 'slackers.' There is a new federal rule, 'work or fight,' which allows arrest of those who are not in the armed forces or working at home. The WWEA is investigated as a possible subversive organization and this destroys the Virginia branch."

Coppens, *What American Women Did*, 213; MCT as quoted in Brown, *Private Politics*, 8. For more on racial discrimination during World War I and the women wage earner associations, see Moore, *Leading the Race*, 156; Materson, *Freedom*, 273n65; Yellin, *Racism*, 194–95; Miller and Pruitt-Logan, *Faithful to the Task*, 67–68; Johnson, *Uplifting the Women*, 150; Harley, "Speaking Up," 45; and Guy-Sheftall, "Introduction," 9.

4. During the Depression, black women struggled to hold onto their jobs as domestic servants. See Harley, "Black Women," 71; Jones, *American Work*, 334; Hine, "Rape," 913; Broussard, "Worst of Times," 105–6; Reich, *Working People*, 87; and Lisio, *Hoover, Blacks, and Lily-Whites*, 199.

5. When she no longer had the representation of a speakers' bureau, Terrell wrote to individuals, organizations, churches, and colleges assiduously soliciting paid speaking engagements for herself. See Terrell's correspondence, MCT Additions; MCT to Thomas A. Church, January 1, 1928, MCT Papers, reel 3; and MCT Diary, July 13, 1936, MCT Additions.

6. Terrell repeatedly requested appointments with publishers and literary agents, traveling to New York City to interest them in publishing her writings, especially her autobiography. Many letters of rejection from publishers can be found throughout the files of her correspondence. For published black women writers, see Robbins and Gates, *Portable Women Writers*; Reed, *Rise of Chicago's Black Metropolis*, 102; and Drake and Cayton, *Black Metropolis*, 400. Eleanor Patterson (*Washington Herald*) to MCT, October 5, 1934; Robert S. Abbott (*CD*) to MCT, October 25, 1934, both in MCT Papers, reel 7; MCT Diary, April 2, October 1, 1931, MCT Additions; Laura Terrell Jones to MCT, May 12, 1935, MCT Papers, reel 2.

7. Gallagher appointed Terrell to the subcommittee, also referred to as the Washington Federation of Churches. In 1942, when she was sixty-two, Georgia Douglas Johnson "found herself hoping for a few hours work in a clerical pool." On Cook and Johnson, see Moore, *Leading the Race*, 125; Terborg-Penn, *African-American Women*, 69–70; Etter-Lewis and Thomes, *Lights of the Spirit*, 71–76; and Hull, *Color, Sex, and Poetry*, 21, 183. MCT Diary, February 24, March 3, 11, December 11, 1931, MCT Additions; Rev. Buell Gordon Gallagher (First Congregational Church, Passaic, N.J.) to MCT, December 9, 1931; and Alice Paul to MCT, February 5, 1934, both in MCT Papers, reel 7.

8. Terrell also supported "laws to promote the welfare of workingmen . . . who are permanently and totally disabled will receive compensation as long as they need it." The Social Security Act of 1935 took seniors out of the job market while providing them with a safety net; it did not cover the great majority of black women who worked as domestic servants or farm laborers. Similarly, the Fair Labor Standard Act of 1938 did not extend the minimum wage and maximum hour law to domestic workers and farmworkers. Van Etteren, *Labor*, 94; Goluboff, *Lost Promise*, 29; Amenta, *When Movements Matter*, 255n23; Domhoff and Webber, *Class and Power*, 232; Brinkley, *Voices of Protest*; Kessler-Harris, *In Pursuit of Equity*, 121, 131, 142, 146, 150, 156; MCT, "Up to Date," *CD*, January 26, 1929, pt. 2, p. 2.

9. Sharon Hartman Strom concludes: "White business people insisted that coworkers and customers would never tolerate the presence of blacks in clerical and management positions." Harley notes that by the end of World War I, "only 2.8 percent . . . of the local black female" workforce had clerical positions. The New Deal was no better; Lucia Pitts, who worked for Clark Foreman, special adviser on the economic status of blacks in the

Interior Department, became "one of the few black women to be employed as a secretary [rather than a clerk] in the federal government." Strom, *Beyond the Typewriter*, 410, 255, 268, 299, 300, 312, 387, 398, 400; Harley, "Black Women," 62, 70; Sullivan, *Days of Hope*, 51, 26; MCT Diary, February 19, 1910, in MCT Diary and Notes, 368, HB; MCT Diary, March 17, 1946, HB.

10. Terrell did what she could to hide her age; in 1949, at the Passport Division, she spoke with the assistant chief, who "had collected all my old passports. In one I said I was born in 1870, on another 1874. I said sometimes I forget dates." Strom, *Beyond the Typewriter*, 138–39; Ingraham, *Foundation of Merit*, 33; Edsforth and Asher, "The Speedup," 83–84; MCT Diary, October 23, 1937, MCT Collection; MCT Diary, April 15, 1949, HB.

11. Congress did not amend the Emergency Relief Act to bar racial discrimination in the distribution of aid and jobs until 1939. Adam Bellow notes that FDR's "establishment of sixty-five new federal agencies has been called 'one of the most spectacular resurgences of the spoils system in American history,' creating a hundred thousand new jobs" exempted from the civil service and used to reward political supporters. Reich, *Working People*, 90–91; Sullivan, *Days of Hope*, 53–54; Sitkoff, *New Deal*, 69, 76; Bellow, *In Praise of Nepotism*, 406–7; Ingraham, *Foundation of Merit*, 46; Tolchin and Tolchin, *To the Victor*, 257; Erie, *Rainbow's End*, 16–17; King, *Separate and Unequal*, 51.

12. Milton A. Lee might have been related to Mollie's high school beau of the same name (see chapter 2). The 1883 implementation of a civil service examination had created a more level playing field by allowing African Americans to compete fairly for government jobs, but the Wilson administration made a series of changes amounting to what Yellin describes as an "attack on black ambition." It systematically segregated federal workplaces in 1913 and the Civil Service Administration began requiring photographs with job applications. Activists William Monroe Trotter and Ida B. Wells-Barnett led a delegation that brought Wilson "an antisegregation petition with the signatures of 20,000 people," but Wilson was unmoved. Yellin, *Racism*, 123, 144, 159; Gatewood, *Aristocrats*, 76–77; King, *Separate and Unequal*, 9, 49; Lisio, *Hoover, Blacks, and Lily-Whites*, 86; Wolters, *Negroes and the Great Depression*, xii–xiii; Harriet A. Lee to MCT, December 7, 1933; Irene Long Dickens to MCT, October 17, 1934; C. Redmond to MCT, September 11, 1934; and Mamie Wilson (Blue Plain Home for the Aged) to MCT, December 18, 1934, all in MCT Papers, reel 7.

13. After almost thirty years in 1940, the "Civil Service stopped requiring application photographs." At the local level, mayors and city officials in northern cities tried to gain black votes by increasing patronage jobs. Leuchtenburg, *White House*, 62; Countryman, *Up South*, 23–24; Sugrue, *Sweet Land of Liberty*, 112–13; Sitkoff, *New Deal*, 69, 76; Reed, *Rise of Chicago's Black Metropolis*, 172–73; Reed, *Chicago NAACP*; Sklaroff, *Black Culture*, 18–19.

14. The one black woman who did get a plum job in the New Deal, Mary McLeod Bethune, was twelve years younger than Terrell and had switched to the Democratic Party after Roosevelt's election. For Bethune's work as a Democrat in the 1936 election, see Plummer, *Rising Wind*, 135; Scroop, *Mr. Democrat*, 120; and Mileur, "The 'Boss,'" 117–18.

15. In 1940, Terrell secured a job for a forty-two-year-old recently widowed friend at the office of the Recorder of Deeds. Her friend had passed the civil service exam several

years earlier but could not then find work "because she was a colored woman and no white woman" was willing to work with her. This time, the Recorder of Deeds was ready to hire her, suggesting that the color line was starting to weaken. MCT Diary, January 11, 1934, MCT Additions; MCT Diary, January 27, February 5, 1940, HB.

16. MCT Diary, January 15, 1934; and Elizabeth K. Peeples (director, Community Center Department) to MCT, January 15, 1934, both in MCT Additions; Miss M. Minton (secretary of LeRoy Halbert) to MCT, April 13, 1934, MCT Papers, reel 7.

17. Leroy Allen Halbert became director of emergency relief in 1932. John E. Hansan, "Leroy Allen Halbert (1875–1958)—Pioneer Social Worker, Director of the Nation's First Department of Social Welfare, Advocate for the Unemployed, Social Reformer, and Author," http://www.socialwelfarehistory.com/organizations/halbert-leroy-allen/; MCT Diary, January 17, 1934, MCT Additions; Peeples to MCT, January 17, 1934, MCT Papers, reel 7.

18. MCT Diary, January 17, 1934, MCT Additions; MCT Diary, May 1, 1948, HB.

19. MCT Diary, January 23, 1934, MCT Additions. See Terrell's 1934 correspondence, MCT Papers, reel 7.

20. This might have been the prominent author and social work expert Ellery F. Reed. MCT Diary, January 25, 1934, MCT Additions.

21. Terrell's yearly salary was $720. At this time, in the mid-1930s, black women tobacco workers made less than $500 a year. The average salary of professionals, including most higher-level federal administrators, ran from $5,000 to $10,000 per year, whereas most "African American urban working women . . . [had] incomes of less than $1,500 per year." Terborg-Penn, "Survival Strategies," 141–42, 148; Amenta, *When Movements Matter*, 164; Janiewski, "Seeking," 164; Poole, *Segregated Origins*, 15–16; MCT Diary, January 25, March 3, 1934, MCT Additions.

22. Muncy, *Relentless Reformer*, 170–71; Anderson, "Last Hired," 86; Hyde, *Arsenal*, 184–86; Frederickson, "'I Know,'" 148; Terborg-Penn, "Survival Strategies," 159; Janiewski, "Sisters under Their Skins," 34; MCT, *Colored Woman*, 250–59.

23. MCT Diary, February 2, 1934, MCT Additions.

24. MCT Diary, February 2, 1934.

25. White, *Too Heavy*, 23, 133; Glenn, *Unequal Freedom*, 129; Higginbotham, *Righteous Discontent*; Carby, *Reconstructing Womanhood*; May, *Unprotected Labor*, 91–93; Alexander, *Army of Lions*, 186; Yellin, *Racism*, 130; MCT Diary, April 16, May 27, 1934, MCT Additions.

26. MCT Diary, January 26, 1934, MCT Additions.

27. MCT Diary, March 23, 24, 1934, MCT Additions.

28. MCT Diary, April 16, May 7, 1934, MCT Additions.

29. Anne Rogers (Division of Emergency Relief) to MCT, March 20, 1934, MCT Papers, reel 7; MCT Diary, March 23, 1934, MCT Additions.

30. Black civil service workers were also refused promotions or pay raises for decades (some were even demoted). Yellin, *Racism*, 127; MCT Diary, April 23, 24, July 31, 1934, MCT Additions.

31. Desmond King notes that black employees were commonly assigned "temporary instead of permanent positions" and then not advanced when vacancies arose. King, *Separate and Unequal*, 75. MCT Diary, April 23–27, May 1, 1934, MCT Additions.

32. MCT Diary, May 2, 1934, MCT Additions.

33. The NAACP was not necessarily perceived as a purely partisan organization. In the first two decades of the twentieth century, most black NAACP members were Republicans, as were the great majority of black voters. Even then, there were a few high-profile exceptions. In 1912, for instance, NAACP leader W. E. B. Du Bois endorsed Democrat Woodrow Wilson for president. Although the group's executive secretary, Walter White, did not endorse FDR in the 1932 election, he built a good relationship with First Lady Eleanor Roosevelt and shifted his allegiance to the Democratic Party by 1933. Terrell's supervisors were unlikely to be objecting to the NAACP on the pretense of its being pro-Republican but because of its civil rights work. Some southern teachers who were NAACP members, especially those involved in suing the school districts over equal pay or the conditions of schools, were fired in the late 1930s. The Supreme Court upheld Alabama's ban on the NAACP in 1956 because "the NAACP had failed to register as an out-of-state corporation doing 'business' in Alabama." The association was considered "subversive and communistic" by the FBI, House Un-American Activities Committee, and eight southern states in the 1950s. Anderson, "Last Hired," 90–91; Gailmard and Patty, *Learning while Governing*, 120; Schramm and Wilson, *American Political Parties*, 172–73; King, *Separate and Unequal*, 45. On the NAACP, see Yellin, *Racism*, 123–24; Tushnet, *Making Civil Rights Law*, 23–24; Randolph, *Rights for a Season*, 138; Morris, *Origins of the Civil Rights Movement*; Felder, *Civil Rights*, 56–62; and Rubio, *History of Affirmative Action*, 126. See Jost, *Supreme Court*, 27–28; Biondi, *To Stand and Fight*, 139–40; and "Alabama Re-Admits NAACP," *The Crisis*, November 1964, 617.

34. In November 1933, "the ILD [International Labor Defense] and the League of Struggle for Negro Rights, initiated by the CP, sponsored their Eastern Conference against Lynching" in Baltimore with 1,500 attendees, including "militant but non-Communist sectors of the freedom movement" such as Mary Church Terrell. Skotnes, *New Deal*, 56–57, 131; Fairclough, *Better Day Coming*, 136–43. See Alice Paul (Women's Consultative Committee on Nationality, created by the Council of the League of Nations) to MCT, January 10, 1936; Dr. Mary F. Waring (president, NACW) to MCT, telegram, January 15, 1936; Rosa M. Wade (National Woman's Party secretary) to Paul to MCT, January 21, 1936; Waring to MCT, January 26, 1936; and Leola Banister to MCT, February 12, 1936, all in MCT Papers, reel 2.

35. Gatewood, *Aristocrats*, 315; Harlan E. Glazier ("with the collaboration of the following sub-committee on education," including MCT), "The Color Line in Our Public Schools: A Study of the Distribution of School Funds and School Opportunities between Negroes and Whites in the District of Columbia," ca. mid-1930s, Inter-Racial Committee of the District of Columbia, NAACP, 1931–41, MCT Papers, reel 15; Nannie H. Burroughs (chair, Speakers Bureau) to MCT, April 3, 1934; Charles Edward Russell to MCT, May 5, 17, 1934; and Lester A. Walton to MCT, June 4, 1934, all in MCT Papers, reel 7; MCT Diary, March 6, 1951, MCT Papers, reel 2.

36. The Committee of the Washington Federation of Churches on Race Relations planned an "Interracial conference" on Lincoln's birthday, February 12, 1935. In late 1933, Terrell was appointed to a Tribunal of Inquiry at an antilynching conference held in Baltimore and sponsored by the Communist Party–supported International Labor Defense and the League of Struggle for Negro Rights. Harriet A. Lee wrote Terrell, "I must first congratulate you upon your very fine manner of presiding at the Anti-Lynching

meeting recently held at John Wesley church. I am delighted to know that the movement is headed by one of your pronounced ability." For more on Anson Stokes, see Goggin, *A Life*, 83–4, 129–37; Skotnes, *New Deal*, 131–35; "Governor [Albert Ritchie] Blamed in Maryland Lynching," *Pittsburgh Courier*, December 2, 1933; James Robert Davis to MCT, December 4, 1933; Harriet A. Lee to MCT, December 7, 1933, MCT Papers, reel 7; Rev. D. Butler Pratt to MCT, January 3, 9, 1934; and "Minutes of the Committee on Race Relations," March 19, October 29, 1934, submitted by MCT, secretary, all in MCT Papers, reel 7; "Our City Beautiful" pamphlet, November 26, 1935, Washington Federation of Churches Committee on Race Relations, 1935–1946, box 102-3, MCT Collection.

37. The Senate restaurant was formally segregated in 1917. The committee wrote a letter of protest against the exclusion of blacks from the House restaurant in the Capitol Building. Each committee member pledged to speak with members of Congress. Howard University students protested at the Capitol. Yellin, *Racism*, 196–99; Poole, *Segregated Origins*, 101–3; "DePriest Appeals for a Square Deal: Speech of Hon. Oscar DePriest of Illinois in the House of Representatives, March 21, 1934," DP. See Asch and Musgrove, *Chocolate City*, 262–63; and Storrs, "Laying the Foundations," 213–35. See correspondence files for 1934 in MCT Papers, reel 7, including to and from Rev. D. Butler Pratt (Committee on Race Relations) to Rep. Lindsay G. Warren and Anson Phelps Stokes (Sub-Committee on Interracial Conference). "De Priest to Force Vote on Color Line: Will Demand Serving of Negroes in Capitol Grill—His Secretary Was Barred," *New York Times*, January 24, 1934, 3; AP, "House Forced to Act on Negro Dining Issue as De Priest Petition Gets 145th Signature," *New York Times*, March 24, 1934, 17.

38. Ambrose Caliver to MCT, January 24, June 1, 1934; and Dean V. E. Daniel to MCT, March 2, April 26, 1934, MCT Papers, reel 7.

39. MCT Diary, May 2, 1934, MCT Additions.

40. MCT Diary, May 2, 3, 1934, MCT Additions.

41. In 1907, Terrell recorded the following incident in Indiana: "'Mrs. Terrell, will you have your meals served in your room or will you eat in the ordinary?' 'Where is the ordinary?' I asked the bell boy. 'Next to the kitchen,' he said. 'Tell the manager I shall eat my meals in the dining room,' I replied." MCT Diary, October 29, 1907, quoted in MCT Diary and Notes, 247, HB; MCT Diary, May 5, 1934, MCT Additions.

42. Terrell conceded: "There are many others in the same fix. That does not help my exchequer a bit, however." Jones to MCT, January 21, 1931, MCT Papers, reel 2; MCT to Church, March 26, 1932, MCT Papers, reel 3.

43. Jones to MCT, January 16, 1934, MCT Papers, reel 2.

44. See chapter 14. Quigley, *Just Another Southern Town*; Caplan, "The Lost Laws," in MCT, *Colored Woman*, 434–45; McCluskey, "Setting the Standard," 47–53; Jones, "Before Montgomery," 144–54; MCT, *Colored Woman*, 419–21.

45. MCT Diary, May 5, 17, 1934, MCT Additions.

46. The National Committee to Defend Negro Leadership fought attacks by anti-communists on civil rights leaders in the 1950s and defended Communists like Claudia Jones and William Patterson along with prominent black spokespeople like Terrell and Bethune. Miller, *Born along the Color Line*, 107; McDuffie, *Sojourning for Freedom*,

114–15; McDuffie, "March of Young Southern Black Women," 95–97; William L. Patterson to MCT, May 10, 1934; Scottsboro Mothers to President Franklin Delano Roosevelt, May 13, 1934, MCT Papers, reel 7.

47. As Thomas J. Sugrue notes, "Activists overcame political, cultural, and social differences, forging a remarkably united front to demand full political and economic citizenship. Devout clubwomen, lawyers, laborers, Democrats, Republicans, Socialists, and Communists marched together on picket lines, lobbied public officials, and joined in lawsuits against segregated housing and schools." Gore, *Radicalism*, 80–81; McDuffie, *Sojourning for Freedom*, 164–66; Horne, *Black and Red*, 58; Sugrue, *Sweet Land of Liberty*, xviii, 9, 22; Patterson to MCT, May 10, 1934; and Scottsboro Mothers to Roosevelt, May 13, 18, 1934, MCT Papers, reel 7; MCT, "Some Facts to Think About," 1936, Election Speech, MCT Papers, reel 22; MCT Diary, March 8, 1952, MCT Papers, reel 2.

48. Hopes for continued funding by the Community Chest sometimes moderated organizations' political stances. Sitkoff, *New Deal*, 248–49; MCT, "Talk for Community Chest over Radio," January 26, 1929, MCT Papers, reel 22; Elwood Street to MCT, January 29, 1934; and "Minutes of Committee on Race Relations of the Washington Federation of Churches," March 19, 1934, submitted by MCT, secretary, both in MCT Papers, reel 7.

49. Elwood Street wrote a letter to President Ernest Hatch Wilkens of Oberlin College in support of granting of an honorary degree for Terrell. MCT Diary, June 1, 1934, MCT Additions; Street to MCT, January 29, 1934; and Ruth B. Hummel (with enclosed letter from Street) to MCT, February 9, 1934, both in MCT Papers, reel 7.

50. MCT Diary, June 21, 23, 1934, MCT Additions.

51. MCT Diary, June 25, 26, 1934, MCT Additions.

52. MCT Diary, July 16, 25, 1934, MCT Additions; MCT, *Colored Woman*, 414.

53. After she was fired, Terrell admitted, "Continually fingering those cards had got on my nerves and I am glad to get away from it but I need the money." Fauntroy notes the "Depression disproportionately damaged blacks. . . . The firing of blacks so that their jobs could be given to whites became accepted policy." Fauntroy, *Republicans and the Black Vote*, 45; MCT Diary, July 26, 31, August 1, 1934, MCT Additions; MCT, *Colored Woman*, 415.

54. MCT Diary, July 31, August 1, 1934, MCT Additions.

55. Street (director of public welfare) to MCT, June 16, 1934; Lawrence A. Oxley to MCT, May 12, June 15, 1934; and Oxley (chief, Division of Negro Labor, U.S. Department of Labor, Bureau of Labor Statistics) to MCT, June 28, 1935, all in MCT Papers, reel 7.

56. Most of the black men who became affiliated with the New Deal, those such as Robert Weaver and William Hastie, were born in the early twentieth century, whereas Terrell was born in 1863. As late as 1949, she was still dreaming about work and her own ambitions: "If I were younger, I would try to get a job to write for the paper." Sullivan, *Days of Hope*, 84; Haber and Gratton, *Old Age*, 110; MCT Diary, August 1, 1934, MCT Additions; MCT Diary, July 30, 1949, HB.

57. "Report of the Conference on the Betterment of Race Relations in Washington, D.C.," Held under the Auspices of the Committee on Race Relations of the Washington

Federation of Churches, February 12, 1935, 11, MCT Papers, reel 14; MCT, *Colored Woman*, 415.

58. MCT, *Colored Woman*, 415.

59. Robyn Muncy notes, "The New Deal government boasted an unusually large number of [white] female executives because President Roosevelt established a better record than any of his predecessors at elevating women to high posts." Rigueur points out that the "programs and agencies of the New Deal were rife with [racial] discrimination; in this sense, the Republican and Democratic parties of this era did not display clear-cut differences in their civil rights policies.'" Muncy, *Relentless Reformer*, 163; Rigueur, *Loneliness of the Black Republican*, 15; Fauntroy, *Republicans and the Black Vote*, 5; Grimshaw, *Bitter Fruit*, 48–49.

60. When Terrell tried to find a government job in 1935, she was told that she would need to take the civil service examination. MCT Diary, June 4, 1949, HB; MCT Diary, July 2, 1935, MCT Papers, reel 2.

Chapter 11

1. Thomas J. Sugrue argues that "across the North, the Democratic Party was largely urban. As their black constituencies grew . . . municipal governments became the employer of first resort for blacks. . . . Their inroads into public employment testified to their newfound electoral clout." Sugrue, *Sweet Land of Liberty*, 112–13.

2. Robert R. Church Jr. campaigned for Hoover in 1928 and then wrote the president detailing his disappointment with his record on race and civil rights. Lenna Yost to MCT, October 12, 1932, MCT Papers, reel 7. R. R. Church Jr. to President Herbert Hoover, November 6, 1929, quoted in Church and Church, *Robert R. Churches*, 263–65.

3. In 1933, Bethune was still "officially a Republican" but "assumed a nonpartisan position" when dealing with the Democratic administration. By 1940, Bethune actively recruited black women as campaign workers and voters for the Democrats. Hanson, *Mary McCleod Bethune*, 121, 124, 152, 154; Nettie Langston Napier to MCT, October 19 (telegram), November 9, 1932, MCT Papers, reel 7 (emphasis in original).

4. Herbert Hoover "appointed almost no blacks to federal office . . . and made fewer public statements on race than any other President in the century." The NAACP organized protests against the appointment of Judge John J. Parker and saw it as a victory when his appointment was scuttled. "DePriest States His Position," ca. 1945, political pamphlet, DP; Sitkoff, *New Deal*, 22, 28, 226–28; Gosnell, *Negro Politicians*, 195; Fairclough, *Better Day Coming*, 147; Davis, *Electing Justices*, 99; Goings, *NAACP*; Burris, *Duty and the Law*; Davis, *Electing Justices*, 21; MCT to Anna A. Lewis, October 10, 1932, MCT Papers, reel 7.

5. MCT, "In Defense of the Republican Ticket," 1932; and MCT, "Why Colored People Should Vote Republican," 1932, both in MCT Papers, reel 22 (emphasis added).

6. Barry, *Rising Tide*; Mizelle, *Backwater Blues*, chap. 3; MCT, "In Defense of the Republican Ticket."

7. MCT, "Speech to the Women of the Eastern Division of the Republican Party," October 1932, MCT Papers, reel 22; Christine S. Smith to MCT, telegram, October 19, 1932, MCT Papers, reel 7.

8. In the mid-1930s, the WILPF was still trying to recruit African Americans by listing its "Inter-Racial Record," which included its work for the Dyer Anti-Lynching Bill and its 1926 recommendation to remove U.S. troops from Haiti and restore self-governance there. Slate, *Colored Cosmopolitanism*, 111; Bennett, *Radical Pacifism*, 27–29; "The W. I. L. Inter-Racial Record" (undated but after 1933), MCT Papers, reel 20; MCT, "Colored People and World Peace, or Colored Women and World Peace," 1932, MCT Papers, reels 20, 22; MCT, "Some Facts for Colored People to Think About," 1932, Women's International League for Peace and Freedom, 1919–1921, and undated, MCT Papers, reel 22; MCT, "In Defense of the Republican Ticket."

9. Martinez, *Long Dark Night*, 152; Renstrom, *Taft Court*, 180, 210–11; Pitre, "*Nixon v. Herndon*," 111–25; Klarman, *From Jim Crow*, 99, 135, 453. MCT, "Some Facts for Colored People"; MCT, "Speech to the Women of the Eastern Division."

10. MCT, "Some Facts for Colored People."

11. See the election results table in Weiss, *Farewell to the Party of Lincoln*, 30; Sitkoff, *New Deal*, 39; Wolf, Pederson, and Daynes, *Franklin*, 147–48.

12. MCT to Norris A. Dodson, October 12, 1932, MCT Papers, reel 7; Phyllis Terrell to MCT, October 31, November 9, 1932, MCT Papers, reel 3.

13. A genealogy website states that "Richard Krishna (Bob {Babu}) SOBRIAN was born on 25 Sep 1892 in San Fernando, Trinidad, W.I. He immigrated on 16 May 1915 to New York City. . . . SOBRIAN and Grace G. MANNEY were married on 15 Jun 1928 in New York. . . . She died cervical Cancer on 15 Oct 1932 in Manhattan." http://www.toolsie.net/b2509.html#P2509. Krishna was about six years older than Phyllis and a widower. Krishna Sobrian to MCT, October 11, 1933, MCT Papers, reel 7; Sobrian to Phyllis Terrell, January 25, February 9, 1934, HB.

14. Terrell did not approve of F. E. Parks, who had been with Phyllis for six years but had not asked her to marry him, even after her divorce from her first husband was finalized. Another Talented Tenth parent, W. E. B. Du Bois, forbade his daughter Yolande from marrying the love of her life, the young jazz musician Jimmie Lunceford. Yolande forever regretted it. Lewis, *Du Bois: Fight for Equality*, 108; Sobrian to MCT, October 11, 1933, MCT Papers, reel 7.

15. John D. Rockefeller Jr. built the Paul Laurence Dunbar Apartments to provide affordable and comfortable housing that would allow African Americans to become property owners in New York City through a rent-to-purchase plan. The Du Bois family moved in 1927 and lived there for about a decade. Gatewood, *Aristocrats*, 144–45; Lubove, *Community Planning*, 53; West and West, "Paul Laurence Dunbar," 260; Lewis, *Du Bois: Fight for Equality*, 212; "Memorandum in re Mrs. Clara Burrill Bruce," in Coordinating Committee for the Enforcement of the D.C. Anti-Discrimination Laws, Miscellaneous, 1949–1954, MCT Papers, reel 14; Roscoe Conkling Bruce to MCT, October 7, 1932, MCT Papers, reel 7.

16. Bruce to MCT, October 12, 14, 17, 1933; and Bruce to Rev. Adam Clayton Powell Jr., October 18, 1933, all in MCT Papers, reel 7.

17. Terrell's friends determined that "at the present time, Postmaster General Farley . . . is backing McKee to the limit. His organization seems to be the only one that will have the [pay] roll. The other organizations, Republicans and Fusionists, are urging their supporters to lend assistance on promises. We all know what that means." Fred D.

McCracken to MCT, October 10, 1933, MCT Papers, reel 7; "Men of the Month: Mr. F. D. McCracken: A Private Secretary," *The Crisis*, September 15, 1915, 222.

18. Bruce to Powell, October 18, 1933; Bruce to MCT, October 26, 1933; Bruce to Hon. Joseph McKee, October 14, 1933; and Powell to Bruce, October 25, 1933, all in MCT Papers, reel 7.

19. Fiorello La Guardia's Fusion ticket won only "13.32 percent of votes in 'Negro Harlem.'" Jeffers, *Napoleon of New York*, 171; Kilson, "Adam Clayton Powell, Jr.," 268; Bruce to MCT, October 14, 19, 20, November 21, 29, 1933, MCT Papers, reel 7.

20. Traveling to New York City in January 1934, Terrell made a final push to find Phyllis a job. She visited Harriet P. Shadd Butcher, who taught at M Street High School from 1905 to 1923 and was working at the Russell Sage Foundation. She gave Terrell a social work application form, but the search petered out. Phyllis and F. E. Parks married in August 1934. MCT Diary, January 10, August 25, 1934, MCT Additions.

21. Robert P. Sellers to MCT, December 26, 1933, MCT Papers, reel 7.

22. Henry, *Eleanor Roosevelt*, 64; Kirby, *Black Americans*, 76–77; Malvinia T. Scheider (secretary to Eleanor Roosevelt) to MCT, May 8, 1933, MCT Papers, reel 7.

23. Correspondence between Eleanor Roosevelt and Bethune, in McCluskey and Smith, *Mary McLeod Bethune*; Kirby, *Black Americans*, 76–77.

24. In 1952, Terrell took credit for Bethune's rise in the NACW: "Wrote letter to National Committee to Defend Negro Leadership. Told about having Mary McLeod speak at Hampton Convention." Terrell resented it when "a picture of the Negro Leadership paper shows two women, Mary Bethune and Charlotte Bass." Referring to herself, she noted: "The colored woman first in her group to be put on a Board of Education, 1st president of 1st large secular national organization of colored women, and the 1st one to represent colored women 3 times is not considered a leader." MCT Diary, September 15, October 7, 24, 1952, MCT Papers, reel 2; MCT Diary, November 15, 1940, December 5, 1948, HB.

25. Terrell did not win an appointment. "American Negro Exposition, 1863–1940: Chicago Coliseum—July 4 to Sept. 2: official program and guide book," https://archive .org/stream/americannegroexpooamer/americannegroexpooamer_djvu.txt; Jane Spaulding to MCT, March 10, 26, April 2, 1936, MCT Additions; MCT Diary, April 30, May 15, 1936, MCT Papers, reel 7.

26. Hanson, *Mary McCleod Bethune*, 162–74, 166; Dossett, *Bridging Race Divides*, 58–59; Hine, *Hine Sight*, 20; Higginbotham, *Righteous Discontent*, 227.

27. Mary E. Switzer (assistant to the assistant secretary of the Treasury) to MCT, July 25, 1935, MCT Papers, reel 7.

28. Hanson, *Mary McCleod Bethune*, 131–37; Smith, "Mary McLeod Bethune," 76–80.

29. Barbara Dianne Savage notes that Nannie H. Burroughs served "as head of the National League of Republican Colored Women. Under fierce attack from some African Americans who switched to the Democratic party in that period, she accused her critics of political opportunism: 'I am not a political rat running from party to party.'" Savage, *Your Spirits*, 167; Hanson, *Mary McCleod Bethune*, 160–61; McNeill, *Groundwork*; MCT Diary, June 26, 1936, MCT Papers, reel 2.

30. By 1938, Bethune "played a substantial part in allocating patronage appointments"

for African Americans. Terrell was less politically active for much of 1937, since she was sidelined by the death of her brother in January, which led to a long, involved, and ultimately successful custody battle for his young son, Thomas A. Church Jr. She became Thomas's legal guardian and placed him in the care of her adopted daughter, Mary, who was his much-older half sister. That occupied her until June, when she sailed to London to participate in the World Fellowship of Faiths international convention. In 1938, Terrell was back on track, attending Bethune's "Conference on the Participation of Negro Women and Children in Federal Welfare Programs" and a host of other civil rights meetings. Hanson, *Mary McCleod Bethune*, 154; Savage, *Your Spirits*, 121; MCT Diary, October 17, 1936, MCT Papers, reel 2. See MCT's diary entries for 1937, MCT Collection; "Conference on the Participation of Negro Women and Children in Federal Welfare Programs," April 4, 1938, MCT Papers, reel 14; MCT Diary, May 4, November 14, 1946, March 4, 6, October 10, 1948, HB.

31. MCT Diary, March 24, October 3, 20, 1934, MCT Additions; Scheider to MCT, April 6, 1935, MCT Papers, reel 7; MCT Diary, January 12, 23, March 30, 1935, MCT Papers, reel 2.

32. MCT Diary, April 14, 1935, MCT Papers, reel 2.

33. In 1944, Oscar DePriest continued to lash out against FDR and the Democrats: "For almost twelve years our President, Franklin Delano Roosevelt . . . has been as voiceless as an iceberg in his cold indifference to these grave wrongs inflicted upon twelve million black souls." DePriest contrasted the Republican Party's 1944 platform, which named the end of segregation in the U.S. military, the establishment of a permanent Fair Employment Practice Commission, the abolition of poll taxes, and an antilynching bill as goals. Savage, *Your Spirits*, 167; Oscar DePriest, "Know the Truth," campaign pamphlet, DP; MCT Diary, April 28, 1935, MCT Papers, reel 2; MCT Diary, October 26, 1936, MCT Collection.

34. This 1935 conference led to the formation of the National Negro Congress. Sitkoff, *New Deal*, 43, 60–65, 56–57, 92–93; Sklaroff, *Black Culture*, 22–23; Gellman, *Death Blow*, 113–14; Sugrue, *Sweet Land of Liberty*, 112–13.

35. Armfield, *Eugene Kinckle Jones*, 57; MCT, "Some Facts for Colored People."

36. When FDR finally spoke out against discrimination, including the poll tax, and supported a permanent Fair Employment Practices Commission in 1944, a large majority of African Americans became Democrats. William J. Grimshaw explains that African Americans' "support for the national Democratic party leaped to 64 percent in 1944, up from 53 percent in 1940, and it continued to rise to the point where 75 percent of the black electorate cast Democratic ballots in 1952." Grimshaw, *Bitter Fruit*, 48–49; Drake and Cayton, *Black Metropolis*, 353–54, 359; Sitkoff, *New Deal*, 94; Plotke, *Building a Democratic Political Order*, 128; Venn, *New Deal*, 62; Oscar DePriest to Gov. Dwight H. Green, April 15, 1941, DP.

37. See Terrell's 1936 diary and MCT Diary, January 8, 1936, MCT Additions.

38. On Julia Grant Cantacuzene, see Rubin, *American Empress*, 278; and Patterson, *Congressional Conservativism*, 20. MCT Diary, January 6, 1936, MCT Additions; MCT to Cantacuzene, January 10, 1936, MCT Papers, reel 7.

39. MCT to Cantacuzene, January 10, 1936.

40. Henry P. Fletcher was chair of the RNC from 1934 to 1936, and Wilma Hoyal was the director of the RNC's Women's Division. Osselaer, *Winning Their Place*, 117; Bass,

Historical Dictionary, 111; Giddings, *When and Where*, 218–19; Cantacuzene to John Hamilton (general counsel, RNC), January 21, 1936, MCT Papers, reel 7.

41. Horton, *Race and the Making*, 123; Manza and Brooks, *Social Cleavages*, 158; Fauntroy, *Republicans and the Black Vote*, 49; Walton, "Political Science," 65–66.

42. Weed, *Nemesis of Reform*, 44, 74; Cantacuzene to Hamilton, January 21, 1936; and Hamilton to Cantacuzene, February 1, 1936, both in MCT Papers, reel 7.

43. Terrell met Mable Jacques Eichel, who became the national director of the Independent Coalition of American Women to defeat Roosevelt and the New Deal, at Cantacuzene's house and then visited her in New York City. See "Coalition Formed by State Women; Campaign to Defeat Roosevelt Enters Pennsylvania," *Scranton (Pa.) Republican*, July 11, 1936, 7; and "Women to Get Out Stay-At-Home Vote; Anti-New Deal Group Prepares for Campaign," *Reading (Pa.) Eagle*, August 29, 1936, 2. Cantacuzene to MCT, March 26, 1936, MCT Papers, reel 7; MCT Diary, March 31, 1936, MCT Additions; MCT Diary, April 1, May 27, June 12, 25, 1936, MCT Papers, reel 2; Mabel Jacques Eichel to MCT, May 8, 1936, MCT Papers, reel 7.

44. For example, Grace Wilson Evans to MCT, April 5, 1936, MCT Papers, reel 7.

45. J. Finley Wilson, head of the Elks, was thrilled to have Terrell speak for the GOP at Elks conventions, writing that he hoped "we can chase these money changers from the Temple next November and finally take care of the 'forgotten man' . . . when we come into power." MCT Diary, April 20, 23, 25, 1936, MCT Papers, reel 2; Perry W. Howard to MCT, April 7, 1936; J. Finley Wilson (grand exalted ruler, Improved Benevolent and Protective Order of Elks of the World) to MCT, April 15, 1936, MCT Papers, reel 7.

46. MCT Diary, June 18, July 13, 14, 1936, MCT Papers, reel 7.

47. In 1936, the GOP offered "African Americans 're-employment' rather than handouts; they promised that the party would integrate the workplace and offer black voters tangible solutions to their economic and racial uncertainties. The Negro Drive had some impact on African American voters in mid-term elections, though it did not stop the growing wave of defections in presidential contests." Rigueur, *Loneliness of the Black Republican*, 20, 42–43. For Coleman, see Freeman, *Room at a Time*, 300n65; and MCT Diary, May 12, 13, 1936, October 28, 1936, MCT Papers, reel 2.

48. This coalition strategy was a mistake. Simon Topping explains: the "GOP's long exile from government was a deeply unhappy one; leaderless, split, and groping for issues, the party staggered from one electoral catastrophe to the next. Consequently, the party's neglect of African Americans can be best understood against the background of its divisions and serious difficulties during the early years of the New Deal." Topping, *Lincoln's Lost Legacy*, 29; MCT Diary, January 6, October 28, 1936, MCT Additions.

49. Topping deems the election of 1936 "the Republicans' nadir." Geoffrey Kabaservice explains, the "virulence of these charges created a backlash that handed the GOP its worst-ever defeat in both the presidential and Congressional elections." Topping, *Lincoln's Lost Legacy*, 33; Kabaservice, *Rule and Ruin*, 5; Patterson, *Congressional Conservativism*, 108–9; Weed, *Nemesis of Reform*, 161; Brinkley, *End of Reform*, 25; MCT Diary, January 8, 1936, MCT Additions.

50. Barbara Dianne Savage notes, "Even in this period of great need, Burroughs expressed deep suspicion and hostility toward public welfare agencies and relief monies not tied to work. She feared they would breed dependency and idleness among African Americans, especially men." Terrell endorsed the GOP claim that its economic policies,

such as a high tariff, would give workers a "full dinner pail." Savage, *Your Spirits*, 172; Brewer and Stonecash, *Dynamics*, 58; Sundquist, *Dynamics of the Party System*, 151; Oscar DePriest, "To the Youth of Illinois," 1934, DP; MCT, "The New Deal," 1936, MCT Papers, reel 22.

51. Clyde P. Weed argues that "bitter denunciations" of the New Deal were typical of RNC operatives in 1936. Weed, *Nemesis of Reform*, 97, 101; Parker, *Articulating Rights*, 177–211; Mayer, *Republican Party*, 428, 440; Topping, *Lincoln's Lost Legacy*, 29; MCT, "New Deal."

52. More southern Democrats joined in open rebellion against FDR and the New Deal after the national Democratic Party sought the black vote in the 1936 presidential election. Sitkoff, *New Deal*, 102, 108–9; Reichley, *Life of the Parties*, 232; Lichtman, *White Protestant Nation*, 98–99; Savage, *Roosevelt*, 30–33; Domhoff and Webber, *Class and Power*, 194; Katznelson, *Fear Itself*, 266; Sitkoff, *New Deal*, 102–16; MCT, "New Deal."

53. Biles, *South and the New Deal*, 137–42; MCT, "New Deal."

54. Quoted in Higginbotham, *Ghosts*, 91; Smith, *Managing White Supremacy*, 150–51; Weed, *Nemesis of Reform*, 191.

55. Bethune was accused of subversion by the Dies Committee in 1943, and Terrell wrote a letter of support for her. Hanson, *Mary McCleod Bethune*, 138; Quigley, *Just Another Southern Town*, 130; Dunn, *Roosevelt's*, 84, 91; Kirby, *Black Americans*, 33; MCT, "Dear Friend," letter, April 2, 1943, MCP, LOC.

56. Graham, *Encore for Reform*, 25, 29.

57. MCT, "New Deal"; Parker, *Articulating Rights*, 177–211.

58. In 1936, DePriest ran in a local Chicago campaign to be reelected as third ward committeeman after he was defeated in his bid to return to Congress. "Pamphlet to reelect 3rd Ward Committeeman DePriest," April 1936, which included a March 13, 1936, editorial in the *Chicago Daily Tribune*, DP.

Chapter 12

1. Berto and Mollie Terrell attended various churches over the years, looking for a good sermon and fellowship. Gatewood, *Aristocrats*, 145; Savage, *Your Spirits*, 128; MCT Diary, September 26, 1909, MCT Papers, reel 2; MCT, *Colored Woman*, 46; MCT Diary, June 13, 1948, HB.

2. See MCT Correspondence 1936, MCT Papers, reel 7; and MCT Diary, 1936, MCT Additions.

3. The only other surviving Terrell diary that contains an opening prayer is for 1911, which has words from a Lutheran hymn focused on social justice for those who have been neglected and scorned by the wider society. Terrell had a prescription for her nerves, MCT Diary, July 27, 1940, HB. MCT Diary, January 1, 1911, MCT Papers, reel 1; second MCT Diary 1936, January 1, 1936 (really April), MCT Papers, reel 2 (she lost the first diary but later found it—that diary is in MCT Additions).

4. Frances Watkins Harper, Nannie Helen Burroughs, Mary McLeod Bethune, and Ida B. Wells-Barnett were among those African American women reformers who used religious language throughout their speeches and writings. MCT Diary, March 26, 1936, MCT Additions.

5. After World War I, Frank Buchman focused on gaining converts among elite young men attending prominent colleges in England and the United States. After the Great Depression, he expanded the movement by convincing prominent whites, usually men, in each community he entered to hold evangelical house parties. Some in the Oxford Group tried reaching out to prominent African Americans as influencers within their own social circles. The most lasting contribution of the Oxford Group to American culture was arguably the 1935 founding of Alcoholics Anonymous, whose principles and procedures were modeled on the Oxford Group, which promoted personal moral scrutiny and honesty. "The five 'Cs' of the Oxford Group—confidence, conviction, confession, conversion, continuance—were subsequently enlarged upon by [William] Wilson [Bill W.] to become the famous 'Twelve Steps.'" Falby, "Modern Confessional," 255–58, 265; Boobbyer, *Spiritual Vision*, 1, 14, 17–18, 78; Sack, "Men Want Something Real," 261–63, 268; Gordon, "Princeton Group," 35, 41; Toy, "Oxford Group," 175, 180; Boobbyer, "B. H. Streeter," 541–67; Woolverton, "Evangelical Protestantism," 59.

6. Boobbyer, *Spiritual Vision*, 135; Woolverton, "Evangelical Protestantism," 65.

7. According to his apologist: "Buchman obviously hoped Himmler might change and in the process help to introduce a new spirit and direction into German life." Boobbyer, *Spiritual Vision*, 137, 148–50; Boobbyer, "B. H. Streeter," 13; Savage, *Your Spirits*, 161.

8. The United Negro Improvement Association also showed an openness to the Oxford Group, although the connection did not develop. Lillian M. Henry, "UNIA News," *Philadelphia Tribune*, November 18, 1937, 10; Boobbyer, "B. H. Streeter," 14; Boobbyer, *Spiritual Vision*, 56, 61, 106; Falby, "Modern Confessional," 259 (emphasis added).

9. Falby, "Modern Confessional," 259; Boobbyer, *Spiritual Vision*, 56, 61; MCT Diary, April 15, 1936, MCT Papers, reel 2.

10. Smith, *Emancipation*, 402–3; MCT Diary, April 20, May 12, 13, 1936, MCT Papers, reel 2.

11. MCT Diary, May 14, 1936, MCT Papers, reel 2.

12. MCT Diary, April 28, May 1, 1936, MCT Papers, reel 2.

13. MCT Diary, May 1, 1936, MCT Papers, reel 2.

14. Asbury Church was founded in 1836 by African American members of Foundry Methodist Episcopal Church who left because of segregation and the paternalism of church leaders. Today, Asbury and Foundry are United Methodist Churches. See Archives and Manuscripts of the United Methodist Churches, 1836–1986, archive.nypl.org. MCT Diary, March 23, May 2, 3, 1936, MCT Papers, reel 2.

15. MCT Diary, May 19, 1936, MCT Papers, reel 2; Phyllis Terrell to MCT, June 7, 1936, MCT Papers, reel 3.

16. MCT Diary, May 29, 30, 31, 1936, MCT Papers, reel 2.

17. MCT Diary, June 1, 1936, MCT Papers, reel 2.

18. MCT Diary, June 5, 6, 7, 1936, MCT Papers, reel 2.

19. MCT Diary, June 2, 1936, MCT Papers, reel 2.

20. Barbara Dianne Savage writes that "toward the end of her life, [Bethune] embraced a controversial new international religious and political movement called 'Moral Re-Armament' because she believed it to be the best hope of the world for unifying and empowering the many diverse peoples of a modern world drawn together by the

threat of atomic annihilation." Savage, *Your Spirits*, 122, 151; Sack, "Men Want Something Real," 274; Gordon B. Hancock, "Between the Lines: The Oxford Group," *New Journal and Guide* (Norfolk, Va.), September 4, 1937, A8; "Many Negroes Join Moral Rearmament," *Atlanta Daily World*, December 24, 1939, A2.

21. MCT Diary, December 1, 1936, MCT Papers, reel 2.

22. The play, and later the movie based on it, depicted "old time" southern black religion in a racially stereotyped way, and some black activists organized boycotts of the film. Other African Americans proudly welcomed it. The 1936 film had an all-black cast, including the actor who played God. In 1933, Terrell was a member of the Committee on Race Relations of the Washington Federation of Churches when she helped organize the protests against the refusal to seat African Americans at the theater where the play was presented. The play had a long impact. As late as the 1960s, critics of Martin Luther King Jr. in the SCLC jokingly referred to him as "De Lawd," the main character in *Green Pastures*. Weisenfeld, *Hollywood*, 80–86; G. S. Morris, "Thank God for Uncle Tom: Race and Religion Collide in *The Green Pastures*," *Bright Lights Film Journal*, January 31, 2008, https://brightlightsfilm.com/thank-god-for-uncle-tom-race-and-religion-collide-in-the-green-pastures/#.XY-8WkZKg2w; Frady, *Martin Luther King, Jr.*, 96. "Minutes: A Meeting of the Committee on Race Relations of the Washington Federation of Churches," February 27, 1933, MCT Papers, reel 14; MCT Diary, October 9, December 1, 1936, MCT Papers, reel 2.

23. MCT, *Colored Woman*, 402–6; MCT Diary, December 8, 23, 1936, MCT Papers, reel 2; MCT Diary, June 7, 1939, MCT Additions.

24. Mollie was not suing for direct custody for herself. Instead, she and her brother Thomas had planned to have his older daughter (and Mollie's adopted daughter), Mary, take care of her much younger half brother in her Chicago home. Mollie's brother Robert R. Church Jr. objected to this plan. MCT, *Colored Woman*, 402.

25. Charles Frederick Weller to MCT, November 21, 1934, MCT Papers, reel 7; MCT, "On the Trip to Europe" for the World Fellowship of Faiths, London, 1937, MCT Papers, reel 22; Laura Terrell Jones to MCT, July 27, 1937, MCT Papers, reel 2.

26. Terrell's ideal was the unification of Christian denominations into one Christian church. Lincoln Congregational Temple still thrives as the Lincoln Temple United Church of Christ. MCT, *Colored Woman*, 114; RHT, "Address to the University Park Temple Church," ca. 1900, RHT Papers, reel 2; MCT, "The Lincoln Memorial Congregational Church," 1901, MCT Papers, reel 22; MCT, "Up to Date," *CD*, November 24, 1928, 2.

27. MCT Diary, May 7, November 26, 1946, November 17, March 22, 1948, HB.

28. Wilmore criticizes early twentieth-century black male ministers as being nonconfrontational and unengaged in the black freedom struggle. Terrell focused her criticism on white ministers. In 1947, Terrell participated in an "Interracial Workshop" protesting "the YMCA's refusal to let an interracial group be served by the restaurant." Terrell had experienced discriminatory treatment in YWCAs. Dorrien, *New Abolition*, 63, 219–20; Wilmore, *Black Religion*, 133–44; Overacker, "True to Our God," 202–3; MCT Diary, March 15, 1908, MCT Papers, reel 1; MCT, "Lucretia Mott: Remarks Made at the Dedication of the New Mott School," May 17, 1909, MCT Papers, reel 2; MCT Diary, November 1, 1947; MCT, *Colored Woman*, 106, 415–16.

29. According to the *Oxford English Dictionary*, the phrase "church militant" has

been in use since at least 1424, meaning "the church on earth, the community of living Christians." Ministers and institutional religion became central to the Civil Rights Movement of the 1950s and 1960s. Overacker, "True to Our God," 201–16; Garrow, *Bearing the Cross*; Reagon, "Women as Culture Carriers," 203–18; MCT, *Colored Woman*, 106; MCT Diary, November 18, 1908, MCT Papers, reel 1.

30. Catsam, "Early Economic Civil Rights," 52–53; Catsam, *Freedom's Main Line*, 21, 77; Scalmer, *Gandhi*, 154–56.

31. MCT, Remarks at Interchurch Fellowship Group, June 9, 1947, MCT Papers, reel 22.

32. MCT, Remarks at Interchurch Fellowship Group.

33. MCT, Remarks at Interchurch Fellowship Group.

Chapter 13

1. Terrell participated in large "interracial meeting[s] of the League of Women Shoppers" and lobbied Congress with the league. She also participated in the Southern Conference for Human Welfare and the Anti-Poll Tax Committee. Smallwood, *Reform*, 61. See, e.g., MCT, "The Race Problem and the War," ca. 1942–45, MCT Papers, reel 22; MCT Diary, January 16, February 15, April 15, October 16, 1946, HB.

2. Only seven branches out of a thousand were integrated by the end of World War II, but Mollie and Nettie might not have known this. In its legal battles, the AAUW did not rely on its status as a private club to be allowed to discriminate because it did not want to undermine its claim to have a public advisory role on higher education policy with federal, state, or local governments. Neumann, "Status Seekers," 90; Levine, *Degrees of Equality*, 107; Leone, "Integrating," 426–27.

3. The NAACP's Walter White also strongly condemned European imperialism. Anderson, *Bourgeois Radicals*, 22; MCT, "Race Problem and the War."

4. The wartime rhetoric of democracy accelerated Indians' demands for independence. Later in the war, Terrell added: "But as between England and Hitler, the Jew hater and Negro hater, Hitler who has persecuted and murdered thousands of innocent men, women, and children . . . there is no doubt that the colored people of the United States . . . are overwhelmingly in sympathy with England." If Hitler won, she warned, American Jews and African Americans would undoubtedly suffer the most in his murderous campaign to destroy "impure" or "inferior" races. Rosenberg, *How Far*, 131–40. For a brief discussion of why some African Americans supported the Japanese at least briefly, see Horne "Race from Power," 53. MCT, "Race Problem and War"; MCT, "Human Relations in Transition to Peace," October 13, 1944, speech to the National Congress of Negro Women, MCT Papers, reel 22. For treatment of African American soldiers during World War II, see Hachey, "Walter White," 333–51. Von Eschen, *Race against Empire*, 28–32; Plummer, *Rising Wind*, 66, 83; MCT, "Race Problem and War"; MCT, "Human Relations."

5. See Bynum, *A. Philip Randolph*; Dudziak, *Cold*, 24–25, 89–90; Reed, *Seedtime*, 11–17; and Kennedy, *Freedom*, 767–68.

6. Reed, *Seedtime*; Lucander, *Winning*, 30–31, 70–71. For black women and work during World War II, see Giddings, *When and Where*, 231–38; Jones, *Labor of Love*, 232–56; and Milkman, *Gender*, 54–55. MCT, "Race Problem and War"; MCT, "Senator

Benton's Appeal to the Senate to Pass the F.E.P.C. (Fair Employment Practices Commission) Bill," 1949, MCT Papers, reel 22.

7. See also MCT Diary, October 31, November 7, 1948, HB.

8. Wynn, *African American Experience*, 40, 66; James, *Double V*, 141; MCT, "Race Problem and War."

9. Southern Democrats in Congress during the Truman administration allowed the FEPC to die. Mitchell, "Epilogue," 562; MCT, "Race Problem and War"; MCT, "Human Relations"; MCT Diary, January 11, 1951, MCT Papers, reel 2.

10. Borstelmann, *Cold War*, 27–41; Wynn, *African American Experience*, 71–75, 83–86; Buckley, *American*, 257–334; Adams and Sanders, *Alienable Rights*, 261–64; MCT, "Race Problem and War"; MCT, "Human Relations."

11. Kempski, "Jim Crow Welcome Home"; Wolcott, *Race, Riots*, 78–82, 246n110; MCT, "Race Problem and War"; MCT, "Human Relations."

12. AAUW general director Kathryn McHale warned an Illinois branch not to invite black teachers to become members because "if some aggressive Negro eligible should insist upon branch membership, which would result in unfortunate publicity.... Branches would rebel." Helen Laville argues, "Many individual white women simply failed to understand racial segregation as a problem they shared with African-American women, and were therefore slow to take collective action against segregation." Laville, *Organized White Women*, 10; Levine, *Degrees of Equality*, chap. 6, 109; Weisenfeld, *African American Women*, 8–9; Lillian E. Smith to MCT, September 4, 1943, MCT Additions.

13. Neumann, "Status Seekers," 89–90; Levine, *Degrees of Equality*, 107; Leone, "Integrating," 426–27.

14. The AAUW was first called the Association of Collegiate Alumnae. Laville, *Organized White Women*, 42, 48; Marvin Caplan, "Mrs. Terrell Reopens a Door," edited by Dorothy Swift, in MCT, *Colored Woman*, 429.

15. It changed its name to the National Association of College Women in 1923, under the leadership of Howard University's dean of women Lucy Slowe, with the same acronym, NACW, as the women's club movement. In 1972 it became the National Association of University Women. Miller and Pruitt-Logan, *Faithful to the Task*, 67–68; Laville, *Organized White Women*, 117; MCT, "Prologue to the Swelling Act: How and When the College Alumnae Club Was Founded," *Journal of the College Alumnae Club of Washington* (1935): 3, MCT Collection.

16. Fannie Barrier Williams also fought to integrate the Chicago Woman's Club. Hendricks, *Fannie Barrier Williams*, 125; MCT Diary, May 24, 1946, HB.

17. Laville, *Organized White Women*, 42–43, 48–50.

18. There is a discussion later in this chapter of Wiley's racist opposition to black members. The AAUW's website confirms that Terrell was listed as a national member in the AAUW directory for 1905–6 and that she was a member of the local branch at that time. AAUW, https://www.aauw.org; Levine, *Degrees of Equality*, 117; MCT Diary, October 6, 8, 10, 1946, November 4, 1948, HB.

19. MCT Diary, October 14, 17, 19, 1946, HB.

20. MCT Diary, October 21, 22, 1946, HB.

21. To make white women aware of the prejudice that existed in their groups, Terrell "told Mrs. Kanzler [of Portland, Ore., Y in 1949] about the YWCA not allowing me to take lunch in the Cafeteria but had Nettie Swift, Dorothy and me eat upstairs (top floor)

with maid to serve us." McDaniel and Julye, *Fit for Freedom*; Austin, *Quaker Brotherhood*, 4; MCT Diary, October 23, 1946, February 23, 1949, HB.

22. MCT Diary, October 28, 1946, HB.

23. Judge Bentley did not turn out to be an ally. Rather, she led the fight to keep branches segregated. MCT Diary, October 28, 30, November 1, 8, 1946, HB.

24. MCT Diary, November 5, 8, 9, 29, 30, 1946, HB.

25. Leone, "Integrating," 429; MCT Diary, November 8, 1946, HB; MCT Diary, October 8, 1947, MCT Additions; MCT Diary, February 14, April 24, June 6, 1949, HB.

26. The AAUW claimed it did not schedule a vote on revised bylaws for its 1947 national convention because it thought the issue was settled. Wanting to fight the case in the court of public opinion through the media, Mollie "asked Nettie about letting the *Star* know about the AAUW mess." AAUW, as quoted in Leone, "Integrating," 429–30, 440; MCT Diary, December 10, 11, 13, 30, 1946, HB; "University Women Reaffirm Democracy," *Afro-American*, December 14, 1946; MCT Diary, January 27, April 30, June 2, October 3, 4, 1947, MCT Additions.

27. Leone, "Integrating," 430; MCT Diary, April 16, 29, 1947, MCT Additions.

28. MCT Diary, June 30, 1947, MCT Additions.

29. Leone, "Integrating," 435; MCT Diary, September 10, October 3, 1947, MCT Additions.

30. MCT Diary, June 30, 1947, MCT Additions.

31. MCT Diary, April 2, 1948, HB.

32. MCT Diary, September 15, 1947, MCT Additions.

33. Helen Laville points out that some branch meetings "took place in member's homes. The domestic setting all too often served as a reminder of the mistress/maid relationship." Laville, *Organized White Women*, 123; MCT Diary, September 18, 1947, MCT Additions.

34. MCT Diary, February 14, 1948, HB.

35. It was a collaborative effort: "Dinner at YWCA with Nettie. Corrected and sent letter she wrote to Dean Hottel." In 1949, Terrell noted an "editorial in *Post* that the Virginia AAUW had voted to accept qualified colored women." For more on the ADA, see Kleinman, *World of Hope*, 227–32. MCT Diary, May 11, 1949, HB; MCT Diary, September 18, 23, October 15, 1947, MCT Additions.

36. Leone, "Integrating," 437.

37. Helen Laville describes a 1948 letter written by Hottel to an AAUW supporter of segregation as "mealy-mouthed"; Hottel attempted to reassure local branches of the national's gradualist approach to integration. Laville, *Organized White Women*, 127, 132; MCT Diary, May 13, June 23, 24, 1948, September 22, 1949, HB.

38. Levine, *Degrees of Equality*, 120; MCT Diary, April 9, June 24, 1948, HB.

39. Hottel "personally visited more than three hundred branches and made speaking appearances in all nine AAUW regions." Hottel, as quoted in Leone, "Integrating," 441–42. Levine, *Degrees of Equality*, 118–19; MCT Diary, June 13, 1949, HB.

40. Anna Kelton Wiley was the member with whom Terrell had lunched in the AAUW dining room when she applied to renew her lapsed membership. Leone, "Integrating," 431–32, 434; Rupp and Taylor, *Survival*, 157.

41. Even at its moment of triumph, the national AAUW shied away from portraying this as a battle against prejudice and for desegregation. The case made the national

news, but the "AAUW did not wish to publicize the Terrell decision. . . . Offered the opportunity to honor Terrell in a joint luncheon with the National Association of Colored Women, the AAUW declined the invitation." On the same day as the affirmative AAUW vote, Terrell spoke in New York as chair of the National Committee to Free the Ingram Family. Laville, *Organized White Women*, 132–33; Leone, "Integrating," 435; Neumann, "Status Seekers," 95–96; Eisenmann, *Higher*, 127–28; MCT, "National Committee to Free the Ingram Family," June 22, 1949, Hotel Theresa, New York, MCT Papers, reel 22; MCT Diary, June 23, 24, 1949, HB.

42. Mollie appreciated Nettie's validating comments. After their final victory, she wrote in her diary that she had received a "letter from Nettie praising me in highest terms. . . . 'Well, Mollie, we have made the test and have won. You have had many honors in your life and won many battles, but as I see it, this is the greatest.'" Nettie was sensitive to the toll the case had taken on Mollie's psyche: "My dear, I know so well how hard it has been and how you have suffered. But you have won the test. . . . And it is no small thing that you have accomplished to secure justice for your group from a large and important national organization." Mollie recorded: "That praise from my old college friend . . . certainly warms the cockles of my heart!" She was particularly pleased with the *Pittsburgh Courier*'s article entitled "'Terrell AAUW . . . Is Victory for Liberals' in large headlines." MCT Diary, October 26, 27, November 4, 1948, June 28, July 4, September 13, 1949, HB.

43. Yet progress was less impressive across the nation. Total branch membership was four hundred. Some branches still only actively recruited white members, and most branches welcomed only a few black women. In the South, even after the 1949 decision, branches pointed to state-level Jim Crow laws that made interracial meetings illegal as an excuse for not integrating. Levine, *Degrees of Equality*, 125–35; MCT Diary, June 26, October 3, 1949, HB; MCT to Mrs. Lowry, NACW, October 1, 1949, MCT Additions.

44. MCT Diary, August 29, 1949, HB.

45. MCT Diary, October 3, 1949, HB.

46. "The fear, distrust, and suspicion created by anti-Communism made women's rights groups more hesitant to bring in large numbers of new members, created fear when conflicts erupted, and dampened enthusiasm for coalitions." Rupp and Taylor, *Survival*, 141.

47. In 1946, Terrell secured a formal reaffirmation of the NACW's early support for the ERA. At the 1946 annual meeting of the National Council of Women in New York City, Terrell seconded a motion to officially endorse the ERA. In retrospect, she worried, as she often did: "Feel white women resent my positive forceful attitude." Back in D.C., however, the Equal Rights Amendment legislative committee, possibly of the NWP, listened as a member appreciatively recounted Terrell's approach: "Mrs. Babcock told what I said in NY about Equal Rights Amendment. 'Am I in the U.S.?' 'You are.' 'Am I in New York State?' 'You are.' 'Am I in New York City?' 'You are.' 'The New York legislature unanimously endorsed the Equal Rights Amendment a year ago. Will the National Council of Women of U.S.A.?'" By 1948, NCW leader Lucia Hanna Hadley testified before a congressional committee that its executive council endorsed the ERA. Hoff, *Law, Gender, and Injustice*, 210; MCT Diary, January 11, 13, 1936, MCT Additions; MCT Diary, May 8, 26, 1946, HB; "Equal Rights Amendment to the Constitution and Commission on the Legal Status of Women," *Hearings before United States*

House Committee on the Judiciary, Subcommittee No. 1 (Judiciary), Eightieth Congress, Second Session, March 10, 12, 1948 (Washington, D.C.: U.S. Government Printing Office, 1948), 40; "Minutes of Meeting, Women's Joint Legislative Committee for Equal Rights," June 30, September 29, 1946, in MCT Papers, reel 20; MCT, "Testimony before the House Judiciary Committee on the Equal Rights Amendment," March 10, 1948, MCT Papers, reel 22.

48. Leila Rupp identified Terrell as the only African American member of the NWP in the 1940s and 1950s. Rupp, "Women's Community," 718. Terrell also testified in favor of the ERA in 1945. MCT Diary, April 29, 1946, HB; MCT "Testimony before the House Judiciary Committee."

49. See Stansell, *Feminist Promise*, 196; Ritter, *Constitution as Social Design*, 146–53. MCT Diary, April 29, October 27, 1946, HB; MCT, "Testimony before the House Judiciary Committee."

50. In 1953, the national AAUW delegates voted to reaffirm their opposition to the ERA. Rupp and Taylor, *Survival*, 142–43; Neumann, "Status Seekers," 117, 120; MCT Diary, May 12, 1951, MCT Papers, reel 2.

51. Lorde, "Uses of Anger," 124–33; MCT Diary, October 3, 4, 1947, MCT Additions.

52. Some prominent African Americans, including Howard University president Mordecai Johnson, joined Terrell in pushing back. MCT Diary, March 16, November 2, 9, 1949, HB.

53. MCT Diary, Wednesday, March 27, 1946, HB.

54. In 1953, leaders of the Council on African Affairs were charged with subversion under the McCarran Act, indicted, and forbidden from traveling abroad, and educational director Alpheous Hunton Jr. was imprisoned for six months. Yergan ultimately endorsed colonialism in Africa. For a copy of the letter signed by Terrell, Henry Arthur Callis, and John Latouche, see Council on African Affairs, letter from Council on African Affairs members to Paul Robeson, May 15, 1948, W. E. B. Du Bois Papers (MS 312), Special Collections and University Archives, University of Massachusetts, Amherst Libraries. Pollack, *Ballad of John Latouche*, 85; MCT Diary, January 24, February 1, 11, 12, March 4, April 13, 20, May 16, September 14, 1948, HB.

55. Aiming to protect radicals' free speech rights, Terrell joined the Committee for Free Political Advocacy. HUAC viewed membership in it as evidence of procommunist sympathies. "Letter from Paul J. Kern, Acting Chairman Committee for Free Political Advocacy . . . asking me to sponsor it and enclosing telegram blank for me to reply collect immediately. Wired 'I will accept with pleasure invitation to be sponsor of Conference in New York, July 16–17, 1949.'" In the inside cover of her 1949 diary, Terrell wrote: "Bishop Dunn says Communism presents more promise than democracy to many people over the world who are still struggling for equal rights, particularly rights denied them because of race." Washington, "History and the Role," 485–86; Storrs, *Second Red Scare*; Dunn, as quoted in MCT Diary, October 11, 1948, 1949 inside cover, May 19, 21, 1949, HB.

56. Returning to her long-standing grievance, she said, "I am praying to my Heavenly Father to give me grace enough to forgive the Republicans in the 80th Congress for not passing an Anti-Lynching Law, which they might easily have done. It grieves me and pains me that the Republican Party I have loved and worked for so long cared so little for our group that it refused to pass a law imposing a penalty upon those who shoot and

burn us to death with impunity, as they do today." MCT, "Remarks Made at the Elks Civil Rights Meeting," February 11, 1949, MCT Collection; MCT Diary, February 11, 1949, HB.

57. Speaking at a conference opposing the new North Atlantic Treaty Organization, Terrell explained: "As a colored woman, I opposed it because the United States would help Great Britain keep colored people in Europe enslaved if they tried to free themselves from her oppression." On May 17, 1950, Terrell signed her name to a press release for the Mid-Century Conference for Peace, declaring "that the American people's insistent demand for peace in the world today is in harmony with our demand for freedom. . . . Our people's battle for full freedom is today the test of our country's reputation, of its claim to leadership." MCT Diary, April 6, 11, 14, 15, 29, May 3, 6, 28, 1949, HB; "College Alumnae Club Washington, D.C., Branch of the National Association of College Women, Report of Activities, 1950–1951," by Florence L. Toms, president, MCT Papers, reel 16; Press Release, "Mid-Century Conference for Peace, Chicago, May 29–30, 1950," MCT Papers, reel 20.

58. The crowd of two thousand cheered Terrell for fighting to integrate the AAUW. Terrell helped to organize and obtain speakers for this CRC meeting at which Paul Robeson was the main draw. Terrell had recruited Senator Neely as a speaker but slyly "failed to mention" that Paul Robeson would also be speaking. Instead, she told the senator, "I knew his record, a liberal," and complimented West Virginia as a "fine state that observes the Constitution." Whether or not Neely regretted attending is unknown. Quigley, *Just Another Southern Town*, 138–41; MCT Diary, September 8, October 4, 13, December 18, 1949, HB.

59. MCT Diary, October 15, 22, 1949, HB.

60. After *Washington Post* columnist Alfred Friendly's talk, Mollie highlighted the global appeal of the Soviet Union's antiracism by asking, "In . . . effort to win the peace, what effect will Russia's well-known friendship for the colored races have?" MCT Diary, October 14, December 28, 1947, MCT Additions.

61. MCT to Hon. J. Howard McGrath (attorney general, Washington, D.C.), February 8, 1951, MCT Additions.

62. "Letter from Daisy Wilkerson asking me to go with delegation of 'non communist Negro leaders' to urge our government to enforce 14th Amendment, Section 2." MCT Diary, November 4, 1947, MCT Additions; Storrs, "Red Scare Politics," 57, 75–76.

63. Kathryn McHale was the AAUW leader. Meyerowitz, *Not June Cleaver*, 85; Neumann, "Status Seekers," 98–99n221; Levine, *Degrees of Equality*, 71–72; Smallwood, *Reform*, 129–30; MCT Diary, May 17, 21, 1949, HB.

64. "I called up Attorney General McGrath's office. . . . Talked to Mrs. Kechen who told me 'American Peace Crusade is not communistic.' She will send me a list of Communist organizations." Lieberman, *Strangest Dream*, 101–11; Horne, *Black and Red*, 186, 199; Horne, *Black Liberation*, 217; MCT Diary, February 23, 24, 1951, MCT Papers, reel 2.

65. Browne-Marshall, *Race, Law*, 156; MCT Diary, February 23, 24, 1951, MCT Papers, reel 2.

66. Neumann, "Status Seekers," 99–98, 101–3n221; Quigley, *Just Another Southern Town*, 168–69; MCT Diary, February 23, 28, 1951, MCT Papers, reel 2.

67. Thanks to Leigh Ann Wheeler for sharing with me the Emergency Civil Liberties

Committee FBI file, November 12, 1952, 29–30. Joan Quigley notes, "HUAC named Mary Church Terrell five times" as a "fellow traveler" for her work with the Stockholm appeal to ban atomic weapons, as well as for sponsoring the World Peace Congress, the Mid-Century Conference for Peace, and the American Peace Crusade. Quigley, *Just Another Southern Town*, 169–70; Neumann, "Status Seekers," 102.

Chapter 14

1. Although President Truman endorsed a permanent FEPC in 1948, conservatives in Congress killed it. MCT, "Human Relations in Transition to Peace," October 13, 1944, speech to the National Congress of Negro Women, MCT Papers, reel 22; MCT, "Senator Benton's Appeal to the Senate to Pass the F.E.P.C. (Fair Employment Practices Commission) Bill," 1949, MCT Papers, reel 22.

2. A year after Terrell's 1950 speech, the Maryland Committee for Peace was investigated for allegedly subversive activities by HUAC. She had a long history of anticolonialism, including when she met with the deposed Ethiopian emperor Haile Selassie, who was living in exile in England after Benito Mussolini's invasion and annexation of his country (they met after she attended the 1937 World Fellowship of Faiths conference). On the Italo-Ethiopian Conflict, see Meriwether, *Proudly We Can Be Africans*, 27–56; Scott, "Black Nationalism"; and Weisbord, "Black America," 134–63. For Harlem women's support for Ethiopia, see McDuffie, "[She] Devoted," 237; and Blain, Leeds, and Taylor, "Women, Gender Politics," 139–43. For red-baiting of the NAACP, see Woods, *Black Struggle*, 49–84. MCT, *Colored Woman*, 402–6; MCT, "On the Trip to Europe" for the World Fellowship of Faiths, London, 1937, MCT Papers, reel 22; MCT, "Address for the Maryland Committee for Peace," October 6, 1950, MCT Papers, reel 22; "Hearings Relating to Communist Activities in the Defense Area of Baltimore, Part I, Hearings before the Committee on Un-American Activities, House of Representatives, Eighty-Second Congress, First Session, Washington D.C.," 1951, 834, https://archives.org/stream/hearingsrelating0102unit; MCT, "Human Relations"; MCT, "Senator Benton's Appeal."

3. For historians who have put forward the long civil rights thesis, see Murphy, *Jim Crow Capital*, 201; Hall, "Long Civil Rights Movement"; Lawson, "Long Origins," 9–38; Lawson, *Civil Rights Crossroads*, 3–28; Crosby, "Introduction," 1–39; Singh, *Black Is a Country*; Joseph, "Black Liberation," 2–19; Kelley, "Stormy Weather," 67–90; Sullivan, *Days of Hope*; Gellman, *Death Blow*; Gilmore, *Defying Dixie*; Sugrue, *Sweet Land of Liberty*, xvi; and Berg, *"Ticket to Freedom."*

4. Tiyi M. Morris points out that a Jackson, Miss., Mary Church Terrell literary club, organized in 1912, encouraged the activist core of the Mississippi group that participated in the 1960s freedom struggle as Womanpower Unlimited. Historians like Morris and Brittany Cooper understand Terrell as the lifelong militant activist she truly was. Morris, *Womanpower*, 3, 10, 27, 110; Cooper, *Beyond Respectability*.

5. Murray became a leading civil and women's rights activist and lawyer. When she was a student at Hunter College, Murray worked at the Harlem branch of the YWCA and heard Terrell speak in its auditorium. Gloria Richardson attended Howard University during World War II and participated in D.C. picketing with her classmates. Howard University was threatened with defunding by the virulent racist, Mississippi

senator Theodore Bilbo, chair of the Senate's District of Columbia Committee. Rosenberg, *Jane Crow*, 36, 134–35; Harley, "'Chronicle,'" 181; Asch and Musgrove, *Chocolate City*, 279–80.

6. The librarian was A. Mercer Daniel. Todd Thomlinson also found the lost laws in the Library of Congress in 1943. Aptheker, *Woman's Legacy*, 148; Caplan, "The Lost Laws," in MCT, *Colored Woman*, 434–35, 444–45; "Background of the Appeal in the Thompson Restaurant Case to Be Heard in the U.S. Court of Appeals, January 7, 1952," in Coordinating Committee for the Enforcement of the D.C. Anti-Discrimination Laws, 1949–1954 files (hereafter cited as Coordinating Committee for Enforcement), MCT Papers, reel 14; Rosenberg, *Jane Crow*, 135–36; Murray, *Autobiography*, 230–31; Fradin and Fradin, *Fight On!*, 125.

7. Stein joined the Young Communist League in 1933 and organized the cafeteria workers' union through the Women's Trade Union League. Terrell was an active member of the League of Women Shoppers during World War II, when Stein chaired the Washington Committee for Consumer Protection. Taylor and Galamison, *Knocking at Our Own Door*, 55–56; Quigley, *Just Another Southern Town*, 148; Parker, "Southern Retail Campaigns," 81, 84.

8. Representative Clare Hoffman. Craig Simpson, "Against the Cold Wind: The 1948 Cafeteria Workers Strike," *Washington Area Spark*, https://washingtonspark.word press/2018/01/02/against-the-cold-wind-the-1948-cafeteria-workers-strike/.

9. "The G. S. I. strikers sent Miss Reed . . . to take me to . . . meet the leaders. Mr. Palmer, Union leader explained the Union won't sign the Communist test because . . . it's not against the law." MCT Diary, January 6, 7, 12, 1948, April 28, 1952, HB.

10. The union was investigated by various congressional committees. In 1951, on Terrell's eighty-eighth birthday, Local 471, Cafeteria and Restaurant Workers, paid tribute to her and gave her a gift. MCT Diary, April 13, 20, 1948, HB; *Congressional Record*, January–March 1948; "Call to a Conference against Jimcrow [*sic*] and Discrimination in the Nation's Capital, at the Cafeteria and Restaurant Workers Union Hall, Initiated by the Washington Trade Union Council for Negro Rights," December 10, 1950, Coordinating Committee for Enforcement, Miscellaneous, 1949–1954, MCT Papers, reel 14; "Union's Friend Honored," Local 471 Cafeteria and Restaurant Workers, *Crusader*, September 1951, 1, 4.

11. In 1952 Terrell recorded that the "cafeteria members invited me to speak at a meeting tonight and gave me a check for $25 for our Coordinating Com." Simpson, "Against the Cold Wind"; Thomas A. Church Jr. to MCT, July 15, 1951, HB; MCT Diary, May 27, 1952, MCT Papers, reel 2. *Hearings Relating to Communist Activities in the Defense Area of Baltimore*, part 1 (Washington, D.C.: U.S. GPO for the Committee on Un-American Activities, U.S. House of Representatives, July 1951), 769–75, 784.

12. In 1946, Terrell participated in a variety of desegregation actions to integrate auditoriums and movie theaters. Coleman, *Counsel for the Situation*, 48; MCT Diary, March 27, October 28, November 4, 1946, March 18, 1948, May 3, 1949, HB.

13. The pamphlet was titled *Segregation in Washington* (1948). Houston had a heart attack in November 1949 and died in April 1950. Murray, *Autobiography*, 230–31; Caplan, "Lost Laws," 434–35, 444–45; Thomas G. Buchanan Jr. to MCT, December 27, 1948, quoted in Quigley, *Just Another Southern Town*, 138.

14. Essie Thompson, a member of Local 471, participated in an interracial test of Thompson's. Terrell recruited the other participants in advance of the executive committee's planning meeting. The main committee members were Terrell, Stein, two black ministers, Arthur Elmes and William Jernagin, the black Red Cross worker Alice Trigg, a black post office employee Verdie Robinson, and white journalist Marvin Caplin. Jones, *Radical Line*, 97–99; Fradin and Fradin, *Fight On!*, 128–30; McDaniel and Julye, *Fit for Freedom*, 238; MCT Diary, May 3, October 3, 1949, HB; "Executive Committee Meeting," January 18, 1950; "Fact Sheet on the Anti-Discrimination Laws of 1872 and 1873," December 1952; and Interview of Mary Church Terrell, April 6, 1954, all in Coordinating Committee for Enforcement, 1949–1954, MCT Papers, reel 14.

15. Terrell had participated in the New Negro Alliance's 1933–34 "Don't Shop Where You Can't Work" picket lines. According to Chris Myers Asch and George Derek Musgrove, by 1938, the group claimed to have "secured more than five thousand nonmenial jobs for black workers." The Supreme Court's decision in *New Negro Alliance v. Sanitary Grocery* (1938) "had a profound impact on the course of social movements nationwide" because it ruled that "'peaceful and orderly dissemination of information' about a labor dispute was lawful, even by people or groups not directly involved in the dispute." It gave "the Court's imprimatur to labor unions, civil rights groups, and other activists seeking to use consumer power as leverage against corporations." CORE led interracial workshops targeting segregated restaurants and theaters in D.C. in 1944, 1947, and 1949. Wolcott, *Race, Riots*, 78; Caplan, "Lost Laws," 436; Asch and Musgrove, *Chocolate City*, 262–63.

16. Terrell recorded, "Phoned Mrs. Stein. She wants delegation of ministers to see the commissioners. She will write and I'll phone them." Caplan, *Farther Along*, 116; Asch and Musgrove, *Chocolate City*, 300–301; MCT Diary, June 18, 1951, MCT Papers, reel 2.

17. Problems with segregation and interracial misunderstandings persisted. In 1951, Terrell described a gathering at a talk by the poet Langston Hughes, whom she had known for decades: "Big colored church. . . . Full of white people. Colored men only appear on platform and open exercises. Colored women sit on one side of the dais, white women on the other." Terrell also continued to encounter white allies who still had trouble understanding her perspective. When dining with two white women active in the coordinating committee, one thoughtlessly insisted that Terrell should not try to enter segregated spaces based on her lighter skin color: "Joan questioned me about going places where dark complexioned people can't go. I told her I go where I want to go and allow no one to forbid me from going anywhere on account of my color. She evidently thinks I shouldn't do it. I told her on the same principle, she shouldn't go anywhere colored people can't go." MCT Diary, March 2, 7, 1951, MCT Papers, reel 2; Caplan, "Lost Laws," 439.

18. Rev. Arthur F. Elmes of the People's Congregational Church participated with Terrell in a second test case at Thompson's Restaurant. Caplan, "Lost Laws," 436.

19. In 1944, HUAC had labeled the NLG, which had several American Communist Party members on staff, as the "'legal bulwark of the Communist Party.'" During the Red Scare, the NLG was repeatedly accused of being a subversive organization and defended people interrogated by HUAC, such as the Rosenbergs and the Hollywood Ten.

Bailey, "Case of the National Lawyers Guild," 146; Caplan, *Farther Along*, 116; Small-wood, *Reform*, 122.

20. MCT, "Concerning the Supreme Court's Decision Opening Southern Institutions to Colored Students," *Our World*, ca. June 1950, MCT Papers, reel 22.

21. Caplan, "Lost Laws,"437.

22. "Minutes, Special Meeting," May 28, 1951, announcing their victory in the Municipal Court of Appeals; and "Minutes of the June 15th Mass Meeting Committee," May 29, 1951, Chairman Mrs. Mary Church Terrell, both in Coordinating Committee for Enforcement, Minutes, 1950–1954, MCT Papers, reel 14.

23. MCT Diary, January 11, April 29, 1951, MCT Papers, reel 2.

24. Caplan, "Lost Laws," 439.

25. It organized groups and individuals "to adopt a restaurant" to monitor all restaurants on the list for compliance. "In June 1950, the Coordinating Committee issued its first list of white-owned District restaurants that served without discrimination—about twenty of them. The list was an immediate best-seller." By 1953, sixty restaurants were on the list. Terrell heralded the NLG in a 1951 press release for taking on the *Thompson* case pro bono and winning it. Caplan, *Farther Along*, 117; Executive Committee Meeting Minutes, April 11, June 13, 1950; and "A Summary of the Status of Things: February 17, 1952," all in Coordinating Committee for Enforcement, Minutes, 1950–1954, MCT Papers, reel 14; MCT Diary, February 21, 1951, MCT Papers, reel 2; MCT, "For Immediate Release," May 25, 1951, Coordinating Committee for Enforcement, 1949–1954, MCT Papers, reel 14.

26. See Executive Committee meetings, June 13, 1950, February 1951, Coordinating Committee for Enforcement, Minutes, 1950–1954, MCT Papers, reel 14 (emphasis added).

27. Caplan, "Lost Laws," 440.

28. Terrell was interviewed on the radio, including on March 18, 1951, which she described as a "great day. Broadcast over Tomlinson Todd's 'Americans All.'" She ended with a critique of the government's persecution of the CRC, whose Ingram and D.C. coordinating committees she chaired. Asch and Musgrove, *Chocolate City*, 302; MCT Diary, January 16, 22, March 18, 1951, MCT Papers, reel 2; "Executive Committee Meeting Minutes," April 18, 1951, Coordinating Committee for Enforcement, Minutes, 1950–1954, MCT Papers, reel 14; MCT Diary, April 26, 1952, MCT Papers, reel 2.

29. Local 471 sent many women to picket, a technique used in their 1948 union strike. The Hecht's boycott started on May 1, 1951, a picket line began on July 20, 1951, and the store changed its policy on January 14, 1952. Terrell traveled to Baltimore "to see Hecht, owner of store." Caplan, "Lost Laws," 441–42; MCT Diary, May 11, 16, 1951, MCT Papers, reel 2; "A Summary of the Status of Things: February 17, 1952," Coordinating Committee for Enforcement, Minutes, 1950–1954, MCT Papers, reel 14.

30. One flyer, "Stay Out of Hecht's," featured a photo of her and stated: "Mrs. Mary Church Terrell, 88 year-old Committee Chairman, says . . . 'I have visited the capitals of many countries, but only in the capital of my own country have I been subjected to this indignity.'" Terrell made the same point in an earlier article. MCT, "What It Means to Be Colored in the Capital of the U.S.," *Independent*, 1906, 181–86; Sample Hecht's Flyers, 1951, Coordinating Committee for Enforcement, Miscellaneous, 1949–1954, MCT Papers, reel 14; MCT Diary, May 11, 1951, October 20, 1952, MCT Papers, reel 2.

31. Green, *Secret*, 297–98.

32. Thomas A. Church Jr. to MCT, July 15, 1951, HB.

33. Thomas continued, "Just be cautious. A lot of people would gladly urge and 'egg you on' to do and say things that they don't have the nerve and courage to say and do themselves." Nonetheless, Thomas shared her values. In 1954, he was stationed in South Korea, wishing he could watch the televised army/McCarthy hearings: "I hope the S. O. B. gets what's coming to him." Church to MCT, July 15, 1951, HB; Church (Taegu, Korea, via San Francisco) to Phyllis Terrell Langston, May 22, 1954, HB.

34. MCT Diary, May 24, 30, 1951, MCT Papers, reel 2.

35. MCT Diary, May 29, 30, 1951, MCT Papers, reel 2.

36. MCT Diary, June 15, 1951, MCT Papers, reel 2.

37. Terrell donated money to the committee, spoke at teas and other fundraisers, and solicited funds from individuals. In 1951, she hosted a party at her Highland Beach home that raised $113.41, one of the largest sums. Lists of contributors (including churches, black politicians, the Barristers Wives, the United Cafeteria Workers, Cooks, Pastry Cooks, #209, and Lambda Kappa Mu Sorority) showed support across economic and social classes. For her birthday in 1951, the committee had a banquet with "over 1000 supporters" who "rallied behind the spirited leadership of Mrs. Terrell. She has headed countless negotiations with restaurant proprietors, has lobbied on Capitol Hill, taken her place on picket lines and addressed hundreds of meetings in the interest of making the inactive [anti-]discrimination laws work." "Anti-Discrimination Laws Annual Statement of Receipts and Expenditures for Year Ending December 31, 1951," and "Executive Committee Meeting Minutes," April 18, 1951, both in Coordinating Committee for Enforcement, Minutes, 1950–1954, MCT Papers, reel 14; MCT Diary, May 28, June 16 1951, MCT Papers, reel 2; Al Sweeny, "Tribute to Mary Church Terrell," ca. September 18, 1951, Coordinating Committee for Enforcement, 1949–1954, MCT Papers, reel 14.

38. Earlier, Terrell reported, "Dinner at People's Cafeteria 11th and G Sts NW. Bad food. Ugly experience." MCT Diary, March 12, June 18, 1951, MCT Papers, reel 2; "A Summary of the Status of Things: February 17, 1952," Coordinating Committee for Enforcement, Minutes, 1950–1954, MCT Papers, reel 14.

39. Terrell wrote a 1952 letter to the *Washington Post* encouraging organizations not to hold their annual meetings in D.C. and praising the American Psychological Association for choosing to refrain from "meeting here again 'until such time as additional progress has been made toward treatment of minority groups.'" The Murphy's picketing ended in success in September 1952. Caplan, "Lost Laws," 443–44; Ransby, *Ella Baker*, 241–43; MCT Diary, July 24, September 14, 1952, MCT Papers, reel 2; "Press Release," Fall 1952; and Interview of Mary Church Terrell, April 6, 1954, both in Coordinating Committee for Enforcement, 1949–1954, MCT Papers, reel 14.

40. Two years later, Terrell testified before the Senate's District Committee, successfully opposing the appointment of Judge Frank Myers to the Municipal Court of Appeals in 1952. From her perspective, he had shown "bias against my group" and did not have "good legal judgment," since his ruling was reversed by the Municipal Court of Appeals. "Press Release," December 27, 1951; "Press Release," January 22, 1953; and "Facts on the Thompson Restaurant Decision" of the U.S. Court of Appeals, February 1, 1953, all in Coordinating Committee for Enforcement, 1949–1954, MCT Papers, reel 14.

41. MCT Diary, November 28, December 8, 1952, MCT Papers, reel 2; Annie Stein to MCT, March 25, 1953, MCT Additions.

42. The Democratic Truman administration and Republican Eisenhower administrations both filed friend of the court briefs on behalf of the committee. So did twenty-two other groups and organizations, including the ACLU, AFL, CIO, and NCNW. As quoted in Caplan, "Lost Laws," 444–45; Dr. Mary Church Terrell, "Testimony Opposing the Appointment of Judge Frank Myers to the Municipal Court of Appeals," Heard by the Senate District Committee, July 4, 1952; "Background of the Appeal in the Thompson Restaurant Case to Be Heard in the U.S. Court of Appeals, Jan. 7, 1952"; and "Coordinating Committee Press Release," June 9, 1953, all in Coordinating Committee for Enforcement, 1949–1954, MCT Papers, reel 14.

43. The coordinating committee created a Mary Church Terrell Fund, and Mamie Eisenhower sent a formal birthday greeting to be read at the party. Mamie Eisenhower to MCT, October 5, 1953, MCT Papers, reel 20; "Committee for Establishing the Mary Church Terrell Fund," September 11, 1953, Coordinating Committee for Enforcement, 1949–1954, MCT Papers, reel 14; MCT Diary, February 8, 1954, MCT Papers, reel 2.

44. "Executive Committee Meeting Minutes," June 25, 1953; and "Theater Test Case Committee Report," September 3, 1953, both in Coordinating Committee for Enforcement, Minutes, 1950–1954, MCT Papers, reel 14.

45. In 1953, Terrell mailed out a letter of support for Julius and Ethel Rosenberg: "I know from my long experience with the troubles of my people, that injustice can exist in America." See McGuire, *Dark End of the Street*; and MCT, letter to friends and associates, 1953, MCT Papers, reel 20.

46. Gore, *Radicalism*, 74–80.

47. The D.C. delegation likely included Terrell. The committee widely distributed a July 1948 *Pittsburgh Courier* interview in which Ingram described her assailant as sexually predatory. Gore, *Radicalism*, 79, 82; MCT Diary, March 10, 1949, HB.

48. Operating out of D.C., Terrell received frequent requests for action and advice from Katz and Jackson in New York. As chair, Terrell monitored the fundraising efforts, making sure the money was well spent. Gore, *Radicalism*, 82; MCT Diary, April 24, 26, May 18, June 30, 1949, HB.

49. The men were Philleo Nash and David K. Niles. MCT Diary, May 24, 27, 31, June 1, 1949, HB. The petition, written by Du Bois (with a long addendum by Terrell), stated: "The undersigned colored women of the United States, legal citizens, voters, wives, and mothers have commissioned Dr. W. E. B. Du Bois to draw up this petition." MCT Diary, May 29, 1949, HB; W. E. B. Du Bois, "A Petition to the Human Rights Commission of the Social and Economic Council of the United Nations; and to the General Assembly of the United Nations, and to the Several Delegations of the Member States of the United Nations," September 19, 1949 (also listed as MCT, "Petitions to the U.N. Protesting Discrimination in the U.S. and the Rosa Ingram Case"), MCT Papers, reel 22.

50. McDuffie, *Sojourning for Freedom*, 166.

51. MCT Diary, September 21, 1949, HB.

52. In 1953, Weltfish was investigated by Senator Joseph McCarthy for writing ostensibly subversive articles and subsequently lost her teaching job at Columbia. Katz, "Learning from History," 82–86; Castledine, "Quieting the Chorus," 57; MCT Diary, June 19, 22, September 21, 1949, HB.

53. In the petition, Du Bois criticized the Commission on Human Rights for declining to confront directly human rights abuses around the globe, especially in democratic countries like the United States. Katz, "Learning from History," 82–86; HB; Du Bois, "Petition to the U.N."; MCT Diary, September 13, 1949, HB.

54. Terrell supported the CRC's "We Declare Genocide" campaign and saw William Patterson speak about it in D.C. MCT, "Petitions to the U.N."

55. MCT, "Petitions to the U.N."

56. MCT, "Petitions to the U.N."

57. Gilmore, *Defying Dixie*, 407–9; Dudziak, *Cold War Civil Rights*, 44–45, 63–66; Anderson, *Eyes Off the Prize*, 160; Plummer, "Introduction," *Window on Freedom*, 4–5; Lauren, "Seen from the Outside," 28–29; Carol Anderson, "Bleached Souls and Red Negroes," 94–95; MCT, "Petitions to the U.N."

58. Shirley Graham married W. E. B. Du Bois in 1951. Diplomat Alva Myrdal, acting assistant secretary general of the Department of Social Affairs of the U.N. Secretariat, was the wife of Gunnar Myrdal, author of the groundbreaking best-seller *An American Dilemma: The Negro Problem and Modern Democracy* (1944). MCT Diary, September 21, 22, 1949, HB; MCT to Phyllis Terrell, September 21, 1949, HB; MCT Diary, 1949 inside cover, HB.

59. Imani Perry argues perceptively that "Terrell's stature allowed her to serve as a bridge between organizations with deep political differences," showing continuing "ties between the mainstream and radical black activists." Perry, *May We Forever Stand*, 137; McDuffie, *Sojourning for Freedom*, 175–76; Gore, *Radicalism*, 85–98; MCT Diary, September 23, October 4, 1952, MCT Papers, reel 2.

60. Stein wanted Terrell to add a chapter to her autobiography: "I wish I were with you and could help to put in the story of your work for Rosa Lee Ingram." Gore, *Radicalism*, 84–94; Annie Stein to MCT, January 9, March 29, 1954, MCT Additions.

61. Dayo F. Gore argues that "the WCEJ suffered a major blow in July 1954 with the passing of Mary Church Terrell. She was a singular figure among black women activists, and her stature and her investment in the work had provided the WCEJ with access to a network of African American organizations." Fradin and Fradin, *Fight On!*, 162; Gore, *Radicalism*, 96.

Conclusion

1. Cooper, *Beyond Respectability*, chap. 2.

2. Quoted in Ross, *Witnessing and Testifying*, 223–24. See Schechter, "'All the Intensity," 48–77; and Lorde, "Uses of Anger," 124–33. MCT Diary and Notes, 1916, 8, HB.

3. Anachebe, "Racial and Ethnic Disparities."

4. Not immune to the threat of assault, when Terrell traveled the lecture circuit throughout the South, local African American women warned her whenever she was in an area in which white men were, at that moment, systematically raping and attacking black women who dared travel at night. McGuire, *Dark End of the Street*, 26–27, 65.

5. Mollie Church Terrell's longevity presents an opportunity to consider the historiography of the entire era from the 1860s through the 1950s. Some scholars identify the 1920s and 1930s as the birth of the Civil Rights Movement. Others point to that time

as simply marking some of its critical antecedents, noting that African Americans did not build a mass movement. Self, *American*, 11; Lieberman and Lang, "Introduction," 4, 6; Sugrue, *Sweet Land of Liberty*, xvi; Lang, "Freedom," 164. MCT Diary, September 23, 1949, HB.

6. "Paul Robeson Extols Mary Church Terrell," news release, July 28, 1954, series E, box 21, Paul and Eslanda Robeson Papers, Moorland-Spingarn Research Center, Howard University, Washington, D.C.

BIBLIOGRAPHY

Archival Sources

Robert R. Church Family Papers, University of Memphis Libraries, Special
    Collections
Oscar Stanton DePriest Papers, Chicago History Museum
W. E. B. Du Bois Papers (MS 312), Special Collections and University Archives,
    University of Massachusetts, Amherst Libraries
National Association of Colored Women's Clubs, New York Public Library,
    Schomburg Center for Research in Black Culture
Paul and Eslanda Robeson Papers, Moorland-Spingarn Research Center, Howard
    University, Washington, D.C.
Mary Church Terrell Collection, Moorland-Spingarn Research Center, Howard
    University, Washington, D.C.
Mary Church Terrell Collection, Oberlin College Archives, Oberlin, Ohio
Mary Church Terrell, Collection Addition, Moorland-Spingarn Research Center,
    Howard University, Washington, D.C.
Mary Church Terrell Papers, Library of Congress.
Robert Heberton Terrell Papers, Library of Congress
[Note: I have standardized Mary Church Terrell's punctuation throughout.]

Private Family Collections

Mary Church Terrell private collection, the Langston/Terrell family, Highland
    Beach, Maryland. Most of these papers are now in the Oberlin College Archives.
Oscar Stanton DePriest private collection, DePriest family, Chicago

Newspapers

Afro-American Ledger (Baltimore)
Atlanta Daily World
Batesville (Ark.) Guard
Bay State Banner (Boston)
Cambridge (Mass.) Chronicle
Chicago Daily Tribune
Chicago Defender
Chicago Press
Chicago Times-Herald

Colored American Magazine
The Crisis
Indianapolis (Ind.) Freeman
Kansas City Plaindealer
Kentucky New Era (Hopkinsville)
Memphis Daily Appeal
Memphis Commercial Appeal
National Association Notes
New Journal and Guide (Norfolk, Va.)

New York Times	*Reading (Pa.) Eagle*
New York World	*Scranton (Pa.) Republican*
North American Review	*St. Louis Republic*
Philadelphia Inquirer	*Voice of the Negro*
Philadelphia Tribune	*Washington Bee*
Pittsburgh Courier	*Washington Star*
Providence (R.I.) Evening Tribune	*Washington Evening Star*
Public Ledger (Memphis)	*Washington Post*

Published Primary Sources

Byers, Mary Adelia. *Torn by War: The Civil War Journal of Mary Adelia Byers.* Edited by Samuel R. Phillips. Introduction by George Lankford. Norman: University of Oklahoma Press, 2013.

Chesnutt, Charles Waddell, Robert C. Leitz, and Joseph R. McElrath, eds. *An Exemplary Citizen: Letters of Charles W. Chesnutt, 1906–1932.* Palo Alto, Calif.: Stanford University Press, 2002.

Church, R. R. "Last Will and Testament of R. R. Church." January 14, 1911. Reprinted in *Journal of Negro History* 65, no. 2 (1980): 158–63.

Cooper, Anna Julia. *A Voice from the South by a Black Woman of the South.* 1892; reprint, Chapel Hill: University of North Carolina Press, 2017.

Davis, James D. *Old Times Papers.* Memphis, Tenn.: Hite, Crumpton and Kelly, 1873.

Du Bois, W. E. B. *The Autobiography of W. E. B. Du Bois: A Soliloquy on Viewing My Life from the Last Decade of Its First Century.* 1968; reprint, New York: Oxford University Press, 2007.

———. "Of the Passing of the First Born." In *The Souls of Black Folk,* edited by Brent Hayes Edwards, 99–102. Oxford World's Classics. New York: Oxford University Press, 2007.

Fogelson, Robert M., and Rubenstein, Richard E., eds. *Mass Violence in America: Memphis Riots and Massacres.* Reprint ed. New York: Arno and New York Times, 1969.

Foner, Philip S., ed. *Frederick Douglass: Selected Speeches and Writings.* Abridged and adapted by Yuval Taylor. Chicago: Lawrence Hill Books, 1999.

Goelet, Augustin H. *The Technique of Surgical Gynecology: Devoted Exclusively to a Description of the Technique of Gynecological Operations.* New York: International Journal of Surgery, 1900.

Jacobs, Harriet. *Incidents in the Life of a Slave Girl.* Edited by Jean Fagan Yellin. Enlarged ed. Cambridge, Mass.: Harvard University Press, 2000.

Jones, Beverly. *Quest for Equality: The Life and Writings of Mary Eliza Church Terrell, 1863–1954.* Brooklyn, N.Y.: Carlson, 1990.

Lee, George W. *Beale Street, Where the Blues Began.* 1934; reprint, College Park, Md.: McGrath, 1969.

Massey, G. Betton. *Conservative Gynecology and Electro-Therapeutics: A Practical Treatise on the Diseases of Women and Their Treatment by Electricity.* Philadelphia: F. A. Davis Co., Publishers, first edition, 1888.

McCluskey, Audrey Thomas, and Elaine M. Smith, eds. *Mary McLeod Bethune:*

Building a Better World; Essays and Selected Documents. Bloomington: Indiana University Press, 1999.

NACW Club Reports, 1906 Convention. "Colored Woman's League." In *Black Women in White America: A Documentary History*, edited by Gerda Lerner, 451. New York: Pantheon, 1972.

Perkins, Kathy A., and Judith L. Stephens, eds. *Strange Fruit: Plays on Lynching by American Women*. Bloomington: Indiana University Press, 1998.

Terrell, Mary Church. *A Colored Woman in a White World*. Washington, D.C.: Ransdell, 1940; reprinted and revised, National Association of Colored Women's Clubs Inc., 1968.

———. "The Duty of the National Association of Colored Women to the Race." In *"We Must Be Up and Doing": A Reader in Early African American Feminisms*, edited by Teresa C. Zackodnik, 254–64. Guelph, Ont.: Broadview, 2010.

———. "The French and Swiss Diaries of Mary Church Terrell, 1888–89: Introduction and Annotated Translation." Edited by Jennifer M. Wilks. *Palimpsest: A Journal on Women, Gender and the Black International* 3, no. 1 (2014): 8–32.

———. "Mary Church Terrell Protests to Jane Addams." In *Social Justice Feminists in the United States and Germany: A Dialogue in Documents, 1885–1933*, edited by Kathryn Kish Sklar, Anja Schuler, and Susan Strasser, 280–82. Ithaca, N.Y.: Cornell University Press, 1998.

———. "What Role Is the Educated Negro Woman to Play in the Uplifting of Her Race?" In *Quest for Equality: The Life and Writings of Mary Eliza Church Terrell, 1863–1954*, edited by Beverly W. Jones, 155–56. Brooklyn, N.Y.: Carlson, 1990.

Washington, Booker T. *Booker T. Washington Papers*, vol. 5: *1899–1900*. Edited by Louis R. Harlan, Raymond W. Smock, and Barbara S. Kraft. Urbana: University of Illinois Press, 1976.

Wells-Barnett, Ida B. *Crusade for Justice: The Auto-Biography of Ida B. Wells*. Edited by Alfreda M. Duster. Chicago: University of Chicago Press, 1972.

———. *Southern Horrors and Other Writings: The Anti-Lynching Campaign of Ida B. Wells, 1892–1900*. Edited by Jacqueline Jones Royster. Boston: Bedford/St. Martin's Press, 1997.

Secondary Sources

Abdur-Rahman, Aliyyah I. *Against the Closet: Black Political Longing and the Erotics of Race*. Durham, N.C.: Duke University Press, 2012.

Adams, Francis D., and Barry Sanders. *Alienable Rights: The Exclusion of African Americans in a White Man's Land, 1619–2000*. New York: HarperCollins, 2003.

Adams, Katherine H., and Michael L. Keene. *Alice Paul and the American Suffrage Campaign*. Urbana: University of Illinois Press, 2008.

Alexander, Adele Logan. *Homelands and Waterways: The American Journey of the Bond Family, 1846–1926*. New York: Pantheon, 1999.

———. *Parallel Worlds: The Remarkable Gibbs-Hunts and the Enduring (In)significance of Melanin*. Charlottesville: University of Virginia Press, 2010.

Alexander, Shawn Leigh. *An Army of Lions: The Civil Rights Struggle before the NAACP*. Philadelphia: University of Pennsylvania Press, 2012.

Ali, Omar H. *In the Balance of Power: Independent Black Politics and Third-Party Movements in the United States.* Athens: Ohio University Press, 2008.

Alldredge, Everett O. *Centennial History of First Congregational United Church of Christ Washington, D.C., 1865–1965.* Baltimore: Port City Press, 1965.

Amenta, Edwin. *When Movements Matter: The Townsend Plan and the Rise of Social Security.* Princeton, N.J.: Princeton University Press, 2008.

Anachebe, Ngozi F. "Racial and Ethnic Disparities in Infant and Maternal Mortality." *Ethnicity and Disease* 16, no. 2, suppl. 3 (Spring 2006): S3–71.

Anderson, Carol. "Bleached Souls and Red Negroes: The NAACP and Black Communists in the Early Cold War, 1948–1952." In *Window on Freedom: Race, Civil Rights, and Foreign Affairs, 1945–1988,* edited by Brenda Gayle Plummer, 93–114. Chapel Hill: University of North Carolina Press, 2002.

———. *Bourgeois Radicals: The NAACP and the Struggle for Colonial Liberation, 1941–1960.* New York: Cambridge University Press, 2015.

———. *Eyes Off the Prize: The United Nations and the African American Struggle for Human Rights, 1944–1955.* New York: Cambridge University Press, 2003.

Anderson, Karen Tucker. "Last Hired, First Fired: Black Women Workers during World War II." *Journal of American History* 69, no. 1 (June 1982): 82–97.

Anthony, Carl Sferrazza. *Florence Harding: The First Lady, the Jazz Age, and the Death of America's Most Scandalous President.* New York: William Morrow, 1998.

Antler, Joyce. "Having It All, Almost: Confronting the Legacy of Lucy Sprague Mitchell." In *The Challenge of Feminist Biography: Writing the Lives of Modern American Women,* edited by Sara Alpern et al., 97–113. Urbana: University of Illinois Press, 1992.

Aptheker, Bettina. *Woman's Legacy: Essays on Race, Sex, and Class in American History.* Amherst: University of Massachusetts Press, 1982.

Armfield, Felix L. *Eugene Kinckle Jones: The National Urban League and Black Social Work, 1910–1940.* Urbana: University of Illinois Press, 2014.

Armstrong, Julie Buckner. *Mary Turner and the Memory of Lynching.* Athens: University of Georgia Press, 2011.

Asch, Chris Myers, and George Derek Musgrove. *Chocolate City: A History of Race and Democracy in the Nation's Capital.* Chapel Hill: University of North Carolina Press, 2017.

Atwater, Deborah F. *African American Women's Rhetoric: The Search for Dignity, Personhood, and Honor.* New York: Lexington Books, 2009.

Austin, Allan W. *Quaker Brotherhood: Interracial Activism and the American Friends Service Committee, 1917–1950.* Urbana: University of Illinois Press, 2012.

Bailey, Percival R. "The Case of the National Lawyers Guild, 1939–1958." In *Beyond the Hiss Case: The FBI, Congress, and the Cold War,* edited by Athan G. Theoharis, 129–75. Philadelphia, Pa.: Temple University Press, 1982.

Bakare-Yusuf, Bibi. "The Economy of Violence: Black Bodies and the Unspeakable Terror." In *Feminist Theory and the Body: A Reader,* edited by Janet Price and Margrit Shildrick, 311–23. New York: Routledge, 1999.

Banner-Haley, Charles T. *The Fruits of Integration: Black Middle-Class Ideology and Culture, 1960–1990.* Jackson: University Press of Mississippi, 2010.

Bardaglio, Peter W. *Reconstructing the Household: Families, Sex, and the Law in the Nineteenth-Century South*. Chapel Hill: University of North Carolina Press, 2000.

Barksdale-Hall, Roland. "Entrepreneurs: Rise of Black Enterprise." In *Encyclopedia of African American History, 1619–1895: From the Colonial Period to the Age of Frederick Douglass*, vol. 2, edited by Paul Finkelman, 476–77. New York: Oxford University Press, 2006.

Barry, John M. *Rising Tide: The Great Mississippi Flood of 1927 and How It Changed America*. New York: Simon and Schuster, 1997.

Bass, Harold F., Jr. *Historical Dictionary of United States Political Parties*. Lanham, Md.: Scarecrow Press, 2009.

Bay, Mia. "The Battle for Womanhood Is the Battle for the Race: Black Women and Nineteenth-Century Racial Thought." In *Toward an Intellectual History of Black Women*, edited by Mia Bay et al., 75–92. Chapel Hill: University of North Carolina Press, 2015.

———. *To Tell the Truth Freely: The Life of Ida B. Wells*. New York: Hill and Wang, 2009.

Beardsley, Edward H. "Race as a Factor in Health." In *Women, Health, and Medicine in America: A Historical Handbook*, edited by Rima D. Apple, 122–31. New York: Garland, 1990.

Beemyn, Genny. *A Queer Capital: A History of Gay Life in Washington, D.C.* New York: Routledge, 2015.

Belknap, Michael R. *Federal Law and Southern Order: Racial Violence and Constitutional Conflict in the Post-Brown South*. Athens: University of Georgia Press, 1995.

Bellinger, Robert A. "The Hope of the Race: African Americans in White Colleges and Universities, 1890–1915." Ph.D. diss., Boston College, 2000.

Bellow, Adam. *In Praise of Nepotism: A History of Family Enterprise from King David to George W. Bush*. New York: Random House, 2003.

Bennett, Scott H. *Radical Pacifism: The War Resisters League and Gandhian Nonviolence in America, 1915–1963*. Syracuse, N.Y.: Syracuse University Press, 2003.

Berg, Manfred. *"The Ticket to Freedom": The NAACP and the Struggle for Black Political Integration*. Gainesville: University Press of Florida, 2005.

Berlin, Ira, et. al. *Slaves No More: Three Essays on Emancipation and the Civil War*. New York: Cambridge University Press, 1992.

Bigglestone, W. E. "Oberlin College and the Negro Student, 1865–1940." *Journal of Negro History* 56, no. 3 (July 1971): 198–219.

Biles, Roger. *The South and the New Deal*. Lexington: University Press of Kentucky, 1994.

Biondi, Martha. *To Stand and Fight: The Struggle for Civil Rights in Postwar New York City*. Cambridge, Mass.: Harvard University Press, 2003.

Blackwell, Joyce. *No Peace without Freedom: Race and the Women's International League for Peace and Freedom, 1915–1955*. Carbondale: Southern Illinois University Press, 2004.

Blackwell-Johnson, Joyce. "Peace without Freedom Is Not an Option: Race and the Women's International League for Peace and Freedom, 1914–1945." In *Living War, Thinking Peace (1914–1924): Women's Experiences, Feminist Thought, and*

International Relations, edited by Geraldine Ludbrook and Bruna Bianchi, 239–63. Newcastle upon Tyne, U.K.: Cambridge Scholars, 2016.

Blain, Keisha N., Asia Leeds, and Ula Y. Taylor. "Women, Gender Politics, and Pan-Africanism." *Women, Gender, and Families of Color* 4, no. 2 (Fall 2016): 139–43.

Blee, Kathleen M. *Women of the Klan: Racism and Gender in the 1920s*. Berkeley: University of California Press, 1991.

Blight, David W. *Race and Reunion*. Cambridge, Mass.: Harvard University Press, 2009.

Blum, Edward J. *Reforging the White Republic: Race, Religion, and American Nationalism, 1865–1898*. Baton Rouge: Louisiana State University Press, 2005.

Blumenthal, Henry. "Woodrow Wilson and the Race Question." *Journal of Negro History* 48, no. 1 (January 1963): 1–21.

Bogdan, Janet Carlisle. "Childbirth in America, 1650 to 1900." In *Women, Health, and Medicine in America: A Historical Handbook*, edited by Rima Dombrow Apple, 101–20. New Brunswick, N.J.: Rutgers University Press, 1992.

Bolt, Christine. *Sisterhood Questioned: Race, Class and Internationalism in the American and British Women's Movements, c. 1880s–1970s*. London: Routledge, 2004.

Bond, Beverly G., and Janann Sherman. *Images of America: Beale Street*. Charleston, S.C.: Arcadia, 2006.

Boobbyer, Philip. "B. H. Streeter and the Oxford Group." *Journal of Ecclesiastical History* 61, no. 3 (July 2010): 541–67.

———. *The Spiritual Vision of Frank Buchman*. University Park: Pennsylvania State University Press, 2013.

Booth, Cynthia J. "The Herculean Task: Anna Julia Cooper and Mary Church Terrell's Struggle to Establish the Black Woman's Voice in the American Feminist and Civil Rights Movement." M.A. thesis, University of Central Oklahoma, 1997.

Boris, Eileen. "The Power of Motherhood: Black and White Activist Women Redefine the 'Political.'" In *Mothers of a New World: Maternalist Politics and the Origins of Welfare States*, edited by Seth Koven and Sonya Michel, 213–45. New York: Routledge, 1993.

Borstelmann, Thomas. *The Cold War and the Color Line: American Race Relations in the Global Arena*. Cambridge, Mass.: Harvard University Press, 2001.

Bredbenner, Candice Lewis. *A Nationality of Her Own: Women, Marriage, and the Law of Citizenship*. Berkeley: University of California Press, 1998.

Brewer, Mark D., and Jeffery M. Stonecash. *Dynamics of American Political Parties*. New York: Cambridge University Press, 2009.

Briggs, Laura. *Reproducing Empire: Race, Sex, Science, and U.S. Imperialism in Puerto Rico*. Berkeley: University of California Press, 2002.

Brinkley, Alan. *The End of Reform: New Deal Liberalism in Recession and War*. New York: Vintage, 1995.

———. *Voices of Protest: Huey Long, Father Coughlin, and the Great Depression*. New York: Alfred A. Knopf, 1982.

Broderick, Francis L. *W. E. B. Du Bois: Negro Leader in a Time of Crisis*. Palo Alto, Calif.: Stanford University Press, 1959.

Broussard, Albert S. "The Worst of Times: African Americans during the Great

Depression." In *Great Depression: People and Perspectives*, edited by Hamilton Cravens, 105–126. Santa Barbara, Calif.: ABC-CLIO, 2009.

Broussard, Jinx C. "Mary Church Terrell: A Black Woman Journalist and Activist Seeks to Elevate Her Race." *American Journalism* 19, no. 4 (October 2002): 13–35.

Brown, Elsa Barkley. "Imaging Lynching: African American Women, Communities of Struggle, and Collective Memory." In *African American Women Speak Out on Anita Hill–Clarence Thomas*, edited by Geneva Smitherman, 100–124. Detroit, Mich.: Wayne State University Press, 1995.

———. "To Catch the Vision of Freedom: Reconstructing Southern Black Women's Political History, 1865–1880." In *Unequal Sisters: A Multicultural Reader in U.S. Women's History*, 3rd ed., edited by Vicki L. Ruiz and Ellen Carol DuBois, 124–46. New York: Routledge, 2000.

———. "'What Has Happened Here': The Politics of Difference in Women's History and Feminist Politics." *Feminist Studies* 18, no. 1 (Summer 1992): 295–312.

Brown, Lois. *Pauline Elizabeth Hopkins: Black Daughter of the Revolution*. Chapel Hill: University of North Carolina Press, 2014.

Brown, Mary Jane. *Eradicating This Evil: Women in the American Anti-Lynching Movement, 1892–1940*. New York: Garland, 2000.

Brown, Nikki. *Private Politics and Public Voices: Black Women's Activism from World War I to the New Deal*. Bloomington: Indiana University Press, 2006.

Browne-Marshall, Gloria J. *Race, Law, and American Society, 1607 to Present*. New York: Taylor and Francis, 2007.

Brumfield, Dale M. *Virginia State Penitentiary: A Notorious History*. Charleston, S.C.: Arcadia, 2017.

Brundage, W. Fitzhugh. "'Woman's Hand and Heart and Deathless Love': White Women and the Commemorative Impulse in the New South." In *Monuments to the Lost Cause: Women, Art, and the Landscapes of Southern Memory*, edited by Cynthia Mills and Pamela H. Simpson, 64–84. Lexington: University of Tennessee Press, 2003.

Buckley, Gail. *American Patriots: The Story of Blacks in the Military from the Revolution to Desert Storm*. New York: Random House, 2001.

Buick, Kirsten P. "The Ideal Works of Edmonia Lewis: Invoking and Inverting Autobiography." In *Reading American Art*, edited by Marianne Doezema and Elizabeth Milroy, 190–207. New Haven, Conn.: Yale University Press, 1998.

Bundles, A'Lelia. *On Her Own Ground: The Life and Times of Madam C. J. Walker*. New York: Simon and Schuster, 2001.

Burris, William C. *Duty and the Law: Judge John J. Parker and the Constitution*. Bessemer, Ala.: Colonial Press, 1987.

Buss, C., et al. "High Pregnancy Anxiety during Mid-Gestation Is Associated with Decreased Gray Matter Density in 6–9-Year-Old Children." *Psychoneuroendocrinology* 35 (2010): 141–53.

Butchart, Ronald E. *Schooling the Freed People: Teaching, Learning, and the Struggle for Black Freedom, 1861–1876*. Chapel Hill: University of North Carolina Press, 2010.

Bynum, Cornelius L. *A. Philip Randolph and the Struggle for Civil Rights*. Urbana: University of Illinois, 2010.

Byrd, W. Michael, and Linda A. Clayton. *An American Health Dilemma: Race, Medicine and Health Care in the United States, 1900–2000.* Vol. 2. New York: Routledge, 2001.

Campt, Tina. *Other Germans: Black Germans and the Politics of Race, Gender, and Memory in the Third Reich.* Ann Arbor: University of Michigan Press, 2004.

Caplan, Marvin Harold. *Farther Along: A Civil Rights Memoir.* Baton Rouge: Louisiana State University Press, 1999.

Carby, Hazel V. *Reconstructing Womanhood: The Emergence of the Afro-American Woman Novelist.* New York: Oxford University Press, 1997.

Carle, Susan D. *Defining the Struggle: National Organizing for Racial Justice, 1880–1915.* New York: Oxford University Press, 2013.

Carson, Carolyn Leonard. "And the Results Showed Promise . . . Physicians, Childbirth, and Southern Black Migrant Women, 1916–1930: Pittsburgh as a Case Study." In *Women and Health in America: Historical Readings,* edited by Judith Walzer Leavitt, 348–62. Madison: University of Wisconsin Press, 1999.

Cash, Floris Barnett. *African American Women and Social Action: The Clubwomen and Volunteerism from Jim Crow to the New Deal, 1896–1936.* Westport, Conn.: Greenwood, 2001.

Castledine, Jacqueline. "Quieting the Chorus: Progressive Women's Race and Peace Politics in Postwar New York." In *Anticommunism and the African American Freedom Movement: "Another Side of the Story,"* edited by Robbie Lieberman and Clarence Lang, 51–79. New York: Palgrave, 2009.

Catsam, Derek Charles. "Early Economic Civil Rights in Washington, D.C.: The New Negro Alliance, Howard University, and the Interracial Workshop." In *The Economic Civil Rights Movement: African Americans and the Struggle for Economic Power,* edited by Michael Ezra, 46–57. New York: Routledge, 2013.

———. *Freedom's Main Line: The Journey of Reconciliation and the Freedom Rides.* Lexington: University Press of Kentucky, 2009.

Chandler, Susan. "Addie Hunton and the Construction of an African American Female Peace Perspective." *AFFILIA* 20, no. 3 (Fall 2005): 270–83.

Chapman, Erin D. *Prove It on Me: New Negroes, Sex, and Popular Culture in the 1920s.* New York: Oxford University Press, 2012.

Childs, John Brown. "Red Clay, Blue Hills: In Honor of My Ancestors." In *Readings for Diversity and Social Justice: An Anthology on Racism, Sexism, Anti-Semitism, Heterosexism, Classism, and Ableism,* edited by Maurianne Adams et al., 100–114. New York: Routledge, 2000.

Chittenden, Elizabeth F. "As We Climb: Mary Church Terrell." *Negro History Bulletin* 38, no. 3 (March 1975): 351–54.

Church, Annette E., and Roberta Church. *The Robert R. Churches of Memphis: A Father and Son Who Achieved in Spite of Race.* Ann Arbor, Mich.: Edwards Brothers, 1974.

Clark, Emily. *The Strange History of the American Quadroon: Free Women of Color in the Revolutionary Atlantic World.* Chapel Hill: University of North Carolina Press, 2013.

Clark-Lewis, Elizabeth. "'This Work Had an End': African-American Domestic Workers in Washington, D.C., 1910–1940." In *"To Toil the Livelong Day": America's*

Women at Work, 1790–1980, edited by Carol Groneman and Mary Beth Norton, 196–213. Ithaca, N.Y.: Cornell University Press, 1987.

Clay, William L. *Just Permanent Interests: Black Americans in Congress, 1870–1991.* New York: Amistad, 1992.

Cobble, Dorothy Sue. *The Other Women's Movement: Workplace Justice and Social Rights in Modern America.* Princeton, N.J.: Princeton University Press, 2004.

Cole, Olen, Jr. *The African-American Experience in the Civilian Conservation Corps.* Gainesville: University of Florida Press, 1999.

Coleman, William T., with Donald Bliss. *Counsel for the Situation: Shaping the Laws to Realize America's Promise.* Washington, D.C.: Brookings Institution Press, 2010.

Collier-Thomas, Bettye. *Jesus, Jobs, and Justice: African American Women and Religion.* New York: Alfred A. Knopf, 2010.

Collins, Patricia Hill. *Black Feminist Thought: Knowledge, Consciousness, and the Politics of Empowerment.* New York: Routledge, 2000.

———. *Black Sexual Politics: African Americans, Gender, and the New Racism.* New York: Routledge, 2004.

Cooper, Brittney. *Beyond Respectability: The Intellectual Thought of Race Women.* Urbana: University of Illinois Press, 2017.

Coppens, Linda Miles. *What American Women Did, 1789–1920: A Year-by-Year Reference.* Jefferson, N.C.: McFarland, 2007.

Cott, Nancy F. "Feminist Politics in the 1920s: The National Woman's Party." *Journal of American History* 71, no. 1 (June 1984): 43–68.

Cox, Karen L. "The Confederate Monument at Arlington: A Token of Reconciliation." In *Monuments to the Lost Cause: Women, Art, and the Landscapes of Southern Memory,* edited by Cynthia Mills and Pamela H. Simpson, 149–62. Lexington: University of Tennessee Press, 2003.

Craig, Douglas B. *Progressives at War: William G. McAdoo and Newton D. Baker, 1863–1941.* Baltimore: Johns Hopkins University Press, 2013.

Crenshaw, Kimberlé, and Andrea J. Ritchie. *Say Her Name: Resisting Police Brutality against Black Women.* New York: African American Policy Forum, 2015.

Crosby, Emilye. "Introduction: The Politics of Writing and Teaching Movement History." In *Civil Rights History from the Ground Up: Local Struggles, a National Movement,* edited by Emilye Crosby, 1–39. Athens: University of Georgia Press, 2011.

Crosby, Molly Caldwell. *The American Plague: The Untold Story of Yellow Fever, the Epidemic That Shaped our History.* New York: Berkeley Books, 2006.

Cott, Nancy F. *The Grounding of Modern Feminism.* New Haven, Conn.: Yale University Press, 1987.

Countryman, Matthew J. *Up South: Civil Rights and Black Power in Philadelphia.* Philadelphia: University of Pennsylvania Press, 2007.

Curwood, Anastasia S. *Stormy Weather: Middle-Class African American Marriages between the Two World Wars.* Chapel Hill: University of North Carolina Press, 2010.

Dagbovie, Pero Galo. *The Early Black History Movement, Carter G. Woodson, and Lorenzo Johnston Greene.* Urbana: University of Illinois Press, 2007.

Danielson, Chris. *The Color of Politics: Racism in the American Political Arena Today.* Santa Barbara, Calif.: ABC-CLIO, 2013.

Dansker, Emil. "William Howard Taft." In *Popular Images of American Presidents*, edited by William C. Spragens, 211–38. Westport, Conn.: Greenwood, 1988.

Davis, Angela. *Women, Race, and Class*. New York: Vintage Books, 1991.

Davis, Deborah. *Guest of Honor: Booker T. Washington, Theodore Roosevelt, and the White House Dinner that Shocked a Nation*. New York: Simon and Schuster, 2013.

Davis, Richard. *Electing Justices: Fixing the Supreme Court Nomination Process*. New York: Oxford University Press, 2005.

———. *Justices and Journalists: The U.S. Supreme Court in the Media Age*. New York: Cambridge University Press, 2011.

D'Emilio, John, and Estelle B. Freedman. *Intimate Matters: A History of Sexuality in America*. New York: Harper and Row, 1988.

Diana, Vanessa Holford. "Narrative Patternings of Resistance in Frances E. W. Harper's *Iola Leroy* and Pauline Hopkins' *Contending Forces*." In *Black Women's Intellectual Traditions: Speaking Their Minds*, edited by Kristin Waters and Carol B. Conaway, 173–91. Burlington: University of Vermont Press, 2007.

Dickerson, Vanessa D. *Dark Victorians*. Urbana: University of Illinois Press, 2008.

Diepenbrock, David. "Black Women and Oberlin College in the Age of Jim Crow." *UCLA Historical Journal* 13 (1993): 27–59.

Dinkin, Robert J. *Before Equal Suffrage: Women in Partisan Politics from Colonial Times to 1920*. Westport, Conn.: Greenwood, 1995.

DiPietro, J. A. "The Role of Maternal Prenatal Stress in Child Development." *Current Directions in Psychological Science* 13, no. 2 (2004): 71–74.

Domhoff, G. William, and Michael J. Webber. *Class and Power in the New Deal: Corporate Moderates, Southern Democrats, and the Liberal-Labor Coalition*. Stanford, Calif.: Stanford University Press, 2011.

Dorrien, Gary. *The New Abolition: W. E. B. Du Bois and the Black Social Gospel*. New Haven, Conn.: Yale University Press, 2015.

Dorsey, Leroy G. *We Are All Americans, Pure and Simple: Theodore Roosevelt and the Myth of Americanism*. Tuscaloosa: University of Alabama Press, 2007.

Dossett, Kate. *Bridging Race Divides: Black Nationalism, Feminism, and Integration in the United States, 1896–1935*. Gainesville: University Press of Florida, 2008.

Drake, St. Clair, and Horace R. Cayton. *Black Metropolis: A Study of Negro Life in a Northern City*. Vol. 2. New York: Harper and Row, 1945; reprint 1962.

Drake, W. Avon. "Booker T. Washington: Racial Pragmatism Revisited." In *The Racial Pragmatism of Booker T. Washington*, edited by Donald Cunningen, Rutledge M. Dennis, and Myrtle Gonza Glascoe, 33–62. Bingley, U.K.: Emerald, 2006.

duCille, Ann. *The Coupling Convention: Sex, Text, and Tradition in Black Women's Fiction*. New York: Oxford University Press, 1993.

Dudden, Faye E. *Fighting Chance: The Struggle over Woman Suffrage in Reconstruction America*. New York: Oxford University Press, 2015.

Dudziak, Mary L. *Cold War Civil Rights: Race and the Image of American Democracy*. Princeton, N.J.: Princeton University Press, 2000.

Duncan, Otis Dudley, and Beverly Duncan. *The Negro Population of Chicago: A Study of Residential Succession*. Chicago: University of Chicago Press, 1957.

Dunlap, Leslie. "The Reform of Rape Laws and the Problem of White Men: Age of Consent Campaigns in the South, 1885–1910." In *Sex, Love, Race: Crossing*

Boundaries in North American History, edited by Martha Hodes, 352–72. New York: New York University Press, 1999.

Dunn, Susan. *Roosevelt's Purge: How FDR Fought to Change the Democratic Party.* Cambridge, Mass.: Belknap Press of Harvard University Press, 2010.

Durham, Walter T. *Nashville: The Occupied City: The First Seventeen Months— February 16, 1862, to June 30, 1863.* Nashville: Tennessee Historical Society, 1985.

DuRocher, Kristina. *Ida B. Wells: Social Activist and Reformer.* New York: Routledge, 2016.

Dye, Nancy Schrom, and Daniel Blake Smith. "Mother Love and Infant Death, 1750–1920." In *Women and Health in America: Historical Readings*, edited by Judith Walzer Leavitt, 91–110. Madison: University of Wisconsin Press, 1999.

Dyer, Thomas G. *Theodore Roosevelt and the Idea of Race.* Baton Rouge: Louisiana State University Press, 1980.

Edgerton, Robert B. *Hidden Heroism: Black Soldiers in America's Wars.* Boulder, Colo.: Westview, 2001.

Edsforth, Ronald, and Robert Asher, with the assistance of Raymond Boryczka. "The Speedup: The Focal Point of Workers' Grievances." In *Autowork*, edited by Robert Asher and Ronald Edsforth, 65–98. Albany: SUNY Press, 1995.

Eisenmann, Linda. *Higher Education for Women in Postwar America, 1945–1965.* Baltimore: Johns Hopkins University Press, 2006.

Elliot, Mark. *Color-Blind Justice: Albion Tourgee and the Quest for Racial Equality from the Civil War to* Plessy v. Ferguson. New York: Oxford University Press, 2008.

Elliot, Orrin Leslie. *Stanford: The First Twenty-Five Years.* Stanford, Calif.: Stanford University Press, 1937.

Ellis, Mark. *Race, War, and Surveillance: African Americans and the United States Government during World War I.* Bloomington: Indiana University Press, 2001.

Emberton, Carole. *Beyond Redemption: Race, Violence, and the American South after the Civil War.* Chicago: University of Chicago Press, 2013.

Engerman, Stanley L. "Changes in Black Fertility, 1880–1940." In *Family and Population in Nineteenth-Century America*, edited by Tamara K. Hareven and Maris A. Vinovskis, 126–53. Princeton, N.J.: Princeton University Press, 1978.

Erevelles, Nirmala, and Andrea Minear. "Unspeakable Offenses: Untangling Race and Disability in Discourses of Intersectionality." *Journal of Literary and Cultural Disability Studies* 4, no. 2 (2010): 127–46.

Erie, Steven P. *Rainbow's End: Irish-Americans and the Dilemmas of Urban Machine Politics, 1820–1985.* Berkeley: University of California Press, 1990.

Ervin, Keona K. *Gateway to Equality: Black Women and the Struggle for Economic Justice in St. Louis.* Lexington: University Press of Kentucky, 2017.

Etter-Lewis, Gwendolyn, and Richard Thomes, eds. *Lights of the Spirit: Historical Portraits of Black Bahai in North America, 1898–2000.* Wilmette, Ill.: Baha'i Publishing, 2006.

Evans, Stephanie Y. *Black Women in the Ivory Tower, 1850–1954: An Intellectual History.* Gainesville: University Press of Florida, 2007.

Fabi, M. Guilia. *Passing and the Rise of the African American Novel.* Urbana: University of Illinois Press, 2001.

Fairclough, Adam. *Better Day Coming: Blacks and Equality, 1890–2000.* New York: Viking, 2001.

Falby, Alison. "The Modern Confessional: Anglo-American Religious Groups and the Emergence of Lay Psychotherapy." *Journal of History of the Behavioral Sciences* 39, no. 3 (Summer 2003): 251–67.

Farr, Britanny. "The Question That Silences Women: An Interview with Gina Clayton, Founder and Executive Director of the Essie Justice Group." *Souls: A Critical Journal of Black Politics, Culture, and Society* 8, nos. 2–4 (April–December 2016): 459–62.

Fauntroy, Michael K. *Republicans and the Black Vote.* Boulder, Colo.: Lynne Rienner, 2007.

Feimster, Crystal N. *Southern Horrors: Women and the Politics of Rape and Lynching.* Cambridge, Mass.: Harvard University Press, 2009.

Felder, James L. *Civil Rights in South Carolina: From Peaceful Protests to Groundbreaking Rulings.* Charleston, S.C.: History Press, 2012.

Felstiner, Mary L. *Out of Joint: A Private and Public Story of Arthritis.* Lincoln: University of Nebraska Press, 2005.

Field, Corinne T. "Frances E. W. Harper and the Politics of Intellectual Maturity." In *Toward an Intellectual History of Black Women*, edited by Mia Bay et al., 110–26. Chapel Hill: University of North Carolina Press, 2015.

Finkelman, Paul. *African Americans and the Legal Profession in Historical Perspective.* New York: Garland, 1992.

Finley, Alexandra. "'Cash to Corinna': Domestic Labor and Sexual Economy in the 'Fancy Trade.'" *Journal of American History* 104, no. 2 (September 2017): 410–30.

Flannagan, Maureen A. *Seeing with Their Hearts: Chicago Women and the Vision of the Good City, 1871–1933.* Princeton, N.J.: Princeton University Press, 2002.

Foner, Eric. *Reconstruction: America's Unfinished Revolution, 1863–1877.* New York: Harper and Row, 1988.

Fontaine, Darcie S. "International League for Peace and Freedom." In *The Oxford Encyclopedia of Women in World History*, edited by Bonnie G. Smith, 600–601. New York: Oxford University Press, 2008.

Ford, Linda. "Alice Paul and the Politics of Nonviolent Protest." In *Votes for Women: The Struggle for Suffrage Revisited*, edited by Jean H. Baker, 174–86. New York: Oxford University Press, 2002.

Foreman, P. Gabrielle. *Activist Sentiments: Reading Black Women in the Nineteenth Century.* Urbana: University of Illinois Press, 2009.

Foster, Gaines M. *Moral Reconstruction: Christian Lobbyists and the Federal Legislation of Morality, 1865–1920.* Chapel Hill: University of North Carolina Press, 2002.

Fox, Stephen R. *The Guardian of Boston: William Monroe Trotter.* New York: Atheneum, 1970.

Fox-Genovese, Elizabeth. "My Statue, My Self: Autobiographical Writings of Afro-American Women." In *The Private Self: Theory and Practice of Women's Autobiographical Writings*, edited by Shari Benstock, 63–87. Chapel Hill: University of North Carolina Press, 1988.

———. *Within the Plantation Household: Black and White Women of the Old South.* Chapel Hill: University of North Carolina Press, 1998.

Fradin, Dennis Brindell, and Judith Bloom Fradin. *Fight On! Mary Church Terrell's Battle for Integration*. New York: Clarion Books, 2003.

Frady, Marshall. *Martin Luther King, Jr.: A Life*. New York: Penguin, 2005.

Francis, Megan Ming. *Civil Rights and the Making of the Modern American State*. New York: Cambridge University Press, 2014.

Frazier, E. Franklin. *Black Bourgeoisie: The Book That Brought the Shock of Self-Revelation to Middle-Class Blacks in America*. 1957; reprint, New York: Free Press, 1997.

Frederickson, Mary. "'I Know which Side I'm On': Southern Women in the Labor Movement in the Twentieth Century." In *Women, Work, and Protest: A Century of U.S. Women's Labor History*, edited by Ruth Milkman, 156–80. 1985; reprint, New York: Routledge, 2013.

Freedman, Estelle B. "Race and the Politics of Identity in U.S. Feminism." In *Unequal Sisters: An Inclusive Reader in U.S. Women's History*, 4th ed., edited by Vicki Ruiz and Ellen Carol DuBois, 1–14. New York: Routledge, 2008.

———. *Redefining Rape: Sexual Violence in the Era of Suffrage and Segregation*. Cambridge, Mass.: Harvard University Press, 2013.

Freeman, Jo. *A Room at a Time: How Women Entered Party Politics*. New York: Rowman and Littlefield, 2000.

Freund, David M. P. *Colored Property: State Policy and White Racial Politics in Suburban America*. Chicago: University of Chicago Press, 2007.

Frymer, Paul. *Uneasy Alliances: Race and Party Competition in America*. Princeton, N.J.: Princeton University Press, 2010.

Gailmard, Sean, and John W. Patty. *Learning while Governing: Expertise and Accountability in the Executive Branch*. Chicago: University of Chicago Press, 2013.

Gaines, Kevin K. *Uplifting the Race: Black Leadership, Politics, and Culture in the Twentieth Century*. Chapel Hill: University of North Carolina Press, 1996.

Gallicchio, Marc. *The African American Encounter with Japan and China: Black Internationalism in Asia, 1895–1945*. Chapel Hill: University of North Carolina Press, 2000.

Gallagher, Gary W., and Alan T. Nolan, eds. *The Myth of the Lost Cause and Civil War History*. Bloomington: Indiana University Press, 2001.

Garrow, David. *Bearing the Cross: Martin Luther King, Jr., and the Southern Christian Leadership Conference*. New York: William Morrow, 1986.

Gatewood, Willard. *Aristocrats of Color: The Black Elite, 1880–1920*. Fayetteville: University of Arkansas Press, 2000.

———. "John Hanks Alexander of Arkansas: Second Black Graduate of West Point." *Arkansas Historical Quarterly* 41 (Summer 1982): 103–28.

Gellman, Erik S. *Death Blow to Jim Crow: The National Negro Congress and the Rise of Militant Civil Rights*. Chapel Hill: University of North Carolina Press, 2012.

Gerson, Noel. *Harriet Beecher Stowe: A Biography*. 1976; reprint, Endeavour Media, 2018.

Giddings, Paula J. *Ida, a Sword among Lions: Ida B. Wells and the Campaign against Lynching*. New York: Amistad/HarperCollins, 2008.

———. "The Last Taboo." In *Race-ing Justice, En-gendering Power: Essays on Anita*

Hill, Clarence Thomas, and the Construction of Social Reality, edited by Toni Morrison, 441–70. New York: Pantheon Books, 1992.

———. *When and Where I Enter: The Impact of Black Women on Race and Sex in America*. 1984; reprint, New York: Amistad/HarperCollins, 2006.

Gidlow, Liette. "The Sequel: The Fifteenth Amendment, the Nineteenth Amendment, and Southern Black Women's Struggle to Vote." *Journal of the Gilded Age and Progressive Era* 17, no. 3 (2018): 433–44.

Gilkes, Cheryl Townsend. "'My Mother's God Is Mine': Finally, the Most Powerful Recognition of the Importance of Women to African American Religion." *Journal of African American History* 96, no. 3 (Summer 2011): 362–69.

Gilman, Sander L. "Black Bodies, White Bodies: Toward an Iconography of Female Sexuality in Late Nineteenth-Century Art, Medicine, and Literature." *Critical Inquiry* 12, no. 1 (Autumn 1985): 204–42.

Gilmore, Glenda Elizabeth. *Defying Dixie: The Radical Roots of Civil Rights, 1919–1950*. New York: W. W. Norton, 2008.

———. *Gender and Jim Crow*. Chapel Hill: University of North Carolina Press, 2013.

Ginzberg, Lori D. *Elizabeth Cady Stanton*. New York: Hill and Wang, 2009.

Glasrud, Bruce A. "Beginning the Trek: Douglass, Bruce, Black Conventions, Independent Parties." In *African Americans and the Presidency: The Road to the White House*, edited by Bruce A. Glasrud and Cary D. Vintz, 17–30. New York: Routledge, 2010.

Glenn, Evelyn Nakano. *Unequal Freedom: How Race and Gender Shaped American Citizenship and Labor*. Cambridge, Mass.: Harvard University Press, 2009.

Godshalk, David Fort. *Veiled Visions: The 1906 Atlanta Race Riot and the Reshaping of American Race Relations*. Chapel Hill: University of North Carolina Press, 2006.

Goethals, George R. *Presidential Leadership and African Americans: "An American Dilemma" from Slavery to the White House*. New York: Routledge, 2015.

Goggin, Jacqueline. *A Life in Black History: Carter G. Woodson*. Baton Rouge: Louisiana State University Press, 1993.

Goings, Kenneth W. *The NAACP Comes of Age: The Defeat of Judge John J. Parker*. Bloomington: Indiana University Press, 1990.

Goluboff, Risa L. *The Lost Promise of Civil Rights*. Cambridge, Mass.: Harvard University Press, 2007.

Gomez-Jefferson, Annetta Louise. *The Sage of Tawawa: Reverdy Cassius Ransom, 1861–1956*. Kent, Ohio: Kent State University Press, 2002.

Gordon, Ann D., with Bettye Collier-Thomas. *African American Women and the Vote, 1837–1965*. Amherst: University of Massachusetts Press, 1997.

Gordon, Ernest. "The Princeton Group." *Princeton History* no. 2 (1977): 34–43.

Gordon, Linda. *The Second Coming of the KKK: The Ku Klux Klan of the 1920s and the American Political Tradition*. New York: W. W. Norton, 2017.

———. *Woman's Body, Woman's Right: A Social History of Birth Control in America*. New York: Viking, 1976.

Gordon, Lynn. *Gender and Higher Education in the Progressive Era*. New Haven, Conn.: Yale University Press, 1990.

Gore, Dayo F. *Radicalism at the Crossroads: African American Women Activists in the Cold War*. New York: New York University Press, 2011.

Gosnell, Harold F. *Negro Politicians: The Rise of Negro Politics in Chicago.* 1935; reprint, Chicago: University of Chicago Press, 1967.

Gould, Lewis L. *The Presidency of Theodore Roosevelt.* Lexington: University Press of Kansas, 1991.

———. *The Republicans: A History of the Grand Old Party.* New York: Oxford University Press, 2014.

———. *Theodore Roosevelt.* New York: Oxford University Press, 2012.

Graham, Otis L., Jr. *An Encore for Reform: The Old Progressives and the New Deal.* New York: Oxford University Press, 1967.

Grant, Donald Lee. *The Way It Was in the South: The Black Experience in Georgia.* Athens: University of Georgia Press, 1993.

Green, Constance McLaughlin. *The Secret City: A History of Race Relations in the Nation's Capital.* Princeton, N.J.: Princeton University Press, 1967.

Green, Elna C. *Southern Strategies: Southern Women and the Woman Suffrage Question.* Chapel Hill: University of North Carolina Press, 2000.

Green, Paul M. "Anton J. Cermak: The Man and His Machine." In *The Mayors: The Chicago Political Tradition,* 4th ed., edited by Paul M. Green and Melvin G. Holi, 111–25. Carbondale: Southern Illinois University Press, 2013.

———. "Mayor Richard J. Daley and the Politics of Good Government." In *The Mayors: The Chicago Political Tradition,* 4th ed., edited by Paul M. Green and Melvin G. Holi, 144–59. Carbondale: Southern Illinois University Press, 2013.

Green, Sharony. "'Mr. Ballard, I Am Compelled to Write Again': Beyond Bedrooms and Brothels, a Fancy Girl Speaks." *Black Women, Gender, and Families* 5, no. 1 (Spring 2011): 17–40.

———. *Remember Me to Miss Louisa: Hidden Black-White Intimacies in Antebellum America.* DeKalb: Northern Illinois University Press, 2015.

Greenwald, Maurine Weiner. *Women, War, and Work: The Impact of World War I on Women Workers in the United States.* 1980; reprint, Ithaca, N.Y.: Cornell University Press, 1990.

Grimshaw, William J. *Bitter Fruit: Black Politics and the Chicago Machine, 1931–1991.* Chicago: University of Chicago Press, 1992.

Guglielmo, Thomas A. *White on Arrival: Italians, Race, Color and Power in Chicago, 1890–1945.* New York: Oxford University Press, 2003.

Gurstein, Rochelle. *The Repeal of Reticence: A History of America's Cultural and Legal Struggles over Free Speech, Obscenity, Sexual Liberation, and Modern Art.* New York: Hill and Wang, 1996.

Gustafson, Melanie Susan. *Women and the Republican Party, 1854–1924.* Urbana: University of Illinois Press, 2001.

Guy-Sheftall, Beverly. *Daughters of Sorrow: Attitudes toward Black Women, 1880–1920.* Brooklyn, N.Y.: Carlson, 1990.

———. "Introduction: The Evolution of Feminist Consciousness among African American Women." In *Words of Fire: An Anthology of African-American Feminist Thought,* edited by Beverly Guy-Sheftall, 1–22. New York: New Press, 2011.

———. "Where Are the Black Female Intellectuals?" In *Harold Cruse: The Crisis of the Negro Intellectual Reconsidered,* edited by Jerry Watts, 229–34. New York: Routledge, 2004.

Haber, Carole, and Brian Gratton. *Old Age and the Search for Security: An American Social History.* Indianapolis: Indiana University Press, 1993.

Hachey, Thomas. "Walter White and the American Negro Soldier in World War II: A Diplomatic Dilemma for Britain." In *Race and U.S. Foreign Policy during the Cold War,* edited by Michael L. Krenn and E. Nathaniel Gates, 333–51. New York: Taylor and Francis, 1998.

Hale, Grace Elizabeth. *Making Whiteness: The Culture of Segregation in the South, 1890–1940.* New York: Vintage Books, 1998.

Haley, Sarah. *No Mercy Here: Gender, Punishment, and the Making of Jim Crow Modernity.* Chapel Hill: University of North Carolina Press, 2016.

Hall, Jacquelyn Dowd. "The Long Civil Rights Movement and the Political Uses of the Past." *Journal of American History* 91, no. 4 (March 2005): 1233–63.

———. *Revolt against Chivalry: Jessie Daniel Ames and the Women's Campaign against Lynching.* New York: Columbia University Press, 1979.

Hanson, Joyce A. *Mary McCleod Bethune and Black Women's Political Activism.* Columbia: University of Missouri Press, 2003.

Harbaugh, William H. *Lawyer's Lawyer: The Life of John W. Davis.* New York: Oxford University Press, 1973.

Harlan, Louis R. *Booker T. Washington,* vol. 2: *The Wizard of Tuskegee, 1901–1915.* New York: Oxford University Press, 1983.

Harley, Sharon. "Beyond the Classroom: The Organizational Lives of Black Female Educators in the District of Columbia, 1890–1930." *Journal of Negro Education* 51, no. 3 (1982): 266–77.

———. "Black Women in a Southern City: Washington, D.C., 1890–1920." In *Sex, Race, and the Role of Women in the South,* edited by Joanne V. Hawks and Sheila L. Skemp, 59–74. Jackson: University of Mississippi Press, 1983.

———. "'Chronicle of a Death Foretold': Gloria Richardson, the Cambridge Movement, and the Radical Black Activist Tradition." In *Sisters in the Struggle: African American Women in the Civil Rights–Black Power Movement,* edited by Bettye Collier-Thomas and V. P. Franklin, 174–96. New York: New York University Press, 2001.

———. "Mary Church Terrell: Genteel Militant." In *Black Leaders of the Nineteenth Century,* edited by Leon Litwack and August Meier, 307–21. Urbana: University of Illinois Press, 1998.

———. "Speaking Up: The Politics of Black Women's Labor History." In *Women and Work,* vol. 6: *Exploring Race, Ethnicity, and Class,* edited by Elizabeth Higginbotham and Mary Romero, 28–45. Washington, D.C.: SAGE, 1997.

Harley, Sharon, and Rosalyn Terborg-Penn. *The Afro-American Woman: Struggles and Images.* Port Washington, N.Y.: Kennikat, 1978.

Harris, Abram Lincoln. *The Negro as Capitalist: A Study of Banking and Business among American Negroes.* New York: Haskell House, 1936.

Hedrick, Joan D. *Harriet Beecher Stowe: A Life.* New York: Oxford University Press, 1994.

Henderson, Mae G. "Toni Morrison's *Beloved*: Re-Membering the Body as Historical Text." In *Comparative American Identities: Race, Sex, and Nationality in the Modern Text,* edited by Hortense J. Spillers, 63–86. New York: Routledge, 1991.

Hendricks, Wanda A. *Fannie Barrier Williams: Crossing the Borders of Religion and Race*. Urbana: University of Illinois Press, 2014.

———. *Gender, Race, and Politics in the Midwest: Black Club Women in Illinois*. Bloomington: Indiana University Press, 1998.

———. "Ida B. Wells-Barnett and the Alpha Suffrage Club of Chicago." In *One Woman, One Vote: Rediscovering the Woman Suffrage Movement*, edited by Marjorie Spruill Wheeler, 263–76. Troutdale, Oreg.: NewSage, 1995.

———. "'Vote for the Advantage of Ourselves and Our Race': The Election of the First Black Alderman in Chicago." *Illinois Historical Journal* 87, no. 3 (Autumn 1994): 171–84.

Henry, Richard. *Eleanor Roosevelt and Adlai Stevenson*. New York: Palgrave Macmillan, 2010.

Herndl, Diana Price. "The Invisible (Invalid) Woman: African-American Women, Illness, and Nineteenth-Century Narrative." In *Women and Health in America: Historical Readings*, edited by Judith Walzer Leavitt, 131–45. Madison: University of Wisconsin Press, 1999.

Herskovits, Melville J. "Race Relations." *American Journal of Sociology* 35, no. 6 (May 1930): 1052–62.

Higginbotham, Evelyn Brooks. "African-American Women's History and the Metalanguage of Race," *Signs* 17, no. 2 (Winter 1992): 251–74.

———. "Beyond the Sound of Silence: Afro-American Women in History." *Gender and History* 1, no. 1 (Spring 1989): 65–75.

———. "Foreword." In *Freedom North: Black Freedom Struggles outside the South, 1940–1980*, edited by Jeanne Theoharis and Komozi Woodard, viii–xiv. New York: Palgrave, 2003.

———. "In Politics to Stay: Black Women Leaders and Party Politics in the 1920s." In *Unequal Sisters: An Inclusive Reader in U.S. Women's History*, 4th ed., edited by Vicki Ruiz and Ellen Carol DuBois, 289–302. New York: Routledge, 2008.

———. "Religion, Politics, and Gender: The Leadership of Nannie Helen Burroughs." In *This Far by Faith: Readings in African American Women's Religious Biography*, edited by Judith Weisenfeld and Richard Newman, 140–57. New York: Routledge, 1996.

———. *Righteous Discontent: The Women's Movement in the Black Baptist Church*. Cambridge, Mass.: Harvard University Press, 1993.

Higginbotham, F. Michael. *Ghosts of Jim Crow: Racism in Post-Racial America*. New York: New York University Press, 2013.

Hill, Patricia Ruth. *The World Their Household: The American Women's Foreign Mission Movement and Cultural Transformation, 1870–1920*. Ann Arbor: University of Michigan Press, 1985.

Hill, Robert A. "Annie Malone." In *Marcus Garvey: Life and Lessons, a Centennial Companion to the Marcus Garvey and Universal Negro Improvement Association Papers*, edited by Robert A. Hill and Barbara Blair, 406. Berkeley: University of California Press, 1987.

Hine, Darlene Clark. "For Pleasure, Profit, and Power: The Sexual Exploitation of Black Women." In *African American Women Speak Out on Anita Hill-Clarence Thomas*, edited by Geneva Smitherman, 168–77. Detroit, Mich.: Wayne State University Press, 1995.

———. *Hine Sight: Black Women and the Re-Construction of American History.* Brooklyn, N.Y.: Carlson, 1994.

———. "Rape and the Inner Lives of Black Women in the Middle West: Preliminary Thoughts on the Culture of Dissemblance." *Signs* 14, no. 4 (Summer 1989): 912–20.

———. "'We Specialize in the Wholly Impossible': The Philanthropic Work of Black Women." In *Lady Bountiful Revisited: Women, Philanthropy, and Power,* edited by Kathleen D. McCarthy, 70–93. New Brunswick, N.J.: Rutgers University Press, 1990.

Hine, Darlene Clark, and Kathleen Thompson. *A Shining Thread of Hope: The History of Black Women in America.* New York: Broadway Books, 1998.

Hodes, Martha. *Sex, Love, Race: Crossing Boundaries in North American History.* New York: New York University Press, 1999.

Hoff, Joan. *Law, Gender, and Injustice: A Legal History of U.S. Women.* New York: New York University Press, 1994.

Hoganson, Kristin L. *Fighting for American Manhood: How Gender Politics Provoked the Spanish-American and Philippine-American Wars.* New Haven, Conn.: Yale University Press, 1998.

Horne, Gerald. *Black and Red: W. E. B. Du Bois and the Afro-American Response to the Cold War, 1944–1963.* Albany: SUNY Press, 1986.

———. *Black Liberation/Red Scare: Ben Davis and the Communist Party.* Wilmington: University of Delaware Press, 1994.

———. *Black Revolutionary: William Patterson and the Globalization of the African American Freedom Struggle.* Urbana: University of Illinois Press, 2013.

———. "Race from Power: U.S. Foreign Policy and the General Crisis of White Supremacy." In *Window on Freedom: Race, Civil Rights, and Foreign Affairs, 1945–1988,* edited by Brenda Gayle Plummer, 45–66. Chapel Hill: University of North Carolina Press, 2003.

Horton, Carol A. *Race and the Making of American Liberalism.* New York: Oxford University Press, 2005.

Horton, James Oliver. "Black Education at Oberlin College: A Controversial Commitment." *Journal of Negro Education* 54, no. 4 (Autumn 1985): 477–99.

Howard, Irene. *The Struggle for Social Justice in British Columbia: Helena Gutteridge, the Unknown Reformer.* Vancouver: University of British Columbia Press, 2011.

Hull, Gloria T. *Color, Sex, and Poetry: Three Women Writers of the Harlem Renaissance.* Bloomington: Indiana University Press, 1987.

Hyde, Charles K. *Arsenal of Democracy: The American Automobile Industry in World War II.* Detroit, Mich.: Wayne State University Press, 2013.

Ingham, John N., and Lynne B. Feldman. "Robert R. Church." In *African-American Business Leaders: A Biographical Dictionary,* 137. Westport, Conn.: Greenwood, 1994.

Ingraham, Patricia Wallace. *The Foundation of Merit: Public Service in American Democracy.* Baltimore: Johns Hopkins University Press, 1995.

Jackson, David H. "Perry Wilbon Howard." In *African American Lives,* edited by Henry Louis Gates and Evelyn Brooks Higginbotham, 417–18. New York: Oxford University Press, 2004.

James, Joy. "Shadowboxing: Liberation Limbos—Ida B. Wells." In *Black Women's*

Intellectual Traditions: Speaking Their Minds, edited by Kristin Waters and Carol B. Conaway, 346–62. Burlington: University of Vermont Press, 2007.

———. *Transcending the Talented Tenth: Black Leaders and American Intellectuals*. New York: Routledge, 1997.

James, Rawn, Jr. *The Double V: How Wars, Protest, and Harry Truman Desegregated America's Military*. New York: Bloomsbury, 2014.

Janiewski, Dolores. "Seeking 'a New Day and a New Way': Black Women and Unions in the Southern Tobacco Industry." In *"To Toil the Livelong Day": American Women at Work, 1790–1980*, edited by Carol Groneman and Mary Beth Norton, 161–78. Ithaca, N.Y.: Cornell University Press, 1987.

———. "Sisters under Their Skins: Southern Working Women, 1880–1950." In *Sex, Race, and the Role of Women in the South*, edited by Joanne V. Hawks and Sheila L. Skemp, 13–35. Jackson: University of Mississippi Press, 1983.

Janney, Caroline E. *Burying the Dead but Not the Past: Ladies' Memorial Associations and the Lost Cause*. Chapel Hill: University of North Carolina Press, 2008.

Jaynes, Gerald D. "Banking and Finance." In *Encyclopedia of African American Society*, vol. 1, edited by Gerald D. Jaynes, 79–81. Troutdale, Oreg.: SAGE, 2005.

Jeffers, H. Paul. *Commissioner Roosevelt: The Story of Theodore Roosevelt and the New York City Police, 1895–1897*. New York: Wiley, 1996.

———. *The Napoleon of New York: Mayor Fiorello LaGuardia*. New York: John Wiley and Sons, 2002.

Jeffries, Hasan Kwame. *Bloody Lowndes: Civil Rights and Black Power in Alabama's Black Belt*. New York: New York University Press, 2010.

Jenkins, Earnestine Lovelle. *Race, Representation, and Photography in 19th-Century Memphis*. New York: Routledge, 2016.

Jensen, Kimberly. *Mobilizing Minerva: American Women in the First World War*. Urbana: University of Illinois Press, 2008.

Jewell, K. Sue. *From Mammy to Miss America and Beyond: Cultural Images and the Shaping of U.S. Social Policy*. New York: Routledge, 1993.

Johnson, Joan Marie. *Southern Women at the Seven Sister Colleges: Feminist Values and Social Activism, 1875–1915*. Athens: University of Georgia Press, 2010.

Johnson, Karen. *Uplifting the Women and the Race: The Lives, Educational Philosophies, and Social Activism of Anna Julia Cooper and Nannie Helen Burroughs*. New York: Routledge, 2001.

Jonas, Gilbert. *Freedom's Sword: The NAACP and the Struggle against Racism in America, 1909–1969*. New York: Rutledge, 2005.

Jones, Beverly W. "Before Montgomery and Greensboro: The Desegregation Movement in the District of Columbia, 1950–1953." *Phylon* 43, no. 2 (1982): 144–54.

———. "Mary Church Terrell and the National Association of Colored Women, 1896 to 1901." *Journal of Negro History* 67, no. 1 (1982): 20–33.

———. *Quest for Equality: The Life and Writings of Mary Eliza Church Terrell, 1863–1954*. Brooklyn, N.Y.: Carlson, 1990.

Jones, Jacqueline. *American Work: Four Centuries of Black and White Labor*. New York: W. W. Norton, 1998.

———. *Labor of Love, Labor of Sorrow: Black Women, Work, and the Family from Slavery to the Present*. New York: Vintage Books, 1985.

Jones, James H. *Bad Blood: The Tuskegee Syphilis Experiment*. New York: Free Press, 1993.

Jones, Martha S. *All Bound Up Together: The Woman Question in African American Public Culture, 1830–1900*. Chapel Hill: University of North Carolina Press, 2007.

———. "'Make Us a Power': African American Methodists Debate the 'Woman Question,' 1870–1900." In *Women and Religion in the African Diaspora: Knowledge, Power, and Performance*, edited by R. Marie Griffith and Barbara Dianne Savage, 128–54. Baltimore: Johns Hopkins University Press, 2006.

Jones, Thai. *A Radical Line: From the Labor Movement to the Weather Underground, One Family's Century of Conscience*. Albany: SUNY Press, 2007.

Jones, William P. *The March on Washington: Jobs, Freedom, and the Forgotten History of Civil Rights*. New York: W. W. Norton, 2013.

Jones-Branch, Cherisse. "Mary Church Terrell (1863–1954): Revisiting the Politics of Race, Class, and Gender." In *Tennessee Women: Their Lives and Times*, vol. 1, edited by Sarah Wilkerson Freeman and Beverly Green Bond, 68–92. Athens: University of Georgia Press, 2009.

Jordan, William. "'The Damnable Dilemma': African American Accommodation and Protest during World War I." *Journal of American History* 81, no. 4 (March 1995): 1562–83.

Joseph, Peniel E. "Black Liberation without Apology: Reconceptualizing the Black Power Movement." *Black Scholar* 31 (Fall–Winter 2001): 2–19.

Jost, Kenneth, ed. *The Supreme Court, A–Z*. New York: Routledge, 2013.

Jules-Rosette, Bennetta. *Josephine Baker in Art and Life: The Icon and the Image*. Urbana: University of Illinois Press, 2007.

Justesen, Benjamin R. *George Henry White: An Even Chance in the Race of Life*. Baton Rouge: Louisiana State University Press, 2001.

Kabaservice, Geoffrey. *Rule and Ruin: The Downfall of Moderation and the Destruction of the Republican Party from Eisenhower to the Tea Party*. New York: Oxford University Press, 2012.

Kahrl, Andrew W. *The Land Was Ours: How Black Beaches Became White Wealth in the Coastal South*. Chapel Hill: University of North Carolina Press, 2016.

Kaplan, Amy, and Donald E. Pease, eds. *Cultures of United States Imperialism*. Durham, N.C.: Duke University Press, 1993.

Kapsalis, Teri. *Public Privates: Performing Gynecology from Both Sides of the Speculum*. Durham, N.C.: Duke University Press, 1997.

Katz, Maude White. "Learning from History—The Ingram Case of the 1940s." *Freedomways* 19 (1979): 82–86.

Katznelson, Ira. *Fear Itself: The New Deal and the Origins of Our Time*. New York: W. W. Norton, 2013.

Kazin, Michael, Rebecca Edwards, and Adam Rothman. "Progressive Parties." In *The Princeton Encyclopedia of American Political History*, edited by Kazin, Edwards, and Rothman, 606. Princeton, N.J.: Princeton University Press, 2010.

Keith, Jeanette. *Fever Season*. New York: Bloomsbury, 2012.

Kelley, Blair L. M. *Right to Ride: Streetcar Boycotts and African American Citizenship in the Era of* Plessy v. Ferguson. Chapel Hill: University of North Carolina Press, 2010.

Kelley, Robin D. G. *Race Rebels: Culture, Politics, and the Black Working Class*. New York: Free Press, 1994.

———. "Stormy Weather: Reconstructing Black (Inter)Nationalism in the Cold War Era." In *Is It Nation Time? Contemporary Essays on Black Power and Black Nationalism*, edited by Eddie S. Glaude Jr., 67–90. Chicago: University of Chicago Press, 2002.

Kellogg, Charles Flint. *NAACP: A History of the National Association for the Advancement of Colored People*, vol. 1: *1909–1920*. Baltimore: Johns Hopkins University Press, 1967.

Kempski, Kara Elizabeth. "A Jim Crow Welcome Home: African American World War Veterans in Knoxville, Tennessee." M.A. thesis, University of Tennessee, Knoxville, 2012.

Kendi, Ibram X. *Stamped from the Beginning: The Definitive History of Racist Ideas in America*. New York: Public Affairs, 2016.

Kennedy, David M. *Freedom from Fear: The American People in Depression and War, 1929–1945*. New York: Oxford University Press, 1999.

Kerr, Audrey. *The Paper Bag Principle: Class, Complexion, and Community in Black Washington, D.C.* Knoxville: University of Tennessee Press, 2006.

Kessler-Harris, Alice. *In Pursuit of Equity: Women, Men, and the Quest for Economic Citizenship in 20th-Century America*. New York: Oxford University Press, 2001.

Kilson, Martin. "Adam Clayton Powell, Jr.: The Militant as Politician." In *Black Leaders of the Twentieth Century*, edited by John Hope Franklin and August Meier, 259–75. Urbana: University of Illinois Press, 1982.

King, Desmond. *Separate and Unequal: Black Americans and the U.S. Federal Government*. New York: Oxford University Press, 1995.

Kirby, John. *Black Americans in the Roosevelt Era: Liberalism and Race*. 1980; reprint, Knoxville: University of Tennessee Press, 1992.

Klarman, Michael J. *From Jim Crow to Civil Rights: The Supreme Court and the Struggle for Racial Equality*. New York: Oxford University Press, 2004.

Kleinman, Mark L. *A World of Hope, a World of Fear: Henry A. Wallace, Reinhold Niebuhr, and American Liberalism*. Columbus: Ohio State University Press, 2000.

Knight, Alisha. *Pauline Hopkins and the American Dream: An African American Writer's (Re)Visionary Gospel of Success*. Memphis: University of Tennessee Press, 2011.

Knupfer, Anne Meis. *The Chicago Black Renaissance and Women's Activism*. Urbana: University of Illinois Press, 2006.

———. *Toward a Tenderer Humanity and a Nobler Womanhood: African-American Women's Clubs in Turn-of-the-Century Chicago*. New York: New York University Press, 1996.

Kohn, Edward P. *Heir to the Empire City: New York and the Making of Theodore Roosevelt*. New York: Basic Books, 2013.

Kornblith, Gary, and Carol Lasser. *Elusive Utopia: The Struggle for Racial Equality in Oberlin, Ohio*. Baton Rouge: Louisiana State University Press, 2018.

Krenn, Michael L., ed. *Race and U.S. Foreign Policy from the Colonial Period to the Present: A Collection of Essays*. New York: Garland, 1998.

Krislov, Samuel. *The Negro in Federal Employment: The Quest for Equal Opportunity.*
   Minneapolis: University of Minnesota Press, 1967.
Kuersten, Ashlyn K. *Women and the Law: Leaders, Cases, and Documents.* Santa Bar-
   bara, Calif.: ABC-CLIO, 2003.
Kuhl, Michelle. "Countable Bodies, Uncountable Crimes: Sexual Assault and the
   Antilynching Movement." In *Interconnections: Gender and Race in American His-
   tory,* edited by Carol Faulkner and Alison M. Parker, 133–60. Rochester, N.Y.:
   University of Rochester Press, 2012.
Kunzel, Regina G. *Fallen Women, Problem Girls: Unmarried Mothers and the Profes-
   sionalization of Social Work, 1890–1945.* New Haven, Conn.: Yale University Press,
   1993.
Lake, Obiagele. *Blue Veins and Kinky Hair: Naming and Color Consciousness in Afri-
   can America.* Westport, Conn.: Greenwood, 2003.
Landau, Emily Epstein. *Spectacular Wickedness: Sex, Race, and Memory in Storyville,
   New Orleans.* Baton Rouge: Louisiana State University Press, 2013.
Lane, Ann J. *The Brownsville Affair: National Crisis and Black Reaction.* Port Wash-
   ington, N.Y.: Kennikat, 1971.
Lang, Clarence. "Freedom Train Derailed: The National Negro Labor Council and
   the Nadir of Black Radicalism." In *Anticommunism and the African American Free-
   dom Movement: "Another Side of the Story,"* edited by Robbie Lieberman and Clar-
   ence Lang, 161–88. New York: Palgrave, 2009.
Lankford, George. *Surprised by Death: A Novel of Arkansas in the 1840s.* Little Rock:
   Butler Center for Arkansas Studies, 2009.
Lauren, Paul Gordon. "Human Rights in History: Diplomacy and Racial Equality
   at the Paris Peace Conference." In *Race and U.S. Foreign Policy from the Colonial
   Period to the Present: A Collection of Essays,* edited by Michael L. Krenn, 99–121.
   New York: Garland, 1998.
———. "Seen from the Outside: The International Perspective on America's Di-
   lemma." In *Window on Freedom: Race, Civil Rights, and Foreign Affairs, 1945–
   1988,* edited by Brenda Gayle Plummer, 21–44. Chapel Hill: University of North
   Carolina Press, 2003.
Lauterbach, Preston. *Beale Street Dynasty: Sex, Song, and the Struggle for the Soul of
   Memphis.* New York: W. W. Norton, 2015.
Laville, Helen. *Organized White Women and the Challenge of Racial Integration,
   1945–1965.* New York: Palgrave Macmillan, 2017.
Lawson, Steven F. *Civil Rights Crossroads: Nation, Community, and the Black Freedom
   Struggle.* Lexington: University Press of Kentucky, 2003.
———. "Long Origins of the Short Civil Rights Movement, 1954–1968." In *Freedom
   Rights: New Perspectives on the Civil Rights Movement,* edited by Danielle McGuire
   and John Dittmer, 9–38. Lexington: University Press of Kentucky, 2011.
Leavitt, Judith Walzer. "Birthing and Anesthesia: The Debate over Twilight Sleep." In
   Mothers and Motherhood: Readings in American History, edited by Rima Dombrow
   Apple and Janet Lynne Golden, 242–58. Columbus: Ohio State University Press,
   1997.
———. "Under the Shadow of Maternity: American Women's Response to Death
   and Debility Fears in Nineteenth-Century Childbirth." In *Women and Health in*

America: Historical Readings, edited by Judith W. Leavitt, 328–46. Madison: University of Wisconsin Press, 1999.

Lee, Chana Kai. *For Freedom's Sake: The Life of Fannie Lou Hamer*. Urbana: University of Illinois Press, 2000.

Leone, Janice. "Integrating the American Association of University Women, 1946–1949." *Historian* 51, no. 3 (Summer 1989): 423–45.

Leuchtenburg, William E. *The White House Looks South: Franklin D. Roosevelt, Harry S. Truman, Lyndon B. Johnson*. Baton Rouge: Louisiana State University Press, 2005.

Levine, Susan. *Degrees of Equality: The American Association of University Women and the Challenge of Twentieth-Century Feminism*. Philadelphia: Temple University Press, 1995.

Lewis, David Levering. *W. E. B. Du Bois: A Biography, 1868–1963*. New York: Henry Holt, 2009.

———. *W. E. B. Du Bois: Biography of a Race, 1868–1919*. New York: Henry Holt, 1994.

———. *W. E. B. Du Bois: The Fight for Equality and the American Century*. New York: Henry Holt, 2000.

Lichtman, Allan J. *White Protestant Nation: The American Conservative Movement*. New York: Grove Press, 2008.

Lieberman, Robbie. "'Another Side of the Story': African American Intellectuals Speak Out for Peace and Freedom during the Early Cold War Years." In *Anticommunism and the African American Freedom Movement: "Another Side of the Story,"* edited by Robbie Lieberman and Clarence Lang, 17–49. New York: Palgrave, 2009.

———. *The Strangest Dream: Communism, Anticommunism, and the U.S. Peace Movement, 1945–1963*. Syracuse, N.Y.: Syracuse University Press, 2000.

Lieberman, Robbie, and Clarence Lang. "Introduction." In *Anticommunism and the African American Freedom Movement: "Another Side of the Story,"* edited by Lieberman and Lang, 1–16. New York: Palgrave, 2009.

Lindsey, Treva B. *Colored No More: Reinventing Black Womanhood in Washington, D.C.* Urbana: University of Illinois Press, 2017.

Link, Arthur S., ed. "Correspondence Relating to the Progressive Party's 'Lily White' Policy in 1912." In *Journal of Southern History* 10, no. 4 (November 1944): 480.

Lisio, Donald J. *Hoover, Blacks, and Lily-Whites: A Study of Southern Strategies*. Chapel Hill: University of North Carolina Press, 1985.

Litwack, Leon F. *Been in the Storm so Long: The Aftermath of Slavery*. New York: Alfred A. Knopf, 1979.

Logan, Rayford W. *The Betrayal of the Negro, from Rutherford B. Hayes to Woodrow Wilson*. 1954; reprint, New York: Da Capo, 1997.

Lommel, Cookie. *Mary Church Terrell: Speaking Out for Civil Rights*. Berkeley Heights, N.J.: Enslow, 2003.

Longmore, Paul K., and Lauri Umansky. "Introduction: Disability History: From the Margins to the Mainstream." In *The New Disability History: American Perspectives*, edited by Longmore and Umansky, 1–29. New York: New York University Press, 2001.

Lorde, Audre. "The Uses of Anger: Women Responding to Racism." In *Sister Outsider:*

Essays and Speeches by Audre Lorde, 124–133. Trumansburg, N.Y.: Crossing Press, 1984.

Lorini, Alessandra. *Rituals of Race: American Public Culture and the Search for Racial Democracy*. Charlottesville: University of Virginia Press, 1999.

Love, Donald M. *Henry Churchill King, of Oberlin*. New Haven, Conn.: Yale University Press, 1956.

Lubove, Roy. *Community Planning in the 1920s*. Pittsburgh, Pa.: University of Pittsburgh Press, 1963.

Lucander, David. *Winning the War for Democracy: The March on Washington Movement, 1941–1946*. Urbana: University of Illinois Press, 2014.

Ludbrook, Geraldine, and Bruna Bianchi, eds. *Living War, Thinking Peace, 1914–1924: Women's Experiences, Feminist Thought, and International Relations*. Newcastle upon Tyne, U.K.: Cambridge Scholars, 2016.

Luker, Ralph E. *The Social Gospel in Black and White: American Racial Reform, 1885–1912*. Chapel Hill: University of North Carolina Press, 1998.

Lumsden, Linda J. *Inez: The Life and Times of Inez Milholland*. Bloomington: Indiana University Press, 2004.

Lunardini, Christine A. *Alice Paul: Equality for Women, 1885–1977*. Boulder, Colo.: Westview, 2013.

———. "Standing Firm: William Monroe Trotter's Meetings with Woodrow Wilson, 1913–1914." *Journal of Negro History* 64, no. 3 (Summer 1979): 244–64.

Lutz, Lara L. *Chesapeake's Western Shore: Vintage*. Charleston, S.C.: Vacationland Arcadia, 2009.

Lynaugh, Joan E. "Institutionalizing Health Care in Nineteenth- and Twentieth-Century America." In *Women, Health, and Medicine in America: A Historical Handbook*, edited by Rima Dombrow Apple, 247–69. New Brunswick, N.J.: Rutgers University Press, 1992.

Mack, Kenneth W. *Representing the Race: The Creation of the Civil Rights Lawyer*. Cambridge, Mass.: Harvard University Press, 2012.

Maclean, Nancy. *Behind the Mask of Chivalry: The Making of the Second Ku Klux Klan*. New York: Oxford University Press, 1994.

Madigan, Tim. *The Burning: Massacre, Destruction, and the Tulsa Race Riot of 1921*. New York: Thomas Dunne Books, 2001.

Mancini, Matthew J. *One Dies, Get Another: Convict Leasing in the American South, 1866–1928*. Columbia: University of South Carolina Press, 1996.

Mann, Kenneth Eugene. "Oscar Stanton DePriest: Persuasive Agent for the Black Masses." *Negro History Bulletin* 35, no. 6 (October 1972): 136–37.

Manza, Jeff, and Clem Brooks. *Social Cleavages and Political Change: Voter Alignments and U.S. Party Coalitions*. New York: Oxford University Press, 1999.

Marable, Manning, and Leith Mallings. *Let Nobody Turn Us Around: Voices of Resistance, Reform, and Renewal: An African American Anthology*. New York: Rowman and Littlefield, 2009.

Marable, Manning. *W. E. B. Du Bois: Black Radical Democrat*. 1986; reprint, Boulder, Colo.: Paradigm, 2003.

Marchand, Roland. *Advertising the American Dream: Making Way for Modernity, 1920–1940*. Berkeley: University of California Press, 1985.

Marks, George P., ed. *The Black Press Views American Imperialism, 1898–1900.* New York: Arno, 1971.

Marsh, Margaret, and Wanda Ronner. *The Empty Cradle: Infertility in America from Colonial Times to the Present.* Baltimore: Johns Hopkins University Press, 1996.

Martinez, J. Michael. *A Long Dark Night: Race in America from Jim Crow to World War II.* New York: Rowman and Littlefield, 2016.

Mason, Mary G. "Travel as Metaphor and Reality in Afro-American Women's Autobiography, 1850–1972." *Black American Literature Forum* 24, no. 2 (Summer 1990): 337–56.

Masur, Kate. *An Example for All the Land: Emancipation and the Struggle over Equality in Washington, D.C.* Chapel Hill: University of North Carolina Press, 2010.

Materson, Lisa G. "African American Women's Global Journeys and the Construction of Cross-Ethnic Racial Identity." *Women's Studies International Forum* 32 (2009): 35–42.

———. *For the Freedom of Her Race: Black Women and Electoral Politics in Illinois, 1872–1932.* Chapel Hill: University of North Carolina Press, 2009.

May, Vanessa H. *Unprotected Labor: Household Workers, Politics, and Middle-Class Reform in New York, 1870–1940.* Chapel Hill: University of North Carolina Press, 2011.

May, Vivian M. *Anna Julia Cooper, Visionary Black Feminist: A Critical Introduction.* New York: Routledge, 2012.

Mayer, George. *The Republican Party, 1854–1964.* New York: Oxford University Press, 1964.

McCluskey, Audrey Thomas. "Setting the Standard: Mary Church Terrell's Last Campaign for Social Justice." *Black Scholar* 29, nos. 2/3 (Summer 1999): 47–54.

McDaniel, Donna, and Vanessa Julye. *Fit for Freedom, Not for Friendship: Quakers, African Americans, and the Myth of Racial Justice.* Philadelphia: Quaker Press of Friends General Conference, 2009.

McDuffie, Erik S. "The March of Young Southern Black Women: Esther Cooper Jackson, Black Left Feminism, and the Personal and Political Costs of Cold War Repression." In *Anticommunism and the African American Freedom Movement: "Another Side of the Story,"* edited by Robbie Lieberman and Clarence Lang, 81–114. New York: Palgrave, 2009.

———. "'[She] Devoted Twenty Minutes Condemning All Other Forms of Government but the Soviet': Black Women Radicals in the Garvey Movement and in the Left during the 1920s." In *Diasporic Africa: A Reader,* edited by Michael A. Gomez, 219–50. New York: New York University Press, 2006.

———. *Sojourning for Freedom: Black Women, American Communism, and the Making of Black Left Feminism.* Durham, N.C.: Duke University Press, 2011.

McElya, Mickie. *Clinging to Mammy: The Faithful Slave in Twentieth-Century America.* Cambridge, Mass.: Harvard University Press, 2007.

McFadden, Margaret H. *Golden Cables of Sympathy: The Transatlantic Sources of Nineteenth- Century Feminism.* Lexington: University Press of Kentucky, 1999.

McGuire, Danielle L. *At the Dark End of the Street: Black Women, Rape and Resistance—A New History of the Civil Rights Movement from Rosa Parks to the Rise of Black Power.* New York: Vintage, 2011.

McHenry, Elizabeth. "Toward a History of Access: The Case of Mary Church Terrell." *American Literary History* 19, no. 2 (Summer 2007): 381–401.

McKay, Nellie Y. "The Girls Who Became the Women: Childhood Memories in the Autobiographies of Harriet Jacobs, Mary Church Terrell, and Anne Moody." In *Tradition and the Talents of Women*, edited by Florence Howe, 105–24. Urbana: University of Illinois Press, 1991.

McKee, Margaret, and Fred Chisenhall. *Beale Black and Blue: Life and Music on Black America's Main Street*. Baton Rouge: Louisiana State University Press, 1981.

McKissack, Patricia, and Fredrick McKissack. *Mary Church Terrell: Leader for Equality*. Berkeley Heights, N.J.: Enslow, 2002.

McMillen, Neil R. *Dark Journey: Black Mississippians in the Age of Jim Crow*. Urbana: University of Illinois Press, 1990.

McNeill, Genna Rae. *Groundwork: Charles Hamilton Houston and the Struggle for Civil Rights*. Philadelphia: University of Pennsylvania Press, 1983.

McVeigh, Rory. *The Rise of the Ku Klux Klan: Right Wing Movements and National Politics*. Minneapolis: University of Minnesota Press, 2009.

Meier, August. *Negro Thought in America, 1880–1925: Racial Ideologies in the Age of Booker T. Washington*. Ann Arbor: University of Michigan, 1963.

Meriwether, James H. *Proudly We Can Be Africans: Black Americans and Africa, 1935–1961*. Chapel Hill: University of North Carolina Press, 2002.

Meyer, Mary K., and Elisabeth Prugl. *Gender Politics in Global Governance*. New York: Rowman and Littlefield, 1999.

Meyerowitz, Joanne J. *Not June Cleaver: Women and Gender in Postwar America, 1945–1960*. Philadelphia: Temple University Press, 1994.

Mileur, Jerome M. "The 'Boss': Franklin Roosevelt, the Democratic Party and the Reconstitution of American Politics." In *The New Deal and the Triumph of Liberalism*, edited by Sidney M. Milkis and Jerome M. Mileur, 86–134. Amherst: University of Massachusetts Press, 2002.

Milkman, Ruth. *Gender at Work: The Dynamics of Job Segregation by Sex during World War II*. Urbana: University of Illinois Press, 1987.

Miller, Carroll L., and Anne S. Pruitt-Logan. *Faithful to the Task at Hand: The Life of Lucy Diggs Slowe*. Albany: SUNY Press, 2012.

Miller, Eben. *Born along the Color Line: The 1933 Amenia Conference and the Rise of a National Civil Rights Movement*. New York: Oxford University Press, 2012.

Miller, Kristie. "Oscar Stanton DePriest." In *African American Lives*, edited by Henry Louis Gates and Evelyn Brooks Higginbotham, 229–30. New York: Oxford University Press, 2004.

———. *Ruth Hanna McCormick: A Life in Politics, 1880–1944*. Albuquerque: University of New Mexico Press, 1992.

———. "Ruth Hanna McCormick and the Senatorial Election of 1930." *Illinois Historical Journal* 81, no. 3 (Autumn 1988): 191–210.

Miller, Sammy M. "Robert Heberton Terrell, 1857–1925: Black Lawyer and Community Leader." Ph.D. diss., Catholic University of America, 1977.

———. "Robert H. Terrell: First Black D.C. Municipal Judge." *Crisis* 83, no. 6 (1976): 209–10.

———. "Woodrow Wilson and the Black Judge." *Crisis* 84, no. 2 (1977): 81–86.

Miller, William D. *Memphis during the Progressive Era, 1900–1917*. Madison, Wis.: American History Research Center, 1957.

Mills, Gary B. *Southern Loyalists in the Civil War: The Southern Claims Commission*. Baltimore: Genealogical Publishing, 1994.

Mitchell, B. Doyle, Jr., and Patricia A. Mitchell. *Industrial Bank*. Charleston, S.C.: Arcadia, 2012.

Mitchell, Clarence M., Jr. "Epilogue: Labor Problems Affecting Negroes." In *The Papers of Clarence Mitchell, Jr.: 1944–1946*, edited by Clarence Maurice Mitchell, Denton L. Watson, and Elizabeth Miles Nuxoll, 559–66. Columbus: Ohio State University Press: 2005.

Mitchell, Michele. *Righteous Propagation: African Americans and the Politics of Racial Destiny after Reconstruction*. Chapel Hill: University of North Carolina Press, 2004.

Mizelle, Richard M., Jr. *Backwater Blues: The Mississippi Flood of 1927 in the African American Imagination*. Minneapolis: University of Minnesota Press, 2014.

Mjagkij, Nina. "Julia Ward Howe Republican Women's Club." In *Organizing Black America: An Encyclopedia of African American Associations*, edited by Nina Mjagkij, 254. New York: Routledge, 2001.

Mollin, Marian. *Radical Pacifism in Modern America: Egalitarianism and Protest*. Philadelphia: University of Pennsylvania Press, 2006.

Moore, Jacqueline M. *Booker T. Washington, W. E. B. Du Bois, and the Struggle for Racial Uplift*. Wilmington, Del.: Scholarly Resources, 2003.

———. *Leading the Race: The Transformation of the Black Elite in the Nation's Capital, 1880–1920*. Charlottesville: University of North Carolina Press, 1999.

Morgan, Francesca. *Women and Patriotism in Jim Crow America*. Chapel Hill: University of North Carolina Press, 2005.

Morris, Aldon D. *The Origins of the Civil Rights Movement: Black Communities Organizing for Change*. New York: Free Press, 1984.

Morris, Tiyi M. *Womanpower Unlimited and the Black Freedom Struggle in Mississippi*. Athens: University of Georgia Press, 2015.

Morton, Patricia. *Disfigured Images: The Historical Assault on Afro-American Women*. Westport, Conn.: Greenwood, 1991.

———. *Leading the Race: The Transformation of the Black Elite in the Nation's Capital*. Charlottesville: University of Virginia Press, 1999.

Moses, Wilson Jeremiah. *The Golden Age of Black Nationalism, 1850–1925*. New York: Oxford University Press, 1988.

Mouser, Bruce L. *A Black Gambler's World of Liquor, Vice, and Presidential Politics: William Thomas Scott of Illinois, 1839–1917*. Madison: University of Wisconsin Press, 2014.

Muncy, Robyn. *Relentless Reformer: Josephine Roche and Progressivism in Twentieth-Century America*. Princeton, N.J.: Princeton University Press, 2015.

Murphy, Mary-Elizabeth B. *Jim Crow Capital: Women and Black Freedom Struggles in Washington, D.C., 1920–1945*. Chapel Hill: University of North Carolina Press, 2018.

Murray, Pauli. *Pauli Murray: The Autobiography of a Black Activist, Feminist, Lawyer, Priest, and Poet*. Knoxville: University of Tennessee Press, 1987.

Murray, Robert K. *Warren G. Harding and His Administration*. Minneapolis, Minn.: American Political Biography Press, 2000.

Neill, Robert. "Reminiscences of Independence County." *Publications of the Arkansas Historical Association* 3 (1911): 348–50.

Neubeck, Kenneth J., and Noel A. Cazenave. *Welfare Racism: Playing the Race Card against America's Poor*. New York: Routledge, 2002.

Neumann, Caryn E. "Status Seekers: Long-Established Women's Organizations and the Women's Movement in the United States, 1945–1970s." Ph.D. diss., Ohio State University, 2006.

Neverdon-Morton, Cynthia. *Afro-American Women of the South and the Advancement of the Race, 1895–1925*. Knoxville: University of Tennessee Press, 1989.

Newman, Louise M. *White Women's Rights: The Racial Origins of Feminism in the United States*. New York: Oxford University Press, 1999.

Ngai, Mae M. *Impossible Subjects: Illegal Aliens and the Making of Modern America*. Princeton, N.J.: Princeton University Press, 2004.

Nielson, David Gordon. *Black Ethos: Northern Urban Negro Life and Thought, 1890–1930*. Westport, Conn.: Greenwood, 1977.

Norrell, Robert Jefferson. *Up from History: The Life of Booker T. Washington*. Cambridge, Mass.: Harvard University Press, 2009.

Odem, Mary E. *Delinquent Daughters: Protecting and Policing Adolescent Female Sexuality in the United States, 1885–1920*. Chapel Hill: University of North Carolina Press, 1995.

Olson, Lynne. "Mary Church Terrell." In *Black Women Activists: Profiles in History*, edited by Karin S. Coddon, 123–30. San Diego, Calif.: Greenhaven, 2004.

Osborn, George C. "Woodrow Wilson Appoints Robert H. Terrell Judge of Municipal Court, District of Columbia." *Negro History Bulletin* 22, no. 5 (February 1959): 111–15.

Osselaer, Heidi J. *Winning Their Place: Arizona Women in Politics, 1883–1950*. Tucson: University of Arizona Press, 2009.

Overacker, Ingrid. "True to Our God: African American Women as Christian Activists in Rochester, New York." In *Gender and the Social Gospel*, edited by Wendy J. Deichmann Edwards and Carolyn De Swarte Gifford, 202–16. Urbana: University of Illinois Press, 2003.

Ovington, Mary White, and Ralph E. Luker. *Black and White Sat Down Together: The Reminisces of an NAACP Founder*. New York: Feminist Press at CUNY, 1996.

Painter, Nell Irvin. "Memoranda and Documents: Jim Crow at Harvard, 1923." *New England Quarterly* 64, no. 4 (December 1971): 627–34.

———. "Soul Murder and Slavery: Toward a Fully Loaded Cost Accounting." In *U.S. History as Women's History: New Feminist Essays*, edited by Linda K. Kerber, Alice Kessler-Harris, and Kathryn Kish Sklar, 15–39. Chapel Hill: University of North Carolina Press, 1995.

Parker, Alison M. *Articulating Rights: Nineteenth-Century American Women on Race, Reform, and the State*. DeKalb: Northern Illinois University Press, 2010.

———. "'The Picture of Health': The Public Life and Private Ailments of Mary Church Terrell." *Journal of Historical Biography* 13 (Spring 2013): 1–44.

Parker, Christopher S. *Fighting for Democracy: Black Veterans and the Struggle against*

White Supremacy in the Postwar South. Princeton, N.J.: Princeton University Press, 2009.

Parker, Traci. "Southern Retail Campaigns and the Struggle for Black Economic Freedom in the 1950s and 1960s." In *Race and Retail: Consumption across the Color Line*, edited by Mia Bay and Ann Fabian, 77–98. Brunswick, N.J.: Rutgers University Press, 2015.

Pascoe, Peggy. *What Comes Naturally: Miscegenation Law and the Making of Race in America*. New York: Oxford University Press, 2009.

Patler, Nicholas. *Jim Crow and the Wilson Administration: Protesting Federal Segregation in the Early Twentieth Century*. Boulder: University Press of Colorado, 2004.

Patterson, James T. *Congressional Conservativism and the New Deal: The Growth of the Conservative Coalition in Congress, 1933–1939*. Westport, Conn.: Greenwood, 1967.

Patton, June O., ed. "Moonlight and Magnolias in Southern Education: The Black Mammy Memorial Institute [Documents]." *Journal of Negro History* 65, no. 2 (Spring 1980): 149–55.

Payne, Phillip G. *Dead Last: The Public Memory of Warren G. Harding's Scandalous Legacy*. Athens: Ohio University Press, 2009.

Pegram, Thomas R. *One Hundred Percent American: The Rebirth and Decline of the Ku Klux Klan in the 1920s*. Chicago: Ivan R. Dee, 2011.

Perdue, Theda. *Race and the Atlanta Cotton States Exposition of 1895*. Athens: University of Georgia Press, 2011.

Perkins, Kathy A., and Judith L. Stephens, eds. "May Miller (1899–1995)." In *Strange Fruit: Plays on Lynching by American Women*, edited by Perkins and Stephens, 174–75. Bloomington: Indiana University Press, 1998.

Perry, Imani. *May We Forever Stand: A History of the Black National Anthem*. Chapel Hill: University of North Carolina Press, 2018.

Pitre, Merline. "*Nixon v. Herndon*, 1927." In *Black Victory: The Rise and Fall of the White Primary in Texas*, edited by Darlene Clark Hine, 111–25. 1979; reprint, Columbia: University of Missouri Press, 2003.

Plastas, Melinda Ann. *A Band of Noble Women: Racial Politics in the Women's Peace Movement*. Syracuse, N.Y.: Syracuse University Press, 2011.

———. "'A Band of Noble Women': The WILPF and the Politics and Consciousness of Race in the Women's Peace Movement." Ph.D. diss., SUNY Buffalo, 2001.

Plotke, David. *Building a Democratic Political Order: Reshaping American Liberalism in the 1930s and 1940s*. New York: Cambridge University Press, 1996.

Plummer, Brenda Gayle. *Rising Wind: Black Americans and U.S. Foreign Affairs, 1935–1960*. Chapel Hill: University of North Carolina Press, 1996.

———, ed. *Window on Freedom: Race, Civil Rights, and Foreign Affairs, 1945–1988*. Chapel Hill: University of North Carolina Press, 2003.

Pollack, Howard. *The Ballad of John Latouche: An American Lyricist's Life and Work*. New York: Oxford University Press, 2017.

Poole, Mary. *The Segregated Origins of Social Security: African Americans and the Welfare State*. Chapel Hill: University of North Carolina Press, 2006.

Pycior, Helena M., Nancy G. Slack, and Pnina G. Abir-Am. "Introduction." In *Creative Couples in the Sciences*, edited by Pycior, Slack, and Abir-Am, 3–35. New Brunswick, N.J.: Rutgers University Press, 1996.

Quadango, Jill. *The Color of Welfare: How Racism Undermined the War on Poverty*. New York: Oxford University Press, 1994.

Quigley, Joan. *Just Another Southern Town: Mary Church Terrell and the Struggle for Racial Justice in the Nation's Capital*. New York: Oxford University Press, 2016.

Randolph, Lewis A. *Rights for a Season: The Politics of Race, Class, and Gender in Richmond*. Knoxville: University of Tennessee Press, 2003.

Randolph, Sherie M. "Not to Rely Completely on the Courts: Florynce Kennedy and Black Feminist Leadership in the Reproductive Rights Battle." In *Toward an Intellectual History of Black Women*, edited by Mia Bay et al., 233–51. Chapel Hill: University of North Carolina Press, 2015.

Ransby, Barbara. *Ella Baker and the Black Freedom Movement: A Radical Democratic Vision*. Chapel Hill: University of North Carolina Press, 2003.

Rauchway, Eric. *The Refuge of Affections: Family and American Reform Politics, 1900–1920*. New York: Columbia University Press, 2001.

Reagan, Leslie J. "Medicine, Law, and the State: The History of Reproduction." In *A Companion to American Women's History*, edited by Nancy A. Hewitt, 348–65. 2002; reprint, Malden, Mass.: Blackwell 2005.

Reagon, Bernice Johnson. "Women as Culture Carriers in the Civil Rights Movement: Fannie Lou Hamer." In *Women in the Civil Rights Movement: Trailblazers and Torchbearers, 1941–1965*, edited by Vicki Crawford, Jacqueline Rouse, and Barbara Woods, 203–18. Bloomington: Indiana University Press, 1990.

Reed, Christopher Robert. *The Chicago NAACP and the Rise of Black Professional Leadership, 1910–1966*. Bloomington: Indiana University Press, 1997.

———. *The Rise of Chicago's Black Metropolis, 1920–1929*. Urbana: University of Illinois Press, 2011.

Reed, Merl E. *Seedtime for the Modern Civil Rights Movement: The President's Committee on Fair Employment Practice, 1941–1946*. Baton Rouge: Louisiana State University Press, 1991.

Reich, Steven A. *A Working People: A History of African American Works since Emancipation*. New York: Rowman and Littlefield, 2013.

Reichley, James. *The Life of the Parties: A History of American Political Parties*. New York: Rowman and Littlefield, 1992.

Renda, Mary A. *Taking Haiti: Military Occupation and the Culture of U.S. Imperialism, 1915– 1940*. Chapel Hill: University of North Carolina Press, 2001.

Renstrom, Peter G. *The Taft Court: Justices, Rulings, and Legacy*. Santa Barbara, Calif.: ABC-CLIO, 2003.

Reverby, Susan M. *Examining Tuskegee: The Infamous Syphilis Study and Its Legacy*. Chapel Hill: University of North Carolina Press, 2009.

Rhodes, Jane. "Pedagogies of Respectability: Race, Media, and Black Womanhood in the Early 20th Century." *Souls: A Critical Journal of Black Politics, Culture, and Society* 18, nos. 2–4 (April–December 2016): 201–14.

Rich, Charlotte J. *Transcending the New Woman: Multiethnic Narratives in the Progressive Era*. Columbia: University of Missouri Press, 2009.

Richardson, H. N., et al. "Exposure to Repetitive versus Varied Stress during Prenatal Development Generates Two Distinct Anxiogenic and Neuroendocrine Profiles in Adulthood." *Endocrinology* 147, no. 5 (2006): 2506–17.

Richardson, Heather Cox. *The Death of Reconstruction: Race, Labor, and Politics in the Post–Civil War North, 1865–1901*. Cambridge, Mass.: Harvard University Press, 2001.

Richardson, Joe M. *A History of Fisk University, 1865–1946*. Tuscaloosa: University of Alabama Press, 1980.

Rief, Michelle. "Thinking Locally, Acting Globally: The International Agenda of African American Clubwomen, 1880–1940." *Journal of African American History* 89, no. 3 (2004): 203–22.

Rigueur, Leah Wright. *The Loneliness of the Black Republican: Pragmatic Politics and the Pursuit of Power*. Princeton, N.J.: Princeton University Press, 2015.

Risjord, Norman K. *Populists and Progressives*. New York: Rowman and Littlefield, 2005.

Ritter, Gretchen. *The Constitution as Social Design: Gender and Civic Membership in the American Constitutional Order*. Palo Alto, Calif.: Stanford University Press, 2006.

Robbins, Hollis, and Henry Louis Gates Jr., eds. *The Portable Nineteenth-Century African-American Women Writers*. New York: Penguin, 2017.

Roberts, Dorothy. *Killing the Black Body: Race, Reproduction, and the Meaning of Liberty*. New York: Vintage Books, 2016.

Robertson, Nancy Marie. *Christian Sisterhood, Race Relations, and the YWCA, 1906–1946*. Urbana: University of Illinois Press, 2007.

Robnett, Belinda. *How Long? How Long? African American Women in the Struggle for Civil Rights*. New York: Oxford University Press, 2000.

Rodrique, Jessie M. "The Black Community and the Birth Control Movement." In *Women and Health in America: Historical Readings*, edited by Judith Walzer Leavitt, 293–305. Madison: University of Wisconsin Press, 1999.

Roediger, David R. *Colored White: Transcending the Racial Past*. Berkeley: University of California Press, 2002.

Roman, Meredith L. *Opposing Jim Crow: African Americans and the Soviet Indictment of U.S. Racism, 1928–1937*. Lincoln: University of Nebraska Press, 2012.

Rosen, Hannah. *Terror in the Heart of Freedom: Citizenship, Sexual Violence, and the Meaning of Race in the Postemancipation South*. Chapel Hill: University of North Carolina Press, 2009.

Rosen, Ruth. *The Lost Sisterhood: Prostitution in America, 1900–1918*. Baltimore: Johns Hopkins University Press, 1983.

Rosenberg, Charles E. *The Care of Strangers: The Rise of America's Hospital System*. New York: Basic Books, 1987.

Rosenberg, Jonathan. *How Far the Promised Land? World Affairs and the American Civil Rights Movement from the First World War to Vietnam*. Princeton, N.J.: Princeton University Press, 2006.

Rosenberg, Rosalind. *Jane Crow: The Life of Pauli Murray*. New York: Oxford University Press, 2017.

Ross, Loretta J. "African American Women and Abortion, 1800–1970." In *Mothers and Motherhood: Readings in American History*, edited by Rima D. Apple and Janet Golden, 259–77. Columbus: Ohio State University Press, 1997.

Ross, Rosetta E. *Witnessing and Testifying: Black Women, Religion, and Civil Rights*. Minneapolis, Minn.: Fortress, 2003.

Rouse, Jacqueline Anne. *Lugenia Burns Hope: Black Southern Reformer.* Athens: University of Georgia Press, 1989.

Rubin, Nancy. *American Empress: The Life and Times of Marjorie Merriweather Post.* New York: Villard Books, 1995.

Rubio, Philip F. *A History of Affirmative Action, 1691–2000.* Jackson: University of Mississippi Press, 2009.

Rucker, Walter C., and James N. Upton. *Encyclopedia of American Race Riots.* Westport, Conn.: Greenwood, 2006.

Rudolph, Kerstin. "Victoria Earle Matthews: Making Literature during the Woman's Era." *Legacy: A Journal of American Women Writers* 33, no. 1 (2016): 103–26.

Rudwick, Elliott M. "Oscar De Priest and the Jim Crow Restaurant in the U.S. House of Representatives." *Journal of Negro Education* 35, no. 1 (Winter 1966): 77–82.

Rupp, Leila J. "Challenging Imperialism in International Women's Organizations, 1888–1945." *NWSA Journal* 8, no. 1 (Spring 1996): 8–27.

———. "The Women's Community in the National Woman's Party, 1945 to the 1960s." *Signs* 10, no. 4 (Summer 1985): 715–40.

———. *Worlds of Women: The Making of an International Women's Movement.* Princeton, N.J.: Princeton University Press, 1997.

Rupp, Leila J., and Verta Taylor. *Survival in the Doldrums: The American Women's Rights Movement, 1945 to the 1960s.* New York: Oxford University Press, 1987.

Sack, Daniel. "Men Want Something Real: Frank Buchman and Anglo-American College Religion in the 1920s." *Journal of Religious History* 28, no. 3 (October 2004): 260–75.

Salem, Dorothy. *To Better Our World: Black Women in Organized Reform, 1890–1920.* Brooklyn, N.Y.: Carlson, 1990.

Sartain, Lee. *Invisible Activists: Women of the Louisiana NAACP and the Struggle for Civil Rights, 1914–1945.* Baton Rouge: Louisiana State University Press, 2007.

Satter, Beryl. *Each Mind a Kingdom: American Women, Sexual Purity, and the New Thought Movement, 1875–1920.* Berkeley: University of California Press, 1999.

Savage, Barbara Dianne. *Your Spirits Walk beside Us: The Politics of Black Religion.* Cambridge, Mass.: Belknap Press of Harvard University Press, 2008.

Savage, Sean J. *Roosevelt: The Party Leader, 1932–1945.* Lexington: University of Kentucky Press, 2015.

Scalmer, Sean. *Gandhi in the West: The Mahatma and the Rise of Radical Protest.* New York: Cambridge University Press, 2001.

Scanlon, Jennifer. *Until There Is Justice: The Life of Anna Arnold Hedgeman.* New York: Oxford University Press, 2016.

Schechter, Patricia A. "'All the Intensity of My Nature': Ida B. Wells, Anger, and Politics." *Radical History Review* 70 (1998): 48–77.

———. *Ida B. Wells-Barnett and American Reform, 1880–1930.* Chapel Hill: University of North Carolina Press, 2001.

———. "Unsettled Business: Ida B. Wells against Lynching, or, How Antilynching Got Its Gender." In *Under Sentence of Death: Lynching in the South,* edited by W. Fitzhugh Brundage, 292–317. Chapel Hill: University of North Carolina Press, 1997.

Schneider, Mark. *Boston Confronts Jim Crow, 1890–1920.* Boston: Northeastern University Press, 1997.

———. *"We Return Fighting": The Civil Rights Movement in the Jazz Age.* Boston: Northeastern University Press, 2002.

Schott, Linda K. *Reconstructing Women's Thoughts: The Women's International League for Peace and Freedom before World War II.* Stanford, Calif.: Stanford University Press, 1997.

Schramm, Peter W., and Bradford P. Wilson. *American Political Parties and Constitutional Politics.* New York: Rowman and Littlefield, 1993.

Schwalm, Leslie A. *A Hard Fight for We: Women's Transition from Slavery to Freedom in South Carolina.* Urbana: University of Illinois Press, 1997.

Schweninger, Loren. *Black Property Owners in the South, 1790–1915.* Urbana: University of Illinois Press, 1990.

Scott, William R. "Black Nationalism and the Italo-Ethiopian Conflict, 1934–1936." In *Race and U.S. Foreign Policy from 1900 through World War II,* edited by Michael L. Krenn and E. Nathaniel Gates, 134–50. New York: Taylor and Francis, 1998.

Scroop, Daniel Mark. *Mr. Democrat: Jim Farley, the New Deal, and the Making of Modern American Politics.* Ann Arbor: University of Michigan Press, 2006.

Self, Robert O. *American Babylon: Race and the Struggle for Postwar Oakland.* Princeton, N.J.: Princeton University Press, 2003.

Sexton, Jared. *Amalgamation Schemes: Antiblackness and the Critique of Multiracialism.* Minneapolis: University of Minnesota Press, 2008.

Shaw, Stephanie J. "Black Club Women and the Creation of the National Association of Colored Women." In *"We Specialize in the Wholly Impossible": A Reader in Black Women's History,* edited by Darlene Clark Hine, Wilma King, and Linda Reed, 433–48. New York: Carlson, 1995.

———. *W. E. B. Du Bois and "The Souls of Black Folk."* Chapel Hill: University of North Carolina Press, 2013.

———. *What a Woman Ought to Be and to Do: Black Professional Women Workers during the Jim Crow Era.* Chicago: University of Chicago Press, 1996.

Sheffer, Debra J. *The Buffalo Soldiers: Their Epic Story and Major Campaigns.* Santa Barbara, Calif.: ABC-CLIO, 2015.

Shepperd, Gladys Byram. *Mary Church Terrell: Respectable Person.* Baltimore: Human Relations Press, 1959.

Shonkoff, J. P., W. T. Boyce, and B. S. McEwen. "Neuroscience, Molecular Biology, and the Childhood Roots of Health Disparities." *Journal of the American Medical Association* 301, no. 21 (2009): 2252–59.

Sigafoos, Robert A. *Cotton Row to Beale Street: A Business History of Memphis.* Memphis, Tenn.: Memphis State University Press, 1979.

Silkey, Sarah L. "The Right to Be a Lady: Ida B. Wells and Social Reform." In *Tennessee Women: Their Lives and Times,* vol. 2, edited by Beverly Bond and Sarah Wilkerson-Freeman, 152–76. Athens: University of Georgia Press, 2015.

Simon, John Y., and Michael E. Stevens, eds. *New Perspectives on the Myths and Realities of the National Conflict.* New York: Rowman and Littlefield, 2001.

Singh, Nikhil Pal. *Black Is a Country: Race and the Unfinished Struggle for Democracy.* Cambridge, Mass.: Harvard University Press, 2004.

Sitkoff, Harvard. *A New Deal for Blacks: The Emergence of Civil Rights as a National Issue*, vol. 1: *The Depression Decade.* New York: Oxford University Press, 1978.

Sklar, Kathryn Kish, and James Brewer Stewart, eds. *Women's Rights and Transatlantic Antislavery in the Era of Emancipation.* New Haven, Conn.: Yale University Press, 2007.

Sklaroff, Lauren Rebecca. *Black Culture and the New Deal: The Quest for Civil Rights in the Roosevelt Era.* Chapel Hill: University of North Carolina Press, 2009.

Skotnes, Andor. *A New Deal for All? Race and Class Struggles in Depression-Era Baltimore.* Durham, N.C.: Duke University Press, 2013.

Slate, Nico. *Colored Cosmopolitanism: The Shared Struggle for Freedom in the United States and India.* Cambridge, Mass.: Harvard University Press, 2012.

Slotkin, Richard. *Lost Battalions: The Great War and the Crisis of American Nationality.* New York: Henry Holt, 2005.

Smallwood, James. *Reform, Red Scare, and Ruin: Virginia Durr, Prophet of the New South.* Bloomington, Ind.: Xlibris, 2008.

Smith, Elaine M. "Mary McLeod Bethune." In *Notable American Women: The Modern Period: A Biographical Dictionary*, vol. 4, edited by Barbara Sicherman and Carol Hurd Green, 76–80. Cambridge, Mass.: Harvard University Press, 1980.

Smith, J. Clay, Jr. *Emancipation: The Making of the Black Lawyer, 1844 to 1944.* Philadelphia: University of Pennsylvania Press, 1993.

Smith, J. Douglas. *Managing White Supremacy: Race, Politics, and Citizenship in Jim Crow Virginia.* Chapel Hill: University of North Carolina Press, 2002.

Smock, Raymond W. *Booker T. Washington: Black Leadership in the Age of Jim Crow.* New York: Ivan R. Dee, 2009.

Sneider, Allison L. *Suffragists in an Imperial Age: U.S. Expansion and the Woman Question, 1870–1929.* New York: Oxford University Press, 2008.

Solinger, Rickie. *Wake Up Little Susie: Single Pregnancy and Race before Roe v. Wade.* New York: Routledge, 1992.

Solomon, Barbara. *In the Company of Educated Women: A History of Women and Higher Education in America.* New Haven, Conn.: Yale University Press, 1985.

Southard, Belinda A. Stillion. *Militant Citizenship: Rhetorical Strategies of the National Woman's Party.* College Station: Texas A&M University Press, 2011.

Stansell, Christine. *The Feminist Promise, 1792 to the Present.* New York: Modern Library, 2010.

Startt, James D. *Woodrow Wilson and the Press: Prelude to the Presidency.* New York: Palgrave Macmillan, 2004.

Steedman, Marek D. *Jim Crow Citizenship: Liberalism and the Southern Defense of Racial Hierarchy.* New York: Routledge, 2012.

Sterling, Dorothy. *Black Foremothers: Three Lives.* New York: Feminist Press and McGraw-Hill, 1979.

———. *We Are Your Sisters: Black Women in the Nineteenth Century.* New York: W. W. Norton, 1984.

———. "Woman Suffrage in Congress: American Expansion and the Politics of

Federalism, 1870–1890." In *Votes for Women: The Struggle for Suffrage Revisited*, edited by Jean H. Baker, 77–89. New York: Oxford University Press, 2002.

Storrs, Landon R. Y. "Laying the Foundations for the Post–World War II Red Scare: Investigating the Left-Feminist Consumer Movement." In *Little "Red Scares": Anti-Communist and Political Repression in the United States, 1921–1946*, edited by Robert Justin Goodstein, 213–35. Farnam, U.K.: Ashgate, 2014.

———. "Red Scare Politics and the Suppression of Left Feminism: The Loyalty Investigation of Mary Dublin Keyserling." In *Liberty and Justice for All? Rethinking Politics in Cold War America*, edited by Kathleen G. Donohue, 51–90. Amherst: University of Massachusetts Press, 2012.

———. *Second Red Scare and the Unmaking of the New Deal Left*. Princeton, N.J.: Princeton University Press, 2013.

Stovall, Tyler. "Love, Labor, and Race." In *French Civilization and Its Discontents: Nationalism, Colonialism, Race*, edited by Stovall and Georges Van Den Abbeele, 297–321. Lanham, Md.: Lexington Books, 2003.

———. *Paris Noir: African Americans in the City of Light*. Boston: Houghton Mifflin, 1996.

Streitmatter, Rodger. "Josephine St. Pierre Ruffin: A Nineteenth-Century Journalist of Boston's Black Elite Class." In *Women of the Commonwealth: Work, Family, and Social Change in Nineteenth-Century Massachusetts*, edited by Susan L. Porter, 147–64. Amherst: University of Massachusetts Press, 1996.

———. *Raising Her Voice: African American Journalists Who Changed History*. Lexington: University Press of Kentucky, 2015.

Strom, Sharon Hartman. *Beyond the Typewriter: Gender, Class, and the Origins of Modern American Office Work, 1900–1930*. Urbana: University of Illinois Press, 1992.

Sugrue, Thomas J. *Sweet Land of Liberty: The Forgotten Struggle for Civil Rights in the North*. New York: Random House, 2009.

Sullivan, Patricia. *Days of Hope: Race and Democracy in the New Deal Era*. Chapel Hill: University of North Carolina Press, 1996.

———. *Lift Every Voice: The NAACP and the Making of the Civil Rights Movement*. New York: New Press, 2009.

Summers, Martin. *Manliness and Its Discontents: The Black Middle Class and the Transformation of Masculinity, 1900–1930*. Chapel Hill: University of North Carolina Press, 2004.

Sundquist, James L. *Dynamics of the Party System: Alignment and Realignment of Political Parties in the United States*. Washington, D.C.: Brookings Institution Press, 1973.

Swain, Gwenyth. *Civil Rights Pioneer: A Story about Mary Church Terrell*. Minneapolis, Minn.: Carolrhoda Books, 1999.

Sylvander, Carolyn Wedin. *Jessie Redmon Fauset: Black American Writer*. Albany, N.Y.: Whitson, 1981.

Taylor, Clarence, and Milton Arthur Galamison. *Knocking at Our Own Door: Milton A. Galamison and the Struggle to Integrate New York City Schools*. Lanham, Md.: Lexington Books, 2000.

Taylor, Ula Yvette. *The Veiled Garvey: The Life and Times of Amy Jacques Garvey*. Chapel Hill: University of North Carolina Press, 2002.

Tepedino, Therese C. "The Founding and Early Years of the National Association of Colored Women." M.A. thesis, Portland State University, 1977.

Terborg-Penn, Rosalyn. "African American Women and the Woman Suffrage Movement." In *One Woman, One Vote: Rediscovering the Woman Suffrage Movement*, edited by Marjorie Spruill Wheeler, 135–56. Troutdale, Oreg.: NewSage, 1995.

———. *African-American Women in the Struggle for the Vote, 1850–1920*. Bloomington: University of Indiana Press, 1998.

———. "Black Male Perspectives on the Nineteenth-Century Woman." In *The Afro-American Woman, Struggles and Images*, edited by Sharon Harley and Rosalyn Terborg-Penn, 28–42. Port Washington, N.Y.: Kennikat, 1978.

———. "Discrimination against Afro-American Women in the Woman's Movement, 1830–1920." In *The Black Woman Cross-Culturally*, edited by Filomina Chioma Steady, 301–16. Rochester, Vt.: Schenkman Books, 1981.

———. "Enfranchising Women of Color: Woman Suffragists as Agents of Imperialism." In *Nation, Empire, Colony: Historicizing Gender and Race*, edited by Ruth Roach Pierson and Nupur Chaudhuri, 41–56. Bloomington: Indiana University Press, 1998.

———. "Survival Strategies among African-American Women Workers: A Continuing Process." In *Women, Work, and Protest: A Century of U.S. Women's Labor History*, edited by Ruth Milkman, 139–55. 1985; reprint, New York: Routledge, 2013.

Theoharis, Jean. *The Rebellious Life of Mrs. Rosa Parks*. Boston: Beacon, 2015.

Thomas, Kruse. *Deluxe Jim Crow: Civil Rights and American Health Policy, 1935–1954*. Athens: University of Georgia Press, 2011.

Thurber, Timothy N. *Republicans and Race: The GOP's Frayed Relationship with African Americans, 1945–1974*. Lawrence: University Press of Kansas, 2013.

Tischauser, Leslie Vincent. *The Changing Nature of Racial and Ethnic Conflict in United States History*. Lanham, Md.: University Press of America, 2002.

Tolchin, Martin, and Susan Tolchin, *To the Victor: Political Patronage from the Clubhouse to the White House*. New York: Random House, 1971.

Topping, Simon. *Lincoln's Lost Legacy: The Republican Party and the African American Vote, 1928–1952*. Gainesville: University of Florida Press, 2008.

Toy, Eckard V., Jr. "The Oxford Group and the Strike of the Seattle Longshoremen in 1934." *Pacific Northwest Quarterly* 69, no. 4 (October 1978): 174–84.

Travis, Dempsey J. *An Autobiography of Black Politics*. Chicago: Urban Research Institute, 1987.

Tsesis, Alexander. *We Shall Overcome: A History of Civil Rights and the Law*. New Haven, Conn.: Yale University Press, 2008.

Tucker, Garland. *High Tide of American Conservatism: Davis, Coolidge, and the 1924 Election*. Bingley, U.K.: Emerald Book, 2010.

Tushnet, Mark V. *Making Civil Rights Law: Thurgood Marshall and the Supreme Court, 1936–1961*. New York: Oxford University Press, 1994.

Tuttle, William M., Jr. *Race Riot: Chicago in the Red Summer of 1919*. New York: Atheneum, 1985.

Tyrrell, Iyan. *Woman's World, Woman's Empire: The Woman's Christian Temperance Union in International Perspective, 1880–1930.* Chapel Hill: University of North Carolina Press, 1991.

Ulrich, Laurel Thatcher. "'The Living Mother of a Living Child': Midwifery and Mortality in Post-Revolutionary New England." *William and Mary Quarterly*, 3rd ser., 46, no. 1 (January 1989): 27–48.

Van Burkleo, Sandra F. *"Belonging to the World": Women's Rights and American Constitutional Culture.* New York: Oxford University Press, 2001.

Van Etteren, Mel. *Labor and the American Left: An Analytical History.* London: McFarland, 2011.

Venn, Fiona. *The New Deal.* Edinburgh: Edinburgh University Press, 1998.

Von Eschen, Penny M. *Race against Empire: Black Americans and Anticolonialism, 1937–1957.* Ithaca, N.Y.: Cornell University Press, 1997.

Wade, Wyn Craig. *The Fiery Cross: The Ku Klux Klan in America.* New York: Oxford University Press, 1987.

Wagner-Martin, Linda. *Telling Women's Lives: The New Biography.* New Brunswick, N.J.: Rutgers University Press, 1994.

Waite, Cally L. "The Segregation of Black Students at Oberlin College after Reconstruction." *History of Education Quarterly* 41, no. 3 (Autumn 2001): 344–64.

Wald, Gayle. *Crossing the Line: Racial Passing in Twentieth-Century U. S. Literature and Culture.* Durham, N.C.: Duke University Press, 2000.

Waldrep, Christopher. *African Americans Confront Lynching: Strategies of Resistance from the Civil War to the Civil Rights Era.* New York: Rowman and Littlefield, 2009.

Walker, Samuel. *Presidents and Civil Liberties from Wilson to Obama: A Story of Poor Custodians.* New York: Cambridge University Press, 2012.

Wall, Cheryl. *Women of the Harlem Renaissance.* Bloomington: Indiana University Press, 1995.

Wallace-Sanders, Kimberly. *Mammy: A Century of Race, Gender, and Southern Memory.* Ann Arbor: University of Michigan Press, 2008.

Wallinger, Hanna. *Pauline E. Hopkins: A Literary Biography.* Athens: University of Georgia Press, 2012.

Walton, Hanes, Jr. *Invisible Politics: Black Political Behavior.* Albany: State University of New York Press, 1985.

———. "Political Science Educational Conditions: Integrating Theory and Practice." In *Ralph Johnson Bunche: Public Intellectual and Nobel Peace Laureate*, edited by Beverly Lindsay, 60–78. Urbana: University of Illinois Press, 2007.

Walton, Mary. *A Woman's Crusade: Alice Paul and the Battle for the Ballot.* New York: Palgrave, 2010.

Ward, Jason Morgan. *Hanging Bridge: Racial Violence and America's Civil Rights Century.* New York: Oxford University Press, 2016.

Ware, Susan. *Why They Marched: Untold Stories of the Women Who Fought for the Right to Vote.* Cambridge, Mass.: Belknap Press of Harvard University Press, 2019.

Washington, Harold R. "History and the Role of Black Law Schools" [1974]. In *African Americans and the Legal Profession in Historical Perspective*, edited by Paul Finkelman, 476–507. New York: Garland, 1992.

Washington, Harriet A. *Medical Apartheid: The Dark History of Medical Experimentation on Black Americans from Colonial Times to the Present*. New York: Doubleday, 2006.

Washington, Mary Helen. "Anna Julia Cooper: A Voice from the South." In *Black Women's Intellectual Traditions: Speaking Their Minds*, edited by Kristin Waters and Carol B. Conaway, 249–66. Burlington: University of Vermont Press, 2007.

Watson, Martha Solomon. *Lives of Their Own: Rhetorical Dimensions in Autobiographies of Women Activists*. Columbia: University of South Carolina Press, 1999.

———. "Mary Church Terrell vs. Thomas Nelson Page: Gender, Race, and Class in Anti-Lynching Rhetoric." *Rhetoric and Public Affairs* 12 , no. 1 (Spring 2009): 65–89.

Weaver, John D. *The Brownsville Raid*. 1970; reprint, College Station: Texas A&M University Press, 1996.

———. *The Senator and the Sharecropper's Son: Exoneration of the Brownsville Soldiers*. College Station: Texas A&M University Press, 1997.

Weed, Clyde P. *The Nemesis of Reform: The Republican Party during the New Deal*. New York: Columbia University Press, 1994.

Weisbord, Robert G. "Black America and the Italian-Ethiopian Crisis: An Episode in Pan-Negroism." In *Race and U. S. Foreign Policy from 1900 through World War II*, edited by Michael L. Krenn and E. Nathaniel Gates, 152–63. New York: Taylor and Francis, 1998.

Weisenfeld, Judith. *African American Women and Christian Activism: New York's Black YWCA, 1905–1945*. Cambridge, Mass.: Harvard University Press, 1997.

———. *Hollywood Be Thy Name: African American Religion in American Film, 1929–1949*. Berkeley: University of California Press, 2007.

Weiss, Nancy J. *Farewell to the Party of Lincoln: Black Politics in the Age of FDR*. Princeton, N.J.: Princeton University Press, 1983.

Welke, Barbara. *Recasting American Liberty: Gender, Race, Law and the Railroad Revolution, 1865–1920*. New York: Cambridge University Press, 2001.

Wellman, Judith. *The Road to Seneca Falls: Elizabeth Cady Stanton and the First Woman's Rights Convention*. Urbana: University of Illinois Press, 2004.

Wertz, Richard W., and Dorothy C. Wertz. *Lying-In: A History of Childbirth in America*. New York: Free Press, 1977.

West, Aberjhani, and Sandra L. West. "Paul Laurence Dunbar Apartments." In *Encyclopedia of the Harlem Renaissance*, 260. New York: Facts on File, 2003.

White, Deborah Gray. *Ar'n't I a Woman? Female Slaves in the Plantation South*. New York: W. W. Norton, 1985.

———. "The Cost of Club Work, the Price of Black Feminism." In *Visible Women: New Essays on American Activism*, edited by Nancy A. Hewitt and Suzanne Lebsock, 249–69. Urbana: University of Illinois Press, 1993.

———. *Too Heavy a Load: Black Women in Defense of Themselves, 1894–1994*. New York: W. W. Norton, 1999.

White, E. Frances. *Dark Continent of Our Bodies: Black Feminism and the Politics of Respectability*. Philadelphia: Temple University Press, 2001.

Wilke, Laurie A. *The Archaeology of Mothering: An African-American Midwife's Tale*. New York: Routledge, 2003.

Wilkerson, Isabel. *The Warmth of Other Suns: The Epic Story of America's Great Migration*. New York: Random House, 2010.

Wilks, Jennifer M., ed. "The French and Swiss Diaries of Mary Church Terrell, 1888–89; Introduction and Annotated Translation." *Palimpsest: A Journal on Women, Gender and the Black International* 3, no. 1 (2014): 8–32.

Williams, Chad L. *Torchbearers of Democracy: African American Soldiers in the World War I Era*. Chapel Hill: University of North Carolina Press, 2010.

———. "Vanguards of the New Negro: African American Veterans and Post–World War I Radical Militancy." *Journal of African American History* 92, no. 3 (Summer 2007): 347–70.

Williams, Kidada E. *They Left Great Marks on Me: African American Testimonies of Racial Violence from Emancipation to World War I*. New York: New York University Press, 2012.

Williams, Lillian S. "Mary Morris Burnett Talbert (1866–1923)." In *Black Women in America: An Historical Encyclopedia*, 1137–39. Bloomington: Indiana University Press, 1994.

Williams, Patricia J. "Spirit-Murdering the Messenger: The Discourse of Fingerpointing as the Law's Response to Racism." In *Critical Race Feminism: A Reader*, edited by Adrien Katherine Wing, 229–36. New York: New York University Press, 1997.

Wilmore, Gayraud. *Black Religion and Black Radicalism*. New York: Doubleday, 1972.

Wintz, Cary D. *Black Culture and the Harlem Renaissance*. College Station: Texas A&M University Press, 1988.

Weisenfeld, Judith. *African American Women and Christian Activism: New York's Black YWCA, 1905–1945*. Cambridge, Mass.: Harvard University Press, 1997.

Wise, P. H. "The Anatomy of a Disparity in Infant Mortality." *Annual Review of Public Health* 24 (2003): 341–62.

Wolcott, Victoria W. *Race, Riots, and Roller Coasters: The Struggle over Segregated Recreation in America*. Philadelphia: University of Pennsylvania Press, 2012.

———. *Remaking Respectability: African American Women in Interwar Detroit*. Chapel Hill: University of North Carolina Press, 2001.

Wolf, Thomas P., William D. Pederson, and Byron W. Daynes, eds. *Franklin D. Roosevelt and Congress: The New Deal and Its Aftermath*. New York: M. E. Sharpe, 2000.

Wolgemuth, Kathleen Long. "Woodrow Wilson's Appointment Policy and the Negro." *Journal of Southern History* 24, no. 4 (November 1958): 457–71.

Wolraich, Michael. *Unreasonable Men: Theodore Roosevelt and the Republican Rebels Who Created Progressive Politics*. New York: Macmillan, 2014.

Wolters, Raymond. *The New Negro on Campus: Black College Rebellions of the 1920s*. Princeton, N.J.: Princeton University Press, 1975.

———. *Negroes and the Great Depression: The Problem of Economic Recovery*. Westport, Conn.: Greenwood, 1970.

Woods, Jeff. *Black Struggle, Red Scare: Segregation and Anti-Communism in the South, 1948–1968*. Baton Rouge: Louisiana State University Press, 2004.

Woolverton, John F. "Evangelical Protestantism and Alcoholism, 1933–1962: Episcopalian Samuel Shoemaker, the Oxford Group, and Alcoholics Anonymous." *Historical Magazine of the Protestant Episcopal Church* 52, no. 1 (1983): 53–65.

Wright, William D. *Black Identity: A Call for a New Historiography.* Westport, Conn.: Praeger, 2002.

Wynn, Neil A. *The African American Experience during World War II.* New York: Rowman and Littlefield, 2010.

Yellin, Eric. *Racism in the Nation's Service: Government Workers and the Color Line in Woodrow Wilson's America.* Chapel Hill: University of North Carolina Press, 2013.

Yurgalite, Karren, and Liette Gidlow. "Biographical Sketch of Mary Eleanora McCoy, 1846–1923." Forthcoming in *Women and Social Movements of the United States,* "Biographical Database of NAWSA Suffragists, 1890–1920." https://documents .alexanderstreet.com/c/1009677121.

Zhang, Ai-min. *The Origins of the African-American Civil Rights Movement.* New York: Routledge, 2014.

Zahniser, Jill D., and Amelia R. Fry. *Alice Paul: Claiming Power.* New York: Oxford University Press, 2014.

INDEX

Note: "MCT" refers to Mary Church Terrell and "RHT" refers to Robert Heberton Terrell. *Page numbers appearing in italics indicate illustrations.*